Springer Textbooks in Law

Springer Textbooks in Law compiles high-quality educational content aimed at undergraduate and graduate students in all areas of law. All self-contained volumes are authored by accomplished academics and suitable for use in class as well as individual study. Many of them include chapter abstracts, definitions of technical terms, cases and self-assessment exercises, as well as recommended reading sections. This series is an invaluable resource for students and lecturers alike and spans the full range of topics in international and European law, including fundamentals of law and comparative law. Special attention is paid to current and emerging topics such as IT law, intellectual property, human rights as well as dispute resolution, mediation, arbitration—and many more.

Fatih Bugra Erdem

The Principles of International Banking, Finance and Investment Law

Global Best Practices from the Group of Twenty (G20)

Springer

Fatih Bugra Erdem
Faculty of Law
Social Sciences University of Ankara
Ankara, Türkiye

ISSN 2509-999X ISSN 2510-0009 (electronic)
Springer Textbooks in Law
ISBN 978-3-032-32504-4 ISBN 978-3-032-32505-1 (eBook)
https://doi.org/10.1007/978-3-032-32505-1

This Springer imprint is published by the registered company Springer Nature Switzerland AG
The registered company address is: Gewerbestrasse 11, 6330 Cham, Switzerland

Dedicated to my dearest wife Gamze and my beloved daughter Öykü –
true companions on every road this life has taken.

Preface

While the global financial system is going through one of the most significant changes since the Bretton Woods Agreement, it is essential to consider of financial law not just as a set of fixed rules, but as a living and constantly changing ecosystem. This publication intends to act as a theoretical compass as well as a strategic roadmap in the maze of contemporary finance. The factor that differentiates this book from similar titles is its capability to liberate itself from the limited perspective of traditional banking law, and to cover a broad range of modern investment partnerships topics by understanding that bank and investment activities have gone beyond local boundaries and are being regulated by a global order shaped by enormous entities such as the G20, the Basel Committee, and the Financial Stability Board.

The newest technological and legislative changes, including digital central bank currencies, crypto asset regulations, and blockchain, based payment systems, are carefully deliberated amongst the pages of this book. It particularly details the sustainable financial models which, under green criteria, have now been the norm in the financial markets, with best practices being showcased. This thorough study for both practitioners and scholars indicates the way in which legal measures, within the delicate balance between financial innovation and regulation, can transform capital into a catalyst for systemic stability and sustainable economic resilience. Based on the principles of trust, stability, and the rule of law, I sincerely hope this work will become a proper source of fundamental reference for anyone seeking to comprehend the future of the worldwide financial system.

Fatih Bugra Erdem

Competing Interests The author has no competing interests to declare that are relevant to the content of this manuscript.

Contents

Abbreviations

ADB	Asian Development Bank
ADR	Alternative Dispute Resolution
AfDB	African Development Bank
AI	Artificial Intelligence
AIFMD	Alternative Investment Fund Managers Directive
AISP	Account Information Service Providers
ALM	Asset and Liability Management
AMC	Asset Management Company
AMF	The Autorité des Marchés Financiers
AML	Anti-Money Loundering
AMLA	Anti-Money Loundering Authority
AMLCO	Anti-Money Loundering Compliance Officer
AMLD6	Sixth AML Directive
AoA	Articles of Association
API	Application Programming Interface
APR	Annual Percentage Rate
ARD	American Research and Development Corporation
ARPA	Australian Prudential Regulation Authority
ASIC	Australian Securities and Investments Commission
BaFin	The Bundesanstalt für Finanzdienstleistungsaufsicht
BCB	Central Bank of Brazil
BCBS	Basel Committee on Banking Supervision
BEPS	Base Erosion and Profit Shifting
BHC	Bank Holding Company
BIS	Bank for International Settlements
BIT	Bilateral Investment Treaties
BoD	Board of Directors
BoE	Bill of Exchange
BoJ	Central Bank of Japan
BRI	Belt and Road Initiative
BRSA	Banking Regulation Supervision Agency
BSA	Bank Secrecy Act

CAC	Collective Action Clause
CAD	Cash Against Documents
CAPM	Capital Asset Pricing Model
CASP	Crypto Asset Service Provider
CBDC	Central Bank Digital Currencies
CBIRC	China Banking and Insurance Regulatory Commission
CBRT	Central Bank of the Republic of Turkey
CCB	Capital Conservation Buffer
CDB	China Development Bank
CDD	Customer Due Diligence
CDIC	Canada Deposit Insurance Corporation
CDS	Credit Default Swaps
CET	Common Equity Tier
CETA	EU-Canada Comprehensive Economic and Trade Agreement
CFPB	Consumer Financial Protection Bureau
CFT	Countering Financing of Terrorism
CIP	Customer Identification Program
CISG	Contracts for the International Sale of Goods
CIRR	Commercial Interest Reference Rate
CJEU	Court of Justice of the European Union
CME	Chicago Mercantile Exchange
CMF	Code Monetaire et Financier
CMN	National Monetary Council
CMU	Capital Markets Union
COD	Cash on delivery
CS	Conditions Subsequent
CSRD	Corporate Sustainability Reporting Directive
CTF	Counter-Terrorism Financing
D-8	Developing Eight
D-8P Card	D-8 Payment System
D/A	Documents against acceptance
DCO	Designated Compliance Officer
DeFi	Decentralised Finance
DIS	Deposit Insurance Systems
DLT	Distributed Ledger Technology
DSB	Dispute Settlement Body
DORA	Digital Operational Resilience Act
D/P	Documents for Payment
EAR	Effective Annual Rate
EBA	European Banking Authority
e-BL	Electronic Bill of Lading
EBRD	European Bank for Reconstruction and Development
EBU	European Banking Union
EC	European Commission
ECA	Export Credit Agencies

ECB	European Central Bank
ECO	Economic Cooperation Organization
ECP	Euro-Commercial Paper
EDC	Export Development Canada
EDD	Enhanced Due Diligence
EEA	European Economic Area
EFF	Extended Fund Facility
EFSI	European Fund for Strategic Investments
EFT	Electronic Fund Transfer
EIB	European Investment Bank
eLC	Electronic Letters of Credit
EMD	Electronic Money Directive
EMH	Efficient Market Hypothesis
EMI	E-Money Institution
EoD	Events of Default
ES	Expected Shortfall
ESF	Environmental and Social Framework
ESG	Environmental, Social and Governance
ESRB	European Systemic Risk Board
ETDB	ECO Trade and Development Bank
ETF	Exchange-Traded Fund
EU	European Union
EUGBS	European Union Green Bond Standard
EURIBOR	Euro Interbank Offered Rate
EVCA	European Venture Capital Association
FAA	Federal Arbitration Act of 1925
FATF	Financial Action Task Force
FBSEA	Foreign Bank Supervision Enhancement Act
FCA	Financial Conduct Authority
FDI	Foreign Direct Investment
FDIC	Federal Deposit Insurance Cooperation
FED	Federal Reserve
FIEA	Financial Instruments and Exchange Act
FinCEN	Financial Crimes Enforcement Network
FinTech	Financial Technology
FINRA	Financial Industry Regulatory Authority
FIU	Financial Intelligence Unit
FLC	Financial Lease Company
FOS	Financial Ombudsman Service
FRB	Federal Reserve Board
FRS	Federal Reserve System
FRTB	Fundamental Review of the Trading Book
FSA	Financial Services Agency
FSAP	Financial Sector Assessment Program
FSB	Financial Stability Board

FSCS	Financial Services Compensation Scheme
FSMA	Financial Services and Markets Act
FSOC	Financial Stability Oversight Council
FSS	Financial Supervisory Service
G-20	The Group of Twenty
GAAP	Generally Accepted Accounting Principles
GBS	Green Bond Standard
GDPR	EU General Data Protection Regulation
GDR	Global Depository Receipts
GEF	Global Environment Facility
GPI	Global Payments Innovation
G-SIB	Globally Systemically Important Banks
HELOC	Home Equity Line of Credit
IAIS	International Association of Insurance Supervisors
IBRD	International Bank for Reconstruction and Development
ICAAP	Internal Capital Adequacy Assessment Process
ICC	International Chamber of Commerce
ICMA	International Capital Market Association
ICS	Investment Court System
ICSID	International Centre for Settlement of Investment Disputes
IDA	International Development Association
IDB	Inter-American Development Bank
IFC	International Finance Corporation
IMF	International Monetary Fund
IOSCO	International Organizaiton of Securities Commission
IPCC	United Nations Intergovernmental Panel on Climate Change
IPE	International Political Economy
IPO	Initial Public Offering
IRB	Internal Ratings-Based
ISDA	International Swaps and Derivatives Association
ISDS	Investor-State Dispute Settlement
IT	Information Technology
ITFA	International Trade and Forfaiting Association
JFSA	Japan Financial Services Agency
JSDA	Japan Securities Dealers Association
KAMCO	Korea Asset Management Corporation
KiFiD	The Klachteninstituut Financiële Dienstverlening
KYC	Know Your Customer
LC	Letters of Credit
LCIA	London Court of International Arbitration
LCR	Liquidity Coverage Ratio
LIBOR	London Interbank Offered Rate
LMA	Loan Market Association
LPR	Loan Prime Rate
LSTA	Loan Syndications and Trading Association

M&A	Mergers and Acquisition
MAC	Material Adverse Change
MAS	Singapore Monetary Authority
MBS	Mortgage-Backed Securities
MDA	Maximum Distributable Amount
MDB	Multilateral Development Bank
MFI	Microfinance Institution
MIC	Multilateral Investment Court
MiFID	Markets in Financial Instruments Directive
MIGA	Multilateral Investment Guarantee Agency
ML	Money Laundering
MLETR	UNCITRAL's Model Law on Electronic Transferable Records
MoU	Memorandum of Understanding
MPE	Multiple Point of Entry
MPT	Modern Portfolio Theory
MS	Member States
NASD	National Association of Securities Dealers
NCA	National Crime Agency
NEXI	Nippon Export and Investment Insurance
NFRD	The Non-Financial Reporting Directive
NFT	Non-Fungible Token
NGFS	Network for Greening the Financial System
NGO	Non-Profit Organisation
NIRP	Negative Interest Rate Policy
NOL	Net Operating Loss
NPL	Non-Performing Loan
NSFR	Net Stable Funding Ratio
NYSE	New York Stock Exchange
LMA	Loan Market Association
OBA	Open Bank Assistance
OBIE	Open Banking Implementation Entity
OCC	Office of the Comptroller of the Currency
OECD	Organisation for Economic Co-operation and Development
OFAC	Office of Foreign Assets Control
OJK	Financial Services Authority of Indonesia
OLA	Orderly Liquidation Authority
OSFI	Office of the Superintendent of Financial Institutions
OTC	Over the Counter
P2P	Peer-to-peer
P&A	Purchase and Assumption
PAI	Principal Adverse Impact
PBoC	People's Bank of China
PISP	Payment Initiation Service Providers
PLS	Profit and Loss Sharing
PLSC	Profit and Loss Sharing Certificate

POCA	Proceeds of Crime Act
PPP	Public-Private Partnership
PPSR	Personal Property Securities Register
PRA	Prudential Regulation Authority
PRB	Principles for Responsible Banking
PSA	Payment Services Act
PSBR	Public Sector Borrowing Requirement
PSD	Payment Services Directive
PTA	Preferential Trade Agreement
RBA	Reserve Bank of Australia
RBI	Reserve Bank of India
RegTech	Regulation Technologies
RTC	Resolution Trust Corporation
RTGS	Real-time Gross Settlement
RWA	Risk-Weighted Assets
SAR	Suspicious Activity report
SBA	Stand-By Arrangement
SBIC	Small Business Investment Corporation
SCM	Subsidies and Countervailing Measures
SCT	SEPA Credit Transfer
SDIF	Savings Deposit Insurance Fund
SDN	Specially Designated National
SDR	Special Drawing Rights
SEC	Securities and Exchange Commission
SFD	Settlement Finality Directive
SEPA	Single Euro Payments Area
SF	Sustainable Finance
SFDR	Sustainable Finance Disclosure Regulation
SFWG	Sustainable Finance Study Group
SIFI	Systemically Important Financial Institution
SME	Small and Medium Enterprises
SOFR	Secured Overnight Financing Rate
SPE	Single Point of Entry
SPV	Special Purpose Vehicle
SRB	Single Resolution Board
SRM	Single Resolution Mechanism
SRO	Self-regulatory Organization
SRR	Special Resolution Regime
SupTech	Supervisory Technologies
SVB	Silicon Valley Bank
SWIFT	Society for Worldwide Interbank Financial Telecommunication
TARGET	Trans-European Automated Real-time Gross settlement Express Transfer
TFA	Trade Facilitation Agreement
TFEU	Treaty on the Functioning of the European Union

TLAC	Total Loss-Absorbing Capacity
TFEU	Treaty on the Functioning of the European Union
TIPS	TARGET Instant Payment Settlement
TLAC	Total Loss-Absorbing Capacity
TPP	Third-party financial Technology Companies
UBO	Ultimate Beneficial Owner
UCP	Uniform Customs and Practice for Documentary Credits
UK	United Kingdom
UKEF	UK Export Finance
UNCITRAL	United Nations Commission on International Trade Law
UNCTAD	United Nations Conference on Trade and Development
UNIDROIT	International Institute for the Unification of Private Law
UNPRB	United Nations Principles for Responsible Banking
URF	Uniform Rules for Forfaiting
URDG	Uniform Rules for Demand Guarantees
US	United States
VaR	Value at Risk
VCLP	Venture Capital Limited Partnership
VEC	Venture Enterprise Centre
WB	World Bank
WTO	World Trade Organization
YCC	Yield Curve Control

Financial System

1

Contents

F. B. Erdem, *The Principles of International Banking, Finance and Investment Law*, Springer Textbooks in Law, https://doi.org/10.1007/978-3-032-32505-1_1

Abstract

This chapter proposes a comprehensive examination of the legal frameworks and operational dynamics of the global financial system. The initial focus is on financial markets, beginning with an overview of the global financial system and exploring key components such as the international money market, monetary exchange, and the intricacies of Eurocurrency markets—including Eurodollar deposits, Eurobond markets, Euroequity markets, and Euro-commercial paper markets. It also delves into the international political economy, the complexities of international financial transactions, and theories of banking and finance. A review of international banking regulations and policies provides context for understanding global financial governance. The chapter then turns to financial institutions, analysing the roles of banks, insurance companies, specialty finance firms, and asset management companies. In the section on banking and finance applications, the chapter explores practical aspects of banking transactions in foreign trade, including international banking transactions, International Chamber of Commerce's (ICC) Uniform Customs and Practice for Documentary Credits (UCP) 600 guidelines, foreign exchange controls, customs procedures, foreign trade operations, letters of credit, and foreign-trade financing. The chapter also addresses the settlement of disputes in the financial sector, focusing on conflict of laws, litigation, alternative dispute resolution methods, and cross-border issues such as insolvencies, sovereign immunity, and international trade finance. Finally, the chapter discusses money and banking, covering theoretical, historical, and legal aspects, with a special focus on central banking issues like autonomy, accountability, governance, and the role of major central banks such as the US Federal Reserve System (FRS), the European Central Bank (ECB), and others. This comprehensive exploration aims to provide a clear roadmap for understanding the legal underpinnings and practical applications of the financial system in a global context.

1.1 Terminology

Markets are the places where demand and supply interact. Markets can be classified into two broad categories: real markets and financial markets. Real markets are the trading of real (hard) assets such as real estate, commodities, and natural resources. Financial markets as places where securities (financial assets) are traded supply the mechanism for the provision of resources (shortages of liquidity) to the real markets by enabling capital accumulation.[1]

Financial markets are capital-raising mechanisms by uniting those needing funds (borrowers) and those supplying them (lenders). This connection, though inherently challenging, is facilitated by money intermediaries such as banks. Banks collect funds from people and institutions with surplus and aggregate the funds together to advance to borrowers requiring funds. Apart from simple bank deposits, more sophisticated finance operations demand disciplined markets wherein borrowers, their agents, lenders, and their agents can transact. These markets allow for the redetermination of outstanding lending or borrowing obligations, offering liquidity and transferability of obligations. An extremely well-publicized example is the stock exchange, where companies raise funds by issuing shares to investors

[1] Georgakopoulos (2017, 1–8).

and these shares are freely transferable to other market participants. In the context of global financial market, it is a framework through which global savings are being mobilized and reallocated to investments via trading venues and stock markets.[2]

It enables capital to cross borders and redistributes consumption potential across countries, facilitating interlinked economic activity worldwide. Global financial market integration, however, is not without restrictions. One of the most significant barriers is 'country risk', which is generated through the inability to enforce international debt contracts in the same legal manner as domestic ones. In contrast to domestic borrowers, sovereign governments cannot be compelled by bankruptcy mechanisms, and thus repayment decisions rest on voluntary cooperation or indirect mechanisms such as sanctions or reputational pressures. In addition, the globalization of capital markets has been fostered by technological changes that have lowered technical transaction costs and by deregulation that has lowered barriers to trade. All this however, the phenomenon of country risk remains a challenge to the free movement of global financial markets, particularly for countries with high economic prospects but lack easy access to international capital due to perceived risks. Financial system is a platform that provides individual and institutional players (household, firms or official institutions) to interact with others with the intention of displacement of funds from the possession of wealth holders to third-party users using various financial payment systems. In between, intermediary functions are performed by financial institutions, which assume the risks of fund transference as well as management.[3]

1.2 Financial System

Financial system is a forum that provides individual and institutional actors (household, corporations or governmental agencies) to interact with others for the sake of displacement of funds from surplus holders to third parties in need via various financial payment systems. In this mechanism, the intermediary activities are held by financial institutions, which run the risks of transferring and managing funds. These risks are basically based on maturities of illiquid assets (e.g. long-term loans) at the time of demanding deposits.

> **Important** The financial system is an environment where surplus funds are transferred from those with excess capital to those with a deficit, through financial instruments and intermediaries. In financial markets, savings are transformed into investments.

[2] Valdez and Molyneux (2016, 2).
[3] Egli (1999, 275–280).

There is a positive correlation between a country's development level and the advancement of its financial system.[4] This is because an efficient financial system enables adjustments in terms of maturity, amount, and risk. Funds can be utilized effectively until the time they are needed. Financial markets not only connect fund suppliers with fund demanders but also process large amounts of capital collected by financial intermediaries. Additionally, there are financial instruments designed to yield higher returns for those willing to take on greater risk.Reference 'Ela Puscasu (2022)' is cited in the text but not provided in the reference list. Please provide the respective references in the list or delete these citations.Ela-Andrada P (2022) The impact of financial systems on economic growth in European Union member countries. Sciendo 16(1):722-731

Ultimately, financial system is to ensure the efficient and uninterrupted transfer or funds between the units supplying funds and the units demanding funds. In the absence of a financial system, savers would be unable to manage their funds under optimal conditions, and those requiring funds would lack a clear means of identifying potential sources. The primary contribution of the financial system to the economy lies in facilitating the connection between creditors and debtors. So, financial markets bring creditors and debtors together.

The financial system also makes it easy to sell assets, and consideration of being able to liquidate is something that is used in assessing the efficiency of the financial system. It is very crucial for investors to own financial assets that are sellable for cash whenever they are required. The well-performing financial system is also able to ensure that investors get an opportunity to diversify risk across sources. The best way of diversifying risk and hence minimizing risk is financial diversification. Diversification is to reduce the aggregate risk of economic agents by spreading their saving in different financial instruments. For example, to finance a large project, spreading the risk to the grassroots level will enable the project to receive sufficient funds. In this way, ownership will be spread over a wide range of financial units, while the entire risk will not be borne by a few individuals or institutions.

Background Information

It is necessary to establish why financial systems differ between countries. That is, why German companies choose bank lending while American companies seek financing through stock markets. The answer must be sought in legal regulations. Whereas Germany imposes some legal barriers to access to financial markets, the US imposes legal regulations that discourage bank intermediation. Most of the German banks went bankrupt when they experienced the 1929 economic crisis, and lacking the necessary reserves in the capital, could not extend credit to financially distressed business organizations. Severe legal measures were enacted to eradicate the widespread distrust of German banks, and banks slowly earned trust by virtue of legal regulations.[5] In the US, following a dramatic occurrence such as the Lehman Brothers' collapse, capital markets were highlighted and placed at the top of the agenda. That is, countries make their economic strategies based on financial systems they have established to respond to economic adversity they face.

[4] Ela-Andrada (2022, 722–731).

[5] Monnet and Quintin (2005).

1.2.1 Fund Flow in Financial Systems

In financial markets, demand and provision of funds are met either indirectly or directly through financial institutions. The main function of financial intermediary institutions is facilitating the flow of funds through easily and efficiently moving funds. There are two distinct mechanisms for fund outflow in the financial system:

(i) Direct Finance: There is no intermediary between the fund providers and the fund demanders. It is the sale of the financial instrument by the fund demanders to the fund demanders directly.

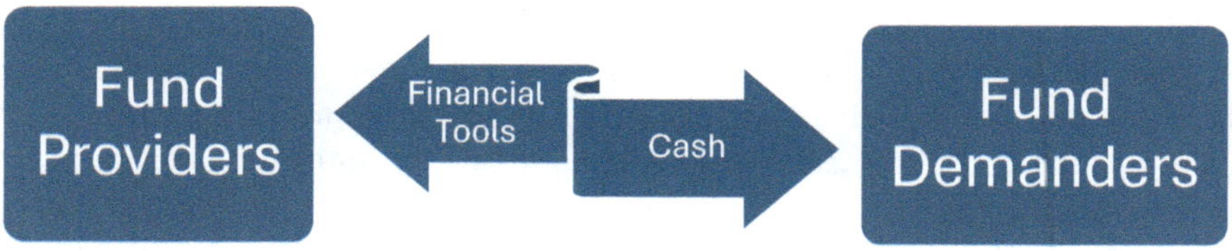

(ii) Indirect Finance: Borrowers reach funds from the financial market through indirect means, such as through a financial intermediary. In such, fund providers and fund demanders do not deal with each other but only with the intermediary financial institution.

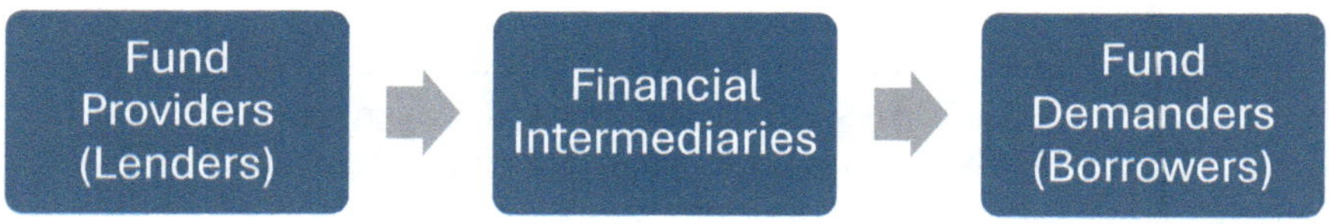

Hence, saving holders and fund-need individuals can transfer funds between them directly or indirectly in the financial system. In direct financing, money is transferred against a financial asset by the lack of any intermediary institution, while in indirect financing, the transfer is carried out through an intermediary institution.

1.2.1.1 Fund Providers

Possibly both individuals and businesses. The financial system relies on fund providers, or lenders, like those saving through banks, insurance premiums, or pensions. There are variations in pension systems across the world: countries like the United States (US), the United Kingdom (UK), Netherlands, Switzerland, and Japan rely mainly on private or employer-based pension funds, while France pays pensions through current taxation, and in Germany, firm pensions are known to reinvest in the company itself. Insurance and pension funds are also major market drivers, as they invest government bonds, corporate bonds, and equities to meet long-term liabilities. Previous shortages of such funds have limited the evolution of securities markets in developing economies. Commercial companies are predominantly borrowers, yet their counterparts who have surplus funds can become short-term money market lenders, which is a manifestation of the dual nature of business firms as lenders and borrowers depending on their cash situation.[6]

1.2.1.2 Fund Demanders

Borrowers include individuals, firms, government agencies, and public corporations. Individuals avail themselves of bank loans for consumption purchases or housing loans for housing finance. Companies take short-term loans for liquidity and long-term loans for growth. Governments, being heavy borrowers, finance budget deficits and state municipal, federal state, public sector institutions, and nationalized industries, all collectively referred to as the public sector borrowing requirement (PSBR). The total volume of such borrowing is the national debt. Money is borrowed by public enterprises, for example, SNCF in France or Deutsche Bundesbahn in Germany, as well as broader public sector bodies like Crédit Local de France or the German Unity Fund.[7]

1.2.2 The Categorisation of Financial System

Some financial instruments are limited to the buying and selling of debt (e.g., bonds), while others establish partnership relationships (e.g., equity). The initial issuance and transfer of these instruments to fund-seekers occur in primary markets. Conversely, the resale of securities purchased in primary markets to meet liquidity needs is facilitated through secondary markets, such as stock exchanges or other financial intermediaries.

In terms of organisation, markets can also be divided into two as organised and over-the counter (OTC) markets. Organised markets are established by law and supervised by government bodies, therefore having their own specific characteristics, e.g. stock markets. The legal liability of inconveniences stemming from transactions carried out in organise markets would be incumbent on organised markets. OTC markets, on the other hand, are decentralized platforms where participants engage in direct trading without the involvement of a central exchange or intermediary. These markets lack physical locations and designated market-makers.

In terms of maturity, money markets include low-risk assets like treasury bonds, certificate of deposits, or short-term corporate bonds with maturities of less than a year. Hence, money market is where short run debts are bought and sold. As to capital markets, they cover long-term securities, like long-term government and corporate maturing in more than one year. Capital market is where companies and governments seek funds for large projects.

---

[6] Valdez and Molyneux (2016, 2–3).

[7] Ibid., 3–4.

1.2.3 Financial Institutions

Financial institutions are the bodies that contribute to the formation of the trust environment required for the well-functioning of the financial system, mediate the transfer of funds between savers and investors through financial assets and thus contribute to economic development. A financial institution acts as an intermediary between fund providers and fund demanders to facilitate financial transactions and enable financial instruments to reach larger investor groups. In this context, banks and other financial intermediaries are the most prominent and important link in the financial intermediation process, ensuring the uninterrupted and efficient flow of funds.[8] One of the most important reasons for using financial intermediaries instead of direct exchange between lenders and borrowers is the fact that investors have incomplete information (asymmetric information). In this regard, the function of the intermediary institution is to bring together order owners whose orders are compatible and complementary to each other. What makes intermediaries valuable in this type of intermediation is their accumulated knowledge and their special skill in interpreting negative and complex data that is not easily observable (or has a high observation cost).[9]

1.2.3.1 Banks: The Cornerstone of the Modern Financial System

Banks are the cornerstone of the current financial architecture. In essence, banks act as financial intermediaries whereby they pool and collect the excess amount of funds from customers, known as savers, and then provide those funds, mainly through the issuance of loans, to customers with deficient funding, known as borrowers.[10] Apart from their role as financial intermediaries, banks undertake various other significant functions, including the facilitation of the payment and settlement process, creation of money through the fractional reserve system, and transforming risks.[11]

1.2.3.1.1 Legal Nature and Scope of Operations

From the legal standpoint, bank is a licensed institution with the exclusive right to accept deposits and other repayable funds and to grant credit on its own account.[12] The presence of both features, namely, accepting deposits and extending credit on the institution's balance sheet, sets banks apart from non-banking financial institutions like finance companies, credit unions, and investment funds, which often lack either one of them or both. Because of the various systemic and public characteristics of deposits, banks are almost universally organized and governed by special laws on banks, as opposed to general company laws. Obtaining a bank license is

[8] Greenbaum et al. (2015, 29) and Stowell (2010, 7).
[9] Greenbaum et al. (2015, 24) and Fabozzi et al. (2009, 23).
[10] Mishkin (2016, 232).
[11] Benlala (2023, 5–30).
[12] Goddard and Wilson (2016, 1–26) and Salievna (2019, 681).

required from either the central bank or, as in many countries, from an authority specializing in bank supervision as a prerequisite for commencing business activities.

1.2.3.1.2 Examples of Legal Frameworks from the Group of Twenty (G-20)

1.2.3.1.2.1 EU

The EU's philosophy emphasizes pre-emptive, ex ante supervision rather than reactive enforcement, thereby considering prudential soundness, transparency, and consumer protection as primary markets' integrity maintainers, a situation that is contrary to the litigation-heavy ones elsewhere. The European Banking Authority (EBA) is the one providing the technical standards and stress tests planned for 2025 as the main instruments by which convergence occurs, while the European Systemic Risk Board (ESRB) continuously monitors the macroprudential risks. The market is characteristically occupied by global banking institutions such as Deutsche Bank, BNP Paribas, and Santander whose interconnected commercial-investment models are balanced by the post-2008 ring-fencing reforms aimed at preventing the spread of risk within the entity.[13] In light of the fact that the authorities involved in the supervision are coordinating and the main banks are carrying out their activities across borders, the financial system in Europe looks like it is moving into a more integrated structure, thus evolution naturally brings the supportive parts of the Banking Union—among which EDIS progress is being the most talked about—into the debate. Nevertheless, a report by AFME in September 2025 underlined that the Banking Union was not complete, and even more, EDIS delays and cross-border barriers were significant hindrances to consolidation and resilience, which eventually led to calls for simplified waivers and fiscal backstops.[14]

1.2.3.1.2.2 Turkey

Turkey's banking framework combines the prudence inspired by the EU with the flexible national adaptations, which underwent post-2001 crisis reforms and Basel alignment to deal with the volatilities of emerging markets. It is based on Banking Law No. 5411, which brings the supervision together under the independent Banking Regulation and Supervision Agency (BRSA) for licensing and enforcement, the Savings Deposit Insurance Fund (SDIF) for resolution and guarantees, and the Central Bank of the Republic of Turkey (CBRT) for monetary and macroprudential measures. Complementary laws, such as Financial Leasing, Factoring, and Financing Companies Law No. 6361.[15]

In a way, Turkey's democratic system has had the growth process through the International Monetary Fund (IMF)-guided overhaul and the EU candidacy pressures as of the already made 2013 hard laws that include the entry of Basel III

---

[13] See, Hardie and Macartney (2016, 503–525), Andenas and Chiu (2014) and ECB (2025).

[14] AFME (2025).

[15] See, Güney (2023).

capital/liquidity ratios limits and related-party curbs in the meantime with the BRSA having broad regulatory powers. By the end of 2025, the digital transformation process shall be a lot faster; the BRSA's "Regulation on Digital Banks and Service Model Banking" directs the branches-less activities and cybersecurity measures. The new open banking rules effective April 2025 will facilitate the sharing of data necessary for the payment initiation, and the digital wallets' growth through the October 2023 updates will be a factor in increasing inclusion alongside the economic revival of 2025.[16]

The supervision is mainly preventive to the BRSA's inspections and SDIF interventions which are both done off-and on-site as the main methods of ensuring the financial stability of the banking sector by avoiding litigation that is going to be costly after the fact.[17] A Global Legal Insights report in September 2025 acknowledges the BRSA's forward-looking fintech licensing as a resilience enhancer, but at the same time the inflation and the debt situation are so intertwined that they strain the adaptability. Turkey's multi-faceted policy—combining conventional, Islamic and digital—illustrates regulatory shrewdness in promoting growth without compromising safeguards.[18]

1.2.3.1.2.3 The US

The US banking structure is a representation of federalism's dual nature, it divides the supervision into federal and state layers which slows down the innovation but at the same time it is a means of an enforcement that is culturally accepted as a barrier against crises.[19] The main character of the scene is the Federal Reserve (FED) which has the role of supervision over the system, and the holding companies, the Office of the Comptroller of the Currency (OCC) which is in charge of national charters, the Federal Deposit Insurance Corporation (FDIC) which deals with insurance and resolutions, and the consumer who is treated justly with the help of the Consumer Financial Protection Bureau (CFPB)—all these are coordinated by the Financial Stability Oversight Council (FSOC) under Dodd-Frank (2010) which tags systemically important financial institutions (SIFIs). U.S. law has been historically reactive and it is marked by events: the National Bank Act (1863) brought about federal chartering; Glass-Steagall (1933) separated activities (repealed 1999); and Dodd-Frank imposed a mix of Volcker Rule separations, stress tests, and liquidity mandates after 2008.[20] Discretionary enforcement and litigation are the mainstays of its operation, while rules-centric counterparts rely solely on these methods; the interpretive latitude granted to the agencies has led to a series of events that are hard to track, such as the FDIC-OCC probes into

---

[16] Aksoy (2025, 1–29), Konca (2025, 142–159) and Daver (2023, 83–108).
[17] Tiryaki and Yılmaz (2012, 69–94).
[18] Bağcı et al. (2025).
[19] Odinet (2021, 1765–1768).
[20] Nofal et al. (2023, 209–234).

the unrealized loss accounting caused by the 2023 Silicon Valley Bank (SVB) collapse.[21]

1.2.3.1.2.4 Singapore

Singapore's integrated approach to law, technology, and finance illustrates how regulatory vision and innovation can drive not only national progress, but also regional leadership in an era of rapid digital transformation. The recent overhaul of Singapore's regulatory framework for the crypto ecosystem marks a pivotal chapter in the region's financial transformation. The Monetary Authority of Singapore (MAS) has demonstrated remarkable ambition by reimagining the financial landscape, not only within its own borders but across Asia. Central to this evolution is the phased implementation of the Financial Services and Markets Act (FSMA) since April 2023, which has fortified Singapore's anti-money laundering (AML) and dispute resolution frameworks. These reforms have cemented Singapore's status as Asia's premier financial centre, simultaneously acting as a catalyst for the broader region's financial modernization. The MAS exemplifies a new breed of central bank—one that innovates with the agility of a technology company while maintaining the prudence of a state regulator.[22] Furthermore, Singapore retains its leadership in Islamic finance by offering Sharia-compliant products, issuing green bonds, and establishing robust digital asset regulations. This unique combination of tradition and innovation has positioned Singapore as the standard-bearer for hybrid financial regimes.[23]

1.2.3.1.2.5 Brazil

In the Brazilian banking sector, the main resilience is a strong domestic one that even continues to be visible during the volatility of emerging markets, and it is represented by the big players, such as Banco do Brasil, Bradesco, and Itaú Unibanco. The complete adherence to Basel III, which has been implemented since 2013 through the resolutions of the National Monetary Council (CMN) and Central Bank of Brazil (BCB) guidelines has not only enhanced the capital adequacy but also reduced the non-performing loans to the lowest levels ever.[24] BCB's 2024 public consultations regarding the components of the Fundamental Review of the Trading Book (FRTB) with January 2026 as the target date for implementation, are meant to make improvements in the process of calculating market risk and to allow for the use of internal models, although the use of such models is still very limited because of the conservatism in the calibration by the supervisory authorities.[25] In the middle of these discussions, Brazil's linking of instant payment systems like PIX with the Basel standards is an example of a mixed approach of innovation

[21] Al-Sari (2025, 661–677).
[22] Phang (2024, 67–104).
[23] Ginting et al. (2019, 235–244).
[24] Pinheiro et al. (2015, 346–361).
[25] Funcao (2024).

and stability, thereby, through the reduction of shadow banking risks, winning the uphill battle of keeping the financial sector to thrive.[26]

1.2.3.1.2.6 The UK

The British banking regime combines full market access with strict regulatory controls—a move that can be tracked back to the financial crisis of 2008. The restructuring after the crisis led to the dismantling of the Financial Services Authority and the creation of the Prudential Regulation Authority (PRA)—part of the Bank of England for macro-prudential supervision—and the Financial Conduct Authority (FCA) which is in charge of protecting consumers and maintaining market integrity.[27] Thus, the "twin peaks" principle enables a One Stop Shop covered by the Banking Act 2009's Special Resolution Regime (SRR), which empowers orderly failure management without triggering contagion.[28] London remains a centre of investment banking, FX trading, and fintech that can still rely on the ring-fencing rule mandating the separation of retail business from speculative activities—a step in the direction of EU structural reforms.[29] In 2025, PRA consultations suggest increasing the Financial Services Compensation Scheme (FSCS) deposit protection from £85,000 to £110,000 effective December and raising temporarily high-balance limits up to £1.4 million, which is coinciding with inflation adjustments and lessons from crises.[30] Regulators, amidst the pressure to grow, have made competitiveness a secondary goal, in line with FCA's plan for 2025/2026 that focuses on artificial intelligence (AI) sprint projects and the resilience of operations for the most critical third parties.[31] Changes like these confirm the UK's flexible model, which gives priority to the stability of the market and at the same time encourages innovation to flourish.

1.2.3.1.2.7 Japan

The Japanese banking system is not only influenced by industrial strategy but also by the interconnections through the traditional keiretsu groups, the whole picture is framed by the Banking Act (1947, as amended) and the Financial Instruments and Exchange Act (2006) which are under the supervision of the Financial Services Agency (FSA) and the central Bank of Japan (BoJ).[32] Giant banks like Mitsubishi UFJ, Sumitomo Mitsui, and Mizuho are responsible for the wholesale finance and project lending market, their restructuring after the 1990s which involved recapitalization and mergers focused on the use of risk-based and macroprudential tools.[33] The BoJ's negative interest rate policy (NIRP) that started in

---

[26] Leal and Haase (2025, 146–171).
[27] Powley and Stanton (2017, 58–80).
[28] Cihak and Nier (2009, 8).
[29] Oppolzer (2019, 122, 137).
[30] Edwards and Lovegrove (2025).
[31] Financial Conduct Authority (2025).
[32] Grabowiecki (2006) and Weber and Devaney (2002, 33–46).
[33] Rosengren (2019).

2016 had an impact on liquidity and lending but was discontinued in March 2024 together with the yield curve control (YCC) which was a part of normalization: the rates were increased to 0.5% by January 2025 thereby increasing net interest margin and profitability.[34] The change of direction, which is predicted to increase rates to 0.75% by the end of the year but at the same time, yen volatility and bond losses are the associated risks.[35] Japan's model is a clear example that the use of unconventional policy could stop the slide down to deflation; now it is moving towards sustainable growth in the face of demographic challenges.[36]

1.2.3.1.2.8 Canada

The reconstructed banking model of Canada is a true representation of the power of prudence. It has the backing of the Office of the Superintendent of Financial Institutions (OSFI) and the support of the Bank of Canada and Canada Deposit Insurance Corporation (CDIC). The "big six" banks—RBC, TD, Scotiabank, BMO, CIBC, and National Bank—are at the forefront of this oligopolistic scenario and are going beyond Basel capital requirements while the vitality of the banking sector is maintained through strict mortgage regulation.[37] There were no significant bank failures during the crisis of 2008 which had a very conservative culture and a mixture of micro and macro prudential policies as its main characteristics; the CET1 ratios were already at 13.5% on average as of the end of April 2025.[38] OSFI's Domestic Stability Buffer (DSB), which has been constant at 3.5% since 2018, requires systemic banks to hold capital buffers; these are reviewed every six months alongside the mortgage renewal and trade tensions—however no measures are taken this time indicating the strength of the sector.[39] With the uncertainties of 2025, OSFI calls for the market to take smart risks in order to keep the flow of credit going, thus putting forward a policy that prioritizes stability over growth.[40]

1.2.3.1.2.9 Australia

The principal regulation of banks in Australia is mainly established in the Banking Act of 1959 and consists of the participation of the Australian Prudential Regulation Authority (APRA) and the Reserve Bank of Australia (RBA), with the Australian Securities and Investments Commission (ASIC) being responsible for banks' conduct. This 'twin peaks' model, which started in 1998, has been imposing capital adequacy, liquidity ratios, and consumer protections globally, affecting even non-European countries.[41] The four major banks: Commonwealth Bank, Westpac,

---

[34] See also, Haba et al. (2025) and Sekhon (2024).
[35] Sugiyama (2025).
[36] Schnabl (2015, 124–150).
[37] Williams et al. (2022, 247–266).
[38] Dobby (2025).
[39] Office of the Superintendent of Financial Institutions (2025).
[40] Liew (2025).
[41] Schmulow et al. (2021, 1–25) and Godwin and Ramsay (2016).

ANZ, and NAB have a powerful influence on the market, but their power has been kept in check by the Basel III regulation that was enforced by APRA plus the post-royal commission reforms that improved the banks' governance.[42] In 2025, APRA's plan will focus on working closely with ASIC on the operational resilience area, with fintech integration and climate risk disclosures being the factors putting pressure on the banks.[43] The transferability of this model has been made possible by the fact that Australia's banking system was not overly affected by the global financial crisis, but the existence of overlapping areas of responsibility between the two regulators calls for clear and strong memorandum of understanding (MoU).[44]

1.2.3.1.2.10 China

The banking system of China being state-controlled mainly serves the country's needs, and it is closely monitored by the People's Bank of China (PBoC) for policy and the China Banking and Insurance Regulatory Commission (CBIRC, now National Financial Regulatory Administration) for supervision. The "big four" banks, including ICBC, Bank of China, China Construction Bank, and Agricultural Bank, possess more than 60% of the banking sector's assets, which are further supported by development banks such as China Development Bank.[45] Gradual reversal in interest rates and the massive tech-driven financial access through Ant Group and WeBank are enhancing inclusion but at the same time, local government debts, real estate depression, and unregulated finance are the factors that threaten the stability of the financial sector.[46] The accommodative monetary stance of PBoC in 2025 with a relatively low loan prime rate (LPR) rate is aimed at reducing risks, and total loss-absorbing capacity (TLAC) requirements for systematically important banks will be increased to 18% by 2028.[47] Such a banking policy has turned the banking sector into a tool for invigorating the economy while the government continues to exercise control along with the gradual liberalization of the economy.

1.2.3.1.2.11 India

The banking situation in India is quite diverse with public, private, and cooperative banks existing side by side the Reserve Bank of India (RBI) through the Banking Regulation Act of 1949. The latter is being complemented by the Companies Act of 2013 and SARFAESI Act of 2002 for the recovery of assets. The Federal Reserve's upper echelons like the State Bank of India (SBI), HDFC, and ICICI banks, which comply with Basel III requirements and have risk-based supervision, are being supported by the Insolvency and Bankruptcy Code, which has decreased resolution timelines.[48] Payment banks and small finance banks together with UPI's

[42] Le et al. (2020).
[43] Australian Prudential Regulation Authority (2025).
[44] Chitimira and Mavhuru (2024, 1–33).
[45] Ren and Lu (2025, 1–32).
[46] Guo et al. (2025).
[47] Fitch Ratings (2024).
[48] World Bank and South Asia Regional Vice Presidency (2025).

peak (over 65,000 crore transactions) are cementing the digital inclusion leadership.[49] The reforms of August 2025 raised the UPI limits to ₹5 crore and set a limit for inquiries to enhance efficiency while PSL adjustments helped MSMEs.[50]

1.2.3.1.3 Socioeconomic Functions

Maturity transformation from an economics perspective, banks, thus, liquidate through the period by reversing the flow of funds from long-term assets to short-term liabilities, thus making it inevitable to incur both types of risks, the study of which led to stringent prudential regulation.[51] Furthermore, they operate the payments system which promotes the smooth flow of business and investment. On the other hand, banks contribute to society by providing financial inclusion, investing deposited money in productive ventures, pushing the development of new businesses, and being the most preferred channel for the implementation of monetary policy through, inter alia, reserve requirements and open market operations.[52]

1.2.3.1.4 Classification and Corporate Governance

The classification of banks can be done based on their functions, ownership, and geographical distribution.

1.2.3.1.4.1 Commercial (Retail) Banks

Their main business activity is to accept deposits and lend money to people and companies. Accordingly, such operations are based on the maturity transformation concept. They accept short-term and liquid deposits and at the same time give out loans for a longer period, thus generating credit in the economy. To ensure depositor protection and systemic stability, they have to comply with very rigid liquidity and capital adequacy regulations such as Basel III standards.[53]

1.2.3.1.4.2 Investment Banks

Mainly concerned with capital markets and issuance activities. The services they provide include advisory for mergers and acquisitions (M&A), underwriting, initial public offering (IPO) or bond issuance, and project finance facilitation.[54] Traditionally they have not accepted retail deposits like commercial banks which is why the liquidity requirements imposed on them are lighter. However, they are under the same strict regulations as commercial banks regarding market abuse, disclosure, and conflict-of-interest rules.

---

[49] Gothi (2025).

[50] India Ministry of Finance (2025, 208).

[51] Diamond and Dybvig (1983, 401–419).

[52] See, Freixas and Rochet (1997).

[53] See, Ben-Oliel (1981, 499–515).

[54] Lejot (2012, 447–458).

1.2.3.1.4.3 Development Banks

Financing infrastructure and key sectors through long-term loans (e.g., World Bank [WB], European Bank for Reconstruction and Development [EBRD]). These financial institutions are supported by government guarantees or capital injections and also get preferential funding conditions (exemptions from certain reserve requirements or access to state guarantees) in return for investing funds in projects which are strategically vital but not commercially attractive due to their nature.[55]

1.2.3.1.4.4 Participation (Islamic) Banks

The standard practices of Islamic banks consists of a prohibition against interest (riba) and the use of various profit-and-loss sharing contracts like murabahah (cost-plus financing), mudabara (profit-and-loss sharing partnership), musharaka, ijara (leasing) and wakala.[56]

1.2.3.1.4.5 Central Banks

The state controller and the ultimate lender, responsible for maintaining both price and financial stability in the economy. Banks are conferred with the power to act as legal persons, they are usually formed as corporations, hence ensuring transparency and facilitating the raising of funds. The governance structure, management boards, and internal controls are also made subject to more stringent rules, as outlined in 'Corporate Governance Principles for Banks', issued by the BCBS in 2015.[57] The members of the board and the top management are expected to perform their duties with care, loyalty, and diligence, and any breach of this may result in the application of administrative, tort, or punitive sanctions.

1.2.3.1.5 International Regulatory Framework

The soft laws produced by different global organizations are the main factor that dictate the global standards for banks. These standards, taken together, offer a regulatory lexicon that is aimed at making the banking system more resilient, more transparent, and more globally consistent.[58] Majority of regulatory framework is surrounded by the following establishments:

- The Basel Accords (I–III): Capital, liquidity ratios (liquidity coverage ratio [LCR] and net stable funding ratio [NSFR]), and leverage ratios (with Basel III final reforms, known as Basel IV, being phased in through 2028).[59]
- The Financial Stability Board (FSB): Oversees coordination of domestic authorities and aspiring for a synchronized execution.[60]

[55] See, Jiang et al. (2023, 995–1024).
[56] Khan (2012, 413–422).
[57] BIS (2015).
[58] Aleem (2022, 1–27).
[59] Kolliopoulos (2025, 840–854).
[60] Pagliari (2014, 143–156) and Weber and Staiger (2014, 82–102).

- The IMF: with the help of Financial Sector Assessment Programs (FSAPs).[61]
- The Bank for International Settlements (BIS): Providing a venue for standard-setting committees.[62]

1.2.3.2 Insurance Companies

Insurance, which plays a very important role in risk management, becomes a significant support system for individuals, institutions, and society at large. It essentially functions as a financial safety measure against unforeseen incidents, transferring the risk of occurrence of the event to the insurance company, for which the individual pays a predetermined premium. The basic idea of insurance is supported by the risk-sharing concept, whereby people who face similar risks combine their funds to mutually aid each other. Insurance firms look for people facing similar risks and make arrangements that ensure the costs of any damage are taken care of when a risk materializes. Pooling the risk of various possible losses makes a person's financial risk manageable, however large it may be.

An insurance company is the organization that provides individuals and organizations with financial security against various risks through insurance contracts. The insurance company undertakes to compensate the insured for the risk if it materializes, and the company receives a specified premium for the service. The insurance company basically plays the role of a risk manager for its insured clients. The basic aim of insurance firms is to ensure a wider reach of insurance services so that people get insured. The more the people who are insured, the more premiums the firms will get, and consequently, the financial position of the firms will improve. Insurance firms therefore develop large networks and structures.

Main activities of insurance companies can be listed under three dimensions. First, insurance companies conduct risk assessment, where insurers assess the risk profile of their insured and then set the premium charges for the risk exposed to them. Second, insurers collect premiums by policyholders periodically to provide source of funds for insurance companies. Third but not least, after the occurrence of the insured event, the insurance companies have the responsibility of paying the loss/value as stipulated in the insurance contract. These functions performed by insurance organizations are of immense significance and play a very important role in managing risks and ensuring a stable economy. This is because these organizations help ensure that the individuals and businesses are financially protected against unexpected events.

1.2.3.3 Investment Trust

An investment trust is a unique financial institution designed to make investing more accessible and rewarding for everyday people. Structured as a private company with a registered capital base, an investment trust pools together the savings of many small investors, giving them the collective strength to participate in a

[61] Zamorski and Choon-Seng Lim (2013, 37–52).
[62] Westermeier (2018, 1–18).

wide range of financial markets. What sets investment trusts apart is their focus on building diversified portfolios that can include not only stocks and bonds, but also gold, precious metals, and other assets traded on both national and international exchanges, as well as organized over-the-counter markets.

The investment trust's mission is to help individuals—who might not have the resources or expertise to manage complex investments on their own—benefit from professional management and the potential returns of a larger, more varied portfolio. Profits earned from these investments are then shared among the members in proportion to their holdings, fostering a sense of partnership and shared success.

Investment trusts are permitted to pursue opportunities across a broad spectrum, from foreign and domestic government and corporate securities to precious metals and innovative financial instruments like forwards and futures. By targeting sectors and assets with high return potential, these trusts strive to enhance their members' wealth while also providing a measure of diversification and risk management that would be difficult to achieve individually. In this way, investment trusts bridge the gap between small savers and the dynamic possibilities of the global capital markets.

1.2.3.3.1 Characteristic Features

1.2.3.3.1.1 Principle of Risk Diversification

Investment partnerships offer individual investors a powerful way to spread out their risks, reaching a level of diversification that would be nearly impossible to achieve alone. By pooling the resources of hundreds or even thousands of people, these partnerships can assemble vast portfolios that include a wide array of assets such as stocks, bonds, and other financial instruments. This collective approach means that the ups and downs of any single investment have less impact on each person, providing greater stability and opportunity for growth.

1.2.3.3.1.2 Professional Management

Navigating the capital markets requires specialised knowledge and constant attention to shifting trends. For most individuals, keeping up with these complexities is a daunting, if not impossible, task. Investment partnerships address this challenge by employing experienced professionals who can respond quickly and wisely to market changes. These teams work to ensure that the partnership's investments are managed efficiently and in the best interests of all members.

1.2.3.3.1.3 Managing a Securities Portfolio

While investment partnerships are allowed to hold cash and precious metals within certain boundaries, their primary focus remains on buying and selling securities to generate income—whether from price changes, dividends, or interest payments. By participating in an investment partnership, individuals gain not only financial returns but also important legal rights, such as the right to receive dividends, vote at shareholder meetings, and sometimes exercise pre-emptive rights. The responsibility for managing the partnership's portfolio is typically assigned to the company's founders, as set out in its governing documents.[63]

1.2.3.3.1.4 Rights of Shareholders

When an investor acquires shares in an investment partnership, this ownership brings a wide array of both financial and non-financial rights. Most notably, investors are entitled to receive a share of the profits through dividend payments, to exercise pre-emptive rights that allow them to participate in new share issuances, and to vote during the general assembly of the company. These rights not only enable investors to benefit from the partnership's financial performance, but also grant them a meaningful role in the governance and strategic direction of the institution. The responsibility for managing the investment portfolio is delegated to the founders or professional managers, as established in the company's articles of association, ensuring that the portfolio is overseen with expertise and aligned with the collective interests of all shareholders. Although investment partnerships may hold cash and precious metals within certain regulatory boundaries, their principal aim remains the acquisition and management of securities—seeking returns through capital gains, dividends, and interest income across a diverse array of financial instruments.

1.2.3.3.1.5 Protection of Assets

A fundamental principle underpinning investment partnerships is the strict separation of the partnership's securities from the personal assets of its founders and portfolio managers. This separation is crucial for maintaining objectivity, impartiality, and the trust of all investors, as it prevents any conflicts of interest from influencing management decisions. Additionally, investment trusts are subject to clearly defined prohibitions that safeguard their integrity and focus: they are not permitted to engage in lending or borrowing transactions (thereby avoiding credit and debt arrangements), cannot accept deposits like banks, are barred from participating in commercial, industrial, or agricultural activities, and are forbidden from acting as securities trading agents for others. These restrictions are foundational to the prudent, transparent, and fiduciary management of the pooled assets, ensuring that investment partnerships remain dedicated to serving the best interests of their members.

1.2.3.3.2 Differences Between Investment Trusts and Investment Funds

Investment trusts and investment funds, while both serving as vehicles for collective investment, are fundamentally distinct in their structures, operations, and investor experiences. Investment trusts are established as joint-stock companies, forming independent legal entities with their own corporate governance structures. By contrast, investment funds are not separate companies but rather pools of assets

[63] Konovalova et al. (2019, 928–937) and Meoqui and Pedraza (2011).

created and managed through contractual agreements. This distinction has significant implications for how each is formed and operated. Investment funds may only be established by certain financial institutions—such as banks, brokerage firms, insurance companies, or pension funds—while investment trusts face no such restrictions on their formation.

Access to these investment vehicles also differs. Investors can purchase participation certificates in investment funds directly from the founding institution or even through automated teller machines, offering ease of access and flexibility. In contrast, shares of investment trusts are bought and sold exclusively through authorized stockbrokers on the stock exchange, giving investors exposure to the dynamics of public equity markets.

Another core difference concerns profit distribution and liquidity. Investment funds do not pay dividends; instead, investors benefit from the appreciation of the fund's value. Investment trusts, however, may declare and distribute dividends to their shareholders, much like other publicly traded companies. When exiting an investment, fund participants redeem their shares by selling them back to the fund, whereas shares in investment trusts are traded between investors on the stock exchange and cannot be sold back to the trust. At their core, both investment funds and investment trusts serve to pool the savings of many individuals and invest them in diversified portfolios managed by professionals. Investment funds, in particular, are accessible and appealing to small-scale investors, offering a straightforward route to market participation. Investment trusts, meanwhile, operate as listed companies, with profits realized primarily through changes in the price of their securities. Both structures offer unique advantages and entry points for investors seeking professional management and diversification in their investment journey.

1.2.3.3.3 The Pros and Con

1.2.3.3.3.1 Advantages

Investment trusts occupy a distinct space within the investment landscape, offering an alternative avenue for those willing to pursue higher potential returns alongside greater risk. Unlike many traditional investment vehicles, investment trusts have the flexibility to allocate capital to a broader range of instruments, including those that may carry more risk but offer the potential for higher yields. This freedom enables them to seek out opportunities that might be inaccessible to more conventional funds.

The regulatory framework governing investment trusts is deliberately flexible, granting these institutions the latitude to pursue profit-maximizing strategies within prudent limits. Such flexibility is particularly valuable in rapidly changing markets, where the ability to respond quickly and decisively to emerging opportunities can significantly improve performance.

A notable feature of investment trusts is their willingness to support early-stage companies. By investing in start-ups and other young enterprises, investment trusts not only diversify their portfolios but also play a vital role in fostering innovation and economic growth. This capacity to channel capital into new ventures helps emerging firms secure the resources they need to expand and thrive.

Above all, investment trusts rely on professional management teams to navigate the complexities of the financial markets. These experts are tasked with maximizing returns while optimizing risk, drawing on their experience and analytical skills to manage portfolios that balance profit with careful risk management. Through this combination of flexibility, professional oversight, and a forward-looking approach, investment trusts stand out as a dynamic option for investors seeking both growth and diversification.

1.2.3.3.3.2 Disadvantages

Investment trusts offer several notable advantages that distinguish them from more conventional investment vehicles. One of the key benefits is the ability for investors to gain access to complex financial instruments—such as derivatives, structured products, or private equity—that are typically beyond the reach of individual investors. This access enables greater diversification and exposure to a wider range of opportunities. In some jurisdictions, investment trusts may also enjoy tax advantages, enabling their profits to be realized more efficiently compared to direct investments.

However, investment trusts also come with certain disadvantages that prospective investors should consider. One challenge is the relative lack of transparency: partners and broader investment communities often have limited information about the trust's detailed business activities and financial statements. Similarly, it can be difficult for outsiders to thoroughly assess fund managers' operations and decisions, which can affect confidence and decision-making.

The pursuit of higher returns in investment trusts often leads to participation in high-risk sectors. While this can yield significant gains, it also exposes investors to the possibility of substantial losses, especially if investments are made in underperforming private equity or venture capital firms. Such losses may be severe enough to offset or even erase previous profits. Additionally, investment trusts tend to attract high-net-worth individuals, which can inadvertently limit accessibility for smaller investors and reduce the overall inclusivity of these institutions. Another dynamic to consider is investors' behaviour: there is a tendency to shift funds toward top-performing trusts and away from those with weaker returns. This pattern can contribute to liquidity challenges for underperforming funds and may amplify volatility in the investment trust sector.

In summary, while investment trusts offer sophisticated investment opportunities and potential tax benefits, they also pose challenges around transparency, risk, inclusivity, and fund stability—factors that all investors should carefully weigh in their financial decision-making.

1.2.3.4 Asset Management Companies (AMC)

The origins of distressed asset management can be traced to the early 1930s. In Austria, following the financial crisis of 1929, the government intervened to manage one of the country's largest banks. After significant financial losses became apparent, the Austrian government established a distressed asset management company, Revisionsgesellschaft, which operated under the central bank's authority. The prominence of distressed asset management increased during the global banking crises of the 1980s and 1990s. These crises had severe economic consequences, prompting widespread government intervention in the banking sector. Supported by the IMF, many governments implemented bank restructuring programs, a key component of which was the sale of distressed assets to specialized asset management firms. One notable model that emerged was the London Approach, a flexible framework developed in the United Kingdom with support from the Bank of England, which provided interim assistance to distressed firms in the banking sector.

Asset management companies are essential to maintaining financial stability and supporting economic recovery. In resolving banking crises, restructuring corporate debt, and managing non-performing loans, these firms contribute significantly to the resilience of financial markets. Through the strategic acquisition, restructuring, and liquidation of distressed assets, asset management companies enable businesses and financial institutions to navigate economic uncertainty more effectively.

In cases of borrower default, financial institutions frequently transfer the debt to an asset management company through a process called debt assignment. Rather than acting as intermediaries for the original lender, these companies acquire the debt and independently pursue repayment. For banks, selling distressed assets to asset management companies is a strategic measure to reduce risk exposure and avoid additional costs associated with debt recovery. By transferring non-performing loans, banks can protect their financial stability and concentrate on core lending operations.

1.2.3.4.1 Asset Management in the US

In the US, government asset management programs emerged during the Great Depression. The FDIC was established in 1933 to enhance banking stability and manage distressed assets through deposit insurance. Both the FDIC and the Resolution Trust Corporation (RTC) primarily employed asset liquidation as their central strategy under three main columns:

i. Purchase and Assumption Transactions (P&A) approach, where financially stable institutions acquire entire failing bank's assets to ensure a smooth transition while minimising disruption of the economy.
ii. Deposit payout, where FDIC was responsible for liquidating failed institutions by selling their assets and distributing remaining funds to shareholders, also responsible for reimbursing insured depositors.
iii. Open bank assistance (OBA), where FDIC provided financial aid to banks on the verge of collapse, offering credit lines, acquiring certain assets, or directly injecting capital to help them remain operational.

1.2.3.4.2 Asset Management in Asia

The Asian financial crisis of 1997 significantly affected countries like Indonesia and South Korea. In Indonesia, nearly three-quarters of corporations became insolvent, prompting many to seek restructuring support from banks. In response, the central bank of Indonesia provided liquidity assistance to institutions that satisfied specific eligibility requirements led to severe financial distress, prompting government intervention. As part of the restructuring efforts, the Korea Asset Management Corporation (KAMCO) was restructured as a publicly traded company tasked with resolving bad debt and stabilising the financial sector.

AMCs are to acquire and manage non-performing loans (NPLs), primarily from banks and other financial institutions. These organisations focus on the recovery and collection of distressed assets by utilising expertise in restructuring processes. The primary objectives of AMCs are as follows: (i) facilitating the settlement of debts for individuals and businesses, thereby enabling their reintegration into the economy; (ii) enhancing liquidity within the financial system through the effective management of distressed assets; and (iii) improving bank balance sheets by removing bad debt and alleviating operational burdens.

1.2.3.5 Portfolio Management Company

A portfolio refers to a collection of multiple financial assets combined into a single investment entity. Portfolio management involves overseeing these assets on behalf of investors, ensuring that investment decisions align with their risk tolerance and time horizon. The primary goal is to optimize returns while minimizing risk exposure. A key concept in portfolio management is diversification, which helps reduce risk by distributing investments across different asset classes rather than concentrating them in a single category—often described as not putting all eggs in one basket.[64]

Determining which assets to buy or sell and at what time requires expertise and responsibility. Therefore, portfolio management services are provided only by banks and authorized financial institutions that have obtained regulatory approval. Firms engaged in portfolio management must adhere to strict regulations to protect investor interests. Some fundamental principles include:

- Employees of portfolio management firms are not allowed to engage in personal trading activities.
- Firms are prohibited from exploiting clients' lack of market knowledge or experience to encourage unnecessary trades for their own benefit.
- Unless otherwise stated in the contract, firms are prohibited from trading assets between their own portfolios and those of their clients. In cases of conflict of interest, they are required to act in favour of the client.

[64] Zhang (2024, 67–72).

- Without a client's written consent, portfolio managers cannot purchase securities at prices above market value or sell securities from the portfolio below market price.
- Companies cannot provide written or verbal guarantees regarding fixed returns, except in cases where legally permitted, such as capital-protected funds.
- Portfolio managers must assess clients' risk-return preferences, document these evaluations, and manage investments accordingly.

Investors typically delegate the management of their portfolios in one of two ways. Non-discretionary Portfolio Management as a first way, the portfolio remains under the investor's control, while the manager acts as an executor of their decisions. This means the manager follows client instructions on asset purchases and sales without independent decision-making authority. Routine activities, such as dividend collection and bond redemptions, are handled automatically. However, a downside of this approach is the potential for missed opportunities or delayed actions due to market fluctuations. On the other hand, discretionary portfolio management is the second way. In this arrangement, full decision-making authority is granted to the portfolio manager through a legally binding agreement. The manager has the flexibility to buy and sell securities, exercise shareholder rights, and manage assets as needed. Although the investor remains the legal owner of the portfolio, the manager operates with autonomy in making strategic investment decisions.

Investors can construct different types of portfolios based on their financial goals and risk tolerance as bond-focused and equity-based portfolios. Bond-focused portfolios are designed for risk-averse investors who prioritize capital preservation, these portfolios typically consist of government and corporate bonds, as well as treasury bills. While they offer lower returns, they provide stability and security. Equity-based portfolios, on the other hand, cater to investors with varying risk appetites, as they include stocks and other securities that fluctuate in value. The composition of such portfolios depends on market conditions and investor preferences, balancing profitability with risk management.[65]

Other investment instruments that can be included in portfolios include:

- Asset-Backed Securities
- Real Estate Investment Certificates
- Gold and Gold Certificates
- Bank Deposits and Deposit Certificates
- Foreign Securities
- Mortgage-Backed Securities
- Mutual Fund Participation Shares
- Foreign Exchange and Forex Accounts
- Repurchase Agreements (Repos)

---

[65] See, Jeong and Babiarz (2025), Huang (2024, 249–256) and Basak and Pavlova (2013, 1728–1758).

- Options and Futures Contracts
- Warrants
- Preferred Shares
- Participation Certificates
- Profit and Loss Partnership Certificates
- Bank Bills and Bank-Guaranteed Bonds
- Commercial Papers
- Treasury Bills
- Precious Metal Bonds

By strategically combining these instruments, investors can create diversified portfolios that align with their financial objectives. Portfolio management firms play a crucial role in structuring and maintaining these portfolios to maximize returns while mitigating risks.[66]

1.2.3.6 Venture Capital Companies

Venture capital (VC) is a form of private equity financing provided to startups and small businesses with high growth potential. The concept of venture capital first emerged in the US, where it played a crucial role in supporting innovative enterprises. The Great Depression of 1929, triggered by the collapse of the New York Stock Exchange (NYSE), resulted in severe economic repercussions across the US, European Union (EU), and the rest of the world. During this period, some influential business figures believed that fostering small, innovative firms could help boost employment and economic recovery in the US.[67]

The first modern venture capital firm, American Research and Development Corporation (ARD), was established in 1946. ARD was founded with four primary objectives: to support new businesses, assist existing companies in organizational development, promote the commercialization of technological innovations, and contribute to economic revitalization, particularly in the New England region. Furthermore, ARD played a key role in popularizing private venture capital funds.[68]

The legal framework for venture capital in the U.S. was first established with the enactment of the Small Business Investment Act in 1958. This law facilitated the creation of Small Business Investment Corporations (SBICs), which received federal government support.[69] Concurrently, the limited partnership model began to be adapted for venture capital investments. The first venture capital limited partnership (VCLP), Draper, Gaither & Anderson, was founded in Palo Alto in 1959. In this structure, investors acted as limited partners with restricted liability, while

66 Munizu et al. (2024, 211–220).
67 Kenney (2011, 1677–1723) and Hsu and Kenney (2005, 579–616).
68 Ibid.
69 Weinmann (1974, 183–206).

venture capitalists served as general partners, assuming management responsibilities despite holding a smaller equity share. This arrangement allowed investors to contribute capital while venture capitalists managed investment decisions.

Unlike other organizational structures, the limited partnership model in venture capital is characterized by contractual freedom, allowing investors and venture capitalists to define their rights and obligations without rigid statutory limitations. While the U.S. pioneered venture capital, its adoption in other regions was relatively slow. In Europe, only a few countries, such as the United Kingdom and Switzerland, developed substantial venture capital ecosystems. To promote venture capital investments, the European Venture Capital Association (EVCA) was established in 1983.

In Asia, Japan led the development of the venture capital industry. In 1963, Japan introduced a Small Business Investment Act similar to the US model, enabling the formation of small business investment corporations. However, unlike in the US, Japanese small business investment firms received significant government support and operated under strict regulatory oversight. This legislation marked the beginning of Japan's venture capital system. Subsequently, the Venture Enterprise Center (VEC) was established in 1974, followed by the Securities Dealers Association of Japan in 1984. From 1985 onward, private-sector venture capital firms emerged, driving further industry growth.

1.2.3.6.1 Venture Capital as a Financial Model

Venture capital financing is designed to support businesses, particularly SMEs with innovative and unproven concepts. It is typically provided during a company's early stages or rapid expansion phase. Since these businesses often lack profitability and a financial track record, venture capital is considered a high-risk investment.[70] However, venture capitalists are attracted to the potential for substantial returns if the company succeeds. In addition to financial backing, venture capitalists often offer strategic guidance and managerial expertise to help the business grow.

Funding sources for venture capital investments include commercial banks, foundations, investment groups, investment banks, and public institutions. These entities allocate funds to venture capital investments with the goal of fostering economic growth and innovation. Venture capital investments play a crucial role in supporting innovative projects and fostering economic development. By financing new technologies, services, and startups, venture capital enables entrepreneurs to enter the market and contribute to the economy. Such investments provide businesses with the necessary liquidity and credit to overcome financial challenges and achieve sustainable growth.

1.2.3.6.2 Types of Venture Capital

1.2.3.6.2.1 Early-Stage Venture Capital

[70] Tannenbaum (2025, Ch 15), Mbhele (2011, 94–11) and Lyasnikov et al. (2017, 111–122).

Capital Seed capital

This is the initial stage of venture capital investment, where a new idea has been developed but has not yet undergone technical research or market validation. Since the entrepreneur has little more than an idea, seed funding carries the highest risk for venture capitalists.[71]

Startup Capital

At this stage, investments are made in businesses requiring substantial fixed capital. This phase involves significant risk but also offers high return potential. Startup financing typically lasts between three to five years.[72]

1.2.3.6.2.2 Early Growth Financing

In this type of financing, the business is already established and has commenced production, but it faces challenges in marketing and branding. Funding is required to improve brand image, secure market presence, and implement marketing strategies. This investment stage usually spans four to six years and involves varying degrees of risk.[73]

1.2.3.6.2.3 Expansion-Stage Venture Capital

Bridge Financing

Sometimes referred to as second-stage financing, bridge financing helps businesses scale from mere production to full-capacity operation and increased market penetration. During this stage, the company aims to become profitable and establish credibility in the market.[74]

Growth Capital

At this stage, businesses have already overcome initial challenges and secured a market position. However, they require additional funding to expand production capacity and market share. Despite achieving moderate financial stability, these companies may still rely on venture capital funding rather than traditional financing sources.[75]

1.2.3.6.2.4 Exit-Stage Venture Capital

Mezzanine Financing

This type of financing supports companies that have established a strong market presence and are experiencing value appreciation. It provides financial backing

[71] Weiss (2025, 1839–1888), Manigart et al. (2015, 175–179).

[72] Sulillari (2024, 21–46) and Eno-Adams (2018).

[73] Lange et al. (2024, 247) and Svetek (2022, 1–34).

[74] Mann and Gonzalez-Uribe (2024) and Oranburg (2015, 397).

[75] Gompers (2010, 1177) and Lattanzino et al. (2023, 75–89).

until the company secures further venture capital funding or proceeds with an IPO. Mezzanine financing typically lasts six months to one year before an IPO.[76]

Replacement Capital
This form of funding is used when companies require immediate liquidity or when disagreements among founders lead to share sales. Investors purchasing shares at this stage also provide financial support to ensure the business continues growing. However, relatively few venture capital firms engage in replacement capital investments.[77]

Buyout Investments
In some cases, existing shareholders may wish to exit the company for various reasons. Buyout investments can occur in multiple forms as indicated below.[78]

Management Buyout (MBO) The company's existing management team acquires ownership.
Leveraged Buyout (LBO) Third-party investors purchase the company's shares.
Management Buy-in (MBI) An external management team takes over the company.
Employee Stock Ownership Plan (ESOP) The company's employees acquire ownership shares.

In sum, VC plays a critical role in financing startups and high-growth companies. While it offers significant return potential for investors, it also involves considerable risk. Venture capitalists typically remain invested until an exit strategy, such as an IPO or acquisition, is executed. By fostering entrepreneurship and economic development, venture capital helps turn innovative ideas into successful businesses and drives overall economic progress.[79]

1.2.4 Financial Assets

1.2.4.1 Overview of Global Financial System

The global financial system consists of institutions, markets, and regulatory frameworks that enable the allocation of capital across borders. This system encompasses central banks, international financial institutions, commercial and investment banks, asset managers, and various market infrastructures, including

[76] Jain and Myburgh (2013, 263–280), Hartmann-Wendels et al. (2011, 464–499) and Vasilescu (2010, 57–67).
[77] Pueyo and Atienzar (2025, 39).
[78] Rauch and Wahrenburg (2013, 281–302) and Renneboog (2012, 89–130).
[79] Zhong (2023, 815–820), Kato and Manchidi (2025), Jeng and Wells (2000, 241–289) and Chang (2004, 721–741).

payment systems and clearing houses. Its primary function is to facilitate international trade, investment, and economic development by supporting the movement of funds and the pricing of financial risk globally. The system operates through a combination of formal regulation, soft-law standards, and market-based discipline, each designed to maintain stability and efficiency in cross-border financial activities.

Over recent decades, globalization and technological integration have greatly increased the scope and complexity of the global financial system. Capital moves at unprecedented speed, generating both opportunities for economic growth and systemic vulnerabilities that extend beyond national borders. Consequently, international coordination, particularly through organizations such as the Basel Committee, the Financial Stability Board, and the International Monetary Fund, has become essential for mitigating contagion risks and ensuring consistent regulatory standards. The ongoing tension between national sovereignty and global market integration continues to shape the structure of international finance.

1.2.4.2 International Money Market

The international money market is a crucial component of the global financial system, enabling the cross-border borrowing and lending of short-term funds, often with maturities of one year or less. This market plays a vital role in supporting the liquidity needs of banks, corporations, and governments by offering access to a variety of short-term financial instruments, such as Eurodollar deposits, commercial paper, certificates of deposit, and short-term government securities. Benchmark interest rates, including those that have replaced London Interbank Offered Rate (LIBOR) and other interbank offered rates, are central to determining the cost of funds in this market. Regulatory oversight of the international money market is complex, involving multiple jurisdictions and diverse legal and supervisory practices. A significant portion of transactions occurs in offshore centres, leading to variations in regulatory standards compared to onshore markets and raising concerns about transparency, systemic risks, and cross-border regulatory effectiveness. Following the 2008 financial crisis, regulators have intensified efforts to reform this segment of the market by introducing stricter liquidity requirements, enhancing risk management, and bolstering the overall stability of global short-term funding channels.

1.2.4.3 International Monetary Exchange

1.2.4.3.1 Eurodollar Deposits

The term "Eurodollar" refers to unsecured US dollar-denominated deposits held at foreign banks or at the overseas branches of American banks. Since these deposits are maintained outside the US, Eurodollars are not subject to regulation by the Federal Reserve Board (FRB), including regulations concerning reserve requirements.[80] When a bank accepts a Eurodollar deposit, it receives a balance

[80] Effros (1968, 629–644) and Bartolini et al. (2008, 193–213).

with a US bank. The recipient bank can then extend dollar-denominated loans to its customers. While most of these loans are used to finance trade, many central banks also participate in the Eurodollar market. For instance, a prominent Japanese company seeking financing in euros may obtain a more favourable loan rate by borrowing in its domestic eurocurrency market, where established banking relationships exist, rather than seeking financing in France. Currently, Eurodollar futures remain available through the Chicago Mercantile Exchange (CME). However, these instruments no longer reference the LIBOR, which has been discontinued. Instead, Eurodollar futures now reference the Secured Overnight Financing Rate (SOFR).[81]

1.2.4.3.2 Eurobond Markets

A Eurobond is a debt instrument issued in a Eurocurrency by a consortium of banks and securities firms, then sold in multiple countries and traded across several international financial centres. The Eurobond market is classified based on the currency of denomination.[82] For example, Eurobonds denominated in US dollars are called Eurodollar bonds, while those denominated in British pounds are known as *Eurosterling* bonds. The term 'Euro' originated in the 1960s to describe US dollar deposits held in continental Europe. Today, a Euro-deposit refers to any deposit of a currency outside its country of origin, regardless of geographic location.[83]

A Eurodollar bond serves as a typical example of a Eurobond. For instance, if a French corporation issues a bond in Korea that is denominated in US dollars, this bond is classified as a Eurobond. Eurobonds are identified by their currency of denomination; for example, a *Euroyen* bond is denominated in Japanese yen.

The Eurobond market has expanded significantly since its inception after World War II. Eurobonds are traded electronically through clearing systems such as Euroclear and Clearstream. They may be issued in any major currency and feature varying maturity periods, depending on whether they are fixed or floating rate instruments. Fixed rate Eurobonds generally mature within 15 years, while floating rate bonds may have maturities of up to 30 years. Eurobonds are typically issued in large denominations, ranging from $100 million to $500 million.[84] Major issuers include entities such as the WB and large multinational corporations. As bearer bonds, Eurobonds are not registered in a central registry.

1.2.4.3.3 Euroequity Markets

The Euroequity market constitutes a segment of the international capital market in which corporations issue shares outside their home country to raise equity capital from a broad base of international investors.[85] In contrast to domestic stock offerings, Euroequity issues are not limited to a single jurisdiction or stock exchange;

[81] Schimpf and Sushko (2019, 29–52), Rashid (2020) and Christensen et al. (2023, 106973).
[82] Choudhry (2008, 271–285).
[83] Swoboda (1968).
[84] Kumar (2014, 97–98).
[85] Rutherford (1992, 235–236).

instead, they are marketed concurrently across several major financial centres, such as London. The emergence of the Euroequity market in the late twentieth century coincided with the liberalization of capital flows and the globalization of securities trading. Multinational corporations, particularly those pursuing international expansion, began issuing equity abroad to diversify their investor base and reduce reliance on domestic markets.[86] Frequently, Euroequity offerings are structured through global depositary receipts (GDRs) or American depositary receipts, enabling foreign investors to trade shares of non-domestic companies on major exchanges in convertible form.[87]

From a legal and regulatory standpoint, Euroequity offerings are subject to intricate cross-border compliance obligations. These offerings generally comply with the listing and disclosure requirements of multiple jurisdictions, coordinated through the International Organization of Securities Commissions (IOSCO) principles and prospectus directives within the European Economic Area (EEA). Lead managers, typically international investment banks, are responsible for structuring the issue, preparing the prospectus, and ensuring due diligence in accordance with both civil and securities law standards.

Euroequity markets play a vital role in global finance by facilitating capital mobility, ownership diversification, and enhanced corporate visibility. These markets grant firms access to larger pools of capital and provide investors with opportunities to invest in international equities without exchange-rate restrictions. Nevertheless, Euroequity offerings also present challenges related to jurisdictional overlap, investor protection, and regulatory arbitrage, which continue to influence the development of international securities law.

1.2.4.3.4 Euro-Commercial Papers Markets

Euro-commercial papers (ECPs) are short-term, unsecured debt instruments issued in a currency other than that of the country in which they are offered. As components of the broader Eurocurrency market, ECPs provide a flexible and cost-efficient financing tool for corporations, banks, and sovereign entities seeking liquidity in the international money market. ECPs generally have maturities ranging from a few days to one year, making them an essential mechanism for managing short-term funding requirements and working The Euro-commercial paper market developed in the 1980s in response to increased global capital mobility and financial innovation. Issuers are drawn to ECPs due to their lower borrowing costs relative to domestic short-term instruments. Institutional investors, in turn, are attracted by the slightly higher yields offered compared to government securities.[88]

Legally, ECPs are typically issued under standardized documentation frameworks, including the International Capital Market Association (ICMA) rules and

86 Smith and Walter (2003, 173–174) and Directorate of Economic and Policy Analysis (1987, 56–59.

87 Kallianiotis (2023).

88 Sunanda Sen, Global Finance at Risk (Palgrave Macmillan 2003), 57–109.

the EEA Prospectus Regulations, which promote transparency and investor protection. Most ECP programs operate on a continuous issuance basis under an ECP Program Agreement, enabling issuers to access funds as required within a predetermined limit. The Euro-commercial paper market connects global liquidity demand and supply by offering a rapid, low-cost financing channel that functions primarily outside domestic regulatory frameworks. This flexibility, however, highlights the necessity for robust oversight and international coordination to mitigate systemic risks associated with unregulated short-term capital flows.[89]

1.2.4.4 International Political Economy

International political economy (IPE) constitutes the intersection of politics, law, and economics, shaping the functioning of financial systems across national borders. It examines the interactions among states, international organizations, and market actors within a global context defined by interdependence, competition, and asymmetrical power relations. A comprehensive understanding of international political economy is essential for analysing how legal frameworks interact with global markets, thereby influencing financial stability, inequality, and the distribution of economic power in the twenty-first century.

IPE fundamentally addresses the allocation of resources by examining who receives *what, when, and how* within the global economic system. Although classical economists such as Adam Smith and David Ricardo emphasized market efficiency and comparative advantage, contemporary IPE recognizes that state intervention, geopolitical interests, and regulatory frameworks play significant roles in shaping global capital flows.[90]

In contemporary global finance, decisions by central banks, the IMF, and the WB shape national economies as well as international credit markets, currency stability, and investment patterns. Since the post-Bretton Woods era, defined by flexible exchange rates and increased capital mobility, financial markets have exerted greater influence over domestic policy-making. As a result, national sovereignty now frequently coexists and at times conflicts with transnational financial governance.

Furthermore, international political economy embodies a fundamental tension between the liberal paradigm, which supports open markets and deregulation, and the realist paradigm, which emphasizes state control, economic nationalism, and capital security.[91] This tension is evident in global regulatory debates, including those surrounding the Basel Accords and capital adequacy standards, as well as in the emergence of regional financial blocs such as the European Monetary Union.

[89] See, Financial Stability Board (2024).
[90] See, Walter and Sen (2009).
[91] Hsueh (2025) and Alami et al. (2021, 995–1023).

1.2.4.5 International Financial Transactions

International financial transactions involve the cross-border transfer of capital, credit, or financial instruments among governments, corporations, and individuals. These activities, which include loans, investments, securities trading, and derivatives, form the foundation of the global financial system. From a legal perspective, international financial transactions are governed by both public international law, which defines the rights and obligations of states, and private international law, which regulates relationships between private entities across jurisdictions. The complexity of these transactions results from the involvement of multiple legal systems, currencies, and regulatory standards.

The principal categories of international financial transactions are as follows: (i) cross-border lending, in which international banks provide credit to foreign borrowers through syndicated loan agreements; (ii) foreign direct investment (FDI), which entails long-term capital commitments to foreign enterprises, frequently protected by bilateral investment treaties (BITs); (iii) portfolio investment, consisting of the acquisition of equity or debt instruments issued by foreign entities; and (iv) derivative contracts, including swaps, forwards, and options, which are utilized to hedge against exchange rate or interest rate volatility.

In practice, these transactions depend on internationally recognized contractual frameworks, such as the International Swaps and Derivatives Association (ISDA) Master Agreement, to manage legal risk and ensure enforceability across jurisdictions.[92] The expansion of electronic trading platforms, offshore financial centres, and decentralized financial instruments has further obscured jurisdictional boundaries, presenting new challenges for regulators.[93] Issues including AML compliance, sanctions enforcement, and data protection have become essential elements of cross-border finance. Therefore, the legal infrastructure governing international financial transactions must balance market efficiency with regulatory oversight to ensure both capital mobility and systemic integrity within the interconnected global economy.

1.2.4.6 The Theory of Banking and Finance

The theory of banking and finance serves as the intellectual foundation for modern financial systems. It elucidates how financial intermediaries allocate capital, manage risk, and support sustained economic growth. Conceptually, banking theory addresses two fundamental functions:

(a) Financial Intermediation: Banks convert short-term liabilities, such as deposits, into long-term assets, such as loans, thereby generating liquidity within the economy.[94]

---

[92] Borowicz (2021, 72–94).

[93] Olanrewaju (2025, 1119–1136).

[94] Werner (2016, 361–379) and Diamond and Rajan (2001, 287–327).

(b) Risk transformation: Banks diversify and redistribute risk through financial instruments, which contributes to the stabilization of the credit system.[95]

In contrast, financial theory examines asset pricing, risk valuation, and investor behaviour under uncertainty. Models, including the Efficient Market Hypothesis (EMH), Modern Portfolio Theory (MPT), and the Capital Asset Pricing Model (CAPM), seek to quantify market price determination and resource allocation efficiency. The banking theory emphasized the link between credit creation and real economic activity.[96] In contrast, the post-Keynesian view highlights the endogenous nature of money and the role of credit cycles in macroeconomic instability. The global financial crises of 2008 and 2020 reinforced the understanding that financial markets are not self-correcting mechanisms but socially constructed institutions requiring robust regulatory frameworks to maintain systemic trust.[97] From a legal perspective, the theory of banking and finance emphasizes the necessity of a robust regulatory framework to maintain systemic trust. Banking law, capital adequacy standards such as Basel III, and central bank policies collectively constitute the institutional foundation supporting modern finance. Hence, the theory of banking and finance constitutes both an economic and legal discourse, examining how financial institutions mediate between risk and reward, liquidity and solvency, and freedom and regulation. This perspective highlights that finance extends beyond quantitative analysis to encompass governance, trust, and the ongoing negotiation between private profit and public interest.

1.3 The Background Information About Banking and Finance Applications

Banking and finance applications constitute the foundation of international economic relations by enabling cross-border payments, capital flows, and trade. Modern banking systems employ advanced instruments and frameworks to facilitate international transactions and mitigate risks such as currency volatility and political instability. Within global finance, banks serve as both financial intermediaries and regulatory agents, ensuring compliance with domestic and international standards. Technological advancements, especially in digital banking and global payment networks, have increased the speed and volume of international financial transactions. Additionally, global institutions such as the IMF, BIS, WTO, and the Organization for Economic Cooperation and Development (OECD) have established standards that promote regulatory convergence among the G20 and other advanced economies. As a result, international banking practices continuously adapt to geopolitical events, sanctions, and global economic crises. Regulatory

[95] Scannella (2016, 4–21) and Chen and Lin (2016, 39–69).

[96] Hodnett (2012, 849–861), Fabozzi and Grant (2011, 11–13) and Fama and French (2004, 18(3) 25–46).

[97] Fontana (2003, 291–314); See also, Rochon and Bougrine (2020).

frameworks introduced by the Basel Committee have further shaped the risk-based approach to international banking.[98] Therefore, international banking and finance applications require evaluation from legal, regulatory, technological, and geopolitical perspectives.

1.3.1 Banking Transactions for Foreign Trade

Banking transactions for foreign trade encompass the financial mechanisms that facilitate the import and export of goods and services across borders. These transactions require a comprehensive legal infrastructure, including Incoterms, documentary requirements, and currency settlement rules. Banks act as intermediaries by securing payments for exporters and providing financing and credit support for importers. Instruments such as letters of credit, documentary collections, and bank guarantees are widely used to reduce payment risks associated with commercial disputes or insolvency. In G20 economies like Germany, the UK, and Japan, specialized commercial banks operate dedicated foreign trade departments that offer trade advisory services and financial instruments. Compliance with anti-money laundering standards, sanctions screening, and enhanced due diligence has become increasingly important in foreign trade banking. Digitalization has further accelerated these transactions through electronic documentation, blockchain-based trade finance solutions, and real-time payment systems. Effective foreign trade banking requires integration with customs authorities, foreign exchange markets, and international supply chains. Overall, banking transactions for foreign trade are essential to global commerce by ensuring trust, liquidity, and operational efficiency.

1.3.2 International Banking Transactions

International banking transactions encompass activities conducted across national borders, such as cross-border payments, international lending, syndicated loans, and correspondent banking. These transactions are regulated by a complex framework of international conventions, supervisory agreements, and domestic compliance requirements. The globalization of banking has led to the rise of multinational financial institutions with branches and subsidiaries in multiple G20 countries. International banking transactions require compliance with AML regulations, sanctions laws, and international reporting standards established by organizations such as the Financial Action Task Force (FATF) and OECD. Additionally, global banks must navigate country-specific restrictions on capital movement, foreign exchange controls, and consumer protection regulations. Technological innovations, including the Society for Worldwide Interbank Financial Telecommunication (SWIFT)

[98] Schuknecht and Siegerink (2020).

networks, digital asset systems, and fintech integration, have transformed international banking operations. International banking is also vital for financing global infrastructure, trade, and investment, particularly through syndicated credit markets. Legally, these transactions demand specialized contractual documentation, sovereign risk assessment, and dispute resolution mechanisms such as arbitration. Consequently, international banking remains a complex yet strategically significant domain within global finance.

1.3.2.1 ICC-UCP 600

ICC-UCP 600, the Uniform Customs and Practice for Documentary Credits developed by the International Chamber of Commerce, serves as the primary global rulebook for letters of credit. UCP 600 establishes standard definitions, obligations, and documentary requirements to harmonize banking practices across jurisdictions. While not legally binding, UCP rules are widely adopted as contractual provisions in nearly all international letters of credit. Banks depend on UCP 600 for consistent document interpretation, clear responsibilities of issuing banks, and effective risk allocation.[99] This framework reduces legal uncertainty caused by differences in domestic banking regulations. Financial institutions in G20 countries, including the United States, China, and Brazil, regularly implement UCP rules in cross-border financing. The transition from UCP 500 to UCP 600 introduced digital compatibility, expedited processing, and clearer definitions of documentary compliance. UCP 600 also interacts with related ICC frameworks such as ISBP and eUCP, which offer further clarification, particularly for electronic documents. Ultimately, UCP 600 supports global trade by creating a consistent transactional environment for banks worldwide.[100]

1.3.2.2 Customs Procedures

Customs procedures govern the movement of goods across national borders and impose requirements for documentation, valuation, and duties. Contemporary customs frameworks utilize electronic filing systems, harmonized tariff schedules, and digital inspection tools. Customs authorities collaborate with central banks and tax agencies to monitor illicit financial flows and prevent trade-based money laundering (ML). G20 members operate advanced customs systems that support real-time clearance and risk-based inspections.[101] Required documents typically include bills of lading, certificates of origin, invoices, and customs declarations. Failure to comply may result in penalties, goods seizure, or administrative sanctions. Customs operations are also linked to World Trade Organization (WTO) trade facilitation agreements, which seek to standardize global customs practices and reduce bureaucratic obstacles. Banks frequently verify customs documentation when processing foreign trade payments or issuing letters of credit. Robust

[99] Bergami (2009, 191–203).

[100] Rodrigo (2011, 1–21) and Low (2010, 193–210).

[101] E.g., Directorate-General for Taxation and Customs Union (2025).

customs procedures enhance transparency and support the efficient operation of international trade.[102]

1.3.2.3 Foreign Trade Operations

Foreign trade operations include the legal, logistical, banking, and administrative activities necessary for international commercial transactions. These processes cover export financing, import payments, customs clearance, insurance, and international transportation. Legal instruments such as Incoterms define responsibilities for transportation, risk transfer, and insurance between buyers and sellers. Effective foreign trade operations require coordination among customs authorities, banks, logistics providers, and international insurers. International sanctions, trade embargoes, and geopolitical conflicts can restrict certain trade activities. Compliance with international trade regulations is overseen by organizations such as the WTO and national trade ministries.[103] Increasingly, foreign trade operations are digitalized through electronic documentation platforms, blockchain, and supply-chain finance technologies. Efficient foreign trade operations enhance national competitiveness and promote global economic integration.

1.3.2.4 Letter of Credit

A letter of credit is a documentary instrument issued by a bank that guarantees payment to a seller upon presentation of specified documents confirming shipment or performance. This instrument provides exporters with assurance by shifting payment risk from the buyer to a reputable issuing bank. International letters of credit are primarily governed by UCP 600, which outlines the responsibilities of issuing, advising, and confirming banks. In cross-border trade, letters of credit help mitigate risks related to distance, differing legal systems, and political instability.[104] Strict adherence to documentary requirements is necessary, resulting in a high incidence of document discrepancies worldwide. Recent innovations include electronic letters of credit (e-LCs) and blockchain-based trade finance platforms, which offer faster and more secure processing.[105] Although letters of credit (LC) can be expensive due to banking fees and compliance costs, they remain among the most reliable instruments for international trade finance.

1.4 Settlement of Disputes

Dispute settlement in international banking and finance encompasses a range of procedural mechanisms aimed at resolving conflicts related to cross-border transactions, financial contracts, and international regulatory matters. The global

[102] See, Azcarraga et al. (2022).
[103] Grainger (2012, 17–30).
[104] Bergami (2009, 191–203), Crozet et al. (2022, 185–211) and Xu (2025, 1–8).
[105] Khalil et al. (2025, 135–159).

nature of financial markets means that disputes frequently span multiple jurisdictions and necessitate complex conflict-of-laws analyses. Such disputes commonly arise in contexts including international payment defaults, insolvency, regulatory sanctions, and breaches of international financing agreements. Contemporary dispute-settlement practices increasingly employ international arbitration and hybrid resolution schemes to promote neutrality and enforceability. The complexity of international banking instruments has led to the creation of specialized arbitral rules for documentary credits, derivatives, and sovereign debt. G20 jurisdictions have implemented institutional reforms to enhance international cooperation among courts, regulators, and financial authorities. Additionally, international dispute settlement now incorporates digital processes, transparency standards, and cross-border enforcement mechanisms. These mechanisms ultimately aim to balance investor protection, regulatory stability, and the autonomy of domestic legislation.

1.4.1 Conflict of Laws

Conflict of laws in terms of private international law involves determining which legal system and jurisdiction govern disputes arising in international financial transactions. This is particularly important in cross-border banking contracts that involve multiple governing laws and different regulatory frameworks. Choice-of-law clauses play a central role in determining applicable law, especially in syndicated loans, international guarantees, and derivatives transactions. Courts and arbitral tribunals typically examine contractual intention, habitual residence of parties, and the place of performance in determining applicable law. Conflict-of-laws rules vary among jurisdictions, although the EU's Rome I Regulation and Rome II Regulation provide a harmonized model for contractual and non-contractual obligations.[106] G20 countries such as the UK and the US adopt common-law approaches emphasizing party autonomy and judicial interpretation. Conflict of laws issues have become more complex due to international sanctions, digital payments, and cross-border insolvencies. In practice, conflict-of-laws decisions aim to protect international predictability while preserving national regulatory interests. The ultimate objective is to mitigate legal uncertainty and enhance stability in global finance.

1.4.1.1 Litigation and Enforcement Actions

Litigation in international banking disputes generally entails complex procedures, such as service of process abroad, recognition of foreign judgments, and resolution of jurisdictional challenges. Financial litigation may proceed before domestic courts, specialized commercial courts, or designated international tribunals. The enforcement of foreign judgments relies on bilateral treaties, regional conventions,

[106] Born and Kalelioğlu (2021, 44).

and the principle of comity in international law. Within the EU, the Brussels I Regulation establishes a uniform framework for the recognition and enforcement of judgments among member states. In contrast, enforcement is more challenging in jurisdictions lacking mutual recognition arrangements, particularly in emerging G20 economies.[107] Enforcement actions may include attachment orders, asset freezing, or seizure of collateral across different jurisdictions. Sovereign defendants and state-owned entities often invoke sovereign immunity, thereby restricting enforcement against sovereign assets. The emergence of digital finance, cryptocurrency disputes, and financial sanctions has further complicated traditional enforcement mechanisms. As a result, litigation in international finance necessitates sophisticated procedural rules and effective enforcement strategies.

1.4.1.2 Alternative Dispute Resolution (ADR) Methods in Financial Disputes

ADR mechanisms, including mediation, conciliation, and international arbitration, have become increasingly significant in resolving financial disputes. ADR methods provide confidentiality, party autonomy, and flexibility, which are essential in sensitive banking matters. International arbitration is frequently chosen for syndicated loans, project finance, investment agreements, and sovereign debt restructuring. Prominent arbitration institutions such as the ICC, the London Court of International Arbitration (LCIA), and International Centre for Settlement of Investment Disputes (ICSID) have developed specialized rules for financial disputes. Mediation is also employed to address cross-border payment issues, contractual renegotiations, and regulatory compliance challenges. G20 economies have promoted ADR by updating arbitration laws in line with the United Nations Commission on International Trade Law (UNCITRAL) Model Law. ADR processes help avoid protracted litigation and minimize the risk of parallel proceedings in multiple jurisdictions. The adoption of digital dispute-resolution methods, such as online mediation platforms, further facilitates the settlement of international financial disputes. Overall, ADR has become a vital tool for preserving commercial relationships and expediting the resolution of complex international banking disputes.

1.4.2 Cross-Border Issues

Cross-border issues arise in international banking when financial transactions involve multiple national legal systems, regulatory authorities, or jurisdictions. These issues include international insolvency, enforcement of foreign judgments, regulatory conflicts, and disputes involving sovereign borrowers. The increasing internationalization of banking business has made traditional domestic legal frameworks insufficient for resolving modern financial disputes. International

[107] See, Hau (2025, 5–14), Shihata (1992, 173–190) and Lupo-Pasini (2018, 1–30).

cooperation among central banks, financial regulators, and judicial institutions is necessary to address systemic financial risk. G20 states employ various harmonization mechanisms through Basel standards, FATF rules, and regional cooperation agreements.[108] Emerging global economic challenges such as sanctions, digital finance, and cyber-risk have further complicated cross-border dispute settlement. Consequently, cross-border issues require a multidimensional perspective incorporating regulatory, contractual, and geopolitical considerations. Cross-border legal coordination remains essential for stability in global financial systems.

1.4.2.1 Cross-Border Insolvencies

Cross-border insolvency refers to situations in which an insolvent debtor or financial institution holds assets or liabilities in multiple jurisdictions. International insolvency raises issues concerning jurisdiction, ranking of creditors, and recognition of foreign insolvency proceedings. The UNCITRAL Model Law on Cross-Border Insolvency provides a harmonized framework that many G20 countries have adopted, including the United States, Japan, and South Korea.[109] International bank failures, including those during the 2008 financial crisis, demonstrated the need for coordinated cross-border insolvency mechanisms. Therefore, resolution regimes for banks—based on FSB Key Attributes—establish procedures for orderly resolution of systemically important financial institutions.[110] Recognition of foreign insolvency judgments remains complex in emerging markets lacking modern insolvency frameworks. Ultimately, cross-border insolvency mechanisms seek to protect creditor equality while preventing systemic disruption in international financial markets.

1.4.2.2 Sovereign Immunity, International Organizations and State Insolvency

Sovereign immunity protects states and state-owned entities from legal proceedings or asset seizure without their consent. Nevertheless, many jurisdictions adopt a restrictive approach, permitting legal action for commercial activities, including sovereign borrowing. G20 economies demonstrate varied approaches: the US enforces the Foreign Sovereign Immunities Act, while the UK implements the State Immunity Act with commercial exceptions. International organizations, including the IMF and WB, play pivotal roles in managing sovereign debt crises, facilitating restructuring negotiations, and administering financial assistance programs. State insolvency lacks formal regulation under international law, necessitating ad hoc negotiations and restructuring agreements. Notable examples include Argentina's restructuring disputes, Greece's sovereign crisis, and negotiations involving emerging-market debt. Enforcement against sovereign assets remains constrained by immunity protections, diplomatic considerations, and

[108] Davis et al. (2023, 75–130).

[109] Olivares-Caminal et al. (2016, 275–358); European Union insolvency regulations further harmonize insolvency administration within the EU. See, Ghio et al. (2021, 1–26).

[110] Cihak and Nier (2009).

public-interest concerns. As a result, sovereign immunity continues to present significant challenges within international financial law and dispute resolution.[111]

1.4.2.3 International Trade Finance

International trade finance encompasses financial instruments that facilitate global trade, such as letters of credit, trade loans, guarantees, and export-credit insurance. Disputes in this area may result from payment defaults, documentary non-compliance, or political-risk events in importing countries. International trade finance transactions are typically governed by UCP 600, ISBP, and relevant ICC rules, which standardize banking practices. Arbitration and commercial courts are commonly utilized to resolve disputes involving international banks and trading companies.[112] G20 export-credit agencies, including Euler Hermes (Germany), EXIM (United States), and Sinosure (China), offer state-supported trade finance facilities. Trade finance disputes frequently involve complex issues related to applicable law, foreign exchange restrictions, and sovereign-risk considerations.[113] Sanctions regimes, particularly those imposed by the United Nations or major G20 economies, have a significant impact on international trade finance operations. Compliance requirements, such as AML and trade-based money-laundering controls, add further complexity to dispute resolution.

1.4.2.4 Foreign Exchange Regulations

Foreign exchange regulations oversee cross-border currency transactions, capital flows, and foreign-currency financing activities. Therefore, disputes often arise from delayed approvals, licensing requirements, sanctions, and restrictions on currency transfers. Several developing G20 economies, such as India and South Africa, implement partial capital controls to safeguard foreign-exchange reserves and deter speculative outflows.[114] In contrast, prevalent liberal discourses indicate free currency convertibility with minimal administrative oversight.[115]

All banks are required to comply with local exchange-control regulations when conducting transactions involving foreign-currency loans, bond issuances, or international payments in the context of global sanctions regimes and AML obligations under FATF standards. Nevertheless, the emergence of digital-currency transactions and crypto-assets has introduced new challenges by bypassing traditional exchange-control mechanisms. As a result, foreign-exchange regulation remains a dynamic and central aspect of international financial law.

[111] See, Paliouras (2017, 115–136), Schwarcz (2016, 1–29), Lienau (2016, 151–214), Brooks (2019, 393–417), Ripple (1971, 369–382) and Weidemaier (2014, 67).
[112] Schmidt-Eisenlohr (2013, 96–112).
[113] Dawar (2023, 61–88) and Bischoff (2014, 25).
[114] Theron (2025, 21–29) and Patnaik and Shah (2009, 157–173).
[115] Abdelal (2007, 40).

1.5 Money and Banking

1.5.1 Theory

The foundations of money and banking are theories that encompass the fields of economics and law, therefore institutions and financial markets. Monetary theory provides explanations of where, how and what form of value is created by money, while banking theory describes how financial intermediaries allocate credit, provide liquidity to the economy, and contribute to economic stability.[116] To properly understand the current global monetary and financial systems requires an understanding of both the economic mechanisms as well as the complex legal and institutional structures that create incentives and define the limits of monetary authority as economies are globalized and become more innovative over time; as well as changes in regulation will create a growing number of new perspectives about digital currencies, systemic risk, macrofiscal links and the role of Central Banks in increasingly complex environments.[117] The sections below provide an overview of key concepts such as the nature of money, evolution of theoretical approaches to money, functions of banks, credit creation process, transmission mechanism for monetary policy, and central banking intellectual foundations.

1.5.1.1 The Nature and Functions of Money

Fundamentally, money is an instrument of exchange and a legal institution that enables exchange and cooperation within society. Each of the essential functions of money allows people and businesses to carry out transactions in an efficient, dependable manner. As a medium of exchange, money removes the obstacles associated with operating under a barter economy, thus allowing larger markets to operate over a broader geographical area and permitting increased specialisation of activity, making it easier to conduct cross-border trade. As a unit of account, money provides a common benchmark for establishing prices, assigning debts, and determining value in commerce or finance, thus making it possible to conduct commercial and financial calculations. By being a store of value, money allows people to move purchasing power over time. However, this requires that the currency remains stable and people have faith in the monetary system.[118] Additionally, money serves as a standard for deferred payment and creates the basis for contracts, loans, and other legal obligations; therefore, money has an important role within both the evolution of the modern economy and its existing legal- and contractual-based architecture. In modern economies, the value of money is primarily derived from public confidence, the legal regime that establishes how money works, and the institutional capacity to maintain the arrangements that support money as a medium of exchange, unit of account, store of value, and standard

[116] Lear (2025, 436–455) and Bhattacharya and Thakor (1993, 2–50).

[117] See, Douglas Arner, Ross Buckley, 'Redesigning the Architecture of the Global Financial System' (2010) 11 Melbourne Journal of International Law 1–56.

[118] Proctor (2023, 3–69), Schwarcz (2025, 1–32) and Spooner (1978, 105–137).

for deferred payment. Such arrangements are representative of the predominance of fiat currencies created by central banks.

1.5.1.2 Theories of Money

Monetary thought has evolved over time as monetary theorists made different assumptions about economic behaviour, types of institutions and the role of government. Generally, classical and neo-classical economists have viewed money as neutral over time, with real economic variables (such as output and employment) experiencing independent adjustments from monetary causes.[119] The primary function of money in these frameworks is to facilitate the exchange of goods and services and the money supply should be regulated to achieve price stability. In this regard, Ricardo stated below:

> Productions are always bought by productions or by services; money is only the medium by which the exchange is effected.[120]

The neutrality of money was challenged by Keynesian and Post-Keynesian theorists who made the claim that money directly impacts real economic activities by way of peoples' expectations about money, their liquidity preferences, and their uncertainty associated with money. The endogenous creation of money (growth of money through the banking industry) is also determined by the demand for credit, and the conditions of the financial marketplace, as opposed to being exogenous to the economy. As Keynes stated:

> The theory which I desiderate would deal, in contradistinction to this, with an economy in which money plays a part of its own and affects motives and decisions and is, in short, one of the operative factors in the situation, so that the course of events cannot be predicted, either in the long period or in the short, without a knowledge of the behaviour of money between the first state and the last. And it is this which we ought to mean when we speak of a monetary economy.[121]

The monetarist school of thought, represented by Milton Friedman, has tended to focus on the connection between money supply and inflation, and advocate for predictable, rule-based monetary policy. There is considerable support for the belief that money has a distinct "institutional" element, namely, the legal status of money based on statutory legal tender provisions, whether contract laws are enforceable, and whether the government has the ability to regulate banks and other financial institutions. Accordingly, the passage below is taken from the joint work of Friedman and Shwartz:

---

[119] Samuelson and Nordhaus (2010, 4).
[120] Ricardo (1928, 193).
[121] Keynes (1936, 408).

> In the long run, money is a veil. The real forces are the capacity of the people, their industry and ingenuity, the resources they command, their mode of economic and political organisation, and the like.[122]

Contemporary theories provide explanations for new forms of digital money and central bank-issued cryptocurrencies that affect consumers, businesses, and governments. Digital currencies create new questions regarding whether the state's authority has authority over consumer transactions or if consumers can only utilize a private currency; whether or not banks should compete with each other, and if banks are required to use their mutual funds, etc.; and, finally, how the state determines who can or cannot have a bank account.

1.5.1.3 Banking as Financial Intermediation

Through banking, the role of banks is to act as a conduit between savers and the productive investments for which they build up savings. Banks do this by converting deposits into loans to aid people in financing their daily lives, while reducing transaction costs and creating a transfer mechanism that allows consumers to access capital at a reasonable cost.[123] As a financial intermediary, the bank converts short-term liquid depositor funds (deposits) into longer-term debt (loans) that finance business activity and household consumptive activities, such as housing, automobiles, and consumer goods. Additionally, banks transform risks associated with lending by diversifying the risk across many different borrowers, loan types, and types of credit risk. However, the most critical aspect of banks is their role as information intermediaries.[124] This is because banks engage in a rigorous process of screening borrowers' ability to repay loans, monitor the performance of those loans, and build their own expertise to evaluate creditworthiness. Consequently, banks are also responsible for the payment systems that enable transactions in our society, working with the central banks and other financial institutions to provide consumers with a mechanism to access their savings and create an integrated banking system. Finally, banking systems create both liquidity and credit to facilitate the growth of an economy.[125] Therefore, banks occupy a key role within the economy by integrating both their operational capabilities and the provision of liquidity and credit with their overall obligation to create a safe and stable environment for depositors. As a result of these systemic functions of banks, the banking industry is embedded within a complex legal and regulatory structure designed to ensure consumer trust, maintaining the liquidity and credit for depositors, and protecting depositors.

---

[122] Friedman and Schwartz (1963, 696).

[123] Carney (2009).

[124] Armour et al. (2016, 118–142).

[125] Beck et al. (2023, 297–336) and Fidrmuc et al. (2015, 151–194).

1.5.1.4 The Credit Creation Process

Money is created by the modern banking system when banks make loans to people and businesses using credit cards or other credit methods. According to economic theory, the traditional view of banks as lenders simply lending out money that they have already collected from depositors does not actually match how banks create deposits through their lending activity for loans they have approved. When a customer of the bank receives an approved loan, an entirely new asset (in this case, the loan) as well as an additional liability (the new deposit credited into the borrower's account) are created at that moment. This entire transaction also increases the money supply and increases the amount of liquidity available in the economy.[126] The ability of banks to create credit through their lending activities is largely affected by not only the amount of demand from potential borrowers for loans but also by factors such as regulatory requirements (including capital requirements and reserve ratios), liquidity regulations imposed by central banks, and general economic conditions. Central banks, in turn, influence these same lending activities by establishing interest rates, regulating what type of reserves and capital banks must keep to support their lending activities, and influencing the general expectations of the financial markets. The process of creating credit through lending generates shock waves through both the economic and financial market systems, resulting in booms and busts in macroeconomic cycles. By being aware of this credit creation mechanism, we can better assess an economy's ability to expand or contract during macroeconomic cycles.

1.5.1.5 The Monetary Transmission Mechanism

The monetary transmission mechanism illustrates how central banks can affect economic activity, financial-market functioning and prices of goods and services, as well as overall economic growth.[127] Policy changes in interest rates will directly change the cost of borrowing, therefore, changing consumer behaviour and investment plans (aggregate demand). The effects of these policy changes are reinforced by the credit channel; that is, the change in the cost associated with borrowing (interest rates) and availability of cash (liquidity) to banks will determine how much money they can lend out and if they choose to extend credit to businesses or consumers. The asset-price channel is also important, as changes in central bank policy will alter the values of (and therefore price) bonds, stocks (equities), real estate and all other forms of financial assets that people hold; this shift in value will affect the wealth of consumers and ultimately, influence their spending behaviour. The exchange-rate channel links monetary policy with the global capital market; changes in interest rates between countries will affect the flow of money across international borders and therefore influence a country's competitiveness within the global marketplace. Most importantly, however, is the expectation channel, which

[126] See, Werner (2014).

[127] Ireland (2005).

serves as a transmission mechanism for all the other channels. Central banks communicate with the market about expected future actions so that investors have a good understanding of the direction that interest rates may take in the future; this communication enhances the credibility of central banks and increases the effect of monetary policy on the economy. These transmission channels work together in a very complex manner; the way that they interact with each other produces different (and sometimes) unexpected outcomes and demonstrate just how complex the relationships between monetary policy and the real economy can be.

1.5.1.6 Theoretical Foundations of Central Banking

From its inception with issuing currencies to supervising the Banking System, the development of the theory of central banking has expanded to include an integrated structure designed to support price stability, financial system stability, macro-prudential regulation, and crisis management. The importance of price stability is a foundational element of central bank theory as it represents the most critical element of monetary policy. Price stability is the foundation for sustainable economic development, reduced uncertainty, and preserved value of money. The debate surrounding whether to implement rules-based or discretionary Monetary Policies and how central bank's should respond to unpredictable economic events is another primary focus of modern central banking theory. Some theorists hold that central banks should adhere strictly to pre-determined policies, while other theorists advocate for greater flexibility in responding to changes in economic conditions.[128]

Central banks have been given the authority to serve as 'lender of last resort' by Walter Bagehot through the theory of crisis management. In Bagehot's view, central banks must provide liquidity to financially sound institutions during periods of market upheaval, subject to provisions to limit potential moral hazard. Modern theories of central banking also include a macro-prudential focus that considers the interconnections and systemic risks that exist within financial markets. As the complexity of financial systems has increased, central bank theories have evolved to include considerations of the need for the design of institutional structures, the necessity for sufficient governance of the financial services sector, and the importance of establishing legal frameworks to provide for central bank independence, accountability, and credibility.[129]

1.5.1.7 Emerging Themes in Modern Monetary Theory

Modern monetary theory is constantly shifting due to an increasing complexity of financial systems, thanks to greater global connectivity, technological innovation, and increased exposure to new sources of risk. A growing literature emphasizes the relevance of macro-financial relationships, showing not only the importance of credit cycles, asset prices, and leverage but also finding stronger-than-expected

---

[128] Balls et al. (2018) and Ugolini (2017).

[129] Bagehot (1999), Muchlinski (2024, 744–764); See also, Mehrling (2010).

influences on the transmission of monetary policy. An increasing role of shadows and market-based finance raises new challenges regarding the limits of regulatory power and the ability to design effectively applicable policy tools.[130] In parallel, the fast pace of technological changes, such as algorithmic trading and AI-based financial architectures, is changing financial landscapes, including financial intermediation, and creates new policy challenges towards control and surveillance.[131] Concurrently to such technological changes, another important source of complexity is due to the growing relevance of climate-related risks to financial systems, suggesting new implications on financial and macroeconomic stability. Another specific relevant issue regards the relation between the role of authorities on either side of fiscal-monetary policy, often faced by high levels of public sector debt and against the background of innovative unconventional tools and measures. These have revived debates on limits and sustainability of fiscal-monetary integration and future architectures of central banking systems under new conditions, such as joint exposure to financial technology, new currencies, and macroeconomic uncertainty.

1.5.1.8 Legal Dimensions of Money and Banking Theory

Given that money constitutes both an economic and a legal institution, the theoretical analysis of monetary systems must be grounded in their legal foundations. Legal tender laws establish the definition of lawful money, enabling states to promote uniformity, stability, and enforceability in commercial transactions. Central bank legislation grants the authority to issue currency, conduct monetary policy, and regulate payment systems, while constitutional provisions delineate the scope of monetary powers and safeguard the independence of monetary authorities. Banking law supplies the structural framework for market entry, licensing, and ongoing prudential oversight, setting requirements for capital adequacy, liquidity, risk management, and consumer protection. In conjunction with contract law, these legal rules provide the institutional certainty required for credit relationships, deposit-taking, and financial intermediation to operate effectively. AML and counter-terrorism financing (CTF) regulations uphold the integrity of the financial system, and international standards such as the Basel Accord, IMF Articles, and FSB principles foster cross-border harmonization and regulatory convergence. Accordingly, the legal dimensions of money and banking theory clarify how the financial system is organized, how trust in monetary instruments is sustained, and how systemic stability is maintained in an increasingly global and complex economic environment.

[130] Murau and Klooster (2023, 1319–1336) and Adrian and Jones (2018, 1).

[131] Vukovic et al. (2025).

1.5.2 History

The story of money and banking is, at its heart, a story about people—our ingenuity, ambitions, and desire to connect across time and distance. From the earliest days of civilization, communities found creative ways to represent value, using grain, metals, or precious stones not simply as objects, but as tokens of mutual trust. When ancient Lydia minted the first coins[132] and precious-metal standards spread, people gained new confidence in their transactions, knowing that money now carried a shared meaning and enduring worth.

In medieval Europe, banking became a distinctly human enterprise, flourishing in the bustling markets of Italian city-states. The Medici Bank and other early institutions did more than invent double-entry bookkeeping and bills of exchange—they fostered relationships, trust, and a sense of shared destiny among merchants and citizens.[133] The birth of central banks like Sweden's Riksbank and the Bank of England in the seventeenth century reflected society's growing need for stability and security, creating public institutions that served the common good by safeguarding currency and managing collective resources.[134]

The nineteenth and twentieth centuries brought waves of change that touched everyday lives—first through the discipline of the gold standard, then the turmoil between world wars, and later the promise of global cooperation at Bretton Woods. As money moved beyond gold to become a matter of collective trust, new challenges and opportunities emerged. Today's world of fiat currencies and digital transactions is shaped not only by technology and regulation but by the enduring human need for stability, connection, and confidence in our shared financial systems.[135]

1.5.3 Law

Banking and monetary law form the backbone of modern economic life, providing the legal framework that shapes how money is created, circulated, and regulated. At its heart, this body of law is a human response to the fundamental need for trust, stability, and fairness in financial relationships. It delineates the state's powers to issue currency and define legal tender, ensuring that money remains a reliable medium of exchange and a store of value. Beyond the core principles of

[132] Before the Lydians, trade was conducted using precious metals like gold and silver. Gold or silver were made into small ingots or coins, and these were used as money. The Lydians were the first to transform a worthless metal, any metal, into a currency and stamp it with the state's seal. In other words, money no longer had any intrinsic value like gold or silver; it was a worthless metal. Yet, the Lydian state claimed and guaranteed that this metal, this coin, was worth a certain amount of money. This is what is meant by the Lydians' invention of money.

[133] Fazzini et al. (2016, 271) and Sangster (2024).

[134] Tekdoğan (2023, 304); See, in general, Haldane and Qvigstad (2016, 627–672).

[135] Peneder (2022, 175) and Vines and Subacchi (2023, 195–209).

monetary law, banking regulation sets the standards by which institutions must operate. These regulations encompass requirements for licensing, capital reserves, liquidity, risk management, and consumer protection—all designed to safeguard the interests of individuals and the broader community. In times of crisis or institutional distress, supervision and resolution frameworks provide mechanisms to maintain confidence, prevent systemic failures, and manage the orderly resolution of troubled banks.

Increasingly, the global nature of finance necessitates international cooperation. Standards developed by organizations such as the Basel Committee on Banking Supervision, the International Monetary Fund, and the Financial Stability Board foster alignment across jurisdictions, promoting both resilience and consistency in banking practices. Legal systems now extend their reach to encompass payment services, electronic money, fintech innovation, and robust AML regimes, responding to technological change and the evolving needs of society.

In sum, the architecture of banking law is not static; it is continually shaped by the interplay of economic realities, technological advances, and the shared aspiration for stability and integrity in the world's financial systems.

1.5.4 Central Banking Issues

Modern central banks are the institutional centres of monetary stability, financial regulation, and macroeconomic management in the overall financial system of the world. The functions of central banks now go beyond issuing notes and acting as a lender of last resort and have expanded into new areas, such as evaluating institutions' soundness from a prudential perspective, preventing systemic risk, overseeing payment systems, and implementing macroprudential policies. Central banks also help to foster the continued growth of the economy through their independence from day-to-day political decision-making. The current debate on the role of a central bank includes many interrelated areas, such as: the appropriate amount and structure of independence; mechanisms for ensuring accountability and transparency; interactions between monetary and fiscal policy; and the evolving legal framework within which central banks will operate in an increasingly interconnected world as a result of technological innovation and globalisation. As central banks undergo major technological shifts, manage geopolitical uncertainty, face increasing climate-related financial risk, and prepare for potential disruption from new digital currencies, the legal and theoretical questions surrounding how to construct and operate modern central banks have never been more significant.

1.5.4.1 Autonomy, Accountability, and Governance

Autonomy of the central bank is an institutional structure creating an environment where the monetary authority can function independently of short-term political influences in creating and executing their monetary policies.[136] The basis for central bank independence is economic theory which recognized the likelihood of monetary decisions being influenced politically. Politicians tend to utilize monetary policies that are expansionary in the short-run, contributing toward creating an inflationary bias due to the political pressure on monetary decisions. By providing a way for policymakers to be insulated from these types of pressures and by enhancing the credibility of monetary institutions, autonomy provides a means to anchor long-term expectations of inflation.[137]

Furthermore, for a central bank to be considered independent, it must have a set of accountability mechanisms that counterbalance the inherent benefits of having its own authority. In a democratic society, there must be some level of accountability that the central bank is still ultimately accountable to their respective elected officials and the public, regardless of how autonomous the central bank may be. Central banks typically have some form of accountability such as required reporting to elected officials, periodic appearance before legislative bodies; public posting of policy decisions, and statutory or constitutional definitions; of their explicit goals.

While governance structures will vary among countries, generally speaking, each country will have formalised processes for how the central bank governor and board members are appointed, how long they will serve, how they can be removed from office, as well as how decision-making committees (monetary policy committees) are created and operated. The purpose of these structures is to provide the monetary policy maker with a mechanism to prevent undue external influence while ensuring that decisions regarding monetary policy are made by committees and not an individual policy maker. Modern governance places major importance on transparency, especially for central banks.[138] To increase their credibility as well as reduce uncertainties and enhance the effectiveness of the monetary transmission mechanism, they now regularly publicly release meeting minutes, inflation forecasts, and explanations or reasoning for their position on various policies.

1.5.4.2 Monetary and Fiscal Policies

One major challenge for central banks today is to maintain independence while meeting the democratic accountability of the public and be seen as not only effective in maintaining price stability but also as legitimate institutions. Monetary and fiscal policies are two of the major components of macroeconomic management, and there are important links between them both theoretically and practically. Monetary policies set by the central banks attempt to influence the macroeconomic environment by manipulating or controlling interest rates, conducting open market transactions, establishing reserve requirements, and using various other tools to affect credit conditions and the money supply. On the other hand, fiscal policies

[136] Arnone et al. (2009, 3–18).

[137] Amtenbrink (2002, 147–163), Elgie (1998, 53–76); See also, Haan and Amtenbrink (2000, 179–190).

[138] Acosta (2023, 49).

refer to the government's actions in areas such as taxation and public spending, and sovereign debt management—each of these has a significant impact on overall or aggregate demand, inflation, and long-term economic growth.[139]

Due to the relationship between the two, questions arise both theoretically and practically. For example, if a fiscal authority embarks on an expansionary budget and funds the expansion through the accumulation of debt, a central bank may feel compelled to maintain an accommodative monetary policy so that the fiscal authority is able to keep costs of borrowing low.

Due to the relationship between the two, questions arise both theoretically and practically. For example, if a fiscal authority embarks on an expansionary budget and funds the expansion through the accumulation of debt, a central bank may feel compelled to maintain an accommodative monetary policy so that the fiscal authority is able to keep costs of borrowing low.

Fiscal dominance refers to a situation where governments dominate central banks and therefore limit their independence from politicians and dampen their ability to achieve targeted inflation. On the other hand, fiscal policy that is overly restrictive limits the ability of monetary policy to act effectively; this is especially true in low-interest-rate environments where an economy may require stimulus measures that can only be achieved through coordination. The global financial crisis and the introduction of various unconventional forms of monetary policy (quantitative easing, large-scale asset purchases and forward guidance) demonstrate that the relationship between fiscal policy and monetary policy is complicated and sometimes fragile.[140]

In a modern economy, effective cooperation between monetary and fiscal authorities will respect institutional boundaries while acknowledging that to achieve economic stability, both policies need to be mutually supportive of each other. This is why an adequate framework of law must separate the monetary and fiscal responsibilities of governments, as this will help to prevent the conflicts of interests, maintain credibility in the financial markets and maintain macroeconomic stability that is required to achieve the long-term goals of monetary and fiscal authorities. Given the many problems that most governments are facing today due to demographics (i.e. the aging population), climate change, geopolitical risk, or rising levels of debt, how monetary and fiscal authorities will coordinate with one another represents a major issue in today's economic governance.[141]

1.5.4.3 Modern Central Bank Law

With the desire of finding solutions to the ongoing, rapid evolution in the environment of modern central banking, they have modernized the legal framework of the central banks to provide clear mandates, autonomy to operate as independent bodies, and hold themselves accountable and disclose their actions. This legal framework

---

[139] Mihaljek (2021, 419–432) and Nusrok (2018, 1–6).

[140] Mihaljek (2021, 419–432) and Kuttner (2018, 121–146).

[141] Yoshino and Miyamoto (2020, 249–255), Radosevic (2024, 99–114) and Wang et al. (2025, 108320).

defines both the roles of the central banks, such as the provision of interest rate policy, the management of currency supply, and the responsibilities for the supervision of financial instability (by monitoring for systemic issues and managing the risk through a macro-prudential approach), and provides other responsibilities including the oversight of the levels of payment system risk, governance of payment system technology, and the intervention process during times of crisis.[142] An important feature of modern central banking law is the establishment of codified governance principles, which promote the integrity, professionalism, and credibility of the institution itself. Governance principles often include explicit anti-political interference provisions, conflict-of-interest policies, communication standards for the general public, and mechanisms for independent, external evaluation.

The evolution of central banking law reflects, to some degree, the global harmonization of central banks as they align themselves with the global standards developed through international organizations, including the IMF, the BIS, and the FSB.[143] Most recently, the development of prudential standards, the establishment of crisis management frameworks, and the creation of macro-prudential tools have followed the establishment of international best practices. As central banks adopt increasingly innovative technologies, including digital currencies, fintech, big data analytics, and climate change-related technologies, the continued development of legal structures governing their operations will remain adaptive, future-oriented, and consistent with the evolving global standards.[144]

1.6 The Road Map

The book approaches the subject of international banking and finance law as a multi-level legal framework aimed at bolstering the stability, integrity, and operational resilience of the global financial system. The key argument presented in this book is that banking and financial activities are no longer governed solely by private contracts and other contractual arrangements, but rather are increasingly impacted (or even governed) by principles of transnational public law, that being the principles, standards and policies that came from the G20, Basel Committee and the FSB.

The book is structured is logically so as to progressively build this multi-level legal framework from the foundational concepts to the broader framework of institutional legal solvency and integrity for the typical bank over the jurisdiction of the global financial system. The study will start by examining the foundational concepts of defining the global financial system, international monetary markets and the function of credit; and then it will move into examining the institutional framework including how banks are established in major jurisdictions; the licensing processes for banks in major jurisdictions; and how banks' corporate governance mechanisms ensure their legal solvency and integrity.

[142] Plosser et al. (2016, 255–297).

[143] Manger-Nestler (2011, 165–227); See also, Satragno (2022).

[144] Martin (2023, 1–12) and Vucinic and Luburic (2024, 5).

In the next stages, the study will look more closely at the Instruments and Mechanisms used for International Financing, which include Syndication Loans, Derivative Products, Trade Financing (L/C or Letter of Credit and Bills of Exchange) and Collateral Arrangement. Detailed analysis of the Systemic Risk(s) created by these Mechanisms will follow shortly after. We highlight the need for Global Oversight Structures as defined by the Basel Accords for Prudential Regulation; the FATF standards regarding AML/CTF; and a global framework for addressing systemic crises. Next, the work will address the Paradigm Shift caused by Digitalization and Sustainability, driven by ESG forms. The analysis of crypto assets will include a legal classification; the consequences of Central Bank Digital Currencies (CBDCs); and the integration of Green Banking into traditional Financial Law. This part will examine the increasing importance of Legal Adaptation in regulation as a response to rapid technological progress.

The book reviews the multiple international dispute resolution mechanisms available to resolve cross-border financial and investment disputes (ICSID, FINRA, International Commercial Arbitration). The delicate balance between safeguarding the investor while respecting the sovereign authority to regulate has been considered in detail. This framework allows the reader to view international banking law not only as a set of technical rules but rather as an evolving legal securitization that ensures global trust and stability. The distinctive feature of this book is that it rigorously documents the internalization of G20 best practice into national and regional laws in order to benefit practitioners, regulators and academics who are interacting and resolving issues in the post-2008 global financial system.

Chapter Summary

This chapter presents a foundational, multi-layered analysis of the global financial system, with particular emphasis on its legal and economic architecture within the G20 framework. The financial system is defined as the primary mechanism for transferring surplus funds from providers to demanders, thereby converting savings into productive investment. This transfer occurs through direct finance, which involves no intermediaries, and indirect finance, which operates via institutions such as banks. The system is categorized by its structure (organized versus over-the-counter markets), maturity (money versus capital markets), and the roles of its various actors.

Financial institutions, which serve as the cornerstones of the system, are analysed for their central role as intermediaries, managing risk and transforming maturities. This section highlights the distinct legal and operational characteristics of these institutions. In this sense, banks are defined by their dual privilege to accept deposits and extend credit and are subject to strict prudential standards such as Basel III. The chapter provides a comparative overview of banking regulations across G20 jurisdictions (including the EU, US, and Turkey) and details the classification of banks, including commercial, investment, central, and participation banks. On the other hand, non-bank intermediaries include insurance companies, investment trusts (which emphasize risk diversification and professional management), asset management companies, and specialized structures such as venture capital companies, which are categorized by funding stage (for example, seed, startup, and expansion).

The chapter subsequently explores financial assets and markets, offering an overview of the global financial system and international money and monetary exchange markets. It specifically examines Eurocurrency markets, including Eurodollar deposits, Eurobonds, Euroequity, and Euro-commercial papers, and defines these as key instruments that operate outside domestic regulation and are influenced by international political economy dynamics.

With respect to banking and finance applications, the chapter details practical legal tools for foreign trade, focusing on letters of credit (governed by ICC-UCP 600) and customs procedures.

A critical section addresses the settlement of disputes, examining conflict of laws (which determines the applicable legal system), litigation, and alternative dispute resolution mechanisms such as arbitration in financial disputes. Cross-border issues, including insolvencies, sovereign immunity, and foreign exchange regulations, are discussed as sources of systemic risk that necessitate harmonized legal frameworks, such as the UNCITRAL Model Law on Cross-Border Insolvency.

Finally, the chapter presented the theory of money and banking, highlighting the functions of money (medium of exchange, unit of account, store of value) and the role of banks as financial and information intermediaries. Key theoretical concepts such as the credit creation process (endogenous money) and the monetary transmission mechanism were explained, culminating in the theoretical foundations of central banking (independence, accountability, and the lender of last resort function, as articulated by Bagehot).[145] The legal dimension emphasizes that financial stability requires a fusion of private contracts with a robust public law framework and governance principles.

Revision Questions

1. Discuss how commercial banks serve both as private businesses and as institutions that hold the public's trust (dual nature of banks). Can you think of ways this dual role shows up in the rules and regulations they must follow, like those in Basel III?
2. What does financial intermediation mean? List three types of risks that come with it—like credit, liquidity, or operational risks. Pick one type of financial institution (for example, a bank or an investment trust) and explain, in simple terms, how its legal structure helps manage one of these risks.

[145] Bagehot (1999).

3. Choose a Eurocurrency market instrument (for instance, a Eurobond) and describe what it is in everyday language. Then, consider how these markets might create challenges for countries trying to control their own money and financial rules in terms of sovereignty. What kind of legal or regulatory issues could come up?
4. Discuss on the traditional money multiplier theory and compare it with today's understanding that banks actually create money when they make loans (the credit creation process). Why does this newer perspective make tools like reserve requirements and capital rules from central banks even more important?
5. In simple terms, what does the Autonomy Principle mean for Letters of Credit (L/C) under UCP 600? Can you think of a situation where a court might step in and make an exception? Why do you think the rules are so strict about not allowing many exceptions?
6. What do you understand by the term 'Conflict of Laws' in international finance? Imagine a dispute over a syndicated loan that's supposed to follow New York law, but with lenders and borrowers from places like Türkiye and Brazil. How do you think the courts decide which country's laws apply, and how is the final decision enforced?
7. List the main stages of venture capital financing, like Early-Stage or Expansion-Stage? What's the difference—both legally and economically—between the money invested at the Seed Capital stage and at the Bridge Financing stage?
8. Why do you think deposit insurance is required by law, both from a legal and an economic standpoint? If a bank runs into trouble, how does the Deposit Insurance Fund (DIF) help protect people's savings and prevent bigger problems in the financial system?◄

References

Abdelal R (2007) Capital rules: the construction of global finance. Harvard University Press

Acosta M (2023) A new measure of central bank transparency and implications for the effectiveness of monetary policy. Int J Cent Bank 19(3):49–97

Adrian T, Jones B (2018) Shadow banking and market-based finance. Dep Pap 18(14):1

AFME (2025) AFME report identifies banking union challenges holding back EU Bank consolidation. https://www.afme.eu/news-insights/press-releases/afme-report-identifies-banking-union-challenges-holding-back-eu-bank-consolidation. Accessed 13 Dec 2025.

Aksoy B (2025) Dijital Finans Ekseninde Finansal Teknolojilerin Dünya'daki ve Türkiye'deki Gelişimi Üzerine Bir Değerlendirme. In: Ergün T (ed) Ergün H. Dijital Finans Alanında Güncel Araştırmalar, Özgür Yayınları, pp 1–29

Alami I, Dixon A, Gonzalez-Vicente R et al (2021) Geopolitics and the 'new' state capitalism'. Geopolitics 27(3):995–1023

Aleem Y (2022) Soft law: the optimal legal framework for global financial regulation. Emory Corp Governance Account Rev 9(1):1–27

Allen F, Qian J (2014) China's financial system and the law. Cornell Int Law J 47(3):499–553

Allen F, Qian J, Zhang C, Zhao, M (2013) China's financial system: opportunities and challenges. In: Fan J, Morck R (eds) Capitalizing China. University of Chicago Press, pp 63–143
Al-Sari A (2025) The collapse of silicon valley bank: a critical analysis of regulatory shortcomings and risk management under Basel III. J Bank Regul 626:61–677
Amtenbrink F (2002) On the legitimacy and democratic accountability of the European Central Bank: legal arrangements and practical experience. In: Arnull A, Wincott D (eds) Accountability and legitimacy in the European Union. Oxford University Press
Andenas M, Chiu I (2014) The foundations and future of financial regulation: governance for responsibility. Routledge
Armour J, Awrey D, Davies P et al (2016) Principles of financial regulation. Oxford University Press
Arner D, Buckley R (2010) Redesigning the architecture of the global financial system. Melb J Int Law 11:1–56
Arnone M, Sommer M, Laurens B et al (2009) Central bank autonomy: lessons from global trends. IMF Staff Pap 56(2):263–296
Australian Prudential Regulation Authority (2025) Annual Report 2024–25. https://www.apra.gov.au/sites/default/files/2025-10/APRA%20Annual%20Report%202024-25.pdf. Accessed 15 Dec 2025
Azcarraga A, Matsudaira T, Montagnat-Rentier G et al (2022) Customs matters: strengthening customs administration in a changing world. IMF
Balls E, Howat J, Stansbury A (2018) Central bank independence revisited: after the financial crisis, what should a model central bank look like? https://www.hks.harvard.edu/sites/default/files/centers/mrcbg/working.papers/x87_final.pdf. Accessed 13 Dec 2025
Bagehot W (1999) Lombart street: a description of the money market. Wiley
Bağcı G, Onar A, Büyüktosun Ö et al (2025) Fintech laws and regulations 2025—Turkey. https://www.globallegalinsights.com/practice-areas/fintech-laws-and-regulations/turkey. Accessed 15 Dec 2025
Bartolini L, Hilton S, Prati A (2008) Money market integration. J Money Credit Bank 40(1):193–213
Basak S, Pavlova A (2013) Asset prices and institutional investors. Am Econ Rev 103(5):1728–1758
Beck T, Döttling R, Lambert T et al (2023) Liquidity creation, investment, and growth. J Econ Growth 28:297–336
Benlala M (2023) Perspectives on fractional reserve banking and money creation/production through the lenses of legal and religious moral precepts and ethics. Perspect Law Public Adm 12(1):5–30
Bergami R (2009) UCP 600 rules—changing letter of credit business for international traders? Int J Econ Bus Res 1(2):191–203
Berger A, Hasan I, Zhou M (2009) Bank ownership and efficiency in China: what will happen in the world's largest nation? J Bank Finance 33(1):113–130
Bhattacharya S, Thakor A (1993) Contemporary banking theory. J Financ Intermediation 3(1):2–50
Ben-Oliel R (1981) Elements for a legal definition of commercial banking: a comparative view. Israel Law Rev 16(4):499–515
BIS (2015) Corporate governance principles for banks. https://www.bis.org/bcbs/publ/d328.htm. Accessed 15 Dec 2025
Bischoff B (2014) ECA-cover in Germany: does foreign content policy need to be reconsidered? Cesifo Forum 15(3):25
Born G, Kalelioğlu C (2021) Choice-of-law agreements in international contracts. Georg J Int Comp Law 50:44–118
Borowicz K (2021) Contracts as regulation: the ISDA Master Agreement. Cap Mark Law J 16(1):72–94
Brooks S (2019) The politics of regulatory design in the sovereign debt restructuring regime. Glob Gov 25(3):393–417

Carney M (2009) What are banks really for? https://www.bankofcanada.ca/wp-content/uploads/2010/03/sp300309.pdf. Accessed 11 Dec 2025
Chang S (2004) Venture capital financing, strategic alliances, and the initial public offerings of internet startups. J Bus Ventur 19(5):721–741
Chen H, Lin K (2016) How do banks make the trade-offs among risks? The role of corporate governance. J Bank Finance 72:39–69
Chitimira H, Mavhuru L (2024) A comparative analysis of the design and implementation of the Twin Peaks Model of financial regulation in South Africa and Australia. Potchefstroom Electron Law J 27:1–33
Choudhry M (2008) The Eurobond market. In: Fabozzi F (ed) Financial markets and instruments. Wiley, pp 271–285
Christensen B, Kjær M, Veliyev B (2023) The incremental information in the yield curve about future interest rate risk. J Bank Finance 155:110973
Cihak M, Nier E (2009) The need for special resolution regimes for financial institutions—the case of the European Union, IMF Working Paper, WP/09/200
Crozet M, Demir B, Javorcik B (2022) International trade and letters of credit: a double-edged sword in times of crises. IMF Econ Rev 70(2):185–211
Daver G (2023) An assessment on bank openness, open banking and open data in Turkey. J Econ Financ Res 5(1):83–108
Davis R, Madaus S, Marcucci M et al (2023) Financial institutions in distress: recovery, resolution, and recognition. Oxford University Press
Dawar K (2023) Export credit agencies: the consequences of non-transparency. In: Manchin M, Puccio L, Yıldırım A (eds) Coherence of the European Union Trade Policy with its non-trade objectives: World Trade Forum. Cambridge University Press
Diamond D, Dybvig P (1983) Bank runs, deposit insurance, and liquidity. J Polit Econ 91(3):401–419
Diamond D, Rajan R (2001) Liquidity creation and financial fragility: a theory of banking. J Polit Econ 109(2):287–327
Directorate of Economic and Policy Analysis (1987) Internationalization of the securities markets: Chapter II—factors affecting the trend toward internationalization of the securities market. https://www.sechistorical.org/collection/papers/1980/1987_IntSecMktRep_05ChapterII.pdf. Accessed 16 Dec 2025
Directorate-General for Taxation and Customs Union (2025) EU-Canada AEO Mutual Recognition Agreement enters into force, boosting trade security and efficiency amid global uncertainty. https://taxation-customs.ec.europa.eu/news/eu-canada-aeo-mutual-recognition-agreement-enters-force-boosting-trade-security-and-efficiency-amid-2025-08-01_en. Accessed 15 Dec 2025
Dobby C (2025) Bank regulator 'Gratified' trade war hasn't hit Canada harder. https://www.bloomberg.com/news/articles/2025-06-26/canada-maintains-bank-capital-level-despite-uncertain-economy?embedded-checkout=true. Accessed 15 Dec 2025
Edwards A, Lovegrove S (2025) PRA consults on proposed increase in FSCS deposit protection limit. https://www.regulationtomorrow.com/eu/pra-consults-on-proposed-increase-in-fscs-deposit-protection-limit. Accessed 15 Dec 2025
Effros R (1968) The whys and wherefores of Eurodollars. Bus Lawyer 23(3):629–644
Egli D (1999) How global are global financial markets? The impact of country risk. https://www.bis.org/publ/confer08n.pdf. Accessed 15 Dec 2025
Elgie R (1998) Democratic accountability and central bank independence: historical and contemporary, national and European perspectives. West Eur Polit 21(3):53–76
Eno-Adams I (2018) Strategies for improving technology startup capital. https://scholarworks.waldenu.edu/cgi/viewcontent.cgi?params=/context/dissertations/article/7292/&path_info=Inibehe_Eno_Adams_Strategies_for_Improving_Technology_Startup_Capital.pdf. Accessed 15 Dec 2025
European Central Bank (2025) 2025 stress test of Euro Area Banks—final results. https://www.bankingsupervision.europa.eu/ecb/pub/pdf/ssm.Report_2025_Stress_Test_202508.en.pdf. Accessed 13 Dec 2025

Fabozzi F, Grant J (2011) Equity portfolio management. Wiley
Fabozzi F, Modigliani F, Jones F (2009) Foundations of financial markets and institutions. Prentice Hall
Fama E, French K (2004) The capital asset pricing model: theory and evidence. J Econ Perspect 18(3):25–46
Fazzini M, Fici L, Montrone A et al (2016) A modern look at the Banco de Medici: governance and accountability. Int Bus Econ Res J 15(6):271–286
Fidrmuc J, Fungacova Z, Weill L (2015) Does bank liquidity creation contribute to economic growth? Evidence from Russia. Open Econ Rev 26(3)
Financial Conduct Authority (2025) AI update. https://www.fca.org.uk/publication/corporate/ai-update.pdf. Accessed 15 Dec 2025
Financial Stability Board (2024) Enhancing the functioning and resilience of commercial paper and negotiable certificates of deposit markets. https://www.fsb.org/uploads/P220524.pdf. Accessed 15 Dec 2025
Fitch Ratings (2024) Chinese G-SIBs on track to meet minimum TLAC requirements. https://www.fitchratings.com/research/banks/chinese-g-sibs-on-track-to-meet-minimum-tlac-requirements-03-12-2024-1#:~:text=Fitch%20Ratings%2DShanghai%2FHong%20Kong,January%202028%2C%20says%20Fitch%20Ratings. Accessed 15 Dec 2025
Fontana G (2003) Post Keynesian approaches to endogenous money: a time framework explanation. Rev Polit Econ 15(3):291–314
Freixas X, Rochet J (1997) Microeconomics of banking. MIT Press
Friedman M, Schwartz A (1963) A monetary history of the United States, 1867–1960. Princeton University Press
Funcao D (2024) FRTB in Brazil—objectives, challenges and impacts for risk teams. https://www.ssctech.com/blog/frtb-in-brazil-objectives-challenges-and-impacts-for-risk-teams. Accessed 15 Dec 2025
Georgakopoulos N (2017) The logic of securities law. Cambridge University Press
Ghio E, Boon G, Ehmke D et al (2021) Harmonising insolvency law in the EU: new thoughts on old ideas in the wake of the COVID-19 pandemic. Int Insolv Rev 30(3):1–26
Ginting L, Ruhana N, Halim N et al (2019) Legal and regulatory framework of Islamic banking and finance: a study in Singapore. Int J Manage Appl Res 26(4):235–244
Goddard J, Wilson J (2016) Banking: a very short introduction. Oxford University Press.
Godwin A, Ramsay I (2016) Twin Peaks—the legal and regulatory anatomy of Australia's system of financial regulation. University of Melbourne Legal Studies Research Paper No 725
Gompers P, Sahlman W (2022) Entrepreneurial finance: A casebook. Wiley
Gothi V (2025) India's digital payment boom drives financial inclusion at scale. https://ibsintelligence.com/ibsi-news/indias-digital-payment-boom-drives-financial-inclusion-at-scale. Accessed 15 Dec 2025
Grabowiecki J (2006) Keiretsu groups: their role in Japanese economy and a reference point (or a paradigm) for other countries. Visiting Research Fellow Monograph Series No. 413
Grainger A (2012) Customs and trade facilitation: from concepts to implementation. World Customs J 2(1):17–30
Greenbaum S, Thakor V, Boot A (2015) Contemporary financial intermediation. Academic Press
Guo Y, Liu X, Zhang M (2025) From advantage to disadvantage: how FinTech impacts small banks? Financ Innov 11
Güney A (2023) Banka Hukuku. Beta
Haan J, Amtenbrink F (2000) Democratic accountability and central bank independence: a response to Elgie. West Eur Polit 23(3):179–190
Haba S, Ito Y, Kasai Y (2025) The impact of negative interest rate policy on interest rate formation and lending. https://www.boj.or.jp/en/research/wps_rev/wps_2025/data/wp25e01.pdf. Accessed 15 Dec 2025
Haldane A, Qvigstad J (2016) The evolution of central banks. In: Bordo M, Eitrheim Ø, Flandreau M et al (eds) Central banks at a crossroads: what can we learn from history? Cambridge University Press, pp 627–672

Hardie I, Macartney H (2016) EU ring-fencing and the defence of too-big-to-fail banks. West Eur Polit 39(3):503–525

Hartmann-Wendels T, Keienburg G, Sievers S (2011) Adverse selection, investor experience and security choice in venture capital finance: evidence from Germany. Eur Financ Manage 117(3):464–499

Hau W (2025) Unified European rules on the recognition and enforceability of third-country judgments. Law Criminol J 2(2):5–14

Hodnett K (2012) Capital market theories: market efficiency versus investor prospects. Int Bus Econ Res J 11(8):849–861

Hsu D, Kenney M (2005) Organizing venture capital: the rise and demise of American research and development corporation, 1946–1973. Ind Corp Chang 14(4):579–616

Hsueh R (2025) Bringing the sector back in and the new political economy: the contextualized comparative sector approach. Perspect Polit

Huang Y (2024) Construction of multiple type assets portfolio based on stocks, options, futures, ETFs, bonds and cryptocurrencies. Adv Econ Manage Polit Sci 105(1):249–256

Ibrahim D (2010) Debt as venture capital. Univ Ill Law Rev 4:1177

India Ministry of Finance (2025) Economic Survey 2024–25. https://www.indiabudget.gov.in/economicsurvey/doc/echapter.pdf. Accessed 21 Jan 2026

Ireland P (2005) The monetary transmission mechanism. Federal Reserve Bank of Boston Working Papers No 6-1

Jain S, Myburgh P (2013) Mezzanine capital. In: Baker H, Filbeck G (eds) Alternative investments. Wiley, pp 263–280

Jeng L, Wells P (2000) The determinants of venture capital funding: evidence across countries. J Corp Finan 6(3):241–289

Jeong D, Babiarz P (2025) Willingness to take financial risks and portfolio choice: the moderating role of financial planners' advice. Financ Plann Rev 8(3)

Jiang S, Xia J, Xu J et al (2023) A theory of national development bank: long-term investment and the agency problem. Econ Theor 76:995–1024

Joseph Y (2008) Competition and cooperation among global and regional financial centres. https://www.bis.org/review/r080514c.pdf

Kallianiotis J (2023) International financial transactions and exchange rates. Springer

Kato A, Manchidi N (2025) Venture capital's role in driving nascent enterprises to industry market leaders. Cogent Bus Manage 12

Kellaf T (2024) Blockchain in trade finance: the good, the bad and the verdict. Mod Financ 2(2):135–159

Kenney M (2011) How venture capital became a component of the U.S. National System of Innovation. Ind Corp Change 20(6):1677–1723

Keynes J (1936) The general theory of employment, interest and money. In: Johnson E, Moggridge D, Robinson A (eds) The collected writings of John Maynard Keynes, vol 7. Cambridge University Press

Khalil M, Padmanabhan R, Hadid M et al (2025) AI driven transformation in trade finance: a roadmap for automating letter of credit document examination. Digit Bus 5(2)

Khan M (2012) Islamic banking practices: Islamic law and prohibition of Riba Islam Stud 50(3):413–422

Kolliopoulos A (2025) Global banking regulation in the era of the new state interventionism. J Bank Regul 26:840–854

Konca Z (2025) Banking 5.0 and the changing dynamics in Turkish banking sector. Int J Econ Polit Humanities Soc Sci 8(2):142–159

Konovalova M, Kuzmina O, Mikhaylov A et al (2019) The management of investment portfolios. TEM J 8(3):928–937

Kumar R (2014) Strategies of banks and other financial institutions: theories and cases. Academic Press

Kuttner K (2018) Outside the box: unconventional monetary policy in the great recession and beyond. J Econ Perspect 32(4):121–146

Lange J, Rezepa S, Zatrochova M (2024) The role of business angels in the early-stage financing of startups: a systematic literature review. Adm Sci 14(10):247
Lattanzino G, Litov L, Megginson W et al (2023) Capitalizing enterpreneurship: the rise of growth equity. J Appl Corp Financ 35(2):75–89
Le C, Shan Y, Taylor S (2020) Executive compensation and financial performance measures: evidence from significant financial institutions. Aust Account Rev 30(3)
Leal A, Haase M (2025) Instant payments and banks: the impact of pix on bank branches in Brazil. Revista Economia Ensaios 40(1):146–171
Lear W (2025) Modern monetary theory and fiscal-monetary policy frameworks. East Econ J 51:436–455
Lejot P (2012) Investment banks. In: Caprio G (ed) Handbook of key global financial markets, institutions, and infrastructure. Academic Press, pp 447–458
Lienau O (2016) The challenge of legitimacy in sovereign debt restructuring. Harv Int Law J 57(1):151–214
Liew C (2025) OSFI to Big Banks: take smart risks and expand lending. https://ca.finance.yahoo.com/news/osfi-big-banks-smart-risks-203000793.html. Accessed 15 Dec 2025
Low H (2010) UCP 600: the new rules on documentary compliance. Int J Law Manage 52(3):193–210
Lupo-Pasini F (2018) Financial disputes in international courts. J Int Econ Law 21(1):1–30
Lyasnikov N, Frolova E, Mamedov A et al (2017) Venture capital financing as a mechanism for impelling innovation activity. Eur Res Stud J 20(2):111–122
Maity S, Sahu T (2022) Financial Inclusion and the role of banking system. Palgrave Macmillan
Manger-Nestler C (2011) Impacts of international law on the restructuring of the global financial system. Max Planck Yearb United Nations Law 15:165–227
Manigart S, Standaert T, Vanacker T (2015) Seed and venture capital. In: Audretsch D, Hayter C, Link A (eds) Concise guide to entrepreneurship, technology and innovation. Edward Elgar, pp 175–179
Mann W, Gonzalez-Uribe J (2024) Venture debt as bridge financing. https://papers.ssrn.com/sol3/papers.cfm?abstract_id=5002114. Accessed 15 Dec 2025
Martin V (2023) New challenges for central banks. Econ Challenges 12(23):1–12
Mbhele T (2011) The study of venture capital finance and investment behaviour in small and medium-sized enterprises. South African J Econ Manage Sci 15(1):94–11
Mehrling P (2010) The new Lombard street: how the Fed became the dealer of last resort. Princeton University Press
Meoqui L, Pedraza J (2011) The importance of adopting a good management strategy. J Current Issues Financ Bus Econ 4(3):221–253
Mihaljek D (2021) Interactions between fiscal and monetary policies: a brief history of a long relationship. Public Sector Econ 45(4):419–432
Mishkin F (2016) The economics of money, banking, and financial markets. Pearson
Monnet C, Quintin E (2005) Why do financial systems differ? History matters. European Central Bank Working Paper Series No. 442
Muchlinski E (2024) Bagehot and the stabilising function of central banks. Eur J Hist Econ Thought 31(5):744–764
Munizu M, Mulyati S, Zikirullaeva N (2024) Portfolio diversification strategy and its influence on investment risk and return in the capital market. Multifinance 1(3):211–220
Murau S, Klooster J (2023) Rethinking monetary sovereignty: the global credit money system and the state. Perspect Polit 21(4):1319–1336
Nofal S, Freddo D, Vargas J (2023) Banking regulation in the United States after the world economic crisis of 2007/2008: economic immunity or false hopes. Braz Keynes Rev 8(2):209–234
Nusrok J (2018) The interplay between monetary policy and fiscal policy. Int J Cent Bank 14(3):1–6
Odinet C (2021) Predatory fintech and the politics of banking. Iowa Law Rev 106:1765–1768

Office of the Superintendent of Financial Institutions (2025) OSFI holds domestic stability buffer rate at 3.5%—June 2025. https://www.osfi-bsif.gc.ca/en/news/osfi-holds-domestic-stability-buffer-rate-35-june-2025. Accessed 15 Dec 2025
Olanrewaju A (2025) Harnessing Decentralized Finance (DeFi) protocols for institutional asset securitization in cross-jurisdictional banking ecosystems. Int J Sci Res Arch 15(1):1119–1136
Olivares-Caminal R, Douglas J, Guynn R et al (2016) Debt restructuring. Oxford University Press
Oppolzer K (2019) Ring-fencing in Europe. Nomos
Oranburg S (2015) Bridgefunding: crowdfunding and the market for entrepreneurial finance. Cornell J Law Public Policy 25:397
Pagliari S (2014) The Financial Stability Board as the new guardian of financial stability. In: Moschella M, Weaver C (eds) Handbook of global economic governance. Routledge, pp 143–156
Paliouras V (2017) The right to restructure sovereign debt. J Int Econ Law 20(1):115–136
Papi L (2005) Central bank autonomy without monetary policy. Trans Stud Rev 12(1):3–18
Patnaik I, Shah A (2009) The difficulties of the Chinese and Indian exchange rate regimes. Eur J Comp Econ 6(1):157–173
Peneder M (2022) Digitalization and the evolution of money as a social technology of account. J Evol Econ 32:175–203
Phang R (2024) Singapore's emerging regulatory approach to stablecoins. Banking Financ Law Rev 40(1):67–104
Pinheiro F, Savoia J, Securato J (2015) Basel III: impact on banks in Brazil. Revista Contabilidade & Finanças 26(69):346–361
Plosser C, Shultz G, Williams J (2016) Panel on independence, accountability, and transparency in central bank governance. In: Cochrane J, Taylor J (eds) Central bank governance and oversight reform. Hoover Institution Press
Powley H, Stanton K (2017) The post-crisis approach and new challenges to banking regulation. Inst Law J 1:58–80
Proctor C (2023) The concept of money. Oxford University Press
Pueyo F, Atienzar M (2025) Private finance market. Comision Nacional del Mercado de Valores
Radosevic D (2024) Geopolitical risks and unconventional RMB internationalization: a reappraisal. In: Wang H, Miao M (eds) Enhancing global governance in a fragmanted world: prospects, issues, and the role of China. Springer
Rashid M (2020) Eurodollar futures, LIBOR and the SFOR, MRPA Paper No. 101760
Rauch C, Wahrenburg M (2013) Buyout funds. In: Baker K, Filbeck G (eds) Alternative investments: instruments, performance, benchmarks, and strategies. Wiley, pp 281–302
Ren C, Lu L (2025) Lender of last resort in China: operating mechanism, legal foundation, and the financial stability implication. Asia Pacific Law Rev 1–32
Renneboog L (2012) Leveraged buyouts and public-to-private transactions. In: Cumming D (ed) The Oxford handbook of private equity. OUP, pp 89–130
Ricardo D (1928) Principles of political economy and taxation. Everyman
Ripple R (1971) Sovereign Immunity vs. Execution of Judgment: a need to reappraise our national policy. Boston College Ind Commer Law Rev 13(2):369–382
Rochon L, Bougrine H (2020) Credit, money and crisis in post-Keynesian economics. Edward Elgar
Rodrigo T (2011) UCP 500 to 600: A forward movement. Murdoch Univ Law Rev 18(2):1–21
Rosengren E (2019) The macroprudential implications of the 1990s Japanese financial crisis, 5th annual macroprudential conference, Eltville, Germany
Rutherford D (1992) Routledge dictionary of economics. Routledge
Salievna A (2019) Analysis and definition of bank-finance terms. Eur J Res Reflect Educ Sci 7(12):681–685
Samuelson P, Nordhaus W (2010) Economics. McGraw-Hill
Sangster A (2024) The emergence of double entry bookkeeping. Econ Hist Rev 78(2):1–19
Satragno L (2022) Monetary stability as a common concern in international law. Brill

Saunders A, Cornett M (2013) Financial institutions management: a risk management approach. McGraw Hill
Scannella E (2016) Theory and regulation of liquidity risk management in banking. Int J Risk Assess Manage 19(1–2):4–21
Schimpf A, Sushko V (2019) Beyond LIBOR: a primer on the new reference rates. BIS Q Rev 29–52
Schmidt-Eisenlohr T (2013) Towards a theory of trade finance. J Int Econ 91(1):96–112
Schmulow A, Mazzola P, Zilva D (2021) Twin Peaks 2.0: avoiding influence over an Australian Financial Regulator Assessment Authority. Federal Law Rev 49(4):1–25
Schnabl G (2015) Monetary policy and structural decline: lessons from Japan for the European crisis. Asian Econ Pap 14(1):124–150
Schuknecht L, Siegerink V (2020) The political economy of the G20 agenda on financial regulation. OECD
Schwarcz S (2016) Sovereign debt restructuring: a model-law approach. J Glob Dev 1–29
Schwarcz S (2025) Money: a functional analysis. Stanf J Law Econ Bus 30(1):1–32
Sekhon M (2024) Japan ends its negative interest-rate policy. https://www.franklintempleton.co.uk/articles/2024/equity/japan-ends-its-negative-interest-rate-policy. Accessed 15 Dec 2025
Sen S (2003) Global finance at risk. Palgrave Macmillan
Shihata I (1992) The settlement of disputes regarding foreign investments: the role of the World Bank, with particular reference to ICSID and MIGA. In: Effros R (ed) Current legal issues affecting central banks volume I. IMF, pp 173–190
Smith R, Walter I (2003) Global banking. OUP
Spooner F (1978) The three functions of money: accounts, exchanges, and assets. Diogenes 26:105–137
Stowell D (2010) An introduction to investment banks, hedge funds, and private equity, the new paradigm. Academic Press
Sugiyama S (2025) BOJ to raise rates once more this year to 0.75%, most likely in Q3. https://www.reuters.com/markets/rates-bonds/boj-raise-rates-once-more-this-year-075-most-likely-q3-2025-02-20. Accessed 15 Dec 2025
Sulillari J (2024) Why start-ups struggle to secure venture capital funding: investigating the factors that shape venture capital investment decisions. Ikonomicheski Izsledvania 33(7):21–46
Svetek M (2022) Signaling in the context of early-stage equity financing: review and directions. Ventur Cap 24(4):1–34
Swoboda A (1968) The Euro-Dollar market: an interpretation. https://ies.princeton.edu/pdf/E64.pdf. Accessed 15 Dec 2025.
Tannenbaum F (2025) Venture capital financing. In: Ennico C (ed) Advising small businesses. Clark Boardman Callaghan
Tekdoğan Ö (2023) Green central banking: a new role for the central banks in the financial system. J Central Bank Law Inst 2(2):301–326
Tiryaki G, Yılmaz A (2012) The relationship of banking regulation and financial stability: case of Turkish economy 1990–2010 period. Marmara Univ J Econ Adm Sci 32(1):69–94
The Association of Business Executives (1999) Corporate finance. https://opac.uma.ac.id/repository/_corpfin1.pdf. Accessed 15 Dec 2025
Theron N (2025) Can South Africa afford full Liberalisation of exchange controls? Some lessons from international experience. South African J Econ 66(1):21–29
Ugolini S (2017) The evolution of central banking: theory and history. Springer
Valdez S, Molyneux P (2016) An introduction to global financial markets. Palgrave Macmilan
Vasilescu L (2010) Financing gap for SMEs and the Mezzanine capital. Ekonomska Istrazivanja 23(3):57–67
Vines D, Subacchi P (2023) From the Bretton Woods system to the global non-system: the trials and tribunals of slow learning. Oxf Rev Econ Policy 39(2):195–209
Vucinic M, Luburic R (2024) Artificial intelligence, fintech and challenges to central banks. J Central Bank Theory Pract 13(3):5–42

Vukovic D, Dekpo-Adza S, Matovic S (2025) AI integration in financial services: a systematic review of trends and regulatory challenges. Humanities and Soc Sci Commun
Walter A, Sen G (2009) Analyzing the global political economy. Princeton University Press
Wang J, Narayan P, Gunadi I, Hermawan D (2025) Climate change and financial risk: Is there a role for central banks? Energy Econ 144:108320
Weber R, Staiger D (2014) Financial stability board: mandate and implementation of its systemic risks standards. Int J Financ Stud 2(1):82–102
Weber W, Devaney M (2002) The global economy and Japanese bank performance. Manag Financ 28(10):33–46
Weidemaier M (2014) Sovereign immunity and sovereign debt. Univ Ill Law Rev 1:67–113
Weinmann E (1974) Venture capital for small business. Univ of Balt Law Rev 3(2):183–206
Weiss G (2025) A theory of seed financing. Univ Ill Law Rev 5:1839–1888
Werner R (2014) Can banks individually create money out of nothing?—The theories and the empirical evidence. Int Rev Financ Anal 36:1–19
Westermeier C (2018) The bank of international settlements as a think tank for financial policy-making. Policy Soc 37(3):1–18
Werner R (2016) A lost century in economics: three theories of banking and the conclusive evidence. Int Rev Financ Anal 46:361–379
Williams R (2022) Regulating Canada's banking system: tackling the 'Big Shall Not Buy Big' problem. In: Linquist E, Howlett M, Skogstad G et al (eds) Policy success in Canada: cases, lessons, challenges. Oxford University Press, pp 247–266
World Bank and South Asia Regional Vice Presidency (2025) India—Financial Sector Assessment. https://documents1.worldbank.org/curated/en/099103025110514063/pdf/BOSIB-606133f7-2e00-4696-9b41-57f3737d140d.pdf. Accessed 15 Dec 2025
Xu Y (2025) Clarifying four key issues regarding letters of credit: the most important international payment method. Asia Pacific Econ Manage Rev 2(5):1–8
Yoshino N, Miyamoto H (2020) How does population aging affect the effectiveness of monetary and fiscal policy? Glob Solut J 5:249–255
Zamorski M, Choon-Seng Lim V (2013) Financial stability insights from recent IMF/World Bank FSAP assessments. Seacen Financ Stab J 1:37–52
Zhang C (2024) The significance of portfolio management in investment and financial decisions. Adv Econ Manage Polit Sci 75(1):67–72
Zhong W (2023) The ongoing importance of venture capital in the economy. BCP Bus Manage 44:815–820

Further Reading

Diamond D, Dybvig P (1983) Bank runs, deposit insurance, and liquidity. J Polit Econ 91(3):401–419
Ela-Andrada, Puşcaşu (2022) The impact of financial systems on economic growth in European Union member countries Abstract Proceedings of the International Conference on Business Excellence 16(1) 722-731 10.2478/picbe-2022-0068
Lastra R (2015) International financial and monetary law. Oxford University Press
Mishkin F, Serletis A (2011) The economics of money, banking, and financial markets. Pearson
Ricks M (2011) Regulating money creation after the crisis. Harv Bus Law Rev 1
Werner R (2016) A lost century in economics: three theories of banking and the conclusive evidence. Int Rev Financ Anal 46:361-379
Wood P (2008) The law and practice of international finance. Sweet & Maxwell

International Banking

2

Contents

F. B. Erdem, *The Principles of International Banking, Finance and Investment Law*, Springer Textbooks in Law, https://doi.org/10.1007/978-3-032-32505-1_2

Abstract

International banking and international trade are fuelled by each other's existence. While World trade has become a single market with technological developments, living standards are changing rapidly, international trade and electronic commerce are being carried out, banks must break the moulds of their working methods and not only keep pace with this change but also lead it. Financial institutions also receive their share from financial globalisation. In connection with globalisation, financial instruments increase, and fund movements accelerate. Banks providing international banking services are generally concentrated in places such as London, Tokyo, New York, Paris and Hong Kong. The most important task of these banks is to provide finance from domestic investors to foreign users or from foreign investors to domestic users. International banking operations include current account, risk capital, retail deposits, business loans, money market instruments, international leasing, European foreign currency deposits, portfolio investment consultancy, consumer loans, reference and guarantee transactions, free zone banking, foreign exchange transactions, future, swap and option transactions, export credit, leasing, factoring, forfaiting, international fund transfers, gold, silver and commodity pledging services. This part of the study aims to provide a legal framework and comparative analysis in the context of international banking.

2.1 Introduction: The Legal and Economic Importance of International Banking

International banking holds a pivotal place in the financial system as a vital component of the present world economic order. Even as free capital mobility across the world has not eroded borders nations physically, it has eliminated them virtually in economic terms. Therefore, international banking still exists as a national and supranational field. This is because the legal framework of international banking affects directly not only the operations of financial institutions, but also the functioning of international trade, capital movements, foreign exchange market stability, and therefore the viability of economic growth.[1]

> **Important**
> The German Herstatt Bank crisis in 1974 demonstrated both the weakness of the international banking system and the inadequacy of the regulatory steps prevalent at the time, as the swap risk arising in the form of a differential in time in foreign exchange transactions in the case of an economy that was small in size caused havoc for the domestic and international financial system. The Basel Committee on Banking Supervision (BCBS) was formed as a result of the crisis, and the financial system was re-formed with Basel I, II and III.[2]

The primary function of banks as financial institutions is to act as intermediaries between those in possession of more money (surplus units of funds) and those who do not have money (deficient units of funds). However, international banking activities do not just limit to funding transfers alone; other activities such as foreign exchange business, trade finance, investment banking, use of derivative products, and international payments system management are also part of international banking activities. Banks hold a pivotal position here both with regard to international financial market stability and security of international economic relations by playing such a wide array of functions. Therefore, regulation under law of international banking operations constitutes a normative framework that not only determines financial stability but also areas of interpenetration of states' sovereignty power.

The international banking sector has made significant progress, particularly due to technological financial innovations and deregulation trends in the financial sector. However, the 2008 Global Financial Crisis demonstrated that this apparent growth could be highly misleading and was built on fragile foundations. The crisis exposed the fragility of a system in which financial institutions were tightly interconnected, but national regulations were insufficient to oversee these connections.[3]

> **Important**
> As a result of the 2008 crisis, the G20 platform has become central to global financial governance and has taken on the task of developing common principles for regulating banking activities. The standards set by the G20 in the areas of financial stability, capital adequacy,

---

[1] Papaioannou (2005); See also, Howells and Bain (2008).

[2] Proxmire (1975) 18; De Rosa (2013) 172.

[3] Admati and Hellwig (2013) 4–12.

risk management and supervision have been integrated into the policy frameworks of national authorities.[4]

The intensification of international bankingactivities is highly significant in terms of distributing risk across different economic regions and, consequently, spreading the risk that may arise over capital. When evaluated from an economic perspective, this situation also contributes to the creation of global liquidity.[5] However, there is no rose without a thorn: the anticipated benefits may also give rise to significant risks such as cross-border insolvencies, arbitration disputes, capital movement controls and ML risks. This demonstrates the necessity for international banking regulations to be very strict.

Due to the international nature of the effects of banking operations, banks are required to follow the decisions and standards of institutions such as the Basel Committee, the IMF, the G20 and the WB, or regional institutions such as the EBU (European Banking Union), particularly in terms of risk assessment.[6] At this point, it is possible to refer to a three-tiered structure in the regulation of international banking as national level (e.g. the FED and OCC), regional level and global level.

This multi-layered structure gives banking law a dynamic character. For example, the financial reform agenda adopted at the 2009 G20 Pittsburgh Summit paved the way for the development of Basel III standards, which were subsequently adapted into the domestic law of many countries.[7] Thus, the effectiveness of soft law instruments in the regulation of international banking has increased. Given that financial systems are becoming increasingly integrated as a result of globalisation, it can be said that the financial systems of developing countries have become highly sensitive to external developments. This situation has increased the importance of the financial inclusion policies pursued by the G20[8] since enhancing the resilience of banking systems has now become a legal requirement. All these changes have directly rendered international banking practices relevant to the sovereign domains of states. Particularly, the free mobility of capital restricts the effectiveness of domestic monetary policy and necessitates the regulation and surveillance of foreign banking operations within the state. This has bred the theory of 'transnational financial governance'.[9]

▶ **Important**

Banking regulations have not only the objective to protect national interest but also to promote the stability of world finance. Therefore,

[4] Schuknecht and Siegerink (2020); Gordon Smith (2011); Nicholas Bayne (2025) 249–263; Claessens and Kose (2018) 15.

[5] Claessens and Van Horen (2014) 32.

[6] BCBS (2011) 5.

[7] BIS (2017).

[8] Khan et al. (2022) 12,688; Maity and Majumder (2025) 14–24.

[9] Goodhart (2011) 22; Nölke (2004) 155–175.

befitting its economic function of international banking, it is necessary that it should also be subject to the law. International banking law can thus be described as an area at the intersection of private law, public law, and economic law.

2.2 Historical Evolution of International BankingActivities

The evolution of international bankingtraces its roots back to the second half of the nineteenth century, a time of the rapid development of international trade and the Industrial Revolution. It was a time when the export of capital, financing of foreign trade, and foreign exchange transactions were the pillars of the modern banking system. London, for example, emerged as the centre of international finance during the late nineteenth century with British banks facilitating foreign investment and funding economic activity in the empire.[10] These phenomena created the genesis of the international bankingsystem as a financial empire which expanded together with world trade.

2.2.1 The Bretton Woods Era and the Genesis of Multilateral Institutions

Following the World War II, when the financial system of the world was being reconstructed, the bases of modern international banking were formed. In 1944, the Bretton Woods system came into place with a regime of fixed exchange rates, linking the US currency to gold and other currencies to the dollar. This system placed the US dollar as the keystone of the stability of the world's finances.[11] Simultaneously, the establishment of the IMF and WB institutionalized global cooperation in finance monitoring and development lending.

One of the Bretton Woods system's distinguishing characteristics was increased predictability that it accorded to banking operations. The fixed exchange rate mechanism simplified the management of foreign exchange risk for banks and provided a firm foundation for cross-border financing growth. But the system's structural vulnerabilities, largely due to increasing US balance of payments deficits, rendered it unsustainable. The Nixon Shock of 1971, which dislinked the dollar from gold, initiated the transition to a postmodern epoch of floating exchange rates and liberalization of international capital.[12]

---

[10] Cassis (2011) 73.

[11] Benassy-Quere and Pisani-Ferry (2011) 12; Eichengreen (2008) 5–6.

[12] Obstfeld and Taylor (2004) 100.

2.2.2 The 1970s: The Emergence of the Eurodollar and Offshore Markets

The 1970s were a turning point in the history of international banking. The liberalization of US capital controls and greater liquidity following the oil shocks fuelled the development of the Eurodollar market. Eurodollars are dollar deposits held outside the US, and these markets soon became an accommodating source of funds largely unshackled by the constraints of regulation.[13] Rising extremely quickly in the centres of London, Paris, and Zurich, these markets extensively widened international banks' cross-border borrowing and lending activity.

Simultaneously, the concept of 'offshore banking' emerged. Low taxation and minimal regulatory burden attracted foreign capital to the offshore centres. Cayman Islands, the Bahamas, and Luxembourg were some of the territories that found themselves playing a significant role in cross-border banking transactions.[14] These developments, as much as they increased finance, also increased the inherent risk of cross-border financial instability due to minimal supervision.

2.2.3 The 1980s–1990s: Financial Liberalisation, Basel Regulations, and Technological Transformation

From the 1980s, numerous countries had systemic financial liberalisation policies through removing capital mobility barriers. During the period, the Basel I standard, published by the BCBS, was the initial global example of regulation of capital adequacy in international banking. Basel I established minimum capital requirements in terms of credit riskand created a common framework of safety for the banking system. With financial globalisation increasing speed during the 1990s, banks became increasingly active in emerging markets, triggering more cross-border banking activity in Asia, Latin America, and Eastern Europe.[15] The Asian Financial Crisis of 1997, however, revealed the weakness created by the uncontrolled expansion of cross-border capital flows.[16]

2.2.4 The 2000s and Beyond: The G20 Era and the Basel III Reform

The most profound disturbance in global banking history was the 2008 Global Financial Crisis. At the heart of the crisis causes were weak implementation of capital standards, uncontrolled spread of financial innovations, and growth of the

[13] Windecker (1993) 383–384.
[14] Fichtner (2016) 1034–1063.
[15] Joyce (2011) 875–895.
[16] Radelet and Sachs (1998).

shadow banking system rapidly.[17] International financial regulation entered the foreground with the G20 in response. The reform agenda that was put into action at the 2009 Pittsburgh Summit paved the way for the creation of Basel III, which introduced sweeping changes like increased liquidity ratios, targeted leverage ratio levels, and required additional capital buffers by SIFIs.[18] The rules improved not only the resilience of the banking sector but the worldwide macroprudential policy coordination as well.

This time also saw much cooperation between G20 countries in such issues as the exchange of financial data, crisis management mechanisms, and bank resolution procedures (bail-in/bail-out).[19] As a result, international bankingwas transformed from being largely market-based to being firmly re-anchored in a multilateral system of financial management.

2.2.5 Digitalisation, Sustainable Finance, and the New Era

From the beginning of the 2010s, digital technology initiated a full-fledged revolution in international banking systems. Mobile banking, artificial intelligence-based risk assessment, and blockchainaccelerated cross-border payment systems, reduced costs, and intensified competition.[20] Meanwhile, environmental and social sustainability policies brought green bankingand sustainable finance concepts to the agenda.

International banking today sits at the crossroads of global regulation and financial integration. While the G20 and the Basel Committee attempt to harmonize technological innovation with the compliance of rules. the legal nature of digital banking and crypto assets remains one of the most debated topics in international financial law.

Briefly, international banking is a system that has developed amid relentless historical progress—starting with the nineteenth-century trade finance, through the Bretton Woods regulated money system, through innovative Eurodollar markets and Basel reforms, and into regulation in the digital age. The evolution demonstrates that banking is not simply undergoing an economic but also an extensive legal evolutionary process.

[17] Cintra and Farhi (2009).

[18] Mashamba (2018) 37–38; BCBS (2011).

[19] Lendermann (2025) 370.

[20] Costa et al. (2025).

2.3 Determinants of the Shift Towards International Banking

International bankinggrowth is not an inevitable by-product of economic growth, but a complex process governed by the inter-penetration dynamics among globalisation, technological innovation, and legal regulation. While determinants of international bank activity vary in terms of background history and geographic conditions, they can be broadly treated under six broad categories of economic liberalisation, technological innovation, widening of trade, corporate strategies for globalisation, liberalisation of capital flows, and transnational law regimes.

2.3.1 Macroeconomic Potential and Economic Policies

Economic liberalisation policies and macroeconomic potential have been the cause of the expansion of international banking. Since the 1980s, the majority of jurisdictions, following neoliberal economic policy, de-controlled their capital, opened their interest rates up to market forces, and later opened up their financial markets to foreign investment. This revolution encouraged banks to play a more active role in international markets.[21]

Macroeconomic stability is also a required starting point for international banking. Reliable low inflation, honest monetary policy, and sustainable public debt open the door for foreign capital flows into a country. That is why macro-economic policy coordination among the G20 countries has become a cornerstone of worldwide financial stability.[22] From the perspective of the global bank, high economic growth potential countries are good new market prospects. For instance, the rapid economic growth of Asia and Latin America since the post-1990 era compelled European and American banks to concentrate on these two continents.[23]

2.3.2 Foreign Trade and Financing Needs Expansion

Foreign financing of trade is among the main driving forces of international banking. Expansion in the value of the trade of goods and services has motivated banks to create specialized products such as foreign exchange operations, letters of credit, and guarantees. Banks are now a pivotal element of global supply chains (through international trade finance flow facilitation. The expansion of foreign trade volume has, on the other hand, brought about additional financing needs, particularly for emerging economies. Financings of energy projects, infrastructure investments, and industrial development in emerging economies have contributed to higher

[21] See, Toporowski (2005) 106–112.
[22] Vines (2010) 157; Triggs (2018) 1309.
[23] Claessens and Horen (2014) 306.

demand for external finance. This has propelled international banks to make the market efficient using sophisticated financial instruments such as syndicated loans and project finance. Further, digitalisation and electronic data interchange systems within trade finance have driven transaction speeds and reduced costs, which has enabled international trade to be made accessible by a more integrated financial system.

2.3.3 Evolution of Transport and Communication Technologies

Technological innovation is one of the most powerful drivers of growth in international banking. Better telecommunications, online banking, and information technology facilitated banks to maintain simultaneous worldwide operations, bridging geographical distances. For example, the SWIFT system was established in 1973, revolutionising cross-border payment systems, allowing banks to transfer money abroad securely, speedily, and in an organized format.[24] Then AI, blockchain, and big data analytics elevate the standards of legal security in global banking operations such as risk assessment, know your customer (KYC) and AML.[25] They not only transformed the operational effectiveness but also the character of financial regulation. Electronic infrastructure makes it easier for supervisory authorities to monitor cross-border transactions in real-time, and that gave rise to the concept of digital regulation.

2.3.4 Corporate Internationalisation Strategies

Internationalization of banking is largely dependent on corporate strategy decisions. Host markets are accessed by domestic banks for diversifying revenue sources and market risk -sharing. The internationalization typically occurs in phases: correspondent bankingarrangements, representative offices and branches, and finally, integration into host markets through subsidiaries or affiliates. Internationalization forms comprise legal as well as operating commitments differences. For instance, US banks' establishment of branches in offshore destinations in London and the Caribbean in the 1960s was a strategic move influenced by both tax advantage and liquidity management.[26] Moreover, the expansion of European banks into Latin American and Middle Eastern markets since the 1990s boosted local competition, further propelling the emergence of a polycentric global banking system.[27]

---

[24] Scott and Zachariadis (2012) 462–483.

[25] Jiao (2023) 302–309.

[26] Schenk (1998) 222–223.

[27] Alvarez (2023) 489.

2.3.5 Capital Movements Liberalisation and Financial Integration

The liberalisation of capital flows after 1950 has been the greatest single driving force behind international banking. Financial liberalisation has exposed investors and borrowers to world sources of funding, thereby boosting international banks' intermediation business.[28] Financial integration has also accelerated through capital account liberalisation, with foreign banks' operations expanding in developing markets. During the process, the G20 and OECD implemented international standards of information exchange to ensure transparency of financial flows.[29] In parallel, liberalisation has further increased the contagion effect of the financial crisis. The 1997 Asian Crisis and the 2008 Global Crisis demonstrated that liberalizing capital flows in the absence of adequate macroprudential arrangements injects systemic risk.[30]

2.3.6 Transnational Regime of Action and Conformance with Regulation

The legal system is significant in international banking for risk diminution caused by differences in the law between jurisdictions. Capital and liquidity standards decided by the Basel Committee, surveillance policy by the IMF, and development programs by the WB make up the institutional regime of action in complying with regulation. Furthermore, the G20 financial regulation agenda has sought solution with a common principle to promote global financial stability. In this case, soft law instruments—such as Basel standards and FSB recommendations—though not legally binding on domestic legal systems, de facto constitute the normative basis of international banking.[31] With the current agenda of digitalisation and sustainability, the future banking law has evolved to have an even broader vision, including financial stability and not merely issues such as data protection, cybersecurity, environmental risk, and ethical governance.

2.4 Organisational Structure in International Banking

The organisational pattern of international banking is inextricably linked with the legal structures and supervisory frameworks of the countries to which banks are affiliated. The organisational form that a bank with overseas activities assumes not only determines efficiency in operations but also juridical liability, supervisory control, and the degree of systemic risk. Hence, organisational structure is

[28] Obstfeld and Taylor (2004) 167–170.
[29] See, OECD (2021).
[30] Besar et al. (2011) 195–300.
[31] Lastra (2015) 552.

a fundamental area of concern in international banking, which requires analysis from economic as well as juridical perspectives. The activities of foreign banks are generally categorized into five broad organisational forms: foreign branches, representative offices, correspondent banks, foreign subsidiaries/affiliates, and consortium banks. The Edge Act Corporation is a special one in the US framework.

2.4.1 Foreign Bank Branches

A foreign bank branch is a banking operation fully integrated into the host country's financial system, sharing the same legal personality as its parent bank. As branches are not separate legal entities, all liabilities fall directly on the parent institution. While this structure offers the advantage of capital efficiency (since the branch relies on the parent's capital base), it introduces complexities in the division of legal and supervisory responsibility. For example, a Frankfurt branch of a British bank is supervised by both the PRA in the UK and Bundesanstalt für Finanzdienstleistungsaufsicht (BaFin) in Germany. This can lead to issues of dual supervision during financial crises.

Example

In the EU, single passport rule allows licensed banks in a member state to establish branches in other member states without acquiring further authorisation. Whilst the rule has accelerated cross-border banking integration, it has simultaneously facilitated the rapid transfer of risks across the border.◀

2.4.2 Representative Offices

Representative offices typically constitute the initial entry stage of a bank into a foreign market. These offices hardly undertake direct banking activities such as lending and taking deposits. Instead, they undertake activities such as market research, developing client relations, and gathering information. Legally, representative offices are associated with a low regulatory risk in that they generally do not require a full operating license. They may, however, have indirect risks through financial crime, ML, and potential shadow banking operations. For this reason, most jurisdictions require representative offices to follow rigorous registration systems involving information sharing.[32] These offices quite literally serve as the advance scout of global expansion plans of major banks, frequently being upgraded to branches or subsidiaries upon success in the market.

[32] See, Byrne et al. (2022).

2.4.3 Correspondent Banking

Correspondent banking is the functional and historical base of the international payment and trade finance system. In it, one bank (the correspondent) holds an account for another bank (the respondent) in another country and conducts payment or collection transactions on the respondent's account. The system funded international trade in most of the mid-twentieth century. The SWIFT system infrastructure significantly enhanced the efficiency of the correspondent banking, creating an inter-linked network among over 120,000 daily messages globally.[33] However, the architecture also permits the formation of complex risk chains. More stringent oversight under AML and CFT regulations in the post-2010 era has led most big international banks to reduce (or de-risk) their correspondent relationships. This risk avoidance has undermined cross-border payment flows, particularly in emerging markets, resulting in problems of financial exclusion.[34] Thus, the G20 and the IMF encourage the upkeep of correspondent banking relationships under a regime of sustainable transparency.

2.4.4 Foreign Subsidiaries and Affiliates

Foreign subsidiary or affiliate is a host country-incorporated bank that has its own independent legal personality. The structure limits the direct liability of the parent bank while providing the host country with full supervisory powers (e.g. The Dodd-Frank Act 2010 gives the Federal Reserve System supervisory powers over those financial institutions that the FSOC, determines to be systematically significant).[35] The model has become increasingly popular in the post-crisis era. Post the 2008 global financial crisis, foreign branches were given a boost by most jurisdictions to convert into subsidiaries through ring-fencingpolicies.[36] This helped local regulators to better protect local liquidity and insulate the local system from foreign parent distress. One advantage of the subsidiary framework is its operation within the host nation's national capital cushions and resolution systems. Systemic risk can still increase, though, if intragroup exposures (risk between the parent and subsidiary) are not monitored and controlled well.[37]

2.4.5 Consortium Banks

Consortium banking is defined as the joint creation of an international bank by a number of banks, commonly based in different countries. This type became

[33] Scott and Zachariadis (2012) 466.
[34] Grolleman and Jutrsa (2017).
[35] Lastra (2015) 49.
[36] Herring and Carmassi (2014) 87.
[37] Landaberry et al. (2021) 100, 032.

successful, particularly in Europe, during the 1960s and 1990s.[38] While the consortium structure facilitated advantages in risk-sharing and market access, managerial decision-making complexity, information asymmetry, and legal differences were inclined to undermine the long-term sustainability of such an arrangement. Today, this structure has been replaced largely by international syndicated lending or more creative strategic alliances.

2.4.6 Edge Act Corporation (the US Example)

The Edge Act Corporation is a type of unique banking institution available exclusively in the US system, authorized under the 1919 Edge Act. They can be engaged to do only international banking and financial activities. The Edge Act structure aided US banks to become involved in international investment financing as well as international trade finance while simultaneously shielding foreign companies from domestic risk. Operating under the umbrella of the Federal Reserve, these companies typically specialize in provision of external financing for international trade to multinational companies. This arrangement provided crucial flexibility during 1980 to the height of international competition, enabling major US banks (e.g., Citibank and Chase Manhattan) to compete for Latin American and Asian businesses.

2.4.7 Assessment: The Organisational Structure with a G20 Focus

In the view of the G20, the organisational structure of international banking is inherently tied to the paramount goals of financial stability and compliance regulation. Cooperation among the different supervisory regimes, particularly for systemically significant international institutions, is decisive for crisis management as well as effective exchange of information. The standards of TLAC, which were reached at the 2014 Brisbane Summit of the G20, established a common legal framework for cross-border bank resolution and restructuring.[39] The cross-border activities of systemically significant banks under this require obligatory coordination among supervisory authorities at the branch and subsidiary levels. This means that the organisational structure of international bankingis not a straightforward internal corporate choice but one of the most fundamental pillars of global financial regulation.

[38] Drach (2024) 287–310.

[39] See, Knight (2015); Abascal and Fraile (2014).

2.5 The Sectoral Impacts and Competition of the International Banks

Global banking expansion has significantly changed not only world financial markets integration, but also the architecture of national banking industries, competition patterns, and efficiency in resource allocation. Banks operating across G20countries have made a great contribution towards deepening capital and credit markets, simultaneously creating structural forces aimed at destabilizing regulatory balance developed by national regulators.

2.5.1 Macroeconomic Effects of International Banks

The most fundamental effect that international banks have is in how they can shape international capital flows. Multilateral banks effectively shift capital from developed, mature economies to developing and emerging economies. This, if stable, has the effect of increasing domestic investment and growth levels.[40] Yet, the growing financial globalization has strongly increased the likelihood that such cross-border flows will lead to financial instability. The Asian crisis of 1997 and the 2008 global financial crisis starkly portrayed how the massive and sudden foreign banks' capital flight could lead to drastic economic downturns in host countries. To that end, the G20 and the IMF strongly recommend regulating and managing capital flows with robust macroprudential measures to counterbalance systemic risk. Apart from that, international banks have a typical influence on exchange rate stability, interest rate spreads, and domestic liquidity conditions. Owing to the fact that their sources of funds are often international in nature, international banks can potentially destabilize the effectiveness of national monetary policiesbecause central banks are exerting decreasing levels of control over traditional instruments.[41]

2.5.2 Competition Dynamics: The Global Banking Race

Competition in international banking is largely shaped by three main strategic dimensions. First, the depth of activities that refers to how broad and far-reaching a bank's products and services are-for example, whether they combine commercial and investment banking. Second, geographic spread, which is about how extensively a bank can reach global markets and build cross-border networks. Third, technological competence that covers a bank's ability to use advanced digital banking channels and data analytics effectively.[42]

[40] See, Bazbauers and Engel (2021).

[41] Bitar (2021).

[42] See, Vives (2016) 57.

Since the 1990s, both deregulation and technological advances have made the banking sector more competitive. In particular, American and European banks have employed cross-border M&A to gain significant economies of scale worldwide.[43] Nevertheless, deregulation has not always had positive effects. For example, the US Gramm-Leach-Bliley Act of 1999 repealed the separation between investment and commercial banking, allowing banks to consolidate these services. While this boosted short-term competitiveness, it also increased long-term systemic risk. Today, G20 countries have a similar perception that competition needs to align with the principle of responsible finance. According to a 2020 OECD report, sustainable competition should support financial stability rather than undermine it.[44]

2.5.3 European, American, and Asian Competitive Models of Banks

Different regions around the world each have their own distinct competitive models in the international banking sector. For instance, European banks are among the most advanced, especially when it comes to designing and implementing Basel standards. The big players, overseen by the ECB, benefit from economies of scale and intense cross-border financial connections within the Eurozone. Nevertheless, the sovereign debt crisis of the 2010s illustrated that high leverage and poor asset quality left some banks struggling to compete.[45] As another example, New York's banks still lead the world in financial innovation, especially in areas likes securitization, derivatives, and other new funding tools. But their rapid, largely unregulated growth was one of the main causes behind the 2008 financial crisis.[46] As a final example, most Asian banks after the 1997 crisis took a more cautious approach to growth. Japan and South Korea have already relied on strict regulations to keep their financial systems stable. In contrast, Chinese banks, have been expanding aggressively abroad over the past decades, most notably with the Belt and Road Initiative (BRI), which has established new markets in Africa and Central Asia.[47]

2.5.4 Post-Crisis Competitive Order and G20Policies

In the post-2008 crisis period, the global competition model shifted towards a model of fewer but stronger banks. While the largest banks were compelled to

[43] Nnadi and Tanna (2013) 848–862.

[44] Jawadi et al. (2025).

[45] Lopez-Penabad et al. (2021) 4.

[46] For the breakdown of 3-6-3 traditional banking business model, see Admati and Hellwig (2013) 53.

[47] Roy-Chaudhury (2019) 153–164.

significantly increase their capital bases, some small and medium-sized banks were threatened by merger or liquidation procedures.[48]

2.5.5 Assessment: Legal Dimension of International Competition

International bank competition is not only an economic competition but also a crucial legal one. The competitive dynamics are immediately affected by banks' authorized activities, licensing systems, taxation systems, and norms for information treatment. The level playing field doctrine, which has been on the G20's agenda since recent years, seeks to lower the regulatory differences between nations that may distort competition.[49] Therefore, there is a new interdisciplinary field at the intersection of financial regulation and competition law: international financial competition law. Lastly, the global banking sectoral impacts have created a multi-level system not only driven by economic size but actually influenced by regulation, technology, and ethical criteria. Most importantly, it is crucial for the G20 countries to steer this multi-level system in such a manner that the banking sector remains a stabilizing force in the world financial system.

2.6 Risks and Supervision in International Banking

International banking activities involve large cross-border flows of capital, complex financial instruments, and transactions involving several jurisdictions, a field where both financial and legal risks are concentrated. Regulation and supervision of these risks are essential not only for the safety and soundness of each bank but also for the stability of the whole global financial system. The most significant risks arising in international banking are discussed under the following major headings, in accordance with Basel Committee standards[50]:

2.6.1 Systemic Risk

The risk of bankruptcy or extreme difficulties of a financial institution threatening the entire financial system and the real economy through a chain reaction. Global Systemically Important Banks (G-SIBs) due to their size and complexity are considered to be the main sources of systemic risk.[51]

[48] Maslak and Senel (2023) 201–220.
[49] Ratnovski (2013).
[50] BIS (2006) 22–27.
[51] Ellis et al. (2022) 31; Qi et al. (2025) 104,298.

2.6.2 Credit Risk

A risk that the borrower (counterparty) will default or be delayed in its contractual payments. In international lending, this risk is compounded when combined with other country risks and sovereign risk factors. Credit risk is the risk that a borrower will fail to meet its obligations. For international banks, credit risk is a double-edged risk due to both foreign exchange rate volatility and cross-border lending. The simple innovation of Basel I was to define the minimum capital requirement against the risk. In Basel II, internal rating-based approaches were introduced to measure credit risk. This method allows banks to use their own risk models while providing supervisory authorities with the authority to approve models. Most recently, the financial implications of climate change have added a new dimension of credit risk to the limelight: environmental and social credit risk.[52] According to the G20Sustainable Finance Working Group report, default risk on carbon-intensive sector debt is now explicitly linked to environmental policy.[53]

2.6.3 Liquidity Risk

The risk that a bank lacks sufficient cash or readily convertible assets to meet the bank's maturing obligations at a reasonable cost and when due. Abrupt disruptions in international markets can quickly increase this risk. Basel III has set two key ratios to measure liquidity risk.[54] While LCR is the ratio of high-quality liquid assets to a 30-day stress scenario, NSFR is the quantity of stable funding relative to a one-year time horizon.

2.6.4 Market Risk

The risk of losing money in a bank's on-balance sheet or off-balance sheet positions due to adverse shifts in financial market prices (interest rates, exchange rates, stock prices). Cross-border transactions particularly exacerbate exchange rate risk. Basel II's Trading Book regulations are based on the Value at Risk (VaR) approach to measuring market risk. However, after the 2008 crisis, this approach was not enough; instead, the Expected Shortfall (ES) measure was introduced.[55]

---

52 Mouti,

53 G20 (2022) 86, 95.

54 Tammenga and Haarman (2020) 367–378.

55 Acerbi and Tasche (2002) 379–388; Tasche (2002) 1519–1533.

2.6.5 Operational Risk

Operational risk is financial loss resulting from human error, system failure, or external events. Basel II proposes three approaches to quantify this risk: the basic indicator approach, the standard approach, and the advanced measurement approach.[56] The most vital component of operational risk presently is cyber risk. With the digitization of banks' systems, cyber-attacks and data breaches have become the factors most directly threatening financial stability.[57] The G20Riyadh Declaration 2020 categorizes cyber risk management as a precedence policy area of the resilience of the financial system.[58]

2.6.6 Reputation Risk

The risk of loss of customer trust and business losses due to loss of reputation of the bank. Cross-border violations in AMLand sanctions compliance are the most significant drivers of this risk. The G20's "Responsible Business Conduct" principles have extended the reporting obligations for banks on their environmental and social footprints.[59] In particular, the EU's Sustainable Finance Taxonomy (EU Regulation 2020/852) has strengthened the legal basis for ethical banking.[60] Reputational risk in this regard is no longer considered simply a public relations issue but also a legal compliance risk.

Global financial crises have demonstrated that effective handling of worldwide banking risks involves a global framework of collaboration beyond national oversight. For example, the BCBS, which sets international risk management and bank capital adequacystandards, forms the cornerstone of international banking.[61] The Basel III framework has introduced higher capital and liquidity standards to render banks more resilient to financial shocks. Especially after the 2008 global financial crisis, it has become a consensus that risks should be managed not only at the micro level (individual bank) but also at the macro level (the financial systemas a whole). Headed by the FSB, the G20 countries have developed a comprehensive macroprudential framework for G-SIBs to reduce systemic risk and solve the 'too big to fail' problem.[62] The framework includes countercyclical Capital Buffers under G-SIBs supervision that impose additional capital requirements on banks during periods when credit growth accumulates risk in the financial system.[63]

56 See, Joosen (2022) 376–402.
57 Vucinic and Luburic (2022) 27–53.
58 Dawe et al. (2021).
59 Dorfmüller et al. (2024) 449–473.
60 Schütze and Stede (2024) 128–160.
61 Kovalenko (2021) 35.
62 Adrieş et al. (2022) 100, 963; Dzhagityan and Orekhov (2022) 48–74; Violon et al. (2020) 95.
63 Drehmann and Gambacorta (2012) 603–608.

2.6.7 Supervisory Structures: G20, Basel, and IMFOversight

The supervision of international banks is carried out by a multi-layered structure[64]:

i. BCBS: BCBS is the primary body that issues micro prudential standards for banks dealing with capital adequacy, liquidity, and risk management. The standards detail how resilient banks individually must be to absorb shocks.
ii. FSB: Macro-prudentially oversees systemic risks, coordinates regulatory reforms in finance globally, and provides policy recommendations to the G20. Among the agenda of FSBis one of its top items, which is the development of a cross-border resolution framework, including tools to prevent the failure of a bank from contaminating the system.
iii. IMFand WB: The two institutions conduct regular examinations of member countries' banking systems and supervisory skills under the FSAP. The reviews are a significant way of assessing the extent to which countries comply with Basel standards and other global principles.

2.6.8 Assessment: Legal Management of Risks

Although the Basel Committee's standards do not constitute a legal obligation (hard law) in the sense of an international treaty, they are soft law. However, thanks to the political support of the G20 and surveillance by the IMF through programs such as FSAP, these standards have been promptly transposed into national legal orders and have become de facto binding. The new era of bank supervision has gone beyond the traditional credit and liquidity risks. Climate risk, cybersecurity risk brought about by digitalization, and data privacy/security issues have become premier agendas of legal compliance in bank supervision.[65] Thus, risk supervision is now a multilateral endeavour that involves not only protecting financial performance and capital, but also conscientiously implementing global financial ethics, sustainability principles, and legal imperatives.

2.7 The Future of International Banking: Digitalization, Sustainability, and the G20Perspective

International bankingis undergoing one of the most profound transformation processes in its history due to technological innovations, environmental transformation, and global regulatory reforms. The wave of reforms that began with the 2008 crisis, combined with the agenda of digitalization and sustainable finance, has accelerated the transition to a comprehensive understanding of finance.[66] The

[64] Chiu and Wilson (2019) 189.
[65] Aguayo and Slusarczyk (2020) 4040.
[66] Arneret al. (2017) 390.

G20 and the Basel Committee now view international bankingnot only as a tool for economic stability but also for sustainable development.[67]

2.7.1 Digitalization and the Technological Evolution of Banking

The banking sector is being revolutionised to its core by the impacts of digitalization that reshaped the entire value chain of conventional banking operations, placing technology at a determining position in every sphere, from customer relations to operations, from risk management to compliance and control mechanisms. The key pillars of the transformation can be listed as financial technologies (FinTech), regulatory technologies (RegTech), new-generation international payment systems, and data-based banking.

FinTech refers to the use of technology to enhance efficiency and reduce the cost of providing financial services. FinTech innovations have enjoyed huge cost reductions, particularly in cross-border transactions, simpler access to service, and enhanced transparency and availability of data. The innovations have created room for new business models (e.g., mobile payment service, crowdfunding) that challenge conventional banking products.[68]

RegTech is a term that describes technology-based solutions which automate the financial institutions' regulatory compliance processes. RegTech solutions enable banks to make intricate reporting obligations easy and decrease errors in obligatory procedures such as risk identification and AML and CFT. This lowers the cost of operations for banks and increases the effectiveness of the regulatory controls.[69]

Cross-border payment platforms and global banking transactions are some of the areas where digitalization is being experienced the most. Blockchain technology, one of the distributed ledger technology (DLT)types, delivers an end solution to this system in terms of reducing or doing away with correspondent banks for cross-border payments. Payment systemsbased on blockchain have the ability to provide faster settlement and reduced cost of transactions. The global financial infrastructure is adapting to support these emerging technologies. For example, SWIFT gpi (Global Payments Innovation) improves the SWIFTmessaging infrastructure both in terms of speed and transparency, while proprietary technology platforms such as RippleNet offer more sophisticated and efficient solutions that define the future of the global payments infrastructure.[70]

Another key focus of digitalization is shifting banking operations to a data-centric model. AI and machine learning algorithms analyse behavioural data such as social media activity, e-commerce shopping habits, and mobile phone usage, in addition to traditional financial data, to make judgments about credit risk. This

---

[67] Rojas-Suarez (2025); Alexander (2015) 1–9.
[68] Almomani and Alomari (2021) 1793–1802.
[69] Jung (2024) 369–396.
[70] Merz (2021) 25–44; Sule et al. (2025) 508–535.

larger set of data gives more financial inclusionby enabling individuals with insufficient credit history to be segmented into the financial system. This data-driven banking progress also comes with a succession of novel and sophisticated legal challenges. Processing and collecting large amounts of customers' personal data are under tight regulation with laws like the General Data Protection Regulation (GDPR). Mirror effects of current imbalances (geographic location, gender, race, etc.) on training sets for AI algorithms can produce lending or service discrimination. This case is threatening legally in the area of equality and fairness doctrines. Also, increased digitalization and interconnectivity have made bank systems vulnerable to cyber-attacks. Protection of financial critical infrastructure has become one of the primary regulators' and banks' responsibilities.

2.7.2 CBDC and the New Money Architecture

One of the most groundbreaking developments in international banking and finance law is the emergence of the concept of CBDC, which refers to a digital currency issued by the central bank of a country and backed by central bank liability. As the BIS' 2024 report indicates, majority of central banks worldwide are currently experimenting with, testing, or trialling CBDC projects.[71] The dissemination of CBDC systems raises fundamental questions to be resolved, particularly regarding international monetary law, rules of conflict of laws, and traditional banking sector role. Among the crucial issues in cross-border digital currency transfers is the manner in which the conventional concept of *lex monetae*(money's law) is to be adapted to CBDC. Particularly in a system where CBDCs from different countries interact (interoperability), whose law (the issuing country's law or the law of the country where the user is located) will prevail? This will determine the legal certainty of cross-border transfers.[72]

Would CBDCswholly displace existing global financial messaging infrastructure, primarily the SWIFT system, or would they be made compatible so that they might exist alongside existing systems in the global payment infrastructure? The majority of central banks would rather have CBDC infrastructures compatible with SWIFT than forswear globally accepted SWIFTstandards completely.[73]

How would the intermediation role of private sector banks be changed by the spread of CBDCs, traditionally involved in the exercise of fund raising and creation of credit? The extensive adoption of CBDC in accounts held at the central bank could lead to the withdrawal of funds from private banks, threatening financial stability (disintermediation). Consequently, most models predict the distribution of CBDC through private banks.[74]

[71] Hofmann et al. (2025); Bayon (2025) 309–347.

[72] See, Glicz (2025) 807–823; Kleiner (2025)130–146.

[73] See, for further discussion, Ruggeri (2025).

[74] Ponce and Taroco (2025).

The need to manage the potential of CBDCs internationally has also been observed by international institutions. In the 2021 Rome Summit, the G20 requested the development of common technical standards and governance principles to enable cross-border interoperability and security of CBDC projects.[75] Such projects, supported by the likes of the BIS and IMF, strive to define the regulatory framework for the new world monetary structure.

2.7.3 Sustainable Finance and the 'Green Banking' Paradigm

Global environmental degradation and climate change are two of the largest macroeconomic risks of the twenty-first century, and the financial sector is undergoing a fundamental transformation as a result of this structural imperative. Financial stability no longer can be addressed in isolation from environmental and social sustainability goals. Green Bankingis a term applied to denote banks that pursue a business model that considers environmental and social impacts, provides a low-carbon economy transition, and invests in green projects.

> **Important**
> This trend is producing fundamental changes to the traditional risk management and reporting standards of international banks. Banks are now forced to examine the carbon footprint, climate resilience, and social impacts of financed projects.

Regulations on sustainable finance are in the high speed of development under the leadership of international institutions. Illustratively, the G20 has spearheaded international standards development in this area under its Sustainable Finance Study Group (SFWG), established in 2016. The SFWG's work has generated principles and standards, including on green bond classification, carbon accounting practices by financial institutions, and ESG reporting expectations for investors. Global standards have also been introduced in line with the European Union's landmark regulation, the Sustainable Finance Taxonomy (EU Regulation 2020/852), which provides a classification system that determines what economic activities are environmentally sustainable based on scientific criteria. The aim is to reduce the risk of greenwashing and channel investment in a more transparent manner.

Physical risks, in the form of direct property or production losses resulting from climate events (floods, droughts, etc.), and transition risks, in the form of devaluation of fossil fuel assets due to policies promoting low-carbon economy transition (e.g., carbon tax), threaten financial stability. The BCBS took a worthwhile step in acknowledging that such risks threaten the financial system and publishing the paper Principles for the Effective Management of Climate-related Financial Risks

[75] Dawe et al. (2022).

in 2022.[76] The Committee recommends banks include climate-related financial risks in corporate governance, risk management procedures, and, most importantly, capital adequacy assessments (stress tests and scenario analysis).

This approach is the foundation for the 'Green Basel' model, which balances financial stability with environmental sustainability and integrates capital requirements with climate risk. This model sends a clear signal that regulators can factor in ESG considerations when establishing banks' risk-weighted assets (RWA) in the future.[77]

2.7.4 The G20's New Regulatory Paradigm: Regulation 4.0

With global financial regulations focusing on digitalization,[78] markets must incorporate dynamic, data-driven, and forward-looking systems of regulation.[79] Following global adoption of Basel standards and the concurrent introduction of a risk-based supervision system, Regulation 4.0, also known as RegTech, has become a new paradigm in the regulatory framework, based on algorithmic regulation and artificial intelligence-backed supervisory systems.[80] The G20's focus in this area is primarily on the implementation of supervisory technologies (SupTech) to enhance the real-time surveillance of data by overseas and merging of RegTechon big data analytics.[81]

2.7.5 The Social Responsibility and Ethical Dimension of Global Banking

It is no longer sufficient now that the banking sector is green, but it must also develop in accordance with ethical values. This is because not only are banks financial intermediaries, but they are also responsible for upholding social values. This could be thought of as the social counterpart to the power they are entrusted with, i.e. the power to provide credit. To that extent, the United Nations Principles for Responsible Banking (UN PRB) and the OECD Due Diligence Guidance for Responsible Business Conduct rules, while non-binding in the G20countries, are seen to have normative impacts.[82] Banks, in that transition, must develop strategies that account for social value as well as financial profitability. The success of the banks in undertaking such ventures will not only be return on capital but also the degree of contribution towards sustainable development.

[76] Suciati (2025) 428.
[77] Lamperti et al (2021).
[78] Mursalov (2021) 62–76.
[79] Sliwa (2018)105–108.
[80] Zetzsche et al. (2020, s. 52).
[81] Kavassalis et al. (2018) 2–4; Jung (2024) 369–396.
[82] OECD (2016) 119–135.

2.7.6 Assessment: The Future Direction of International Banking

In light of the foregoing considerations, it can be anticipated that international banking evolution in the not-too-distant future will be concentrated on three main axes. The first of these is digitalization due to the increasing depth of technology-based financial services; the second is sustainability due to the convergence of environmental/social risks into financial stability; and the third is global governance concepts with the increasing prominence of regulatory frameworks such as the G20 and Basel Regulations. These developments have led to the evolution of international banking from its past definition to becoming a global financial ecosystem. Therefore, ere long, international banking will be assuming responsibility not only for capital flows but also for maintaining global financial stability.[83]

Chapter Summary

Chapter 2 provides a legal and economic overview of international banking, focusing on how the sector has changed over time, how it is organized, the main risks it carries, and possible future directions under the global regulatory framework set by the G20. The chapter begins by outlining how international banking developed over time, starting with the Bretton Woods period and the founding of multilateral bodies like the IMF and the World Bank. The next section looks at how the Eurodollar market and other offshore markets grew during the 1970s. This process reached a peak in the G20 period, with the adoption of Basel III after the 2008 Global Financial Crisis, and it moved financial governance toward a multilateral approach that puts financial stability at the centre.

Several factors help explain why banking has become more international. These include macroeconomic liberalization, growth in cross-border trade and the need for financing to support it, firms adopting strategies that span multiple countries, and the rise of a shared transnational set of expectations and practices through soft law shaped by bodies such as the Basel Committee and the FSB. This section examines how banks organize their activities across borders by separating four common arrangements. A foreign branch operates as part of the parent bank and does not have its own legal identity. A representative office gives the bank a local presence for liaison and information purposes, but it does not carry out banking business. Correspondent banking supports cross-border payments by allowing banks to access services through other banks, while it also raises serious AML and CTF risks. Foreign subsidiaries or affiliates are set up as separate legal entities, and they

[83] Stoliarchuk E (2023) 13.

are often preferred when supervisors want ring-fencingbetween the local unit and the parent bank.

This chapter focuses mainly on the key risks and the oversight measures used to monitor and manage them. International banks face several types of concentrated risk. These include systemic risk, especially among global systemically important banks; credit risk, which can rise with country and sovereign exposures; liquidity risk, which Basel III addresses through the liquidity coverage ratio and the net stable funding ratio; and operational risk, where cyber risk is taking a larger share. Global banking oversight is layered across several bodies. The Basel Committee on Banking Supervision sets core supervisory standards, the Financial Stability Board-coordinates macro-prudential policy, and the International Monetary Fund reviews national systems through Financial Sector Assessment Programs. Together, their guidance often moves from soft-law expectations to rules that countries apply in practice as binding domestic regulation.

The chapter ends with a discussion of where international banking may head next, focusing on several developments that are likely to shape its direction. Digitalization is driving the expansion of FinTech and RegTech, along with newer payment systems such as SWIFTglobal payments innovation and possible solutions based on distributed ledger technology. Sustainable finance refers to green banking and to treating climate-related financial risks, both physical and transition, as part of governance frameworks and prudential standards, as shown by the Green Basel model. Basel IV sets out the requirements for this section. This period is marked by a G20-led shift toward supervisory work that is more dynamic and data-driven, with a stronger focus on future risks, including the growing use of SupTech.

Revision Questions

1. Explain how Basel III responded to the weakness in the global banking system exposed by the 2008 financial crisis by particularly focusing on the LCR and NSFR. Also explain how these ratios help control liquidity risk and assess the role of the FSB in macro-prudential oversight.
2. Compare and contrast the legal status and liability implications for a foreign bank operating through a branch and a subsidiary in the host country and determine which mode is more favoured by the host country regulators for retail operations and the grounds for such preference.
3. Discuss the notion of soft law measures such as the Basel Accords or FSB recommendations in the framework of international bankingregulations. Discuss the processes through which these non-binding documents attain de facto legal powers within the jurisdictions of the G20.
4. What is the green banking paradigm? What is the legal difference between physical risks and transition risks in relation to global change? How

will banks be mandated to incorporate these risks in their overall risk management approach in accordance with new global banking standards?

5. Examine the continued regulatory importance of two major historical events in international banking: (a) the collapse of the Bretton Woods monetary system in 1971 and (b) the Global Financial Crisis of 2008.
6. What is regulatory technology (RegTech)? Explain the potential use of RegTech in assisting bank compliance functions in high-risk areas like AML and CTF. What is the impact of digitalisation, e.g. through use of the SWIFT gpi network or DLT, on the legal notion of payment security?
7. Explain the main role of correspondent banking within the global system for the exchange of payments. Scrutinise the legal risks that include AML and CTF that contribute to the trend of de-risking. Discuss the broader implications of de-risking for financial inclusion in emerging markets.◄

References

Abascal M, Fraile A (2014) Brisbane G20 summit: substantial progress on the regulatory reform. https://www.bbvaresearch.com/wp-content/uploads/2014/11/Flash14114_i.pdf. Accessed 15 Dec 2025.

Acerbi C, Tasche D (2002) Expected shortfall: a natural coherent alternative to value at risk. Econ Notes 31(2):379–388

Admati A, Hellwig M (2013) The bankers' new clothes: what's wrong with banking and what to do about it. Princeton University Press

Aguayo F, Slusarczyk B (2020) Risks of banking services' digitalization: the practice of diversification and sustainable development goals. Sustainability 12(10):4040

Alexander K (2015) Banking regulation and environmental sustainability. Amicus Curiae 104:1–9

Almomani A, Alomari K (2021) Financial technology (FinTech) and its role in supporting the financial an banking services sector. International Journal of Academic Research in Business and Social Sciences 11(8):1793–1802

Alvarez S (2023) Latin American banks and Euromarkets: a view on the process of early bank globalization from the periphery. Jahrbuch Für Wirtschaftsgeschichte 64(2):489–527

Andrieş A, Ongena S, Sprincean N, Tunaru R (2022) Risk spillovers and interconnectedness between systematically important institutions. J Financ Stab 58(100):593

Arner D, Berberis J, Buckley R (2017) FinTech, RegTech, and the reconceptualization of financial regulation. Northwest J Int Law Bus 37:371–413

Bayne N (2025) The Decline of the G8 Summit and Lessons for the G20. In: Bayne N, Woolcock S (eds) The decision-making and negotiation in international economic relations, new economic diplomacy. Routledge

Bayon P (2025) Current and future central bank digital currency (CBDC) projects. In: Sempere C (ed) Governance and control of data and digital economy in the European single market: legal framework for new digital assets, identities and data spaces. Springer, pp 309–347

Bazbauers A, Engel S (2021) The global architecture of multilateral development banks: a system of debt or development? Routledge

BCBS (2011) Basel III: A global regulatory framework for more resilient banks and banking systems. https://www.bis.org/publ/bcbs189.htm. Accessed 31 Jan 2026.

Bénassy-Quéré A, Pisani-Ferry J (2011) What international monetary system for a fast-changing world economy. Bruegel Working Paper, No. 2011/06.

Besar D, Booth P, Chan K, Milne A, Pickles J (2011) Systemic risk in financial services. Br Actuar J 16(2):195–300
BIS (2006) Core principles methodology. https://www.bis.org/publ/bcbs130.pdf. Accessed 31 Jan 2026.
Bitar J (2021) Foreign currency intermediation: Systemic risk and macroprudential regulation. Latin American Journal of Central Banking 2(2).
Byrne J, Marxen K, Kozakowski M, Byrne M (2022) Trade based financial crime compliance. Institute of International Banking Law and Practice.
Cassis Y (2011) Capitals of capital: a history of international financial centres, 1780–2005. Cambridge University Press
Cedillo P, Loya M, Hernandez D (2023) The 2008 financial crisis and the consolidation of the G20. Revista Mexicana De Politica Exterior 126:11–27
Chiu I, Wilson J (2019) Banking law and regulation. Oxford University Press
Cintra M, Farhi M (2009) The financial crisis and the global shadow banking system. Revue De La Regulation 5(5):347–368
Claessens S, Horen N (2014) Foreign banks: trends and impact J Money, Credit, Bank 46(1):295–326
Claessens S, Kose A (2018) Frontiers of macroeconomic research on the global financial cycle. Annual Review of Economics 10:1–25
Costa D, Querci F, Santulli R (2025) Competition or cooperation? Disentangling the bank-FinTech interaction through a hybrid literature review. Res Int Bus Financ 78(102):993
Dawe K, Noh M, Ignatov A (2021) 2020 G20 Riyadh summit interim compliance report, https://www.g20.utoronto.ca/compliance/2020riyadh-interim/2020-g20-compliance-interim.pdf. Accessed 30 Jan 2026.
Dawe K, Dobson S, Ignatov A (2022) 2021 G20 Rome summit final compliance report, https://www.g20.utoronto.ca/compliance/2021rome-final/04-2021-g20-compliance-final-digital.pdf. Accessed 30 Jan 2026.
Drach A (2024) An early form of European champions? Banking clubs between European integration and global banking (1960s–1990s). Bus Hist 66:287–310
DeRosa D (2013) Foreign exchange operations: master trading agreements, settlement, and collateral. John Wiley and Sons
Drehmann M, Gambacorta L (2012) The effects of countercyclical capital buffers on bank lending. Appl Econ Lett 19(7):603–608
Dorfmüller H, Kimotho W, Ebert I, Dey P, Wettstein F (2024) Responsible business conduct in commodity trading—a multidisciplinary review. J Bus Ethics 195(3):449–473
Dzhagityan E, Orekhov M (2022) Global systemically important banks: do they still pose risks for financial stability? Int Organ Res J 17(3):46–74
Eichengreen B (2008) Globalizing capital: a history of the international monetary system. Princeton University Press.
Ellis S, Sharma S, Brzeszczyński J (2022) Systemic risk measures and regulatory challenges. J Financ Stab 61(100):960
Fichtner J (2016) The anatomy of the Cayman islands offshore financial center: Anglo-America, Japan, and the role of hedge funds. Review of International Political Economy 23:1034–1063
G20 (2022) Sustainable finance report. https://g20sfwg.org/wp-content/uploads/2022/10/2022-G20-Sustainable-Finance-Report-2.pdf. Accessed 31 Jan 2026.
Goodhart C (2011) The basel committee on banking supervision: a history of the early years 1974–1997. Cambridge University Press
Herring R, Carmassi J (2014) Complexity and systemic risk: what's changed since the crisis. In: Berger A, Molyneux P, Wilson J (eds) The Oxford handbook of banking. Oxford University Press, pp 77–112
Hoffmann B, Tang X, Zhu F (2025) Central bank and media sentiment on central bank digital currency: an international perspective. https://www.bis.org/publ/work1279.pdf. Accessed 31 Jan 2026.

Howells P, Bain K (2008) The economics of money, banking and finance: A European text. Pearson.
Jawadi F, Pondie T, Cheffou A (2025) New challenges for green finance and sustainable industrialization in developing countries: a panel data analysis. Energy Economics 142(108):120
Jiao M (2023) Big data analytics for anti-money laundering compliance in the banking industry. Highlights in Science Engineering and Technology 49:302–309
Joosen B (2022) Operational risk in the capital requirements framework for banks. In: Joosen B, Lamandini M, Tröger T (eds) Capital and liquidity requirements for European banks. Oxford University Press, pp 376–402
Joyce J (2011) Financial globalization and banking crises in emerging markets. Open Economics Review 22(5):875–895
Jung J (2024) RegTech and SupTech: the future of compliance. In: Madir J (ed) FinTech: law and regulation. Edward Elgar
Kavassalis P, Stieber H, Breymann W, Saxton K, Gross F (2018) An innovative RegTech approach to financial risk monitoring and supervisory reporting. The Journal of Risk Finance 19(1):39–55
Khan N, Zafar M, Okunlola A, Zoltan Z, Robert M (2022) Effects of financial inclusion on economic growth, powerty, sustainability, and financial efficiency: Evidence from G20 countries. Sustainability 14(19):12,688.
Kleiner C (2025) The applicable laws to cross-border payments in central bank digital currencies. In: Zatti F, Barresi R (eds) Digital assets and the law: Fiat money in the era of digital currency, Routledge, p 130–146.
Knight M (2015) Completing the G20's program to reform global financial regulation. https://www.cigionline.org/static/documents/no55_web.pdf. Accessed 31 Jan 2026.
Kovalenko V, Sheludko S, Radova N, Murshudli F, Gonchar K (2021) International standards for bank capital regulation. Financial and Credit Activity Problems of Theory and Practice 1(36):35–45
Lamperti F, Bosetti V, Roventini A, Tavoni M, Treibich T (2021) Three green financial policies to address climate risks. Journal of Financial Stability 54.
Landaberry V, Caccioli F, Rodriguez-Martinez A, Baron A, Martinez-Jaramillo S, Lluberas R (2021) The contribution of the intra-firm exposures network to systemic risk. Latin American Journal of Central Banking 2(2).
Lastra R (2015) International financial and monetary law. Oxford University Press
Lendermann U (2025) Automated ball-in: eliminating regulatory restraints. J Bank Regul 26(3):370–391
Lopez-Penabad M, Iglesias A, Neto J (2021) Competition and financial stability in the European listed banks. SAGE Open 11(3).
Maity S, Majumder A (2025) A comparative study on the financial inclusion status of G20 countries. Journal of Decision Analytics and Intelligent Computing 5(1):14–24
Glicz M (2025) Selected conflict-of-law issues related to digital curency. Prawo i Wiez 53(6):807–823
Mursalov M (2021) Regulation of the banking sector: pandemic challenges and digital solutions. In: Shaposhnykov P (ed) Transformation of the economy, finance and management in a pandemic: the development of digital technologies. Kielce, p 62–76.
Mashamba T (2018) The effects of basel III liquidity regulations on banks' profitability. Journal of Governance and Regulation 7(2):34–48
Maslak G, Senel G (2023) Bank consolidation and systemic risk: M&A during the 2008 financial crisis. Journal of Financial Services Research 63(2):201–220
Merz M (2021) Contemporaneous financial intermediation: how DLT changes the cross-border payment landscape. In: Härdle W, Dai M, Kou S (eds) Digital finance: smart data analytics, investment innovation, and financial technology. Springer, pp 25–44
Nnadi M, Tanna S (2013) Analysis of cross-border and domestic mega-M&As of European commercial banks. Manag Financ 39(9):848–862

Nölke A (2004) Transnational private authority and corporate governance. In: Schirm S (ed) New rules for global markets: public and private governance in the world economy. Palgrave Macmillan, pp 155–175
Obstfeld M, Taylor A (2004) Global capital markets: integration, crisis, and growth. Cambridge University Press
OECD (2016) The sustainable development goals as business opportunities. OECD Publishing.
OECD (2021) Transparency and exchange of information for tax purposes: multilateral co-operation changing the world. https://www.oecd.org/content/dam/oecd/en/networks/global-forum-tax-transparency/global-forum-10-years-report.pdf. Accessed 31 Jan 2026
Ponce J, Taroco S (2025) CBDC's design implications for financial stability. Latin American Journal of Central Banking. https://www.sciencedirect.com/science/article/pii/S2666143825000262. Accessed 30 Jan 2026
Porter T (2001) The transnational agenda for financial regulation in developing countries. In: Armijo L (eds) Financial globalization and democracy in emerging markets. Palgrave Macmillan, p 91–116
Proxmire W (1975) Compendium of major issues in bank regulation. US Government Printing Office
Radelet S, Sachs J, Cooper R, Bosworth B (1998) The East Asian financial crisis: diagnosis, remedies, prospects. Brook Pap Econ Act 1:1–90
Papaioannou E (2005) What drives international bank flows? Politics, institutions and other determinants. Journal of Development Economics 88.
Qi M, Zhang J, Shi D, Feng S, Xu J (2025) Systemic risk contagion and bailout effects in the global financial system. Int Rev Econ Financ 102(104):298
Ratnowski L (2013) Competition policy for modern banks, IMF Working Paper WP/13/126
Rojas-Suarez L (2025) Aligning international banking regulation with the SDGs. Policy Paper 351:1–13
Roy-Chaudhury S (2019) China, the belt and road initiative, and the hambantota port project. St Antony's International Review 15(1):153–164
Ruggeri E (2025) Is the world ready for a cryptocurrency standard?, https://papers.ssrn.com/sol3/papers.cfm?abstract_id=5374830. Accessed 31 Jan 2026.
Schenk C (1998) The origins of the Eurodollar market in London: 1955–1963. Explor Econ Hist 35(2):221–238
Schuknecht L, Siegerink V (2020) The political economy of the G20 Agenda on financial regulation. European Journal of Political Economy 65(6):101,941.
Schütze F, Stede J (2024) The EU sustainable finance taxonomy and its contribution to climate neutrality. Journal of Sustainable Finance and Investment 14(1):128–160
Scott S, Zachariadis M (2012) Origins and development of SWIFT, 1973–2009. Bus Hist 54(3):462–483
Sliwa R (2018) Governance of Industrie 4.0. Contribution to the Discussion. International Scientific Journal "Industry 4.0" 3(2):105–108.
Smith G (2011) G7 to G8 to G20: Evolution in global governance. https://www.files.ethz.ch/isn/132561/G20No6.pdf. Accessed 31 Jan 2026.
Stoliarchuk Y, Ilnytskyy D, Ilnytska N (2023) Global financial ecosystem and processes of unshadowing of business activities: the role of the FATF. Journal of Innovations and Sustainability 7(1):13
Suciati R (2025) The role of financial stability in mitigating climate risk: a bibliometric and literature analysis. Journal of Risk and Financial Management 18(8):428
Sule A, Eyo-Udo N, Onukwulu E, Agho M, Azubuike C (2025) Implementing blockchain for secure and efficient cross-border payment systems. International Journal of Research and Innovation in Applied Science 9(12):508–535
Tammenga A, Haarman P (2020) Liquidity risk regulation and its practical implications for banks: the introduction and effects of the liquidity coverage ratio. Maanblad Voor Accountancy En Bedrijfseconomie 94(9–10):367–378
Tasche D (2002) Expected shortfall and beyond. J Bank Finance 26(7):1519–1533

Toporowski J (2005) 'A haven of familiar monetary practice': the neoliberal dream in international money and finance. In: Johnston D, A, Saad-Filho (eds). Pluto Press, pp 106–112
Triggs A (2018) Macroeconomic policy cooperation and the G20. The World Economy 41(5):1309–1341
Vines D (2010) The global macroeconomic crisis and G20 macroeconomic policy coordination. Margin J Appl Econ Res 4(2):157–175
Violon A, Durant D, Toader O (2020) The impact of the designation of global systematically important banks on their business model. Int J Cent Bank 16(5):95–142
Vučinić M, Luburić R (2022) Fintech, risk-based thinking and cyber risk. Journal of Central Banking Theory and Practice 11(2):27–53
Windecker G (1993) The eurodollar deposit market: strategies for regulation. American University International Law Review 9(1):357–384

Further Reading

Arner D, Barberis J, Buckley R (2017) FinTech, regtech, and the reconceptualization of financial regulation. Northwest J Int Law Bus 37(3):371–413
BIS (2017) Basel III: Finalising post-crisis reforms, undefined
Diamond D, Dybvig P (1983) Bank runs, deposit insurance, and liquidity. J Polit Econ 91(3):401–419
Dikau S, Ulrich V (2021) Central bank mandates, sustainability objectives and the promotion of green finance. Ecol Econ 184:107022
Eichengreen B (2008) Globalizing capital: a history of the international monetary system. Princeton University Press
Goodhart C (2011) The basel committee on banking supervision: a history of the early years 1974–1997. Cambridge University Press
Grolleman D, Jutrsa D (2017) Understanding Correspondent Banking Trends: A Monitoring Framework IMF Working Papers (216), https://doi.org/10.5089/9781484323625.001
Lastra R (2015) International financial and monetary law. Oxford University Press
Schuknecht L, Siegerink V (2020) The Political economy of the G20 agenda on financial regulation. Eur J Polit Econ 65:101941
Vives X (2016) Competition and Stability in Banking The Role of Regulation and Competition Policy. Princeton University Press
Zetzsche, D Arner, D Buckley, R & Weber, R (2020) The Evolution and Future of Data-Driven Finance in the EU, *Common Market Law Review 57:331–360*

3 Alternative Methods in Foreign Trade Financing

Contents

F. B. Erdem, *The Principles of International Banking, Finance and Investment Law*, Springer Textbooks in Law, https://doi.org/10.1007/978-3-032-32505-1_3

Abstract

This chapter explores alternative financing methods used in foreign trade, highlighting how they can provide flexibility, security, and efficiency for international transactions. It starts with an in-depth examination of factoring, outlining its key beneficiaries and purposes. The section covers the advantages of factoring, such as providing instant down payments, facilitating the collection of forward receivables, and offering intelligence on debtors. It also describes how, in cases of financial difficulties, the debtor bears the loss, providing a form of guarantee. The chapter identifies various types of factoring according to scope, including non-notification, notified, old-line, with recourse, non-recourse, bulk, back-to-back, undisclosed, maturity, and full-service factoring. It also categorizes factoring based on the place of issue into domestic, export, and import factoring. Next, the chapter delves into forfaiting, covering its origins and the establishment of forfaiting agreements. It outlines the process of forfaiting, detailing the steps involved before and after exporting, including notifying the forfaiting organization, receiving offers, and the transfer and purchase of receivables by contract. The discussion includes the pearls and pitfalls of the forfaiting process for both the exporter and the forfaitor, as well as the applicable law governing forfaiting agreements. The chapter also explores financial leasing, detailing the form and registration of financial lease agreements, and the liabilities of the parties involved. It examines the obligations of the lessor and the tenant, emphasizing the responsibilities for providing, transferring, and maintaining the leased property, as well as ensuring its careful use and protection. The chapter concludes with a look at leasing-barter, offering insight into this unique alternative financing method in foreign trade.

3.1 Factoring

3.1.1 The Concept

The basis of the factoring is the legal nexus that is developed between a financial institution, that is, a bank or a specialized factoring entity that becomes the factor, and a commercial enterprise, in this case, the client. Under the auspices of this contractual relationship, the client transfers its due receivables, current and prospective to the factor, usually at a discount to its nominal value. The factor presupposes, in its turn, the statutory obligation of collecting the said receivables hence ensuring that the debtors pay on the due date.[1] This means that the client obtains the liquidity instantaneously and bypasses the maturity date of its receivables where the factor tries to make a profit margin out of the above transfers. The client, in return, is required to pledge its receivables with the factor as a block, and consequently, the title of creditor will be conveyed to the factor. The assigned receivables are recognised as an active entry in the balance sheet of the factor and after this, the factor takes up the responsibility of accounting as well as the collection of the same.

3.1.2 The Mechanism

In its broadest usage, Factoring is the use of deferred receivables, which arise out of the commercial transaction of goods and services, to a factoring institution through an assignment of title after which such receivables are then controlled by the factoring institution in a systematic manner. Using this structure, it is possible to broadly break down the factoring relationship into three service elements as indicate below:[2]

i. Collection and management of receivables: It is the process that starts with the assignment of receivables arising from sales of goods and services to the factoring institution. The factoring institution that assigns the receivables undertakes the collection of these receivables, keeps receivable records, and also carrying out of procedure activities like issue of notices and warnings in a bid to ensure that they are paid in a timely manner. Moreover, the factor can take on supporting roles, i.e., the market research and provision of the pertinent market intelligence to the client.[3]
ii. Insurance of receivables: Where the debtors who have been assigned to a factor get into solvency, the factor risks non-payment. This means that the

[1] Spasić et al. (2012) 157-173.
[2] Milenkovic-Kerkovic and Dencic-Mihajlov (2012) 428-435.
[3] Bakker et al. (2004) 4.

client which sets its receivables can be hedged against the insolvency of the institutions to which it sells its goods.[4]

iii. Financing: The factor provides an advanced payment to its client based on a portion of receivables. In return, the debtor pays the full amount of the receivable directly to the factor at maturity.

3.1.3 Advantages

Factoring is a financial service which provides businesses, more particularly those engaged in forward sales, with an opportunity to obtain liquidity by assigning their receivables. It provides a bundled financing, collection and risk-management services.[5] In this respect, factoring is aimed at both controlling the cash flow and professionalising the trade receivable management. All creditor companies that sell goods and services on credit can benefit from factoring transactions. Especially small and medium-sized enterprises (SMEs) resort to this method to accelerate their cash flows.[6] Through early collections of receivables, liquidity is increased and risk is reduced by passing the collection tasks to the factoring company; and operating expenses are reduced by professional follow-up of receivables management. All these benefits lead to better and more stable balance-sheet performance.

3.1.3.1 Instant down payment

Factoring provides businesses with the ability to transform receivables arising from forward/credit sales into cash prior to maturity.[7] Thus, businesses are able to accelerate their cash flows and sustain operations seamlessly without encountering liquidity constraints.

3.1.3.2 Collection of Forward Receivables

It can be said that factoring companies can take the responsibility of collecting not just current receivables but also those that are bound to be realised in future. This ability expands the range of financing opportunities of the enterprises by the further designation of future revenues. In line with this, the supervision, collection and management of receivables are left to the professional thereby reducing the risk of collection in question.

---

[4] ibid.

[5] Factoring can provide a healthier financial outlook by enabling the conversion of current assets in company balance sheets. This may lead to results such as reducing indebtedness ratios and increasing creditworthiness, especially in the financial statements of SMEs. However, since factoring transactions can also be used as a form of secret borrowing between companies, they should be supported by accurate reporting and transparency principles.

[6] Castellano (2023); Istuk (2015) 212-234.

[7] Michalski (2009) 570.

3.1.3.3 Debtor's Intelligence

Factoring companies carry out comprehensive credit and payment-stroke checks on whom the debtors will be gathering payments. By so doing, risks are minimised under evaluation of the collectability of the receivables and debtor profile. Therefore, the business minimises the losses that could be encountered due to inadequacy of information about the debtor.

3.1.3.4 Diversification of Default Risk

Factoring transactions can generally be structured in such a way that the factoring company assumes the financial risk of the debtor in case the receivables purchased by the factoring company are not collected (non-recourse factoring). As a result, the business obtains funding with no default risk. This assurance would reduce the financial losses and facilitate risk management.

3.1.4 Factoring Agreement

Factoring agreements cover the factor and client relationship by provisions on the assignment of receivables, financing and collection services. Factoring agreements are commercial hybrid commercial contracts with features of assignment, loan and service agreements. This multilateral structure necessitates careful drafting of the agreements and the balancing of the interests of the parties in each clause. Although the content of these contracts is shaped according to the needs of the parties and the contract law of the country in which they are applied, some basic elements are common in international practices. Since the freedom of contract and assignment provisions differ in the domestic law of each country, there are legal and contractual risks to be considered in factoring agreements. Based on these, the subsequent fundamental aspects, which are considered as crucial in the formulation of the factoring agreements are set out below:

i. Identity and titles of the parties: The contract shall clearly identify the party providing the factoring service and the party benefiting from the service. In addition, the identity of the debtor (especially for assignments with notice) is also important.
ii. Nature and scope of assigned receivables: It should be clearly stated in the agreement which receivables are assigned to the factor, the commercial transactions from which these receivables arise, invoice information and maturities, if any. In addition, it should be stated whether the assigned receivables are current or future receivables.
iii. Financing terms: The extent and conditions under which the factor will provide financing to the client (e.g. advance rate, payment terms, interest rate, etc.) are regulated in this agreement.
iv. Collection and risk management provisions: Determine who will collect the receivables, the procedure to be followed in case of default of the debtor, and

the payment risk to be assumed by the factor (e.g. the risk of non-performance by the debtor).

v. Notification and effectiveness of assignment: It should be clearly stated in the contract whether the receivables have been notified to the debtor, i.e. whether the assignment was made with or without notice. This issue is particularly important in terms of the debtor's obligation to pay.

vi. Fees and expenses: The calculation and payment of commissions, interest, filing fees and similar items that the factor will receive in return for this service should be clarified. The cost of factoring transactions consists of two items: commission and/or factoring fee, depending on the type of service provided. Factoring companies collect factoring commission on the assigned receivables in return for the follow-up, collection and management of the assigned receivables. The commission rate varies according to the transaction volume, the number of invoices and the maturity of the receivable.[8] For international transactions, the number of buyers in a country, the creditworthiness of the buyers, the number and size of invoices, and the annual transaction volume and maturity are determinative.

vii. Collaterals: Issues such as whether collateral will be requested from the client in return for the factoring transaction, the type of collateral and the conditions for its return should be regulated.

viii. Applicable law and dispute resolution: The legal framework upon which the contract will be performed and the manner in which the dispute resolution will be settled (e.g. arbitration, court jurisdiction, international chamber of commerce rules, etc.) must be clearly stated.

3.1.5 Differences Between Factoring and Guarantee Agreements

Although factoring agreements and guarantee agreements, which are frequently used in international commercial transactions, contain mechanisms whereby one party provides assurance to the other party against a certain risk, they show significant differences in terms of their legal qualifications, purposes and performance relationships. The determination of these differences is of great importance in terms of determining the legal rules applicable to these contracts and determining the obligations of the parties.

On one hand, a factoring contract comprises a multilateral hybrid contract under which a factor provides a spectrum of services such as collection, financing and administration of current or future receivables emerging by the commercial activities of the client. Conversely, in guarantee agreements, especially independent guarantee or first-demand guarantees, the guarantor agrees to perform a duty without reference to the underlying debt relationship. Such a contract is aimed that

[8] Sayer (2024).

the beneficiary would be guided towards a certain performance and to repay any devastation caused by such performance.

Especially in non-recourse factoring transactions, those known as ‘del credere’ factoring, the factor assumes the debtor’s default risk and waives the recourse to the customer. Whereas, in a guarantee agreement, the guarantor assumes the risk to induce the guarantor to undertake a certain undertaking, usually without receiving any consideration. In such contracts, risk taking is independent and often gratuitous. The liability to the guarantor in the event of the materialisation of the guaranteed event is imposed but this risk is mostly based on the relationship of trust between the parties, not on commercial interest.[9]

The consideration element in the Factoring agreement is one of the constituent elements of the agreement. The factor is entitled to various fees and commissions (e.g. factoring fee, del credere commission) in return for taking over and collecting receivables, providing financing and assuming the risk. In this respect, factoring is clearly a contract for commercial gain. In a guarantee agreement, the consideration element is not the basis, but an exception. The guarantor is generally expected to undertake liability without any economic interest and often gratuitously. Especially in the Anglo-American legal system, although there is an element of consideration in guarantee contracts, the weight of this element is quite weak compared to the consideration in factoring contracts.

In the factoring relationship, the customer has receivables arising under legally binding sales contracts previously established with the debtors. The factor takes over the assignable receivables arising after the customer fulfils these contracts. In this respect, factoring is not based on an independent trust relationship; it is based on the existing commercial transaction flow. In the guarantee agreement, the receivable relationship has not yet arisen in most cases. The guarantor provides a guarantee to encourage to take a certain legal action (e.g. entering into a contract, participating in a tender, ordering goods). In this respect, the guarantee agreement guarantees the risks that may arise from the main contract; however, it can also be valid without being a party to that contract.

Lastly, it should be mentioned that these two kinds of contracts are governed by separate regulatory texts in international transactions. For instance, standardizing the assignment, collection, and financing connection between the factor and the client at the global level is the goal of the UNIDROIT factoring Contract Convention on factoring transactions. However, guarantee contracts are typically drafted in accordance with local legal systems or the ICC Uniform Rules for Demand Guarantees (URDG 758). In particular, independent guarantee types are crucial to international banking and commercial arbitration procedures.

[9] Spasić et al. (2012) 161.

Important

Despite the fact that both suretyship and factoring agreements are tools for risk management and financial assurance in business dealings, their outcomes and legal structures differ. A suretyship agreement is an ancillary security agreement. If the principal debtor defaults on its duty, the surety agrees to personally pay the obligation to the creditor. The surety and the creditor are the parties to the contract in this connection; the major debtor's knowledge or assent is not required. However, only if a legitimate primary debt relationship exists does the surety become liable. In contrast, a factoring agreement is a three-way legal arrangement whereby receivables are assigned for consideration. The customer gives a factor its receivables from business operations, and the factor collects them, gives the customer money, and, if required, takes on the risk of collection. The parties to the contract are the customer and the factor; there is no direct contractual relationship with the debtor, and the debtor need not even be aware of the transaction. In a suretyship agreement, the surety's liability is strictly bound to the existence and validity of the principal debt, and if the principal debt is terminated, the surety is released from its obligation. The surety is obliged to make a payment to the creditor if and only if the debtor fails to fulfil its obligation. The main purpose is to guarantee the creditor's receivable, in other words, to act as a guarantee. In non-recourse factoring, the factor is fully responsible for the collection of the receivable and the customer cannot be held liable for the debtor's non-payment. In recourse factoring, the customer assumes liability to the factor only in case of non-payment of the receivable. However, this liability does not arise within the scope of a surety relationship; it arises as a side obligation of the assignment of receivables agreement. Therefore, the guarantee function is not directly in question in factoring. Factoring is essentially a financing method; liquidity is provided by transferring the receivables of the customer to the factor. In the international arena, factoring transactions are generally evaluated within the framework of the UNIDROIT 1988 Factoring Convention or the factoring rules of the IFC, while suretyship agreements are mostly handled within the framework of the Rome I Regulation, the UNIDROIT Principles or the national law rules chosen by the parties.[10] This is because the formal requirements, validity conditions and performance responsibility of suretyship vary from country to country. Especially in the Anglo-American system, a distinction is made between guarantee and suretyship; in some systems, the independence of personal guarantees is discussed.

[10] Spasić et al. (2012) 165.

3.1.6 Types of Factoring

3.1.6.1 According to the scope

3.1.6.1.1 Non-Notification Factoring

Non-notification factoring - also known as 'confidential invoice discounting' - is a special form of financing in which the process of transferring receivables to the factoring company is not notified to the buyer. The business immediately cashes a large part of the invoices issued, while it carries out the collection itself and transfers the proceeds to the factor; the debtor does not notice this process and continues its normal payment rhythm. Factoring with non-notification ensures that customer relationships are not affected by aggressiveness, brand image is protected, and a solution that complies with confidentiality agreements or agreements with the buyer that do not distort forecasts. Non-notification programmes are subject to stricter acceptance criteria such as stronger credit history, high volume of receivables and at least one year of performance.[11] Since this model is more complex than traditional factoring, it is mostly preferred by large and well-financed companies.

3.1.6.1.2 Notified Factoring

In notified factoring transactions, the debtor is explicitly notified that the receivable has been transferred to the factoring company. The buyer shall make the payment directly to the factoring company. This makes the collection process transparent and reduces the risk.[12] Since the factoring company carries out the collection itself, it has more financial control. It is frequently used for small and medium-sized enterprises.

3.1.6.1.3 Old-Line Factoring

Old-line factoring is a service in which only the collection and management of receivables is undertaken.[13] Hence, the main purpose is not to provide financing, but to monitor receivables in a professional manner. The factoring company follows the payment habits of the debtors, sends warnings and carries out the collection. The seller is generally not prepaid.

3.1.6.1.4 With Recourse Factoring

The factoring company reserves the right of recourse to the seller in case the debtor buyer fails to pay its debt. So, the risk is not completely transferred to the factoring company; the seller is held responsible if the debt cannot be collected. Therefore, lower commission rates are applied. It is generally preferred by parties who want to share the risk. The seller may be under the burden of repayment if the collection fails.

---

[11] Beale et al. (2016) 208; Puja (2022) 399; Nagy (2008) 131-152.

[12] Pigula and Paduszynska (2015) 105.

[13] Silverman (1949) 597-98.

3.1.6.1.5 Non-Recourse Factoring

The factoring company fully take the risk that the debtor will default on a payment obligation. There is no recourse to the seller even if the debtor fails to make the payment. This protects the seller from financial risks, but the service fee is higher. It is especially preferred in cases where there is concern about the financial situation of the debtors. The factoring company analyses the credit risk very meticulously.

3.1.6.1.6 Bulk Factoring

In this type, the factoring company agrees to take over a large number of receivables in bulk. The seller does not have to process each receivable separately. The collection is usually made by the seller and transferred to the factoring company. The debtor does not have to be notified of the assigned receivables. This method is suitable for high volume transactions.

3.1.6.1.7 Back-to-back Factoring

In this model applied in international trade, there are two collaborating factoring companies - one in the exporter's country and one in the importer's country to obtain more secure transactions in cross-border trade under the provision of bilateral guarantee and supervision. The exporter assigns its receivables to the factoring company in its own country, which in turn assigns them to the foreign factor.[14] Thus, both the exporter and the importer can be supervised more effectively.

3.1.6.1.8 Undisclosed Factoring

In this type of factoring, the factoring transaction is performed, but the buyer (debtor) is not notified of the assignment. In other words, the collection and relationship continues completely through the seller. The collection is realised by the customer and transferred to the factoring company. This model is suitable for companies that want to protect the customer-debtor relationship.

3.1.6.1.9 Maturity Factoring

In this system, the factoring company does not make payment immediately but waits for the receivable to become due. This structure is more suitable for businesses that want to provide receivable management and guarantee services. Since guarantee and collection services are at the forefront rather than financing, the commission rate is less than other models.[15]

3.1.6.1.10 Full-Service Factoring

This comprehensive type of factoring includes all components such as financing, collection, accounting services and guarantee. The factoring company provides both prepayment and collection and risk management services. It is one of the

---

[14] Marak and Pillai (2021) 320-337; Mizan (2011) 248-251.

[15] Pylypenko et al. (2018) 253.

highest-priced types of factoring, but the scope of services is also broad. It is especially preferred by SMEs looking for professional outsourcing. The entire receivable process of the seller is transferred.

3.1.6.2 According to the place of issue

3.1.6.2.1 Domestic Factoring

In domestic factoring transactions, the buyer, seller and factoring company are located in the same country. It is generally used for the assignment and management of receivables arising from forward sales of companies operating in the domestic market.

3.1.6.2.2 International Factoring

Factoring is a versatile financial instrument that provides financing, collection and risk management services to businesses through the assignment of receivables. With the application of this service to international trade relations, a special system called 'international factoring' has emerged. International factoring offers an important solution especially for small and medium-sized exporters to organise their cash flows and reduce the collection risks that may arise from foreign buyers. Hence, international factoring becomes a prominent financial way when the buyer and seller are in different countries. It is basically based on the principle that the exporter transfers its receivables from the foreign buyer to the factoring company in its own country. In this system, factoring companies (or banks) belonging to both the exporter and the importer country come into play and the transaction takes on a multilateral structure.

In this respect, international factoring is a cross-border dimension of traditional factoring transactions. However, the fact that different country laws, foreign exchange regimes and payment risks are involved requires international factoring to be carried out based on special regulations and contractual infrastructures. There are typically four parties involved in an international factoring transaction as exporter (client), exporter factor, importer (borrower) and importer factor.

The transaction begins with the exporter, who sells goods or services to a buyer abroad and assigns the invoice arising from this sale to the exporting factor in its own country. Then, the exporter factor transfers this receivable to the importer factor in the debtor's country or co-operates with it for collection. The importing factor subsequently assesses the financial position of the debtor and assumes the risk of non-payment of the debtor within a certain limit. On the due date, the debtor makes payment, which is transmitted from the importing factor to the exporting factor and then to the exporter. This structure is often referred to as the 'two-factor system' and is the most common form of international factoring. In particular, member organisations of international factoring chains such as Factors Chain International (FCI) adopt this operating model.

One of the most important functions of international factoring is the collection risk mitigation mechanism. In this context, especially the importing factor may assume responsibility for the debtor's ability to perform. This responsibility, limited to a predetermined credit limit, includes the factoring company's payment to the exporter in the event of non-payment by the debtor. However, exchange rate risk, transfer risk (e.g. non-payment due to foreign exchange controls) and political risks are generally excluded from the responsibility of factoring companies. Additional insurance mechanisms may need to be put in place for such risks. Since the importing factor is generally more familiar with the local legislation and commercial practices of the buyer, it can more accurately assess the financial structure and payment habits of the debtor. Therefore, a significant portion of the risk management functions in the factoring chain are fulfilled by the importing factor.

The International Factoring Convention of 1988 prepared by UN International Institute for the Unification of Private Law (UNIDROIT) as one of the most vital legal texts on international factoring is designed to ensure legal security in cross-border factoring relationships, especially in the assignment of receivables, rights and obligations of the parties, and cross-border factoring relationships.[16] The agreement clearly states that factoring is specifically related to trade receivables and does not cover consumer receivables. It is also stipulated that the agreements between the parties must be in writing and contain certain standard elements.

Example

A manufacturer in Turkey sells to a buyer in Germany with a 90-day maturity. The manufacturer assigns its receivables to an export factor in Turkey. This company realises the collection through the import factor in Germany and provides early payment to the manufacturer.◄

3.1.7 Factoring Applications in G-20 Countries

Factoring originated in the 17th century and emerged especially in the English legal system. This method has gained an important place in international trade and was initially used extensively in the textile trade between the UK and the US.[17] Since then factoring practices have been playing an important role in trade finance on a global scale, and legal regulations in this field vary significantly from country to country. An analysis of G20 countries reveals that multidimensional factors such as assignment of receivables, regulatory oversight, sharia compliance, digitalisation and fintech integration are decisive on factoring systems. In this context, regulatory approaches to factoring activities in both developed economies and

[16] The Rome Convention of 1980 on the law applicable to contractual obligations and the United Nations Convention of 2001 on the assignment of receivables in international trade are other sources in global dimension.

[17] Paraschiv (2013) 138-142.

emerging markets vary according to the nature of economic structures, legal systems and financial markets. In Table 3.1, the main findings of this comparative study are presented in a systematic manner.

As seen in the above table, the transfer of receivables in factoring transactions is secured in different ways among legal traditions. Some of these jurisdictions, which follow Anglo-Saxon legal tradition (e.g. the US, the UK and Australia), it is deemed sufficient to notify the debtor for the assignment of receivables to the factor and the consent of the buyer is not required. In contrast to this, in continental Asian legal systems such as Japan and China, the consent of the buyer is important in terms of the effectiveness of the assignment and this consent may be made a contractual prerequisite, especially in corporate commercial relations.

Some of the G20 member countries, where the influence of Islamic jurisprudence is very strong, factoring transactions are designed in accordance with the Sharia principles. The factoring models developed in Saudi Arabia and Indonesia are based on an interest-free transaction structure and risk sharing between the parties. In these countries, factoring is designed through Islamic finance instruments based on trade in goods and services, rather than conventional debt financing. Therefore, factoring has taken on a special form in accordance with religious norms by separating from conventional finance systems.

Whether factoring activities are subject to public supervision varies depending on the intensity of regulation in the financial systems of countries. In emerging markets such as Türkiye, India and China, factoring companies are under the direct supervision of the relevant public authorities. In these countries, regulation and supervision mechanisms are strict to maintain financial stability. In contrast, in market-oriented economies, such as the US, Canada and the UK, factoring transactions have a relatively liberalised environment, and the regulation is held at a rather muted level to promote entrepreneurial behaviour and stimulate financial innovations.

To increase the level of transparency in receivable assignments, as well as to clarify the rights of the third party, some members of the G20 have established the mechanism of electronic registries. In the case of Personal Property Securities Register (PPSR) adopted in Australia, the legal security is enhanced by the electronic registration of the assignment transactions. Similarly, important steps have been taken in the EU countries to digitise notifications regarding assignment of receivables. These systems consequently have one significant impact to the financial markets in that they hasten and enhance the effectiveness of factoring transactions.

The emergence of financial technology has brought new regulatory demands in the field of factoring sector. An Indian Directive allowed FinTech companies to engage in factoring activities and created a great digitalisation momentum in this field. This legislative spur enabled traditional non-banking financial institutions to engage in trade receivables financing and also the expansion of the credit access, especially to the SMEs. The resulting innovation shows that there are both financial and technological innovations that are welcome in factoring practices.

Table 3.1 Factoring applications in G-20 countries

	Regulations	Relevant Authority	Distinctive Features
Türkiye	6361 Financial Leasing, Factoring and Funding Companies Law	Banking Regulation and Supervision Board	Factoring companies are subject to licensing requirements and operational supervision
The US[18]	Uniform Commercial Code (UCC) - Article 9 (Secured Transactions)	State-based financial authorities	Factoring transactions are regulated as "secured transactions" – hence, creditors must register (perfection/filing) under UCC
Germany	Bürgerliches Gesetzbuch (BGB) & Handelsgesetzbuch (HGB)	Bundesanstalt für Finanzdienstleistungsaufsicht (The Federal Financian Supervisiory Authority)	Non-bank financial institutions are not subject to licensing
France	Code Monétaire et Financier & Code de Commerce	Autorité de Contrôle Prudentiel (ACP)	Factoring is carried out through a special assignment system called *cession dailly*[19]
The UK[20]	Common law & Receivables Financing Regulation	FCA (Financial Conduct Authority)	Assignment of invoices is permitted. "Confidential invoice discounting" is common[21]
Italy	Civil Code & Legislative Decree No. 231/2002	Bank of Italy	Factoring companies have specific licensing and transparency rules
Canada	Common Law & Provincial PPSA (Personal Property Security Acts)	Provincial regulators	It is regulated at the state level; the rules for granting property vary from state to state

(continued)

[18] See Tatge et al. (2017).

[19] Cession Dailly is a special and simplified system under French law for the assignment of both present and future receivables as per Articles L313-23 and L313-35 of the Code monétaire et financier (CMF). It takes its name from the Dailly Act of 1981, which introduced this regulation. This system is used in particular by banks to obtain collateral through assignment of receivables when lending to businesses. The assignment of the receivable does not require the consent of the debtor, the assignment is made only by means of a simplified written notice.

[20] See, Ruddy and Mills (2020).

[21] In confidential invoice discounting, businesses assign their invoices to factoring companies, but the debtors (buyers) are not informed about these assignments. Therefore, the collection is still made by the seller and transferred to the factoring company. In this model, financing is usually provided but no service is provided (this is the difference from full factoring). The Receivables Financing Regulations (SI 2018 No. 1254), which came into force in 2018, invalidate contractual provisions that prevent the free assignment of receivables.

Table 3.1 (continued)

	Regulations	Relevant Authority	Distinctive Features
Japan	Japanese Civil Code	Financial Services Agency (FSA)	The assignment of ownership is usually subject to the buyer's consent. Limited regulations exist
China	Civil Code of the RPC, Regulations on Non-Bank Financial Institutions, Commercial Bank Law of the RPC	CBIRC (China Banking and Insurance Regulatory Commission)	Non-bank factoring companies have been subject to strict regulations since 2020[22]
India	Factoring Regulation Act, 2011	Reserve Bank of India (RBI)	With the 2021 Factoring Regulation (Amendment) Act, fintech-based factoring companies were granted authorization[23] 2021 değişiklikleriyle fintech tabanlı faktöring şirketlerine yetki verilmiştir 2021 değişiklikleriyle fintech tabanlı faktöring şirketlerine yetki verilmiştir
Australia	Personal Property Securities Act 2009	ASIC (Australian Securities and Investments Commission)	Assignment notifications are made electronically. Transparency is paramount
Brazil	Civil Code & Central Bank Regulation	Banco Central do Brasil	Factoring usually operates under the name of fomento mercantil[24]
Argentina	Codigo Civil y Comercial de la Nacion	BCRA (Banco Central de la Republica Argentina)	Factoring and assignment of receivables are carried out through official documents; the notary system is effective

(continued)

[22] Zhang (2025) 12-20.

[23] Mittal (2022).

[24] *Fomento mercantil* refers to services that provide financing and collection support to businesses in exchange for the transfer of their receivables arising from the sale of goods/services. Factoring activities are not subject to a bank licence in Brazil, but have a special contractual nature as a *fomento comercial* activity. It is considered as a receivable transfer and management service, not lending (therefore not subject to credit regulations).

Table 3.1 (continued)

	Regulations	Relevant Authority	Distinctive Features
Mexico	Ley General de Títulos y Operaciones de Crédito	CNBV (Ulusal Banka ve Finansal Kurul)	Banka dışı faktöring şirketleri piyasada yaygındır
Russia	Sivil Kanun & Mikrofinans Kanunu	Merkez Bankası	Faktöring devlet destekli KOBİ finansman aracı olarak öne çıkar
Saudi Arabia	Regulations are developed within the framework of Islamic finance	SAMA (Saudi Arabian Monetary Authority)	Sharia-compliant factoring is common. Consent is essential in assignment transactions
Indonesia	Directives and Regulations by Otoritas Jasa Keuangan (OJK)	OJK (Financial Services Authority)	Sharia-compliant factoring products have also been developed
South Korea	Commercial Act & Financial Services Commission kuralları	FSC (Financial Services Commission)	Transactions are conducted by private companies linked to banks
South Africa	National Credit Act & Common Law	NCR (National Credit Regulator)	Assignment and collection transactions are recorded
EU	EU Financial Services Directives (PSD2, CRR/CRD)	European Central Bank & National Authorities	No binding directive at EU level; regulations are country-based

3.1.8 Some Legal Disputes Arising from Factoring Agreements

3.1.8.1 Distinction between True Sale and Secured Debt

In factoring transactions, whether the transfer of receivables is a true sale or a secured debt is of critical importance, especially in bankruptcy proceedings. If the transaction is not a true sale, the rights of the factoring company may be jeopardised as the transferred receivables may be included in the debtor's bankruptcy estate. For this reason, it is important to use expressions that clearly indicate that the transaction is a sale (e.g. transfer of ownership, transfer of risk) in factoring agreements.[25]

3.1.8.2 Conflicts of Priority on Receivables

Although factoring agreements, by their very nature, obligate the client not to make commitments that conflict with other creditors, the order of priority may become unclear if more than one party (factoring company, banks or other creditors) claims

[25] Tatge et al.(2017); Kurtz (2022).

the same receivables. This may jeopardise the collection rights of the factoring company. Therefore, it is important to carry out a detailed due diligence to check the existence of other security rights (liens) prior to the assignment of receivables.

3.1.8.3 Status of Receivables in Bankruptcy

When the debtor goes bankrupt, it may become uncertain whether the receivables taken over by the factoring company will be included in the bankruptcy estate. In addition, the automatic stay may prevent the factoring company from making collections. In this context, an exemption from the automatic stay may be requested by co-operating with the bankruptcy court. In addition, prior to bankruptcy, the factoring company must protect its rights on receivables by registering a perfected interest.

3.2 Forfaiting

3.2.1 Origin and Conceptual Foundations

The term 'forfaiting' comes from the verb forfaire, meaning to forfeit in its current usage in law jurisdiction when exchanging rights or obligation against a fixed lump-sum rock. Post cold war trade finance, forfaiting is used as the non-recourse purchase of export receivables: a bank/financial institution (the forfeiter) buys medium/long-term obligations from an exporter in another country at a discount, freeing him from risk of non-payment.

> **Important**
> Forfaiting is the process of purchasing and discounting receivables arising from the export of goods and services on credit, which are to be collected according to a specific payment schedule, by a bank or a specialized financial institution without any recourse (unconditionally and irrevocably) against those who previously held this right.
>
> This method became popular in Europe after World War II, especially in Switzerland. During that moment in history, the demand of developing and Eastern Bloc countries was rising but required a 3-10 year purchase under credit to the exporters of Western European capital goods. The loans obtained by commercial banks were typically of short-term and recourse nature which was unpalatable by exporters. Swiss banks as well as the Zurich Kantonalbank, Union Bank of Switzerland (since renamed UBS) and Credit Suisse, converted it into a risk-transference instrument through forfaiting, and transformed it into a pure risk-transference instrument. Bills of exchange (avalised by a first-class bank) or letters of credit usually represented the debt paper, and were also secured in the country of the importer.
>
> Unlike traditional discounting method, where there would usually be the recourse to the exporter, forfaiting, by virtue of its legal novelty,

being true sale, vests the title and the risk of the debts in the forfaitor. This aspect alters the legal status of other parties to the same. The exporter becomes the seller of a sale on deferred payment, the forfaitor (usually a bank) transfers the credit risk of the importer (or its guarantor) to itself. The importer obtains the benefits of the longer payment terms and continuity of delivery. Under the international economic law, a forfaiting is positioned between factoring and securitisation. It only takes part in international, medium, long-term capital transactions that also obtained bank guarantees to promissory notes hence contrasting with factoring which also has credit sale principle.

Important
In terms of the emergence, forfaiting was firstly observed in Swiss Banks, which became mediators between the US and the Soviet Union in the 1960s, when the conflict between the two countries had turned to standstill as the US was demanding cash payments and Russia was demanding payments in instalments. Under this system, Swiss banks purchased the American receivables at a discount, made the payment immediately, thereby meeting the American demand, and allowing the Soviet Union, which insisted on to pay by instalments.

3.2.2 Establishment of the Forfaiting Agreement

On endorsement and delivery of the debt instruments, which are usually avalised bills of exchange, promissory notes, or deferred letters of credit, all claims and all the risks attaching to it, credit, country, currency, and interest-rate—are transferred to the analyser and the exporter is not involved. Overwriting the forfaiting multi-layer contract under law has the following form:

i. the exporting contract, whereby the seller that is exporter obtains the receivables;
ii. payment instrument (i.e., promissory notes or bills of exchange), which typically includes the bank guarantee of the importer;
iii. assignment or sale of the receivables, under which the exporter sells the receivables and the forfaitor receives it;
iv. payment guarantee, either an aval or a guaranteed letter, which is directed to the forfaitor.

In such cases, transfer of the receivables is under the assignment law (civil law jurisdiction) or assignment law (common law jurisdiction) the latter being controlled by the Bills of Exchange (BoE) Acts or Article 3 of the UCC. The forfaiting contract is always non-recourse. To this effect the contract should expressly declare that the forfaitor- or the holder of the receivables, is taking the default risk, except for the cases of fraud, breach of warranty, or the voiding of underlying obligation. Practically, forfaiting agreements have the ICC Uniform Rules for Forfaiting (URF 800) of 2013, which the International Chamber of Commerce edits as the paradigm of standardised documentation, risk distribution and dispute resolution. URF 800 offers a solid framework of legal predictability in cross-border dealings by accurately clarifying and standardising expressions without recourse, assignment of receivables and the enforceability of the guarantee.

3.2.3 The Process of Forfaiting

The forfaiting process in the field of international trade finance is followed by a sequential process that carefully takes into account the management of the credit risk, thorough documentation and on the legal enforceability of the facility. This methodology could be outlined into two major phases that are the pre-export stage and the post-export stage, after which execution and transfer processes are implemented.

3.2.3.1 Beginning of the Forfaiting Process

3.2.3.1.1 Before Exporting

The forfaiting process begins with steps taken in the pre-export phase, when the exporter and importer agree on a forward sale contract based on deferred payment. The contract should clearly specify the payment amount and currency, the maturity and number of instalments, the payment instruments to be used (e.g., BoE or promissory note), and the bank or guarantor that will support the importer's obligation. While contract negotiations are ongoing, the exporter evaluates both the importer's creditworthiness and the acceptability of the guarantee to be provided from the perspective of potential forfaitors; this is because the forfaitor's risk appetite largely depends on the legal infrastructure and credit rating of the guarantor's country. For example, a promissory note governed by German or Swiss law and backed by a bank aval is generally more readily accepted than documents governed by weaker and more uncertain legal systems due to the high degree of legal predictability. To reduce these uncertainties, the exporter may obtain a 'forfaiting commitment letter' from the forfaitor before finalizing the export contract. This commitment guarantees that the receivables will be purchased at predetermined discount terms once the goods are shipped and the receivables arise. From a legal perspective, this commitment is considered a binding conditional offer, subject to the condition that the receivables are properly documented and presented.

3.2.3.1.2 After Exporting

After the shipment is completed and commercial and financial documentation such as invoices, transport documents, and, if necessary, inspection/expertise certificates are prepared, the exporter presents the receivables to the forfaitor for purchase. At this stage, the forfaitor examines the submitted documents in terms of form and content, assessing their conformity with the contract, their authenticity, and their legal validity according to applicable law; in practice, this examination is often carried out on bills of exchange and promissory notes subject to the Geneva Uniform Bills of Exchange and Promissory Notes Act of 1930. If the documents are found to be in order, the forfaitor pays the amount to the exporter after deducting the discount amount and any fees and takes ownership of the receivables. From this moment on, the exporter is legally completely released from the debt relationship; the right to demand payment on the due date passes directly to the forfaitor and can be asserted against the importer or their bank/guarantor. This transfer is not a secured loan but a true sale, a distinction that is critically important from both legal and financial perspectives. A true sale removes receivables from the exporter's balance sheet, increasing liquidity and improving leverage ratios. Indeed, under accounting and prudential regulations (particularly IFRS 9 and Basel III), this off-balance-sheet accounting depends on a substantial transfer of risks, and forfaiting fulfils this condition by eliminating recourse against the exporter.

3.2.3.2 Course of Proceeding

3.2.3.2.1 Notifying

In the continuation of the forfaiting process, the notification stage is of great importance in terms of legally completing the transfer of receivables and protecting the rights of the forfaitor. Generally, in civil law systems, for example, according to Article 184 of the Turkish Code of Obligations, the transfer of a receivable is not legally binding on the debtor unless it is notified to the debtor. In this context, the notification in a forfaiting transaction aims to ensure that the importer recognizes the forfaitor, not the exporter, as the new creditor and makes the payment directly to them. However, if the receivable is based on negotiable instruments such as bills of exchange or promissory notes, the proper endorsement and delivery of the instrument is generally sufficient for the transfer of the receivable; further notification is not legally required. In contrast, in transactions based on letters of credit, the bank notifying or confirming the letter of credit must be informed to ensure the payment is directed to the correct party. Otherwise, if the importer or the relevant bank is not notified of the transfer, the importer may make payment to the exporter in good faith, which could expose the forfaitor to the risk of double payment and weaken their rights. Therefore, notification, although not formally mandatory in some instruments, is considered a critical step in practice to safeguard the forfaitor's interests.

3.2.3.2.2 Forfaiting Organization's Offer

Following the completion of the notification phase, the forfaiting entity prepares a formal offer form or discount agreement outlining the terms of the transaction. This document clearly states the nominal amount and currency of receivables, the applicable discount rate and maturity structure, fees to be collected, withholding taxes and other expenses, applicable law and competent court, and that the transaction is without recourse. Thus, the rights and obligations between the forfaitor and the exporter become concrete and binding. Upon the exporter's acceptance of this offer, a fully binding forfaiting agreement is established, subject to general contract law provisions and, if agreed upon by the parties, the ICC's URF 800 (Uniform Rules for Forfaiting). The determined discount rate is generally based on current market references such as the Euro Interbank Offered Rate (EURIBOR) or the SOFR (historically LIBOR has also been used); however, this rate is subject to upward adjustments taking into account factors such as the risk of the importer's country, the credit risk of the guarantor bank, and the maturity period. From a legal perspective, the discount rate can affect not only the economic cost but also the legal nature of the transaction; in some legal systems, applying an excessive discount may risk reclassifying the transaction not as a genuine sale of receivables, but as a disguised lending arrangement.

3.2.3.2.3 Transfer and Purchase of Receivables by Contract

In forfaiting transactions, the assignment and purchase of receivables are carried out through a deed of assignment signed between the parties, or, if negotiable instruments are involved, through proper endorsement and delivery. At this stage, the exporter explicitly declares and undertakes that the receivables subject to assignment are valid, unconditional, and enforceable; that the goods have been delivered in accordance with the sales contract; that there are no claims, counterclaims, or third-party rights to the receivables; and that the exporter is the full owner authorized to assign said receivables. In return, the forfaitor agrees to waive its right of recourse against the exporter, except in cases of fraud or breach of these declarations and undertakings. The assignment takes effect immediately upon the signing of the deed of assignment and delivery of the relevant instruments; thus, ownership of the receivables instantly passes to the forfaitor. From this point onward, the forfaitor legally acquires the status of a "holder in due course," entitled to demand full payment from the importer or their guarantor, and is unaffected by disputes arising from the underlying contract between the exporter and the importer. This principle is explicitly set out in Article 16 of the ICC's URF 800 rules and is also consistent with generally accepted principles of commercial law, including those under the 1930 Geneva Convention on BoE.

3.2.4 Pearls and Pitfalls of the Forfaiting Process

3.2.4.1 For the Exporter

The forfaiting process offers both significant advantages and some drawbacks for exporters. The most important advantage is that the exporter receives immediate cash upon sale of receivables; this completely eliminates credit risk related to the importer. Similarly, removing receivables from the balance sheet provides balance sheet relief and contributes to improved debt and leverage ratios. Furthermore, since not only commercial risks but also political and transfer risks are transferred to the forfaiter, there is a comprehensive risk transfer for the exporter. Knowing cash flows in advance significantly facilitates the exporter's liquidity and financial planning.

However, forfaiting also brings some disadvantages. Firstly, the applied discount rates can be higher compared to secured loans, especially when dealing with long-term and high-risk countries, increasing financing costs. Secondly, by transferring receivables, the exporter waives any potential interest or return they might have earned until maturity. Due to the legal structure of the transaction and the payment instruments used, the paperwork is relatively heavy; the creation of collateral and the preparation of contracts often require expert legal and financial advice. Finally, since the forfaitor's willingness to enter the transaction largely depends on the credit rating of the importer's bank or guarantor, the exporter has limited control over this element. From a legal perspective, the exporter's main risk is concentrated in the areas of reputation and contractual liability; because in cases such as misrepresentation, incomplete disclosure, or breach of guarantee, liability may arise again despite the non-recourse nature of the transaction.

3.2.4.2 For the Forfaitor

From a forfaitor's perspective, forfaiting is an attractive investment vehicle offering certain and predictable returns. Since the purchased receivables provide a fixed and predetermined return, the cash flow and return calculations are relatively clear for the forfaitor. Furthermore, because these receivables are often backed by bank guarantees or guarantees from governments or state-backed institutions, the risk becomes secured. Including cross-border receivables from different countries and counterparties in the portfolio helps the forfaitor diversify its portfolio by distributing country and counterparty risk.

However, the forfaitor faces various risks, particularly those inherent in the nature of international transactions. Sovereignty and political risks, such as payment moratoriums, currency transfer restrictions, or nationalization, can make collection virtually impossible. In addition, differences in national laws regarding negotiable instruments can make the legal assertion and enforcement of receivables more difficult. Deficiencies in the form or content of documents—for example, an invalid guarantee, incomplete endorsement, or an improperly prepared promissory note—can even render the receivable entirely void. To mitigate these risks, forfeiters seek risk insurance through export credit agencies (ECAs), the Multilateral Investment Guarantee (MIGAs), or private insurance companies, and include choice of law and jurisdiction clauses in their contracts, preferring jurisdictions with high legal predictability.

3.2.4.3 Applicable Law to the Forfaiting Agreement

Determining the applicable law to a forfaiting contract is of particular importance due to the multifaceted and multi-legal nature of the transaction. Forfaiting, by its very nature, has an international legal framework encompassing different areas such as contract law, bill of exchange law, assignment of receivables, and banking regulations. Therefore, both international private law rules and the contractual intentions of the parties (lex contractus) are considered together in determining the applicable law.

3.2.4.3.1 Choice of Law

In practice, the parties often choose English or Swiss law due to its legal predictability, impartiality, and developed case law. According to the Rome I Regulation, such a choice of law is generally valid; however, this choice must not contradict the mandatory provisions of a country more closely connected to the transaction. In cases where the parties do not explicitly choose a law, the law of the forfaitor's habitual place of residence or the law of the place where the payment is to be made usually applies, as the economic centre of gravity is often concentrated in these areas.

3.2.4.3.2 Public Law Aspects

Forfaiting transactions are not limited solely to private law rules; regulations of a public law nature, such as foreign exchange regimes, AML, financing of terrorism, and sanctions, apply independently of the parties' intentions and limit contractual freedom. For example, the European Union's AML Directives mandate customer identification and transaction monitoring obligations in receivables assignment transactions, while the OFAC sanctions may completely prohibit payments in specific individuals, countries, or currencies. Similarly, in Turkey, Decree No. 32 on the Protection of the Value of the Turkish Currency contains mandatory rules regarding the repatriation of export proceeds and foreign exchange transactions. Therefore, even a forfaiting agreement established entirely within the realm of private law between the parties must be implemented within the framework of these regulations concerning public order.

3.2.4.3.3 Dispute Resolution

In terms of dispute resolution, ICC arbitration is frequently used in forfaiting transactions to ensure impartiality and international enforceability. The ICC's URF 800 Rules also explicitly support the resolution of disputes arising from forfaiting contracts in accordance with the ICC Arbitration Rules, designating centres such as Paris or Geneva as the *de facto* default venues for arbitration. However, national courts retain residual jurisdiction with regard to urgent and temporary legal protection measures such as provisional injunctions, provisional attachments, or asset freezes.

3.2.4.4 Interaction with Other Legal Instruments

Forfaiting is not a closed legal regime in itself, but interacts with various international regulations. The 2001 UNCITRAL Convention on the Assignment of Receivables provides a general framework for cross-border assignment transactions, while the 1930 Geneva Convention on Bills of Exchange forms the basis for forfaiting transactions based on negotiable instruments. On the other hand, Basel III regulations classify forfaiting receivables backed by bank guarantees as relatively low-risk assets, directly affecting the capital adequacy calculations of financial institutions. In this respect, forfaiting is a hybrid legal institution that combines contractual, negotiable instrument law-based, and regulatory elements.

3.2.5 Conclusion

In conclusion, forfaiting, initially a niche financing technique centred in Europe, has become a globally standardized tool for risk-free export financing. Its legal strength lies in combining assignment of receivables, guarantee mechanisms, and discounting principles into a single structure, thereby both creating liquidity and maintaining legal certainty. Essentially, forfaiting represents the conversion of a term-bound credit relationship into capital through legal instruments; in other words, the law eliminates the commercial tension arising from the time difference between delivery and payment, immediately transforming deferred promises into economic value.

3.3 Financial Leasing

3.3.1 Form of Financial Leasing Agreement

Financial leasing agreements must be in writing because they impose legally binding obligations on the parties and involve the transfer of significant rights of use and possession over the leased asset. Today, financial leasing has become a fundamental tool of global commercial financing, offering a flexible and effective alternative to traditional bank loans for asset acquisition At the heart of this structure are financial leasing companies (lessors) whose primary activity is providing asset-based financing. The essence of financial leasing lies in the functional separation of ownership rights: the rights to use and benefit from the asset are transferred to the lessee, while the right of disposal and ownership remains with the lessor. Thus, the main purpose of the contract is to secure financing for an asset that will generate economic return.

In practice, a financial leasing relationship consists of three legally independent but economically and functionally linked contracts: the sales (supply) contract between the supplier and the lessor, the financial leasing contract between the lessor and the lessee, and, where necessary, an insurance or guarantee contract. While each contract is subject to its own legal regime, this interoperable structure forms the characteristic 'tripartite' structure of financial leasing. This structure is explicitly regulated in Article 1 of the 1988 UNIDROIT International Financial Leasing Agreement, ensuring that the lessor is positioned solely as the financier, not the seller, of the asset, while the lessee is directly accountable to the supplier for defects and performance risks.

On the other hand, in common law systems, particularly in English and American law, certain formal elements are required for the validity of a financial leasing contract. These include a clear definition of the leased asset, the duration of the contract, and the determination of rental payments, all of which must comply with the formal requirements stipulated in UCC Article 2A. The absence of such mandatory elements may lead to the contract being deemed invalid or, considering its true nature, may be reclassified by the courts not as a lease but as an implicit loan or credit agreement. Therefore, compliance with the formal and substantive requirements of financial leasing agreements is critically important not only for legal validity but also for ensuring the transaction is classified correctly under the appropriate legal category.

3.3.1.1 The Scheme of Things

A financial lease constitutes a tripartite arrangement among the financial lease company (FLC) as lessor, the end-user as lessee, and the equipment supplier as vendor. The FLC serves as the financier, structuring transactions that separate legal ownership of the asset from its economic use. At the end of the lease term, the lessee typically has the option or obligation to acquire legal title to the asset for a nominal or residual value. This feature distinguishes a financial lease from an operating lease. The FLC's participation generally involves a four-stage process as demonstrated below:

i. Lessee Selection: The prospective lessee identifies the required asset, such as machinery, vehicles, or equipment, and selects an appropriate supplier.
ii. Lease Agreement: The lessee enters into a long-term, non-cancellable financial lease agreement with the FLC. This contract specifies periodic rental payments intended to cover the FLC's initial purchase price, related costs, and a profit margin throughout the lease term.
iii. Acquisition (supply agreement): The FLC acquires the asset from the supplier and obtains legal title.
iv. Delivery and Use: The supplier delivers the asset directly to the lessee, who generally assumes the rewards and risks of ownership, such as maintenance, insurance, and the risk of loss, an retains the right to use the asset for the majority of its economic life.

3.3.1.2 Functions

One of the key functions of the FLC is efficient risk management, which allows it to offer financing where traditional lenders might be hesitant. Because the FLC retains legal ownership, the asset itself serves as an inbuilt security. This retention provides the lessor with a superior and easier right to repossession in the event of lessee default, making it an instrument with higher *debt capacity* than secured lending, especially valuable for financially constrained firms. In many jurisdictions (such as the US Bankruptcy Code), the FLC's property interest (reversionary interest) provides better protection in the lessee's insolvency compared to a mere security interest. The lessor is typically immune from the general haircut taken by unsecured creditors, as the leased asset is generally not treated as part of the insolvent lessee's estate. FLCs protect their financing interest by employing hell or high water clauses in the lease contract. These clauses stipulate the lessee's unconditional obligation to continue making rental payments for the full term, regardless of defects in the equipment or disputes with the supplier, effectively shifting performance risk away from the FLC (the financier).

> **Important**
> FLCs are critical financial institutions that translate the abstract concept of asset financing into concrete, legally structured commercial relationships. Their continued success relies on their ability to navigate complex tax and accounting rules, maintain superior security rights, and adapt to the diverse economic and regulatory environments of global commerce.

3.3.1.3 Classification

The financial leasing industry typically exhibits an oligopolistic market structure, with dominance by subsidiaries of major banking groups or captive finance divisions of large manufacturers. FLCs can be classified into three primary categories:

i. Bank-related FLCs: These subsidiaries of commercial banks benefit from the parent bank's established reputation, substantial capital resources, and extensive customer network.
ii. Producer-Related (Captive) FLCs: These finance subsidiaries are established by manufacturers, whose primary function is to lease the parent company's products, thereby supporting sales and managing the secondary market for used assets.
iii. Independent FLCs: These entities are specialised firms unaffiliated with bank or manufacturers. Although they are less dominant overall, they serve an essential function within niche market segments.

3.3.2 Registration and Annotation of the Financial Lease Agreement

The registration and annotation of a financial leasing agreement serve a fundamental function, both in ensuring transparency and in protecting the lessor's rights against third parties. Since ownership rights remain with the lessor in financial leasing, while possession and actual use are transferred to the lessee, conflicts of rights with third parties such as creditors, pledgees, or bankruptcy administrators are possible. The registration mechanism prevents such conflicts, ensuring that the lessor's real rights are visible and enforceable.

This matter is explicitly regulated in Turkish law. According to Article 23 of Law No. 6361 on Financial Leasing, Factoring, and Financing Companies, financial leasing agreements relating to movable property must be registered in the register maintained by the Association of Financial Leasing, Factoring, and Financing Companies; agreements relating to immovable property must be registered in the land registry. This registration confirms the lessor's ownership rights, provides priority against subsequent real and personal rights such as liens, attachments, or mortgages, serves as legal notification to third parties, and secures the lessor's rights over the property in the event of the lessee's bankruptcy or insolvency.

Internationally, Article 7 of the 1988 UNIDROIT International Financial Leasing Agreement acknowledges that, provided the leased property is distinguishable, the lessor's ownership rights can, as a rule, be asserted against third parties without registration. However, considering the differences in approach between different legal systems, particularly in cross-border transactions, registration is strongly recommended for legal certainty and enforceability. In the European Union, regulations concerning consumer credit and asset-backed finance, along with various national registry systems, serve a similar function of transparency and protection; In the United States, in order for a lessor's interest to be asserted against third parties, a "financing statement" (UCC-1) must be registered under UCC Article 9, meaning the security right must be properly fulfilled.

3.3.3 Liabilities of the Parties Arising from the Financial Leasing Agreement

A financial leasing agreement creates reciprocal and complementary obligations between the lessor and the lessee; the lessor's primary obligation is to finance the asset and make it available for the lessee's use, while the lessee's primary obligation is to pay the lease payments and to use and maintain the leased asset in accordance with the agreement. These obligations stem not only from the provisions agreed upon by the parties in the contract but also from mandatory legal regulations specific to financial leasing. In this respect, a financial leasing agreement differs from classic lease or sales contracts, creating a *sui generis* debt relationship that strictly defines the rights and obligations of the parties both contractually and legally.

3.3.3.1 Obligations of the Lessor

3.3.3.1.1 Lessor's Obligation to Provide the Leased Property Subject to the Contract Determined by the Tenant

In a financial leasing agreement, one of the lessor's most fundamental obligations is to provide the leased asset, which meets the specifications and characteristics determined by the lessee. This obligation stems from the principle of 'lessee's freedom to choose the asset', a distinguishing feature of financial leasing. In this model, the lessee determines the type, technical specifications, and supplier of the asset; the lessor then purchases the asset according to these preferences and makes it available for the lessee's use. Therefore, the lessor's role is shaped more as a financier than a seller. If the lessor fails to provide the asset specified by the lessee at all, or fails to deliver it in accordance with the contract, this is considered a material breach of contract. Such a breach gives the lessee the right to terminate the contract for just cause and claim compensation for the damages incurred.

3.3.3.1.2 Tenant's Obligation to Transfer the Possession of the Goods Subject to the Contract to the Tenant

Under a financial leasing agreement, the lessor is obligated to transfer possession of the asset to the lessee after acquiring it. This transfer of possession does not refer to a transfer of ownership, but rather to the granting of legally permissible actual control and the right to use the asset to the lessee. Delivery is a critical turning point in a financial leasing relationship, as the lease term and the obligation to pay lease payments generally begin with delivery. If the lessor fails to deliver the asset or delays delivery, the lessee has the right to suspend lease payments or terminate the contract for just cause (rescission). In practice, however, delivery is often made directly by the supplier to the lessee, not through the lessor. This is consistent with Article 8 of the 1988 UNIDROIT International Financial Leasing Agreement, which stipulates that delivery made by the supplier to the lessee is legally considered equivalent to delivery made by the lessor. Thus, the lessor's absence from the actual delivery does not mean that the delivery obligation has not been fulfilled, and a solution consistent with the tripartite structure of financial leasing is achieved.

3.3.3.1.3 Lessor's Liability for Damages to the Leased Property

In financial leasing agreements, the lessor's liability for damage and loss to the leased asset is, as a rule, significantly limited by the contractual provisions. Since the lessor is essentially the financier, not the seller or operator of the asset, in accordance with the structure of financial leasing, they are generally not held liable for defects or technical and operational problems arising during use. However, if the damage results from the lessor's fault—for example, neglecting obligations such as obtaining insurance, maintenance, or supervision explicitly undertaken in the contract—this limited exemption from liability disappears, and the lessor may face liability for damages.

Timing is crucial in determining who bears the risk. The risk of damage or loss to the leased asset before delivery generally rests with the lessor, as possession has not yet passed to the lessee at this stage. After delivery, the risk passes to the lessee according to a clause commonly found in financial leasing practice and known as the hell or high water clause. This principle means that even if the asset is damaged, rendered unusable, or loses its economic value for any reason, the lessee's obligation to pay the lease payments in full and on time continues. In this respect, this provision is one of the fundamental mechanisms that strengthens the credit-like nature of financial leasing and minimizes the lessor's risk.

3.3.3.1.4 Responsibility of the Lessor for Defects of the Leased Property

In financial leasing agreements, liability for defects in the leased asset is, as a rule, directed not to the lessor, but to the supplier of the asset. Indeed, according to Article 8(2) of the UNIDROIT International Financial Leasing Agreement, the lessee can assert their rights and claims arising from the defective asset directly against the supplier; this mechanism allows the lessee to directly address the issue by bypassing the lessor. Therefore, under normal circumstances, the lessor is not held liable for defects in the asset. However, this exemption from liability may exceptionally be lifted if the lessor interferes with the selection of the asset, effectively eliminates the lessee's freedom of choice, or fails to transfer to the lessee the rights arising from warranties and defects that the lessor has against the supplier.

In several jurisdictions, the lessor is obliged to transfer to the lessee the rights relating to defects and warranties that the lessor has against the supplier. This regulation aims to protect the lessee not through the lessor's direct liability, but through subrogation and assignment of claims. Therefore, in financial leasing relationships, the lessee's legal protection against defective goods is based not on the lessor's liability for damages, but on transferable or directly usable rights that can be directed against the supplier.

3.3.3.1.5 Lessor's Obligation to Avoid the Tenant from Evasion

Another important obligation of the lessor under a financial leasing agreement is to ensure the lessee's safe and secure use of the leased property, in other words, to refrain from any interference that would infringe upon the lessee's possession. This obligation is an adaptation of the guarantee against eviction principle in classical lease law to financial leasing and covers situations such as eviction, obstruction of use, or claims of ownership or limited real rights by third parties.

In this context, if a third party claims a superior right over the leased property—for example, if the supplier asserts a retention of title or if a pre-existing real right exists over the property—the lessor is obligated to protect the lessee's possession. The lessor must defend the lessee against such claims, take legal action, or, if necessary, secure the lessee by compensating for any damages incurred. Otherwise, the lessor may face liability for breach of contract due to the infringement of possession.

3.3.3.1.6 Lessor's Obligation not to Transfer the Ownership of the Goods in the Tenant's Possession to a Third Party

In a financial leasing relationship, ownership of the leased asset constitutes the fundamental security element for the lessor. However, the lessor's transfer of ownership of the asset in the lessee's possession to a third party, or the establishment of a pledge, assignment, or similar real right on the asset during the lease term, seriously jeopardizes the lessee's contractual rights. Therefore, in financial leasing law, the transfer of ownership to third parties during the lease term is generally prohibited or at least considered inviolable against the lessee. Many national regulations and international agreements consider such transactions null and void for the lessee, thus protecting the lessee's right of use and possession.

If the lessor breaches this obligation, the lessee may claim compensation for damages suffered due to the breach; depending on the severity of the breach, the lessee may also have the right to terminate the contract for just cause. In this context, this prohibition functions as a fundamental safeguard mechanism protecting not only the lessee's actual use but also the economic stability and legal security of the financial leasing relationship.

3.3.3.2 Obligations of the Lessee (Tenant)

3.3.3.2.1 Duty of Paying the Price

In a financial leasing agreement, the lessee's most fundamental and primary obligation is to pay the agreed lease payments on time and in full. These payments are often structured to amortize the acquisition cost of the leased asset while simultaneously providing a certain return to the lessor; in this respect, financial leasing is a long-term and asset-based financing technique from an economic perspective. If the lessee defaults on their payment obligation, acceleration clauses, commonly found in contracts, come into effect, and even lease payments not yet due can be demanded immediately; in addition, the lessor is granted strong collateral and property rights such as the right to repossession of the asset.

According to the hell or high water clause, the lessee cannot evade their obligation to pay lease payments even if the leased asset becomes defective, unusable, or no longer provides economic benefit. The legal options available to the tenant in such situations are not limited to suspending rent payments, but rather to exercising their rights against the supplier based on defects and failure to perform. Thus, the contract deviates from a classic lease relationship, acquiring a structure specific to financing agreements that makes the tenant's payment obligation almost unconditional.

3.3.3.2.2 Obligation to Use Carefully According to the Terms and Provisions Provided in the Financial Rental Contract

Under a financial leasing agreement, the lessee is obligated to use the leased asset with care and only for the purposes agreed upon in the contract. This obligation is an adaptation of the general duty of care in contract law to financial leasing and prohibits the lessee from misusing the asset, operating it for purposes other than its intended use, or exceeding the limits stipulated in the contract. Contrary to the contract or negligent use of the leased asset constitutes a breach of contract for the lessor and may lead to various legal sanctions, including termination, depending on the severity of the breach.

This obligation is not limited to an abstract duty of care but also includes the lessee's compliance with technical user manuals, manufacturer's instructions, and license terms. Furthermore, compliance with local and mandatory legislation, such as environmental, occupational health and safety, or sectoral regulations, is an integral part of the lessee's duty of care. Violation of such rules may not only give rise to contractual liability but also subject the lessee to administrative or criminal sanctions.

3.3.3.2.3 Obligation to Provide All Kinds of Maintenance and Protection of the Leased Property

In a financial leasing agreement, unless otherwise stipulated, all obligations regarding the maintenance and protection of the leased asset belong to the lessee. This includes not only performing routine maintenance arising from the normal use of the asset, but also carrying out preventative and protective maintenance to prevent future malfunctions and depreciation. This maintenance obligation is consistent with the economic logic of financial leasing and is based on the fact that the lessee is the party directly benefiting from the asset. Failure of the lessee to properly fulfill their maintenance and protection obligations constitutes a breach of contract and may give rise to liability for damages resulting from unusual wear and tear, depreciation, or damage to the asset at the end of the lease term. In this context, the lessee is obligated to return the asset in the condition in which it was received, excluding wear and tear from normal use, in accordance with the contract; otherwise, compensation for the damages incurred may be claimed.

3.3.3.2.4 Obligation to Survive Damages and Losses of the Leased Property

According to financial leasing principles, the risk of damage and loss to the leased asset passes to the lessee upon delivery. This transfer of risk includes events independent of the lessee's fault, such as the total destruction of the asset by fire, theft, natural disaster, or accident. Even in such cases, as per the regulations commonly found in financial leasing agreements, the lessee's obligation to pay the lease payments generally continues; in other words, the asset becoming unusable does not automatically extinguish the payment obligation. However, if the damage is covered by insurance, the insurance compensation comes into play to compensate for the economic loss, and in practice, this compensation is directed to the lessor or to the settlement of the debt as stipulated in the contract.

This risk distribution is justified by the structural characteristics of financial leasing. The lessee is the party that chooses the type, technical specifications, and supplier of the leased asset; the lessor is only in the position of providing the financing in accordance with these choices. Therefore, the transfer of the risk of the asset failing to provide the expected economic benefit to the lessee, who aims to obtain that benefit, is considered consistent with the financing-oriented nature of financial leasing.

3.3.3.2.5 Obligation to Pay Insurance Premiums Related to the Property

In financial leasing agreements, ensuring the leased asset is a mandatory obligation. Insurance coverage is generally arranged to cover physical risks such as theft, damage, and fire, as well as damages that may be caused to third parties due to the use of the asset. The payment of these insurance premiums is, as a rule, the responsibility of the lessee; however, the insured or beneficiary status in the insurance contract is often given to the lessor, since the ownership right remains with the lessor. The lessee's failure to pay the insurance premiums or to obtain the necessary insurance constitutes a breach of contract and provides the lessor with various legal remedies. In this case, if stipulated in the contract, the lessor can obtain the insurance themselves and demand the premium costs from the lessee, or add these amounts to the lease debt. Thus, the insurance obligation functions as a fundamental risk management tool that both protects the economic value of the leased asset and secures the lessor's collateral interest.

3.3.3.2.6 Tenant's Obligation for not Transferring the Possession of the Rented Property to a Third Party Without the Written Permission of the Lessor

Under a financial leasing agreement, the lessee cannot transfer possession of the leased asset to a third party or grant the right of use through subleasing without the written consent of the lessor. This prohibition aims to protect the lessor's ownership rights and security interests in the asset; because the unauthorized transfer of possession to third parties can make it difficult to actually control the asset and complicate the repossession process in the event of termination of the contract. Failure to comply with this obligation is considered a material breach of contract and is often subject to severe penalties in financial leasing agreements. In practice, contracts may stipulate that unauthorized transfer of possession will be considered grounds for immediate termination and that the lessee will also be liable to pay pre-agreed liquidated damages or compensation. This provision serves as a fundamental safeguard mechanism protecting the element of personal trust and the economic stability of the financial leasing relationship.

3.3.3.2.7 Tenant's Obligation to Return the Rented Property to the Lessor at the End of the Contract Period

Upon termination of a financial lease agreement, the lessee is obligated to return the leased asset to the lessor, unless they have exercised a purchase option stipulated in the agreement. This return obligation includes delivering the asset in good condition, conforming to the contract, excluding wear and tear resulting from normal use. This obligation is a natural continuation of the lessee's duties of care and maintenance undertaken during the lease term. If the lessee fails to return the leased asset at the end of the term or delivers it in a severely damaged or non-conforming condition, the lessor has the right to pursue legal action. In this case, the lessor may demand compensation based on the current market value of the asset, or, if agreed upon in the contract, may demand payment of any unpaid lease balances or residual value. Thus, the return obligation functions as one of the fundamental mechanisms for maintaining economic balance between the parties upon termination of a financial lease relationship.

3.3.3.2.8 Obligation to Review the Rented Property After Receiving It and to Notify Any Defects Detected, if any, to the Lessor

Under a financial leasing agreement, the lessee is obligated to inspect the leased goods within a reasonable time upon delivery and to immediately notify the lessor of any clearly discernible defects or deficiencies. This notification obligation is a requirement of both the principle of contractual fidelity and the effective exercise of rights arising from defects. If the lessee delays an inspection that could be carried out at the time of delivery or fails to notify detectable defects in a timely manner, it implies acceptance of the goods in their current state. In this case, the lessee largely loses the ability to subsequently assert claims against the lessor based on these defects; in other words, delayed notification results in an implicit waiver of claims related to the defect. However, for hidden defects, the obligation to notify within a reasonable time at the time the defect becomes apparent continues. This regulation serves to clarify the moment of delivery and transfer of risk in the financial leasing relationship and to reduce legal uncertainties between the parties.

3.3.3.2.9 Regulatory Framework and Recognition (G20 Context)

Financial leasing is a regulated financial service in most G20 nations, with FLCs typically required to obtain licenses or register as financial institutions. The legal framework governing financial leasing is generally distributed across multiple legislative domains. For instance, in the US, the UCC Article 2A distinguishes a true lease from a secured transaction, or disguised sale, by assessing whether the lease term is shorter than the asset's economic life.[26] In Germany, the primary legal framework for financial leasing is shaped by tax law and commercial practice. Financial leasing serves as a leading source of external finance for SMEs.[27] In China, financial leasing companies are regulated under both the contract law and the financial leasing law. The Chinese market is a dominant growth in Asia, with expansion frequently driven by large infrastructure projects and state-backed entities.[28] As a different approach, France employs specific statutory instruments, such as the credit-bail, which explicitly recognizes the financial lease as a financing transaction distinct from an ordinary rental (louage).[29] Internationally, the UNIDROIT Convention on International Financial Leasing, though adopted by few countries, has served as a template for domestic reform and recognizes the tri-partite structure of financial leasing.

3.3.3.2.10 Specialised FLC Structures

FLCs have innovated specific structures to manage complex assets and financial risks as indicated below:

i. Leaseback (sale and leaseback): This two-party transaction involves a firm selling an already-owned asset to an FLC and immediately leasing it back. The firm gains an immediate cash infusion (liquidity) while retaining use of the asset. Legally, this can be controversial, as courts would likely to view it as a prohibited loan secured by a commercial sale, rather than a genuine lease.[30]
ii. Leverage leasing: A structure for financing high-cost, risky assets (e.g., aircraft, ships). It involves three parties: the lessee, the FLC (which provides only a portion of the equity, typically up to one-third), and a third-party lender (providing the debt financing). The FLC uses the borrowed funds to acquire

[26] Paglia (1988) 69-82.
[27] Friedrich (2019) 113-136.
[28] Liu and Huang (2023) 228-230; Stein (2010) 26-33.
[29] Brebisson (2018) 9-33.
[30] Peponis et al. (2024) 25-27; Notes (1972) 1221-1250; Notes (1949) 482-499.

the asset, and the lender's security is secured by the asset itself and an assignment of the future lease payments. This structure is prominent in the US and the Anglo-Saxon legal tradition.[31]

iii. Social leasing: An emerging model (e.g., France's EV program) aimed at achieving public policy goals, such as sustainability and social inclusion. FLCs are involved in providing assets (like electric vehicles or heat pumps) to low-income users at subsidized, affordable rates, often requiring government guarantees or grants to manage the credit risk.[32] For instance, France launched a social leasing program in 2024, enabling low-income individuals to rent electric vehicles at a subsidised rate of 100 Euros per month. As demand exceeded initial projections, the program was suspended at the same year, but it was subsequently relaunched in the autumn of 2025.[33]

3.4 Barter Leasing

The convergence between leasing and barter is a significant development reflecting the evolution of modern trade finance, pointing to hybrid structures where monetary and non-monetary transactions are increasingly intertwined. In this context, leasing-barter arrangements refer to transactions where leased goods become part of a reciprocal, cashless trade agreement, either in place of or in addition to cash payment. As Shestakovscaia points out, barter leasing is a type of material leasing where the lessee pays the lease payments with their own goods; in other words, the lease debt is fulfilled by providing goods or services instead of money.[34] In practice, this structure is particularly preferred in international trade and in markets where there are currency constraints, liquidity shortages, or commodity surpluses. For example, an exporter may lease industrial machinery to a foreign company through financial leasing; the lessee may then pay all or part of the lease payment by providing commodities, energy, production output, or specific services instead of cash. Such arrangements preserve the financing function of leasing while providing payment flexibility through the logic of barter, enabling the parties to establish a more multifaceted exchange relationship that is more compatible with their commercial needs.

3.4.1 Legal Structure

Businesses can extend their loan terms owing to the barter leasing system. This model establishes a hybrid legal structure combining the principles of financial

[31] See, Fabozzi (2008) 825-835.

[32] Unger et al.(2025).

[33] EAFO (2025); Lundberg et al. (2026); Cheron and Mathieu (2024).

[34] Shestacovscaia (2017) 332.

leasing and countertrade. The financial leasing contract functions as the primary financing mechanism, while the barter clause determines the methods and means by which the obligations between the parties will be fulfilled. Within this framework, instead of payment in cash, payment is stipulated to be made entirely or partially in kind, and this in-kind payment replaces or complements the cash lease payment. However, payment in kind requires a high degree of legal and financial certainty. The type, quantity, quality standards, and especially the monetary equivalent of the goods or services to be paid for must be clearly regulated in the contract. Otherwise, disputes may arise regarding whether the lease payment has been fulfilled. Furthermore, such arrangements must be compatible with mandatory public law regulations such as foreign exchange legislation, export-import regimes, customs rules, and taxation. Therefore, leasing-barter structures are subject to more complex legal oversight compared to classic financial leasing, requiring the consideration of both private law and regulatory law aspects in contract design.

3.4.2 Practical and Legal Challenges

Despite the flexibility of barter leasing, it carries substantial risks—chiefly valuation risk. Without objective valuation of in-kind payments, disputes often arise over obligation fulfillment. Contracts must explicitly state the market value, valuation method, and reference date of non-cash consideration. Taxation is another critical area of concern. Income earned through barter and cash rental payments may be subject to different VAT, corporate tax, or income tax regimes. This can create unexpected tax burdens or double taxation risks for the parties. Furthermore, the lessor must ensure that the payment of the in-kind rental does not infringe upon the principle of maintaining ownership of the property; otherwise, the incorrect structuring of the in-kind payment could lead to claims of implicit transfer of ownership.

Finally, compliance is a particularly sensitive aspect of leasing-barter transactions. Since barter transactions are frequently used in high-risk countries and sectors with currency restrictions or financial sanctions, full compliance with AML and CFT regulations, as well as export control and sanctions legislation, is mandatory. Non-compliance with these regulations may jeopardize the validity of the contract and may result in serious administrative and criminal penalties for the parties.

3.4.3 International Relevance

Leasing-barter arrangements have gained significant importance, particularly during periods of economic crisis and in trade with countries facing foreign exchange restrictions. In such environments, limited access to liquidity and restricted international payment channels can render classic cash-based financing models ineffective. Leasing-barter structures, however, stand out as hybrid financing tools that allow these obstacles to be overcome, enabling transactions that would be difficult or impossible under normal circumstances.

In this respect, leasing-barter combines the financing advantage of financial leasing, which facilitates asset acquisition, with the function of barter in balancing foreign trade and reducing foreign exchange needs.[35] Ultimately, this model exemplifies how legal creativity transforms into economic adaptability; that is, it embodies the capacity to produce flexible and innovative solutions that overcome the constraints imposed by market conditions at the intersection of law, finance, and trade.

Chapter Summary

Chapter 3 provides an exhaustive legal and operational analysis of the main non-bank financing and guarantee instruments used in international trade, focusing especially on Factoring, Forfaiting, and Financial Leasing. The discourse takes a philosophical approach and places each tool in the context of the global commercial law and practice.

Factoring is described as a complex financial service whereby a client or exporter sells its outstanding debts, which are short term in nature, at a discounted price to a factor. The major benefits that have been identified are the acquisition of instant fund, the professional handling of debts, and the reduction of default risk especially in non-recourse models. The chapter classifies factoring agreements as notified vs. non-notified, recourse vs. non-recourse, and international factoring with the two-factor system. It also examines legal challenges that are occasioned by a clear differentiation of a bona fide sale and secured debt, which is based on jurisprudential and doctrinal studies. The UNIDROIT Convention on International Factoring is the statutory basis of international law emphasized as offering a unified legal foundation.

Forfaiting is presented as a non-recourse and medium-term financing mechanism dedicated to capital goods exports. Here, trade receivables (usually formalised into bills of exchange or promissory notes) are sold to the forfeiter at a discounted price, thus shifting all the commercial, political and transfer risks to the exporter. It requires considerable paperwork, e.g. avalized note or bank guarantee to prove a real sale, and is often regulated by the ICC Uniform Rules for Forfaiting (URF 800). It involves both pre-export and post-export, and salient legal issues in the process include the enforceability of the aval and barring of recourse against the exporter.

Financial Leasing is introduced as a three-party contract between a lessor, lessee and supplier when financing an asset. In this type of structure, the legal ownership of assets, which are legally retained by the lessor or the financial leasing company, are separated in legal terms, and the right of use

[35] Hew (1992) 11-16.

is given to the lessee. Under the 'hell or high water' clause maintenance and loss risk are transferred to the lessee. The contract is normally written and registered to provide notice to the public that the lessor owns the property in case of insolvency. The chapter lists the legal obligations of the two parties: the lessor is under an obligation to deliver the asset without evading but the lessee has a duty to pay rent, use the asset prudently and finally, dispose of the asset, which is also required. Other specialized structures are also discussed like Leaseback and Leverage Leasing structures.

Lastly, the chapter briefly scouts over Leasing-Barter that constitutes a hybrid system where the lease payments are made partially or wholly through the release of goods or services and therefore, are an in-kind payment. This example is illustrating how financial instruments are flexible in law regarding currency limitations and how the relationship between ingenuity in contract and regulation is changing.

Revision Questions

1. Compare and contrast factoring with forfaiting, using three observable characteristics of each funding instrument: recourse to the customer, the maturities or time frames of receivables, and whether or not bills of exchange or promissory notes are utilized in their respective creation.
2. Differentiate between a "true sale" of a receivable and a secured debt for purposes of factoring; what is the major legal difference between a true sale and a secured debt; why is this difference important to the factor in the event that the customer files for bankruptcy.
3. Explain the tripartite nature of the financial leasing contract, and the role played by an FLC within the context of a true lease between a lessor and lessee. Explain how the registration or annotation of the financial lease provides the lessor with a pre-emption right.
4. Describe how the risk of payment default for a bill of exchange from an exporter to an importer is transferred under a "no recourse" principle in forfaiting. What are the main categories of risk that are transferred to the naliz ng? How is it possible to complete the transfer of such risks when the parties to the forfaiting transaction utilize bills of exchange as part of the transaction?
5. Explain the lessee obligations and risk of the "hell or high water" clause in financial lease agreements by specifically identifying the party to whom the clause most shifts the risk, how the clause relates to the lessor's limited liability due to equipment defects.
6. What are the main advantages of the two-factor system?
7. Briefly explain the leasing-barter system.◄

References

Bakker M, Klapper L, Udell G (2004) Financing Small and Medium-size Enterprises with Factoring: Global Growth in Factoring- and Its Potential in Eastern Europe. The World Bank

Beale H, Gullifer L, Paterson S (2016) A Case for Interfering with Freedom of Contract? An Empirically-informed Study of Bans of Assignment. Journal of Business Law 3:203–230

Brebisson H (2018) Finance Leases and the Principle of Substance-over-form in France. Audit Comptabilite Controle: Recherches Appliquees 2018(1):9–33

Castellano G (2023) Knowledge Guide on Factoring Regulation and Supervision. https://www.ifc.org/content/dam/ifc/doc/2024/knowledge-guide-on-factoring-regulation-and-supervision-ifc-2024.pdf. Accessed 31 Jan 2026

Cheron M, Mathieu L (2024) Social Leasing: A Key Measure for National Social Climate Plans: A Targeted Support to Promote Access to Electric Vehicles for Middle and Low Income Households. https://www.transportenvironment.org/uploads/files/2024_10_Social_leasing_briefing.pdf. Accessed 31 Jan 2026

EAFO (2025) France Launches 2025 Round of Social Leasing for electric Cars, European Alternative Fuels Observatory. https://alternative-fuels-observatory.ec.europa.eu/general-information/news/france-launches-2025-round-social-leasing-electric-cars. Accessed 31 Jan 2025

Fabozzi F (2008) Handbook of Finance: Financial Markets and Instruments. Wiley

Friedrich J (2019) The Effect of Academic Literature on Accounting Regulation: Evidence from Leases in Germany. Accounting History Review 30:113–136

Hew R (1992) Barter Leasing. Journal of Equipment Lease Financing 10(1):11–16

Istuk I (2015) The Potential of Factoring for Improving SME Access to Finance. In: Dahan F (ed) Research Handbook on Secured Financing in Commercial Transactions. Edward Elgar, pp 212–234

Kurtz S (2022) True Sale of Accounts in Bankruptcy – A Different Perspective. https://magazine.factoring.org/magazine-articles/true-sale-of-accounts-in-bankruptcy-a-different-perspective. Accessed 31 Jan 2026

Liu J, Huang R (2023) The Development of the Financing Leasing System in China. Saudi Journal of Business and Management Studies 8(9):228–230

Lundberg L, Bengtsson G, Sprei F, Fernqvist N, Zetterholm J (2026) Transportation Research Part D. Transport and Environment 151:105126

Marak Z, Pillai D (2021) Relationship between International Factoring and Cross-border Trade: A Granger Causality Approach. Margin The Journal of Applied Economic Research 15(3):320–337

Michalski G (2009) Influence of the Accounts Receivable Factoring on the Firm Value. Research Papers of Wroclaw University of Economics 48:566–574

Milenkovic-Kerkovic T, Dencic-Mihajlov K (2012) Factoring in the Changing Environment: Legal and Financial Aspects. Procedia – Social and Behavioral Sciences 44:428–435

Mittal M (2022) Factor's Registration Regulations: Going Back to Square-on?. https://vinodkothari.com/2022/01/factors-registration-regulations-going-back-to-square-one. Accessed 31 Jan 2026

Mizan A (2011) Factoring: A Better Alternative of International Trade Payment Methods. ASA University Review 5(9):247–264

Nagy Z (2008) Theoretical Principles of the Classification of Factoring Deals. Public Finance Quarterly 53(1):131–115

Notes (1949) Disclosure Problems in Sale and Leaseback Transactions. The University of Chicago Law Review 16(3):482–499

Notes (1972) The Expanding Definition of "Security": Sale-Leasebacks and Other Commercial Leasing Arrangements. Duke Law Journal 6:1221–1250

Paglia L (1988) U.C.C. Article 2A: Distinguishing between True Leases and Secured Sales. St. John's Law Review 63(1):69–82

Paraschiv C (2013) Factoring Agreement – Instrument for Credit Institutions. Agora International Journal of Juridicial Sciences 7(4):138–142
Peponis M, Reaves K, Reynolds D, Lanzkron J (2024) Sale-Leasebacks: A Tool for the Times. Real Estate Finance Journal 40(2):25–27
Pigula E, Paduszynska (2015) Factoring as a Special Means of Financing SMEs' Activities – The Case of Enterprises in the Lodz Area. Journal of Finance and Financial Law 2(3):103-117
Puja A (2022) Sustaining Access to Finance for Africa's Small and Medium Enterprises During and Post COVID-19 Crisis: Factoring to the Rescue. Speculum Juris 36(2):387–409
Pylypenko S, Udovenko Y, Cherneha V (2018) Legal Description of the Factoring Contract in Romania. Baltic Journal of Economic Studies 4(5):251–255
Ruddy N, Mills S (2020) Sallinger on Factoring. Sweet and Maxwell
Sayer B (2024) Understanding Factoring Rates, Fees, and the Total Cost of a Factoring Agreement. https://ecapital.com/blog/understanding-rates-fees-and-the-total-cost-of-a-factoring-agreement. Accessed 31 Jan 2026
Shestacovscaia A (2017) Specific of the Development of Leasing Activity in the Republic of Moldova. Scientific Papers Series Management, Economic Engineering in Agriculture and Rural Development 17(2):331–336
Silverman H (1949) Factoring as a Financing Device. Harvard Business Review 27:594–611
Spasić I, Bejatović M, Dukić-Mijatović M (2012) Factoring - Instrument of Financing in Business Practice –Some Important Legal Aspects. Economic Research-Ekonomska Istraživanja 25(1):157–173
Stein G (2010) Commercial Leasing in China: An Overview. Cornell Real Estate Review 8:26–33
Tatge D, Tatge J, Flaxman D (2017) American Factoring Law.. Bureau of National Affairs
Unger N, Kreye K, Seibert D (2025) Assessing the Need for Social Support and Designing Social Leasing as Part of the Transition to Electric Vehicles in Europe. https://www.oeko.de/fileadmin/oekodoc/Social-leasing-tech-report.pdf. Accessed 31 Jan 2026
Zhang W (2025) Coordinating Financial Regulation and Financial Technology of China: Current State and Internal Mechanisms. Journal of Education Humanities and Social Sciences. 61:12–20

Further Reading

ICC (2012) Uniform Rules for Forfaiting - URF 800 (Including Model Agreements)
Maulidiana L (2018) Implementation of Leasing Contract in Non-banking Finance Institutions. European Research Studies Journal 21(4):255–267
Merrill T (2020) The Economics of Leasing. The Journal of Legal Analysis 12:221–272
Milenkovic-Kerkovic T, Dencic-Mihajlov K (2012) Factoring in the Changing Environment: Legal and Financial Aspects. Procedia – Social and Behavioral Sciences 44:428–435
Schroth P (2010) Financial Leasing of Equipment in the Law of the United States. The American Journal of Comparative Law 58:323–351
Silverman H (1948) Factoring: Its Legal Aspects and Economic Justification. Law and Contemporary Problems 13(4):593–608
Spasic I, Bejatovic M, Dukic-Mijatovic M (2012) Factoring – Instrument of Financing in Business Practice – Some Important Legal Aspects. Economic Research 25(1):157–173
UNCITRAL (2017) Model Law on Electronic Transferable Records (MLETR)

Establishment of Banks

4

Contents

F. B. Erdem, *The Principles of International Banking, Finance and Investment Law*, Springer Textbooks in Law, https://doi.org/10.1007/978-3-032-32505-1_4

Abstract

This chapter explores the intricate legal framework governing the establishment and operation of banks, emphasizing their nature as corporate entities. Incorporation legally transforms a bank into a distinct legal entity, equipped with its own organs and attributes as prescribed by law. This requirement applies universally to various types of banks, including deposit, participation, development, investment, and offshore banks. The chapter begins by outlining the essential conditions for establishing banks, such as obtaining an establishment license or official authorization, ensuring capital adequacy, and understanding the grounds for license revocation. It also covers the necessary elements of a banks articles of association and the specific conditions under which foreign banks can open branches in third countries. This section delves into the legal provisions related to deposit and participation fund collection, detailing the processes for opening and withdrawing from deposit and participation fund accounts. It also addresses the prescription of deposit money, the insurance of deposits and participation funds, and the legal aspects of safe-deposit boxes. The chapter discusses the restructuring mechanisms available to banks, including mergers (with a focus on foreign bank mergers), takeovers, and cross-border reorganizations. It highlights the reasons for mergers in the banking sector, such as value maximization through increased efficacy, monopoly power, competition, and the influence of governmental policies. Additionally, the chapter examines other factors that accelerate the merger process, including technological advancement, deregulation, and globalization. The chapter concludes by exploring the process of bank insolvencies, covering enforcement provisions, the foreclosure of pledged property, bankruptcy proceedings, and the follow-up on public receivables. It also discusses the process of insolvency and the role of deposit insurance in protecting the financial system.

4.1 Establishment of Banks: Legal Genesis and Regulatory Framework

Banks hold a significant place within the financial system as financial institutions that facilitate the lending of funds collected from those with surplus funds to those who demand funds. In other words, banks ensure the most efficient exchange between savings and investments. Beyond facilitating the flow of funds in the economy, banks also have other important economic functions, such as creating fiat money, assisting in the implementation of monetary and fiscal policies, and influencing income and wealth distribution.

There is a balancing mechanism regarding the approval of bank establishments. This balance is sought between the public will, which aims to ensure macroeconomic stability by protecting depositors, and the will of private enterprises established for profit, expected to create value in financial markets. This explains the requirement for banks to obtain operating licenses from public administrations in all developed countries under the influence of liberalization. Only in this way can the public administration filter whether the relevant banking establishments meet financial standards.

> **Important**
> 'Too big to fail' is a term frequently cited in the 2008 US banking crisis, which emphasizes the importance of the banking system but also shows how harmful bank failures can be within the macroeconomic order. It is based on the idea that when large banks in a financial system fall into difficulty and fail to meet their obligations, this can have devastating and contagious effects on the whole economic order, and the state will ultimately suffer the consequences.[1]

Therefore, the commencement of banking operations is subject to a licensing or authorization process conducted by competent supervisory authorities. While this regulatory prerequisite is universally accepted, the scope, intensity, and procedural architecture of supervisory discretion vary significantly across legal systems. In this regard, to determine the financial adequacy and reliability of banks to be established for authorization, they are expected to meet specified capital adequacy.

Banks must have a certain level of payment capacity and in this regard, they are assessed based on whether they meet their financial obligations, specifically in terms of their RWA and whether they meet the minimum capital adequacy requirements. Under the Basel III standards, which were introduced after the 2008 crisis to strengthen banks' financial adequacy and, as a result, make the financial system more resilient, banks are required to hold sufficient and high-quality capital against the risks they bear. Capital adequacy is measured by the level of capital a bank holds relative to its RWA.[2]

According to Basel III, the most fundamental capital item that banks must hold is Common Equity Tier (CET) 1 capital. This capital consists of paid-in capital, retained earnings, and other high-quality equity elements. To enable banks to absorb losses, the CET1 ratio must be at least 4.5% of risk-weighted assets. However, in addition to CET1, Basel III also regulates the Tier 1 capital ratio, which includes additional primary capital instruments (Additional Tier 1) with specific characteristics. Accordingly, banks' Tier 1 capital must be at least 6% of their risk-weighted assets.[3] Basel III also sets a minimum threshold for banks' total regulatory capital. The total capital adequacy ratio includes Tier 1 capital along with Tier 2 capital elements, which are of lower quality but have loss-absorbing capacity. This total capital must be at least 8% relative to risk-weighted assets.

---

[1] Omarova (2019) 2495.

[2] Cecchetti and Kohler (2014) 205–231.

[3] BIS (2011) 12.

This ratio is the fundamental minimum threshold that has long been maintained under Basel regulations.[4]

In addition, Basel III introduced the Capital Conservation Buffer to encourage banks to build up capital during good times. This buffer consists entirely of CET1 capital and is set at a minimum of 2.5%. The purpose of this buffer is to ensure that banks can continue to lend when economic conditions deteriorate. Therefore, in practice, a bank must have a CET1 ratio above 4.5%, reaching a total of approximately 7%, in order to operate without restrictions. Another tool to be applied during periods of increased macroeconomic risk is the countercyclical capital buffer.[5] National regulatory authorities can set this buffer between 0% and 2.5% during periods of excessive credit growth. This buffer is also covered by CET1 capital and aims to limit the impact of financial cycles on the banking system. Finally, Basel III introduced the leverage ratio as a simple safety mechanism that does not rely on risk weights. This ratio represents the bank's Tier 1 capital relative to its total risk-free assets and has been set at a minimum of 3%.[6] The aim is to limit excessive borrowing by banks against potential errors in risk measurements.

In summary, while the legal minimum total capital ratio for banks under Basel III is 8%, when the capital conservation buffer and possible cyclical buffers are taken into account, the actual expected capital adequacy ratio reaches a level of 10.5% or higher in most countries. National regulators may impose additional requirements on top of these standards.[7]

▶ **Important**

Under the Basel III framework, banks in G-20 countries are generally required to maintain the following minimum ratios:

- CET1 $\geq$ 4.5%,
- Tier1 $\geq$ 6.0%,
- Total Capital $\geq$8.0%.

Consequently, the legal and regulatory design of bank establishment frameworks within G20 economies reflects a commitment to *prudential proportionality*: ensuring that market entry fosters innovation and competition without compromising systemic stability. Best practices promoted by the FSB and the BCBS emphasize the need for rigorous licensing criteria, transparent assessment procedures, and continuous supervisory oversight to prevent regulatory arbitrage and maintain financial soundness. In sum, the establishment of banks embodies not

[4] ibid. 59.

[5] ibid. 57–60; Drehmann et al. (2011) 189–240; Drehmann and Gambacorta (2012) 603–608.

[6] BIS (2011) 63.

[7] ibid. 21.

merely the inception of a private enterprise but the legal institutionalization of public trust.[8] It represents a constitutive act that situates private financial activity within the normative architecture of economic governance—anchored in the rule of law, prudential regulation, and market discipline.

4.2 Foundational Requirements for Bank Authorization in G20 Jurisdictions

The establishment of a commercial bank underpins the legal and institutional framework of the banking system because banks safeguard the public's funds and play a central role in financial stability, regulators in every G20 jurisdiction closely review applications before granting authorization. National regulatory systems reflect each country's legal history and institutions, yet many are moving in the same direction by bringing their rules closer to widely accepted international standards. This convergence is mainly shaped by standards set by the BCBS, the FSB, and the OECD, especially in areas such as governance, capital adequacy, and basic licensing rules.

Across G20 countries, a common requirement for setting up a bank is to incorporate it as a separate legal entity, most often in the form of a joint-stock company or a public limited company. This legal form is chosen for a reason: it protects owners through limited liability and supports public oversight by relying on established corporate governance rules. For example, in Turkey, Article 7 of Banking Law No 5411 addresses the point that a bank can be set up only as a joint-stock company. In the UK, the FSMA requires a firm to be formally incorporated under the Companies Act before it can submit an authorization request to the Prudential Regulation Authority PRA. In the EU, including Germany, CRD IV and the CRR require a firm to be incorporated under national company law before it can apply for authorization from the competent supervisory authority. In the US, a bank must first obtain a charter, either from the Office of the OCC at the federal level or from a state regulator, before it can meet the requirement to obtain deposit insurance from the FDIC.

4.2.1 Fit and Proper Requirements for Founders and Management

Across G20 countries, prudential regulators treat the fit and proper test as a basic requirement for assessing whether individuals are suitable for key roles. This assessment examines the ethical conduct, financial stability, and professional ability of the founding shareholders (promoters) as well as the proposed senior management and board members. The purpose of this test is to stop unqualified or

[8] Butzbach (2016) 304.

dishonest people from taking control of systemically important institutions.[9] For instance, the EBA issues shared guidelines intended to align how suitability assessments are carried out across EU member states. In places such as Japan, Article 4 of the Banking Act states that executive officers must have enough knowledge and experience, and it requires that the planned ownership structure supports sound and prudent management rather than weakening it. In a similar way, the RBI uses its licensing guidelines to stress clear disclosure of ownership and a credible track record for promoters.

4.2.2 Foundational Requirements for Bank Authorization in G20 Jurisdictions

Setting up a commercial bank is a basic step that supports the legal and institutional structure of the banking system. Since banks play a central role in the economy and hold the public's trust, every G20 jurisdiction places close regulatory scrutiny on the bank authorization process. National regulatory approaches are shaped by domestic legal traditions, but many are moving toward shared international standards. This alignment mainly reflects the standards set by the BCBS, the FSB, and the OECD, with a focus on governance, capital adequacy, and key licensing requirements. Across the G20, a common requirement for setting up a bank is that it must be incorporated as its own legal entity, most often in the form of a joint-stock company or public limited company. This legal structure is intentional rather than arbitrary. It helps protect owners through limited liability and supports careful public oversight through established corporate governance practices.

In Turkey, Article 7 of the Banking Law No. 5411 serves as a clear example. It states that a bank can be formed only as a joint-stock company. In the UK, the FSMA requires a firm to be incorporated under the Companies Act before it may apply for authorization from the PRA. In the EU, including Germany, the CRD IV and the CRR set out a process where a firm must first be incorporated under national company law and then obtain authorization from the relevant competent authority. In the US, a bank must first obtain a charter, either from the Office of the OCC at the federal level or from a state authority, before it can meet the separate requirement of obtaining deposit insurance from the FDIC. Across G20 countries, a core part of prudential regulation is the fit and proper test. This assessment examines the ethics, financial stability, and professional qualifications of the founding shareholders (promoters) and the proposed senior management and board members. The purpose of this test is to ensure that people who lack the necessary competence or integrity do not gain control of institutions that are critical to the stability of the financial system. For instance, the EBA issues common guidelines that aim to make suitability assessments more consistent across MS of the EU. In Japan, Article 4 of the Banking Act states that executive officers must have enough

[9] Hopt (2013); BIS (2012); Palm-Steyerberg (2025) 573–595.

knowledge and experience. The rule is meant to ensure that the planned ownership structure does not weaken the bank's ability to be managed in a safe and careful way. In a similar way, the RBI, in its licensing guidelines, stresses that ownership should be transparent and that promoters should have a reputable track record.

Capital adequacy is the most important financial requirement when setting up a bank. Minimum capital requirements matter because they give banks a basic cushion against unexpected operational or credit losses, and they also help banks meet international rules, especially those set out in the Basel III framework.[10] The level of initial capital required is usually set based on the bank's planned activities and the risks linked to those activities. Directive 2013/36/EU (CRD IV) requires credit institutions in the EU to start with at least EUR five million in initial capital, but other major economies set different minimum capital requirements.[11] Under Article 14 of China's Commercial Bank Law, a national commercial bank must have at least RMB 1 billion in registered capital.[12] In Canada, OSFI expects a bank's capital level to match the risks in its proposed business plan.[13] These different numbers point to the same basic point: a firm needs enough start-up capital to qualify for an operating license. One key regulatory issue after the financial crisis is making sure that core capital is lawful and that its source can be tracked.

Consistent with guidance from the FATF, most G20 jurisdictions require detailed disclosure of UBO as a way to reduce the risk of ML and terrorist financing. Regulators such as the UK PRA and US supervisory agencies set expectations for how firms manage risk, report information, and meet capital and governance standards.[14] The OCC and Australia's APRA review shareholding structures closely and require full disclosure of the true, original source of funds. This requirement is essential to maintaining the integrity of the financial system. Regulatory approval depends on the applicant submitting a clear, workable business plan. This plan should clearly set out the proposed activities, explain the governance structure in detail, describe the internal controls, and present a risk management framework. This shows that the institution can operate in a sustainable way from the first day. Australia's Restricted ADI Framework is a useful case: it lets new banks enter the market with a staged licence, so they can begin operating while they build and put in place the full governance and risk systems required for a standard ADI licence.[15] Similarly, the South African Prudential Authority requires institutions to submit a detailed operational plan that provides clear, verifiable evidence of compliance with all prudential standards.[16]

[10] Obadire et al. (2022) 57.

[11] Binder (2023) 99.

[12] Leigh and Podpiera (2007).

[13] Pan (2017).

[14] Federal Reserve System (2014).

[15] Davies et al. (2021) 332–354.

[16] Lange and Petros (2010).

4.3 The Licensing Process: Authorization, Capital, and Revocation

In modern financial law, granting a bank licence is the main legal filter that limits market entry to institutions that can show adequate financial strength and sound governance before they are allowed to take deposits and make loans. In practice, this process serves two regulatory aims: it works as a prudential safeguard to support system-wide stability, and it also sets standards for business conduct that help sustain public trust. Across G20 jurisdictions, the main reasoning is similar, but the steps usually follow a required two-stage process: first, an in-principle approval before the bank is set up, and then a final licence that allows it to begin formal banking operations. After a bank is granted a license, it can keep that license only if it continues to meet required standards for capital adequacy and governance. Regulators can revoke a license as the strongest sanction when a firm no longer meets fit and proper standards or does not keep the required minimum capital buffers. This step is rare and severe, but it is used to protect customers and the wider financial system when continued operation is not acceptable. In this high-stakes setting, a banking license is not a permanent right; it is a conditional privilege that depends on continued compliance and ongoing review by regulators.

4.3.1 Capital Adequacy as the Core Licencing Principle

Capital adequacy is central to deciding whether to grant a license. Regulators treat required capital as an indicator of an institution's financial health and its capacity to absorb losses from operational, credit, and market risks.

4.3.1.1 International Standards

Basel III pushes banks toward more consistent rules across countries by setting a minimum Common Equity Tier 1 capital ratio of 4. The requirements specify a minimum leverage ratio of 5%, a Tier 1 ratio of 6%, and a total capital ratio of 8%, with extra capital conservation and countercyclical buffers added on top. In most G20 countries, these requirements are already built into national law or reflected in supervisory practice. In the EU, the Capital Requirements Regulation (CRR) sets the core rules on bank capital and how banks measure and manage risk. Regulation EU No 575/2013 and the CRD IV Directive require banks to meet Basel III standards as a condition for obtaining and maintaining a licence. In a similar way, the US uses the Dodd-Frank Act to assess banks' capital adequacy at the outset and over time, using tools such as CCAR stress tests.[17] In Asia, Japan (through the Financial Services Agency, JFSA) and South Korea (through the Financial Supervisory Service, FSS) have also adopted risk-based capital frameworks that closely follow the Basel approach.

---

[17] Krettek (2025).

4.3.1.2 National Practices and Supervisory Evaluation

Even with international harmonization, national regulators can still set higher thresholds when they think local risk tolerance or market conditions call for it. In Canada, the OSFI often takes a super-equivalent approach. In practice, it expects new entrants to hold capital above the Basel minimum to account for potential concentration risk in a relatively small domestic market.[18] In a similar way, Australia's APRA uses a two-stage licensing approach under the Restricted ADI Framework.[19] It first gives a limited approval for the pilot stage, and that approval depends on meeting minimum capital requirements. This shows a careful use of capital requirements. Capital adequacy is not reviewed on its own. Regulators usually apply a fit and proper plus capital assessment that looks at both the firm's financial strength and the quality of its risk governance, internal controls, and liquidity management. In many jurisdictions, regulators can require supervisors to submit capital restoration plans, and they may also refuse or revoke a license if the firm's capital structure is judged to create unacceptable systemic risk.

4.3.2 Revocation of License: Conditional Authorisation

A banking license is not a permanent right. It is permission to operate that continues only as long as the bank keeps meeting the required conditions. Regulators may suspend or withdraw a license when there is a serious breach of prudential requirements, a clear risk of insolvency, or a credible threat to financial stability.

4.3.2.1 Legal Frameworks and Due Process

Across the G20, the legal grounds for revoking citizenship are set out in primary legislation, which helps protect due process and supports proportionate decision-making. Article 18 of the EU's CRD IV sets out the reasons a competent authority may revoke an authorisation, including when an institution does not start operating within 12 months or no longer meets prudential requirements on an ongoing basis. In the US, the FDIC and the OCC have statutory authority under the Federal Deposit Insurance Act to end a bank's deposit insurance and revoke its charter if the bank engages in unsafe or unsound practices.[20] The authority to revoke should be matched with basic procedural safeguards so that administrative decisions remain lawful and accountable. In many jurisdictions, regulators must give advance notice, allow the institution a chance to respond or fix the problems, and preserve the right to appeal the decision to an administrative body or a court.

---

[18] Peihani (2023) 419.

[19] Australian Prudential Regualation Authority (2018).

[20] Menand (2021).

4.3.2.2 Post-Revocation Measures

When a license is revoked, the firm is typically required to enter resolution or liquidation right away, usually under the direction of a deposit insurance agency or a specialized resolution authority. The EU's Single Resolution Mechanism (SRM), led by the Single Resolution Board (SRB), coordinates bank resolution actions across participating member states,[21] while in the United States similar responsibilities are mainly handled by the Federal Deposit Insurance Corporation under the bank resolution framework. When a bank fails, the FDIC may serve as receiver to keep essential operations running. In a similar way, Turkey's Savings Deposit Insurance Fund carries out comparable duties. These resolution mechanisms aim to keep to the "no creditor worse off" principle by protecting depositors and limiting the moral hazard that can arise when bailouts are expected.[22]

4.3.3 Essential Elements Mandated by Prudential Standards

Banking regulation requires that a bank's internal constitution is more than a set of standard corporate rules. In practice, it works as a core part of the regulatory system, setting the basic controls and responsibilities that help protect financial stability and the bank's integrity. A bank's articles of association should include the required provisions that align with international prudential rules and corporate governance standards.[23] This framework starts with a clear definition of the institution's corporate identity and purpose, and it requires the articles to restrict the corporate object to the banking and financial services the institution is authorized to provide.[24] This is often done by using restrictive purpose clauses that bar banks from non-financial activities or from taking on overly speculative business. The share capital and ownership structure should be set out in clear terms, including specific limits on the transfer of shares. Consistent with the EU's CRD IV rule that requires regulators to approve any acquisition of more than 10% of voting rights in advance, these provisions are meant to prevent control from becoming concentrated in the hands of owners who are not suitable or who are not transparent.[25]

The institution's structure is strengthened when its governance and management bodies are clearly defined. In line with Basel Committee best practices, the articles should require a clear separation between supervisory and executive roles and should also require the appointment of independent directors with relevant expertise. Including audit, internal control, and compliance in the bank's corporate constitution makes them formal parts of the governance structure, not just day-to-day operational tasks. Integrating legal requirements in this way keeps compliance

[21] Busch (2017) 447.
[22] Lunetti and Feller (2026) 355–371.
[23] BIS (2020).
[24] Black (2013) 69–87.
[25] Alexander (2015) 227–253.

at the centre of the bank's corporate governance and supports confidence in the financial system and the integrity of the market.

4.3.4 Conditions for Foreign Banks to Open Branches

Setting up banks across national borders, either as branches or as subsidiaries, is a common and important part of today's international financial system. It supports international trade, but it also exposes host jurisdictions to risks that arise from foreign institutions. To limit this exposure, G20 countries rely on structured supervisory arrangements that rest on cooperation between home and host regulators, reciprocity, and assessments of prudential equivalence. In general, opening a foreign bank branch or setting up a subsidiary requires approval in advance from the host country's banking regulator. In most cases, this approval depends on the consent of the bank's home-country supervisor, consistent with the idea of mutual reliance among supervisors set out in the Basel Concordat (1983). This two-step approval process is necessary, especially in the US context. Before granting approval under the International Banking Act, the Federal Reserve reviews whether the bank's home regulator provides adequate consolidated supervision.[26]

Under reciprocity, a foreign bank may enter a country's market only if its home country offers comparable access to that country's banks that want to operate abroad. This factor is central to whether third-country firms can access the EU market under Article 47 of CRD IV. A related idea is prudential equivalence, which asks whether the home supervisor's rules and oversight work in practice much like international standards, such as the Basel principles.[27]

Under the Foreign Bank Supervision Enhancement Act (FBSEA), the US follows a national treatment approach, meaning foreign banks are treated the same as domestic banks, but they are not given any special advantages.[28] Brazil and India use a case-by-case approach to reciprocity, in which their central banks assess whether the other country provides comparable access to its financial markets.

Background Information

Foreign banks can enter a host country either by opening a branch, which remains part of the parent bank under the same legal entity, or by setting up a subsidiary, which is a separate legal entity incorporated in the host country. Branch model: often chosen for efficiency, but it can raise control and risk issues because the parent entity abroad remains responsible for the branch's liabilities. In the US and Canada, foreign bank branches are usually limited to wholesale banking activities unless they meet extra regulatory requirements. Under a subsidiary model, the host country has clearer regulatory oversight, and local assets can be ring-fenced within the subsidiary. In many emerging markets such as China, India, and Indonesia, firms that plan to run retail financial operations are often required to form locally incorporated subsidiaries, which regulators view as a way to better protect depositors. Some jurisdictions follow hybrid or transitional approaches. In this regard,

[26] Nakagawa (2011) 215.
[27] Hildner and Struckmann (2024) 123–141.
[28] Kress (2021) 951; Belton et al. (2021).

South Korea and Mexico, foreign banks may begin operating as branches only with limits on their allowed exposures. If the branch later exceeds set thresholds, such as a deposit-volume cap or a measure of systemic importance, it must convert into a locally incorporated subsidiary. Host regulators may also require capital to be held locally, meaning foreign branches must keep a set amount of assigned capital or meet asset maintenance ratios.

4.4 Deposits and Fund Management of Banks

Across G20 legal systems, a deposit is generally understood as money paid into a bank that the bank agrees to repay, either immediately on request or at an agreed later date, with or without interest. It functions both as a civil law contract and as a regulated financial transaction. Deposits are central to how banks operate, since they provide the main pool of funds that banks rely on for lending and other core activities. Their legal status and strict oversight mark the line between the officially regulated financial sector and the often-opaque world of shadow finance.[29] This section compares the legal nature of standard bank deposits and participation funds in Islamic banking. It explains that both generally require authorization, then sets out the distinct rules that apply to opening these accounts and to withdrawing funds under the relevant regulatory frameworks.

Background Information

In common law systems like the United Kingdom and the United States, taking deposits is usually treated as a debtor–creditor relationship between the bank and the depositor.A traditional reading of this point comes from earlier case law, including *Foley v.As Hill* (1848) explains, when money is deposited the bank takes ownership of the funds, while the depositor holds a right to be repaid,[30] so the deposit is treated as a general liability of the bank.In many civil law systems, such as Germany, France, and Turkey, deposits are usually treated as a contractual arrangement, similar to a loan obligation. Even with these legal differences, the basic regulatory point is the same: when an institution takes deposits, it takes on fiduciary duties that require ongoing solvency, clear disclosure of its financial condition, and strict supervisory control by regulators.

Across most G20 countries, banking is commonly defined as taking funds on the basis that they will be repaid, and the law generally reserves this activity to licensed banks. This rule limits the right to take deposits from the public to licensed credit institutions, aiming to protect depositors and support financial stability by keeping unregulated intermediaries out of the deposit market and reducing risks linked to shadow banking.[31]

In some G20 jurisdictions, including Saudi Arabia and Indonesia, local law allows participation funds, which are treated as the Sharia-compliant alternative to conventional bank deposits. These funds follow a profit-and-loss sharing (PLS)

[29] Iwanicz-Drozdowska et al. (2021) 19–38; Craig and Dinger (2013) 3605–3622.
[30] Benlala (2022) 638–649.
[31] Levitin (2016).

model, usually based on mudaraba or wakala contracts.[32] This creates a clear legal difference from conventional deposits: participation funds do not promise repayment of the principal or any fixed return. Instead, the fund provider's returns depend on the bank's investment results, so the provider faces risk closer to an equity investor than a lender. Even though these contracts differ, regulators apply prudential and consumer protection rules similar to those for standard deposits, focusing mainly on clear disclosure and strong transparency in accounting.

Indonesia's Financial Services Authority (OJK) provides a clear example of this dual-system approach by requiring institutions to keep profit-sharing pools separate and to operate under the oversight of a Sharia Supervisory Board to ensure compliance.[33] These frameworks show that countries with both conventional and Islamic banking try to give consumers similar levels of protection, while still respecting the different contract rules and religious principles built into their legal systems. This means that, no matter what type of contract is used—whether it is a debt-based deposit or a risk-sharing participation fund—the shared aim of maintaining financial integrity is still upheld.

▶ **Important**

Requiring a banking license to accept deposits is a basic rule in financial regulation around the world. It sets a clear line between licensed banks and other financial firms, and it helps limit deposit-taking by entities that are not supervised or held to the same standards. Accepting deposits without clear authorization is not only a breach of financial regulation; in most major jurisdictions it is treated as a criminal offense. In the EU, Article 9 of CRD IV limits deposit-taking to authorized credit institutions. A similar rule applies in the US, where taking deposits without authorization is treated as a criminal offense under § 378 of the 12 U.S.C. Similar legal bans appear in Japan's Banking Act (Article 3) and Korea's Banking Act (Article 8), and Turkey's Banking Law No. 5411 Article 150 contains a related restriction, sets a prison sentence for collecting funds without authorization. These strict bans aim to stop the growth of shadow banks and to protect less experienced investors from the broader systemic risks created by firms that operate outside formal regulation. When the law allows only licensed institutions that meet strict capital and liquidity requirements to hold public funds, it helps protect market integrity and limits the growth of illegal financial arrangements.

[32] Al-Rasyid (2025) 102–111.

[33] Syamlan (2017) 81; Susanti et al. (2024) 49–55.

4.5 Bank Account

4.5.1 Account Opening and Customer Due Diligence

Opening a deposit or participation fund account creates a formal contract with the institution, and the agreement is recorded and reviewed under relevant regulatory requirements. A contract should clearly state who the depositor is and confirm KYC compliance, identify the account type, set out the repayment terms or the profit-sharing arrangement, and record the customer's consent to data processing.[34] Across the G20, countries have incorporated FATF Recommendations 10–12 on customer due diligence (CDD) into their domestic legal and regulatory frameworks. Banks must confirm the customer's identity, identify the beneficial owners, and document the purpose of the banking relationship.[35] For higher-risk customers, such as politically exposed persons, banks should apply enhanced due diligence (EDD).Regulatory oversight helps keep contracts clear and open to review; for instance, in the United States, agencies may require standard disclosures and set rules on how key terms must be presented, e.g. the Truth in Savings Act (Regulation DD) of the US requires banks and other deposit-taking institutions to clearly disclose account terms and fees so consumers can understand and compare them.[36]

4.5.2 Withdrawal Conditions and Systemic Stability

Deposits are usually repayable either on request or at an agreed maturity date, so the depositor has a legally enforceable claim under the contract. This right is limited by regulations, especially in times of financial distress. During a crisis, regulators may set short-term limits on withdrawals, or temporarily suspend them, on the grounds that doing so serves the public interest and helps preserve stability across the financial system. The EU's Bank Recovery and Resolution Directive (BRRD) allows authorities to temporarily suspend payment obligations during a resolution, and similar powers appear in the banking frameworks,[37] also implemented by Turkey's BDDK, India's RBI, and China's CBIRC. Because participation funds are set up through contractual terms, the agreement may limit or block withdrawals until the fund's investment period ends, and it can also place extra conditions on early withdrawal. Followingly, BRRD II strengthened crisis management in a way that was more effective and put public funds at less risk; in particular, it increased the capacity of large banks to absorb losses and improved cross-border applicability. Member states transposed this into national

[34] Jun and Ai (2009) 406–416; BIS (2001); Lyman et al. (2019).

[35] FSB (2015).

[36] Schneider and Ben-Sharar (2011) 647.

[37] Mabrouki and Vaudoit (2026) 333–353.

law by December 28, 2020.[38] Similarly, this regulation was adapted for the UK despite Brexit.[39]

4.5.3 Management of Dormant Accounts and Prescription of Deposit

Prescription of deposit money refers to a legal process in which money in bank accounts that have remained inactive for a long time is treated as unclaimed and transferred to a public authority or a specified fund, but only when the law's stated conditions are met. In the G20, these regimes usually aim to do three things: remove old problem assets from banks' balance sheets, set up one central process to repay consumers and, where relevant, their heirs, and build a capital fund that some jurisdictions can direct toward projects meant to serve the public interest.

Looking across global legal approaches, practices have three common principles. The first is Transparency and Warning, which means banks must notify customers through more than one channel before any transfer is made. This is supported by a pro-consumer right to reclaim, which keeps the option of perpetual reclaim available even after the funds are no longer in the bank's control. The principle of fair treatment sets clear limits on charging interest and taking administrative fees while an account is dormant, so the customer's principal is not reduced during that period.[40] By balancing these aims, the regulatory framework allows banks to run accounts efficiently while safeguarding each person's basic property rights for as long as the account remains open.

4.5.4 Trigger Conditions: Dormancy and Statutory Periods

Dormancy occurs when a customer does not start any transactions within the statutory time period set by law. The duration of this period and the exact threshold levels differ across G20 members, which reflects differences in how risk is viewed and in national legal traditions (see Table 4.1).

In many cases, the trigger is defined narrowly as no activity started by the customer. Other events can also speed up the timeline, such as failed contact attempts (for example, returned mail) or the transfer of accounts after a bank closes branches. In the US, escheat laws are set by each state, and they require banks to make a reasonable effort to notify the account holder before turning unclaimed funds over to the state. This segment offers a clear comparison of how G20 jurisdictions handle dormant or unclaimed deposits, focusing on the prescription of deposit money. It gives a clear overview of both conventional and Islamic finance

38 ISDA (2021); Poulle et al. (2024) 111–132; Putnis and Hurn (2020) 291–312.

39 Bank of England (2020).

40 European Commission (2019).

Table 4.1 Statutory dormancy periods and reclaim mechanisms: a cross-country analysis

Jurisdiction	Dormancy Period	Designated Recipient/Fund	Reclaim Status
The UK	15 years	Reclaim fund ltd.	Perpetual reclaim
Canada	10 years	Bank of Canada	Perpetual reclaim
Turkey	10 years	Saving deposit Insurance fund	Reclaim possibility preserved
India	10 years	Depositor education and awareness fund	Perpetual reclaim
The US	Approx. 3–5 years	State unclaimed property programs	Perpetual reclaim (state-dependent)
Australia	7 years	Austalian securities and investments commission	Online reclaim available
Japan	10 years	Unclaimed deposits utilisation mechanism	Reclaim possibility preserved

and explains the need to balance administrative efficiency with the protection of consumer rights.

4.5.5 Procedural Obligations: Notification, Archives, and Evidence

In most G20 jurisdictions, supervisors require banks to follow strict procedures to protect customers' rights before any limitation period expires. These rules are meant to ensure that moving unclaimed private assets to the state or a designated fund happens only after all other steps have been taken. The process starts with a required notice step. Banks must send the customer one or more formal warnings, usually at least one in the last six to twelve months, using several channels such as mail, email, and SMS.[41] This notice is not just a formality. It is part of a due diligence requirement that banks must follow by law. Under this requirement, banks must keep customer contact details up to date and make a reasonable effort to find the account holder before any transfer takes place. Even after the funds have been transferred, the institution still has duties to meet. These include strict recordkeeping rules that require it to keep detailed transaction records and related documents for a long period, often about seven to ten years. In practice, the legal framework for these regimes places the burden of proof mainly on the transferring bank, which must show that it followed each required procedural step before treating the deposit as dormant. This step-by-step process of giving notice, doing due diligence, and keeping records works as a legal safeguard. It sets clear duties for the bank while also protecting the basic idea that the owner should be able to get their property back with reasonable effort.

[41] Fang and Quintos (2023) 47–77.

4.5.6 The Insurance of Deposits and Participation Funds

Deposit and participation fund insurance is a key measure for sustaining public trust and supporting stability in the international banking system. These mandatory protection schemes have three main aims: to protect small savers without conditions and lower the risk of bank runs, to limit panic during system-wide crises by ensuring payouts are orderly and quick, and to align the scheme with the wider regulatory rules for bank resolution. This coordination is necessary to manage payouts, move assets, and set up bridge banks when an institution fails.[42] In G20 countries, the general rule is that these schemes are run by a public authority with legal approval, such as the FDIC in the United States and the FSCS in the United Kingdom.[43] Coverage limits are a key legal feature of deposit insurance, since they usually protect eligible deposits only up to a set maximum for each customer at each institution. Eligible instruments generally include checking, savings, and payment accounts. Fiduciary or trust accounts may also qualify for pass-through protection, but only if certain conditions are met. Protection does not apply to instruments that involve built-in investment risk, such as securities, shares in investment funds, and cryptocurrency assets. To reduce moral hazard, most schemes do not cover large shareholders, related parties, or deposits linked to illegal activities. In countries that run both Islamic and conventional banking systems, such as Saudi Arabia, and Indonesia, participation funds are covered by insurance schemes that operate in the same way as the schemes that insure conventional bank deposits. Although Islamic finance contracts are built around sharing profits and losses, these schemes still protect each saver separately, with limits that are like those used in other systems. This approach meets the main goal of protecting depositors while still respecting the separate legal status of the fund pools. In doing so, it also helps keep fair competition between conventional banks and participation banks.

4.6 Safe-Deposit Box

A safe-deposit box service is usually treated as a mixed type of agreement, with features of both a lease and a bailment. In practice, the bank provides the customer with a secured space, and the customer's access and use of that space are limited by the terms the bank sets. This arrangement is different from a deposit. When money is deposited, the bank becomes the owner of the funds. By contrast, the bank does not own, and has no property right in, whatever is kept inside a safe-deposit box. It is important for customers to understand that standard deposit insurance schemes usually cover only monetary claims and do not cover the physical items stored in these boxes.[44]

---

[42] Jameaba (2018); Nikolaj et al. (2022) 5632.
[43] Demirguc-Kunt, Kane and Laeven (2015).
[44] Stein (1972) 45–59; Soe (1974) 289–295; Lord (1983) 263.

The parties' arrangement is governed by a specific lease agreement that sets out the rights and duties of both sides and makes clear that the bank holds the space as a bailee, not as the owner of the assets. The bank's main duties relate to due diligence and security. This includes keeping the facility secure and using dual-authority controls for access, such as a system that requires two keys or biometric checks. A bank generally owes its customers a duty to keep account information confidential, but the law can require disclosure in certain cases, such as when there is a court order or a regulatory investigation. To meet these standards, the bank should apply strict access controls. It should verify the identity of the customer or any approved representative, and it should require valid documents that prove inheritance rights or legal authority when the customer has died or no longer has capacity. In contrast, the customer must follow certain restrictions, including a rule against storing hazardous or illegal materials. Since the bank's general liability limits are usually low, customers should state a declared value and obtain separate insurance coverage on their own. If the required fees are not paid, this is treated as a failure to meet financial obligations and may lead to formal steps to end the contract and open the box. These steps should be carried out with witnesses present and recorded in an official report, and any recovered items should be kept in escrow until payment is made or the claimant proves ownership.

When property is left unclaimed for a long period, national law usually sets out the steps for selling it at auction or disposing of it through a court order. These rules also keep tighter controls for sensitive items, such as jewellery and legal documents, which often require added documentation, oversight, or secure handling. In today's regulatory setting, safe-deposit box providers face growing exposure to cross-border activity and sanctions-related risks. Under AML/CTF rules, entering into or continuing a contract with a person or organization on a sanctions list may be prohibited, and any such contract may be ended without notice. In comparative legal practice across the UK, the US, and the EU, a breach of sanctions rules generally requires a prompt freeze of the relevant assets and a report to the relevant authorities. Even when a bank does not claim ownership of the funds, it is still expected to take control of them in practice and apply measures that prevent any transfer or use. To manage these complexities, standard guidance recommends that banks set clear limits on liability, require a dual-signature registration chain for each entry, and keep emergency contingency plans, such as flood and fire protection, to protect the service's physical and legal integrity.

4.7 Restructuring of Banks

Restructuring in banking law—driven by mergers, acquisitions, takeover, court-led reorganisations, and insolvency or resolution proceedings- serves as a vital set of legal mechanisms. These ways allow banks to adapt to shifting economic conditions, rectify operational inefficiencies, and reallocate capital in the most strategic way. Hence, they facilitate an orderly market exit when viability is no longer sustainable. By doing so, these mechanisms bolster sector-wide resilience and mitigate the risk of systemic contagion during periods of financial distress. The 2008 global financial crisis demonstrated that traditional insolvency regimes are ill-suited for large, complex financial institutions due to their deep interconnectedness. In response, the G20 served as a primary forum for international coordination, tasking the FSB with developing robust reform standards. A cornerstone of this agenda is the FSB's Key Attributes of Effective Resolution Regimes for Financial Institutions, endorsed at the 2011 Cannes Summit.[45] These attributes provide authorities with a structured tool kit to wind down failing institutions without relying on taxpayer-funded bailouts or triggering wider systemic instability.

Current legal outlines stick with structured flexibility to empower authorities to customise interventions based on its systemic importance in accordance with the national interests. Nevertheless, this elasticity should not be interpreted as carte blanche; it requires to be applied pursuant to market discipline and the rule of law. Therefore, at the outset, the authority shall paid attention to hierarchy of claims by ensuring that shareholders bear the primary risk before creditors are affected, i.e. equity holders must absorb losses first.[46] Besides, the 'no creditor worse off than in liquidation' test should be run to ensure that no creditors receive less in resolution than they would have under a standard liquidation route.[47] Other things, but not least, that needs to be taken into consideration are depositor protection and cross-border fair treatment of creditors.

Indeed, when examining developed economies, such precautions have already been placed into law. For instance, the EU implemented Bank Recovery and Resolution Directive (BRRD) and the SR); the US presented the Dodd-Frank Act's Orderly Liquidation Authority (OLA) and the FDIC's dedicated toolset; the UK updated its Banking Act of 2009 to bring into line with FSB principles.[48] Beyond these, several unnamed countries have also adopted similar frameworks by modelling IMF and WB guidelines on their domestic law.

In conclusion, mentioned mechanisms facilitate well-functioning market consolidation and provide continuance of vital economic transactions of payment services and lending. What is important, these mechanisms aim to provide a market discipline with systemic stability to ensure fairly predictable, and there for sustainable, international banking applications.

4.7.1 Mergers

Background Information

In the banking sector, mergers and acquisitions are often presented as a way to raise shareholder value, with expected efficiency gains cited as a main reason for these deals. When institutions merge and work at a larger scale, they can reduce the cost per unit of information technology,

[45] Nolle (2015) 46.

[46] Grünewald (2025) 70; Rutledge et al. (2012) 14.

[47] Schillig (2021) 239; Baker (2021) 335.

[48] Ventoruzzo and Sandrelli (2019).

regulatory compliance, and payment systems. These mergers can lead to economies of scope by allowing banks to offer both retail and corporate products through the same distribution channels. They may also lower funding costs, since a larger merged firm can receive a better credit rating and may find it easier to access collateral. Diversifying a credit portfolio can lower risk-weighted assets and, along with any cost savings, reduce the amount of capital the bank is required to hold. Firms may still try to gain monopoly power and raise prices by making markets more concentrated, but antitrust law and public interest tests restrict the extent to which they can do this.

If a planned merger is likely to reduce competition, regulators often approve it only if the parties accept specific conditions. These conditions may require a firm to sell specific business units or to agree to defined purchase-and-assumption terms to maintain competition in the market. Two other factors to consider are what senior executives do and how government policies shape outcomes. Managers may support consolidation to raise their own prestige, compensation, or authority, often described as empire-building. This can lead to agency costs when managers' private incentives outweigh the goal of maximizing shareholder value. To limit these risks, it is common to rely on independent board oversight, a careful and well-documented fair valuation process, and a formal fairness opinion prepared by an external adviser.

Important

Governments sometimes support bank mergers, particularly in a financial crisis, to address weak zombie banks, strengthen the scale and stability of domestic banks, or align the banking system with regional development goals. These measures may also involve temporary public funding to support the process and keep it moving forward. The merger is moving faster partly because new technology has shortened key steps in the process. Since digital core banking systems and cybersecurity require large up-front spending, banks often need a larger operating scale to spread these fixed costs. This change is tied to deregulation, which lowers barriers for firms to enter and exit markets, and to globalization, which pressures institutions to support multinational clients through payment and custody networks that cross national borders. Managing these complex transitions requires clear process management and established best practices.

Banking merger law and the approval process run on two separate regulatory tracks, and the level of review is much stricter than what most corporate mergers face. Since the sector poses macroeconomic risk, the proposed merger should go ahead only after it receives explicit approval from prudential supervisors (e.g., the Fed/OCC, PRA/SSM, or RBI) and the required approval from competition authorities.[49] This regulatory review places most weight on the public interest, asking how the merger could affect financial inclusion, access to credit, and whether essential services will continue, especially when the deal may lead to branch closures.

These mergers usually have set procedural steps, such as required notice periods and change-in-control filings, and they often include a public period when third parties may submit formal objections.At this stage, regulators review whether

[49] Grischkan (2024) 557–612; Kress (2020) 435–498; Scherer (2013); Carletti et al. (2021).

the incoming managers meet fit-and-proper standards and check that the funding sources are legitimate, so the combined entity can remain stable. Approval is often granted only if regulators set clear conditions, such as requiring capital injections, limiting how assets can be moved, and putting in place ring-fencing measures or detailed IT transition plans. When institutions merge, they usually must revise their resolution plans (living wills) so they match the new entity's structure, complexity, and systemic footprint.[50] In practice, these transactions can take different forms, depending on the goals the parties are pursuing. In a statutory merger or amalgamation, the parties combine into one legal entity, and that entity takes on all rights and obligations. By contrast, an asset or business transfer, often set up as a P&A, can be structured so only chosen assets, liabilities, or portfolios are transferred. Some institutions instead choose a holding company model by setting up a Bank Holding Company (BHC) that owns and manages several subsidiaries.[51] This setup can make internal restructuring within the group easier while keeping different types of risk separated across entities.

Foreign bank mergers are more complex because supervisors in both the bank's home country and the host country must approve the deal, so the merger requires approval from two regulators. These cross-border mergers depend on supervisors working together through supervisory colleges and on treating different regulatory systems as equivalent. In these situations, an important strategic choice is whether the bank should operate as a branch or set up a subsidiary. In many jurisdictions, regulators prefer a locally incorporated subsidiary for retail banking so they can supervise the entity under local law and better protect domestic depositors.

For G-SIBs, any merger should align with cross-border resolution plans and include a clear choice between a single point of entry (SPE) model and a Multiple Point of Entry (MPE) model. This choice determines how TLAC requirements are allocated across the group and whether protected deposits are excluded from bail-in.[52] In practice, the legal framework for bank mergers is meant to permit consolidation while keeping depositor protection and the stability of the financial system intact.

4.7.2 Takeover

In corporate restructuring, bank takeovers stand out because regulators play a much closer role, mainly to protect the stability of the financial system.[53] These transactions usually take one of two forms. In a friendly takeover, the acquiring bank moves forward with the approval and cooperation of the target bank's management. In a hostile takeover, the acquirer proceeds without the board's support and instead makes its offer directly to the shareholders. Hostile takeovers are fairly

[50] Carmassi and Herring (2013) 361–387.
[51] Klein and Saidenberg (2010) 127.
[52] Allemand (2015); Philippon and Salord (2017).
[53] Beccalli and Frantz (2016) 79–95; Powell and Yawson (2007) 1169–1192.

common in corporate law, but they are very rare in the banking sector.[54] This is rare mainly because the licensing rules are strict and regulators must approve the deal in advance. That approval can act as a regulatory shield for the target, making a hostile takeover hard to carry out in practice and difficult to defend under the law. Banking law sets extra, sector-specific limits that are stricter than the rules that apply under general corporate law. Acquirers must manage change-in-control thresholds, often set at 10, 20, 30, or 50 percent, that trigger prior approval requirements and a fit and proper review of the incoming owners. In this review, regulators require full disclosure of the Ultimate Beneficial Owner (UBO) and the source of funds so they can screen for ML and confirm that the buyer has adequate financial capacity.[55] The transaction must also clear local competition reviews that assess how it may affect market concentration, and regulators often attach conditions to protect depositors and ensure that day-to-day services continue without disruption.

In many industries, firms can adopt aggressive takeover defences such as poison pills, but banks have far less room to use these kinds of measures. In most legal systems, a firm usually needs approval from the relevant regulator before taking defensive steps, because regulators give priority to the public interest and the stability of the wider financial system over a board's wish to keep the company independent.[56] This helps make sure the bank remains stable and is not put at risk by a long-running dispute between companies. In this context, securities law protects minority shareholders by requiring a mandatory bid, also called a mandatory tender offer. These rules state that once an investor's ownership stake passes a set threshold, the investor must make a mandatory offer to buy the remaining shares at a fair price. This process is based on equal treatment. It aims to ensure that minority shareholders are not put at a disadvantage and that they receive full disclosure documents so they can decide, with adequate information, whether to sell their shares and leave. The legal framework aims to keep bank takeovers orderly and open by limiting the acquirer's power, protecting minority shareholders, and giving regulators a clear role. These rules are meant to support financial integrity.

4.7.3 Cross-Border Reorganization

In cross-border bank reorganizations, the law often reflects a trade-off between keeping operations efficient across countries and meeting local rules meant to protect the stability of each banking system. These reorganizations can take several forms, especially cross-border mergers. In the EU, single passport rules can make these mergers easier, but transactions that involve firms from outside the EU still require full approval from the relevant regulators. Institutions may change their structure, for example by turning branches into subsidiaries, to meet ring-fencing

[54] Scholz (2023) 3–7; Baradwaj et al. (1990) 1229–1242.
[55] Radon et al. (2019) 159; Clancy (2025) 20–23.
[56] Barry and Hatfield (2012); Sunder (2013) 47–66.

rules intended to protect local depositors. In some cases, a bank may shift from subsidiaries to branches to reduce administrative steps and make wholesale banking operations easier to manage. These moves often come with internal changes to the group structure, such as setting up a holding company or shifting specific assets and liabilities within the group to improve its legal and financial structure. Carrying out these changes means meeting strict regulatory requirements that depend on coordination between home and host authorities. A key part of this work is setting up MoUs and involving supervisory colleges so that the selected cross-border resolution strategy, whether SPE or MPE, can be carried out in practice. In this setting, legal compliance includes allocating TLAC to the right entities and keeping key functions running through clear intra-group service level agreements.[57]

Cross-border reorganizations are shaped not only by structural and resolution issues, but also by tax rules, accounting standards, and data governance requirements. When assets are transferred, it is important to review book values and amortization schedules and to consider how the transfer may affect Net Operating Losses (NOLs), since these factors can change the tax outcome. At the same time, legal duties to protect data privacy can conflict with the practical need to move data across borders, which often means getting specific permits for data localization and international transfers. In the end, these reorganizations are not just internal business changes. They are complex legal processes that need to align international banking standards with the binding rules in every involved country, so that the institution stays sound and the wider financial system remains stable.

4.7.4 Insolvencies

The rules for handling bank insolvency and resolution differ from standard corporate bankruptcy because they focus on protecting the wider financial system and keeping essential banking services running, rather than mainly selling assets to pay creditors.[58] The process starts with enforcement rules that let banks seek debt recovery through faster procedures, either after a court judgment or without one. In secured transactions, this usually means selling the pledged property after default. The law sets detailed steps for appraisal and a public sale, and those steps should be followed in a way that still protects consumers and avoids taking collateral far beyond what the debt reasonably requires. When a bank becomes insolvent, administrative resolution regimes usually take the place of ordinary court-based adjudication.[59] These frameworks rely on tools such as bridge banks, good bank/bad bank separation, and sale-of-business arrangements to support orderly resolution and preserve market integrity.

---

[57] Allemand (2015) 305–324.

[58] Pulgar (2024) 71–98; Stef and Dimelis (2020) 480–495.

[59] Hüpkes (2005) 471.

Before a firm enters formal insolvency proceedings, it is often required to take early steps such as drafting a plan to restore capital and accepting tight limits on management decisions or dividend payments. If these steps do not work and the bank is judged to have no viable private sector alternative, the resolution triggers are turned on to keep essential system-wide services running and to limit broader risks. To limit spillovers across the market, authorities often carry out these steps over a resolution weekend, a short window designed to keep payment systems running and to finish the transfer of assets and liabilities, often through purchase and assumption agreements, before markets open again. During the restructuring, the order of claims is tightly controlled so that the collection of public receivables follows depositor preference, which helps protect retail savings from losses.

Deposit insurance brings these efforts together by acting as a system-wide stabilizer during the resolution phase. Alongside quick payouts to depositors, insurance funds work with resolution authorities to provide temporary bridge financing and to support public confidence through clear, planned communication.[60] This kind of coordination helps prevent bank runs by assuring people that they can still reach their accounts and that payment cards will keep working without interruption. In cross-border cases, the legal issues become more complicated because regulators need to align how protected deposits are ranked in the host country with the repayment agreements that exist between national deposit insurance funds. These reforms point to a shift toward a living will approach, where the legal system gives priority to orderly management of debt and maintaining confidence in the financial system rather than treating liquidation as the fixed end point.

Chapter Summary

This chapter sets out a detailed legal and regulatory review of how banks are formed, run, reorganized, and resolved in modern financial systems, drawing comparisons across G20 jurisdictions. It treats banks not just as private firms that seek profits, but as public-trust institutions whose actions shape financial stability, how monetary policy reaches the economy, and overall economic well-being. The chapter opens by describing banks as incorporated bodies and notes that incorporation makes a bank a separate legal person. It also explains that this status places banks under closer public regulation. In many legal systems, banks are required to operate as joint-stock or public limited companies so that liability is limited, governance is open to scrutiny, and regulators can supervise them more clearly. Entering the banking market requires an establishment license or other formal approval from the relevant regulatory authority, which aims to balance open market access with the need for overall economic stability. Capital adequacy is the main criterion used when granting a license. Using the Basel III framework as its main reference point, the chapter sets out how minimum capital ratios (CET1, Tier 1, and

[60] Alam et al. (2021) 52.

total capital), capital conservation buffers, countercyclical buffers, and leverage ratios are meant to limit the risk of bank failure and reduce spillovers to the wider financial system. Basel III sets global minimum standards, but national regulators often require higher thresholds to reflect their prudential judgment and local market conditions.

This chapter reviews the fit and proper requirements that apply to founders, shareholders, and senior management. In G20 countries, regulators review a person's integrity, competence, financial soundness, and the transparency of ownership to reduce the risk that unsuitable individuals gain control of systemically important institutions. In academic discussions of AML and corporate governance, disclosing UBO and the lawful source of capital is often treated as a key measure for transparency and oversight. The analysis also considers the legal status of banks' articles of association, which have a role that goes beyond that of standard corporate documents. These documents should set out prudential standards, limit activities outside core banking, control how shares can be transferred, specify the bank's governance bodies, and make risk management, internal audit, and compliance part of the bank's formal constitutional rules.

The chapter subsequently examines how foreign banks enter a market, drawing a clear distinction between operating as a branch and setting up a subsidiary. It sets out key ideas such as reciprocity, prudential equivalence, and consolidated supervision. In most cases, approval depends on cooperation between the home and host regulators. In many countries, regulators prefer retail banking to be done through locally incorporated subsidiaries. This structure is meant to protect local depositors and to make it easier for authorities to resolve a bank if it fails.

Much of this chapter focuses on deposit-taking and participation funds, and it compares conventional deposits with Islamic finance arrangements built on profit-and-loss sharing. Even though the contracts differ, both arrangements are still governed by strict licensing rules, consumer protection law, and prudential oversight. Taking deposits without authorization is generally illegal and, in many jurisdictions, treated as a criminal offense. This is why licensing is a key safeguard for maintaining trust and integrity in the financial system.

This chapter explains how accounts are opened, what customer due diligence is required under FATF standards, how withdrawals may be limited during a crisis, and which legal rules apply to dormant accounts and time limits on claiming deposits. In different legal systems, these frameworks try to keep administrative processes workable while still protecting property rights, including rules that allow property to be reclaimed without a time limit.

The chapter also reviews deposit and participation fund insurance schemes and explains how they can lower the risk of bank runs, sustain public trust, and help with orderly resolution. This section reviews coverage limits, exclusions, and how insurance schemes work with resolution authorities. The law treats safe-deposit boxes as a separate matter. It makes clear that a safe-deposit box is not the same as a bank deposit, and that the bank's role is limited to custody rather than managing the contents. The rules also set limits on when the bank can be held liable, and they note that banks may face stricter duties under AML and sanctions requirements when offering safe-deposit box services.

The chapter ends by discussing how banks can be restructured, focusing on mergers, takeovers, cross-border reorganizations, and insolvency procedures. It describes how reforms after 2008, shaped by the FSB's key attributes, have pushed insolvency law toward dedicated resolution regimes. These frameworks focus on protecting depositors, keeping critical functions running, ensuring that shareholders and creditors absorb losses, and applying the no creditor worse off principle. Mergers and takeovers are reviewed by both prudential regulators and competition authorities, and the assessment can place greater weight on public interest concerns than on the parties' private aims. Overall, the chapter argues that both the creation of banks and the way they operate over time are shaped by a dense set of legal rules meant to secure public trust. Banking law sits between private business and public oversight, shaping how banks compete and innovate while keeping the financial system stable, protecting depositors, and supporting the rule of law.

Revision Questions

1. Why do banks need a regulatory license to be set up and operate, instead of being formed through the usual company registration process?
2. Assess, in a critical and balanced way, how capital adequacy requirements shape the decision to authorize a bank, including why regulators treat them as a key entry condition and what limits or drawbacks arise when authorization relies heavily on capital thresholds.
3. Explain the rationale for 'fit and proper' requirements for founders, shareholders, and senior management of banks.
4. Compare the legal treatment of deposits and participation funds or profit-loss sharing funds.
5. Explain how current bank resolution regimes alter the long-standing law of bank insolvency.
6. How do resolution tools of bail-in, bridge banks, or forced mergers differ from shareholders' and creditors' rights in normal corporate law?
7. Examine the economic implications of an open-ended structure of a mutual fund as opposed to a closed-ended structure of a traditional investment trust, particularly in respect of liquidity and the possible divergence between the price of shares in a fund and its net asset value.

8. Explain the legal role of the custodian bank in a collective investment scheme. Discuss how the distinction between the roles of the fund manager (portfolio management company) and the custodian bank reduces the risk of fraud from a legal perspective.
9. Describe the duty of care and the duty of loyalty as they apply to the portfolio manager. Explain how the concepts of suitability and appropriateness, as defined by the regulator, apply to the investment recommendation to the retail client.
10. Identify the two main legal differences and the two main economic differences between the regulated open-ended mutual fund and the unregistered hedge fund.
11. Explain the process of creation and redemption of an Exchange Traded Fund (ETF). Analyze the process of creation and redemption of an ETF and the alignment of the ETF's market price with its Net Asset Value (NAV), with the involvement of the Authorized Participants (APs).
12. Analyze the economic trade-offs between active and passive investment strategies. Explain how the disclosure of fees and expenses allows the investor to make an assessment of the legal rationale for the higher fees charged by active investment strategies.
13. Explain why the valuation of the illiquid assets of the fund, such as private equity investments, creates more regulatory and legal challenges than the valuation of the publicly traded securities of the same fund.◄

References

Al-Rasyid C (2025) Sharia financial services products based on Muradabah contract as a form of Unvestment. Journal of Economicate Studies 9:102–111

Alam N, Sivarajah G, Bhatti M (2021) Do deposit insurance systems promote banking stability? International Journal of Financial Studies 9(3):52

Alexander K (2015) Regulation the structure of the EU banking sector. Eur Bus Organ Law Rev 16:227–253

Allemand F (2015) The ECB, the SSM and Differentiated Integration: the Legal Triangle of Incompatibility?. In: European Central Bank (ed) From Monetary Union to Banking Union, on the way to Capital Markets Union: New opportunities for European integration, p 305–324

Australian Prudential Regualation Authority (2018) ADI Licensing: Restricted ADI Framework. https://www.apra.gov.au/sites/default/files/information-paper-adi-licensing-restricted-adi-framework-20180504.pdf. Accessed 30 Jan 2026

Baker C (2021) Clearinghouse shareholders and "no creditor worse off than in liquidation" claims. Transactions: The Tennessee Journal of Business Law 22:335–353

Bank of England (2020) Bank Recovery and Resolution Directive II. Consultation Paper CP18/20

Baradwaj B, Fraser D, Furtado E (1990) Hostile banking takeover offers: analysis and implications. J Bank Financ 14(6):1229–1242

Barry J, Hatfield J (2012) Pills and Partisans: Understanding Takeover Defenses. Univ Pa Law Rev 160:633–713

Beccalli E, Frantz P (2016) Why are some banks recapitalized and others taken over? J Int Financ Mark Inst Money 45:79–95

Belton D, Gambacorta L, Kokas S, Minetti R (2021) Foreign banks, liquidity shocks, and credit stability. The Review of Corporate Finance Studies 12(1):1–35

Benlala M (2022) The characterization of the demand deposit as a loan under fractional reserve banking: a critical legal analysis. Perspectives of Law and Public Administration 11(4):638–649

Binder J (2023) Not equivalent (yet?): the current EU third country regime for credit institutions and incoming changes. Eur Bus Organ Law Rev 25(1):99–116

BIS (2001) Customer Due Diligence for Banks. https://www.bis.org/publ/bcbs85.pdf. Accessed 30 Jan 2026

BIS (2011) Basel III: A Global Regulatory Framework for More Resilient Banks and Banking Systems. https://www.bis.org/publ/bcbs189.pdf. Accessed 30 Jan 2026

BIS (2012) Core Principles for Effective Banking Supervision. https://www.bis.org/publ/bcbs213.pdf. Accessed 30 Jan 2026

BIS (2020) Convergence in the Prudential Regulation of Banks—What is Missing?. https://www.bis.org/fsi/publ/insights24.pdf. Accessed 30 Jan 2026

Black J (2013) Prudential regulation of banks. In: OECD (ed) International Regulatory Co-operation: Canada-US Co-operation, EU Energy Regulation, Risk Assessment and Banking Supervision. OECD Publishing, p 69–87

Busch D (2017) Governance of the European banking Union's single resolution mechanism. European Business Law Review 28(4):447–498

Butzbach O (2016) Trust in Banks: a tentative conceptual framework. Schmollers Jahr 136(4):303–330

Carletti E, Ongena S, Siedlarek J, Spagnolo G (2021) The impacts of stricter merger legislation on Bank mergers and acquisitions: too-big-to-fail and competition. J Financ Intermed 46:100859

Carmassi J, Herring R (2013) Living wills and cross-border resolution of systematically important banks. Journal of Financial Economic Policy 5(4):361–387

Cecchetti S, Kohler M (2014) When capital adequacy and interest rate policy are substitutes (and when they are not). Int J Cent Bank 10(3):205–231

Clancy A (2025) Unexplained wealth orders and the UK's anti-corruption regime. Oxford University Press, pp 20–23

Craig B, Dinger V (2013) Deposit market competition, wholesale funding, and Bank risk. J Bank Financ 37(9):3605–3622

Davies C, Walpole S, Pearson G (2021) Australia's licensing regimes for financial services, credit, and superannuation: three tracks toward the twin peaks. Companies and Securities Law Journal 38:332–354

Demirguc-Kunt A, Kane E, Laeven L (2015) Deposit insurance around the world: a comprehensive analysis and debate. J Financ Stab 20(7):155–183

Drehmann M, Borio C, Tsatsaronis K (2011) Anchoring countercyclical capital buffers: the role of credit aggregates. Int J Cent Bank 7(4):189–240

Drehmann M, Gambacorta L (2012) The effects of countercyclical capital buffers on Bank lending. Appl Econ Lett 19(7):603–608

European Commission (2019) Options and National Discretions under the Deposit Guarantee Scheme Directive and Their Treatment in the Context of a European Deposit Insurance Scheme. https://finance.ec.europa.eu/system/files/2019-11/191106-study-edis_en.pdf. Accessed 30 Jan 2026

Fang L, Quintos D (2023) Security measures applied on digital banking towards service improvement proposal. Journal of Business and Management Studies 5(5):47–77

Federal Reserve System (2014) Enhanced Prudential standards for Bank holding companies and foreign banking organizations: final rule. Fed Regist 79(59):17240–17388

FSB (2015) Report to the G20 on Actions Taken to Assess and Address the Decline in Correspondent Banking. https://www.fsb.org/uploads/Correspondent-banking-report-to-G20-Summit.pdf. Accessed 30 Jan 2026

Grischkan J (2024) Regulating Bank Mergers: Past and Present. Univ Ill Law Rev 2:557–612

Grünewald S (2025) The handling of the credit Suisse failure in light of the FSB's key attributes for global systematically important banks. European Business Organizations Law Review 26:67–87
Hildner A, Struckmann J (2024) The EU market access for third-country undertakings following CRD 6. Zeitschrift für Bankrecht und Bankwirtschaft 36(2):123–141
Hopt K (2013) Better Governance of Financial Institutions. https://personal.lse.ac.uk/schustee/hopt%20governance.pdf. Accessed 30 Jan 2026
Hüpkes E (2005) Insolvency-Why a Special Regime for Banks?. In: IMF (ed) Current Developments in Monetary and Financial Law, Vol 3. IMF, p 471–513
ISDA (2021) ISDA Resolution Stay Jurisdictional Modular Protocol BRRD II Omnibus Jurisdictional Module. https://www.isda.org/a/xaggE/ISDA-BRRD-II-Omnibus-Jurisdictional-Module.pdf. Accessed 30 Jan 2026
Iwanicz-Drozdowska M, Penczar M, Kujawski L, Liszewska M (2021) Deposits as a stable source of Bank funding. Did the global finance crisis influence the banks' funding structure? Argumenta Oeconomica 1:19–38
Jameaba M (2018) Deposit insurance and financial intermediation: the case of Indonesia deposit insurance cooperation. Cogent Economics and Finance 6(1):1–32
Jun T, Ai L (2009) The international standards of customer due diligence and Chinese practice. Journal of Money Laundering Control 12(4):406–416
Klein P, Saidenberg M (2010) Organizational structure and the diversification discount: evidence from commercial banking. J Ind Econ 58(1):127–155
Kress J (2020) Modernizing Bank Merger Review. Yale Journal on Regulation 37:435–498
Kress J (2021) Domesticating foreign finance. Florida Law Review 73:951–1031
Krettek J (2025) Market reactions to the Basel reforms: implications for shareholders, creditors and taxpayers. Q Rev Econ Finance 101:101990
Lange N, Petros M (2010) Prudential supervision of banks in the South African—the supervisory review and evaluation process. https://www.bis.org/ifc/publ/ifcb33o.pdf. Accessed 30 Jan 2026
Leigh L, Podpiera R (2007) The rise of foreign investment in China's banks: taking stock. IMF Working Paper 6(292):1–14
Levitin A (2016) Safe banking: finance and democracy. Univ Chic Law Rev 83:357–455
Lord R (1983) The legal relationship between the bank and its safe deposit customer. Campbell Law Review 5(2):263–303
Lunetti C, Feller J (2026) NCWO and its application. In: Kozinska M (ed) Marano P. The Insurance Recovery and Resolution Directive, A Commentary. Edward Elgar, pp 355–371
Lyman T, Koker L, Meier C, Kerse M (2019) Beyond KYC Utilities: Collaborative Customer Due Diligence for Financial Inclusion. https://documents1.worldbank.org/curated/en/961341625138843266/pdf/Beyond-KYC-Utilities-Collaborative-Customer-Due-Diligence-for-Financial-Inclusion.pdf. Accessed 30 Jan 2026
Mabrouki S, Vaudoit V (2026) Resolution stay powers (arts. 48-53). In: Marano P, Kozinska M (eds) the insurance recovery and resolution directive: a commentary. Edward Elgar, p 333-353
Menand L (2021) Why supervise banks? The foundations of the American monetary settlement. Vanderbilt Law Review 74:951–1022
Nakagawa J (2011) International harmonization of economic regulation. Oxford University Press, pp 215–278
Nikolaj S, Drazenovic B, Buterin V (2022) Deposit insurance, banking stability and banking indicators. Econ Res 35(1):5632–5649
Nolle D (2015) Who's in charge of fixing the World's financial system? The un[?]der-appreciated Lead role of the G20 and the FSB. Financial Markets, Institutions and Instruments 24(1):1–82
Obadire A, Moyo V, Munzhelele N (2022) Basel III capital regulations and Bank efficiency: evidence from selected African countries. International Journal of Financial Studies 10(3):57
Omarova S (2019) The "too big to fail" problem. Minnesota Law Review 103:2495–2541
Palm-Steyerberg I (2025) Sustainability and fit and proper testing in the boards of banks, insurers and investment companies. In: Alexander K, Gargantini M, Siri M (eds) The Cambridge

handbook of EU sustainable finance: regulation. Cambridge University Press, Supervision and Governance, pp 573–595
Pan N (2017) Opportunities for better systemic risk Management in Canada. Institut C.D, Howe Commentary, No, p 490
Peihani M (2023) Resolution of small and medium-sized deposit-taking institutions: Back to basics? Am Bus Law J 60(2):419–475
Philippon T, Salord A (2017) Bail-ins and Bank Resolution in Europe. https://elischolar.library.yale.edu/cgi/viewcontent.cgi?params=/context/ypfs-documents2/article/3067/&path_info=60176_geneva_special_4_bail_ins_and_bank_resolution_in_europe.pdf. Accessed 30 Jan 2026
Poulle J, Kannan A, Spitz N, Kahn S, Sotiropoulou A (2024) EU banking and financial regulation. Edward Elgar
Powell R, Yawson A (2007) Are corporate restructuring events driven by common factors? The implications for takeover predictions. J Bus Financ Acc 34(7–8):1169–1192
Pulgar J (2024) Bank resolution and insolvency law: interactions and frictions. Financial Stability Review 47:71–98
Putnis J, Hurn C (2020) Bank recovery and resolution directive (BRRD). In: Herbst J, Lovegrove S (eds) Brexit and financial regulation. Oxford University Press, pp 291–312
Radon J, Achuthan M, Ravichandran N (2019) Beneficial ownership: filling the gap in transparency and accountability in the extractive industries and improving governance. In: Krøvel R (ed) making transparency possible: an interdisciplinary dialogue. Cappelen Damm Forskning, p 159-180
Rutledge V, Moore M, Dobler M, Bossu W, Jassaud N, Zhou J (2012) From bail-out to bail-in: mandatory debt restructuring of systemic financial institutions. IMF Staff Discussion Note 12/03
Scherer F (2013) Financial mergers and their consequences. Harvard Kennedy School Faculty Research Working Paper, RWP13–019
Schillig M (2021) EU Bank insolvency law harmonisation: what next? International Solvency Review 30(2):239–266
Schneider C, Ben-Sharar O (2011) The failure of mandated disclosure. Univ Pa Law Rev 159:647–749
Scholz P (2023) Hostile takeovers: are banks threatened by FinTechs? Corporate Finance 1(2):3–7
Soe M (1974) The legal position of safe deposit boxes in banks. Malaya Law Review 16(2):289–295
Stef N, Dimelis S (2020) Bankruptcy regime and the banking system. Econ Model 87:480–495
Stein A (1972) The safety deposit vault or leased metal box: the responsibility of a Bank to its customers. McGill Law Journal 18(1):45–59
Sunder D (2013) The controversial 'poison pill' takeover Defense: how valid are the arguments in support of it? NMIMS Management Review 23:47–66
Susanti E, Andrini R, Fathoni M (2024) System of supervision and control of Syariah banking. International Journal of Information System and Innovation Management 2(2):49–55
Syamlan Y (2017) Does dual banking system in Indonesia differentiate investment account requirement? Tazkia Islamic Finance and Business Review 11(1):81–106
Ventoruzzo M, Sandrelli G (2019) O tell me the truth about bail-in: theory and practice. European Corporate Governance Institute Working Paper No 442

Further Reading

Barrios V, Blanco J (2003) The effectiveness of Bank capital adequacy regulation: a theoretical and empirical approach. J Bank Financ 27(10):1935–1958
Black F, Scholes M (1973) The pricing of options and corporate liabilities. J Polit Econ 81(3):637–654

Britz V, Gersbach H, Haller H (2021) Deposit insurance and reinsurance. Ann Finance 17:425–470
Chronopoulos D, Wilson J, Yilmaz M (2023) Regulatory oversight and Bank risk. J Financ Stab 64:101105
Hofmann C (2020) The role of deposit Insurance in Bank Resolution. Journal of Financial Regulation 6(1):148–158
Kladakis G, Chen L, Bellos S (2022) Bank regulation, supervision and liquidity creation. J Int Money Financ 124:102629
Malkiel B (2016) A random walk down Wall street: the time-tested strategy for successful investing. W.W, Norton and Company
Rivera T (2025) Bank regulation, investment, and capital requirements under adverse selection. Review of Finance 29(2):415–465
Zhou X, Li X, Zhou Y, Kara A (2025) Deposit insurance and Bank liquidity creation: evidence from a natural experiment in China. J Financ Serv Res 67:101–137

Corporate Governance of Banks 5

Contents

F. B. Erdem, *The Principles of International Banking, Finance and Investment Law*, Springer Textbooks in Law, https://doi.org/10.1007/978-3-032-32505-1_5

Abstract

The most important difference of banks from other companies is that they have the privilege of collecting money from the public and granting loans. The fact that banks are institutions of trust, the role they assume in the economic system, the functioning of the payments system, the power to create dematerialised money, the encouragement of savings and investments, and the provision of a wide range of financial products to the society also reveal the economic and social importance of banks. Therefore, failing to establish or implementing insufficient corporate governance and risk management policies in banks will strengthen the possibility of undesirable consequences both in the financial sector and in the society as a whole in the following processes and a domino effect will be created. Corporate governance in banks refers to a structure in which business and activities are managed by the board of directors and senior management. The structure of corporate governance in banks includes setting corporate objectives, protecting the rights of depositors, regulating corporate activities and behaviours with the expectation that the banking system can operate more reliably and effectively in compliance with existing laws and regulations, and protecting the interests of shareholders. Corporate governance in banking is defined as the management of the bank by the bank's senior management in a manner that protects the rights and interests of all stakeholders, shareholders and savers in line with the set objectives, the law and regulations issued on the basis of the law and other relevant legislation, the articles of association, internal regulations and banking ethical rules. In this context, this part of the study will focus on the obligations that the bank must fulfil legally.

5.1 Introductory Remark

This chapter focuses on banking corporate governance from a legal/normative perspective, acknowledging the specific nature of banking entities as fiduciaries of public trust. While common corporations, tend to be regarded from a corporate governance perspective, banking entities occupy a pivotal role within the financial system, exercising the privilege of receiving deposits, granting credits, and generating non-physical money. As such corporate governance of banks assumes a more elevated status, as banking entities need to comply with prudential regulation and supervision, as well as adhere to ethical standards, which not only concentrate on profit maximisation but also uphold financial stability as a primary goal. Initially, this chapter identifies historical developments concerning banking corporate governance, pointing to banking regulation as defined by Basel II, which specifies sound banking regulation on three important pillars: capital adequacy, supervisory review, and market discipline as the three pillars of sound banking regulation. Following, there is a definition of corporate banking governance on a legal level, identifying arbitration of authority between boards, senior managements, and governing entities. Particular attention is devoted to risk management, internal controls, and auditing mechanisms as instruments of legal compliance and public accountability.

Finally, this chapter investigates the legal provisions which restrict and govern banks, such as capital requirements, transactions between closely-related parties, and the obligation of transparency. Through this section, it becomes apparent that an effective system of governance in banking organizations extends beyond efficiency considerations, as it becomes a legal mandate with significant legal effects in the financial sphere.

Background Information

While the debtor-creditor relationship is traditionally contractual under general company law, banking law treats depositors as key stakeholders in corporate governance — even though they are not shareholders in the bank's capital structure. The primary reason is that depositors bear the bank's risk directly, as bank failures can transmit losses to public finances (e.g., through deposit insurance schemes or government bailouts). It is in this context that the scope of the fiduciary duties owed by bank directors and managers becomes particularly relevant.

The notion of corporate governance in banks is a distinct phenomenon within the realms of law and finance. Thus, whereas corporate governance generally illustrates the manner within which organizations are steered and administered, bank corporate governance portrays a more complex process. This complexity stems from the dual character of banks: as private enterprises seeking profit and as quasi-public institutions entrusted with safeguarding public savings and ensuring financial stability. This duality explains why the legal expectations imposed on banks—especially regarding internal control, risk management, and transparency—are more stringent than those applied to ordinary corporations.

5.1.1 Legal and Economic Foundations of Bank Regulation: From Liquidity Transformation to Negative Externalities and Systemic Contagion

The legal and economic rationale underpinning the specific regulation of banks has to do with their distinctive 'liquidity-transformation' role. Banks act as the bridge connecting short-term funding sources (deposits) and long-term uses of these funds (loans). By their very nature, this implies a structural vulnerability. From a legal perspective, this implies a deviation from the 'shareholder primacy' principle. The legal system is aware that, as banks function under a high level of leverage, which can differ markedly from leverage ratios in non-financial companies, thereby exacerbating moral hazard risks. The greater the risks taken by bank managers, the higher their potential personal gains (via rising stock prices), while the adverse consequences disproportionately affect depositors and, ultimately, taxpayers.

Thus, bank corporate governance reconciles two distinct legal regimes: private law, governing contractual and fiduciary relations among the bank, its shareholders, and clients; and public law, imposing mandatory prudential standards to safeguard monetary and financial stability. This chapter explores this hybrid nature, focusing on the concept of intrusive supervision in G20 jurisdictions. For example, in countries such as Canada and Australia, often cited for their sound banking stability, the law grants supervisors intervention powers in the internal governance of a bank well before the onset of insolvency-a legal mechanism commonly known as early intervention powers.

The economic rationale also addresses the "Negative Externality"problem. In a routine corporate failure, the consequences are usually confined to investors and employees of the company. In banking, however, the interconnectedness of the payment system means that the failure of one institution can trigger a domino effect, shutting down the credit markets and undermining the rule of law in commercial transactions. Accordingly, the legal duty of bank regulation is not only to maximize corporate value but to operate as a 'regulatory anchor' precluding systemic contagion.

In most G20 nations, the legal system mandates a level of fitness and propriety for bank directors that goes significantly beyond the common level of care for directors under general corporate law. This obligation is far from a mere formality; it constitutes a substantive legal requirement. It guarantees that those who are in authority over public savings have, in addition to the appropriate level of professional expertise (knowledge), the right qualities (character) for integrity in fulfilling their fiduciary obligations. In the UK and Singapore, failing this standard can mean personal disqualification from the financial sector, thus emphasizing the personal legal responsibility for bank management.

5.1.2 Emergence of Basel II and the Evolution of Prudential Regulation

The Basel I to Basel II transition represents the beginning of an entirely new paradigm in the philosophy of the law as it relates to banking regulation. Basel I represented, first and foremost, the establishment of the so-called quantitative risk capital ratio, while with Basel II, the law adopted, for the first time, what could well be described as the risk-sensitive legal approach. This new focus started to translate the bank's balance sheet into its process-related decision-making structures. Basel II systematically identified the bank's corporate governance standards as the first determinant in establishing its legislated capital charges. This was translated into the so-called internal ratings-based (IRB) framework in G20 countries, where the law gives the banks the flexibility to make their risk assessments based on their internal risk-modelling approaches, as long as their respective corporate governance structures have passed through the supervisors with flying colours.

The three pillars of Basel II introduced a three-fold legal framework that restructured the obligations of banking directors. According to Pillar 1 (Minimum Capital Requirements) in regard to risk-based capital, there is the legal requirement in this pillar to ensure, as a board responsibility, that the level of the bank's capital is appropriate to its true risks, such as credit and market risks, and, in specific terms, operational risk, which encompasses legal and governance risk. Pillar

2 (Supervisory Review Process), on the other hand, gives the authorities the discretionary power to interfere with the bank's management. This process includes the internal capital adequacy assessment process (ICAAP), which is the legal document through which the board must demonstrate its awareness and ability to manage risk to the concerned authority. This means that, in the event the concerned authority finds the governance framework of the bank to be weak, the authority may impose Pillar 2 Add-ons consolidations requiring the bank to maintain more capital than the statutory requirement. Finally, Pillar 3 (Market Discipline) enforces the conversion of transparency from a voluntary matter within the corporation to a legal requirement. In this way, the legislation makes possible private monitoring by the market, namely investors, rating agencies, and major depositors, as a secondary control mechanism through the utilization of market power.[1]

Countries in the G20, such as France and Italy, have incorporated the principles of Basel II not as guidance, but as a norm within their banking codes.[2] This implies that a failure in the area of internal audit or risk management does not only represent a managerial failure but could result in a breach of a regulation, which could lead to fines, removal from boards, or revocation of a banking license. One of the most important best practices that have developed during Basel II and have been adopted by G20 countries (in particular, ECB's SSM framework for European banks) is that of formalization of so-called supervisory dialogue.[3] In this case, unlike common firms that communicate with the government only via tax or general checks, banks have an ongoing legal dialog that involves deep dive inspections with regard to board minutes and structures of this kind on a constant basis. In this regard, the legal meaning of this context consists in that so-called business judgment rule, which normally protects managers against liability for honest mistakes, being greatly limited for banks, since it can be expected that managers have made efforts in taking part in this kind of dialog and correcting potential issues regarding internal structures and procedures, based on this dialog.

5.1.3 Capital Adequacy and Legal Oversight

Capital adequacy represents the main regulatory constraint on the banking firm's balance sheet, thus constituting a legal buffer that embodies the costs of risk-taking. Normatively speaking, capital regulation represents the embodiment of the banking firm's obligation to be solvent. Capital regulation differs from the limited liability company principle in the following way: whereas the latter shields shareholders from the company's debt obligations within the context of the corporation law, capital regulation standards necessitate a skin in the game element. This assumes that banking firm shareholders and managers feel the initial shock of

[1] Al-Eideh (2011) 5–19.
[2] Bellis (2025) 91–115.
[3] Busch et al. (2021) 48.

the risk results before they reach the depositors or the exchequer. The regulation of capital adequacy is marked by a dynamic and intrusive approach. In G20 countries like Japan and Brazil, the regulation does not specify a mere ratio, and in fact, the regulator adopts a mandatory stress test, which is a legal process where the regulator hypothetically poses negative economic outcomes to assess whether the bank's corporate governance and capital base are fit.[4] Failure in stress testing results in corrective action constraints that derogate substantially from private laws, as they enable the state to disregard the shareholders' votes to impose additional capital, halt dividend distribution, and even replace the boards of directors.

Moreover, capital adequacy elevates the standard of care that the bank directors must exercise. In a typical corporation, the business judgment rule often insulates directors from liability for risky decisions that result in losses. However, in the banking context, exceeding the bank's risk appetite or falling below capital thresholds is often treated as prima facie breach of the fiduciary duty of oversight. This shift heightens the status of capital management to a legal core responsibility of the board.[5]

Modern banking law introduces a sophisticated legal mechanism in G20 nations and under the Basel III Capital Conservation Buffer (CCB). When a bank's capital levels fall into the buffer zone, the law automatically triggers maximum distributable amount (MDA) restrictions.[6] In other words, by operation of law, the bank is forbidden from paying bonuses to executives or dividends to shareholders. This erects a self-executing legal penalty that aligns the interests of management with the long-term solvency of the institution without requiring a court order or a specific administrative act.

5.1.4 Market Discipline and Transparency

Market Discipline is the decentralized part of banking supervision, where the law uses the market mechanism itself to discipline banking behaviour. Pillar 1 and Pillar 2 require the direct intervention of the law, whereas in Pillar 3 (Market Discipline), a legal framework is established in which transparency becomes the silent supervisor.[7] From a legal point of view, the transparency requirement turns banking data into a public good. By the mandatory disclosure of a bank's RWA, liquidity risks, and remuneration policies, the law seeks not only to report, but to require a discursive practice to empower 'private supervisors,' such as institutional investors, credit rating agencies, and highly knowledgeable lenders, to sanction excessive risk-taking.[8]

[4] Jobst et al. (2013); Llorent-Jurado et al. (2024).
[5] Hargovan (2016) 33–51.
[6] Dicanio and Montesi (2021) 34–35.
[7] Boot (2011) 167–183; Dewatripont et al. (2010) Press; Weber (2010) 783–869.
[8] Frolov (2007) 177–191; Longo (2025) 37–54.

The legal function of transparency will now be explained in two: ex-ante, that is preventive, and ex-post, that is corrective. Preventively, the law applies strict disclosure requirements-as the IFRS 9 expected credit loss model-which impede management from concealing non-performing loans or inflating capital levels by window dressing. The threat of market de-valuation acts as a legal deterrent against moral hazard.[9]

Correctively, once information is in the public domain, the law facilitates market-based sanctions. If a bank's disclosures reveal a deteriorating risk profile, the resulting increase in its cost of funding or the decline in its share price serves as a corrective signal that often precedes formal regulatory intervention. For example, based on EBA guidelines or SEC rules in the United States, banks are expected to disclose not just financial data but also what is known as a Governance Statement.[10] The statement is expected to include details such as board meeting frequency, knowledge of board members, as well as risk culture of bank, thereby ensuring that non-financial aspects of governance are also amenable to legal scrutiny. One of the most common best practices, especially among G20 countries such as the UK or Australia, is related to bank executive pay, which is mandated to emphasize transparency. According to this, banks are expected to disclose details of how bonus incentives are connected to risk-adjusted performance as opposed to mere profit. Done under say on pay, this practice enables shareholders or the marketplace to review if there is a reckless way of working as a result of bank pay incentives. In some countries, regulators have the authority to demand bonus paybacks, thus relying on transparency as a component of accountability.[11]

5.1.5 The Normative Framework of Bank Governance

The regulatory architecture of banking supervision has entered a multi-layered world of normativity, where the lines between hard law and soft law have been blurred. Because of this diversity, the standards of governance will be able to keep pace with the dynamic nature of financial markets while ensuring a measure of stability and predictability.

5.1.5.1 Statutory National Laws

At the top of its national system is a series of primary banking acts and company laws that are considered to grant legal personality to banks and express their principal organs' core functions. In G20 countries, many such statutes have started to incorporate mandatory governance clauses, such as an obligatory Risk Committee or fiduciary duty relating to systemic risk. The Italian banking sector, for example,

[9] Gontareva and Stepaniuk (2020) 126–131.

[10] Jedrzejowska-Schiffauer et al. (2019) 432–456.

[11] See, Fisch et al. (2018) 101–129; Lu (2022) 207–227; Marcinkowska (2014) 41.

serves as an excellent example of how national legal systems implement mandatory corporate governance and risk management provisions. In Italy, governance and risk management requirements for banks are not just soft-law principles but are also included within the body of law governing banking activity and as part of supervision. The legal personality of a bank in Italy is derived from the Italian Civil Code and the Testo Unico Bancario (Consolidated Banking Act), which detail the key corporate organs of the bank and allocate governance, management and oversight responsibilities among them, thereby establishing a structure for a bank that has risk governance embedded into it. In Italy, the introduction of mandatory internal control and risk committees has strengthened the role of Boards of Directors in the oversight of risk in response to the global financial crisis as well as the Basel Committee and EU Level reforms. These Committees create definitions for the bank's risk appetite; ensure that the bank's risk appetite is consistent with the bank's business strategy; and assess how effective the bank's internal control system is. Additionally, the presence of an independent risk management process with a Chief Risk Officer who reports directly to top management and the Board is now a regulatory requirement and not merely a best practice. The Italian regulation goes further than requiring that board members act in the interest of shareholders by also holding them accountable to depositors and the overall stability of our entire financial system—which is especially important for banks due to their systemic relevance noted above. In essence, this broader view of fiduciary duty allows for better alignment between corporate governance objectives and macro-prudential objectives as they affect financial institutions and their related business interests. As such, risk management is part of the governance responsibility rather than strictly a technical function, as it also incorporates both financial (credit, market, etc.) and non-financial risks (including operational risk and the potential for financial systemic risk) into how individual firms devise and implement strategic initiatives. Therefore, Italy's experience clearly illustrates how G20 member nations have taken international standards related to corporate governance and developed enforceable governance mechanisms for compliance by local entities through the adoption of the Italian regulation and similar legal frameworks. For instance, the recently enacted Italian regulation requires that (1) all member companies establish a formalized Risk Committee, (2) all board members be more accountable for their decisions, and (3) member companies establish a documented risk appetite that will determine how much risk a company is able to tolerate under its governance framework, ultimately promoting an environment of systemic risk prevention.[12]

5.1.5.2 Administrative-Supervisory Regulations

Administrative-supervisory regulations are considered as secondary regulations. They are issued by bodies such as the ECB or the FED. From a legal perspective, their importance exists in their operative character. They are a way of putting a

---

[12] Cerrone (2019) 58–69.

general legal provision into a specific form (for example, the exact requirements for a personal auditor). These regulations have the force of *lex specialis* in the legal field.[13] They are considered to outweigh general corporate law.

5.1.5.3 International Schemes (Basel II, III, IV)

Although international schemes, namely Basel II, III and IV, do not have direct effect in the domestic law of nations, they nonetheless constitute global administrative law. Because they are enacted and thus applied either through national legislation or supranational directives-at the EU level, most notably, through its CRD/CRR-Basel has become the de facto global standard. Basel III and IV have recently set higher standards for the so-called leverage ratio and liquidity coverage, which are now legally binding standards of good governance.[14]

5.1.5.4 Soft-Law and Ethical Codes

Instruments such as the OECD Principles of Corporate Governance or the Banking Standards Board guidelines in the UK represent a move to reflexive law.[15] Though not enforceable directly before a court of law as a statute, they are frequently employed by judges and regulators as interpretative tools to decide whether or not a director has acted with the required standard of care.[16]

5.1.5.5 Concluding Remarks

The interaction between these layers creates a governance ecosystem in which a breach of an ethical code-which amounts to so-called soft law-can then be used as evidence of failure regarding fit and proper requirements, hard law, thus enabling administrative sanctions. A key area of divergence within the normative framework amongst the G20 countries is the enforcement mechanism. Whereas the UK traditionally championed the 'comply or explain' model, which allows flexibility if a bank can justify deviation,[17] this has given way to a more comply or penalise approach for banks in the US and post-2008 Europe.[18] Within this more stringent normative environment, governance requirements are considered absolute duties. For instance, the Dutch Banking Code incorporates a moral/ethical statement known as the *banker's oath*, which has legal form and force, so failure to adhere to an ethical standard may lead to professional disqualification.[19]

In summary, the introductory framework establishes that the corporate governance of banks is a legal necessity rather than a managerial preference. It is designed to safeguard public confidence, protect depositors, and ensure that banks

---

[13] Levi (2013) 51–101; Duran (2015) 97–125; Hayden (2022) 1011–1050.

[14] Sterzel (2020) 81–122; Atik (2014) 283–341.

[15] Zhang (2018) 272–278; Cox and Soobiah (2018) 120–134; Alexander (2004) 991–1034; Chisnall (2010) 7–8.

[16] Nelemans (2019) 21–32; Thakor (2021) 47–77; McGrath and Walker (2023) 791–809.

[17] Roberts et al. (2020) 602–626; MacNeil and Esser (2022) 1–56.

[18] Amariles and Winkler (2018) 497–536.

[19] Laaper and Busch (2019) 444–467; Zaring (2020) 555–577; Hobt (2021) 13–37.

contribute to financial stability rather than endanger it. The subsequent sections of this chapter will examine the legal dimensions of governance in greater depth—starting with definitional aspects, the structure of internal governance processes, and finally, the statutory provisions and limits imposed for the protection of banks.

5.2 The Concept of Corporate Governance

5.2.1 Definition

Bank corporate governance goes well beyond the shareholder focus of a typical company to being essentially a legal instrument through which systemic stability and public trust are secured.[20] The management of a normal industrial company concentrates on limiting the agency problem between managers and shareholders, however, a bank corporate governance has to incorporate wider fiduciary duties not only to depositors but also to the overall integrity of the payment system.

Being trust intermediaries, banks operate under a governance framework where the strategic and operational decisions are, to a large extent, determined by the law and regulations that aim at reconciling private interests with the public good. This means moving from a simple administrative framework to a strict system of normative compliance that requires not only lawfulness but also the highest standards of corporate conduct and transparency in the banking business. This framework's legal aspects rest on fiduciary duty and full accountability.[21]

The leadership has to be loyal and careful not only to their shareholders but also to creditors and the community at large. Besides, an accountability requirement that forces companies to explain their actions to the governing bodies and the general public strengthens this notion, thus governance is being used as an instrument of prudence. Therefore, the corporate governance of a bank is an exceptional combination of corporate law, banking regulation, and professional ethics where the main goal is the upholding of trust of the entire system by means of careful and clear decision, making.

5.2.2 The Legal Nature of Governance in Banking

The legal character of governance in banking hinges on it being *lex specialis*, a specialized set of rules distinguishing financial institutions from regular corporations due to their systemic importance and their susceptibility to contagion risk. Generally, banks are viewed as regulated entities across most countries' legal systems and, therefore, the governance within them is subject to supervisory approval and continuous monitoring. Through this regulatory system, the roles of directors and

[20] Alexander (2006) 17–40; Omarova (2017) 1029–1070.

[21] Ungureanu (2008) 1–19; Levi (2013) 51–101; Heremans and Pacces (2023) ch 13.

senior management exceed the usual requirements of loyalty and care under corporate law and incorporate prudential obligations necessary for the safeguarding of financial stability.

Among the principal duties that the board and management have to undertake are guaranteeing sufficient capital and liquidity at the bank, implementing an effective internal control and risk management framework, and averting conflicts of interest between the management and customers. Also, the top executives have a legal duty to inform the regulators about the significant risks, large exposures, as well as compliance breaches. These kinds of rules derive from public law doctrines of depositor protection and systemic risk prevention. As a consequence, bank governance can be seen as an intricate mixture of the private law aspect that governs the company's internal relations, and the public law that constitutes the states supervisory authority. This duality makes governance a hybrid legal regime that is both contractual and regulatory. Thus, the courts and regulators are increasingly recognizing that the failures correspond not only to the breaches of the corporate fiduciary duties but also to the banking regulation statutory obligations.[22] This alignment of responsibilities is a reflection of the changing view of the judiciary according to which banks are considered as private entities that carry out crucial public functions in the market environment and therefore their governance should be oriented to the public interest along with the shareholder value.

5.2.3 The Legal Principles of Corporate Governance in Banks

The legal principles of corporate governance in banks are essentially a mixture of international standards, for instance, those laid down by the BCBS and the OECD, as well as national laws. These sets of rules together essentially change the way bank governance is viewed, from being merely an internal administrative issue to a major legal accountability that comes with high stakes.

Transparency is a major principle of this legal system which basically requires that the bank's financial condition, risk exposure, and governance framework should be open not only to the regulators but also to the general public.[23] Sound financial statements certified by an independent accountant and a capital adequacy ratio are examples of disclosures for transparency under the law. This in turn helps making the market discipline and enables the regulator to perform an anticipatory control.

Furthermore, there is the principle of accountability which, apart from being a moral commitment, is turned into a legal requirement for the firm officials to give a proper account of their actions. This principle is backed up by a top, down system mainly: internally a situation where the board of directors controls the

[22] BIS (2015).

[23] Szalay (2019) 21–28.

management through review of its performance; externally the supervisory authorities which have been given the legal power to impose sanctions for negligence or mismanagement.[24]

Moreover, the legal requirement for fairness serves as a further reason to extend the concept of governance by only the consideration of the interests of the shareholders, depositors, and employees. The implementation of this principle at the operational level can be seen in the prohibitions of statutory lender insider, conflict of interest, and the preferential treatment of the related parties that must be very strictly adhered to.[25]

Last but not least, prudence as one of the main legal concepts imposes on the management the obligation to behave in a prompt manner and with the mind of a cautious person. In contrast to the general corporate law, which may give more freedom for risk, taking, banking law implements prudence by setting the most stringent capital adequacy requirements and proper asset quality management.[26] If the implementation of risk, taking through certain governance practices starts to falsify the reality of the banks and the real prudential soundness, then the supervisors are the ones who will be empowered by the law to take control over the situation direct intervention.

5.2.4 Governance as a Legal Safeguard for Depositors and the Public

Corporate governance in the banking industry serves a crucial legal shield which allows a bank to align its internal workings with its main social purpose, that is, the protection of depositors. This protective function is a consequence of the implicit fiduciary pact that is established through deposit, taking, whereby depositors, unlike shareholders, have no say in the institution's strategic decisions and yet they are the most to be affected in the case of financial failure. In order to solve this inequality, the law of banking uses governance as a control tool in the wider framework of protection, conjuring alongside prudential regulation and deposit insurance. Thus, corporate governance standards help in decreasing the risk of insolvency through ensuring proper decision, making and transparency, hence, they preserve the soundness of the deposit insurance scheme and prevent public funds from being unnecessarily exposed to risk.[27] Besides the protection of individual account holders, law also sees governance as a means to keep the economy stable. Since banks are the main channels through which savings are converted into investments and the ones that maintain the payment infrastructure, their lack of good governance may lead to systemic risk, that is, the risk of the whole financial system's failure, which can spread very quickly to the rest of the economy. Thus,

---

[24] See, in general, Akuffo (2020).

[25] Vegholm and Silver (2008) 352–364.

[26] Buck (2010); Arif et al. (2024); Ditchkus et al. (2011) 447–464.

[27] White (2012) 302–322.

the enforcement of laws on governance standards is nothing else but the embodiment of the public interest principle in banking law. The doctrine goes beyond the private contractual relations of the firm, effectively stating that the question of governance in a bank is an issue of public concern as the stability of the entire financial system is reliant on the responsible and transparent management of each institution.

5.2.5 Ethical and Legal Dimensions

Although at its core governance is largely a legal concept, the effectiveness of governance, however, is deeply connected to the ethical foundation of the institution's operations. The Basel Committee highlights this link by using the term *tone at the top* which essentially means that the board and senior management should lead by example and create a culture of integrity, compliance, and risk awareness throughout the organization.[28]

The fact that legal rules are not enough to control human behavior in complex financial environments is increasingly accepted by regulators, who are, therefore, more and more turning to "comply or explain" as their regulatory tool. This approach combines the binding statutory rules with a principles, based framework, thereby opening up the possibility for banks to adapt governance structures that fit their particular business models while at the same time holding them responsible for any deviations from the accepted standards.[29]

In such a hybrid setting, the ethical codes, which are implemented as internal policies, aim at closing the gap between what is legal and what is right. They essentially set the moral criteria not only for directors but also for the employees. This aspect of ethics is progressively coming to intersect with the boundary that is being pushed out by the environmental, social and governance (ESG) factors of the regulatory landscape. To the extent that the law is incorporating ESG into banking governance, it is, in fact, attributing a new role to banks as stewards of society's capital. In the light of the changing paradigm, the fiduciary duty of a bank is not just about its financial solvency in the short term but is more broadly about sustainability, social welfare, and the bank's governance role in ensuring the co, evolution of the system and society over the long term.

5.3 The Dual Nature of Bank Corporate Governance

Corporate governance in banking is among the most complex and hybrid concepts in contemporary legal systems. Contrary to governance frameworks of other corporations, bank governance goes beyond the mere internal organization of corporate

[28] Sheedy and Canestrari-Soh (2023) 4093–4124; Kabuye et al. (2019)1–24; Burdon and Sorour (2020) 47–80; Zaring (2017) 187–209.
[29] Hopt (2021) 14; Schemmel (2016) 455–504.

power. Rather, it fulfills a public regulatory function, combining the principles of private fiduciary law with public prudential supervision. This twofold character corresponds to the double role of the bank in the economy. A bank is firstly a private legal person created under company law, whose objective is profit and competitiveness. Secondly, it holds public funds and is a vital part of the financial system, the stability of which has an impact on macroeconomic stability and social welfare. Hence, bank governance is both a matter of private accountability and public order. Law, in acknowledging this dichotomy, puts forward duties going beyond the interests of shareholders. Directors and managers should act not only to please owners but also to safeguard depositors, creditors, and the broader economy. Their obligations of loyalty, care, and prudence assume a public character, which is further strengthened by the supervisory authorities, who are given powers of prevention and correction.

5.3.1 The Relationship Between Governance and Financial Stability

Banking crises, such as the 1997 Asian crisis, the 2008 global financial crisis, and more recent cases of institutional failure, show that bad corporate governance is a system, wide risk. Inadequate board supervision, risky behaviour, and lack of transparency in financial reporting have been the chief causes of bank failures that have required government rescue. After 2008, there have been legal changes that focus on using governance as a tool for macroprudential stability. Both national and international regulators now agree that good governance helps to prevent contagion and makes the system more resilient.[30] Under this view, governance is turned into a public commodity. The stability of the financial system is not solely dependent on macroeconomic policy but also on the trustworthiness and responsibility of the individual institutions. As a result, the governance of banks gains a constitutional status within the overall structure of economic governance.

5.3.2 Accountability, Ethics, and the Rule of Law

A major topic in today's bank governance is how accountability is connected to the rule of law. In democracies, it is a must that economic power is used under the confines of law and morality. Banks, due to their large size and influence, are on the hook for being highly accountable.[31] However, law is just one side of the coin and cannot do without a ethical framework. The essence of governance is a culture of trust in which one sees compliance as something coming from within rather than something forced from without. The idea of "ethical banking" which is

[30] Nakatani (2020) 1169–1186.
[31] Kulmie and Ibrahim (2024) 1917–1932.

considered both a legal and a moral standard, refers to honesty, fairness, and social responsibility being at the forefront of business practice.[32] Governance failure is judged by the courts and regulators not only in terms of financial losses but also in terms of violation of the trust.[33] Therefore, governance can be seen as a branch of the rule of law going into the economic field: it limits private power through public responsibility.

5.3.3 The Future of Governance: Digitalization, ESG, and Resilience

The future of banking governance will mainly depend on three major changes: digitalization, sustainability, and resilience. Each of these will bring along new legal and ethical issues. The digital transformation has significantly changed how banks operate offline banking services have been replaced by online ones, loans are now mostly processed by algorithms, and risk assessment is increasingly done by artificial intelligence.[34]

Legal provisions should also cover security duties online, responsibility of the algorithms, compliance with data protection rules, and overall digital resilience. Governance here refers not only to financial prudence but also to technological diligence or the legal obligation to efficiently handle technological risks as one would handle financial risks.[35] ESG standards are now a central part of any company's ethical and environmental responsibility. For banks, ESG is more than just concern over image; it is a regulatory challenge. From a legal perspective, ESG governance involves boards integrating sustainability goals into the overall bank strategy, climate, related risks being factored into the banks financial assessment, standards for disclosure being broadened to include sustainability metrics, and banking loan policies being aligned with environmental and social criteria.[36] Banking supervisory authorities have incorporated the evaluation of banks climate risk exposure into their overall prudential review. Hence ESG has evolved to a legal aspect of governance as well-establishing a connection between financial stability and the two other major components: ecological and social sustainability.[37]

The pandemic of COVID, 19, unstable markets, and especially continuing geopolitical conflicts serve as a good reminder of the necessity of having sturdy governance frameworks in place. Resilience, in short, refers to the ability to foresee, withstand, and adjust to turbulent events without the turmoil spreading to the entire system. Compliance with rules has been at the core of resilience from a

---

32 Thakor (2021) 47–77.

33 Muslim (202515–29.

34 Fernandez (2025) 1558–1571; Alam et al. (2025) 46–55; Gaviyau and Godi (2025) 48; Popa (2024) 74–82.

35 Mohammed (2025) 338–350; Mahdi (2024) 130–149.

36 Lamanda and Tamasne (2025); Boafo et al. (2025) 1–32.

37 Brindelli et al. (2022) 25–35; Feridun and Güngör (2020) 5325.

legal point of view. It entails business continuity planning as a regulatory requirement, recovery and resolution frameworks to deal with possible failures, as well as stress testing and scenario analysis as part of governance practices. Therefore, the evolution of governance is in adaptive legality a framework that keeps changing with new risks/substantiates the core values of prudence, accountability, and transparency.

5.3.4 Reconciling Autonomy and Regulation

A perennial challenge in the governance of banks is reconciling the need for institutional autonomy with the imperatives of regulatory oversight.[38] Excessive regulation can impede innovation and operational vitality, while insufficient oversight may foster imprudence and threaten financial stability. The law's task, then, is to exercise discernment and proportionality—intervening only to the extent that the scale of systemic risk warrants.[39] The aim is not to subordinate banks under the full authority of the state, but to bring their private incentives into constructive harmony with the public good. When governance is thoughtfully designed, it cultivates prudential values within the institution itself, allowing them to shape corporate judgment from the inside out. In this way, regulation ceases to function merely as an external constraint and instead becomes a support for a discipline that is already internally grounded. In the ideal conception, the law does not displace corporate autonomy; it affirms and strengthens it—by ensuring that autonomy unfolds within an architecture of integrity, fairness, and accountability.

5.3.5 Governance as Legal Architecture for Trust

At its core, the governance of banks is anchored in the human quality of trust, a trust bestowed by depositors on their banks, by investors on the financial system, and by society on the very stability of money.[40] While trust cannot be directly mandated by statute, its cultivation and preservation are fundamentally shaped by law. The intricate network of legal provisions ranging from capital requirements and liquidity standards to disclosure obligations, ethical norms, and supervisory oversight, which constitutes an architecture designed to inspire and sustain that trust. When thoughtfully conceived and rigorously enforced, this legal architecture elevates private financial enterprise into a public trust, governed not by arbitrary power but by the rule of law.

Corporate governance in banking, therefore, transcends mere managerial efficiency or regulatory compliance.[41] It is, above all, about safeguarding the moral

[38] Moenninghoff, Ongena and Wieandt (2015) 221–236.

[39] Gai et al. (2019) 32–41.

[40] Colombo (2010) 577–602.

[41] Zulfikar et al. (2020) 137.

and legal legitimacy of finance ensuring that institutions entrusted with public confidence operate with responsibility, openness, and fairness. This endeavour is not mechanical, but deeply humanistic: it recognises that the law's ultimate aim is to serve the common good, mediating between the imperatives of profit and the demands of justice.

5.3.6 Final Observation

In summation, the corporate governance of banks stands at the crossroads of law, economics, and ethics. It reveals how legal systems transform economic rationality into normative order. By embedding prudential discipline within corporate structures, the law channels the pursuit of profit toward socially responsible outcomes. Banks that internalize these governance principles not only comply with legal requirements but also exemplify them, serving as agents of stability and trust in an increasingly uncertain environment. Thus, sound corporate governance constitutes both a legal obligation and a moral imperative, reflecting the rule of law within the financial sector.[42]

Chapter Summary

This chapter approaches corporate governance of banks from a legal, normative perspective, and thus concentrates on banks as fiduciaries of public trust. The chapter also highlights the differences between banks and other companies that primarily focus on shareholder value and profit maximization. Banks, on the other hand, are at the very core of the financial system playing a systemic role. Banks are the institutions that accept deposits, extend credit, create money, and perform liquidity transformation (converting short, term liabilities into long, term assets), hence, they are structurally exposed to vulnerabilities, high leverage, moral hazard, negative externalities, and contagion risks. Consequently, a failure of a bank may result in the costs being passed onto the depositors, deposit insurance, taxpayers, and the overall economy.

Therefore, bank governance is seen as a hybrid legal regime where private law (fiduciary duties, contractual relations among shareholders, managers, and clients) is combined with public law (mandatory prudential regulation and intrusive supervision to protect financial stability). This dual nature of banks is a departure from the traditional shareholder primacy principle: directors and managers here have extended fiduciary duties not only to the shareholders but also to the depositors, creditors, and the community at large.

[42] Hopt (2021) 13–37.

The level of legal expectations in banks is far higher than in non, financial firms as they cover risk management, internal controls, auditing, capital adequacy, transparency, and restrictions on related, party transactions.

The chapter highlights a greater emphasis on risk management and internal controls in banks' corporate governance. It also charts the evolution of key historical and regulatory events focusing on Basel II and its three pillars which are structural of bank governance changes:

(i) Pillar 1 Minimum capital requirements (risk, based, including credit, market, and operational risks), making directors legally accountable for capital being consistent with the bank's real risk profile.
(ii) Pillar 2 Supervisory review process (including ICAAP), giving regulators the power to enforce additional capital buffers or early intervention measures in case of governance weaknesses.
(iii) Pillar 3 Market discipline through mandatory transparency and disclosure, turning information into a public good that investors, rating agencies, and depositors can use to put corrective pressure.

Further Basel III/IV reforms added several tools like the Capital Conservation Buffer, Maximum Distributable Amount (MDA) restrictions, leverage ratios, liquidity coverage, stress testing, etc., that lead to automatic sanctions (e.g., dividends/bonus restrictions) once the limit is violated. These instruments make capital and risk management a fundamental legal obligation of the board, thus restricting the extent to which the business judgment rule can offer protections and considering such violations as either fiduciary failures or regulatory breaches.

The normative framework has several layers: national banking laws, administrative regulations (e. g. ECB, FED), international Basel standards (BCBS standards, incorporated into domestic law in G20 countries), and soft, law instruments (OECD principles, codes of ethics). In countries such as Italy, the UK, Canada, Australia and Singapore, supervisors have been granted powers to intervene early, enforce the "fit and proper" standards with the risk of disqualification, require risk committees and Chief Risk Officers, and engage in regular supervisory dialogue.

Effective bank governance, therefore, is not just about efficiency or voluntary adoption of best practices; it is a legal requirement aimed primarily at the protection of depositors, the prevention of systemic contagion, the maintenance of public confidence, and the alignment of private profit motives with macroprudential stability. It serves not only as a protective framework for the trust but also as a means of integrating prudence, accountability, transparency, and ethical behavior in banking institutions.

Revision Questions

1. Discuss the place of the supervisory review process (Pillar II) in the Basel framework. How did this pillar change bank governance from being just an internal managerial issue to a permanent legal compliance requirement?
2. What are the main duties and legal liabilities of the BoD and senior executives in guaranteeing the adequacy of a bank's risk management plan? How does the internal audit system support the Board's oversight duties?
3. Examine the legal justification for limiting a bank's exposures to risk groups (related parties) and credit concentration (credit ceiling). In what ways do these limits safeguard depositors and reduce moral hazard?
4. Explain how poor bank governance can lead to systemic risk. Give two examples of legal penalties or regulatory powers, capital or licensing related, that can be used by the regulators to hold accountable and prevent the escalation of such failures.
5. What differentiates the legal obligation of banks regarding bank secrets and client secrets? How do the GDPR and similar laws affect the traditional banking practice of client confidentiality?
6. What is legal significance of a bank keeping fully paid stock and meeting the capital adequacy ratio? How is this obligation different from, yet supportive of, having to meet the LCR/NSFR?
7. What are the anticipated legal and ethical implications of digitalisation and/or ESG factors on bank governance?◀

References

Akuffo J (2020) Corporate governance and accountability of financial institutions. Palgrave Macmillan

Al-Eideh B (2011) The three pillars of Basel II: a diffusion model with jumps of banking regulation. Journal of Money, Investment and Banking 19:5–19

Alam Y, Azizah S, Caroline C (2025) Digital transformation in banking management: optimizing operational efficiency and enhancing customer experience. International Journal of Management Science and Information Technology 5(1):46–55

Alexander K (2004) UK corporate governance and banking regulation: the Regulator's role as stakeholder. Stetson Law Review 33:991–1034

Alexander K (2006) Corporate governance and banks: the role of regulation in reducing the principal-agent problem. J Bank Regul 7:17–40

Amariles D, Winkler M (2018) U.S. economic sanctions and the corporate compliance of foreign banks. The. International Lawyer 51(3):497–536

Arif S, Donovan J, Gopalan Y, Morris A (2024) Pay for prudence. J Account Econ 77(1):101619

Atik J (2014) EU implementation of Basel III in the shadow of euro crisis. Review of Banking and Financial Law 33:283–341

Bellis M (2025) Adaptation and endorsement: the incorporation of global standards for banking and accounting in the EU. In: Eliantonio M, Volpato A, Röttger-Wirtz S (eds) Global standards and EU law. Edward Elgar, pp 91–115

BIS (2015) Corporate Governance Principles for Banks. https://www.bis.org/bcbs/publ/d328.pdf. Accessed 31 Jan 2026.

Boafo J, Maclean E, Danzerl N, Amoafo-Danquah K (2025) Sustainable banking and ESG integration: a systematic review of green finance practices in global banking systems. Interdisciplinary Journal of Management Sciences 2(1):1–32

Boot A (2011) Banking at the crossroads: how to Deal with marketability and complexity? Review of Development Finance 1(3–4):167–183

Brindelli G, Bruno M, Citterio A, Fuso U (2022) Banks' governance and risk management frameworks: how to integrate ESG and climate risks. Risk Management Magazine 17(1):25–35

Buck F (2010) Managerial Prudence under Banking Regulation. https://www.econstor.eu/bitstream/10419/37204/3/VfS_2010_pid_991.pdf. Accessed 31 Jan 2026

Burdon W, Sorour M (2020) Institutional theory and evolution of 'a legitimate' compliance culture: the case of the UK financial service sector. J Bus Ethics 162:47–80

Busch D, Ferrarini G, Hurk A (2021) The European Commission's sustainable finance action plan and other international initiatives. In: Busch D, Ferrarini G, Grünewald S (eds) Sustainable finance in Europe: corporate governance. Palgrave Macmillan, Financial Stability and Financial Markets, pp 19–61

Cerrone R (2019) Risk management as increased corporate governance requirement in Italian banks and insurance companies. Corporate Board: Role, Duties and Composition 15(3):58–69

Chisnall P (2010) Corporate governance in UK banks. Corp Ownersh Control 7(4):7–8

Colombo R (2010) The role of Trust in Financial Regulation. Villanova Law Review 55(3):577–602

Cox P, Soobiah D (2018) An empirical investigation into the corporate culture of UK listed banks. Journal of Financial Regulation and Compliance 26(1):120–134

Dewatripont M, Rochet J, Tirole J (2010) Balancing the banks: global lessons from the financial crisis. Oxford University Press

Dicanio A, Montesi G (2021) Banks in time of Covid-19: loss absorption capacity, lending and market valuation. Bancaria 2:31–58

Ditchkus L, Sierra G, Reed B (2011) The role of managerial prudence in Bank loan loss provisioning. J Manag Issues 23(4):447–464

Duran C (2015) The framework for the social accountability of central banks: the growing relevance of the soft law in central banking. European Journal of Legal Studies 8(2):97–125

Feridun M, Güngör H (2020) Climate-related Prudential risks in the banking sector: a review of the emerging regulatory and supervisory practices. Sustainability 12(13):5325

Fernandez J (2025) The architecture of sustainable banking: financial, institutional and risk patterns behind environmental performance. Borsa Istanbul Rev 25(6):1558–1571

Fisch J, Palia D, Solomon S (2018) Is say on pay all about pay? The impact of firm performance. Harvard Business Law Review 8:101–129

Frolov M (2007) Why do we need mandated rules of public disclosure for banks? J Bank Regul 8(2):177–191

Gai P, Kemp M, Serrano A, Schnabel I (2019) Regulatory Complexity and the Quest for Robust Regulation. https://www.esrb.europa.eu/pub/pdf/asc/esrb.asc190604_8_regulatorycomplexityquestrobustregulation~e63a7136c7.en.pdf. Accessed 31 Jan 2026

Gaviyau W, Godi J (2025) Banking sector transformation: disruptions. Challenges and Opportunuties FinTech 4(3):48

Gontareva V, Stepaniuk Y (2020) Mission Impossible: The True Story of Ukraine's Comprehensive Banking Reform and Practical Manual for Other Nations. https://www.lse.ac.uk/iga/assets/documents/publications/2020/Mission-Possible-the-true-story-of-Ukraines-comprehensive-banking-reform-and-practical-manual-for-other-nations.pdf. Accessed 31 Jan 2026

Hargovan A (2016) Directors' duties to consider creditor interests: a solution in search of a problem? In: Omar P (ed) Parry R. Banking and Financial Insolvencies, The European Regulatory Framework. INSOL-Europe, pp 33–51

Hayden H (2022) Enforcement of fines and other pecuniary obligations imposed by the ECB (part I): European level. European Company and Financial Law Review 18(6):1011–1050

Heremans D, Pacces A (2023) Regulation of banking and financial markets. In: Geest G (ed) Encyclopedia of law and economics, ch. 13

Hopt K (2021) Corporate governance of banks and financial institutions: economic theory, supervisory practice, evidence and policy. Eur Bus Organ Law Rev 22(1):13–37

Jedrzejowska-Schiffauer I, Schiffauer P, Thalassinos E (2019) EU regulatory measures following the crises: what impact on corporate governance of financial institutions? European Research Studies Journal 22(3):432–456

Jobst A, Li O, Schmeider C (2013) A framework for macroprudential bank solvency stress testing: application to S-25 and other G-20 country FSAPs. IMF Working Paper 13(68)

Kabuye F, Bugambiro N, Akugizibwe I, Nuwasiima S, Naigaga S (2019) The influence of tone at the top management level and internal audit quality on the effectiveness of risk management practices in the financial services sector. Cogent Business and Management 6:1–24

Kulmie D, Ibrahim M (2024) Bank corporate governance: shield against fraud. Journal of Ecohumanism 3(3):1917–1932

Laaper P, Busch D (2019) The Dutch Banker's oath and the Dutch banking disciplinary committee. In: Busch D, Ferrarini G, van Solinge G (eds) Governance of financial institutions. Oxford University Press, pp 444–467

Lamanda G, Tamasne Z (2025) Is banks' ESG disclosure associated with financial depth and economic growth? Evidence from the Visegrad four countries. Environ Dev 55:101233

Levi L (2013) The European banking authority: legal framework, operations and challenges ahead. Tulane European and Civil Law Forum 28:51–101

Llorent-Jurado J, Ordaz-Sanz J, Melgar-Hiraldo M, Guerrrero-Casas F (2024) A review of the discussion proposal on changes to the EU-wide stress test. Central Bank Review 24(3):100161

Longo S (2025) Disclosure in banking: the role of financial reporting in Bank behaviours and investor decision-making. Springer

Lu L (2022) Market or state: differences in the regulations and practices of bankers' remuneration in the UK and China. Cambridge University Press

MacNeil I, Esser I (2022) The emergence of 'comply or explain' as a global model for corporate governance codes. European Business Law Review 33(1):1–56

Mahdi M (2024) Shared cybersecurity responsibilities in the banking sector: a case studies online banks and their customers in data security protection. Journal of Education for Pure Science 14(4):130–149

Marcinkowska M (2014) Remuneration of Bank managers—problems and potential solutions. Argumenta Oeconomica 32(1):41–74

McGrath J, Walker C (2023) Regulating ethics in financial services: engaging industry to achieve regulatory objectives. Regulation and Governance 17(3):791–809

Moenninghoff S, Ongena S, Wieandt A (2015) The perennial challenge to counter too-big-to-fail in banking: empirical evidence from the new international regulation dealing with global systemically important banks. J Bank Financ 61(C):221-236

Mohammed A (2025) Data privacy: research on how banks handle customer data in compliance with regulations like GDPR. International Journal of Advances in Engineering and Management 7(5):338–350

Muslim M (2025) The failure of governance and internal controls in preventing fraud in the company. Advances in Managerial Auditing Research 3(1):15–29

Nakatani R (2020) Macroprudential policy and the probability of a banking crisis. J Policy Model 42(6):1169–1186

Nelemans M (2019) Financial regulation and corporate governance in banks. Challenges and opportunities. European Journal of Commercial Contract Law 2:21–32

Omarova S (2017) Bank governance and systemic stability: the "Golden share" approach. Alabama Law Review 68(4):1029–1070

Popa V (2024) Identification and use of sustainability and resilience indicators within banking institutions. Journal of Financial and Monetary Economics 12(1):74–82

Roberts J, Sanderson P, Seidl D, Krivokapic A (2020) The UK corporate governance code principle of 'comply or explain': understanding code compliance as 'subjection'. ABACUS A Journal of Accounting, Finance and Business Studies 56(4):602–626

Schemmel J (2016) The ESA guidelines: soft law and subjectivity in the European financial market—capturing the administrative influence. Indiana Journal of Global Legal Studies 23(2):455–504

Sheedy E, Canestrari-Soh D (2023) Does executive accountability enhance risk management and risk culture? Account Finance 63(4):4093–4124

Sterzel A (2020) Reforming the regulatory treatment of sovereign exposures in banking regulation. Credit and Capital Markets 53(1):81–122

Szalay G (2019) The impact of the lack of transparency on corporate governance: a practical example. Corporate Law and Governance Review 1(2):21–28

Thakor A (2021) Ethics, culture, and higher purpose in banking: post-crisis governance developments. Int J Cent Bank 17(5):47–77

Ungureanu M (2008) Banks: regulation and corporate governance framework. Journal of Ownership and Control 5(2):1–19

Vegholm F, Silver L (2008) The impact of corporate fairness on the Bank-SME relationship. Journal of Financial Regulation and Compliance 16(4):352–364

Weber R (2010) New governance, financial regulation, and challenges to legitimacy: the example of the internal models approach to capital adequacy. Adm Law Rev 62(3):783–869

White L (2012) Corporate governance and Prudential regulation of banks: is there any connection? In: Barth J, Lin C, Wihlborg C (eds) Research handbook on international banking and governance. Edward Elgar, pp 302–322

Zaring D (2017) The international campaign to create ethical bankers. Journal of Financial Regulation 3(2):187–209

Zaring D (2020) Regulating banking ethics: a toolkit. Seattle University Law Review 43:555–577

Zhang C (2018) Can we tame the bankers? A critical review of the functions of the UK's banking standards board. Journal of International Banking Law and Regulation 33(8):272–278

Zulfikar R, Lukviarman N, Suhardjanto D, Ismail T, Astuti K, Meutia M (2020) Corporate governance compliance in banking industry: the role of the board. J Open Innov: Technol Mark Complex 6(4):137

Further Reading

Admati A, Hellwig M (2024) The bankers' new clothes: What's wrong with banking and what to do about it. Princeton University Press

Anginer D, Demirgüç-Kunt A, Huizinga H, Ma K (2018) Corporate governance of banks and financial stability. J Financ Econ 130(2):327–346

Armour J, Awrey D, Davies P, Enriques L, Gordon J, Mayer C, Payne J (2016) Principles of financial regulation. Oxford University Press

Beltratti A, Stulz R (2012) The credit crisis around the globe: why did some banks perform better? J Financ Econ 105(1):1–17

Bordo M, Eitrheim Ø, Flandreau M, Qvigstad J (2016) Central banks at a crossroad: what can we learn from history? Cambridge University Press

Capriglione F, Masera R (2016) Bank Corporate Governance: A New Paradigm. https://openreviewmbf.org/2016/12/23/bank-corporate-governance-a-new-paradigm. Accessed 31 Jan 2026

De Haan J, Vlahu R (2016) Corporate governance of banks: a survey. J Econ Surv 30(2):228–277

Fahlenbrach R, Stulz R (2011) Bank CEO incentives and the credit crisis. J Financ Econ 99(1):11–26

Laeven L, Levine R (2009) Bank governance, regulation and risk taking. J Financ Econ 93(2):259–275

Macey J, O'Hara M (2003) The corporate governance of banks. Federal Reserve Bank of New York Economic Policy Review 9(1):91–107

Institutions Related to Foreign Payments and Financing

6

Contents

Abstract

This chapter offers a thorough analysis of institutions involved in foreign payments and international financing. It examines international institutions such as the EU, WTO, OECD, WB, and IMF in relation to their functions, roles, and consequences for, and within, the global financial system. The chapter also

F. B. Erdem, *The Principles of International Banking, Finance and Investment Law*, Springer Textbooks in Law, https://doi.org/10.1007/978-3-032-32505-1_6

analyses prominent regional institutions such as IFC, EIB, ECO, and D-8 Organization with regards to their contributions to regional or international financial stability and development. This section studies the interaction of these institutions in terms of their impact on foreign payment mechanisms and financing practices. In today's economic landscape, which is characterized by growing international trade and capital flows, foreign payments and international financing mechanisms serve as important proxies for the economic independence and financial stability of foreign payment channels and the economic independence and financial the parties making payment. This section will systematically assess institutions, areas of influence, and tools that impact or assist foreign payments and financing channels, whether directly or indirectly, on both the international and regional level.

6.1 Development of Foreign Payments

With the establishment of systems for electronic funds transfer, the notion of foreign payments has evolved to include both reserve movements across central banks of different countries and commercial and financial transactions through banks of the private sector. This has generated acceptable velocity of international money movement while also introducing new standards of security, supervision and identity verification in banking law. With the rise of financial technology and decentralized finance, the architecture offered by digital wallets and mobile payment systems and CBDCs from governments is layering this infrastructure further and making it technologically complicated.[1] While digital wallets offered by fintech companies or digital currencies from governments require the system to be much more layered, international payments are generally processed through the SWIFT network which is regarded as secure, and identity is verified.[2]

6.2 International Organizations

As previously noted, institutions such as the EU, the WTO, the OECD, the WB and IMF are key organisations with respect to the stability of payment systems, the movement of capital, crisis prevention and development assistance. This section will evaluate the influence of these organisations on foreign payments, financing and banking practices analytically.

[1] Allen et al. (2022) 1; Reslow et al. (2025).
[2] Robinson et al. (2025) 237–249.

6.2.1 The EU

The pursuit of economic integration by the EU has led to substantial increases in speed, reliability and cost-uniformity regarding regional payments by centralising monetary and payment systems among its Member States. This has been executed through infrastructure such as the SEPA, the TARGET2 and the TIPS.[3] The regulatory framework for infrastructure such as SEPA and TARGET2 provides a clear specification of the obligations of the member banks with respect to the accounts of their participants and the provision of payment services. The rights of payers and payees are also defined under payment services legislation, together with transaction settlement times and transaction cost transparency.

As an illustration, the SEPA Credit Transfer (SCT) rules compel that the payment orders are settled on the business day it is received and transferred to the account of the payee within maximum of one business day; also, per the cost-sharing principle 'SHA', the costs of any transaction must be shared by the parties involved. The TARGET2 system obliges participating banks to obligations such as revocation of payment orders; error correction and liquidity provision separately, settled through the participation agreement with the ECB.[4] These EU legislation harmonised to the national payment legislative schemes of member states also require banks to agree to regulators, competent authorities and regulatory bodies, such as ECB and EBA. In this context, the overall legal framework is based upon the three EU regulatory framework laws of the payment systems infrastructure comprising respectively Payment Services Directive (PSD 2); settlement finality directive; electronic money directive regulation. PSD2 has also ushered in a new era of open banking, that requires payment service providers to facilitate and provide access financial technology companies for third-party payment (TPP). This has generated fresh discussions in banking law relating to both customer information protection (compliance with the GDPR) and liability for unauthorized transactions. For instance, TPPs' access to customer information under open banking expands the risks of information security and privacy breaches, but also creates uncertainty over how the liability for unauthorized transactions is shared between banks and TPPs.[5]

The SFD guarantees payment finality of payments in systems such as SEPA and TARGET2. The directive indicates that once a payment order is permitted into the system, it is non-revocable, meaning payments are deemed 'final and irrevocable' in all instances, even in the event of insolvency. Therefore, with the principle of payment finality in EU law, banks have an essential basis to manage their liquidity and default risks.[6]

---

[3] Cipollone (2025).

[4] Iglesias-Rodriguez (2025); Ciani and Masi (2014) 7–40; Jesse (2018) 322–327.

[5] Petrovic (2020) 1–14; Mai (2018); Gounari et al. (2024) 5(1) 1–42.

[6] Athanassiou (2020) 711–735; Murphy and Braithwaite (2017) 291–325.

The Electronic Money Directive (EMD) regulates the behaviours of electronic money institutions, establishes the legal framework for digital payment mechanisms throughout the EU, and is in line with the European Commission (EC)'s aim to promote the use of electronic Money.[7] The EMD states that electronic money means a digital representation of value, that can be accepted in place of cash, stored electronically, issued by electronic money institutions.[8] Electronic money institutions are required to obtain a license, worn minimum capital requirements, safeguard customer funds, perform audit and reporting responsibilities, and comply with AML/KYC regulations.[9]

6.2.2 The WTO

The WTO is a global institution that gives the rules for international trade, runs negotiations and provides dispute settlement. The WTO does not have a payment system, but its work affects the speed and predictability of goods and thus payment flows by formalizing trade policies, streamlining customs processes and mechanisms, such as the TFA. Institutional stability related to trade affirms payment risk, and WTO processes shape relationships for international payments and financing among its member states. When a member country simplifies its customs procedures under the auspices of WTO agreements, exporters receive revenue faster, and banks have less need for short-term financing, thus changing the use of collateral, letters of credit, rediscounting, etc. in this example.

The WTO is a global institution that establishes the framework for international trade, administers the multilateral trade negotiations process, and administers international disputes. While the WTO does not have a direct payment or financing process to the system, it greatly affects the speed and predictability of goods flows, and thus, subsequently payment flows, by standardising trade policies, streamlining customs procedures, and other mechanisms such as the TFA. The indirect nature of these effects reduce payment risk by promoting institutional stability in trade while shaping its member states' relationships toward international financing. For example, when a member country simplifies its customs procedures in accordance with a WTO Agreement, exporters will receive revenue faster; this will reduce short-term demand for bank financing and will change the use of trade instruments such as letters of credit, collateral, and rediscounting. Likewise, faster customs processing assists with making payments to exporters, which is fundamental to restructure the banks guarantee and letter of credit obligations; WTO regulations, such as the TFA, prompt banks to make risk assessments on commercial documents and delivery documents.

---

[7] Miriyeva (2022) 47–53.

[8] Panova and Makhinchuk (2020) 100–104.

[9] EC (2013).

The WTO's input into trade financing, while often indirect, has very clear economic impacts. The TFA in particular aims to reduce trade costs significantly by facilitating the digitisation of customs procedures, such as pre-declaring documents, and also reducing border crossing times. Article 10 of the TFA enables documents, for example, to be supplied electronically, resulting in significant time savings and money savings to banks engaging in documentary credit processes; thereby reducing the financial risk in import-export processes and speeding up capital flows. A realistic TFA implementation could reduce import customs clearance time by 3.7 days and export time by about 1.9 days[10]; these gains, in terms of trade finance, makes access to finance easier, especially in developing economies.

The WTO's Aid for Trade project coordinates financing support arrangements to assist in strengthening the trade capacity and trade infrastructure of low and least-developed countries. Since its launch in 2005, nearly $650 billion in resources have been mobilised under the initiative. Aid for Trade aims to enhance trade capacity and help developing countries overcome trade obstacles. In particular, investments in infrastructure and capacity building help facilitate trade finance, improve the transit of payments, and promote longer-term financial stability. Together with organisations like the OECD, the Aid for Trade initiative helps promote sustainable economic growth through better alignment of donor and recipient country strategies.[11]

The WTO Dispute Settlement Body creates inter-state trust through the non-discriminatory, expedited resolution of disputes between countries on trade-related issues. The impact of the DSB is not limited to sustaining financial flows; rather, it reduces uncertainty related to international trade activities, thus lowering country risk premiums from banks for allocating international credit and increasing national debt capital flows.[12] In this way, the settlement body facilitates trust in financial markets by extending the interpretation of trade agreements.

6.2.3 The OECD

The OECD serves as an international forum to provide policy analysis, data collection, and guidance to its member and partner countries. In the role, it disciplines export financing that is officially supported, most notably through the Arrangement on Officially Supported Export Credits. The Arrangement has been in force since the 1978 and seeks to ensure that the implementation of credit and guarantee programs supported by the state does not distort fair competition; thus, the export financing models of banks and other financial institutions are governed under the standards of the OECD. The Arrangement only considers officially supported export credits for official financing that matures beyond two years, and aims

[10] Melo et al. (2025) 265.
[11] Hoekman (2014).
[12] Maggi and Staiger (2011) 475–515.

to balance the competitive advantages of the exporting country where appropriate and possible, except artificially in the case of military equipment.[13]

For example, creditworthiness assessments of exporting and importing banks are conducted according to the OECD Arrangement's minimum commercial interest reference rates (CIRR) and rules relating to payment schedules. State-guaranteed export credits can enhance capital adequacy by providing banks with low-risk positions; however, international compliance requirements can have implications for financial institutions and their risk management practices. The latest update to the Regulation, with its 2023 and 2024 revision, has made trade finance work more efficiently via enhanced transparency and flexible funding arrangements.[14]

The OECD is a global standard-setting body regarding matters beyond export credit, such as international financial transparency, tax compliance and ethical financing principles. The Organisation has a close connection with the FATF, and the FATF's 40 Recommendations on combating ML, and terrorist financing form the basis of banks' customer due diligence, i.e. KYC, obligations and transaction monitoring.[15] These standards promote reduced illicit flows in trade finance by, among other things, requiring financial institutions to have a risk-based approach.

Additionally, the OECD Anti-Bribery Convention (1997) addresses the issue of the party providing bribes in international commercial transactions and involves controls to mitigate anti-corruption risk on banks and other financial institutions. The Convention allows companies to be held liable for bribery offences and those offences are treated as an element of ML offences, which adds compliance costs in the context of cross-border financing transactions.[16] The OECD's Base Erosion and Profit Shifting (BEPS) initiative seeks to limit the ability of multinational companies to exploit opportunities in the rules of taxation to shift profits. The project initiated in 2013, in conjunction with the G20, promulgated 15 action plans. Banks are now required to rethink and re-organise their cross-border financing structures with tax risk in mind; for example, the introduction of transfer pricing rules and hybrid mismatch prevention increases the transparency of trade finance. In 2025, minimum standards will begin being legislated with the cooperation of 140 countries and jurisdictions.[17]

6.2.4 The WB

The World Bank Group is a multilateral organization that involves international development finance with a number of institutions, including the IBRD, the IDA, the IFC and the MIGA. The Group seeks to promote economic development

[13] See, OECD (2023).
[14] OECD (2024).
[15] FATF (2025); Koker (2014) 281–295; Levi and Reuter (2006) 289–375.
[16] Rose-Ackerman and Palifka (2016); Moran (2002) 141–150.
[17] OECD (2021).

through loans, grants, guarantee mechanisms, and technical assistance services (to both public and private sectors). The WB has the ability to provide funding or guarantees, which creates opportunities to partner with the banking sector, particularly in developing countries, which will further enhance the feasibility of infrastructure and development projects.[18]

The IBRD extends long-term loans to middle-income countries at interest rates similar to market conditions while the IDA directs low-interest or interest-free loans and grants to low-income countries. The IFC provides support to facilitate private sector investment, and MIGA provides foreign investors with insurance to cover against political risk from issues related to expropriation, foreign exchange transfer restrictions, and breaches of contract. For instance, the combined use of an IBRD loan and MIGA insurance on an infrastructure project provides long-term financing while reducing the risks of payment for investors and allowing financial institutions to lend to the projects more easily. World Bank guarantees protect payment risk for borrowing countries and project financiers. In this case, the loan and project agreements provide legal collateral to for banks.[19]

A sovereign guarantee mechanism is commonly employed in World Bank projects to bolster legal certainty. Even with the adoption of the mechanism, the risk of borrower default is ultimately reduced by the operational funds of a sovereign borrower, and it can reinforce credit guarantees. Also, the World Bank's Environmental and Social Framework (ESF) standards are incorporated into loan agreements as a way to ensure practices are followed to manage environmental and social risks that might accrue from projects. The standards establish an internationally law-based monitoring framework on issues such as environmental protection, human rights, and employee safety, and aim to ensure sustainability in the practice of the project. The terms of contract increase the obligations of the banks in relation to monitoring credit related performance by establishing compliance obligations between the debtor and the external environments.[20]

The WB has, in recent years, sought to mobilize financing from the private sector to enhance its climate change initiatives through its climate finance and green bond programs. The backing of the green bond markets assists in financing environmentally friendly investments, benefiting both the countries that issue them and the investing parties. This process supports the establishment of new financing structures intended to address environmental issues worldwide.[21] Its capacity building services facilitate the alternative enhancement of national banking regulations and improve the safety and efficiency of international payments systems. These components are an essential part of supporting financial stability and the effectiveness of development projects for the long term.

---

[18] Stiglitz (2002); Bird and Rowlands (2007) 856–870.

[19] Mathiasen and Aboneaaj (2023); Gamso and Dimitrova (2024) 159–172.

[20] Morley et al. (2021) 1–6.

[21] Martin (2023) 197; Trompeter (2017) 5.

6.2.5 The IMF

The IMF is the global organization created to encourage international monetary cooperation, promote exchange rate stability, and provide assistance to countries with balance of payments problems. The IMF's main purposes are to help maintain macroeconomic stability, provide policy advise, and maintain global financial stability.[22] The IMF uses a range of important tools to achieve these goals, such as lending programs, policy advice, and allocations of special drawing rights (SDRs). SDRs are an international reserve asset that can be used by member countries to supplement their own foreign exchange reserves and increase global liquidity. The value of the SDR comes from a basket of major currencies including the US dollar, euro, Chinese yuan, Japanese yen, and British pound.[23]

The IMF's lending arrangements, including the Stand-By Arrangement (SBA) and Extended Fund Facility (EFF), offer short- and medium-term financial assistance to countries facing external financing issues.[24] Lending activities under these arrangements are typically conditional on the implementation of certain policies and reforms, which aim to restore economic stability in the borrowing country. Although the policies in question are intended to address structural imbalances, their implementation may create temporary disruptions in the availability of domestic credit and liquidity. The IMF also carries out economic surveillance through the Article IV Consultations process, whereby it systematically reviews each member country's economic policies and performance. The consultations provide a written summary of economic policies, risk considerations, and policy recommendations for each member country, which governments and central banks can use to promote economic stability and prevent economic crises.

In conjunction with the WB, IMF undertakes the FSAP, which assesses the resilience of countries' financial systems. The FSAP provides recommendations to enhance the regulation and supervision of banks, which provides a safe system of international payments and promotes stable capital flows.[25] Through its lending facilities, its reserve assets, and its expertise in policy advice, IMF is key to global liquidity, correcting payment imbalances, and confidence in the international financial system. IMF also fosters coherence in global financial governance through its engagement with organizations such as the WB and the FSB.

[22] Abbakumova (2019) 26.

[23] Rangarajan and Patra (2012) 41–51.

[24] Chahine et al. (2025) 1–18.

[25] Zamorski and Lim (2013) 37–52.

6.3 Regional Institutions

Regional financial institutions serve as important complementary components of the global financial system. While global institutions, like the IMF and WB, typically emphasize macroeconomic stability, regional institutions consider infrastructure investments, trade collaboration, and promoting financial inclusion in particular geographic areas. The idea of regional development banks is one of the important mechanisms to represent such institutions. Significant examples of RDBs are the Asian Development Bank (ADB), African Development Bank (AfDB), EIB, and Inter-American Development Bank (IDB). Given the ability to assess local needs with increased depth, regional banks are better able to make financial decisions as flexibility can more easily be attained. This inherent flexibility may matter significantly in a seamless advance of regional economic solidarity and integration.

6.3.1 The IFC

The International Finance Corporation, a member of the WB Group, is the main institution providing finance for private sector development in any emerging market. IFC supports the private sector in emerging markets through investments, loans, guarantees, and advisory services. Additionally, IFC partners with banks to offer syndicated loans, assist the banks with risk sharing, and create guarantees to share risks with commercial banks. For example, if IFC co-finances energy projects, it can reduce local banks' risks and lead to project financing; any guarantees offered by IFC will reduce people's credit costs or improve the predictability of cash flows for communities. When dealing directly with IFC's own investments, banks must adhere to approved environmental and social standards known as the IFC performance standards, which are evaluated and incorporated into the loan agreement after the commercial bank has completed its own due diligence. In addition to conventional lending, IFC is involved in measures such as the Global Trade Finance Program, which provides bank guarantees to facilitate trade flows in developing markets. IFC participates in supplying credit to borrowers using syndicated loan structures for advancing risk sharing by pooling credits from multiple private banks. In recent years, IFC has prioritized green finance and public-private partnerships (PPPs). In the context of energy and infrastructure, it supports financial models that bring the public and private sector together to provide financing. IFC's blended finance approach combines some development funding with private sector investments to balance risks.

6.3.2 European Investment Bank (EIB)

An institution that provides low-cost project financing to enable long-term investment policies for the EU is the EIB. It lends money for projects in strategic areas such as transport, climate change mitigation, digital infrastructure and energy using funds raised from the capital markets. The EIB helps facilitate access to finance, especially in EU MS.[26] For instance, its loans for a railway project help to strengthen the financial structure of the project by allowing private sector lenders to provide longer-term funding and allowing projects to develop repayment schedules that fit their needs. EIB supported projects require the establishment of legal frameworks for PPPs; contract law, guarantee regimes and repayment mechanisms physically affect banking law. For example, even policy shifts in certain areas, such as defence financing policy can completely change the channels and risk management for banks financing projects.

Supporting economic growth and sustainability in the EU is one of the EIB's primary responsibilities. Consequently, it provides guarantees and co-financing to help fund both high-risk and strategically necessary investments via the European Fund for Strategic Investments (EFSI) and InvestEU. Moreover, the EIB raises capital by issuing EIB environmental impact bonds in the international bond markets which are attractive to investors due to the EIB's AAA credit rating and considered a low-risk investment.[27] The bank is also financing climate-neutral investments through its involvement in the European Green Deal and environmental sustainable financing via the Climate Bank Roadmap Phase 2 (2026–2030).[28] This will require banks to create new types of contracts compliant with green finance law, especially in the area of environmental and social standards.

6.3.3 Eco

The Economic Cooperation Organisation (ECO) is a regional body focused on increasing economic integration and regional collaboration amongst its memberships in Central, South and West Asia. The ECO operates in the fields of trade, transport, energy, and the planning of infrastructure projects. The ECO fosters an increase in economic relationships between member states by promoting regional payment facilities, and coordinating financial cooperation. For example, regional energy pipeline projects are funded through international credit and guarantee systems to align payment systems. Because financing these types of projects involve horizontal relationships between member countries, country risk illustrated by contractual rights can become even more complicated for banks. ECO's incentives for payment in local currencies are to reduce foreign exchange risk and increase access to swap markets.[29]

The ECO Trade and Development Bank (ETDB) is one of the pillars of ECO's financial activities. The ETDB advances regional economic growth by focusing on

[26] Clifton et al. (2014) 63–71.
[27] Spielberger (2025) 37–54; Trotta (2024) 1–8; Tiikkainen et al. (2022) 170–182.
[28] EIB (2025); Mertens and Thiemann (2023) 68–82.
[29] Yawar (2025) 75–79.

the financing of transport infrastructure, energy, and cross-border trade in particular. The regional payment clearing systems the bank has developed also provides additional payment security for member countries, enhancing financial inclusion.[30] Together, these efforts deliver a number of benefits by supporting ECO's regional integration agenda and also encouraging the development of new financial products and services for banks.

6.3.4 D-8 Organization

The D-8 Organization for Economic Cooperation (D-8), which includes eight founding members; Bangladesh, Egypt, Indonesia, Iran, Malaysia, Nigeria, Pakistan and Turkey, has grown to include Azerbaijan as a full member in 2024.[31] The D-8 aims to promote economic cooperation among developing countries that are predominantly Muslim and seeks to stimulate internal trade through a variety of means, including customs facilitation, preferential trade agreements, and integration into local supply chains. Consequently, in recent years, but particularly in 2021 or so, the option of transactions with payments based on preferential trade agreements (PTAs) or local currency have been on the table as a means of facilitating increased payment flows with reduced use of foreign exchange.

The D-8 PTA encourages trade through the elimination of customs duties on select products among members, while also aiming to increase intra-regional trading volume to US$500 billion by 2030.[32] The provisions of the agreement mandate the establishment of innovative products within import-export financing provided there is a regulation of rules of origin and payment facilities- for example, local currency exchange lines and reciprocal swap products are used in this regard. These arrangements have reduced banks' foreign exchange dealing and have made local liquidity instruments more prominent, requiring whiplash to review currency selection clauses and collateral arrangements in contracts. To the extent that direct linkages were established between banking systems in the member countries, all elements of legal infrastructure (pari passu clauses, netting arrangements, and third-party guarantees) must be considered.

The essential provisions of the D-8 PTA address definitions, objectives, and trade facilitation provisions, while also covering rules of origin as well as payment systems. Further, the D-8 Payment System (D-8P Card), which was introduced in

[30] ECO Trade and Development Bank (2025).

[31] The D-8 Financial Cooperation Working Group promotes information sharing and regulatory convergence among the central banks of member countries, with Turkey and Malaysia playing a leading role in these initiatives. These efforts aim to strengthen the position of developing countries in global trade by supporting the organization's overall economic integration goals.

See, Zeynalova (2025) 177–192.

[32] Abubakar (2025).

2023 as a pilot, aims to create a shared digitized payment method and infrastructure in the member countries so that foreign exchange costs can be reduced as part of cross-border transactions and payments made in local currencies.[33]

6.4 Inter-Institutional Interaction and its Effects on Foreign Payments

Coordination between institutions in the international financial architecture is developing rapidly. Institutions like the G20, the FSB and the BIS are pivotal in overseeing payment systems and harmonising macroprudential policies. For example, the Basel III and IV standards developed by the BIS govern banks' capital adequacy and liquidity ratios, with support from policy institutions like the IMF and the OECD. Creditor groups like the Paris Club and London Club help sustain international payments by implementing debt restructuring plans under the supervision of the IMF. This complex architecture means that national banking law is constantly having to interact with international norms.

6.4.1 Liquidity and Payment Security

Central financial institutions are enhancing liquidity management and security safeguards within the international payment infrastructure. Real-time gross settlement (RTGS) systems such as TARGET2, operated by the ECB and instant payment infrastructures such as TARGET Instant Payment Settlement (TIPS) enables payments to be processed in euro quickly and securely, therefore enhancing the efficiency of liquidity flows. Institutions such as the IMF and WB provide macro-level liquidity support and guarantee mechanisms that help to manage country-specific payment challenges. Collectively, these layers of infrastructure and macro-financing mechanisms reinforce banks' cross-border payment capability while providing safety from systemic risks.

6.4.2 Trade Finance and Export Loans

International institutions' regulations and its support instruments direct trade finance. The OECD's regulations on officially supported export credits set out the financing conditions for exporter countries by producing a level playing for competition of the international banking system. WB and IFC guarantees incite trade flows in developing countries through increased risk capacity of the private sector. These instruments enable banks to manage export credits using both publicly supported and private mechanisms to support the sustainability of global trade.

[33] Incekaya (2019).

6.4.3 Regional Currencies and Local Payment Systems

Regional cooperative organizational arrangements also reduce foreign exchange reliance through trade and payments in local currencies. D-8, for example, along with the ECO, changes banks' foreign exchange position management and swap access through local currency payment systems. Local currency payment systems enhance the security of cross-border transactions as a result of a strengthened legal infrastructure (e.g., default provisions, time of performance and regional economic integration).

> ► International institutions are changing payments by driving the development of digital finance. The proliferation of CBDCs, smart contracts and digital assets reduce cross-border payment costs and create new regulatory needs. Institutions like the IMF and BIS help to steer banking law to digital assets by creating global standards for these technologies, thereby addressing the need for future financial stability.

6.5 Case Studies

6.5.1 The Impact of SEPA and TARGET Applications on Bank Operations

By introducing the SEPA framework, cross-border retail euro payments have become as convenient and seamless as domestic payments. On the other hand, TARGET2 and TIPS provide for settlement in central bank money for high-value and instant payments.[34] The shift to this more interconnected environment has compelled banks to reformulate their treasury liquidity reserves, hourly net obligations, and payment guarantees. From a legal perspective, there is a need for integration of the respective bank contracts and payment service agreements. For instance, to allow for seamless liquidity management between retail payments made by a bank though the SEPA infrastructure and high-value payments made though TARGET2 or TIPS, it has now become necessary to align both customer contracts and central bank settlement provisions with the same account.[35]

[34] The SEPA system has reached an average daily transaction capacity of 50 million as of 2023. In the TARGET2 system, more than 5500 banks are actively conducting transactions in 2024. This volume has made data protection and transaction finality issues even more important in payment law.

[35] Duca-Radu and Friz (2020).

6.5.2 IMF Programme and Local Bank Liquidity

Programs supported by the IMF are aimed at preventing capital outflow in the short term in order to ultimately achieve macroeconomic stability. However, the stringent monetary policies that may be implemented as part of these programs can subsequently result in a decline in local credit volumes. To ensure banks mitigate risk in this scenario, contingent price mechanisms in credit agreements and maturity provisions against liquidity risk becomes very significant. Essentially, the 'IMF event clause' or 'market disruption clause' added to variable-rate agreements allows for renegotiating interest rates to diminish the negative impact of abrupt funding cost increases for banks.[36]

Moreover, since IMF-supported programs can enhance the liquidity pressures to bank balance sheets, credit agreements frequently incorporate material adverse change (MAC) or liquidity adjustment clauses which grant repricing authority. In other words, in Turkey's 2001 (stabilization) IMF program or Argentina's 2018 IMF program, banks invoked revision clauses that indexed loan interest rates to the funding cost in the market. These contractual arrangements allowed banks to address their liquidity risks and provide flexibility to stabilize credit markets but also helped debtors avoid paying disconnected market interest rates.[37]

▶ **Important**

MAC is a protective provision used in international loan contracts to deal with material adverse changes that impact financial conditions, business operations, and assets of the debtor. The bank has the right to withdraw its loan, seek additional and/or better collateral security, and/or waive loans previously uncovered in case of MAC in financial conditions, business operations, and assets of the debtor. The provision is very valuable to the bank in relation to sudden changes in economies in countries under IMF programs.

6.5.3 D-8 PTA and Local Currency Trials

Since the D-8 Economic Cooperation Organisation's preferential trade agreements and trade arrangements involving local currencies, pilot uses of local currency payment models have occurred in selected trade pairs, requiring banks to set swap lines to transact in local currencies instead of US dollars, which have occurred in

[36] Turkey's 2001 IMF stand-by programme envisaged the recapitalisation of the banking sector and the cleaning up of public banks' balance sheets. These reforms revitalised international financial flows.

[37] Gelpern and Powell (2023); Ibish and Ferhad (2023) 5–12.

Turkey-Pakistan and Iran-Malaysia trade contexts. In these instances, both agreements and collateral agreements between central banks are updated always, and provisions concerning exchange rate risk, currency of payment in a contract, and default risk are updated by commercial banks to facilitate local currency transactions between engaged parties. For example, in TL-PKR transactions, the parties have introduced a clause than when referencing the official cross rate on the payment date, that rate will be according to what is published by the CBRT and that in the case of liquidity challenges, payment can be made in the equivalent value of US dollars.[38]

6.5.4 Private Sector Credit Catalyst with IFC Guarantee

IFC's co-financing and guarantee of an energy project functioned as a risk-sharing instrument to catalyse private bank lending. In these arrangements, through a guarantee and a loan participation agreement, IFC shared part of the payment default risk, which allowed private banks to be comfortable aligning their lending terms with IFC's 2012 Environmental and Social Performance Standards. IFC guarantees serve as a 'credit catalyst' for long-term private sector financing, especially in developing countries. The guarantees, allocated in Turkey under the Renewable Energy and Energy Efficiency Project, which was established in partnership with the Global Environment Facility (GEF) and IFC, helped reduce local banks' capital adequacy considerations, thus enabling them to pursue long-term financing for projects. In light of IFC's Performance Standards (PS 1–8),[39] banks integrated elements such as environmental impact assessment, occupational health and safety, and social consultation and grievance mechanisms into their contracts as part of the overall credit monitoring.

6.6 Practical Consequences and Recommendations from the Perspective of Banking Law

Banking law, as part of the system of international finance, is one crucial part of a legal framework for the regulation of payments and for dispute resolution. Banks need to create effective legal and operational processes to manage those issues. One of the most important forms of legal remedy for disputes about international payments is arbitration.[40] One of the principal fora for states and investors to arbitrate those disputes is the ICSID, associated with the WB.[41]

---

[38] Under the D-8 PTA, some pilot payments in Turkey-Malaysia trade were made in local currency; this experience has demonstrated that currency risk can be reduced.

[39] Finnfund (2025).

[40] Hudson (2017).

[41] Schreuer et al. (2021).

Banks need to strengthen governance internally by improving compliance functions as part of broader control systems. A robust compliance program generally includes: (1) written policies and procedures; (2) employee training programs; (3) risk-based monitoring programs; (4) independent internal audits; and (5) reporting and feedback mechanisms. This is essential for governance related to AML, CFT, and sanctions compliance.

In terms of banking law, building legal and institutional infrastructures is essential to provide predictability in cross-border financial transactions. International contracts need to clearly state the currency of payment as well as the governing law and methods of performance and enforcement. In addition, elements such as jurisdiction and recognition of each others' judgments are important to reduce uncertainty in foreign payment flows and dispute resolution. Further, contractual provisions on access to RTGS systems or central clearing may need to be considered against banks' obligations in relation to finality of payment and settlement risk.[42]

Oversight and compliance functions support the legal soundness of today's banking systems. Laws and regulations related to AML, CFT, and sanctions represent the largest sources of legal risk for banks. Banks should adopt recommendations from multinational organizations like the IMF, the OECD, and the FATF into their internal audit functions.[43] In transactions involving multilateral guarantees or rediscount facilities through the WB group (i.e., the IBRD, IFC, and MIGA), banks should consider the option of a simplified legal framework and documents in relation to collateral and guarantee enforcement.[44]

Regional monetary frameworks of cooperation - including the D-8 and ECO arrangements - require clear mechanisms for the management of counterparty risk, defaults, and netting arrangements, which must also be consistent with tax, exchange control, and capital flow regulations.[45] As financial institutions are developing cross-border digital payments and CBDCs, the banking and legal profession must address issues of data protection, customer verification, and consumer rights in accordance with best practices and with developing regulations.

6.7 Conclusion and Future Trends

International and regional institutions influence foreign payments and financing channels using mechanisms through both direct (credit, guarantees, SDR allocations) and indirect (trade facilitation, regulatory frameworks, payment infrastructures) means. The main issues from a banking law perspective are compliance,

[42] See, Proctor (2023)
[43] Alexander (2019).
[44] Zettelmeyer et al. (2013) 513.
[45] Lastra (2015).

contractual law, collateral and guarantees regimes, and evolution through the digital transformation. Trends in this space include CBDCs, regional local currency frameworks, climate financing, and digital trade financing solutions.[46]

International payment systems have been structurally altered as a result of digital transformation.[47] One example includes a pilot project called Project mBridge administered by the BIS which may radically change the correspondent banking system, and is testing interoperability between CBDCs and cross-border payments. The initial central banks from Hong Kong, Thailand, United Arab Emirates, and China lead this initiative to allow cross-border payments that leverages CBDCs in a multilateral framework providing a new aspect of payment systems allowing direct digital payments.[48]

In addition to facilitating consistency in data among financial institutions globally, the introduction of the ISO 20022 messaging standard is promoting transparency of cross-border risks. This standard increases traceability of payments, both technically and legally by rendering every transaction traceable through identified data fields.[49] Another important trend globally is the increased significance that green finance and sustainable banking concepts have taken on in the context of foreign financing relationships. International organisations, particularly the World Bank, OECD and EIB, are increasingly making criteria related to environmental and social impact in their credit allocation processes. These developments have resulted in the introduction of new types of contractual provisions in banking law, such as 'environmental covenants', and 'green clauses', as already provided for in the Loan Market Association (LMA) Green Loan Principles, and ICMA Green Bond Principles.[50]

> **Important**
> Environmental covenants are contractual provisions that require the borrowing company to manage its environmental performance to specified standards.
>
> Example: In a project financing agreement, borrower agrees to keep emissions under a specified limit as part of the construction phase and agree to file an annual environmental update report.
>
> Green clauses are provisions that condition the granting, use of, and/or change in interest terms of a loan, with respect to an assessment of the sustainability of the borrower.
>
> Example: A provision of a green loan agreement indicating that if the target for renewable energy investment is met, the interest rate will be reduced by 0.25%.

[46] Alexander (2023) 1–3; Soana and Arruda (2024) 467–486.

[47] Aurazo et al. (2024); Mirzaye and Mohiuddin (2025) 421.

[48] WB (2021).

[49] BIS (2023).

[50] Lee (2020) 577–586; Fdhila (2024); Hermawan and Khoirunisa (2023) 96–124; Gharleghi et al. (2024) 208–215.

In conclusion, digital trade documents and smart contracts facilitate the electronic execution of international financing documents. Legislation, including the Electronic Trade Documents Act, which became effective in the UK in 2023, has made the electronic bill of lading (e-BL) and digital letters of credit legally valid.[51] All of these developments will not only accelerate international payment systems, but also restructure them into a more transparent, traceable and sustainable format. As part of this re-structuring process, the role of banking law is now being redefined to be compatible to technology, to cover cross-border transactions, and to be inclusive to digital assets.

Chapter Summary

Chapter 6 explores how financial actors shape the real-world landscape of cross-border payments and financing. It also assesses the influence of key institutions—including the EU, WTO, OECD, World Bank, IMF, and various regional organizations—on the banking systems and legal structures of different countries. In the process, the authors see how external payments have evolved from humble bank wire payments into complex systems, including SWIFT and Digital Currencies, and are now entering the "age of Central Bank Digital Currencies". These international bodies set the terms of this change. The EU, on the other hand, has developed an integrated payments market infrastructure with initiatives such as SEPA and TARGET2, coupled with legislation that is driving developments in the Open Banking space with PSD2 and seeks to consolidate transaction certainty with the Payment Certainty Directive (SFD). The WTO is working on improving risk for cross-border trade under the Trade Facilitation Agreement (TFA), and the OECD is promoting financial integrity with the standardization of export credits and AML/CFT best practices under the FATF.

The WB and IMF are one of the cornerstones of the international finance system, providing essential resources for maintaining stable and sustainable financing. In addition, through its arms, IBRD, IDA, and MIGA, it delivers financing for projects and invests in Environmental and Social Framework criteria, which are a prerequisite for borrowing. The IMF, ensuring the sustainability of the international finance system, manages countries' reserves through conditional lending, including Stand-By Arrangements and Special Drawing Rights, and examines countries' resilience in the finance sector through the Financial Sector Assessment Program. Finally, in addition to the main framework, the IFC encourages private sector lending, the European Investment Bank offers cheap financing for strategic investments, and ECO & D-8 help countries trade using their common currencies.

This international flow of rules in finance is integrated through harmonized standards: Basel III is a good example that is guided by bodies such

[51] Antoniou (2023) 25–28; Zhao (2025) 159–180; Krebs (2023) 323–338.

as the Financial Stability Board. The reality on the ground is that international agreements, such as those with IMF programs, have a direct impact on loans to banks. Meanwhile, future trends for international finance include developments such as the use of CBDCs and digital trade finance within the framework set out in MLETR. Additionally, environmental factors have been incorporated into loan agreements through criteria set out under ESG. Banks have had to get out of FX swap lines and now use green finance provisions within international finance.

Revision Questions

1. Describe the principal object of the EU Settlement Finality Directive (SFD). Consider how PSD2, also known as the Payment Services Directive 2, together with the Open Banking framework, has legal effect to transform the classical bank-customer relationship with regard to data as well as payments.
2. Distinguish the primary financial roles of the IMF and the World Bank Group relating to the international support for financial stability and development financing. Describe how the World Bank or IFC guarantee plays the role of credit catalyst for the private banks.
3. Explain the legal and economic implication of IMF conditional lending arrangements, for example, the Standby Arrangement (SBA) and the Extended Fund Facility (EFF). Describe how membership in an IMF program could lead to the addition of material adverse change (MAC) and liquidity adjustment clauses into loan agreements between banks and their customers.
4. Investigate the role of WTO, in broad, and the Trade Facilitation Agreement (TFA) and the OECD Arrangement on Officially Supported Export Credits, and its influence on risk evaluation and financial structuring between borders by banks.
5. Discuss the rationale for, and explain the commercial and legal reasons for, the-importance of trade in local currency placed upon both D-8 and ECO countries, and enumerate the key risk against which the strategy is engineered to protect commercial banks.
6. Define and distinguish between the "Environmental Covenant" and the "Green Clause" in modern trade finance contracts and discuss how these relate to the Environmental and Social Framework of the World Bank.
7. Think about how CBDCs might impact the existing correspondent banking system. Analyse how new messaging formats, such as ISO 20022, could enhance the ability to track payments from a legal perspective.◄

References

Abbakumova D (2019) The role of World Bank and the IMF in the international financial system and the human rights sphere. Baltic Journal of Economic Studies 5(4):25–33

Abbakumova D (2019) The role of World Bank and the IMF in the international financial system and the human rights sphere. Baltic Journal of Economic Studies 5(4):26

Abubakar A (2025) D-8 Preferential Trade Agreement Targets $500 Billion in Intra-trade by 2030. https://www.bilaterals.org/?d-8-preferential-trade-agreement. Accessed 31 Jan 2026

Alexander K (2019) Principles of banking regulation. Cambridge University Press

Alexander K (2023) Sustainability in commercial and financial law. Law Financ Mark Rev 17(1):1–3

Allen F, Gu X, Jagtiani J (2022) Fintech, cryptocurrencies, and CBDC: financial structural transformation in China. J Int Money Financ 124:1

Antoniou A (2023) UK digitalisation of trade finance: the new loan on electronic trade documents. Documentary Credit World 27(4):25–28

Athanassiou P (2020) Payment systems. In: Amtenbrink F, Herrmann C (eds) The EU law of economic and monetary union. Oxford University Press, pp 711–735

Aurazo J, Frost J, Kosse A (2024) Faster Digital Payments: Global and Regional Perspectives. https://www.bis.org/publ/bppdf/bispap152.pdf. Accessed 31 Jan 2026

Bird G, Rowlands D (2007) The IMF and the mobilisation of foreign aid. J Dev Stud 43(5):856–870

BIS (2023) Harmonised ISO 20022 Data Requirements for Enhancing Cross-border Payments. https://www.bis.org/cpmi/publ/d218.pdf. Accessed 31 Jan 2026

Chahine S, Panizza U, Suedekum G (2025) IMF programs and borrowing cost does size matter? Eur Econ Rev 177:1–18

Ciani D, Masi P (2014) Integration of the EU payment systems: a “tolerable straight line”? Quaderni 2014:7–40

Cipollone P (2025) Enhancing cross-border payments in Europe and beyond. Speech (1 April 2025) https://www.ecb.europa.eu/press/key/date/2025/html/ecb.sp250401~9e1ee05e88.en.html?utm_source; Accessed 31 Jan 2026

Clifton J, Diaz-Fuentes D, Revuelta J (2014) Financing utilities: how the role of the European Investment Bank shifted from regional development to making markets. Util Policy 29:63–71

Duca-Radu I, Friz L (2020) Liquidity Distribution and Settlement in TARGET 2. https://www.ecb.europa.eu//press/economic-bulletin/articles/2020/html/ecb.ebart202005_03~4a20eae0c8.en.html. Accessed 31 Jan 2026

EC (2013) Commission Staff Working Document Impact Assessment - Accompanying the document Proposal for a Directive of the European Parliament and of the Council on the prevention of the use of the financial system for the purpose of money laundering, including terrorist financing and Proposal for a Regulation of the European Parliament and of the Council on information accompanying transfers of funds. (2013) SWD/2013/021 final

ECB (2024) Target Annual Report 2023. European Central Bank

ECO Trade and Development Bank (2025) Doing Business with ETBD. https://www.etdb.org/Content/WorkWithUs/e-Brochure.pdf. Accessed 31 Jan 2026

EIB (2025) Climate Bank Roadmap Phase 2: 2026–2030. https://www.eib.org/attachments/lucalli/20250240-eib-group-climate-bank-roadmap-phase-2-en.pdf. Accessed 31 Jan 2026

FATF (2025) International Standards on Combating Money Laundering and the Financing of Terrorism and Proliferation. https://www.fatf-gafi.org/en/publications/Fatfrecommendations/Fatf-recommendations.html. Accessed 31 Jan 2026

Fdhila I (2024) Green finance Bank-sustainability and innovation. LAP Lambert Academic Publishing

Finnfund (2025) IFC Environmental and Social Performance Standards. https://www.finnfund.fi/en/impact/sustainability/risk-assessment/ifc-environmental-and-social-performance-standards. Accessed 31 Jan 2026

Gamso J, Dimitrova A (2024) Rewarding a friend: does the World Bank direct non-commercial risk insurance to countries that support US foreign policy interest? New Political Economy 29(1):159–172
Gelpern A, Powell A (2023) Sovereign debt restructuring: the need for a new approach. Inter-American Development Bank discussion paper no IDP-DP-11022
Gharleghi B, Shafighi N, Nawaser K (2024) Green finance and its role in sustainability in the EU. Journal of Economy and Technology 2:208–215
Gounari M, Stergiopoulos G, Pipyros K, Gritzalis D (2024) Harmonizing open banking in the European Union: an analysis of PSD2 compliance and interrelation with cybersecurity frameworks and standards. Int Cybersecur Law Rev 5(1):1–42
Hermawan S, Khoirunisa Z (2023) The emergence of green banking: a sustainable financing strategy for protecting against deforestation in ASEAN. J Environ Dev 33(1):96–124
Hoekman B (2014) The WTO Trade Facilitation Agreement: Milestone, Mirage, or Mistake?. https://sais.jhu.edu/sites/default/files/Hoekman.pdf. Accessed 31 Jan 2026
Hudson A (2017) Law on financial derivatives. Sweet and Maxwell
Ibish M, Ferhad S (2023) Understanding the challenges of the IMF through the case studies of Greece, Argentina and Turkiye. Journal of Law and Politics 1(4):5–12
Iglesias-Rodriguez P (2025) The future of instant payments in the EU: Bank ownership, market contracting costs, and the accomplishment of financial regulation objectives. J Bank Regul 26:911–931
Incekaya G (2019) D8 Countries to Use Single Payment Card in Trade. https://www.aa.com.tr/en/energy/finance/d8-countries-to-use-single-payment-card-in-trade/23146. Accessed 31 Jan 2026
Jesse M (2018) TARGET instant payment settlement: the Eurosystem's response to an evolving payments landscape. Journal of Payments Strategy and Systems 12(4):322–327
Koker L (2014) The FATF's customer identification framework: fit for purpose? Journal of Money Loundering Control 17(3):281–295
Krebs T (2023) Electronic bills of lading, transnational and English law: blocking the blockchain? Uniform Law Review 28(3–4):323–338
Lastra R (2015) International financial and monetary law. Oxford University Press
Lee J (2020) Green finance and sustainable development goals: the case of China. Journal of Asian Finance Economics and Business 7(7):577–586
Levi M, Reuter P (2006) Money Loundering. Crime Justice 34:289–375
Maggi G, Staiger R (2011) The role of dispute settlement procedures in international trade agreements. Q J Econ 126(1):475–515
Mai H (2018) PSD2, Open Banking and the Value of Personal Data. https://www.dbresearch.com/PROD/RPS_EN-PROD/PROD0000000000471102/PSD_2%2C_open_banking_and_the_value_of_personal_data.pdf?&realload=uZ7TLfD5D3tbNycAl/EHFwBxOkW51S7lSVL1gwqFoulNSOwpujcDbddiV/2raYhU. Accessed 31 Jan 2026
Martin V (2023) Green finance: regulation and instruments. Journal of Central Banking Theory and Practice 12(2):185–209
Mathiasen K, Aboneaaj R (2023) MIGA: the little engine that should. Center for Global Development, Policy Paper 309. https://www.cgdev.org/sites/default/files/miga-little-engine-should.pdf. Accessed 31 Jan 2026
Melo J, Sorgho Z, Wagner L (2025) Reducing wait times at customs to boost trade: how implementing the trade facilitation agreement can expand trade among AfCFTA countries? J Afr Econ 34(2):265–294
Mertens D, Thiemann M (2023) The European Investment Bank: the EU's climate Bank? In: Rayner T, Szulecki K, Jordan A, Oberthür S (eds) Handbook on European Union climate change policy and politics. Edward Elgar, pp 68–82
Miriyeva N (2022) European payments in the digital age. Elte Law Journal 2:35–60
Mirzaye S, Mohiuddin M (2025) Digital transformation in international trade: Opportunuties, challenges, and policy implications. Journal of Risk and Financial Management 18(8):421

Moran J (2002) Bribery and corruption: the OECD convention on combating the bribery of foreign public officials in international business transactions. Business Ethics: A European Review 8(3):141–150

Morley J, Buchanan G, Mitchard E, Keane A (2021) 'Implications of the World Bank's environmental and social framework for biodiversity. Conserv Lett 14(1):1–6

Murphy D, Braithwaite J (2017) Central counterparties (CCPs) and the law of default management. J Corp Law Stud 17(2):291–325

OECD (2021) OECD/G20 Inclusive Framework on BEPS: Progress Report July 2020—September 2021. https://www.oecd.org/content/dam/oecd/en/publications/reports/2021/09/oecd-g20-inclusive-framework-on-beps-progress-report-july-2020-september-2021_4b4684a0/4e30e26d-en.pdf. Accessed 31 Jan 2026

OECD (2023) Arrangement on Officially Supported Export Credits. https://one.oecd.org/document/TAD/PG(2023)7/en/pdf. Accessed 31 Jan 2026

OECD (2024) Arrangement on Officially Supported Export Credits. https://one.oecd.org/document/TAD/PG(2024)6/en/pdf. Accessed 31 Jan 2026

Panova L, Makhinchuk V (2020) The civil law nature of electronic money. Baltic Journal of Economic Studies 6(1):100–104

Petrovic M (2020) PSD2 influence on digital banking transformation—banks' perspective. Journal of process management—new technologies. International 8(4):1–14

Proctor C (2023) Mann and Proctor on the law of money. Oxford University Press

Rangarajan C, Patra M (2012) Can the SDR become a global reserve currency? Econ Polit Wkly 47(11):41–51

Reslow A, Soderberg G, Tsuda N (2025) Cross-Border Payments with Retail Central Bank Digital Currencies: Design and Policy Considerations. IMF NOTE/2024/002

Robinson G, Dörry S, Derruder B (2025) Trusted infrastructure for infrastructures. In: Westermeier C, Campbell-Verduyn M, Brandl B (eds) The Cambridge handbook of financial infrastructure. Cambridge University Press, pp 237–249

Rose-Ackerman S, Palifka B (2016) Corruption and government: causes, consequences, and reform. Cambridge University Press

Schreuer C, Sinclair A, Reinisch A, Malintoppi L, Schill S (2021) The ICSID convention: a commentary on the convention on the settlement of investment disputes between states and nationals of other states. Cambridge University Press

Soana G, Arruda T (2024) Central Bank digital currencies and financial integrity: finding a new trade-off between privacy and traceability within a changing financial architecture. J Bank Regul 25:467–486

Spielberger L (2025) EIB policy entrepreneurship and the EU's regulation of green bonds. J Econ Policy Reform 8:37–54

Stiglitz J (2002) Globalization and its discontents. W.W, Norton and Company

Tiikkainen O, Pihlajamaa M, Akerman M (2022) Environmental impact bonds as a transformative policy innovation: frames and frictions in the construction process of the nutrient-EIB. Environ Innov Soc Trans 45:170–182

Trompeter L (2017) Green is good: how green bonds cultivated into wall Street's environmental paradox. Sustainable Development Law and Policy 17(2):4–43

Trotta A (2024) Environmental impact bonds: review, challenges, and perspectives. Curr Opin Environ Sustain 66:1–8

WB (2021) Central Bank digital currencies for cross-border payments: a review of current experiments and ideas. International Bank for Reconstruction and Development

Yawar M (2025) Study of the member states of the economic cooperation Organization in International law Based on trade. GRS Journal of Arts and Educational Sciences 1(2):75–79

Zamorski M, Lim V (2013) Financial stability insights from recent IMF/World Bank FSAP Asssessments. SEACEN Financial Stability Journal 1:37–52

Zettelmeyer J, Trebesch C, Guladi M (2013) The Greek debt restructuring: an autopsy. Econ Policy 28:513–563

Zeynalova A (2025) Azerbaijan's membership in the D-8 economic cooperation: process and impacts. The Journal of International Relations and Politics 5(2):177–192
Zhao L (2025) UK electronic trade documents act: problems of reliable system and exclusive control. International Trade Law and Regulation 3:159–180

Further Reading

Arner D, Buckley R (2010) Redesigning the architecture of the global financial system. Melbourne Journal of International Law 11:1–56
Lastra R (2015) International financial and monetary law. Oxford University Press
Levit J (2004) The dynamics of international trade finance regulation: the arrangement of officially supported export credit. Harv Int Law J 45:65–182
Sule A, Eyo-Udo N, Onukwulu E, Agho M, Azubuike C (2025) Implementing blockchain for secure and efficient cross-border payment systems. International Journal of Research and Innovation in Applied Science 9(12):508–535

7 Digital and Cryptoasset Laws

Contents

F. B. Erdem, *The Principles of International Banking, Finance and Investment Law*, Springer Textbooks in Law, https://doi.org/10.1007/978-3-032-32505-1_7

Abstract

This chapter provides a comprehensive analysis of the legal and regulatory landscape surrounding digital and crypto assets. It begins by exploring the modern barter system and the growth of P2P payment networks, highlighting key Supreme Court cases related to the Coinage Clause and legal tender. The chapter delves into the development of blockchain technology and the creation of Bitcoin, followed by an examination of the application of securities and commodity laws and related key cases. The chapter also covers the money transmission laws, exemptions, and cases concerning cryptocurrency. It discusses the custody of digital assets, including pertinent laws and regulations. Significant attention is given to SEC and CFTC enforcement cases, FinCEN guidance for virtual currency businesses, and key AML laws and regulations. Other crucial topics include the New York Bit License framework, DeFi, stablecoins, NFTs, and CBDCs, and the international regulatory ecosystem. The chapter concludes with an overview of crypto and banking policies, bank regulations, and the roles of electronic Money institutions and nonbank issuers in the digital age payment systems, as well as a look at various national approaches.

7.1 Introduction

The emergence of digital assets and blockchain-based systems marks a significant transformation in finance and banking law, presenting both positive and negative implications.[1] Initially conceived as a decentralized experiment in peer-to-peer value transfer, these technologies have developed into a complex regulatory

[1] Rejeb et al. (2021) 93–118; Joebges et al. (2025) 473–502.

environment that connects technological innovation, monetary sovereignty, and systemic stability.[2] This chapter analyses the legal framework governing crypto assets, the policy approaches of financial authorities, and the development of case law related to digital currencies. It investigates the intersections between established banking regulations and new crypto ecosystems, with particular attention to the definition of money, the boundaries of private issuance, and the extent of regulatory oversight. Key areas of focus include the legal monopoly of government-issued currency, the Coinage Clause, and the classification of cryptocurrencies under securities, commodities, and payments law. The chapter also reviews recent case law in the United States, the European Union, and other jurisdictions, as well as enforcement actions by the SEC, CFTC, and FinCEN. Licensing and compliance regimes, such as the New York BitLicense, are discussed alongside the rise of stablecoins, non-fungible tokens (NFTs), decentralized finance (DeFi), and CBDCs. The implications of these developments for banks, e-money institutions, and non-bank issuers are considered within the broader context of global payment systems. Ultimately, the chapter contends that digital assets constitute a legal redefinition of value, signalling a new phase in the evolution of monetary law that necessitates both regulatory adaptation and a reassessment of foundational concepts such as money, property, and trust.

7.2 Crypto and Banking—Policy and Regulatory Issues

7.2.1 From Coinage to Code

Historically, the printing and issuance of money have constituted fundamental sovereign functions of the state, with this authority enshrined in the coinage clause of the US Constitution and analogous provisions in other legal systems. The doctrine of legal tender ensures that only state-authorized currencies may settle public and private debts. Cryptocurrencies, however, challenge this state monopoly by enabling private entities to create and circulate units of value independently of central authority.[3]

The emergence of Bitcoin in 2009 represents both a technological revolution and a legal challenge to the monetary sovereignty of the state. From the perspective of banking law, cryptocurrencies blur the boundaries between established legal categories. Debates persist regarding whether these assets should be classified as money, securities, commodities, or intangible property, and whether they fall under the jurisdiction of central banks or market regulators. The approaches to managing deposit, custody, and transaction processes for such assets differ significantly

[2] Atzori (2017) 45–62.
[3] McGinnis (2020) 59–66.

across jurisdictions, reflecting divergent legal philosophies between market liberalization and regulatory conservatism. This uncertainty constitutes a major legal obstacle to the integration of digital assets into existing banking frameworks.

7.2.2 The Modern Barter System and P2P Networks

Digital currencies initially emerged as a contemporary form of barter, enabling individuals to exchange value without the involvement of intermediaries.[4] The advent of blockchain technology has introduced transparency and immutability by substituting the trusted third parties of traditional finance with cryptographic consensus mechanisms. As a result, peer-to-peer (P2P) payment networks have developed into alternative monetary ecosystems. This technological shift prompts significant public policy considerations, including whether governments should permit parallel currencies, the risk that private digital tokens may undermine financial stability, and the necessary adaptations to monetary law in an environment where trust is increasingly algorithmic rather than institutional.[5] Currently, central banks and lawmakers generally recognize that crypto assets do not qualify as legal tender; instead, these assets are typically classified as private digital property and are subject to taxation, consumer protection regulations, and AML requirements.

7.2.3 Monetary Sovereignty and the Legal Tender Doctrine

Legal tender status requires that money be accepted in the fulfilment of debt obligations, whereas cryptocurrencies do not possess this legal mandate and instead operate as discretionary means of exchange rather than state-backed instruments.[6] In the US, courts and regulators invoke the Coinage Clause of the Constitution to uphold the federal monopoly over money issuance. The 1871 case United States v. Van Auken established that only Congress holds the authority to create legal tender.[7] Comparable frameworks exist internationally: the European Union designates the euro as the sole legal tender under Article 128 of the Treaty on the Functioning of the European Union (TFEU); the UK Treasury defines legal tender narrowly, thereby excluding crypto assets[8]; and most Asian jurisdictions classify cryptocurrencies as digital commodities rather than as money.[9] Despite these distinctions, the functional equivalence of crypto assets as a store of value, medium of exchange, and unit of account has renewed debates regarding the constitutional definition of money in a decentralized context.

---

[4] Singh and Faisal (2019) 221–224.
[5] Bongini et al. (2025).
[6] Nandakumar (2022) 160.
[7] United States v. Van Auken, 96 U.S. 366 (1877); Natelson (2008).
[8] Held et al. (2025); Huang (2021) 336–351.
[9] Sufian et al. (2024) 1–14.

7.2.4 Financial Stability and Systemic Risk

The pronounced volatility of cryptocurrencies and DeFi protocols introduces additional systemic risks to the financial system. Liquidity mismatches and significant price fluctuations within these ecosystems pose direct threats to investor protection.[10] Stablecoins may foster a shadow banking environment in the absence of adequate prudential safeguards.[11] In addition, operational risks and cyber threats endanger the stability of payment systems. Regulatory authorities increasingly recognize the interconnectedness of crypto markets and traditional finance, especially as banks engage in custody, lending, and derivative activities involving digital assets. In response, as per the prudential standards for crypto asset risks issued by BCBS, it aims to impose elevated capital requirements for unsecured tokens and establish a distinct regulatory framework for tokenized traditional assets.[12]

7.2.5 Public Policy Considerations

From a policy perspective rules for new financial technologies should balance limiting systemic risk with keeping space for innovation so that these technologies can develop and be adopted. This debate centres on how to maintain financial integrity and protect consumers, mainly by applying AML/CTF policies strictly so they reduce fraud and other security incidents. Regulatory bodies should work to keep markets stable and limit speculative bubbles, while also making sure that the shift to digital platforms does not create room for regulatory arbitrage or new institutional vulnerabilities.

This is primarily achieved through the doctrine of technological neutrality, which adopts a function-not-form approach. Under this framework, the legal requirements governing the transfer of funds, investment advisory services, and custodial duties remain unchanged, regardless of whether the underlying infrastructure relies on blockchain technology or conventional centralised database system. Another important aspect of this functional equivalence is demonstrated by global FATF standards. According to these standards, VASPs are required to follow the same strict compliance standards as traditional financial institutions to ensure that the global perimeter remains impervious to unique vulnerabilities presented by decentralized innovation.[13]

[10] Naifar (2025) 329.
[11] Bertsch (2023).
[12] BIS (2022).
[13] Aidoo (2025).

7.2.6 Juridical Nature of Cryptoassets

The conceptual metamorphosis of crypto-assets from transient cyber forms of data to a formally ascertained form of legal property marks a paradigm-shifting moment in modern financial legal jurisprudence, reflecting a transformative moment in the constitutive underpinning of private property law. The traditional bipolar system of classifying personal property as merely comprising choses in possession and choses in action could not effectively capture the distinct features of decentralised ledger assets, which are neither tangible property, nor represent a debt or contractual right. However, current judicial incursions in the principal common law regimes have wrought a judicial expansion to incorporate crypto assets under the rubric of proprietary interests, recognizing that the lack of tangible quality does not per se render the existence of proprietary interests impossible. The positioning of crypto assets under the property rubric thus maintains the needful continuum between the cryptographic reality of self-executing code and judicial recognition. The present redescriptive step, rather than merely notational, is thus an operational requirement to facilitate the transfer of ownership interests, provide a foundation for recoverability in insolvency litigation, and implicate a legal framework for fiduciary obligations. The subsequent sections will thus identify the judicial standards informing crypto assets as digital property and its implications on secured transactions in the overall financial regulatory framework.

7.2.6.1 The Ainsworth Criteria and the Judicial Determination of Property

This shift in jurisprudence regarding the nature of crypto assets, to transform them from transitory digital information to a formalized form of legal property, is mainly based on the application of the Ainsworth test, as encapsulated in the influential decision in the case of National Provincial Bank v. Ainsworth. The application of the test in the most influential decision in the case of *AA v. Persons Unknown* established that Bitcoin fulfils the required elements to constitute property, in the sense that it is capable of being defined in a way that has a clear conceptual limits, is capable of being identified by third parties, in the sense that third-party identification is possible, capable of being assumed by third parties, in the sense that third-party assumption is possible, and exhibits a degree of permanence during the life cycle.[14] Through the fulfilment of the above-referred elements, crypto assets have transcended the binary classification between choses-in-action and choses-in-possession to a more evolved concept of intangible property, as they provide the gesture to proprietary relief, in the form of freezing orders and injunctions, to the judiciary, and as such, to the judiciary, to fall within the shelter of private law.

[14] Temelini (1966) 133–141; Brown and Pawlowski (2022) 305–316.

7.2.6.2 Collateralization and Secured Transactions in the DeFi Framework

Formal legal recognition of crypto-assets as digital property acts as the critical catalyst for a step in the evolution of collateralization and secured transactions within the DeFi ecosystem in the path from algorithmic execution to statutory enforcement. Qualifying these assets as property makes them eligible for perfection under modernized commercial codes, such as the UCC Article 12 in the US or the Financial Collateral Arrangements Directive in the European Union, which enable creditors to obtain senior priority over digital collateral.[15] Such legal status ensures that technical asset lock-in in a smart contract is bolstered by a robust proprietary claim, enabling sophisticated financial applications, such as re-hypothecation and cross-protocol credit facilities, while maintaining a clear fiduciary responsibility framework. Ultimately, this allows seamless liquidation of assets in case of default, making decentralized protocols legally recognized venues for institutional-grade secured lending.

7.3 Bank Regulations on Cryptocurrencies

7.3.1 The Position of Central Banks

The global central banks have taken a quite jubilant regulatory approach toward cryptocurrencies, struggling to strike the perfect balance between promoting financial innovations and effective management of complex risks. As has been repeatedly highlighted in the communiques issued by the BIS, due to the complex innate risks in the crypto markets, especially illiquidity, excessive price volatility, and inadequate consumer protection, strict prudence requirements need to be imposed upon banks. However, the legal treatment of these tools is currently very disperse, being identified merely as speculative assets for the ECB,[16] while being identified as virtual commodities for the PBoC[17]; in contrast, for the JFSA, these assets are private digital property, and for the FINMA of Switzerland, these assets are merely a potential trigger for innovative payments, which are subject to close monitoring of regulatory oversight.[18] Though most central banks have now allowed commercial banks to act as settlement agencies for custody services, an overall ‘consensus’ exists against retaining such uncollateralized crypto assets for proprietary purchases.

[15] See, Mandhan (2024) 199–231; Bruce et al. (2022) 1073–1160; Ezike (2022); Keijser et al. (2014) 429.

[16] Khatavkar (2025) 2712–2745.

[17] Zhou et al. (2025) 29–33; Hilpert and Tokarski (2024).

[18] Ochrymowicz et al. (2024) 22–26.

7.3.2 Basel Committee Guidance

The prudential framework on crypto assets issued by the Basel Committee on Banking Supervision in 2023 aims to ensure the stability of finances by classifying exposure to crypto assets by commercial banks into two groups in a prudent manner. Group 1 involves crypto assets that are tokens on traditional assets, including tokens on bonds, stablecoins that have sufficient mechanisms to stabilize the value within the boundaries stipulated in the prudential framework, and are assigned risk weights based on the risk characteristics of the underlying traditional assets. On the other hand, Group 2 involves unbacked crypto assets such as Bitcoin that are not backed by any form of stabilization mechanisms to ensure that commercial banks back them with equity to avoid any potential risk to depositors in case of exposure to speculative instruments by commercial banks, hence ensuring that technological innovation does not modify the inherent characteristics of financial risk in any form whatsoever.[19]

7.3.3 Custody of Digital Assets

Holding digital assets can create legal issues because philosophies like possession and control are harder to define when the asset has no physical form. Unlike physical securities, digital assets are kept and accessed through private keys. This raises practical and legal issues about how asset ownership is determined when a custodian controls the private key, what a custodian may be responsible for if assets are lost or stolen, and how digital assets are kept separate if the custodian enters bankruptcy. To address these uncertainties, the US SEC's Custody Rule (17 CFR § 275.206(4)-2) under the Investment Advisers Act is being modernized to better cover digital assets, with recent no-action relief allowing state trust companies to serve as qualified custodians for crypto assets.[20] In the same way, the EU's MiCA regulation requires Crypto Asset Service Providers (CASPs) to follow strict rules on keeping customer assets separate and putting cybersecurity measures in place.[21] The custody of digital assets is governed by the same trust-based duty of loyalty that applies to traditional property. This means that having technical control over the assets is treated as a legal duty to keep them safe. Banks that handle cryptocurrency-related services must comply with strict AML/CTF rules, even though many cryptocurrency transactions are pseudonymous.

[19] Wilmarth (2023); Buch (2023) 54.
[20] Plaze (2025) 59.
[21] Zetzsche and Woxholth (2025) 77–94; Zetzsche et al. (2024) 207–229; Zetzsche et al. (2021) 203–225.

7.3.4 AML/CTF Obligations for Banks in Crypto Transactions: No Room for Pseudonymity Excuses

Banks that deal in crypto assets shall meet strict AML/CTF requirements, even though many digital assets allow users to act under pseudonyms. These institutions should record the wallet addresses of both the originator and the beneficiary, monitor transactions on an ongoing basis using blockchain analytics tools, and file reports on any suspicious activity as required under FATF Recommendation No16.[22] All transactions must be screened against international sanctions lists, including those maintained by OFAC, the EU, and the UN. Regulators note that the pseudonymous nature of cryptocurrency transactions is not a reason to relax compliance requirements. The US sanctions against BitMEX, Binance, and Bittrex show how banking oversight is tied to efforts against financial crime and how costly it can be when firms fail to meet compliance duties. Regulators have noted that even though cryptocurrencies are pseudonymous, firms still need to meet very high compliance standards when they handle them.US sanctions against BitMEX, Binance, and Bittrex show that banking oversight and efforts to combat financial crime are closely tied in how regulators frame their concerns.[23]

7.3.5 Integration into Banking Infrastructure

Banks are increasingly integrating blockchain technology into their operations. This trend is evident in the development of consensus networks such as JPMorgan's Onyx network and JPM Coin, digital bond issuances utilizing DLT exemplified by the EIB's 2021 initiative, and the provision of digital asset custody services for institutional investors.[24] These developments suggest the emergence of hybrid banking systems in which digital and traditional assets coexist under unified oversight. It is essential that regulatory frameworks are structured to ensure that such technological innovations do not compromise core banking principles, including prudent soundness, deposit insurance, and consumer protection.

7.4 Electronic Money Institutions and Issuance of Electronic Money

7.4.1 Concept and Legal Definition

Electronic money, e-money, is defined as a monetary value stored electronically, issued in exchange for funds, representing a claim on the issuer, and accepted as a means of payment by parties other than the issuer. From a legal perspective,

[22] Pocher (2025) 197–220; Kim et al. (2021) 78.
[23] Bittrex Global [2025] SC (Bda) 78civ; Emmert (2024).
[24] Possenti (2021).

e-money serves as a digital representation of fiat currency and is distinct from crypto assets in two principal respects. First, e-money is issued by a central institution and consistently guarantees repayment or redemption at par value. Second, it is subject to licensing requirements and prudential regulatory standards. The European Union's Electronic Money Directive 2009/110/EC establishes the most comprehensive regulatory framework in this area. The directive defines e-money as a monetary value stored electronically, including magnetically, issued in exchange for funds for the purpose of carrying out payment transactions, accepted by natural or legal persons other than the issuer, and constituting a right over the issuer. This definition underpins global e-money regulation and clearly differentiates regulated digital money from decentralised crypto assets.

7.4.2 Legal Nature of Electronic Money

E-money constitutes a hybrid financial instrument. Unlike bank deposits, e-money is not representing a to the issuer; instead, the received funds must be safeguarded and are prohibited from being used by the issuer for credit transactions. This distinction enhances the protection of consumer funds, including when the issuer becomes insolvent. From the standpoint of legal theory, e-money bridges the conceptual divide between private law obligations, such as debt and receivables, and public law requirements, including authorization, capital, and consumer protection. This change can be viewed as a digital manifestation of how banking has developed over time.

7.4.3 Licensing and Authorization of E-Money Institutions (EMIs)

E-money law builds trust in digital payments by stating that value stored electronically must be treated as the same as money in ordinary form, and by giving users legal protection that this value can be accepted and redeemed as money. Licensing and prudential regulation of EMIs are generally intended to meet four main legal aims. These goals include protecting consumers by ensuring that e-money can be redeemed at its face value, setting prudential requirements to limit spillover from a provider's failure, safeguarding the system through AML/CTF rules and transaction traceability, and supporting competition by reducing regulatory arbitrage while still allowing room for innovation.[25]

EMIs are legal entities authorized to issue, distribute, and receive electronic money. In the EU, EMIs must be licensed by the relevant national authorities, such as the FCA in the UK or BaFin in Germany, and are required to hold a minimum initial capital of EUR 350,000 as per Article 4 of the Directive 2009/110/EC. By

---

[25] See, Central Bank of Ireland (2025).

law, customer funds must be kept separate from an institution's own assets. Operational resilience, consumer protection, and AML/CTF measures remain central to ongoing compliance. Under PSD2, EMIs are licensed to provide payment services, which allows them to work with both traditional banks and fintech firms.[26] This interoperability exemplifies how banks and non-bank financial intermediaries are functioning in similar ways, which is a central feature of open banking ecosystem.

7.4.4 Distinction from Cryptocurrencies and Stablecoins

E-money and stablecoins may be built on similar technology, but the legal basis for each is different. E-money can be described as a regulated form of digital fiat.[27] It is issued by licensed financial institutions and must be redeemable on demand for fiat currency at its full-face value. By contrast, stablecoins are often treated as market-based private money, issued by firms that are unregulated or subject to only limited oversight.[28] From a legal standpoint, e-money is treated as a replacement for fiat currency, and it gives the holder a legal right to redeem it at its full face value. On the other hand, stablecoins are tokens that are backed by assets and may be supported by fiat currency, crypto assets, or other holdings. The rules for refunds depend on the terms set out in a contract or on the issuer's discretion. This basic distinction shapes current regulatory approaches that try to reduce shadow banking risks by following the idea of same risk, same regulation.[29]

7.5 Nonbank Issuers of Electronic Money

7.5.1 Emergence of Nonbank Issuers

The financial services sector has been revolutionized by the digitalization process, and this has led to the rise of a new wave of non-bank payment and money issuance services offered by fintech companies, telecom players, and general technology platforms, and which now increasingly perform the role of quasi-bank institutions in the form of digital money, prepaid instruments, and payment tokens.[30] Although this has contributed immensely to the expansion of the role of financial inclusion and enhanced efficiency in the market, it has, however, challenged the conventional legal monopoly over deposit-taking functions traditionally and comprehensively exercised by the conventional banking sector, and has therefore brought about a paradigm shift in the constitutional architecture underpinning financial laws. In response to this, the legal systems have therefore erected a set of specialized

---

[26] Harasim and Klimontowicz (2018) 50–73; Riefa (2017) 146–176; Poulle et al. (2024) 538–542.

[27] Acuna and Pullas (2016) 176.

[28] Bruce, Odinet and Tosato (2022) 1073–1160; Wilmarth Jr. (2021) 1–21.

[29] Hockett (2020) 345 et seq.

[30] See, in general, Robinson et al. (2023) 478–493.

licensing and tiered regulatory frameworks, carefully crafted to balance the need to keep abreast with the role of innovation in the tech sector and the need to keep consumers safe and protected.

7.5.2 Legal Framework

The legal architecture governing non-bank issuers reveals a complex convergence of regional and international mandates. These frameworks increasingly emphasise the economic substance of financial activities over their formal institutional labels. In the EU, this is mainly created out of the Electronic Money Directive 2009/110/EC and the PSD2, both of which demarcate the operational boundaries for issuance and payment services, whereas the requisite framework for rigorous AML is provided by the AMLD5 and AMLD6 directives.[31] On the other hand, the US takes a decentralized approach where, by and large, regulation proceeds at the state level through the acquisition of Money Transmitter Licenses; exemptions include the 2015 New York BitLicense, which, for its part, serves as an innovative hybrid model in that it integrates cryptographic and fiat-based digital assets under one regulatory roof.[32] However, this diversity in jurisdictions is being gradually homogenized through the strategic suggestions of the FSB and the BIS, which both promote same activity, same risk, same regulation, arguing that non-bank issuers are obliged to conform to the same prudence standards applicable to conventional banking institutions if and only if the functional outcome is economically indistinguishable from conventional banking services.

7.5.3 Safeguarding of Funds

Protecting the funds of customers is thus a key fiduciary and legal requirement for the issuer, acting as an absolute prerequisite for enshrining the broader integrity of the new digital finance environment. Within this context, the financial institution is strictly obligated to safeguard the customers' assets through a multi-defence mechanism, starting from the mandatory segregation of customers' accounts at licensed credit institutions, thus ensuring that customers' funds are kept segregated from the issuer's own operational balance sheet, and supplemented by the procurement of insurance contracts or bank guarantees as an indemnification defence mechanism against the risk of insolvency.[33]

While such protocols might be merely nominal, safeguarding procedures undergo periodic audits and independent verification mechanisms to allow for

[31] Breszkovics (2024) 69; See also, Tosza and Voordeckers (2024) 405–424.
[32] DeWaal and Dempsey (2015) 59–65.
[33] Rank and Tome (2020) 620–623.

necessary transparency to regulatory oversight. The need for stringent governance, therefore, underlined the 2020 Wirecard collapse-a watershed event that showed very clearly the very real risks of poor asset isolation, thus compelling the European Union to up the ante on supervisory reach and fortify cross-border institutional cooperation.[34] As a result, failure to adhere to these safeguarding standards is no longer a procedural issue but has been classified as a core regulatory breach with serious legal consequences, which include the immediate revocation of operating licenses all the way to full corporate and individual liability.

7.5.4 AML/CTF and Consumer Protection

The strict implementation of AML and CTF standards to non-bank issuers represents one of the most important regulatory imperatives of our times, determined as it is to safeguard the integrity of the global financial architecture and foster systemic trust. In turn, this normative framework has required entities to perform granular due diligence on customers in line with the KYC principle, involving the ongoing monitoring of transaction flows and transparent identification of ultimate beneficial owners to prevent illicit financial activity from taking place. Meanwhile, another dimension of this regime-consumer protection- requires a high degree of informational symmetry: regulators require complete disclosure of fee and contractual terms, the institutionalization of effective dispute resolution mechanisms, and strict adherence to the GDPR to guard data sovereignty. These diversified requirements together ensure that the arc of technological progress does not sidestep foundational legal principles of accountability, transparency, and fairness, thereby aligning rapid fintech evolution with established prudential standards.

7.5.5 Role in Financial Inclusion

Non-bank electronic money issuers significantly contribute to advancing financial inclusion, especially within developing economies. Mobile money platforms such as M-Pesa in Kenya, GCash in the Philippines, and bKash in Bangladesh exemplify how streamlined regulatory frameworks can broaden access to payment and savings services. International organizations, including the IMF, WB, and FATF, advocate for proportionate regulation that aligns compliance requirements with risk levels to balance financial integrity and inclusion.[35] Within this framework, non-bank issuance activities constitute a legal innovation by permitting private entities, subject to public oversight, to undertake quasi-monetary functions.

[34] Jo et al. (2021) 96–106; Jakubeit (2021).

[35] Tarazi and Breloff (2010) 1–10; Hove and Dubus (2019) 568; Velez (2025) 390–397; See also, Rubini (2024).

7.6 Payment Systems in the Digital age

7.6.1 Conceptual Foundations

Payment systems constitute the core infrastructure of the financial sector, facilitating the final and irreversible transfer of value. In the digital era, these systems include both centralized, bank-based networks and decentralized frameworks such as blockchain and DLT.[36] Although technological advancements have altered the distinctions between private and public money, interbank and peer-to-peer (P2P) transactions, as well as domestic and cross-border transfers, the legal objective remains consistent: to ensure finality, reliability, and systemic stability in transactions.[37]

7.6.2 Legal Principles of Payment Systems

The legal framework of payments systems is intrinsically grounded in a trilateral approach that relies on finality, netting applicability, and oversight of the system, which together provide for operational certainty and reduce systemic risks in the financial environment. Finally, while the principle of finality, enshrined in the EU 98/26/EC Settlement Finality Directive, ensures that processed transactions are definitive and irreversible, and netting, recognized in law, enables efficient and simultaneous fulfilment of obligations, these two principles, although being equally valid for traditional e-infrastructure and the new DLT architectures, also require an essential re-assessment of conventional principles, particularly with respect to the meaning of accountability, governance, and oversight in the decentralized framework of the latter, which, instead of relying on the mediation of the 'central clearinghouse,' guarantees the validity of consensuses via decentralized means of interpretation and verification, specific to this technology and achieved through its own distributed and peer-to-peer architecture of consensus.[38]

7.6.3 DLT and Legal Implications

DLT is revolutionising financial law in terms of decentralization of record-keeping infrastructure. The legal framework, on the other hand, is dependent on the legal principle of legal accountability, which requires legal entities. There is thus a conflict in terms of the issue of responsibility in cases of error or fraud on decentralized networks.[39] The issue of responsibility in relation to error or fraud in decentralized networks still exists. There is a debate on whether code meeting the

[36] Jimenez-Gomez (2023) 665–678.
[37] Arner et al. (2024); Putrevu and Mertzanis (2023) 476–500.
[38] Annunziata et al. (2023) 145.
[39] Zaccaroni (2022) 601.

regulatory requirement is possible. The 2022 EU DLT Pilot Regime, on the other hand, aims to close the gap.[40]

7.6.4 DeFi and Stablecoins

7.6.4.1 DeFi

The recent proliferation of DeFi platforms, which effectively emulate conventional financial instruments such as lending, exchange-mediated trading, and derivatives through autonomous smart contract architectures, has precipitated a fundamental disruption to traditional regulatory paradigm, predicated upon centralized intermediaries as the locus of oversight. As the removal of these intermediaries fundamentally challenges core conceptions of institutional authorization and legal accountability, regulatory authorities are increasingly pivoting toward a functional equivalence approach to bridge this normative gap.[41] This transition involves the probable reclassification of smart contract operators as regulated service providers, a foisting of fiduciary responsibilities upon governance token holders on account of their decisional influence over protocol trajectories, and a compulsion to integrate protocol compliance layers designed to facilitate automated AML and enforcement screening within the codebase itself.

7.6.4.1.1 The EU: The MiCA and Pilot Regime Paradigm

One of the key roles played by the EU is that of global standard-setter, using the framework of the Markets in Crypto-Assets Regulation, or MiCA, which came into its strong enforcement phase in 2026. This regulatory body gives precedence to the concept of legal certainty, which requires that issuers and service providers have real-world, physical, and authorised presences inside the EU. On the concept of DeFi, the EU applies the framework of the DLT Pilot Regime, which is also considered to be 'a regulatory sandbox' approach, as it permits market infrastructure to test trading and blockchain-based trading systems, which are temporarily relief from traditional requirements.[42]

7.6.4.1.2 The US: From Litigation to Legislation (GENIUS Act)

The traditional US approach was marked by jurisdictional fragmentation and reliance on the 1946 Howey Test as a means of determining whether or not tokens are considered securities. Fast forward to 2026, though, and the legislative landscape has significantly matured in line with the GENIUS Act of 2025.[43] In contrast to the EU's model, which is state-directed, the US framework places great emphasis on corporate legal rights and insolvency protection for consumers. A very important difference involves the "dual banking system" logic wherein,

[40] Tomczak (2024) 32–39; Zetzsche and Woxholth (2025) 189–202; Zaccaroni (2022) 601–613.

[41] Oreskovic and Bajakic (2024) 59; Bakare et al. (2024) 3075–3089.

[42] Ahern (2021) 395–432; Zaccaroni (2022) 601–613; Tomczak (2024) 32–39.

[43] Oranburg (2025) 81.

once a stablecoin issuer surpasses a threshold of $10 billion, they need to "graduate" from state-level licensing into the direct federal oversight of either the Federal Reserve or the OCC.[44] This is a more modular and reactive approach, whereby the code applied changes with scale and risk profile rather than imposing a universal code from the outset.

7.6.4.1.3 The Convergence: Functional Equivalence

Despite these different starting points, global regulatory expectations increasingly coalesce around the principle of functional equivalence. In both jurisdictions, regulators increasingly look past the decentralised label in search of control points-such as front-end operators, governance token whales, or core developer groups-and hold them to the same AML/KYC and fiduciary standards as traditional financial institutions.[45] By 2026, embedded regulation-where compliance mechanisms are programmatically integrated directly into the protocol's smart contracts-has become the primary bridge between these two major legal systems.

7.6.4.2 Stablecoins

The legal classification and oversight of stablecoins evolved from a period of *laissez-faire* experimentation to a strict, codified framework, crafted to fetter systemic fragility. At the very centre of this taxonomy lies the dichotomy between asset-backed tokens, whose value is derived from tangible reserves of fiat or commodities, and e-money tokens-one currency digital surrogates with a right of redemption at par.[46] Algorithm-based stablecoins, on the other hand, which try to maintain parity through programmatic supply-demand adjustments rather than exogenously held reserves, have been under harsh scrutiny-the collapse of TerraUSD in 2022 was a clarion call that these models are essentially high-risk, and international regulators would classify it as such.[47] Accordingly, the MiCA Regulation raises the legal threshold for issuers within the EU to the level where formal institutional authorization, robust capital buffers, and the publishing of a standardized whitepaper to ensure transparency are now required. This reflects a growing sense that there is a developing global view that stablecoins as functional equivalents of traditional deposits or money market products must be held to the same prudent standards of liquidity and solvency to avoid financial contagions.

7.6.5 Central Bank Digital Currencies (CBDCs)

CBDCs function as public law alternatives to private digital assets and constitute sovereign digital money issued by central banks that combines state-backed trust with technological efficiency. Two principal models are identified in this context

[44] Wilmarth Jr (2025).
[45] Filippi and Mannan (2025) 151–177.
[46] Su (2025) 1–10.
[47] Emmert (2023) 21.

as retail and wholesale CBDCs. While retail CBDCs are designed for use by the public with prominent examples of China's digital yuan (e-CNY) and Nigeria's eNaira. On the other hand, wholesale CBDCs are accessible only to participants operating under interbank agreements.[48]

It is also worth noting that CBDCs alter the relationship between citizens and central banks, redefine the scope of monetary sovereignty, and modify payment privacy and oversight mechanisms. Implementing CBDCs requires comprehensive legal reforms to clarify legal tender status, establish rigorous data protection standards, and ensure interoperability with private financial systems. International coordination, led by the BIS Innovation Centre and the IMF, aims to harmonize cross-border CBDC frameworks.

7.6.6 NFTs and Tokenized Assets

Qualified intellectual property rights in the context of Non-Fungible Tokens (NFTs) expand digital asset law to encompass unique representations of value linked to art, media, or specific rights. Legally, NFTs serve as certificates of authenticity for the underlying asset rather than conferring ownership, unless explicitly specified. This distinction introduces significant legal challenges, including the transfer of intellectual property and copyrights, consumer protection within digital marketplaces, and the taxation and valuation of digital assets.[49] Regulatory authorities such as the Securities and Exchange Commission (SEC) and the European Securities and Markets Authority (ESMA) assess NFTs individually based on their economic function as collectibles, securities, or utility tokens.[50] Notably, marketing an NFT with a promise of return on investment or issuing NFTs in series to enhance liquidity may result in their classification as securities, thereby subjecting them to conventional capital market regulations.

7.7 Various National Approaches

7.7.1 The US

The United States employs a fragmented yet effective regulatory framework. The Securities and Exchange Commission (SEC) applies the Howey Test to determine when a crypto asset qualifies as a security, as demonstrated in SEC v. W.J. Howey Co. (1946) and SEC v. Ripple Labs (2023). The Commodity Futures Trading Commission (CFTC) classifies Bitcoin and Ether as commodities under the Commodity Exchange Act. The Financial Crimes Enforcement Network (FinCEN) recognizes virtual currency businesses as money transmitters under the Bank Secrecy Act.

[48] Hebert et al. (2023).
[49] Mao (2023) 21 et seq.
[50] Benson et al. (2024) 37–61.

The Office of the Comptroller of the Currency (OCC) authorizes national banks to provide limited custody and settlement services. Additionally, state-level regimes such as the New York BitLicense impose parallel licensing and AML obligations. This multi-agency approach exemplifies the pluralistic structure of US financial law, seeking to balance innovation with robust enforcement mechanisms.[51]

7.7.2 The EU

The EU is pursuing a comprehensive legislative strategy to ensure harmonization in the field of digital finance. At the heart of this strategy is the Crypto Asset Market Regulation (MiCA) of 2023, which establishes uniform rules for crypto asset and stablecoin issuers and Crypto Asset Service Providers (CASPs), regulating transparency, governance, and reserve requirements.[52] Together with the Funds Transfer Regulation (TFR), MiCA integrates crypto assets into the EU's financial integrity framework, ensuring full AML/CTF compliance. Furthermore, the Electronic Money Directive and PSD2, which form the basis of digital payment law, are currently being consolidated under the proposed PSD3 and the Payment Services Regulation (PSR).[53] Ultimately, the EU model represents a comprehensive and risk-based regulatory approach focused on consumer protection and market stability.

7.7.3 The UK

In the post-Brexit period, the United Kingdom has adopted a measured and innovation-oriented approach to crypto assets. These assets are classified as exchange tokens, which are similar to Bitcoin and remain largely unregulated except for AML requirements; utility tokens, which provide access to specific services; and security tokens, which are subject to FCA oversight. The Financial Services and Markets Act 2023 broadens the regulatory framework by authorizing the Treasury to designate crypto assets as regulated activities.[54] Concurrently, the Bank of England is conducting comprehensive consultations on privacy and financial inclusion, and is assessing the potential implementation of a Digital Pound as a CBDC.[55]

[51] Donovan (2023) 2309; Collins (2025) 71–103.

[52] Zetzsche and Sinnig (2025) 157.

[53] Divissenko (2023) 665–687.

[54] Wronka (2024) 417–426; Singh and Yadav (2025) 999.

[55] Bank of England (2024).

7.7.4 Asia-Pacific and Emerging Economies

Regulatory models in the Asia-Pacific region reflect each jurisdiction's monetary philosophy and risk tolerance. Japan recognized cryptocurrencies as legal tender and introduced exchange licensing through the Payment Services Act of 2017. Singapore unified digital payment activities under the Payment Services Act (PSA) of 2019. China has banned private cryptocurrency trading but leads in CBDC development with the Digital Yuan, a.k.a. e-CNY.[56] India is drafting comprehensive digital asset legislation and has started regulating exchanges under AML laws. Australia applies its financial services law to crypto activities and is developing sector-specific regulations.[57] These varied approaches highlight the diverse legal foundations of digital finance worldwide.

7.7.5 International Coordination

International coordination is essential to prevent regulatory arbitrage at the global level. The FSB, the IMF, and the BIS have undertaken measures such as developing common taxonomies for crypto assets, enhancing cross-border supervisory cooperation, ensuring consistent application of AML/CTF standards, and establishing prudential limits for banks' exposure to crypto asset risks. International soft law instruments, including the FATF Recommendations, IOSCO Principles, and BIS standards, form a transnational regulatory framework for digital finance. These instruments indicate a gradual convergence toward judicial universality, where diverse systems share a single normative foundation, thereby establishing trust through legal consistency.

7.7.6 Concluding Remarks

The legal treatment of digital and crypto assets signifies a fundamental redefinition of money in the information age. This evolution merges technological innovation with legal principles by integrating algorithmic consensus mechanisms and sovereign regulatory authority. Banks, nonbank issuers, and regulators now operate along a spectrum where code assumes legal functions, while legal frameworks continue to regulate technological processes. The future of financial regulation relies on this dynamic synthesis, embedding transparency, accountability, and human oversight into technological systems that increasingly facilitate the transfer and storage of value. Digital asset law does not eliminate traditional banking law but instead represents its digital transformation. It preserves the essential objectives of

[56] Chen (2020) 101–121; Jahan et al. (2022); Ni and Yu (2025) 287–299.
[57] Pearson (2022).

stability, fairness, and integrity within a legal framework adapted for the digital era.

Chapter Summary

Chapter 7 reviews recent changes in the laws and rules that govern digital assets and crypto assets. It focuses on the central tension between governments' control over money and private systems that run without a central authority. This chapter argues that cryptocurrencies put pressure on the state's control over issuing money, a control that is usually justified by legal and constitutional principles, such as those in the coinage clause and the legal tender doctrine: what the Constitution allows Congress to do with money, and where the limits may be.

In most discussions, crypto assets are treated as privately held digital property or as commodities, not as legal tender. How the law classifies them matters because, if they are treated as property (a chose in action), they can be enforced and seized, and this can also create duties to hold or safeguard them. Regulators often take a technology-neutral stance by focusing on the activity itself, such as money transmission or the issuance of securities, instead of the specific technology used to carry it out. In this context, the FATF has expanded its standards to cover Virtual Asset Service Providers (VASPs) and requires them to apply AML/CTF controls, including the travel rule, which requires that originator and beneficiary information be sent with the transfer.

In the US, regulation is split across federal and state levels and across many agencies, so the overall system is fragmented. The SEC uses the Howey Test to decide whether a token should be treated as a security, the CFTC may regulate certain tokens as commodities, and FinCEN oversees related activity under its rules for Money Services Businesses, or MSBs. State-level licensing rules, such as New York's BitLicense, also shape how these activities are regulated. In its guidance on how crypto assets should fit within the banking framework, the Basel Committee sets a very high capital requirement for unbacked cryptoassets. These assets fall under Group 2 and are assigned a 1250% risk weight, which leads banks to hold a large amount of capital against them. This requirement limits the bank's exposure to speculative tokens. Banks that offer digital asset custody still have to follow fiduciary duties and keep customer assets separate from the bank's own holdings, as required by rules in the US. This approach aligns with the SEC Custody Rule and the EU MiCA Regulation and aims to reduce the risk tied to managing private keys. In the range of digital payment options, e-money is centrally issued digital fiat that is a liability of the issuer and can be redeemed one-for-one at face value. It is governed by strict rules under frameworks like the European Union E-Money Directive. Nonbank issuers must follow safeguarding rules and keep the required level of capital.

The chapter discussed stablecoins, which aim to keep their value close to fiat currency, while noting that their legal treatment is not the same as e-money. They are classified as asset-referenced tokens and will need authorization under upcoming rules, including the EU MiCA Regulation. In academic writing, CBDCs are often described as a public-law alternative to private cryptocurrencies, intended to update state-issued money for use in a digital economy. Their introduction raises new legal questions about privacy and how the role of private banks may change.

Revision Questions

1. Define legal tender doctrine and coinage clause. Examine how cryptocurrency issued by private entities challenges state sovereignty over money, and argue why cryptocurrencies are not recognized as money in major jurisdictions.
2. Explain what is meant by the principle of functional regulation in digital finance. How does the US SEC use the Howey Test to determine whether a digital token is a security? What are the implications for regulatory requirements?
3. What is the rationale behind the 1250% risk weight given to unbacked crypto assets by the Basel Committee under Group 2? How does it impact the ability of traditional banks to participate in direct cryptocurrency speculations?
4. Distinguish e-money from stablecoins in terms of three aspects of their legality, namely their centralised issuance, their redeemability, and their regulation.
5. Describe the legal purpose behind the FATF's travel rule for virtual asset service providers (VASPs). Assess the effectiveness of this rule on tackling the issue of pseudonymity used for blockchain-based transactions for AML compliance.
6. Analyze the major legal and regulatory issues that are being raised by the emergence of decentralized finance protocols, specifically in relation to issues of authorization, supervision, and liability. Consider how the principle of functional equivalence is being used by regulators to deal with such issues.
7. Identify and discuss two critical issues in law and policy that must be considered before full implementation of a retail Central Bank Digital Currency (CBDC), with specific reference to its implications on consumer privacy and on the role of commercial banking institutions.◄

References

Acuna G, Pullas A (2016) The digital currency challenge for the regulatory regime. Revista Chilena de Derecho y Tecnologia 5(2):173–209

Ahern D (2021) Regulatory lag, regulatory friction and regulatory transaction as FinTech Disenablers: calibrating an EU response to the regulatory sandbox phenomenon. Eur Bus Organ Law Rev 22:395–432

Aidoo S (2025) Anti-money Laundering Challenges and Compliance in Decentralized Finance: A Comparative Analysis of Regulatory Frameworks in the U.S., EU, and Singapore. https://www.researchgate.net/publication/393686912_Anti-Money_Laundering_Challenges_and_Compliance_in_Decentralized_Finance_A_Comparative_Analysis_of_Regulatory_Frameworks_in_the_US_EU_and_Singapore. Accessed 20 Jan 2026

Annunziata F, Chisari A, Amendola P (2023) DLT-based trading venues and EU capital markets legislation: state of the art and perspectives under the DLT pilot regime. The Italian Law Journal 9(1):141–161

Arner D, Animashaun S, Cai Y, Charamba K (2024) Building digital payment ecosystems: digital financial infrastructure, financial inclusion, and the UN sustainable development goals. California Western International Law Journal 55(1):1–66

Atzori M (2017) Blockchain technology and decentralized governance: is the state still necessary? Journal of Governance and Regulation 6(1):45–62

Bakare F, Omojola J, Iwuh A (2024) Blockchain and decentralized finance (DeFi): disrupting traditional banking and financial systems. World Journal of Advanced Research and Reviews 23(3):3075–3089

Bank of England (2024) Enhancing the Privacy of a Digital Pound. https://www.bankofengland.co.uk/-/media/boe/files/digital-pound/mit-report-enhancing-the-privacy-of-a-digital-pound.pdf. Accessed 20 Jan 2026

Benson V, Adamyk B, Chinnaswamy A, Adamyk O (2024) Harmonising cryptocurrency regulation in Europe: opportunities for preventing illicit transactions. Eur J Law Econ 57:37–61

Bertsch C (2023) Stablecoins: adoption and fragility. Sveriges Riksbank working paper series no 423

BIS (2022) Prudential Treatment of Cryptoasset Exposures. https://www.bis.org/bcbs/publ/d545.pdf. Accessed 20 Jan 2026

Bongini P, Mattassoglio F, Alessia P, Vismara S (2025) Crypto ecosystem: navigating the past, present and future of decentralized finance. J Technol Transf 50(5):20254–22075

Breszkovics B (2024) NFTs under the framework of MiCA. In: Rodina A, Russo T (eds) Kostic J. Regional Law Review, Institute of Comparative Law, pp 65–76

Brown J, Pawlowski M (2022) The challenge of identifying private property under English law. Conveyancer and Property Lawyer 3:305–316

Bruce K, Odinet C, Tosato A (2022) The private law of stablecoins. Arizona State Law Journal 54:1073–1160

Buch C (2023) Are Cryptoassets a threat to financial stability? World Commerce Review 17(2):46–57

Central Bank of Ireland (2025) Electronic Money Institutions. https://www.centralbank.ie/regulation/industry-market-sectors/electronic-money-institutions. Accessed 20 Jan 2026

Chen C (2020) Regulation of derivatives in Asia: when technology meets financial engineering. In: Werner D, Wan W, Godwin A, Shen W, Gibson E (eds) Research handbook on Asian financial law. Edward Elgar, pp 101–121

Collins J (2025) Cryptocurrencies and Financial Crimes: The Role of Decentralized Cryptocurrency in Facilitating Money Laundering and the Challenges Posed on Anti-Money Laundering Regulations 34(1):71–103

DeWaal G, Dempsey G (2015) New York BitLicense regulations virtually certain to significantly impact transactions in virtual currencies. Journal of Investment Compliance 16(4):59–65

Divissenko N (2023) Regulation of crypto-assets in the EU: future-proofing the regulation of innovation in digital finance. European Papers 8(2):665–687
Donovan M (2023) Ripple effect: the SEC's major questions doctrine problem. Fordham Law Rev 91:2309–2352
Emmert F (2023) Smart money for the people: using financial innovation and technology to promote ESG. Duke Law and Technology Review 22:21–70
Emmert F (2024) The regulation of cryptocurrencies in The United States of America. European Journal of Law Reform 25(1/2):27–122
Ezike O (2022) The EU financial collateral directive: the distinguishing features of a security financial collateral arrangement? Uniform Law Review 27(3):1–12
Filippi P, Mannan M (2025) Regulatory equivalence in blockchain systems: the role of public values and legitimacy. In: Goossens J, Keymolen E, Stanojevic A (eds) Public governance and emerging technologies: values, trust, and regulatory compliance. Springer, pp 151–177
Harasim J, Klimontowicz M (2018) Regulations as a tool to increase consumer protection on the European retail payment market. Journal of Economics and Management 31(1):50–73
Hebert J, Moshammer E, Barth H (2023) Wholesale central Bank digital currency—the safe way to debt capital market efficiency. European Stability Mechanism Discussion Paper Series No 22
Held A, MacPherson A, Ripley B (2025) United Kingdom (UK) (England and Wales). In: Lehmann M, Morishita T (eds) Cryptocurrencies in National Laws: a global survey. Brill
Hilpert H, Tokarski P (2024) The Digitalisation of Central Bank Money: China Advances While Europe Hesitates SWP Comment, 48/2024. https://www.econstor.eu/bitstream/10419/305241/1/1906343020.pdf. Accessed 20 Jan 2026
Hockett R (2020) The capital commons: digital money and citizens' finance in a productive Commercial Republic. Review of Banking and Finance Law 39:345–498
Hove L, Dubus A (2019) M-PESA and financial inclusion in Kenya: of paying comes saving? Sustainability 11(3):568
Huang S (2021) Crypto assets regulation in the UK: an assessment of the regulatory effectiveness and consistency. Journal of Financial Regulation and Compliance 29(3):336–351
Jahan S, Loukoianova E, Papageorgiou E, Che N, Goel A, Li M, Rawat U, Zhou Y (2022) Towards central Bank digital currencies in Asia and Pacific: result of a regional survey. IMF
Jakubeit R (2021) The Wirecard Scandal and the Role of BaFin: A Case for Unifying Capital Markets Supervision in the European Union. Luiss SEP Working Paper 5/2021. https://leap.luiss.it/wp-content/uploads/2022/09/WP5.21-The-Wirecard-scandal-and-the-role-of-Bafin.pdf. Accessed 20 Jan 2026
Jimenez-Gomez B (2023) Distributed ledger Technology in Financial Markets. The European Union Experience Cuadernos de Derecho Transnacional 15(2):665–678
Jo H, Hsu A, Llanos-Popolizio R, Vergara-Vega J (2021) Corporate governance and financial fraud of Wirecard. European Journal of Business and Management Research 6(2):96–106
Joebges H, Herr H, Kellermann C (2025) Crypto assets as a threat to financial market stability. Eurasian Econ Rev 15:473–502
Keijser T, Kyrkousi M, Bakanos A (2014) Financial collateral: the legal framework of the European Union and UNIDROIT compared. Uniform Law Review 19(3):429–458
Khatavkar P (2025) Stablecoins and the law: global regulatory approaches, legal challenges, and cross-border implications. International Journal of Management and Humanities 8(4):2712–2745
Kim D, Bilgin M, Ryu D (2021) Are suspicious activity reporting requirements for cryptocurrency exchanges effective? Financ Innov 7(1):78
Mandhan S (2024) Confronting the DeFi revolution: a comparative analysis of the application of new Zeland's personal property securities act 1999 to Cryptoassets. Victoria University of Wellington Law Review 55:199–231
Mao C (2023) Imperfect digital certificate of provenance: a categorical risk-based approach to non-fungible tokens (NFTs). Colorado Technology Law Journal 21:21–84

McGinnis J (2020) Bitcoin's nature and its future. Harvard Journal of Law and Public Policy 43(1):59–66
Naifar N (2025) Mapping systemic tail risk in crypto markets: DeFi, stablecoins, and infrastructure tokens. Journal of Risk and Financial Management 18(6):329
Nandakumar G (2022) The political economy of global private currencies. PhD Thesis, Political Science and Geography, Old Dominion University
Natelson R (2008) Paper money and the original understanding of the coinage clause. Harvard Journal of Law and Public Policy 31(3):1017–1081
Ni Y, Yu H (2025) The integration of digital payments within the Asia-Pacific region in the age of artificial intelligence. Eximia 14(1):287–299
Ochrymowicz M, Celebi R, Stefanoski D (2024) Legal, regulatory and tax environment in Switzerland relevant for blockchain based businesses. The International Journal of Blockchain Journal of Blockchain Law 9:22–26
Oranburg S (2025) Function over form: toward a Safe Harbor framework for DeFi regulation of utility tokens. Louisiana Law Review 86(1):81–166
Oreskovic L, Bajakic I (2024) Regulating DeFi: safeguarding market integrity while managing high expectations. Crotian Yearbook of European Law and Policy 20:59–90
Pearson B (2022) Crypto governance: Australia's need for regulation in crypto markets. University of South Wales Law Journal Student Series 21:1–37
Plaze F (2025) Regulation of Custodial Practices under the Investment Advisers Act of 1940 Rule 206(4)-2. https://business.cch.com/srd/RegulationofCustodialPracticesUnderInvestmentAdvisersAct11132025.pdf. Accessed 20 Jan 2026
Pocher N (2025) Traceability to crypto-asset transfers under the new EU AML/CTF regime: the crypto travel rule between challenges and open issues. In: Lee J, Darbellay A (eds) A research agenda for financial law and regulation. Edward Elgar, pp 197–220
Possenti E (2021) EIB Issues Its First Ever Digital Bond on a Public Blockchain. https://www.eib.org/en/press/all/2021-141-european-investment-bank-eib-issues-its-first-ever-digital-bond-on-a-public-blockchain. Accessed 20 Jan 2026
Poulle J, Kannan A, Spitz N, Kahn S, Sotiropoulou A (2024) EU banking and financial regulation. Edward Elgar:538–542
Putrevu J, Mertzanis C (2023) The Adoption of Digital Payments in Emerging Economies: Challenges and Policy Responses 26(2):476–500
Rank P, Tome M (2020) PSD2 and the safeguarding of clients' funds: a comparative analysis with respect to funds of payment service users in The Netherlands and Brazil. Butterworths Journal of International Banking and Financial Law:620–623
Rejeb A, Rejeb K, Keogh J (2021) Cryptocurrencies in modern finance: a literature review. ETIKONOMI 20(1):93–118
Riefa C (2017) Directive 2009/110/EC on the taking up, pursuit and prudential supervision of the business of electronic money institutions and directive 2015/2366/EU on the control of electronic payments in the EU. In: Lodder A, Murray A (eds) E-regulation of E-commerce. Edward Elgar, pp 146–176
Robinson G, Dörry S, Derudder B (2023) Global networks of money and information at the crossroads: correspondent banking and SWIFT. Global Netw 23(2):478–493
Rubini A (2024) Fintech in a flash: financial technology made easy. De Gruyter Brill
Singh B, Faisal M (2019) Cryptocurrency: an analysis of growth of bitcoin and its future. International Journal of Innovative Science and Research Technology 4(6):221–224
Singh B, Yadav S (2025) Comprehensive analysis of cryptocurrency and regulations, legal implications, and economic consideration in the UK. Int J Environ Sci 11(19):999–1012
Su Z (2025) Evolution and financial implications of stablecoins—a literature review. SHS Web of Conferences 218:1–10
Sufian M, Syahril N, Ghapa N (2024) Regulatory framework for cryptocurrency: a comparative analysis of Malaysia, Indonesia and Singapore. Malaysian Journal of Social Sciences and Humanities 9(11):1–14

Tarazi M, Breloff P (2010) Nonbank E-money issuers: regulatory approaches to protecting consumer funds. CGAp Focus Note 63:1–10

Temelini P (1966) National provincial bank v. Ainsworth, [1965] 2 all E.R. 472. Osgoode Hall Law Journal 4:133–141

Tomczak T (2024) 'Advantages' of distributed ledger technology and the DLT pilot regime. Business Law Journal 5:32–39

Tosza S, Voordeckers O (2024) An anti-money laundering Authority for the European Union: a new Center of Gravity in AML enforcement. ERA Forum 25:405–424

Velez G (2025) A systematic review of Mobile banking, fintech innovations, and regulatory gaps to achieve financial inclusion in The Philippines. Journal of Interdisciplinary Perspectives 3(3):390–397

Wilmarth A (2023) We must protect investors and our banking system from the crypto industry. Wash Univ Law Rev 101:233–324

Wilmarth A Jr (2021) It's time to regulate stablecoins as deposits and require their issuers to be FDIC-insured banks. Banking and Financial Services Policy Report 41(2):1–21

Wilmarth Jr A (2025) Policy Brief: The Hagerty-Scott-Lummis-Gillibrand Stablecoin Bill Would Cause Great Harm to Consumers, Investors, Our Financial System, and Our Economy. https://scholarship.law.gwu.edu/cgi/viewcontent.cgi?article=3035&context=faculty_publication. Accessed 20 Jan 2026

Wronka C (2024) Crypto-asset regulatory landscape: a comparative analysis of the crypto-asset regulation in the UK and Germany. J Asset Manag 25(4):417–426

Zaccaroni G (2022) Decentralized finance and EU law: the regulation on a pilot regime for market infrastructures based on distributed ledger technology. European Papers 7(2):601–613

Zetzsche D, Annunziata F, Arner D, Buckley R (2021) The Markets in Crypto-Assets Regulation (MiCA) and the EU digital finance strategy. Capital Markets Law Review 16(2):203–225

Zetzsche D, Sinnig J (2025) The EU approach to digital currencies. Law Contemp Probl 87:157–183

Zetzsche D, Sinnig J, Nikolakopoulou A (2024) Crypto custody. Capital Markets Law Journal 19(3):207–229

Zetzsche D, Woxholth J (2025) The EU law on crypto-assets: a guide to European FinTech regulation. Cambridge University Press

Zhou L, Hu B, Zheng L (2025) Disruptive impacts of central Bank digital currencies on the traditional financial system: a regulatory framework perspective. Journal of Fintech and Business Analysis 2(1):29–33

Further Reading

Allen H (2023) DeFi: Shadow Banking 2.0? William and Mary Law Review 64(4):919–968

Basel Committee on Banking Supervision (2022) Prudential Treatment of Cryptoasset Exposures

Buckley R, Arner D, Zetzsche D, Selga E (2020) Techrisk. Singap J Leg Stud 35-62

Buckley R, Zetzsche D, Arner D, Tang B (2021) Regulating artificial intelligence in finance: putting the human in the loop. Sydney Law Review 43(1):43–81

EU (2023) Markets in Crypto-Assets Regulation

Ferrari V (2020) The regulation of crypto-assets in the EU—investment and payment tokens under the radar. Maastricht Journal of European and Comparative Law 27(3):1–18

International Capital Market Instruments

8

Contents

F. B. Erdem, *The Principles of International Banking, Finance and Investment Law*, Springer Textbooks in Law, https://doi.org/10.1007/978-3-032-32505-1_8

Abstract

This chapter provides an extensive overview of the legal framework governing international capital market instruments. It starts with an analysis of the international stock market and then delves into various capital market instruments and securities. The discussion includes stock certificates, differentiating between bearer and registered share certificates, preferred and ordinary stocks, paid and non-paid shares, as well as premium and non-premium stocks. It further explores non-voting shares, participating shares, debt instruments such as bonds and securities, profit and loss sharing certificates, real estate certificates, and asset-backed and guaranteed securities. Additional topics include corporate warranties, covered warrants, lease certificates, and the derivatives exchange. The chapter also examines international securities, depository receipts, and various types of funds like investment funds, hedge funds, pension funds, and ETFs. Lastly, it discusses microfinance and microcredits, including insurance, crowdfunding, financial conglomerates, and informal remittance, alongside common disputes in capital markets, such as unauthorised transactions and misleading investment advice.

8.1 Introduction

This chapter examines global capital market instruments by analysing the structural design of international stock exchanges and the legal characteristics of financial securities. It contextualizes the development of capital markets as mechanisms for allocating corporate resources, with particular attention to corporate governance law and financial innovation. The discussion further explores how legal frameworks constrain and guide market participants within these institutions to foster trust and confidence during periods of innovation.

The chapter first addresses the international stock market, focusing on cross-border trading, listing requirements, and regulatory convergence among international authorities. It then outlines the taxonomy of capital market instruments, including equity-based instruments such as stocks and stock certificates, as well as debt-based and hybrid instruments such as bonds, asset-backed securities, and covered warrants. Additionally, the chapter considers collective investment schemes—including funds, exchange-traded funds (ETFs), and hedge or pension funds—and alternative financing mechanisms such as microfinance, crowdfunding, and informal transfer systems, which extend the capital market structure beyond traditional entities.

The chapter assesses financial markets by presenting case studies of contested issues in financial transactions, illustrating how irresponsibility and investor protection manifest in practice. Ultimately, it demonstrates that capital market instruments represent not only financial assets but also legal embodiments of public trust and economic order, balancing investment freedom with systemic stability.

8.2 International Stock Market

8.2.1 The Nature of the Global Stock Market

The global stock market comprises a transnational network of exchanges and trading systems that enable the issuance of stock shares and related securities, as well as the trading of corporate ownership and investment products.[1] Unlike domestic capital markets, international stock markets function within a pluralistic legal environment in which multiple national legislations coexist alongside global standards, such as those established by the IOSCO, the OECD Principles of Corporate Governance, and the IMF codes of financial transparency.

From a legal perspective, the stock market serves both as a contract market that facilitates private transactions and as an institution governed by public law[2]

[1] Slimane (2012) 61.

[2] Kahan (1997) 1509–1519; Pistor (2013) 315–330; Chan (2021) 219–251; See also, Roe (2006) 462–518.

and subject to government regulation. The effective operation of the global market depends on several key guarantees, which are outlined below[3]:

(i) Market integrity, maintained through anti-manipulation and insider trading laws,
(ii) Transparency, achieved through comprehensive disclosure and reporting requirements,
(iii) Investor protection through controlling and overseeing intermediaries, and
(iv) Systemic stability, supported by a robust understanding of market dynamics.

Collectively, these guarantees form a coherent system of interdependent commitments that support the orderly and fair operation of this legally pluralistic environment. The effectiveness of the global stock market therefore depends significantly on continued convergence toward rigorous worldwide standards of both national and global regulation, which maintain the market as both a contracting mechanism for private interests and a well-regulated system under public mandates.

8.2.2 Cross-Border Listing and Trading

Cross-border listings enable corporations to access capital in foreign markets, subjecting them to multiple regulatory frameworks.[4] For instance, a German company listed on the New York Stock Exchange (NYSE) must comply with both domestic corporate law and US securities disclosure requirements under SEC Form 20-F. This multi-jurisdictional context presents significant legal challenges, such as prospectus liability for false or misleading statements in offering documents, complexities in reconciling accounting standards like IFRS and Generally Accepted Accounting Principles (GAAP), jurisdictional and enforcement conflicts regarding regulatory authority in transnational misconduct, and the necessity for corporate governance equivalence to meet host-country listing standards. Legislators must balance investor protection with market accessibility, seeking to prevent regulatory arbitrage while facilitating global capital flows.

8.2.3 International Cooperation and Harmonization

Global institutions seek to reduce jurisdictional conflicts by promoting regulatory harmonization. The international stock market exemplifies a juridical ecosystem characterized by soft law and mutual recognition, integrating national sovereignty

[3] Moloney (2012) 111–202.
[4] Coffee Jr. (2002) 1770–1775.

with global norms.[5] These harmonization efforts are implemented through initiatives such as the IOSCO Multilateral Memorandum of Understanding (MMoU), which facilitates cross-border enforcement and information sharing among regulators.[6] G20 and FSB initiatives also promote convergence in key areas by establishing shared standards for disclosure, prudential oversight, and market conduct. Additionally, regional efforts such as the EU's Capital Markets Union (CMU) aim to integrate European financial markets through legislative harmonization of directives and regulations, including MiFID II, the prospectus regulation, and the market abuse regulation.

8.3 Capital Market Instruments and Securities

8.3.1 Concept and Classification

Capital market instruments represent ownership (equity) or credit (debt) interests in corporations or other financial entities. Unlike money market instruments, they have longer durations and are intended for long-term financing and risk allocation.[7] These instruments are considered securities because they are standardized, transferable, and enforceable claims regulated by public authorities. The legal form—whether certificate, book-entry, or dematerialized record—determines the method of transfer, ownership rights, and liability for loss or fraud.

8.3.2 Stock Certificates

8.3.2.1 Bearer Vs. Registered Share Certificates

A bearer share certificate confers ownership to the individual who physically possesses the certificate. Transfer of ownership is effected through delivery, without the need for registration.[8] Although bearer shares facilitate anonymity and liquidity, they present significant AML and transparency challenges. Consequently, nearly all major jurisdictions have abolished or restricted bearer shares, rendering conversion to registered-nominative form mandatory. In contrast, a registered share certificate documents ownership in a share register, and legal transfer requires both endorsement and registration. The transition from bearer shares to registered shares signifies a broader shift in corporate law from anonymous capital to traceable ownership.

[5] Emeziem (2025) 35.
[6] Austin (2015) 1–24; Cunha (2010) 677–691; Silvers (2020).
[7] Stosic-Mihajlovic (2016) 30–38.
[8] Constantin and Crisan (2019) 9–15.

8.3.2.2 Preference/Ordinary Shares

In corporate law, two fundamental forms of corporate ownership are represented by preference shares and ordinary shares. The legal distinctions between these share types provide investors with a trade-off between managerial control and security of return. Preferred shareholders typically forgo participation in management in exchange for reduced risk, whereas ordinary shareholders assume greater risk in return for the potential to benefit most from the company's ultimate success.[9]

	Preference shares	Ordinary shares
Yield priority	Priority ownership rights in dividends and liquidation balances	Residual ownership rights after all priority rights have been satisfied
Right to vote	Usually absent or limited	Grants full voting rights (active control over company management)

Legal frameworks typically require that privileges, or preferential rights, attached to shares are clearly and specifically articulated in the company's articles of association (AoA). The articles delineate the scope of these privileges, such as specifying a fixed dividend rate. The issuance of preferred shares establishes the concept of class rights within the company, which are safeguarded, particularly from unilateral alterations. For instance, Section 630 of the UK Companies Act 2006 mandates that any modification affecting the rights of share classes must undergo additional procedures, including obtaining the consent of the affected class or court approval.[10]

8.3.2.3 Paid-up and Partly Paid Shares

Shares, in relation to company capital contribution, are classified as either paid-up or partly paid. This distinction is significant for both the company's balance sheet capital strength and the legal obligations of investors. Paid-up shares are those for which shareholders have fully satisfied their capital commitments, thereby forming the company's existing, fully contributed capital. In contrast, partly paid shares indicate that shareholders have only partially met their capital contribution obligations. The unpaid portion of partly paid shares is considered a debt owed by the shareholder to the company and becomes payable upon demand by the Board of Directors (BoD).

Example

The 2023 revision of China's Company Law introduces more stringent capital contribution requirements for partially paid-up shares. The reform abolishes partially paid-up capital for publicly listed companies and imposes a mandatory five-year contribution period for unpaid shares in private companies. Because

[9] Ferran, Howell and Steffek (2023) 167–198; Raz (2018) 255.
[10] Cahn and Donald (2010) 259–272.

unpaid capital constitutes a future payment obligation upon which creditors may depend after company operations begin, these stricter rules are regarded as justified to safeguard creditor interests.[11] ◀

▶ **Important**
In the context of international banking regulations, the status of paid-in shares is crucial for maintaining the stability of financial institutions. According to the Basel regulations, fully paid-in shares constitute capital that directly and reliably reinforces a bank's capital base. Consequently, the Basel framework generally prohibits financial institutions from issuing partially paid-up shares to enhance their capital adequacy. This restriction is intended to mitigate risks and uncertainties within the banking system.[12]

▶ **Important**
securities regulators mandate clear disclosure of the payment status of shares. Such transparency is essential to facilitate the flow of information to investors and to enable accurate share valuation. When an investor acquires a partially paid share, they must be informed of any potential future payment obligations that may be imposed by the BoD.[13]

8.3.2.4 Premium and Non-Premium (at Par) Shares

In the issuance of capital shares, the situation of the issue price relative to the nominal value of the share divides the shares into two categories: Premium and Non-Premium (At Par). No-par value shares represent the nominal issue price. This means that the shares are issued at the nominal value specified in the articles of association. They are generally used to establish a company's initial capitalization. On the other hand, premium shares are those where the issue price differs from the share's par value. The issuance of premium shares indicates market confidence in the company and a surplus valuation of the company's net assets.[14]

The amount by which the issue price of shares exceeds their nominal value is known as the share premium, and it is recorded in a separate legal reserve account on the company's balance sheet. The primary legal rationale for maintaining the share premium as a distinct reserve is to uphold the principle of capital maintenance. Preserving this premium prevents concealed distributions that could diminish the company's equity, thereby protecting the interests of creditors.

---

[11] Li and Cai (2025) 923–946.
[12] Greenwood et al. (2017) 479–565.
[13] Li and Cai (2025) 931.
[14] See, Dudycz and Brycz (2021) 16.

According to legal regulations, the share premium may be used for issuing bonus shares or for repaying preliminary expenses.

8.3.3 Non-Voting Shares

Non-voting shares constitute a class of capital shares that do not grant holders the right to vote at company general meetings. These instruments allow companies to raise external capital without diluting existing control structures. Family-owned and state-controlled corporations frequently employ non-voting shares to maintain management control while obtaining additional financing. Nevertheless, the use of non-voting shares raises substantial corporate governance concerns, particularly in relation to minority shareholder protection and transparency. Shareholders without voting rights face an elevated risk of having their interests undermined, as they lack the ability to influence management decisions.[15]

In the US, non-voting shares and dual-class share structures are prevalent and largely unregulated, especially among technology and growth-oriented companies. Because corporate law is determined at the state level, with Delaware being particularly influential, companies possess significant flexibility to issue non-voting shares. Major technology firms such as Google (Alphabet), Meta (Facebook), and Snapchat have adopted these structures to go public while preserving founders' control.[16] Although regulators recognize that these arrangements allow founders and entrepreneurs to pursue long-term strategic objectives, market indices such as S&P Dow Jones exert indirect governance pressure by restricting or relaxing the inclusion of companies with such structures. This dynamic illustrates how market mechanisms, rather than formal legal restrictions, can promote governance standards.

Germany has historically enforced the 'one share, one vote' principle, largely prohibiting structures that permit non-voting shares or multiple voting rights. This approach was intended to provide robust protection for minority shareholders and to ensure proportionality between capital investment and control. New regulations now permit multiple-vote share structures in limited proportions and for a period of ten years, subject to possible extension. This reform represents a measured effort to facilitate capital increases without diluting control. Unlike the approach to non-voting shares, legislators have maintained minority protection by imposing strict limitations and sunset clauses.[17]

Company law under the UK Companies Act 2006 does not strictly prohibit the issuance of non-voting shares or the creation of different share classes, allowing flexibility through articles of association. However, companies seeking a listing on the London Stock Exchange's "Premium" segment must comply with stricter FCA

[15] Lund (2019) 687–745.
[16] Battocletti et al., (2023) 541–576.
[17] Mock (2025) 71–79.

requirements regarding the "one share, one vote" standard. These indirect restrictions on non-voting share issuance are designed to enhance international investor confidence and uphold market integrity. As a result, some companies may opt for alternative listing segments with more flexible rules. This framework demonstrates how stock exchange regulations, rather than statutory law, can align with investor expectations.[18]

8.3.4 Participating Shares/Dividend Right Certificates

Participating shares, also known as dividend right certificates, are financial instruments that entitle holders to a share of the company's profits without conferring ownership or voting rights. These instruments enable companies to distribute revenue to investors or employees while maintaining their existing capital structure.

> **Important** profit participation shares are legally classified as hybrid instruments, combining features of both debt and equity.

Given their complex legal structure, the issuance terms for these instruments must clearly define the profit participation formula, duration, redemption conditions, and liquidation priority to ensure transparency regarding investor rights.

Example

Several advanced legal systems have established specific regulations to address the uncertainty associated with hybrid financial instruments and to enhance investor protection. In Germany, profit participation shares, known as Genussrechte, are typically issued under contract law rather than company law. The primary challenge concerning these instruments is their classification as either debt or equity. German regulations set forth explicit criteria for this classification, which become especially significant during insolvency proceedings. Genussrechte are considered debt if they have priority over common shareholders in the liquidation balance; conversely, if they are subordinate to shareholders or participate in loss sharing, they are regarded as equity-like.[19] this distinction is crucial for both tax treatment and capital adequacy assessments.◄

---

[18] See, Reddy (2021) 515; Jin (2024) 124.

[19] AktG, § 221 paras. 3 and 4.

8.3.5 Debt Instruments

Debt instruments are financial assets that create creditor relationships, distinguishing them from instruments that grant ownership rights. These instruments document the debtor's obligation to repay principal and, in most cases, interest to creditors. Common examples include bonds, notes, commercial paper, and other securities that require repayment. For issuers, debt instruments facilitate borrowing, while for investors, they provide the right to receive predetermined future cash flows. Investors do not acquire ownership of the issuer's assets; instead, they hold the right to enforce repayment obligations.

8.3.5.1 Bonds

A bond is a negotiable debt security in which the issuer, or borrower, agrees to pay interest to the holder, or creditor, at specified intervals and to repay the principal at maturity. Bonds represent one of the most prevalent and standardized types of debt instruments. They can be classified based on the issuing entity, the interest payment mechanism, and structural features. For instance, bonds may be categorized as corporate bonds issued by companies, sovereign bonds issued by central governments, or municipal bonds issued by local governments. Bonds are also classified by interest rate structure, including fixed-rate bonds with unchanging interest rates, floating-rate bonds with rates that adjust according to market indicators, and discount bonds, which are sold below face value and repay principal plus interest at maturity.

> ▶ **Important**
> Convertible bonds, which are exempt from certain regulatory distinctions, provide bondholders with the right to convert their bonds into shares of the issuing company or other financial instruments under specific conditions.

During bond issuance, the legal relationship between the issuer and bondholders is governed by an intermediary institution that represents the interests of bondholders. The trustee or fiscal agent serves as this intermediary, safeguarding bondholder rights and ensuring the application of collective enforcement and resolution procedures in the event of issuer default. This structure offers investors protection against information asymmetry.

8.3.5.2 Securities

Securities is a broad term referring to financial instruments that possess monetary value and are transferable. While the legal definition varies across jurisdictions, securities generally encompass instruments that facilitate investment and capital transfer.[20]

---

[20] Dybinski and Oplustil (2024) 263–310.

The principal categories of instruments classified as securities include the following:

(i) Equity and Debt Instruments as Shares and bonds;
(ii) Investment certificates, including funds, real estate certificates, and other instruments intended for investment purposes; and
(iii) Derivative Instruments as Options, futures, and swaps.

The legal definition of securities determines the jurisdiction of the relevant regulatory authority and the applicability of investor protection mechanisms. In the European Union, the concept of securities is codified by the MiFID II Directive (2014/65/EU), which establishes a legal standard across member states by introducing comprehensive rules regarding trading, transparency, and market infrastructure.[21] In the United States, the classification of an instrument as a security is generally guided by the Howey Test under the Securities Act of 1933.[22] This test assesses whether an investment constitutes an investment contract by evaluating if funds are invested in a common enterprise with the expectation of profits derived from the efforts of others.

8.3.6 Profit and Loss Sharing Certificates

Profit and Loss Sharing Certificates (PLSCs) is a type of joint venture in which the entrepreneur and investor contribute to the operation, including both capital and expertise, and profits and losses are shared as complying with Islamic finance principles. These certificates grant investors the right to participate in both the profits and losses of a project or venture. The key distinguishing feature of PLSCs is that they do not involve interest payments, in accordance with Islamic law's prohibition on interest (riba). Thus, PLSCs do not include a predetermined and guaranteed return payment, which makes them compliant with the prohibition on riba. The return is based on the actual economic performance of the underlying asset or project.[23]

From a legal perspective, PLSCs exhibit a hybrid structure. While they resemble traditional equity in terms of their economic substance, they possess certain characteristics that differ from a typical stock structure. Similar to equity, investors participate in the project's ultimate success or failure to the extent of the capital they invest. Unlike shares, PLSCs are usually issued with a fixed maturity. At maturity, the certificates are either liquidated or extended.

---

[21] See, for a general discussion, Comana, Previtali and Bellardini (2019).
[22] Albert (2011) 5.
[23] Terebessy (2021) 41–43.

PLSCs are recognized as an alternative financing instrument under traditional capital market legislation in various jurisdictions where Islamic finance is prevalent, such as Malaysia and the UAE. In these countries, religious principles (Sharia rules) are intertwined with secular financial rules, enabling PLSCs to be used as a regulated instrument for both Islamic investors and traditional market players.[24]

8.3.7 Real Estate Certificates

Real estate certificates represent a specialized investment vehicle that facilitates the transformation of ownership or income rights in real estate projects into financial instruments through securitization. These certificates convert illiquid real estate assets into tradable securities and permit fractional investment. Consequently, the legal structure of real estate certificates exhibits a dual character, as they are grounded in both financial instruments and physical assets. As a result, in most jurisdictions, these securities are regulated under both capital markets law and real estate law.[25]

To securitize a real estate project, a SPV must first be established to issue the certificates. The real estate asset or its associated income rights are then transferred to the SPV or leased for an extended period. The SPV issues securities, known as real estate certificates, to investors based on the value of the real estate or its projected cash flows. Proper valuation is the most critical step in this process, as independent and reliable assessment of the underlying real estate is essential for transparency and informed investor decisions. Additionally, the issuance and trading of real estate certificates are secured through supervision and registration by the relevant Capital Markets Board or equivalent authority. This comprehensive legal oversight safeguards property rights and the integrity of physical assets.

8.3.8 Asset-Backed Securities

Securitisation enables banks and other financial institutions to convert illiquid assets on their balance sheets into securities and offer them to investors. This process is carried out through the capital market instruments of Asset-Backed Securities (ABS).[26]

> **Important**
> Securitisation is as a mechanism for risk transfer and liquidity provision by pooling illiquid assets (loans, receivables, mortgages etc.) and issuing securities based on this pool.

---

[24] See, in general, Lutsyshyn (2023).
[25] Tilquin (2017) 67.
[26] Riddiough (1997) 121–152; FSB (2024).

ABS are financial instruments based on cash flows derived from a pool of underlying assets that consists of homogenous assets, such as individual or commercial loans, promissory notes, auto loans, credit card receivables, or mortgage-backed securities (MBSs). The legal validity of the ABS structure relies on the legal certainty of transfering assets to the intermediary institution, namely SPV, which issues the securities in the securitisation process. This whole transaction is referred to as the true sale principle.[27]

> **Important**
> The true sale principle guarantees that the transferred assets are legally isolated from the originator's bankruptcy estate, thereby ensuring the originator's legal isolation. This isolation ensures that ABS investors' rights to the underlying assets are protected even in the event of the originator's bankruptcy, thereby securing the "bankruptcy remote" structure of the securities.[28]

The 2008 Global Financial Crisis exposed the moral hazard risks in securitization markets. In particular, originators securitizing low-quality assets, failing to exercise due diligence, and not retaining risks played a role in deepening the crisis. Significant legal reforms were implemented to reduce these risks and increase market security. For example, in the US, Section 941 of the Dodd-Frank Act introduced a risk retention rule requiring originators to retain a portion (e.g., 5%) of the assets they securitize. The EU Securitisation Regulation requires originators to retain a significant economic interest in the risk and imposes comprehensive due diligence obligations on investors. These regulations form the basic legal framework aimed at preventing moral hazard in securitization markets and ensuring that risks are priced correctly.[29]

8.3.9 Blanked Capital Market Instruments

Blanked instruments are incomplete certificates in which certain essential elements necessary for the validity of the security (e.g. the name of the holder, amount, or maturity date) are left blanked to be filled in afterwards. Under securities law, the blank sections must be filled in with the issuer's consent; otherwise, unauthorized filling constitutes forgery or fraud. The principle of bona fide acquisition, a fundamental principle of commercial law, protects bona fide purchasers who are unaware of irregularities, thereby ensuring the secure circulation of securities in

27 Agarwal et al. (2010) 101–115; Sabarwal (2006) 258–265.
28 Vygovskyy (2019) 1–11.
29 Cheng (2023); Senarath (2017) 153–166.

the market. This principle is widely accepted in commercial paper and securities law and is a mechanism that supports market confidence and speed.[30]

8.3.10 Corporate Warranties and Covered Warrants

Warrants are financial instruments that grant the holder the right to purchase shares of the issuing company at a fixed price for a specified period. Essentially, they are long-term call or put options. Corporate warrants are issued directly by the issuing company and typically represent the company's own equity shares.[31] These warrants are often issued alongside bonds to reduce issuance risk and increase investor appeal. This structure is called a bond-cum-warrant.[32] Covered Warrants, unlike corporate warrants, are issued by a financial institution (usually a bank or brokerage firm) and use third-party securities as the underlying assets. These warrants are fully collateralized (covered) to secure the exchange. The issuing institution holds the underlying assets or maintains the relevant derivative position to fulfil the warrant's obligations. Collateralized warrants are usually exchange-traded to provide high liquidity.

8.3.11 Lease Certificates (Sukuk)

Sukuk are Islamic capital market instruments that grant investors the right to represent undivided ownership of a leased asset designated as the underlying asset. Like PLSCs, Sukuk must comply with Sharia law's prohibition on interest (riba). Therefore, the returns provided to Sukuk holders consist of rental income from the underlying assets (returns from rentals) rather than interest on debt.[33]

Sukuk has a complex structure that combines commercial legal structures with religious compliance. Therefore, to ensure global acceptance, it is subject to specific regulatory frameworks: it is regulated in accordance with religious compliance frameworks established by institutions such as the AAOIFI Sharia Standards and IFSB Guidelines.[34] As a result, it is now recognized globally as a financing instrument, and sovereign Sukuk are traded on major exchanges such as the London Stock Exchange, Nasdaq Dubai, and Borsa Istanbul, demonstrating the integration of Islamic finance into international capital markets.[35]

---

30 Allcock (1982) 18–33; Neuenschwander (1951) 150–159.
31 Choudhry (2004) 221–225.
32 Theisen and Wenz (2003) 185; Roon and Veld (1998) 1481–1998; Bundgaard (2017) 382–383.
33 Noorali (2025).
34 Balibek (2017).
35 COMCEC Coordination Office (2018).

8.3.12 International Securities and Depositary Receipts

Depositary Receipts, including American Depositary Receipts and Global Depositary Receipts, are essential financial instruments that allow investors to hold shares of foreign companies in a domestic format. It basically serves as a legal mechanism for securitized global share ownership, as they are negotiable certificates issued by a depositary bank. These certificates represent shares of a foreign company as the underlying asset, with the underlying shares held in custody by the depositary bank responsible for the securitization process. This arrangement facilitates cross-border investment by addressing local share registration barriers that investors face when acquiring foreign shares directly.[36]

Depositary receipts exemplify the legal globalization of equity, as they are governed by the regulations of both the home and host jurisdictions. The issuing company must adhere to its home-country corporate law regarding the fundamental legal status and internal governance of its shares. To enable trading of depositary receipts in the host market, the company is also required to meet the host country's disclosure standards. For instance, in the US, American Depositary Receipts must be registered with the US Securities and Exchange Commission (SEC) before they can be publicly offered.[37] This hybrid structure constitutes a complex mechanism through which legal frameworks and capital interact to regulate international capital flows.

8.3.13 Collective Investment Schemes and Funds

8.3.13.1 Investment Funds

Investment funds are financial vehicles that aggregate capital from numerous investors to invest in securities and other assets, thereby creating diversified portfolios. These funds are managed under two primary legal structures. The first structure is a contractual arrangement, in which investors enter into a contractual relationship with the fund manager. The second structure is a trust arrangement, where assets are held and managed by an agent or trustee for the benefit of the investors.[38]

Investment funds operate under stringent regulations intended to safeguard investors. These regulations promote transparency and reliability. Funds are required to diversify their assets to mitigate exposure to any single asset or issuer,

---

36 Blessymol, Parvathy and Nazar (2023) 3029–3037.

37 Royston (1985) 87–106.

38 Morley (2014) 1228.

to disclose comprehensive and regular information regarding investment strategy, fees, risks, and performance, and to uphold a fiduciary duty, obligating fund managers to act in the best interests of investors.[39]

Example

Within the European Union, the undertakings for collective Investment in Transferable Securities (UCITS) directives have established uniform standards for funds targeting retail investors. Due to their liquidity, asset diversification, and regular disclosure requirements, UCITS funds are readily tradable across the EU and are considered highly reliable.[40] ◀

8.3.13.2 Hedge Funds

Hedge funds are alternative investment vehicles designed to achieve high returns by employing flexible and aggressive strategies that differ from traditional investment approaches. Common practices include the use of leverage, derivatives, and short selling to enhance portfolio returns. Compared to retail funds, hedge funds are generally subject to less stringent regulation, as they primarily serve qualified, risk-tolerant, and professional investors.[41]

After the 2008 Global Financial Crisis, the role of hedge funds in contributing to systemic risk was acknowledged, leading to increased regulatory oversight. In the European Union, the Alternative Investment Fund Managers Directive (AIFMD) introduced requirements for transparency, risk management, and reporting for managers operating or marketing funds within the EU. In the United States, the Dodd-Frank Act mandates that large hedge fund managers register with the SEC and provide enhanced disclosures. These regulatory measures seek to address the inherent risks of hedge funds and promote systemic stability.[42]

8.3.13.3 Pension Funds

Pension funds manage retirement assets in accordance with fiduciary principles, requiring fund managers to prioritize the interests of participants. Regulatory frameworks emphasize prudence, diversification, and solvency, establishing a foundation for funds to meet long-term obligations.[43] The OECD Core Principles of Private Pension Regulation serve as global benchmarks in this context.

---

[39] ibid.

[40] Alshaleel (2016) 14–22.

[41] See, Stowell (2010).

[42] Kaal (2015) 163–193; Awrey (2011) 119–128; Schwarcz and Zaring (2016) 1813–1881.

[43] Johnson and Graaf (2009) 44–51.

8.4 Microfinance and Microcredits

8.4.1 The Legal Concept of Microfinance

Microfinance refers to the provision of diverse financial services, including credit, savings, insurance, and payment systems, to individuals or micro-enterprises excluded from the formal banking sector. Although it originated as a development initiative, microfinance has evolved into a well-regulated domain within financial law.[44] The core rationale for microfinance is financial inclusion, a principle now acknowledged by international organizations such as the World Bank, the IMF, and the United Nations as essential to economic justice and sustainable development. Hence, microfinance lies at the intersection of banking regulation, consumer protection, and social policy. However, the implementation of microfinance gives rise to several fundamental legal and ethical questions.[45] such as:

(i) Can profit objectives be pursued concurrently with the advancement of social justice?
(ii) In what ways can regulators balance prudential soundness with the need to expand access to finance?
(iii) What governance standards are appropriate for application to Microfinance Institutions (MFIs)?

A primary legal challenge in microfinance is achieving an ethical balance between profitability and social justice. Microfinance institutions (MFIs) must maintain sustainability without contributing to financial exclusion through excessive borrowing or high interest rates. Regulators should mitigate systemic risk by enforcing prudential soundness requirements, such as capital adequacy, while also safeguarding access to finance by avoiding regulations that could exclude the intended beneficiaries.[46] Governance standards for MFIs should reflect their hybrid structure and incorporate transparent, accountable rules that monitor both financial performance and the achievement of social objectives.

► **Important**
Most jurisdictions regulate microfinance institutions through specialized licensing regimes or tiered supervisory frameworks that acknowledge their hybrid nature. This hybrid character arises because private initiatives are designed to deliver public goods.

[44] Hunt (2015); Meki and Quinn (2024) 1–7.
[45] Milana and Ashta (2020) 257–266.
[46] ibid.

8.4.2 Microcredit: Contractual and Regulatory Dimensions

Microcredit refers to the provision of small loans to low-income borrowers. This system employs simplified procedures and alternative collateral mechanisms, such as group guarantees, in contrast to traditional banking. In this model, borrowers collectively assume responsibility for each other's debts, which serves to manage credit risk and promote repayment.[47]

Microcredit agreements retain the essential elements of legal lending transactions, including consent, consideration, and repayment obligations. However, they differ from traditional loans in risk management and enforcement. Rather than relying solely on conventional interest, microcredit may implement interest caps or profit-sharing arrangements to promote social justice. In certain jurisdictions, microcredit may not be governed by conventional banking law. Nevertheless, it is not entirely unregulated, as microcredit is generally subject to consumer lending statutes and usury regulations. A primary challenge is to prevent social lending from evolving into predatory micro-debt, as observed in unregulated markets. Regulators must therefore balance the promotion of access to credit with the protection of borrowers.

8.4.3 Institutional Models of Microfinance

Microfinance services are generally delivered through three primary institutional models. The first model comprises non-profit organisations (NGOs) supported by donors, which primarily focus on development and social objectives. The second model involves microfinance banks, which are licensed institutions subject to comprehensive banking supervision and are capable of conducting more complex financial transactions. The third model includes cooperative and community-based schemes, which are mutual organizations owned by their members. Regulatory frameworks typically employ a tiered approach, adjusting requirements based on institutional complexity. For instance, capital adequacy is required for microfinance banks, simplified reporting may suffice for NGOs, and prudent oversight is mandated for all deposit-taking institutions. The overarching objective of this phased regulatory approach is to achieve functional equivalence among financial service providers, thereby ensuring minimum standards for service integrity and consumer protection.[48]

[47] See, European Microfinance Network (2024); European Commission (2007).

[48] D'Espallier et al. (2017) 19–33; Uddin et al. (2020) 95–118.

8.4.4 Insurance in Microfinance

Microinsurance functions as a significant risk mitigation tool that complements microcredit by providing low-premium, low-coverage insurance products specifically designed for low-income populations. The legal framework of microinsurance is shaped by the necessity to reduce the complexity inherent in the insurance sector. This is achieved through the use of simplified contracts, which are often arranged on a group basis. Additionally, insurers are subject to proportional disclosure obligations, reflecting the nature of these policies. In practice, partnerships between insurance companies and MFIs are prevalent. Regulatory organizations, including the International Association of Insurance Supervisors (IAIS) and the WB, advocate for a proportionate regulation approach to microinsurance. This strategy seeks to balance effective supervision with the need to maintain accessibility. Consumer protection remains central within this regulatory framework, necessitating transparent disclosure and equitable claims processes.[49]

8.4.5 Crowdfunding: An Innovation in Capital Markets

Crowdfunding serves as an intermediary between microfinance and traditional capital markets by allowing the public to finance ventures via internet-based platforms. This process establishes a legal tripartite relationship among the Investor (funder), the Project Owner (beneficiary), and the Platform (intermediary). Crowdfunding structures include donative funding, which encourages donations without expectation of return, and reward-based funding, which offers non-monetary benefits. Financial models encompass lending-based (peer-to-peer) funding and equity-based funding, the latter involving the issuance of securities.[50] Equity-based crowdfunding is subject to securities regulations and requires prospectus exemption frameworks (such as the EU Crowdfunding Regulation 2020/1503), platform licensing, conduct rules, and investor protection mechanisms including investment limits and risk warnings.[51] Although crowdfunding democratizes access to capital, it also introduces risks such as fraud, misrepresentation, and data misuse, which necessitate robust regulatory oversight.

8.4.6 Financial Conglomerates

Financial conglomerates are corporate groups providing diversified financial services, including banking, insurance, securities and investment activities, under common control. This broad range of activities makes them effective in many

[49] Biener, Eling and Schmit (2014) 21–40; Balkenhol and Churchill (2002) 90–93.
[50] See, Cattelan and Neumann (2022) 7–53.
[51] Ortolani and Louisse (2021) 3–4; Sasso (2023) 137–147.

areas of the financial system at the same time and distinguishes them from other corporate structures. It is worth noting that conglomerates epitomize institutional integration of finance and blur the conventional boundaries between banking and capital markets. They operate across many sectors and jurisdictions, raising consolidated supervision challenges. The most common regulation established to effectively supervise conglomerates due to their complex structures is the EU Financial Conglomerates Directive[52] and Basel/IAIS/IOSCO Joint Forum Principles, which require group-wide capital adequacy, risk concentration and intra-group exposure limits and cross-sector supervisory coordination. This complexity also increases systemic risk, making corporate governance and disclosure obligations central to their legal regulation. Therefore, strengthening both the internal governance mechanisms and external transparency obligations of such groups becomes critical for maintaining financial stability.

8.4.7 Informal Value Transfer Systems

Informal money transfer systems, including methods such as Hawala and Fei-Ch'ien, facilitate cross-border fund transfers outside formal banking channels. These mechanisms depend on trust-based networks among intermediary institutions, known as brokers, and utilize ledger balancing instead of telegraphic transfers. While these systems fulfil significant social roles, especially for migrant workers and unbanked populations, they also present substantial legal and regulatory challenges. Operating outside official channels, they raise concerns regarding AML and CTF due to limited traceability and oversight of funds.[53] Regulatory authorities typically employ a dual strategy to address the risks associated with these systems. Money transfer providers are either required to register and operate under supervision, or unlicensed operators transferring illicit funds face criminal penalties.

> **Important**
> FATF recommendation 14 (financial action task force) establishes that all money or value transfer services, regardless of whether they are formal or informal, must adhere to identical regulatory requirements.

8.4.7.1 Hawala

Hawala is a method used to transfer money obtained through illegal channels, due to its advantages such as low cost, fast processing, reliability, lack of bureaucracy, and the inability to trace the money even during detailed investigations.[54]

[52] Council Directive 2002/87, Financial Conglomerates Directive, 2002 O.J. (L 35).
[53] Shah (2007) 193–218.
[54] Schaeffer (2008) 95–117.

The Hawala system begins when a person who wants to transfer money from their country of origin to a foreign country (the destination country) applies to a Hawala broker to arrange the transfer. Hawala Agent 1 contacts another Hawala Agent 2 in the target region by phone, fax, or email, providing the amount to be transferred and the transfer code. The final recipient then contacts Hawala Agent 2, provides the transfer code, and receives the money. This process takes only a few hours (or a few days in the case of very distant regions), and Hawaladars receive a small commission ranging from 2 to 5 percent of the transferred amount. Once a transfer is complete, all traces of the transaction are erased. Unpaid debts between Hawaladar 1 and 2 are settled through reverse transfers, parallel goods trading, or cash via couriers.[55] Thus, in Hawala, money is not transferred physically or electronically between different geographical locations. Instead, a series of exchange transactions takes place. Any pair of Hawaladars must periodically cancel their mutual financial obligations.[56]

Hawala networks historically facilitated secure money transfers for merchants along the Silk Road in Asia. The contemporary evolution of Hawala is associated with the 1947 partition of India and Pakistan, when currency controls rendered cross-border money transfers illegal and Hawala emerged as an alternative mechanism.[57] Today, Hawala remains prevalent among migrant worker communities in Europe, North America, and the Gulf region, who use it to remit funds to families in South Asia, Africa, and Latin America.[58]

Example

The United Kingdom utilizes a simplified registration regime, guided by the "light touch" principle, to discourage the migration of the sector into the informal economy. In recent years, compliance requirements have been strengthened to align with European Union directives. Conversely, Germany mandates that money transfer operators comply with the same rigorous licensing standards as banks, including a requirement for managers to have at least three years of professional experience and to submit a comprehensive business plan. Despite these regulatory differences, the overarching trend across Europe is toward simplified registration procedures, particularly following the implementation of the EU payment services directive (PSD) in 2010, to facilitate the integration of hawala businesses into the formal economy.[59] ◀

---

55 Lambert (2002) 358; Vaccani (2010) 5.

56 Lambert (2002) 358–369; Razavy (2005) 277–299; Van de Bunt (2008) 691–702.

57 De Goede (2003) 513.

58 El Qorchi (2002) 31–33; Wang (2011) 210–224.

59 Wang (2011) 210–224.

8.4.7.2 Fei-Ch'ien

Fei Ch'ien, meaning 'flying money' in Chinese, refers to a historical money transfer system primarily utilized for trade.[60] These networks generally operated through gold shops, trading companies, and currency exchange offices, employing minimal record-keeping and encrypted communication methods. Over time, Fei Ch'ien evolved to address the financial needs of migrating Chinese workers remitting funds to their families. Trust is a fundamental aspect of Fei Ch'ien. The system is embedded within guanxi, a comprehensive social framework governing relationships and behaviour, which ensures both the secrecy and integrity of transactions. Historically, these networks relied on rice merchants and, subsequently, shipping routes to transport remittances. In contemporary practice, a physical token such as an authenticated chop or a coded phone call or email serves to demonstrate ownership and legitimacy, functioning similarly to a receipt.[61]

Currently, Fei Ch'ien enables individuals and businesses to bypass the Chinese central government's capital controls, which restrict citizens to withdrawing approximately $50,000 annually. Illicit financial outflows from China were estimated at $1.08 trillion between 2002 and 2011. This system facilitates capital flight, tax evasion, and the laundering of criminal proceeds for organizations such as Chinese triads. The US Department of State identifies the use of indigenous Chinese underground financial systems for illicit outbound transfers and capital flight as a significant concern.[62]

> **Important**
> Chits and chops serve as essential tools for establishing trust within the Fei Ch'ien system. These physical, low-technology instruments preserve both anonymity and reliability in informal value transfers. A chit is a coded message, note, or internal voucher that records the transaction between the sender and the broker. Such notes typically employ specific codes or agreed-upon passwords, functioning as receipts or letters of transfer without generating a paper trail detectable by conventional financial authorities. The chop is an authenticated seal or stamp, commonly used by the Fei Ch'ien broker to validate the chit or the entire transaction. The application of a chop authenticates the transfer note, providing security and trust grounded in the broker's personal reputation and guanxi, or relationship network. Collectively, chits and chops enable rapid and secure cross-border value transfers while maintaining customer anonymity, which contributes to the system's frequent exploitation for ML and capital flight.[63]

[60] Donner et al. (2008) 318–322.
[61] Cassara (2015) 73–83.
[62] ibid.
[63] Buencamino and Gorbunov (2002).

8.5 Common Disputes on Capital Markets

8.5.1 Overview

Disputes in capital markets often arise from information asymmetry, intermediary misconduct, or systemic errors. The occurrence of such disputes reflects not only individual mistakes but also highlights structural weaknesses within the financial system. In contrast to straightforward contract disputes, these cases involve regulated relationships subject to public law obligations, including requirements for transparency and integrity.

8.5.2 Disputes Arising from Unauthorised Transactions

8.5.2.1 Nature of the Problem

An unauthorised transaction arises when a broker executes a trade in a client's investment account without explicit authorization. Such trades circumvent the client's decision-making autonomy and undermine the foundational agent-principal relationship. Consequently, these actions constitute a breach of the mandate contract governing broker-client relations, resulting in both contractual violations and potential regulatory offenses. In many jurisdictions, these transactions also prompt supervisory scrutiny, as they threaten market integrity and erode investor confidence.

8.5.2.2 Legal Framework

Securities law establishes that brokers possess a fiduciary duty to act strictly within the parameters of the client's instructions, as their authority derives solely from the investor's consent and expectations. Unauthorised transactions are therefore voidable, and any resulting client losses may give rise to claims for damages. Beyond private remedies, these violations also have a public dimension, as market regulators may impose administrative penalties to uphold the integrity of trading systems.

This dual structure, combining private liability with public oversight, is present in most legal systems, though it appears in various doctrinal forms. In civil law jurisdictions, such conduct results in agency liability, as exemplified by Article 506 of the Turkish Code of Obligations and §665 BGB in Germany, emphasizing breaches of the representative's mandate. In common law systems, these actions are classified as unauthorized dealings, leading to restitutionary or tort claims. Despite doctrinal differences, the underlying principle remains consistent: unauthorized trading is fundamentally incompatible with the normative and axiological foundations of capital market intermediation.

8.5.2.3 Evidentiary Issues

E-trading gives rise to new evidentiary problems related to digital authentication of orders, record-keeping responsibilities of the intermediary, and apportionment of the burden of proof in cases of dispute.[64] Since electronic systems displace human, face-to-face instructions, the law needs to decide how to authenticate intent and authority in a dematerialized world. Accordingly, regulators require traceable audit trails and retain appropriate communications electronically as building blocks for accountability. Their function is not only to enable reconstruction after the trade has taken place but also to act as a preventive device because the risk of detection of unauthorized dealings is much higher. In cases of doubt, the rule of interpretatio pro investitore often applies-an interpretation that favors the investor-which reflects the protective ethos underlying securities regulation today. This presumption respects the imbalance between professional intermediaries and retail clients and prevents technological complexity from undermining substantive investor protection.

8.5.3 Problems Caused by Investment Recommendations ("Bum Steer")

8.5.3.1 The Legal Nature of Investment Advice

Investment advisory services elevate a commercial relationship to a fiduciary one, as clients depend not only on transaction execution but also on the advisor's professional judgment. Upon establishing this relationship, the advisor assumes obligations of suitability, competence, and good faith, reflecting the expectation that advice should advance the client's financial interests rather than the advisor's. Deceptive or inadequate advice constitutes both a breach of contract and a violation of legal regulations, as these actions undermine the trust foundational to fiduciary norms. In European Union law, MiFID II (Articles 24 and 25) codifies the fiduciary principle through comprehensive conduct rules, including suitability assessment, conflict of interest disclosure, and product governance.[65] Comparable standards are imposed in the United States by the Investment Advisors Act of 1940 and the FINRA Rules under the "best interest" doctrine. Although regulatory frameworks differ, both regimes reach the same normative conclusion: investment advice must be competent, honest, and tailored to the client's needs.[66]

8.5.3.2 Elements of Liability

Claims for damages suffered by investors typically require four interrelated fundamental elements. The first is the duty of care, which arises from an advisory relationship and establishes the required standard of care. The second element, breach, involves the provision of misleading information, incomplete statements, or inappropriate advice that violates this standard. Establishing liability also requires proof of causation, demonstrating that the investor relied on the advice

---

64 UNCITRAL (2009); Ruslijanto (2021) 664–681.

65 Rinaldo (2023) 309–340; Mezzanotte (2023) 843–897; Wagner (2024).

66 Steinberg et al. (2020); Dombalagian (2011) 1265; Bunting (2011) 993–1074; Haslem (2010) 23–30.

and that this reliance directly resulted in a loss. The final element, damage, requires evidence of quantifiable financial harm, thereby completing the compensation framework. These elements are cumulative; the claimant must demonstrate not only the existence of a fault but also that this fault materially influenced the investment decision and resulted in a measurable loss. Judicial bodies assess the investor's level of knowledge and experience, often referred to as sophistication, during this process. Professional investors are expected to exercise independent judgment due to their expertise and access to information, whereas individual (retail) investors receive greater protection because of their relative vulnerability. This distinction ensures that legal liability appropriately reflects both the advisor's conduct and the investor's reasonable expectations.[67]

8.5.3.3 Misrepresentation and Omission

In investment advisory cases, legal liability now includes both affirmative misstatements and the omission of material information that may influence investment decisions. The failure to disclose conflicts of interest, such as commissions received by advisors or financial incentives tied to product sales, constitutes a significant breach of fiduciary duty. Regulatory authorities, including the SEC in the US and the FCA in the UK, regularly sanction professional misconduct such as churning, recommending high-risk products inconsistent with a client's risk profile, or providing advice that favors the advisor's interests over those of the client.[68] When investors seek financial compensation through legal proceedings, the assessment of damages is based on established legal doctrines. The tort of negligent misstatement is central in Anglo-Saxon (common law) jurisdictions, while the principle of *culpa in contrahendo* (pre-contractual fault) is foundational in Continental European (civil law) systems.

8.5.4 Remedies and Dispute Resolution Mechanisms

The enforcement of legal standards in capital markets depends on a comprehensive framework of redress intended to restore market integrity and compensate affected parties. Given that financial disputes frequently involve complex instruments and broader systemic consequences, the law offers a range of mechanisms, including private litigation, regulatory intervention, and specialized alternative dispute resolution. The following sections examine how these mechanisms, such as individual civil remedies, regulatory sanctions, expert-led arbitration, and ombudsman schemes, operate to address breaches of duty while preserving the efficiency and reputation of the financial system.

[67] See, Kleineman (2001) 393–419; Laby (2020) 954–1022; Sanders (2014) 535–579.

[68] See, Becker (2024) 791.

8.5.4.1 Civil Remedies

Investors can seek private remedies including but not limited to rescission of the transaction, restitution (return of consideration) and payment of compensatory damages, interest and costs.[69] Courts usually expect the investor to mitigate its loss i.e. act reasonably and take appropriate steps to reduce its loss after becoming aware of the breach. If the breach was fraudulent or by gross negligence, however, full restitution may be awarded.

8.5.4.2 Regulatory Enforcement

Regulators can use their coercive powers to impose administrative sanctions and remove market licences, disgorgement orders and public shaming through censure and bans from market participation.[70]

8.5.4.3 Arbitration and Ombudsman Schemes

Capital market contracts typically contain arbitration clauses or provide for referral of disputes to specialist financial ombudsman schemes. This is because their resolution often requires knowledge and experience of financial markets and instruments. Furthermore, confidentiality is seen as important for market reputation and preserving commercial relationships by providing a quicker, less costly alternative to ordinary courts. On an international level, it makes even more sense for the ICSID and UNCITRAL frameworks to provide a mechanism to bring investment treaty arbitration claims between states and foreign investors. The private law arena is no different, with specialist investor redress schemes such as FINRA Arbitration in the US and the Financial Ombudsman Service in the UK to help investors and intermediaries.[71]

8.5.5 Broader Implications: Law, Trust, and Market Ethics

Capital market conflicts extend beyond material damages between individuals. They represent complex processes that challenge the ethical foundations of finance and emerge from the intrinsic dynamics of modern financial systems. In this context, law serves not only as a mechanism for remedy but as the primary factor in establishing and maintaining market confidence. A robust legal framework that both constrains and legitimizes financial behaviour is essential for establishing a sustainable environment of market trust. Investor confidence, which is central to capital formation, depends on the consistent application of the rule of law. The ongoing examination of legal norms through disputes illustrates that market obligations and expectations have tangible consequences. Consequently, dispute resolution processes are crucial for upholding the market's moral economy.

---

[69] Swenson (1969) 337; Maitra (2024) 64–79; Feldman (2013) 399.
[70] See, IOSCO (2013).
[71] Hober (2015) 58.

8.6 Concluding Remarks

The global capital market with its economic functionalities is a legal creature. This legal aspect comes to the fore in all constitutive elements of the system, as, every share, bond, warrant and fund is a bundle of contracting, regulative and moral relationships. The pressure between those relationships will lead to the kind of frictions — disputes that show a legal system's stress points, where its forms must evolve to keep pace with financial innovation. Further the current struggles also inform the search for an organic future, and here is where we find flesh on the bones that point toward the salvation of capital market law, being one in which there will be integration but not homogenization: uniform standards with diverse appeal. In this, the law faces a new challenge and the same old duty — to regulate capital, not the other way around. As technological innovation is further integrated into financial markets, the law still must ensure capital serves society.

Chapter Summary

Regulating international capital markets takes place in a setting of legal pluralism, where national laws overlap with global standards set by bodies such as IOSCO and with regional efforts such as the EU's CMU. In this setting, legal issues arise when aligning disclosure rules under IFRS and GAAP, and when managing cross-border listings and enforcement. Securities are generally grouped by their legal form into equity interests and debt interests. In equity markets, many jurisdictions are moving toward registered shares to improve transparency and meet AML requirements, which is gradually replacing anonymous bearer shares. Specialized instruments such as preferred stock, which gives priority to dividends while limiting voting rights, and participating shares, which provide a share of profits without full ownership, show how corporate structures can be set up with a wider range of rights and obligations.

Debt instruments such as corporate and government bonds set up a lender–borrower relationship. Investor protection is usually provided through trust deeds and restrictive covenants. As financial engineering has expanded, it has led to structured products such as asset-backed securities. In these transactions, the underlying assets are transferred through a true sale to a SPV so they are separated from the originator and are less subject to the originator's bankruptcy risk. This differs from Islamic finance tools such as Sukuk, which give investors shared ownership in leased assets and pay returns based on rental income rather than interest. Collective investment schemes such as ETFs and hedge funds pool investors' money to spread risk through diversification. Hedge funds often face stricter regulatory scrutiny because they may rely on leverage and higher-return strategies. New microfinance and crowdfunding platforms need clear licensing rules and well-defined exemptions so they can support social goals while still meeting basic prudential standards.

Disputes in these markets often arise when parties do not have the same information and when intermediaries engage in misconduct. Unauthorized transactions can make an agency liable because they break fiduciary duties and the terms of the mandate agreement. Misleading investment recommendations, often called bum steers, also breach a broker's duties, including suitability and the obligation to act in good faith. Since these disputes are often technical, they are usually handled through arbitration or an ombudsman scheme, since both can bring subject-specific expertise and a process that fits the needs of international commercial settings.

Revision Questions

1. Describe how Bearer Shares differ from Registered Shares in respect to transferability of ownership and anonymity. Describe why full Bearer Shares have been eliminated or severely limited by big international countries.
2. Define Asset-Backed Securities (ABS) by explaining the true sale principle and its implications in securitization, and assess the extent to which the true sale principle protects investors of Asset-Backed Securities from the risk of bankruptcy of the loan originator institution.
3. Discuss the meaning of legal pluralism in the global stock market. Identify two specific international efforts (for example, IOSCO or EU) that extend the drive for harmonization of regulations in order to eliminate conflict in cross-market transactions.
4. Compare the legal features of Participating Shares (Dividend Right Certificates) and Lease Certificates (Sukuk). Discuss the alignment of the structure of Sukuk in relation to the prohibition of Riba in Sharia.
5. Describe two major fiduciary responsibilities that the broker breaches under Unauthorised Transactions (unauthorized trading). Analyse the two-component legal regime that is applied in dealing with the problem.
6. Describe the legal obligation of Suitability as it applies to investment advice. Summarize the typical four links the investor must make in order to place the burden of liability for deceptive or unsuitable advice upon an advisor for a bum steer.
7. Discuss the reasoning underlying Microfinance (financial inclusion). The regulatory challenge faced by regulators to achieve a "proportionate regulation" approach regarding Microfinance Institutions (MFIs).◀

References

Agarwal S, Barrett J, Cun C, Nardi M (2010) The asset-backed securities markets, the crisis, and TALF. Federal Reserve Bank of Chicago 4:101–115

Albert M (2011) The Howey test turns 64: are the courts grading this test on a curve? William & Mary Business Law Review 2(1):1–50

Allcock B (1982) Documents signed in blank. The Modern Law Review 45(1):18–33

Alshaleel M (2016) Undertakings for the collective Investment in Transferable Securities Directive V: increased protection for investors. European Company Law 13(1):14–22

Austin J (2015) The power and influence of IOSCO in formulating and enforcing securities regulations. Asper Review 15:1–24

Awrey D (2011) The limits of EU hedge fund regulation. Law Financ Mark Rev 5:119–128

Balibek E (2017) Establishing a legal framework for sovereign sukuk issuance: a public debt management perspective. MFM Global Practice Discussion Paper No. 18

Balkenhol B, Churchill C (2002) From microfinance to micro health insurance. In: Preker A (ed) David Dror. Social Reinsurance, A New Approach to Sustainable Community Health Financing. World Bank, pp 75–102

Battocletti V, Enriques L, Romano A (2023) Dual-class shares in the age of common ownership. The Journal of Corporation Law 48(3):541–576

Becker Z (2024) With whom is your issue? Use of investor sophistication in defining the scope of seller liability under § 12(a)(2) of the securities act of 1933. Columbia Business Law Review 2:791–823

Biener C, Eling M, Schmit J (2014) Regulation in microinsurance markets: principles, practice, and directions for future development. World Dev 58(c):21-40

Blessymol M, Parvathy B, Nazar A (2023) Understanding global depository receipt (GDR) and American depository receipt (ADR). International Journal of Law, Management and Humanities 6(6):3029–3037

Buencamino L, Gorbunov S (2002) Informal money transfer systems: opportunities and challenges for development finance. United Nations

Bundgaard J (2017) Hybrid financial instruments in international tax law. Walters Kluwer

Bunting W (2011) The trouble with investment banking: cluelessness, not greed. San Diego Law Review 48:993–1074

Cahn A, Donald D (2010) Comparative company law: text and cases on the Laws governing corporations in Germany, the UK and the USA. Cambridge University Press

Cassara J (2015) Trade-based money laundering: the next frontier in international money laundering enforcement. Wiley

Cattelan S, Neumann T (2022) Status artis: research in the law and practice of crowdfunding. Nordic Journal of Commercial Law 12(2):7–53

Chan J (2021) The relevance of public law to private ordering: the consequences of uncertain judicial review for stock exchange self-regulation. J Corp Law Stud 21:219–251

Cheng Y (2023) Mandatory retention rules and Bank risk. Bank of Canada staff working paper 2023-3

Choudhry M (2004) Corporate bonds and structured financial products. Butterworth-Heinemann

Coffee J (2002) Racing towards the top?: the impact of cross-listing and stock market competition on international corporate governance. Columbia Law Rev 102:1770–1775

Comana M, Previtali D, Bellardini L (2019) The MiFID II framework: how the new standards are reshaping the investment industry. Springer

COMCEC Coordination Office (2018) The Role of Sukuk in Islamic Capital Markets. https://www.sbb.gov.tr/wp-content/uploads/2018/11/The_Role_of_Sukuk_in_Islamic_Capital_Markets.pdf 20–21. Accessed 30 Jan 2026

Constantin D, Crisan E (2019) Special purpose entities and companies with bearer shares—a comparison. Managerial Challenges of the Contemporary Society 13(1):9–15

Cunha R (2010) The IOSCO multilateral memorandum of understanding (MMoU): an international benchmark for securities enforcement. Uniform Law Review 15(3–4):677–691
D'Espallier B, Goedecke J, Hudon M, Mersland R (2017) From NGOs to banks: does institutional transformation Alter the business model of microfinance institutions? World Dev 89:19–33
David C, Michielse G, Theisen M, Wenz M, Tiley J (2003) The tax treatment of financial instruments. Kluwer Law International
De Goede M (2003) Hawala discourses and the war on terrorist finance. Environ Plann D: Soc Space 21:513–532
Dombalagian O (2011) Investment recommendations and the essence of duty. American University Law Review 60(5):1265–1337
Donner J, Tellez C (2008) Mobile banking and economic development: linking adoption, impact, and use. Asian J Commun 18(4):318–322
Dudycz T, Brycz B (2021) Why the par value of share matters to investors. International Journal of Financial Studies 9(1):16
Dybinski J, Oplustil K (2024) Defining 'securities' in the European capital markets code. In: Veil R (ed) Regulating EU capital markets union: volume I: fundamentals of a European code. Oxford University Press, pp 263–310
El Qorchi M (2002) Hawala Finanzas Desarrollo 39:31–33
Emeziem C (2025) Soft international economic law: a new sovereign? University of Bologna Law Review 10(1):35–92
European Commission (2007) The Regulation of Microcredit in Europe. https://eur-lex.europa.eu/legal-content/EN/TXT/HTML/?uri=CELEX:52007DC0708. Accessed 31 Jan 2026
Feldman S (2013) Rescission, restitution, and the principle of fair redress: a response to professors brooks and Stremitzer. Valparaiso University Law Review 47(2):399–477
Ferran E, Howell E, Steffek F (2023) Principles of corporate finance law. Oxford University Press
FSB (2024) Evaluation of the Effects of the G20 Financial Regulatory Reforms on Securitisation. https://www.fsb.org/uploads/P020724.pdf. Accessed 18 December 2025
Greenwood R, Stein J, Hanson S, Sundream A (2017) Strengthening and streamlining Bank capital regulation. Brookings papers on economic activity 479-565
Haslem J (2010) The new reality of financial advisors and investors. J Invest 19(4):23–30
Hober K (2015) Investment treaty arbitration and its future—if any. Yearbook on Arbitration and Mediation 7:58–65
Hunt K (2015) The law and economics of microfinance. Journal of Law and Commerce 33(1):1–78
IOSCO (2013) Investigating and Prosecuting Market Manipulation. https://www.iosco.org/library/pubdocs/pdf/ioscopd103.pdf. Accessed 31 Jan 2026
Jin D (2024) Shattering the fetter of Main markets on the London stock exchange: is it a benign start for the dual-class share structure in the UK? Business Law Review 45(5):124
Johnson K, Graaf F (2009) Modernizing pension fund legal standards for the twenty-first century. Rotman International Journal of Pension Management 2(1):44–51
Kaal W (2015) The systematic risk of private funds after the Dodd-frank act. Michigan Business and Entrepreneurial Law Review 4(2):163–193
Kahan M (1997) Some problems with stock exchange-based securities regulation. Va Law Rev 83(7):1509–1519
Kleineman J (2001) Adviser's liability in connection with duty to inform—a problem inventory. Stockholm Institute for Scandianvian Law 41:393–419
Laby A (2020) Advisors as fiduciaries. Florida Law Review 72(5):954–1022
Lambert L (2002) Asian underground banking scheme: a field note. J Contemp Crim Justice 18:358–369
Li F, Cai Q (2025) An examination of partly-paid shares in China's new company law and lessons for comparative company law. European Business Law Review 36(6):923–946
Lund D (2019) Nonvoting shares and efficient corporate governance. Stanford Law Rev 71:687–745
Lutsyshyn Z (2023) Islamic finance in the reconfiguration of the global financial system: a structural analysis and potential implication. Bielsko-Biala

Maitra C (2024) Restitution as remedy in disputes between investor and state. Utrecht Law Review 20(1):64–79
Meki M, Quinn S (2024) Microfinance: an overview. Oxf Rev Econ Policy 40:1–7
Mezzanotte F (2023) EU sustainable finance: complex rules and compliance problems. Review of Banking and Financial Law 42:843–897
Milana C, Ashta A (2020) Microfinance and financial inclusion: challenges and opportunities. Strateg Chang 29(3):257–266
Mock S (2025) Multiple voting shares in Germany. European Company Law 22(3):71–79
Moloney N (2012) The legacy effects of the financial crisis on regulatory design in the EU. In: Ferran E, Moloney N, Hill J, Coffee J (eds) The regulatory aftermath of the global financial crisis. Cambridge University Press, pp 111–202
Morley J (2014) The separation of funds and managers: a theory of investment fund structure and regulation. Yale Law J 123:1228–1287
European Microfinance Network (2024.) Microcredit Regulation in Europe: An Overview https://www.european-microfinance.org/wp-content/uploads/2025/04/mainReport_NEW_2024_FINAL-1.pdf. Accessed 31 Jan 2026
Neuenschwander G (1951) Negotiable instruments incomplete when delivered. Case West Reserv Law Rev 3(2):150–159
Noorali S (2025) An introduction to sukuk: the Islamic finance debt instrument that has transcended global capital markets. Columbia. Business Law Review. https://journals.library.columbia.edu/index.php/CBLR/announcement/view/767. Accessed 31 Jan 2026
Ortolani P, Louisse M (2021) Introduction: keep calm and continue crowdfunding. In: Ortolani P, Louisse M (eds) The EU crowdfunding regulation. Oxford University Press, pp 3–24
Pistor K (2013a) A legal theory of finance. J Comp Econ 41(2):315–330
Raz A (2018) Share law: toward a new understanding of corporate law. University of Pennsylvania Journal of International Law 40(1):255–321
Razavy M (2005) Hawala: an underground haven for terrorists or social phenomenon? Crime Law Soc Chang 44:277–299
Reddy B (2021) Up the Hill and down again: constraining dual-class shares. Cambridge Law Journal 80(3):515–551
Riddiough T (1997) Optimal design and governance of asset-backed securities. J Financ Intermed 6(2):121–152
Rinaldo C (2023) Automation in investment advice. A European perspective. Revista de derecho Privado 45:309–340
Roe M (2006) Legal Origins and Modern Stock Markets. Harv Law Rev 120:462–518
Roon F, Veld C (1998) Announcement effects of convertible bonds loans and warrant-bond loans: an empirical analysis for the Dutch market. J Bank Financ 22(12):1481–1506
Royston J (1985) The regulation of American depository receipts: Americanization of the international capital markets. North Carolina Journal of International Law 10(1):87–106
Ruslijanto P (2021) Validity of digital signature as evidence in electronic commerce. Indonesian Journal of International Law 8(4):664–681
Sabarwal T (2006) Common structures of asset-backed securities and their risks. Corp Ownersh Control 4(1):258–265
Sanders W (2014) Resolving the conflict between fiduciary duties and socially responsible investing. Pace Law Review 35(2):535–579
Sasso L (2023) Bridging entrepreneurial finance in the EU: the new crowd funding regulation. Frontiers in Law 2:137–147
Schaeffer E (2008) Remittances and reputations in hawala money-transfer systems: self-enforcing exchange on an international scale. The Journal of Private Enterprise 24(1):95–117
Schwarcz D, Zaring D (2016) Regulation by threat: Dodd-frank and the nonbank problem. University of Chicago Law Review 84(4):1813–1881
Senarath S (2017) Securitisation and the global financial crisis: can risk retention prevent another crisis? International Journal of Business and Globalisation 18(2):153–166

Shah A (2007) The international regulation of informal value transfer systems. Utrecht Law Review 3(2):193–218
Silvers R (2020) Cross-border cooperation between securities regulators. J Account Econ 69(2):101301
Slimane F (2012) The structural evolution of stock exchanges. Recherches en Sciences de Gestion 6:61
Steinberg M, Couture W, Kaufman M, Morrisey D (2020) Securities litigation: law, policy, and practice. Carolina Academic Press
Stosic-Mihajlovic L (2016) Functioning of financial and Capital Markets in Modern Conditions. Journal of Process Management New Technologies 4(4):30–38
Stowell D (2010) An introduction to investment banks, hedge funds, and private equity. The New Paradigm
Swenson K (1969) Remedies for private parties under rule 10b-5. Boston Coll Law Rev 10(2):337–359
Terebessy L (2021) Alchemy of "Islamic" finance: turning usury into profit. Amazon Digital Services LLC
Tilquin T (2017) Les Certificats Immobiliers Jurimpratique 3:67
Uddin N, Hamdan H, Embi N, Kassim S, Saad N (2020) Governance structure of microfinance institutions: a comparison of models and its implication on social impact and poverty reduction. Journal of Ibn Haldun Studies 5(1):95–118
UNCITRAL (2009) Promoting confidence in electronic commerce: legal issues on international use of electronic authentication and signature methods. United Nations
Vaccani M (2010) Alternative remittance systems and terrorism financing: issues in risk management. World Bank Working Paper No. 180
Van de Bunt H (2008) A case study on the misuse of hawala banking. Int J Soc Econ 35:691–702
Vygovskyy O (2019) Re-characterization risk and true Sale principle within the context of asset securitization. Global Jurist 20(1):1–11
Wagner F (2024) Determinants of conventional and digital investment advisory decisions: a systematic literature review. Financ Innov 10(1):1–32
Wang J (2011a) Regulating hawala: a comparison of five National Approaches. Journal of Money Laundering Control 14(3):210–224
Wang R (2011b) Regulating hawala: a comparison of five National Approaches. Journal of Money Laundering Control 14:210–224

Further Reading

Caldararo N (2011) The theory of banking: why banks exist and why we fear them. Int J Sociol Anthropol 5(4):116–132
Georgakopoulos N (2017) The logic of securities law. Cambridge University Press
Omarova S, Steele G (2024) Banking and antitrust. Yale Law J 133:1162–1253
Pistor K (2013b) A legal theory of finance. J Comp Econ 41(2):315–330

Alternative Payment and Guaranteeing Procedures

9

Contents

Abstract

The chapter deals with the complex legal frameworks and business customs underpinning alternative methods of payment and assuring mechanisms in global trade. International trade is not an issue of simple physical transfer of good, it is also about the smooth transfer of value and the proper allocation of risks, which has been achieved through a complex set of financial structures interwoven in an interface of contractual and regulatory structures. The analysis begins with a Bill of Exchange, which is the basic negotiable instrument in

F. B. Erdem, *The Principles of International Banking, Finance and Investment Law*, Springer Textbooks in Law, https://doi.org/10.1007/978-3-032-32505-1_9

the law of bills and notes, embodying the core principles of transferability and holder-in-due-course protections. It then proceeds to an examination of letters of credit and letters of guarantee, highlighting their autonomous character vis-à-vis the underlying sales contract, while also stressing the important role of the ICC in standardising these instruments through UCP 600 and URDG 758. The following sections examine the Bill of Lading as a composite legal instrument functioning simultaneously as a receipt, evidence of the contract of carriage, and a document of title transferable by endorsement, thus bridging the commercial practice with maritime law. In addition to transport documents, this part further scrutinises trade finance facilities commonly employed in international commerce. In this context, bankers' acceptances are examined as short-term credit enhancement instruments grounded in bank creditworthiness and primarily used for discounting purposes. The analysis then proceeds to forfaiting, which is addressed as a medium-term, non-recourse financing technique based on the assignment of export receivables. The chapter deconstructs the modalities involved in counter-trade, including barter—a direct exchange without any monetary intercession, counter-purchase involving reciprocal commitments by the parties to purchase goods from the counterparty, and industrial offset commitments coupled with technology transfer or local content requirements—and more complex versions such as Buyback, which entails a repurchase agreement linked to capital goods exports, and switch trading, triangular clearing of imbalances through third-party intermediaries. These mechanisms are especially relevant when it comes to currency inconvertibility, trade imbalances, and financing constraints in agents in emerging and transitional economies. Overall, the chapter argues that the alternative payment together with guaranteeing procedures play a dual role, namely, being both juridical architectures of trust based on the autonomy of domestic law duties and economic conduits of liquidity that coordinate different national regimes in the name of international commercial uniformity. This interaction also contributes to enhanced transactional efficiency and strengthens the resilience of global trade networks against geopolitical and financial volatilities.

9.1 Bill of Exchange

9.1.1 Concept and Legal Nature

The Bill of Exchange (BoE) has remained to hold a preeminent place as one of the most fundamental negotiable instruments of the framework of international trade and finance. Instead of being a clerical device, it functions as a sophisticated socio-legal mechanism that combines payment, credit, and security services into one cross-border commercial instrument. As per Section 3(1) of the Bills of Exchange Act (BEA) 1882, the bill can be defined as an unconditional written order, that is addressed by one party to another and signed by the drawer, on which the drawee is obligated to pay a sum certain in money on demand or at a specified future date.[1] In this legal perspective, the instrument is an embodiment of the hallmark features of transferability and independence, which are critical to the mobility of international markets.

The global governance of this tool is determined by an ancient split into two major normative patterns. The Geneva Uniform Law on Bills of Exchange and Promissory Notes 1930 continues to be master on one hand, but across civil law jurisdictions; on the other, the BEA 1882 is the principle of commercial practice in common law countries and the Commonwealth. This dualism bears the description of Murray, who describe it as a comparative duality with the formalist autonomy dominant in Geneva-based systems and the contractual autonomy characteristics of the common-law model.[2] Although these are the divergent foundations in the philosophical nature, the two models have a teleological goal of ensuring the smooth and efficient flow of credit instruments across international frontiers. To obtain such a safe circulation, both legal systems provide the strict observance of certain formal conditions since the validity of the bill is inseparably connected with its form. This brings difficulties and therefore, such an unconditional payment should be signed by the drawer with the promise of giving a sum certain of money to create commercial certainty at maturity.

To achieve this secure circulation, both legal regimes mandate strict adherence to specific formal requirements, as the validity of the bill is inextricably linked to its form. Central to these requirements is the existence of an unconditional order in writing, meaning the instruction to pay must remain absolute and entirely insulated from external contingencies. Furthermore, the instrument must bear the signature of the drawer for authentication, state a sum certain in money to ensure commercial reliability, and specify a definite maturity—either on demand or at a determinable future time. Finally, the parties involved, including the drawer, drawee, and payee, must be clearly identifiable to ensure the instrument's integrity. Such formalities are not just ritual based as cogently, but they are the foundation of negotiability in that they guarantee the independence between the instrument and the contract in the ordinance.[3] It is precisely this autonomy that converts the bill into a *chose in action*, a proprietary right to payment which may be transferred without reference to the commercial transaction in which it was originally granted.[4]

Eventually, this legal framework enables the bill to have a triadic economic function that is indispensable to contemporary trade. It is an essential tool of credit since it allows payment to be deferred, which funds the international trade. Simultaneously, it acts as an efficient payment instrument to replace the movement of money across the borders. Last but not least, through the rigorous chain of

[1] Belovski et al. (2016, 39–49) and Mihai (2016, 15–21).
[2] Murray (1994, 189–225).
[3] Maduegbuna (1994, 338–362).
[4] Baxter (1979, 197–213).

endorsements, the bill functions as an instrument of security, providing an enforceable guarantee to its holders. Thus, the bill of exchange remains an indispensable synthesis of legal form and economic utility.

9.1.2 Parties, Endorsement, and the Dynamics of Circulation

The efficacy of a bill of exchange as a financial instrument is predicated upon a sophisticated tripartite relationship comprising the drawer, the drawee, and the payee. However, this structure is not static; rather, the legal standing and liabilities of these parties evolve dynamically as the instrument moves through the stream of commerce. Central to this evolution is the act of "acceptance." When the drawee—the party to whom the payment order is addressed—formally accepts the bill, they undergo a legal transformation into the acceptor. In this capacity, they assume primary liability for the payment, effectively becoming the principal debtor. Conversely, the drawer and subsequent endorsers maintain a secondary or contingent liability, ensuring that the holder has recourse should the primary obligor default.[5]

This framework of liability is activated and expanded through the mechanism of endorsement, which serves as the primary engine for the bill's circulation. Far from being a uniform process, endorsement can be tailored to meet specific commercial objectives through various forms. A blank endorsement, consisting merely of the endorser's signature, strips the instrument of its specificity and renders it payable to the bearer, thereby maximizing its fluidity. In contrast, a special endorsement designates a specific endorsee, maintaining a controlled chain of title. Furthermore, parties may employ a restrictive endorsement—such as "for collection only"—to truncate the negotiation process and limit the bill's use to specific agency functions.

Linking these legal formalities to the broader economic landscape, it becomes evident that these processes collectively sustain the bill's negotiability. It is precisely this quality that allows financial institutions to intervene in the life cycle of the instrument through the process of discounting. By purchasing a bill at a discount rate prior to its maturity, a bank effectively transforms post-dated receivables into immediate liquidity for the trader. This transformation is an indispensable function in international trade finance, bridging the temporal gap between the dispatch of goods and the receipt of payment. Consequently, the circulation of the bill is not merely a transfer of paper, but a sophisticated mobilization of credit that fuels global economic activity.References 'Accominotti and Ugolini (2024) and Andrew et al. (2024)' are cited in the text but not provided in the reference list. Please provide the respective references in the list or delete these citations.No reference needed.

A bill of exchange involves three parties: the drawer, the drawee, and the payee. As the bill is transferred between holders, each party's legal responsibility may change. When the drawee accepts the bill, the drawee becomes the *acceptor*,

[5] Accominotti et al. (2021, 892).

assuming primary liability, while the drawer and endorsers remain secondarily liable, and their liabilities arise only if the acceptor does not pay. Endorsement establishes the transfer mechanism and appears in three forms: (a) blank endorsement (signature only, making the bill payable to bearer), (b) special endorsement (specifying a new endorsee), and (c) restrictive endorsement (limiting negotiation, e.g., 'for collection only').

> **Important**
> These alternatives keep the bill negotiable and allow banks to discount the instrument before it matures. When a bank purchases a bill for less than its face value, it converts a post-dated receivable into cash right away, which is a key practice in international trade finance.[6]

9.1.3 Holder in Due Course (HIDC) Doctrine and Conflict of Laws

The HIDC principle is a key basis for treating the bill as reliable for credit purposes. *Section 29 of BEA 1882* and *Article 16 of the Geneva Convention* state that a bona fide holder who takes a bill for value, in good faith, and without notice of a defect in the transferor's title has a right to be paid that cannot be challenged. This doctrine cuts of *personal defences*, such as breach of the underlying agreement or fraud that led a party to sign, but it does not block real defence. So, real defences still apply, including forgery, fraud in the factum, duress, illegality, lack of capacity, material alteration, and discharge in bankruptcy.[7]

The HIDC doctrine puts into practice what Bridge et al. (2024) call a transferable credit trust, where the instrument itself carries the assurance that lets parties rely on it in cross-border finance.[8] If the bill is dishonoured through non-payment or non-acceptance, the holder may seek recourse against earlier endorsers, so long as any required protest is made and timely notice is given.[9] The protest procedure, often handled by a notary, is still required for foreign bills, which reflects the emphasis civil law systems place on careful documentary proof. Conflict of laws remains a key factor in how legal decisions are enforced between countries. In jurisdictions that follow the Geneva system, the governing law is usually *lex loci solutionis*, meaning the law of the place where the bill must be performed. In common law jurisdictions, courts tend to apply the proper law of the bill, which is often identified by where the bill was drawn or accepted. The 1988 UNCITRAL

---

[6] Accominotti et al. (2021, 892–921).
[7] Clarkson et al. (2009, 504–522).
[8] See, in general, Bridge et al. (2024, 28).
[9] Tan (2021, 28) and Epstein (1987, 9).

Convention on International Bills of Exchange and Promissory Notes aimed to harmonize the rules in this area, but many states have still not ratified it.

9.1.4 Contemporary Challenges: Digital Transformation and Normative Convergence

As trade instruments move away from paper, researchers and practitioners have shown renewed interest in the digital bill of exchange. The UNCITRAL MLETR of 2017 uses the idea of functional equivalence to treat an electronic bill in a way that matches key legal features of a paper bill, including possession and endorsement. In e-documents, the legal requirement of exclusive control replaces physical possession and supports interoperability across digital trade platforms.[10] Accominotti and Ugolini argue that even as technology changes, the bill keeps the same basic legal features—autonomy, negotiability, and formalism. In their view, this continuity links the older lex mercatoria with the digital lex mercatoria of the 21st century.[11]

9.1.5 Intermediate Result

The bill of exchange still serves as a legal document that supports trust between parties and as a tool that helps move funds through the financial system. It draws on centuries of trade practice, but digital change now shapes it, combining legal self-rule with economic ties across markets. Under the Geneva and English approaches, the instrument seeks to balance clear legal rules with the flexibility that commercial practice requires, which helps explain why it remains widely used in international trade finance and in cross-border payment systems.

9.2 Letters of Credit

9.2.1 Concept and Function

A *Letter of Credit (L/C)* is still a widely used payment method in international trade. It is a written promise from a bank, issued at the buyer's request, that the bank will pay the seller if the seller submits the documents listed in the letter of credit and those documents meet its stated terms. The bank's duty to pay depends on the documents presented, not on the underlying sales contract. In documentary credit law, this framework is central because it supports predictability in transactions and clarifies how risk is shared between the buyer and the seller.[12]

[10] Yu (2022, 1–27).

[11] Accominotti et al. (2021) and Emeasoba (2025, 314–339).

[12] Mann (2000, 2494).

Under the Uniform Customs and Practice for Documentary Credits (UCP 600), Article 4 states that a documentary credit is independent of the underlying sale or other contract, even when the credit is issued because of that contract. This arrangement shifts the buyer's commercial risk from the buyer to the bank's credit standing, which helps address both credit risk and performance risk in cross-border trade.[13]

> **Important**
> For the buyer, payment is due only after the required documents are presented (e.g., the documents specified in the credit). Under a letter of credit, the bank pays when the seller presents the required documents, such as the bill of lading and the insurance certificate. For the seller, this makes payment more predictable because it is not tied to the buyer's solvency or willingness to pay. Confirmed credits provide extra protection when a local bank in the exporter's country adds its confirmation, which reduces both country risk and transfer risk.

9.2.2 Legal Nature and the Autonomy Principle

The L/C rests on the autonomy principle: the issuing bank's duty to pay the beneficiary comes from the credit itself and is separate from the sale contract or any dispute about the underlying deal.[14] According to Article 5 of the UCP 600, "*banks deal with documents and not with goods, services or performance to which the documents may relate*". Therefore, disputes regarding the performance of the underlying contract cannot affect the bank's duty to honor payment if the presented documents conform facially to the credit's terms. This documentary independence forms the legal foundation for the L/C's reliability in international trade.[15] The fraud exception is the only accepted limit on the autonomy principle. The preservation of strict autonomy is to ensure commercial efficacy, except in cases of manifest fraud or abuse of right. A court will usually order to suspend a payment only if there is clear proof that the beneficiary knowingly submitted fraudulent or forged documents, and that the bank knew about the fraud before it made the payment.[16]

[13] Bergami (2009, 191–203).

[14] *United City Merchants (Investments) Ltd v Royal Bank of Canada* [1983] 1 AC 168 (HL).

[15] Jancikova and Pasztorova (2021, 27).

[16] *Alternative Power Solution Ltd v Central Electricity Board* [2014] UKPC 31.

9.2.3 The Strict Compliance Rule

Alongside the autonomy principle, the strict compliance rule (in French, principe de conformité stricte) requires that in a letter of credit, the documents presented must match the credit's terms exactly, with no differences.[17] This rule keeps the bank's duties mechanical, automatic, and predictable, which helps maintain the security and reliability of the transaction for everyone involved. This strict rule is often traced to the 1927 English case *Equitable Trust Co of New York v Dawson Partners Ltd*, where the court made the point that near matches are not enough: it said there is no place for documents that are almost the same or that would work just as well.[18] Put simply, partial compliance is not enough; the documents must meet every requirement, or they are rejected.

Today, this doctrine is set out in UCP 600, which applies to most commercial letters of credit used in international trade. Article 14 sets out that banks must review the presented documents with reasonable care and confirm that the information in them is consistent, both across the documents and with the terms of the credit. Article 16 supports this point by requiring an issuing bank that rejects the documents to send one notice of refusal, and that notice must clearly list every discrepancy the bank has found. Using a clear, step-by-step procedure saves time, keeps key points clear, and lowers the chance of disputes during the examination process.[19] This formal approach also appears in ISP98 (International Standby Practices), which is the standard most often used for standby letters of credit. ISP98 treats standby credits as independent commitments that require strict compliance with the terms and conditions stated in the credit. This strict standard lowers the risk of improper or bad-faith demands and supports confidence in standby instruments, which are usually issued as performance or financial guarantees rather than as a method for paying for goods.[20]

All in all, the strict compliance rule requires that a bank can only pay when the documents presented match the credit's stated requirements exactly. Small inconsistencies may be enough for the submission to be rejected. At first, the rule can seem rigid, but it shields banks from uncertain liability, gives clear instructions to those who present documents, and supports the predictability and confidence that international trade relies on.

9.2.4 Letters of Guarantee and ICC Rule Frameworks

A letter of guarantee (LG), or demand guarantee, serves a purpose similar to a L/C, but it is enforced under a different legal basis. In this arrangement, the L/C serves as the main payment method, while the LG is a backup duty that only

[17] Ay (2022, 125–133) and Kwaw (2021, 51–87).
[18] *Equitable Trust Co of New York v Dawson Partners Ltd* (1927) 27 Ll L Rep 49.
[19] ICC Banking Commission (2016) and Ferrero (2014).
[20] Mijatovic (2023).

becomes due if the applicant fails to meet its obligations. Article 5 of the Uniform Rules for Demand Guarantees (URDG) 758 states that a demand guarantee is independent from the underlying contract. In other words, the guarantee stands on its own, much like a letter of credit.[21] Together, these instruments make up a lex mercatoria for trade finance that the ICC recognizes. In practice, the ICC sets common rules through UCP 600 for commercial documentary credits, URDG 758 for demand guarantees and counter-guarantees, and ISP98 for standby letters of credit. Although these rules are based on contract terms, their common inclusion in credit agreements and acceptance by courts has given them an authority that resembles legislation.

> **Important**
> Smart L/Cs—executed through blockchain—automatically verify documentary compliance via coded conditions, enhancing speed and reducing fraud risk. However, the *autonomy* and *strict compliance* doctrines continue to apply, now adapted to algorithmic verification mechanisms, ensuring continuity with traditional norms.

9.3 Bill of Lading

9.3.1 Nature, Legal Functions, and Quasi-Negotiability

In maritime and trade law, the bill of lading is central because it does three related things at once: it records that the carrier received the goods, it serves as proof of the contract for carriage, and it functions as a document of title that can be transferred through endorsement and delivery. Since the bill of lading serves these three roles, it has a partly negotiable character.[22] This sets it apart from fully negotiable instruments, such as bills of exchange. The bill of lading has changed over time as trade practices changed. A key point in this development was the English case *Lickbarrow v Mason*,[23] which treated the bill of lading as a document of title. The case accepted that constructive possession of the goods could pass to another party through endorsement and delivery of the document. Later case law, including The *Delfini*,[24] reaffirmed this point by treating the title of a bona fide endorsee as independent. In current legal practice, bills of lading sit within a layered framework shaped by common law rules and international conventions, which aims to balance the carrier's liability, their value as evidence, and their role as negotiable documents.[25] The recent shift to electronic formats has broadened

[21] Affaki and Goode (2021).
[22] Spanjaart (2022) and Pejovic (2020).
[23] [1775-1802] All ER Rep 1 (KB); Francis (2006, 25) and Mitchelhill (1990, 3–5).
[24] (1990) Lloyd's Rep 252.
[25] Panesar (2004, 196–199) and Tong-Jiang and Peng (2009, 345–351).

the bill of lading's legal scope while keeping its traditional role as a document of title intact.

9.3.2 Legal Framework and Evidentiary Status

International rules for Bills of Lading have developed through a series of conventions intended to set common standards for carrier duties and liability in global shipping. The Hague-Visby Rules of 1968 are still widely cited in English law and in international shipping practice because they set a baseline for a carrier's duties and cap liability using SDR per package or unit. Under Article III(4) of this regime, the bill of lading is treated as initial evidence that the carrier received the goods in the quantity and condition stated. If the bill of lading is later held by a good-faith third party, the carrier may be prevented from denying what the document says about the goods. Later court decisions and new laws tried to clarify and adjust how authority and responsibility were shared between shippers and carriers. The Hamburg Rules (1978) set a stricter system of liability for damage and delay, and they also shifted the burden of proof so it was more favourable to cargo interests.[26] More recently, the Rotterdam Rules (2009) offer the latest attempt to bring these rules together. They are not yet in force, but they would extend the legal coverage beyond sea carriage to include door-to-door transport across different modes. Articles 8–10 of the Rotterdam Rules expressly accept electronic transport records and align their use with traditional maritime roles, so the legal rules can still work in electronic commerce.[27]

9.3.3 Transfer, Negotiability, and Security Interests

Sorting Bills of Lading by the transfer rules written into them matters because it shapes how ownership can pass between parties and how goods and payment are handled in international trade and maritime finance. Bills of lading are usually grouped into three types: order bills of lading, which can be transferred through endorsement and delivery; bearer bills of lading, which transfer by delivery alone; and straight bills of lading, which are not transferable and are issued to a named consignee.

When an order bill of lading is endorsed, the transferee takes a derived title. This gives the transferee proprietary rights in the goods even while they are still in transit, as confirmed by the *Chikuma*.[28] This legal framework makes the bill of lading a key document for financing under Article 20 of the UCP 600, especially in letter of credit transactions. Banks often require the borrower to submit

[26] Adascalitei (2024, 83–91).
[27] Krebs (2024, 328–338) and Andrew et al. (2024, 23–36).
[28] [1981] 1 WLR 314.

a complete set of original bills of lading, usually endorsed in blank, as collateral for the transaction. Because a bill of lading serves both as evidence of the carriage contract and as a document of title, it allows lenders in trade finance to take a possessory pledge over the goods. To protect the cargo interest, the law treats a carrier as strictly liable for misdelivery if it hands over the goods without being shown an original bill of lading, and recent cases continue to apply this rule, including the *Yue You*.[29]

9.3.4 Interim Result

Whether issued on paper or as an electronic record, the bill of lading remains a central document in maritime shipping and in the financial arrangements that support international trade. It is a hybrid document: it works as evidence, a contract, and a document of title, and it shows where *lex mercatoria* and *lex maritima* meet. Recent legal frameworks, including the MLETR and the Rotterdam Rules, carry these ideas into modern digital trade by keeping the long-standing rules on possession, negotiability, and trust at the center of global logistics and trade finance.

9.4 Banker's Acceptances

A Banker's Acceptance (BA) is a financial instrument in which a bank accepts responsibility for paying a trade bill, turning a private trade obligation into a negotiable claim on the bank that can be sold in the market. A BA is a time draft that is drawn on a commercial bank and accepted by that bank. Under UCC §3-104(a), it is treated as a draft that is payable at a definite time, signed by the bank as the drawee, and that includes an unconditional order to pay.[30]

Once the bank accepts the instrument, it takes on primary responsibility for payment. As a result, payment at maturity depends on the bank's obligation rather than on whether the underlying commercial transaction is completed or disputed. Under UCC Article 3, this status gives a good-faith transferee the rights of a holder in due course, which lowers the risk of nonpayment and makes it easier to sell the instrument at a discount in secondary money markets.[31]

In international trade finance, a banker's acceptance can both strengthen the credit behind a transaction and provide a short-term instrument that investors can hold or trade. It helps cover the time between shipping goods and receiving the final payment by turning trade receivables into bank-backed paper that can be sold for cash with little delay. A banker's acceptance usually starts with a sales transaction in which goods are shipped under a time draft. After shipment, the

[29] [2019] 902 SGHC 305.

[30] Anderson (2009, 1–2) and LaRoche (1993, 75–85).

[31] Floyd (2018, 33).

draft is presented for acceptance, and the bank accepts it so that payment rests on the bank's credit rather than the buyer's. After it is accepted, the instrument moves into the discounting stage, where it can be sold in the money market to obtain cash right away. The process ends at maturity, when the bank pays the face value to whoever holds the instrument at that time.

This mechanism is recognized internationally in the ICC Uniform Rules for Collections (URC 522) and UCP 600, both of which treat bankers' acceptances as an acceptable way to settle payments under documentary credits. The economic value of the BA comes from turning illiquid trade obligations into liquid financial assets. Historically, central banks, including the FED, have used this mechanism to transmit liquidity through the financial system. The bill of acceptance has long been handled on paper, but it is now shifting toward digital forms. Pilot projects that draw on the UNCITRAL MLETR, along with distributed ledger platforms such as Contour and Komgo, are testing e-Acceptances. These digital versions are designed to mirror the main endorsement and maturity features of a traditional banker's acceptance, while keeping it negotiable and able to support interbank liquidity and financial market efficiency.

9.5 Conclusion

Regulatory harmonization in trade finance marks the transition from fragmented paper-based regimes to an integrated digital legal order. The synergy among ICC, UNCITRAL, UNIDROIT, and WTO frameworks demonstrates a unique blend of *soft law cooperation and public law endorsement.* Future governance will depend on maintaining interoperability, digital enforceability, and cross-border recognition—ensuring that the principles of *autonomy, trust, and uniformity* continue to underpin the legal architecture of global trade finance.

Classical instruments such as the *Bill of Exchange, Letter of Credit,* and *Bill of Lading* institutionalized the autonomy principle, ensuring that documentary obligations could operate independently of underlying contracts. Their codification under frameworks such as the Geneva Convention and UCP 600 marked the first global harmonization of commercial law. Subsequent developments, such as *factoring* and *banker's acceptances,* extended this logic into credit risk distribution and liquidity transformation, transforming receivables into negotiable assets and facilitating the rise of global trade finance markets. In the twenty-first century, the emergence of electronic trade instruments under the UNCITRAL MLETR, eUCP, and URDTT (2021) represents a doctrinal and technological renaissance. The principles of *functional equivalence* and *technological neutrality* now bridge traditional paper-based systems with digital infrastructures such as blockchain, tokenization, and smart contracts. These innovations have not only enhanced speed and transparency but also redefined legal concepts such as possession, endorsement, and control—embedding them within cryptographic frameworks.

At the regulatory level, institutions such as ICC, UNCITRAL, UNIDROIT, and WTO are converging toward a unified digital trade order. This global lex mercatoria seeks to harmonize private commercial practices with public international law, ensuring that cross-border digital transactions enjoy the same enforceability as traditional instruments. The future of trade finance thus lies in regulatory interoperability, where national laws, model conventions, and technological standards coalesce into a coherent legal architecture.

Ultimately, the transformation of trade finance is not merely technological but jurisprudential—it reaffirms the enduring adaptability of commercial law to evolving modes of exchange. As legal instruments become digital, their legitimacy must remain rooted in transparency, predictability, and trust. In this synthesis of law and technology, the future of international trade finance stands poised between continuity and innovation—a testament to the resilience of global commerce and the universality of its legal foundations.

Chapter Summary

This chapter provides an extensive legal and functional evaluation of the major payment and guarantee systems that are applied in international trade acting as legal constructs of allocating risks and ensuring liquidity. The chapter firstly defined bill of exchange as the basic negotiable instrument that secures an unconditional command to pay. It has three main functions: payment, credit and security. The doctrine of HIDC, which is held in both the Geneva Convention and common law, gives an indefeasible right to payment, thus preserving the negotiability and insensitivity of the instrument to the contract itself. In terms of banker acceptances (BAs), they are type of time draft endorsed by a commercial bank, which transforms a personal obligation of trade into a negotiable and short-term bank liability.

The chapter also covers L/C as a bank payment commitment, which is irrevocable and conditional as the bank pays the seller when the seller presents the required documents. It is stated that their effectiveness is based on the principle of autonomy guaranteeing that they are not subject to the underlying sale and strict compliance rule to provide strict adherence to the contractual terms in the documents. In this regard, the most important governing structure is ICC-UCP 600. On the other hand, letters of guarantee (LGs) are standalone primary obligations that come into effect in the event of default by the applicant. They are subject to the ICC Uniform Rules for Demand Guarantees (URDG 758). The only principle that has been recognised to be limited is the principle of autonomy by the fraud exception.

Afterwards, the chapter includes bill of lading (B/L) as an essential document that simultaneously serves as a receipt of goods, as an evidentiary instrument under the carriage contract and a document of title, that transfers possessory rights. The transferability of the B/L makes it a necessity to use as a collateral to letters of credit. In addition to that other financing methods, namely forfaiting and countertrade, are presented. Accordingly, forfaiting is a medium term, non-recourse financing way that entails the discounted assignment of export invoices, usually avalised notes or bills, hence assigning commercial, political and transfer risks. Countertrade, whereas is a reciprocal arrangement obligation that is a substitute product of currency settlements by joint performance obligations (such as barter, counter-purchase, buyback and offset) to conserve foreign exchange or promote industrial policy aims.

During the chapter, recent developments in relation to digital transformation of payment system are quoted. Particularly, the UNCITRAL MLETR permits the use of electronic trade-finance instruments, including e-BL, eUCP and URDTT. This legal system creates a functional equivalence and a monopoly of digital power so as to reproduce the negotiability of traditional tools.

Revision Questions

1. Examine the legal connection between the autonomy principle, which is provided to the letters of credit and demand guarantees, and the strict compliance rule.
2. Compare forfaiting and a conventional bank loan using the criteria of recourse and type of instrument used. Provide justifications as to why forfaiting is mostly preferred in capital-goods exports, which are medium-term.
3. Discuss and describe the three key legal roles played by the B/L. Report on what is the role that makes the B/L indispensable to banks issuing letters of credit.
4. Explain the doctrine of holder in due course (HIDC) of a bill of exchange.
5. Discuss how the UNCITRAL MLETR can be relevant to modern trade finance. Explain how the principle of functional equivalence authorises e-BL to act as a legal replacement of a paper document of title.
6. Explain the legal effect on an instrument of acceptance by a bank of a time draft and the improvement of its credit quality. Discuss the way this process enhances instantaneous liquidity to the exporter.
7. Define countertrade and give two examples, e.g. barter and offset. Examine the key economics and policy incentives such as currency factor and market access that underpin its use.◄

References

Accominotti O, Lucena-Piquero D, Ugolini S (2021) The origination and distribution of money market instruments: sterling bills of exchange during the first globalization. Econ Hist Rev 74(4):892–921

Adascalitei O (2024) Shipper's obligations under the Rotterdam Rules. A comparison with the Hague-Visby Rules 1968 and Hamburg Rules 1978. Int Invest Law J 4(1):83–91

Affaki G, Goode R (2021) Guide to ICC uniform rules for demand guarantees URDG 758. ICC

Anderson R (2009) Bankers' acceptances: yesterday's instrument to restart today's credit markets? Econ Synopses 5:1–2

Andrew F, Purwanto HF (2024) The position of bills of lading in the carriage of goods at sea. J Indep 12(1):23–36

Ay Y (2022) The interpretation of the principle of strict compliance in letters of credit in international commercial law. Facta Univ 20(2):125–133

Baxter I (1979) The bills of exchange act and conflict of laws. Revue de droit de l'Universite de Sherbrooke 10(1):197–213

Belovski V, Majhosev A, Dujovska I (2016) The bill of exchange as a means of payment and security. J Process Manage New Technol 4(3):39–49

Bergami R (2009) UCP 600 rules—changing letter of credit business for international traders? J Econ Bus Res 1(2):191–203

Bridge M, Gullifer L, Lomnicka E (2024) The law of security and title-based financing. Oxford University Press

Clarkson K, Miller R, Jentz G, Cross F (2009) Business law: text and cases—legal, ethical, global and e-commerce environment. South-Western Cengage Learning, pp 504–522

Emeasoba G (2025) The law on electronic trade documents: applying functional equivalence in the model law on electronic transferable records and comparable Common Law Jurisdictions. Unif Law Rev 30(3):314–339

Epstein A (1987) Inducement of breach of contract as a problem of ostensible ownership. J Leg Stud 16:9

Ferrero S (2014) Some considerations on the doctrine of strict compliance and the autonomy principle in documentary credit. https://www.businessjus.com/wp-content/uploads/2014/05/Some-considerations-on-the-doctrine-of-strict-compliance-and-the-autonomy-principle-in-documentary-credit.pdf. Accessed 30 Jan 2026

Floyd M (2018) Mastering negotiable instruments (UCC Articles 3 and 4) and other payment systems. Carolina Academic Press

Francis N (2006) Transferring right of Suit under Bill of Lading: the conflict of laws implications. Australian & New Zealand Maritime Law J 20:25

ICC Banking Commission (2016) Notes on the principle of strict compliance. https://www.icc-switzerland.ch/images/8.Notes-On-The-Principle-Of-Strict-Compliance.pdf. Accessed 30 Jan 2026

Jancikova E, Pasztorova J (2021) Legal aspects of letters of credit. Perspect Law Public Adm 10:18–31

Krebs T (2024) Electronic bills of lading, transnational and English Law: blocking the blockchain? Unif Law Rev 28(3-4):328–338

Kwaw E (2021) Strict or substantial compliance in letters of credit: crafting guidelines for verifying documentary compliance. E-J Law 7(1):51–87

LaRoche R (1993) Bankers acceptances. Econ Q 79(1):75–85

Maduegbuna S (1994) The effects of electronic banking techniques of the use of paper-based payment mechanisms in international trade. J Bus Law 1994.338–362

Mann R (2000) The role of letters of credit in payment transactions. Mich Law Rev 98(8):2494–2536

Mihai G (2016) Bill of exchange—a modern and efficient instrument of payment within the commercial relations. J Euro Compet 3(7):15–21

Mijatovic M (2023) Standby letter of credit as a means of security in international contractual relations. Pravo – teorija i praksa 40(4):1–16

Mitchelhill A (1990) Bills of lading: law and practice. Springer

Murray D (1994) The U.N. Convention on international bills of exchange and international promissory notes with some comparisons with the former and revised article three of the UCC. Miami Inter-Am Law Rev 25(2):189–225

Panesar S (2004) Is a straight bill of lading a document of title? Bus Law Rev 25(8):196–199

Pejovic C (2020) Transport documents in carriage of goods by sea: international law and practice. Informa Law
Spanjaart M (2022) The straight bill of lading in a paperless future. https://law.nus.edu.sg/cml/wp-content/uploads/sites/8/2022/09/CML-WPS-2204.pdf. Accessed 31 Jan 2026
Tan Z (2021) The 'Property' paradigm in torts protecting contractual interests. In: Eldridge J, Douglas M, Carr C (eds) Economic torts and economic wrongs. Hart, pp 9–37
Tong-Jiang S, Peng W (2009) Carrier's liability under international maritime conventions and the UNCITRAL draft convention on contracts for the international carriage of goods wholly or partly by sea. Transport 24(4):345–351
Yu G (2022) Functional equivalence to a piece of paper: a comment on the UNCITRAL model law on electronic transferable records. International Commercial Law. Dispute Resolution, Digital Economy and Contemporary Issues in Harmonisation of International Commercial Law 26:1–27

Further Reading

Bridge M (2019) The sale of goods. Oxford University Press
Hare C, Neo D (2021) Trade finance: technology, innovation and documentary credits. Oxford University Press
Lupton C, Huneberg S (2023) Issuance of independent guarantees by insurance companies. J Juridical Sci 48(1):16–39
Mugasha A (2022) Technological innovation in trade finance and the law: from the bank payment obligation and blockchain to the uniform rules on digital trade transactions. Bank Financ Law Rev 38:217–243

Credits

10

Contents

F. B. Erdem, *The Principles of International Banking, Finance and Investment Law*, Springer Textbooks in Law, https://doi.org/10.1007/978-3-032-32505-1_10

Abstract

This chapter provides a comprehensive overview of the legal aspects of credit and loan agreements. It begins by discussing loan reserve requirements, which are crucial for maintaining financial stability and liquidity. The chapter then delves into the loan contract, outlining its legal nature, terms, scope, and conditions. It highlights the importance of the loan agreement for the parties involved and explains the limits and additional provisions that may be included in credit agreements. The chapter categorizes bank loans into personal and commercial loans. Personal loans are further broken down into various types, including personal finance credit, real estate loans (such as mortgages, home equity lines of credit, and fixed-interest loans), and auto loans (covering secured, unsecured, and specialized loans). Commercial loans are detailed with types such as collateralized commercial credit, spot loans, revolving credit, and non-cash credits. Lastly, the chapter examines international banking credit agreements, focusing on legal proceedings and the collection of receivables, essential for cross-border financial operations.

10.1 Introductory Remark

All economic transactions that are based on deferred payment or future delivery must necessarily be accompanied by a system of credit and enforceability. Therefore, credit is an integral concept of the modern financial system. The essential meaning of credit etymologically originates from the word of credere in Latin, meaning to believe. Thus, credit is actually about establishing trust between parties rather than immediate exchange of goods or money. From an economic point of view, credit is merely a mechanism of intertemporal transfer of resources. It makes possible the transfer of capital from units that have surplus capital (savers or suppliers of credit) to units that have deficit capital (borrowers of credit or capital). In the absence of a stable legal system that provides for the rights and duties of the parties, credit and speculation would be identical concepts. Credit, from a legal standpoint, can be understood through two connected aspects that continuously interact. First, there is a private law aspect. Credit is a two-sided obligation governed by contract. It requires a lawful cause, consent, and enforceable consideration. The second aspect is public law because creating credit is a semi-sovereign act. Through fractional reserve banking, private institutions increase the money supply with public approval.

The history of credit law shows the gradual development of trust. In the Middle Ages, credit relations followed customary law and mercantile practices. The Church's ban on usury limited lending to specific situations.[1] In Renaissance Italy, the emergence of bills of exchange and powerful banking houses (such as those of the Medici, Bardi, and Peruzzi) reflected and drove the move toward a more formalized, contract-based system of commerce and credit.[2]

By the nineteenth century, credit became a key part of industrial capitalism, leading to its inclusion in civil codes, such as the French Code Civil and the German BGB §§ 488–490, as well as specialized banking laws. The legal definition of credit should reflect a balance of autonomy and control. Parties can negotiate terms freely, but their freedom is guided by mandatory rules that protect the system's integrity. In this way, credit represents what legal theorists refer to as regulated freedom, where private arrangements and public rules meet.

[1] Baker and Cohanier (2025, 341–362).

[2] Angeli (2018, 37).

10.1.1 The Legal-Economic Function of Credit

The economic rationale for credit is to facilitate investment and consumption by bridging the temporal gap between production and realization. The legal system, however, ensures that this rationale operates within predictable and regulated boundaries. The fundamental inquiry in any lending relationship lies the question of which party bears the financial burden in the event of default or failure. Traditionally, the onus falls on the lender who puts up the money. Prevailing legislation spreads that risk in different ways-through collateral, insurance, swaps, and other instruments-shaping who bears it, and sometimes shifting it onto third parties. How risk is allocated is not just about freedom to contract; legal realities, information gaps, and power dynamics between parties also steer the balance. Subsequently, there are the legal avenues and solutions in case of borrower default. The law provides the creditor with his tool kit: insisting on performance, turning collateral into cash, exercising liens, or damages for the losses suffered. Those remedies need to be weighed with due care against protection of the lender's rights while ensuring a fair and orderly liquidation that doesn't wipe out the borrower's entire economic footing. But beyond individual loans, broader institutional structures are important to the health of the credit system as a whole. Since credit is a contagious risk, the system depends on central banks as lenders of last resort, regulators setting capital adequacy standards-as Basel does-and macroprudential safeguards such as deposit insurance. These elements combined give the legal and economic backbone to keep the credit cycle running on trust, where one default cannot spiral into wider crisis.

Credit turns risk into a phenomenon capable of legal treatment. In effect, credit risk is dispersed and allocated between debtor and creditor and beyond them to the wider community, or made social, through the use of interest, collateral, guarantees, and prudential regulation. Absent legal enforceability, credit reverts to morals and chance.[3] In this vein, one of the central myths of modern social science is the reduction of premodern economies to systems of credit, interpreted through modern economic categories rather than indigenous cosmologies.[4] Nonetheless, some conceptualizations of modern credit have highlighted the need for modern credit systems to be based not on trusting persons but on trusting systems mediated via impersonal institutions.[5] "A debtor is credible, in other words, for creditworthy qualities that can be measured in any case." Of course, this implies that credit relationships are conditioned on credit quality, and in this scenario, the credit contract becomes a private and social sign.

---

[3] Ahmed et al. (2024, 95–110).

[4] Sahlins (2000, 412–455).

[5] See, Simmel (2011, 94–107) and Holton and Turner (1989).

10.1.2 Credit and Financial Stability

Every credit extension made by banks increases the risk of systemic exposure. Any default at any given node can spread credit exposure and funding risks. Therefore, credit law cannot be grasped in any manner that is only private in nature. There must be legal regulation in addition to private credit regulation. Basel Accords (Basel I, II, III, and now Basel IV Regulations) have made the prudent approach toward credit risk the de facto international credit law standard. Banks are also required to hold sufficient capital in relation to their risk-weighted assets (RWAs), and that credit risk should never potentially damage public confidence in banks.[6] Credits work like hybrid institutions—apparently private contracts with public effects. Non-fulfilment of credit commitments can trigger the insolvency of banks, which in turn endangers funds held in banks and the payment system in general. Consequently, credit law enforceability must be balanced in relation to the need for prudential control.

10.1.3 The Normative Structure of Credit Relations

In understanding from an abstract point of view, the credit relationship consists of five steps: (i) obligation of payment (debt); (ii) right of interest (compensation for the time factor); (iii) security interest (collateral pledge); (iv) event of default (solving remedies); and (v) public supervision (supervision of banks). All of them emerge in contemporary systems of law. In the Civil Law tradition, credit agreements are based on mutuum (loan for consumption) and are governed by the Code Civil and the BGB, whereas in the common law traditions, credit agreements are grounded in contract and equity and are supplemented by consumer protection legislation. In any case, the debtor's side is personal and unconditional, and the lender binds himself or herself conditionally on payment/disbursement. Thus, the difference between promise and performance sets the framework of the theory of trust.

10.2 Loan Reserve Requirements

10.2.1 Concept and Historical Development

Reserve requirements are some of the oldest tools of monetary control. Banks are required to maintain a certain fraction of their deposits in reserves, in cash (also known as vault cash) or on account at the central bank.[7] There are two purposes: securing withdrawals and preventing the banks from engaging in speculative and

[6] Parchimowicz and Spence (2020, 13–27), Feridun and Özün (2020, 7–24), Binder and Lehner (2019, 183–205), and Barth and Miller (2018, 77).

[7] Hardy (1997).

uncontrolled money creation. Historically, reserve requirement systems were introduced as a consequence of bank runs in the nineteenth-century crisis situations when banks' liquidity crisis led to the bankruptcies of apparently sound banks due to huge withdrawals of funds in case of expected runs. Reserve requirements were formally introduced for the first time in the United States within the National Banking Act of 1864 and later improved within the Federal Reserve Act of 1913. In Europe, similar systems were introduced within central banking laws. Reserve requirement systems were codified in the mid-20th-century developments as central elements of monetary control and supervision of banks. Being dual-purpose systems—means of control and of monetary policy—remains one of the defining areas of contemporary banking law.[8]

10.2.2 Legal Foundation

In most countries, reserve requirements are defined by a hierarchy of legal instruments. At the highest level, primary legislation-specifically central bank laws or general banking acts-lay down the statutory framework for imposing and enforcing reserve obligations. The monetary authorities issue secondary regulations spelling out operational rules, methods of calculation, and reporting arrangements. Finally, binding circulars and/or macroprudential guidelines frequently spell out the technical aspects of reserve requirement adjustments, allowing central banks to hone their reserve policy in line with evolving financial conditions.

A set of concrete examples is used to show how different regulatory systems implement these requirements. In the US, Federal Reserve Regulation D (12 CFR 204) deals with the reserve ratios applicable to transaction accounts. In the European Union, Regulation (EU) 2021/378 sets the framework for the minimum reserve system of the European Central Bank. In a similar vein, national bodies, such as the Banking Regulation and Supervision Agency in Turkey or the Prudential Regulation Authority from the Bank of England, issue equivalent mandates but adapted to their respective domestic banking sectors. Taken together, these instruments are an integral part of the public law of banking. The reserve requirements are binding in nature, and non-compliance with them may entail administrative sanctions because of their core position in safeguarding monetary stability as well as the stability of the financial system.

10.2.3 Economic and Legal Function

Loan reserve requirements stand at the juncture of economic stability and legal obligation. Economically, these reserves represent very important liquidity buffers that help safeguard the stability of financial institutions. By forcing banks to keep

[8] See, Carlson (2015, 191–224), Vaz (1988), and Jamilov et al. (2025).

a portion of their assets in reserve, the system ensures at least a minimum degree of solvency against unanticipated bank shocks. It is a kind of inbuilt safety valve that mixes the independent operation of individual banks with the greater need for overall financial stability. Reserve requirements also represent prudence in action and serve as a legal means for regulating the money supply. Because the fractional reserve system allows banks to lend far beyond their actual deposit base, the reserve ratio becomes the critical factor in determining the credit multiplier. The state curtails that magic by locking away part of deposits, dampening, in turn, the cyclical surge of lending that could otherwise overheat the economy.[9] These reserves are legally framed as a public obligation rather than a private debt. They do not just sit as direct liabilities owed to each individual depositor but form part of the broader financial system's architecture. The distinction is important because it promotes reserve maintenance from a bookkeeping rule to a compliance rule. In such a light, the law of reserve is the invisible boundary of private lending freedom, which enables profit-seeking not to undermine the public interest. This obligation has its seriousness underlined by strict enforcement on the part of the central bank. For a bank, noncompliance is not only a breach of contract but also a regulatory one that can trigger harsh penalties. These penalties may involve interest charges, limitations in banking activities, or-in the worst cases-suspension or revocation of a banking license. In a nutshell, the given legal framework ensures monetary stability through sound administrative control and strict penalties in case of failure to satisfy reserve requirements.

10.2.4 The Basel Framework and Capital Adequacy

The structure of the financial regulatory architecture is more or less Basel-like presently, but it has evolved from the traditional concept of reserves to a much more complex construct for Capital Adequacy.[10] The attention in liquidity, within traditional reserves, is mostly on the short term, however in capital adequacy, the focus is on long term. Nevertheless, both notions have a similar macro-goal, which is to absorb shocks without denting market confidence.

In Basel III, this rationale is encapsulated in the framework through the two key ratios discussed below. Banks must always have sufficient high-quality liquid assets on hand to cover the period of 30-days severe stress. That's what Liquidity Coverage Ratio (LCR) demands from them. Apart from that, net stable funding ratio (NSFR) requires banks to have funding that is sufficiently stable in relation to their assets and off-balance sheet activities.[11] These ratios do differ from central bank reserves. But they are also aimed at the same target. This target is to ensure that lending and related activities do not outrun the stability factors in a bank.

---

[9] See, Espinosa et al. (2023, 221) and Sheard (2013).

[10] Atuahene et al. (2021, 45–54) and Barghouthi and Bayyoud (2016, 102–115).

[11] BIS (2013).

A transposition process involves taking such global standards and converting them into a law of the land for example, EU's Capital Requirements Regulation (CRR) or the Dodd-Frank Act of the U.S. When cost-effective interfaces are available, a universal approach towards substance may be costlier than imposing local rules and standards. By statutorily requiring liquidity ratios, the state strengthens the belief that financial stability is a public good by aligning private risk management with the common good of resilience.

10.2.5 Judicial and Administrative Enforcement

The regulatory force of reserve requirements resides primarily within the ambit of administrative law, where central banks enjoy substantial discretionary powers. In practice, courts often exhibit a high degree of judicial deference to the technical expertise of regulators, seldom intervening in compliance disputes. However, this administrative independence is not absolute. When a failure to maintain adequate reserves culminates in insolvency or the erosion of depositor equity, the legal landscape shifts from mere administrative non-compliance to civil liability.[12] At this juncture, the door opens for litigation against the financial institution, grounded in allegations of supervisory negligence or the failure to implement prudent reserve practices as a proximate cause of the systemic crisis.

On the one hand, the equivalent truism circumscribes wickedness, and on the other hand, it does not. It is possible banks contest challenges to excessive reserve requirements on the basis that those restrictions adversely affect the property rights and economic liberty of banks. Legal trials assess the power of national governments when it comes to freezing private capital. In practice, national courts support national reserve requirements on the basis of a legitimate national interest. When analysing these sets of obligations, the courts often refer to the principle of proportionality. The judiciary generally examines whether these reserve requirements are proportionate and necessary and appropriate for the preservation of monetary stability, not unduly burdensome to the viability of a bank. The regularity of backing by the judicial system in upliftment of systemic stability generally implies support of the judiciary that the statutes in the reserve are not rules but the pillar of the financial system.

10.2.6 Contemporary Debates

The swift transformations in the financial environment, which are marked by the surge of liquidity and the growing number of central bank digital currencies, have resulted in a change in the status of required reserves. Legal tender ratios in advanced economies such as the US, the UK, and Canada have been reduced

[12] Andenas and Fairgrieve (2002, 757–780).

to almost zero, while market-based measures of liquidity have multiplied.[13] This leads to the conclusion that reserve requirements are no longer needed due to the availability of modern monetary policy tools, while the other side warns that extremely low reserve requirements or complete disregard for them could disrupt the economic system. The setting of a mandatory reserve ratio is still, however, a legal requirement that limits an otherwise unrestricted government power to expand the money supply.

10.2.7 Relationship Between Reserves and Credit Creation

Reserves and credit expansion are interconnected in a way that is not simple to understand, nevertheless the situation has been and still is greatly influencing the whole process. Traditional approaches have not and cannot explain it. In fact, banks today are engaging in one of the most powerful forms of future-oriented investments—the branch of credit creation that is at the heart of modern finance being a bank lending before it reserves. Simply put, the law acts as a stabilizer after the credit has been made, not before. As a result of this credit expansion-law connection, there arises a paradox of modern finance. The credit creation process becomes private money while law grants the money its quality. From a legal perspective, reserve requirements signify a conditional legality. Banks have the power to create money (which is not unlimited) provided that they comply with the guarantees laid down by the government.[14] Hence, there exists a mutual relationship in the sphere of law where the extra-legal power of banks to lend money is conditioned by the public duty to maintain guarantees. The final outcome regarding reserve regulation is very simple. The issuance of credit authority necessarily comes along with a duty to keep liquidity. By establishing this framework of rules and regulations, the rule of law as institutionalized by the legal system ensures that the increase in the money supply is traceable.[15] On top of that, reserve regulation is not merely controlling banking operations; these regulations, in fact, are the very foundation upon which the credit system could be transformed into a trustworthy currency.[16]

The use of reserve requirements in a dynamic and counter-cyclical manner is the most prominent feature among G20 countries. For instance, in Brazil and Türkiye, reserve requirements are used as a tool to take control over credit expansions.[17] Conversely, in the US or EU, they rely more on Basel III requirements—the Liquidity Coverage Ratio or Net Stable Funding Ratio—for managing systemic liquidity.[18] It is an exemplary practice of full incorporation of these ratios into the

[13] Meaning et al. (2021, 1–42) and Dionysopoulos et al. (2024)

[14] Starkey (2018). See also Shahizam (2023).

[15] Werner (2014, 71–77).

[16] See in general, Menand (2021, 951–1022).

[17] Cantu et al. (2024).

[18] Du (2017, 1–18), Hartlage (2012, 453–484) and Khalifeh et al. (2025).

national law (as in the cases of CRR or Dodd-Frank regulations). That way, liquidity management becomes a regular action instead of a discretionary one. Another good practice would be to make reserves more diversified and connect them to incentive schemes. This would mean the guiding of reserve management of most of the G20 members towards social and economic development goals via lower reserve requirements for 'green' projects or SMEs. In this way, managing reserves is less a punishment than a means of working with. The judicial transparency and predictability are the major requirements among the standards the G20 has set forth. The best practices on the part of the central banks would entail using the stress test outcomes to adjust the reserve ratio per a pre-determined schedule. This facilitates the market players' ability to foresee the compliance costs. The G20 cooperation in this area has resulted in the creation of a supervisory framework that strengthens not only the local but also the global financial sector's ability to withstand disturbances.

10.3 Loan Contract

10.3.1 Legal Nature of the Contract

A loan agreement (also known as mutuum in the legal language of civil law) is the oldest tool in the private law arsenal. It provides for the relationship between the creditor, who either gives or undertake to give to the borrower a certain amount of money, and the debtor, who önder the terms of the contract, agrees to pay back an equal sum of money. Even though it may look like a straightforward transaction between two parties, in the world of banking law, it is still subject to a highly regulated framework of trust duties, cautionary obligations, and monetary discipline. In the case of civil law systems, traditionally, the loan was a real contract, effective through the actual delivery of money. This principle, coming from Roman law, underlines the physical cash transfer as the basis for obligation.[19] The French Code Civil, Article 1892, and German BGB §488, are still examples of this perspective. But in modern banking, where credit lines, overdrafts, and digital disbursements are common, the concept of delivery is more of a symbol rather than a physical action—it is an accounting or electronic credit. On the other hand, a loan in common law jurisdictions is treated as a consensual contract that can be enforced upon agreement and not on the delivery of the money. Lending is enforceable if it is backed by consideration.[20] The lender's duty to provide the money is derived from the contract, not the payment action. In both systems, the main point is the same: a promise to repay, conditioned by the terms agreed upon and enforceable by law.

[19] Selmani (2015, 142–151).

[20] Foakes v. Beer [1884] UKHL 1; Purdue (1941, 42–48), Pearce (2008, 630–636).

10.3.2 The Structure and Components of Loan Contracts

Loan agreements constitute the foundational instruments of credit intermediation and are therefore properly characterized as consensual, bilateral, and—except in rare gratuitous cases—onerous contracts. The core element of any loan contract is the principal amount: a definite sum of money advanced by the lender to the borrower. In addition, the interest rate serves as the legal price of credit, compensating the lender for the opportunity cost of capital, inflation risk, administrative expenses, and—most importantly—the borrower's individual credit risk. The repayment schedule establishes the temporal framework of the obligation, providing the primary benchmark against which a state of default is assessed.

Modern loan agreements address credit risk and information asymmetries through sophisticated risk-allocation mechanisms. Collateral grants the lender a priority (secured) claim over the borrower's specified assets or property, ensuring preferential recovery in the event of default or insolvency. Covenants impose ongoing obligations on the borrower, such as maintaining prescribed financial ratios (e.g., debt-to-equity or interest coverage), restricting additional indebtedness, prohibiting major asset disposals without consent, or requiring timely delivery of financial statements.[21] Breach of these covenants typically triggers acceleration clauses, allowing the lender to declare the entire outstanding principal, accrued interest, and fees immediately due and payable. Finally, choice-of-law and jurisdiction (or forum-selection) clauses specify the governing legal system and the venue for dispute resolution—provisions that are especially critical in cross-border transactions to reduce legal uncertainty and forum-shopping risks.

For a loan contract to be valid and enforceable, several essential conditions must be satisfied. First, both parties must possess the legal capacity to contract. In the case of natural persons, this requires full legal age and mental competence; for legal entities, it necessitates verification that the signatories are duly authorized under corporate documents (articles of association, board resolutions, or powers of attorney) to borrow and bind the entity. Second, the agreement must pursue a lawful purpose and must not contravene mandatory laws or public policy (e.g., prohibitions on usury, ML, or financing illegal activities).

While freedom of contract prevails in commercial lending, many jurisdictions impose formal requirements for certain types of loans. Residential mortgages and some consumer credits are frequently required to be in writing—and in some cases notarized or registered—to ensure enforceability and protect vulnerable borrowers. Moreover, lenders are generally obliged to provide full and transparent pre-contractual disclosure, including the effective interest rate (or APR), all fees and charges, the total cost of credit, repayment schedule, and material risks. Failure to comply with these disclosure obligations can render the contract voidable, trigger regulatory sanctions, or expose the lender to civil liability (including rescission, damages, or administrative fines).

---

[21] Ioannidou et al. (2022, 93–121).

10.3.3 Regulatory Context of Loan Contracts

Although loan contracts appear to be purely private, consensual agreements between lender and borrower, their economic and systemic consequences frequently extend far beyond the immediate parties and engage core public interests. Banks occupy a privileged and heavily regulated legal position: they operate under state-issued licenses that authorize them to accept public deposits and—through the fractional reserve mechanism—create credit and money. Consequently, each loan extended by a bank is not merely a bilateral contract; it is also an act that influences the broader economy through its effects on money supply, credit expansion, risk concentration, and overall financial stability.[22]

Modern legal regimes therefore refuse to treat lending as an exclusively private matter. Instead, they subject it to comprehensive prudential oversight designed to contain harmful externalities and prevent unchecked credit growth from jeopardizing the resilience of the financial system. This public-interest dimension manifests in concrete statutory limits and supervisory frameworks that qualify the scope of private contractual freedom. In the EU, the Capital Requirements Directive IV (CRD IV) and its implementing Regulation (CRR) impose strict large-exposure limits under Article 395, capping exposures to a single counterparty or connected group at 25% of eligible capital (with tighter restrictions for certain systemically important entities) in order to mitigate concentration risk. In the United States, the Dodd–Frank Wall Street Reform and Consumer Protection Act introduced enhanced disclosure obligations, stress-testing requirements, and prohibitions on abusive lending practices, aiming to close information asymmetries and protect both borrowers and the financial system from excessive risk-taking. In Turkey, Articles 48–54 of Banking Law No. 5411 establish detailed prudential rules governing record-keeping, collateral valuation, loan classification, non-performing loan provisioning, and per-borrower/per-group exposure limits (typically aligned with Basel standards and enforced by the Banking Regulation and Supervision Agency—BRSA/BDDK). These provisions impose clear public-law boundaries on private freedom of contract, ensuring that banks maintain sufficient capital and asset quality to absorb institution-specific and systemic shocks.

A fundamental shift has occurred in the regulatory conception of the duty of care. The traditional commercial principle of caveat emptor ("let the buyer beware") has largely given way to a modern supervisory ethos of caveat creditor ("let the lender beware"). Banks are now required to act proactively as responsible lenders: they must conduct thorough creditworthiness assessments, provide clear and transparent disclosure of the effective interest rate, total cost of credit, and associated risks, and implement measures to prevent borrowers—particularly consumers and small businesses—from assuming unsustainable debt burdens.

In this framework, the bank is no longer viewed solely as a profit-oriented private actor; it is also treated as a gatekeeper of financial soundness. Prudential

[22] Qian and Strahan (2007, 2803–2834).

regulation obliges lenders to exercise diligence and restraint as a precondition for participating in the credit market. By embedding these obligations in law, regulators seek to align private incentives with the broader public goal of preserving financial stability and protecting depositors, taxpayers, and the economy from the adverse consequences of imprudent lending.

10.3.4 Term, Scope, and Conditions of the Contract

10.3.4.1 The Temporal Dimension of Credit: Maturity Structures and Formal Requirements

The legal consequences and formal requirements of a loan vary significantly according to its duration. As the time horizon lengthens, the law generally demands greater formality, clearer documentation, and stronger safeguards to protect both parties and third-party interests. Short-term lending is often conducted with relative informality. Repayment may rely on implied security (such as the borrower's ongoing business cash flows), personal guarantees, or the lender's assessment of the borrower's creditworthiness, with documentation frequently limited to a simple promissory note or short-term credit agreement.

As the exposure period increases, however, so does the probability of default and the potential for competing claims on the borrower's assets. Consequently, longer-term loans are subject to stricter legal frameworks. In many civil law jurisdictions, obligations exceeding a certain duration or amount must be documented in writing, and in some cases recorded in a public register, to be fully enforceable. These formalities are not mere administrative requirements; they serve essential economic and protective functions.

For example, long-term loans secured by real property typically require a formal mortgage deed, which must be executed before a notary and registered in the land registry. This public registration achieves two critical objectives: first, it preserves the lender's priority over the collateral vis-à-vis subsequent creditors; second, it creates a transparent public record of encumbrances, thereby protecting third parties, such as future buyers or other lenders, from hidden claims on the asset.

10.3.4.2 The Doctrine of Purpose: Functional Constraints and "Use-of-Proceeds"

The scope of a credit facility is far more than a descriptive outline of the agreement; it constitutes a binding legal limit that defines the permissible boundaries for the use of the borrowed funds. In complex credit agreements—particularly syndicated facilities, project finance arrangements, and large corporate loans—this restriction is operationalized through use-of-proceeds clauses (also known as purpose clauses).[23] These provisions require the borrower to apply the loan proceeds

---

[23] Lambillon (2026, 25–41).

exclusively to the specific purposes expressly listed in the contract (e.g., financing a particular acquisition, capital expenditure project, working capital needs, or refinancing existing debt). In contractual terms, the borrower's representation and covenant regarding the intended use of funds form a core and material obligation. Any deviation—such as diversion of proceeds to unauthorized purposes—constitutes a purpose breach, which is typically classified as a material event of default. This entitles the lender (or agent on behalf of the syndicate) to accelerate repayment, suspend further drawdowns, terminate the facility, or enforce security.

The legal rationale for these restrictive covenants extends well beyond the lender's private interest in risk mitigation. In publicly traded debt markets (e.g., bonds and notes) and syndicated loan markets, use-of-proceeds clauses serve as a critical compliance and due-diligence tool. By tying disbursement to verifiable, specific purposes, lenders can more effectively screen borrowers, monitor fund flows, and demonstrate adherence to mandatory regulatory obligations—most notably under AML and CTF regimes (such as the EU's AML Directives, FATF Recommendations, and national implementations like Turkey's Law No. 5549 and MASAK regulations). This linkage helps prevent the financial system from unwittingly facilitating illicit capital flows, sanctions evasion, or activities in the shadow economy.

The inclusion and evolution of purpose clauses illustrate the deepening convergence between private contract law and public policy objectives. In contemporary finance—particularly with the rapid growth of green bonds, sustainability-linked loans (SLLs), and ESG-aligned facilities—the use-of-proceeds clause has transcended its traditional role as a defensive risk-management device. It has become an active instrument for enforcing compliance with environmental, social, and governance standards. For example, in green or sustainability-linked financing, proceeds must be allocated to eligible green projects (as verified by external second-party opinions or frameworks such as the ICMA Green Bond Principles or LMA Sustainability-Linked Loan Principles), with ongoing reporting and verification obligations to maintain the facility's sustainability credentials.[24] Breach of these purpose restrictions can trigger step-up interest margins, mandatory prepayments, or reputational and regulatory consequences.

Ultimately, the scope of a loan is no longer purely an internal matter between contracting parties. It now occupies the intersection of private contractual freedom and international expectations for financial integrity, transparency, and sustainable development. By constraining the application of credit, purpose clauses reconcile the pursuit of economic efficiency with the broader societal imperatives of risk containment, regulatory compliance, and responsible finance.

[24] Loan Market Association (2019) and PWC (2021).

10.3.4.3 Operational Efficacy: The Mechanics of Conditions Precedent and Subsequent

A credit facility becomes available, and remains available over time, only when the agreed conditions are satisfied at the required points in the facility's lifetime. These conditions are far more than routine administrative tasks; they are contractual safeguards that protect both parties between signing the agreement and the actual transfer of funds. Conditions precedent (CPs) are prerequisites that the borrower must fulfil before the lender becomes obliged to disburse funds or permit drawdowns. In high-stakes commercial lending, these usually include delivering formal legal opinions, providing valid insurance certificates, and obtaining the required regulatory approvals.

Requiring these pre-closing verifications ensures that the lender does not assume credit or legal risk until the borrower's legal capacity, corporate authority, and operational readiness have been independently confirmed. If any CP remains unsatisfied at the scheduled drawdown date (or by the long-stop date), the lender is entitled to withhold funding without breaching the agreement. Once the initial disbursement has occurred, conditions subsequent (CS) and ongoing covenants take effect. These govern the borrower's conduct throughout the life of the facility and maintain the lender's risk position over time. Typical ongoing obligations include regular reporting duties, like filing audited financial statements, and meeting financial covenant terms, such as keeping the debt-to-equity ratio at an agreed level. Conditions precedent set the requirements a borrower must meet before funds are released, while conditions subsequent set the ongoing requirements that keep the credit arrangement in place after the loan begins.[25]

Conditions precedent thus establishes the threshold requirements for initial funding, whereas conditions subsequent and covenants impose continuing obligations that preserve the integrity of the credit arrangement after the facility becomes operative. Failure to satisfy these conditions can lead to legal consequences. Non-fulfilment of a condition precedent generally allows the lender to refuse to advance funds without incurring liability for breach of contract. By contrast, a breach of a condition subsequent or a covenant is often treated as an event of default. This allows the lender to pursue several remedies, such as suspending any further drawdowns, charging a higher default interest rate, or ending the agreement and requiring immediate repayment of the full facility. In a credit relationship, these conditions serve as safeguards that let the lender change the terms or end the exposure if the borrower's risk profile worsens.

[25] Proksch (1982, 333–353).

10.3.5 The Dialectics of Credit: Asset Creation, Risk Allocation, and Regulatory Integration

The loan agreement is a formal legal instrument that carefully balances trust and risk between the parties. For the borrower, it provides access to liquidity that supports everyday operating needs, planned investments, or the growth and development of a small or medium-sized enterprise. For the lender, the contract fulfils a dual role: it represents the principal earning asset (generating interest income) while simultaneously constituting a potential source of loss that demands vigilant risk management and mitigation.[26] This dual character means the loan agreement is never static. Rather, it functions as a dynamic framework that enables continuous monitoring of changing economic conditions, the borrower's financial health, and evolving risks throughout the life of the facility.

The loan agreement draws a clear distinction between categories of rights and remedies. At origination, the loan creates a personal (*in personam*) claim: the lender holds a contractual right to demand repayment from the borrower's general estate, without any proprietary interest in specific assets. By contrast, when the borrower pledges assets as collateral, the lender acquires a real (in rem) right—a proprietary security interest in the designated property.[27] This distinction becomes decisive upon default or insolvency. An unsecured creditor ranks as a general claimant and must share pro rata with other unsecured creditors in the debtor's estate. A secured creditor, however, enjoys priority over the encumbered assets (or their proceeds), enabling recovery ahead of the general body of creditors and thereby significantly improving the likelihood and quantum of repayment.[28]

Beyond defining the bilateral relationship between lender and borrower, the loan contract serves as the foundational unit for prudential reporting, risk assessment, and regulatory capital calculation. In modern regulatory frameworks—most notably the Basel Accords (Basel III and Basel IV)—a private loan is no longer treated solely as a confidential commercial transaction. It is a reportable exposure that directly influences the amount of regulatory capital a bank must hold against credit, market, operational, and other risks.

Each loan must therefore be classified according to its type (e.g., corporate, retail, sovereign), maturity, collateral status, credit quality, and risk parameters. These classifications feed into the calculation of RWA) under the standardized or IRB approaches, determining the minimum capital charge the institution must maintain. In this way, what begins as a private contractual arrangement acquires a significant public dimension: it affects the bank's overall risk profile, contributes to system-wide credit monitoring, and—through aggregated exposures—helps shape the stability of the broader financial system. Ultimately, the loan agreement transcends its role as a mere bilateral instrument. It operates at the intersection of private law (contractual rights, security interests, enforcement remedies) and public

---

[26] Tur et al. (2021, 1–13).

[27] Bridge (1996, 141–162).

[28] Wessels and Madaus (2020, 211–225) and Kasak (2019, 112–121).

law (prudential regulation, capital adequacy, financial stability oversight), ensuring that individual credit decisions remain compatible with the resilience and soundness of the banking sector and the economy at large.

10.3.6 Interest: Legal and Economic Dimensions

The borrower pays interest for two reasons: suspending the payment and the risk of nonpayment. Therefore, interest is often treated as the price of shifting scarce capital across time. Therefore, interest rate depends on the lender's flexibility in date of redemption: the rate would be higher to reschedule to a later date.

The setting of interest rates is not determined only by market forces; rather, the credibility of both lenders and borrowers is also a determinant for rates. This points to a long-running historical debate about the doctrine of usury.[29] Modern finance is often based on the idea that parties are free to agree on loan terms, yet many legal systems, through civil codes and consumer protection laws, set interest caps to limit predatory lending.[30] These limits reflect a public policy choice meant to protect a debtor's basic financial dignity and to keep the credit market stable for everyone involved.

Interest is usually split into two types: (i) compensatory interest, which is the agreed payment for using someone else's money, and (ii) default interest, which applies when the debtor does not pay or perform as required and serves both as compensation and as a penalty. Under contract law, the first term is central to the contract's financial return, and the second term works as a deterrent to keep the payment schedule intact. Interest is not just a number; it also sits at the point where goals like economic efficiency meet concerns about distributive justice.

10.3.6.1 Taxonomy of Interest: From Contractual Autonomy to Statutory Restraint

In a credit relationship, labelling a payment interest is more than a calculation; it depends on the legal character of the obligation that gives rise to it. In modern financial law, interest is usually grouped into a few main categories based on how it works in practice, and each category is treated under its own set of regulatory rules. The interest rate is mainly shown in three forms.

The first form is contractual (nominal) interest that expressly agreed upon in the loan contract. It is the main payment the borrower makes in return for receiving credit from the lender. The interest rate stated in the loan agreement reflects what both parties understood the cost of the funds to be at the time the loan was made. Even though it reflects the parties' freedom to contract, its validity is now more often questioned unless the terms are clear and the effective annual rate (EAR)

---

[29] Glaeser and Scheinkman (1994) and Lee (2017, 227–263).

[30] European Parliament (1999).

is disclosed as required.[31] The second form is default interest, sometimes called mora interest or late-payment interest. It arises when the debtor fails to perform on the agreed maturity date. It serves two purposes: it sets a pre-agreed monetary amount as compensation for the delay, and it encourages timely performance by making late payment more costly. Since default interest can be coercive, legal systems, especially in civil law jurisdictions, often set statutory limits on default rates.[32] These caps stop debts from growing so large that they cannot reasonably be repaid, and they help make sure that legal penalties do not push borrowers into complete financial collapse. The third form is compound interest, a.k.a. anatocism or interest on interest as charging interest on unpaid interest. For a long time, both legal scholars and theologians treated anatocism with suspicion, and most modern legal systems now ban it outright or allow it only under narrow conditions. When it is allowed, it usually depends on a clear written agreement between the parties.[33] In many cases, it applies only to certain commercial accounts, or it is limited to a defined time period. Such limits aim to keep debt from compounding, so repayment obligations do not grow faster than the borrower can reasonably cover through income and other resources.

Finally, variable interest rate have become widespread in medium- and long-term financing as a way to respond to swings in global markets. These rates are tied to external reference indices such as EURIBOR and SOFR, and in the past LIBOR. The legality of variable interest rates rests on transparency and fairness, meaning the lender should base the rate on a benchmark it cannot change on its own.[34] The move from bank-set rates based on judgment to market-based indices reflects a regulatory effort to protect borrowers from arbitrary increases in borrowing costs.

10.3.6.2 The Limits of Accumulation: Usury, Transparency, and the Doctrine of Unconscionability

The principle of *pacta sunt servanda* (agreements must be kept) as a basic rule in contract law is not absolute. There would be interventions when credit terms shift from standard market returns to exploitative practices.[35] In both past and present settings, this kind of intervention appears in usury laws, which set limits on interest rates to protect borrowers from financial harm. These ceilings are not just economic price controls; they reflect states' police power to curb predatory practices that could push many people into insolvency and create broader social instability.[36]

Usury rules vary widely across countries, so a global overview needs to compare how each jurisdiction sets interest-rate limits and enforces them. In the EU,

[31] See, Rundo and Stallo (2019, 91).
[32] Gunnarsson (2017, 765–788).
[33] McNiece (1946, 71–79) and Gioia-Carabellese (2016, 174–200).
[34] Geronimo and Baclay (2021, 267–268) and Kovacs and Tertak (2025, 140).
[35] Witzleb (2023, 1), Gebhardt (1947, 160), Kesuma and Mahduf (2023, 432–440), and Zhifeng (2022, 745–801).
[36] Vandenbrink (1982, 44–55).

national usury laws apply alongside Directive 2008/48/EC on consumer credit agreements, so both EU rules and domestic statutes shape how consumer lending is regulated.[37] This two-level approach lets member states hold the reins of power to set their own interest rate caps while still maintaining a shared baseline of consumer protection across the single market. In the US, likewise, lending rules are shaped by both state and federal law. States set usury caps, and these interest-rate limits differ across jurisdictions. At the federal level, statutes such as the TILA set disclosure requirements for credit terms. In the US, the main approach is protection through disclosure: the idea is that clear, detailed information helps borrowers recognize and avoid unfair or exploitative interest rates.[38] In Islamic finance under Sharia law, charging or paying riba (interest or usury) is not permitted.[39] This principal shapes financial contracts so they avoid the interest-based lending model that is widely used in Western banking systems. In this framework, capital is not treated as a commodity that earns a fixed return over time; it is invested through profit-sharing arrangements such as Musharakah or Mudarabah. In this case, the lender should bear part of the project's risk if they want to share in its returns, which shifts the ethical basis of the credit arrangement.

Alongside statutory caps, many courts now rely on the doctrine of unconscionability to review credit agreements. Courts may also review contract terms for hidden charges, poor transparency, or provisions so one-sided that they shock the conscience of the court. In efforts to reduce information asymmetry, the APR serves as an important measure. APR is a standard measure that includes both the stated interest rate and any required fees or other costs tied to the loan.[40] In many legal systems, failing to state the APR correctly is not just a minor technical mistake. It is a substantive breach that may make the contract voidable and can expose the lender to serious administrative sanctions.

10.3.7 Credit Limits and the Framework of Ancillary Covenants

A credit limit sets the numeric cap in a lending arrangement and states the highest level of exposure a lender is willing or permitted to accept. Beyond its contractual function, it serves as a key safeguard for prudent risk control. Under Basel III and corresponding national laws, these limits prevent excessive concentration of risk in a single borrower, a related group, or a specific industry sector. In most cases, the bank sets these exposure limits as a percentage of its Tier 1 capital so that a single borrower's default does not put the bank's solvency at risk.[41]

[37] Cherednychenko (2024, 241–270), Ferretti and Livada (2016, 15).
[38] Levitin (2024, 425–484).
[39] Zaman (2008, 1–15).
[40] Posner (1995, 283), McCullough (2016, 779–825), Lonegrass (2012), and Russell (2019, 965–1026).
[41] BIS (2010).

In practice, a credit facility agreement is seldom an isolated instrument; it usually sits at the center of a wider set of related contracts. This framework is supported by several types of related agreements and clauses that are meant to protect the lender's position.

Covenant packages are the practical rules that set the boundaries for how the agreement is carried out. These terms can include financial ratios, such as a debt-to-EBITDA limit, detailed reporting requirements, and negative pledge clauses that prevent the borrower from placing liens on assets to secure other creditors.[42]

10.3.8 The Jurisprudence of Default: Contingency, Enforcement, and Equitable Constraints

A credit agreement can be understood as a written record of what will happen if certain conditions arise. Although the contract is mainly meant to guide and secure performance, its legal strength is usually assessed only when one party fails to perform. In a loan agreement, the default clause is the provision that allows the lender to activate and enforce its contractual remedies. They are put into practice through a set list of events of default (EoD), which covers more than just a failure to make a payment.

Default can occur in several ways. First of all, monetary default is the standard reason where a borrower does not pay the required principal or interest when it is due.[43] That being said, the debtor may default in case of covenant breaches,[44] i.e. the operational or financial limits specified in the contract are exceed, e.g. exceeding a leverage cap, falling below an interest coverage ratio, or missing a minimum liquidity requirement. Insolvency and bankruptcy are also cases of debtor default.[45] If a creditor waits until the due date, their debt will become difficult to collect, giving them the right to demand payment directly. Cross-default clauses might be involved in credit agreement that if a borrower fails to meet such obligations under any other external debt, that failure also counts as a default under the current agreement.[46] The purpose is to let the lender respond at the same time as other creditors rather than waiting until recovery options are reduced. Also, if borrowers' statements, representations and warranties are inaccurate (misrepresentation), the debtor would be in default.[47]

Once an EoD occurs, the lender may take the remedies available under the agreement. These include an acceleration clause, under which the lender may demand immediate payment of the full remaining balance, bringing the credit

[42] Ivashina and Vallee (2025, 9998–10,021).
[43] Vu (2023, 242–260) and Li et al. (2015, 1638).
[44] Freudenberg et al. (2017, 540–565).
[45] Shubhan (2019, 76).
[46] Childs et al. (1996, 511–536), Huang and Yin (2025, 215–225), and Johan, Sudiro and Gunadi (2022, 1–13).
[47] Dorman (2012, 35–43).

arrangement to an end. In such cases, the lender may enforce its rights by realizing the collateral through foreclosure or sale of pledged assets, calling on any personal or corporate guarantees, and starting litigation or arbitration to obtain a court or tribunal judgment for the debt.

The exercise of these rights is subject to limits and is not absolute. In public policy and modern consumer protection law, enforcement is limited by the need to be proportionate and to follow due process. Courts and regulators are paying closer attention to aggressive enforcement tactics. For example, predatory foreclosure occurs when a lender seeks to seize collateral based on a minor or purely technical breach, which courts may treat as an abuse of right (*abus de droit*). If a lender goes too far, he may face legal liability for damages and regulatory sanctions from banking supervisors. Therefore, the default phase involves balancing the creditor's right to recover what is owed with the borrower's right to a fair exit from the contract that does not rely on predatory terms.

10.3.9 The Digital Frontier: Algorithmic Governance and the Rise of Smart Loan Contracts

Currently, numerous loan agreements are no longer signed only on paper; they are made and stored through digital systems, which raises questions about how traditional contract law rules apply. Blockchain-based lending and smart contracts, which run automatically with the agreement terms written in code, shift trust away from human judgment and toward rules enforced by cryptographic math. In this framework, the credit process—from algorithm-based scoring and automatic pay-out to ongoing, real-time tracking—is increasingly run by self-directed systems, which raises basic questions about informed consent, who is responsible when things go wrong, and when courts should step in.[48]

Moving credit systems into digital formats raises legal questions that older civil law and common law rules were not built to deal with. The enforceability of electronic signatures and automated click-wrap consent is supported by legal instruments such as the UNCITRAL Model Law on Electronic Commerce and the EU eIDAS Regulation.[49] These tools make digital contracts function much like paper contracts, but courts and researchers still closely examine whether the parties had an intent to be bound when the agreement is formed in an automated setting.[50]

As credit scoring moves from human judgment to machine learning, regulators are increasingly concerned that opaque black-box models can hide discriminatory decisions. Protecting borrowers from biased algorithms calls for updated data protection laws that hold lenders responsible for automated credit decisions and

48 Bassan and Rabitti (2024) and Levy (2017, 1–15).
49 Lima (2023, 108).
50 Wolff (2018, 151–181).

require a clear, human explanation when an application is denied. The view that smart contracts enforce themselves, often summed up as code is law, can undermine the state's exclusive role in enforcing legal rules. When a smart contract is set up to take collateral automatically once it detects a default, courts are no longer deciding the issue before the seizure. Instead, they may only be able to review after the fact whether the code ran as intended, which can make it harder to enforce these digital obligations across national borders.[51]

Even with these limits, moving credit processes online can cut processing time and lower administrative costs. Real-time data feeds, often called oracles, let financial systems adjust interest rates as conditions change and react quickly to market swings. This can lower transactional friction compared with many traditional banking processes that update rates slowly or rely on manual steps. As trust becomes built into software through formal rules, the legal system needs to make sure that error-correction processes and fair safeguards are still included in the code, rather than removed by design. A digital loan contract is more than a new tool. It marks a shift in credit law by bringing computational methods into legal analysis and changing how borrowers and lenders set terms and manage obligations.

10.3.10 The Loan Contract as the Genetic Code of Global Finance

The loan contract sits in a tense space between the parties' freedom to set their own terms and the state's rules for overseeing financial activity. It captures a key tension in the modern financial system: each deal draws its legal and ethical force from the parties' consent, yet public law steps in to protect the wider public by supporting the stability and sound functioning of the economy. This tension shows how credit shifted from an informal favour between individuals to an institutional asset governed by strict rules and oversight. Loan agreements are sine qua non for the continuation of the financial system, since it sets out the core terms that shape how the transaction works. This is not just a metaphor; it describes how the structure works. Even the most complex financial products, such as credit default swaps, sovereign bonds, and structured securities, rest on the same basic idea: a two-party commitment that sets the terms for payment and responsibility. A loan contract is a basic building block in finance. Its main terms, such as the principal, the interest rate, and the maturity date, set out the structure that supports much of the global capital market.

[51] Goodness et al. (2025) and Umeaduma and Adeniyi (2025, 6647–6661).

Example

The legal continuity of the loan contract perhaps ranks as the most profound characteristic, spanning centuries of financial evolution. While the modern facilities of credit are now determined by digital signatures and blockchain smart systems, their doctrinal essence remains astonishingly consistent with the great international fairs of pre-modern Europe. To take just one example, the international fairs of the 12th, 15th, and sixteenth centuries, and specifically those in Champagne, functioned as a "forcing house" for the creation of the tools that now support credit law. These were, in effect, not just centres of goods exchange, but also of money, credit, and exchange in general. The development of these forms of legal regulation can be traced to a series of important milestones in the past. For example, there has been a scarcity of precious metals (the Bullion famine), hence the need to innovate ways of providing liquidity without the use of cash. There was also a certificate, namely *lettre de foire*, that was given to a seller that stated that they legally deserved to receive payment at a future fair. This is basically like a secure credit system without money. Another example was *instrumentum ex causa cambii*, which notarized document that represents the merchant's promise to repay a debt in the future. It is a prototype for the modern-day credit agreement. Last but not least, there was a scontration (clearing) mechanism. By 1180, the Champagne Fairs had developed an advanced method of 'scontration', which enabled the mutual clearing of accounts between partners without the actual medium of cash. The emergence from the "lettra di pagamento," an informal letter of advice, to the bill of exchange, or "lettera di cambio," in the fourteenth century marked the beginning of payment orders that facilitated the transfer of debt through an array of international correspondents. This autonomy from physical metal and "money of account" formed the monetary security to facilitate trade over distance. The modern credit facilities with intricate covenants and various international enforcement practices trace back to the aforementioned 'capital markets' before the Industrial Revolution. Thus, it becomes evident that the most enduring instrument in managing risks in international commerce remains the legally enforceable promise to repay.[52] ◄

10.4 Types of Bank Loans: The Bifurcation of Personal and Commercial Lending

In modern banking, credit is not a single tool; it covers many products designed for different economic uses, levels of risk, and regulatory requirements. In legal theory, classifying loans is meant to set the rules, not just to describe the product. Once a credit facility is put in a given category, that label determines the legal

[52] Denzel (2025, 245–270).

regime that applies, including how much consumer protection is required, how strict the collateral rules are, what limits apply to interest rates, and how detailed the required prudential reporting must be.

The credit market is often split into two main categories: personal (retail) loans and commercial (corporate) loans. Both rest on the same basic contract—money provided now in return for a commitment to repay later—but the legal consequences differ in important ways. Personal loans are aimed at individuals who need funds for everyday spending or housing-related costs. In many cases, the lender has much more bargaining power than the borrower. For this reason, the law steps in with asymmetric regulation to protect the borrower first. This requires the bank to disclose the APR, allow consumers cooling-off withdrawal rights, and comply with a stricter duty of explanation when presenting the terms. In this context, the rule of caveat emptor is largely replaced by a social policy designed to protect buyers.[53] Commercial loans are credit facilities designed to meet the operating and investment needs of businesses. They can cover short-term working capital needs as well as longer-term funding for projects that require structured financing.[54] As a matter of law, the parties are treated as sophisticated commercial actors with comparable bargaining power.

As a result, the law gives parties more freedom to set the terms of their contract, including custom covenant packages, complex security structures, and interest rules that are less restrictive. This discussion centres on how reliably the rules are enforced and how well capital is allocated, not on social protection. This split allows the financial system to do two things at the same time: keep credit safe and transparent for most people, while still providing flexible financial instruments that support industrial and commercial expansion. Classifying a loan is the first step in deciding which legal rules will apply throughout the credit relationship.

10.4.1 Personal Loans

A personal loan is a credit agreement between a bank and an individual, taken mainly for private purposes rather than for the borrower's trade, business, or profession. Whether they are used for consumption, education, health care, or personal investment, these facilities fall under two sets of legal rules: general civil law principles and the specific requirements of consumer protection law. This overlap shows that the state recognizes an inherent asymmetry of power, both economic and informational, between an individual borrower and an institutional lender.

Rules for personal lending have increasingly been shaped by international legal instruments, many of which aim to place the main duty to provide clear information on the creditor. The EU Consumer Credit Directive (2008/48/EC) sets out key rules for consumer credit in the EU and is widely treated as a main reference

[53] Flagg and Hannon (2023).
[54] Ellias and Fontenay (2025, 779–857).

point in retail finance. In general, it applies to consumer loan agreements up to €75,000. The directive formalizes the Standard European Consumer Credit Information (SECCI), requires lenders to disclose the Annual Percentage Rate (APR), and gives borrowers a legal right to withdraw from the agreement within 14 days during a cooling-off period.[55]

From an Anglo-American point of view, the UK takes a clear statutory approach. The Consumer Credit Act 1974 allows courts to examine whether a credit agreement has created an unfair relationship between the lender and the borrower, and to order remedies if it has.[56] In the US, there is no single equivalent rule across the whole system. Courts and regulators instead rely on a mix of state contract doctrines such as unconscionability, state consumer protection statutes, and federal disclosure rules such as the Truth in Lending Act to address unfair lending practices. The TILA helps protect borrowers from misleading credit pricing by requiring clear, consistent disclosures and restricting fees that are not plainly disclosed.[57]

A key part of the modern lending framework is the doctrine of responsible lending, meaning that a bank's duty is not limited to making money; it also has to check, before lending, whether the borrower can realistically repay without facing undue hardship. This legal standard is supported by key case law from the Court of Justice of the European Union. In Case C-449/13 (CA Consumer Finance), the Court made clear that failing to carry out a proper creditworthiness assessment is not just a procedural mistake; it amounts to a breach of public policy.[58]

From this perspective, personal credit is no longer treated as only a private matter between the parties to a contract. This is a social activity in which the law aims to ensure that access to credit does not turn into predatory debt. In this context, the bank acts as a gatekeeper, and if it does not act with due care, the contract may end up being unenforceable or the bank may face serious administrative penalties.

10.4.1.1 Personal Finance Credit

In personal finance, a credit loan is an unsecured form of debt offered to individuals for general uses such as paying for education, travel, or everyday spending. From a risk management point of view, what sets this instrument apart is that it has no specific collateral, so the lender does not hold any in rem right over the borrower's assets. Rather than requiring collateral, the bank bases its decision solely on the borrower's expected future income and overall credit profile. Since unsecured lending carries a higher risk that the borrower will not repay, many legal systems have moved away from a broad freedom of contract approach and toward stricter regulation that places demanding, fiduciary-like duties on lenders. In personal finance credit law, lender duties are usually grouped into three main areas:

---

[55] Porras and Boom (2012).

[56] Goode (1975).

[57] Griffith (2007, 611–676) and Pridgen (2012, 615–639).

[58] Ferretti (2021, 102–121) and Grundmann et al. (2021, 205).

The first duty is the duty to provide information (mandated disclosure) where the lender must, by law, provide clear disclosure of the full cost of the loan. This goes beyond stating the nominal interest rate; it also calls for stating the Annual Percentage Rate (APR) and accounting for all fees, insurance costs, and any penalties.[59] The aim is to remove hidden pricing so the borrower can make a rational economic decision.

The second duty to assess credit affordability test since it requires lenders to check whether a borrower can realistically afford the credit before it is approved. Lenders should rely on reliable, objective data, such as credit bureau reports and verified income statements, to assess whether a borrower can repay the loan over time. In European practice, this is treated as a procedural rule for how business is conducted, not as an optional recommendation.[60]

Advisory duty could be regarded as the final essential duty because lending is not only a matter of calculating risk and repayment; it can also involve an obligation to warn borrowers when the terms or the likely outcomes could cause foreseeable harm. This means informing the borrower about the long-term risks of taking on too much debt, especially with revolving credit or loans with high interest rates.[61]

In many legal systems, failing to follow these duties can lead to more than administrative fines; it can also change the balance of the contract in a meaningful way. As a clear example is §505a of the German Civil Code (BGB), if a lender seriously neglects the creditworthiness assessment, it can lose its claim to interest and, in very severe cases, even its right to repayment of the principal.[62] This sanction through loss of profit works as a deterrent by giving the bank a clear financial reason to act as a prudent gatekeeper in the credit market, rather than behaving in a predatory way.

10.4.1.2 Real Estate Loans

10.4.1.2.1 Mortgage in General

A mortgage is one of the oldest tools used in credit, operating where contract law and property law come together. A mortgage differs from personal finance arrangements because it gives the lender a real right in rem over immovable property. This

---

[59] Ben-Shahar and Schneider (2011, 647–749).

[60] Cherednychenko and Meindertsma (2019, 483–519) and Fairweather (2012, 84–110).

[61] Pavlovich and Sante (2024).

[62] According to Section 505a of the BGB titled obligation to perform a creditworthiness assessment for consumer credit agreements, "Prior to concluding a consumer credit agreement, the lender is to assess the creditworthiness of the borrower. The lender may conclude the consumer credit agreement only if the creditworthiness assessment shows that no significant doubts exist, where a general-purpose consumer credit agreement is concerned, and that it is likely, where a consumer credit agreement relating to immovable property is concerned, that the borrower will comply with their obligations in connection with the credit agreement as stipulated by the contract. If the net loan amount is significantly increased following conclusion of the credit agreement, the creditworthiness is to be newly assessed on an updated basis, unless the amount by which the net loan was increased already had been included in the original creditworthiness assessment."

legal structure means the asset, not just the borrower's personal promise, stands as the final guarantee that the debt will be repaid. If the borrower commits a material default, the lender may foreclose and request a court-ordered sale of the property, with the sale proceeds applied to the unpaid debt.[63]

In civil law systems, a mortgage is generally valid and enforceable only when it has been made public through the required registration or other publicity rules. For a mortgage to be enforceable against third parties and to set its priority among competing claims, it must be recorded in the official land registry. In common law systems, a similar practical outcome is reached by using charges or deeds of trust. Across legal systems, the basic rule on priority is prior *tempore potior jure*, meaning first in time, stronger in right. In insolvency proceedings, the order in which interests are registered generally decides which creditor has the higher-ranking claim.[64]

Modern mortgage law is not simply a tool that favours creditors. It is a balanced set of rules that aims to protect homeownership and support the stability of the housing system. For this reason, the foreclosure process is controlled by strict procedural safeguards. Mandatory notice and grace periods require lenders to follow the timelines set by law and to give the debtor a final chance to fix the default before further action is taken.[65] Courts can rely on their supervisory jurisdiction to limit abusive conduct, such as accelerating a debt in a way that is unfair or predatory. Deficiency judgment limitations refer to state laws that restrict when, or how much, a lender can collect from a borrower after a foreclosure sale. If the sale price is less than the amount owed, these rules may prevent the lender from suing for the remaining balance or may cap what can be recovered. In practice, this limits a borrower's post-foreclosure liability and reduces the risk of severe long-term financial harm.

From a macroprudential viewpoint, regulators often focus closely on mortgage portfolios when assessing risks in the financial system. Under Basel III, housing loans that are fully secured by collateral are usually given lower risk weights than unsecured loans. This regulatory approach reflects the long record of real estate as a relatively stable asset class and is meant to encourage banks to keep their mortgage portfolios well managed.[66] In this sense, mortgages are a central part of the financial system because they turn land's fixed value into a steady source of long-term funding.

10.4.1.2.2 Endowment Mortgage

An endowment mortgage is a hybrid form of borrowing that pairs a standard mortgage with an endowment policy, so it does not fit neatly into the usual categories of home loans.[67] Unlike a standard repayment mortgage, this arrangement is an

[63] Tsintsadze (2015, 106–111).
[64] Ibid.
[65] Odinet (2021, 89) and Bubb and Krishnamurthy (2015, 1539–1630).
[66] See, BIS (2021, 38) and Liu and Molise (2019, 264–279).
[67] Pereira et al. (2003, 197–221).

interest-only loan in which the borrower's regular payments to the bank cover only the interest on the amount borrowed. The principal is not repaid during the loan term. Instead, the full principal is due at maturity and is expected to be paid from the proceeds of a separate life insurance or investment policy set up alongside the loan. This setup creates three linked contracts: the main loan agreement, the insurance or investment policy, and a separate assignment agreement that gives the lender a security interest in the policy's future value at maturity. Since the return of principal depends on how the underlying investment performs, this instrument carries a real risk that the investor will receive less than the amount initially invested. Because these products are complex, courts have often looked closely at cases where they were mis-sold or where advisers may have failed to meet their duty to give proper advice. Under current financial conduct rules, the lender must do more than standard checks and carry out a suitability assessment to confirm that the loan fits the borrower's circumstances.

Simply disclosing the terms is not enough; the lender should take reasonable steps to confirm that the borrower understands the risks and that those risks fit the borrower's tolerance and level of financial knowledge, given the volatility of an investment-linked repayment option. How regulators handle endowment mortgages reflects the fact that they combine features of both a mortgage loan and an investment product. Under the UK Financial Services and Markets Act (FSMA) and, in the EU, under MiFID II, these products are more often being treated as investment-linked loans.[68] This classification creates a dual regulation regime, meaning firms must follow mortgage lending rules and also meet strict investment disclosure requirements. Lenders must provide investors with a Product Disclosure Statement (PDS) and a clear explanation of the risks, including that the endowment policy may not reach the target amount needed to repay the principal debt.[69] The endowment mortgage is a useful case study for examining how contractual coupling can raise a lender's exposure to liability and shift legal attention away from the value of the security toward how clear and transparent the advice was.

10.4.1.2.3 Assumption of Mortgage

A housing loan transfer happens when the original borrower sells the mortgaged property to another person, and the buyer takes over the remaining loan and the duty to repay it.[70] This transaction should not be treated as a straightforward sale. It may amount either to a novation or to an assignment of debt, depending on how the relevant jurisdiction classifies it. The legal issue is that the mortgage, as a security right attached to the land, stays with the property when it changes hands, while the debt is a personal duty of the borrower. Because of that difference, the borrower cannot transfer the debt on their own without the creditor's agreement, since doing so could weaken the creditor's security.

---

[68] Busch (2017, 340–380).

[69] Bamford (2001, 84).

[70] Ramadhani (2020, 31–37) and Hunt et al. (2013, 1529–1586).

In civil law, a key point is that transferring an asset is treated separately from transferring the related liability. The original debtor can be released only if the lender gives clear, express consent. If the required approval is not obtained, the initial borrower still has legal responsibility for meeting the contract terms under the rule of privity of contract, even if the property has been transferred to someone else. This requirement protects the lender from debtor risk by preventing a borrower with strong credit from being replaced by a weaker borrower unless the lender can review the change and give approval in advance. In today's global financial market, these transfers often fall under conflict-of-law rules. In the EU, Article of the Rome I Regulation sets out the basic rule for choosing which national law applies to a contract in cross-border cases. Clause 14 sets out the main test for deciding which national law applies to the transferability of these obligations and to the legal relationship between the assignor and the assignee.[71] The legal validity of a loan transfer depends on whether it is recorded in the land registry. The relationship between the borrower's personal obligation under the loan and the mortgage on the property should stay aligned. If they split, legal fragmentation can occur, meaning the property owner and the loan debtor are different parties with no clear contract tying the debt to the security. Transferring a home loan is a formal process that involves the seller, the buyer, and the lender working together so the loan and its collateral remain in place without interruption.

10.4.1.2.4 Home Equity Line of Credit (HELOC)

This section examines the Home Equity Line of Credit, or HELOC, as a credit device that brings together two features that are often treated separately. On the one hand, it operates as revolving debt, since the borrower may draw funds up to a set limit, repay, and borrow again during the draw period. On the other hand, it is backed by in rem security over the borrower's home, which gives the lender a property-based claim that stands apart from the borrower's personal duty to pay.[72]

The revolving structure raises questions about how the outstanding balance is quantified, how interest and fees are charged, and when unilateral amendments are allowed. The in-rem security feature raises questions about creation and perfection of the security interest, priority against other creditors, and the steps required for enforcement if payment is not made. Since the secured amount can change with each draw and repayment, a HELOC also tests how well traditional rules on mortgages and secured credit fit a fluctuating debt. The discussion focuses on the legal nature of the HELOC agreement, the allocation of risk between borrower and lender, and the role of disclosure and consumer protection rules. It also considers how default and enforcement operate in practice, including notice, acceleration, and foreclosure, and how these rules interact with bankruptcy and competing liens.

---

[71] Hartley (2011, 29–56), Ferrari (2020, 58) and Dougherty and Killen (2020, 108–111).

[72] Day (2005).

The aim is to clarify how revolving credit and in rem security work as one arrangement, and where this structure creates legal uncertainty that courts and lawmakers must address.

HELOC is credit backed by your home that lets you borrow, repay, and borrow again up to a set limit, much like other revolving credit, while still being secured by a mortgage lien on the property. A traditional term loan gives the borrower a lump sum that is repaid on a fixed schedule. A HELOC works more like a revolving credit line: the borrower can draw funds up to a set limit, repay them, and borrow again, with the equity in a primary residence serving as collateral. In doctrinal terms, this functions as a revolving security interest: the mortgage acts as a floating form of security that follows a debt balance that goes up and down over time.[73]

Since a HELOC can be drawn on and repaid over time, it raises legal and safety concerns that are different from those found in fixed, closed-end mortgage loans. A key concern is gradual over-indebtedness: when money is easy to obtain, borrowers may draw down their home equity and spend it on consumption rather than on activities that generate future income. Modern financial rules set strict loan-to-value (LTV) caps, meaning the combined amount of the first mortgage and any HELOC cannot be more than a set percentage of the home's appraised value. This buffer is required by law to help keep the lender financially stable and reduce the risk that borrowers lose their homes when market conditions change.[74] In jurisdictions that allow more than one encumbrance, re-advancing funds under a HELOC may create priority disputes between later lenders. To protect the accuracy of the land registry, many legal rules require the secured interest to be formally confirmed each time it is renewed, or they restrict the priority of later advances when other creditors have entered in the meantime.

Because most HELOCs have variable interest rates, consumer protection concerns support requiring lenders to give borrowers clear, regular updates about rate changes and their likely cost impact. Lenders must provide periodic statements that explain any changes in interest rates and how those changes affect future repayment amounts. In this setting, a HELOC shows how credit law has changed over time. It lets homeowners turn what is usually a fixed home value into a source of usable cash. At the same time, it calls for closer, ongoing oversight by regulators because the borrowing and repayment can shift quickly and create risk.[75]

10.4.2 Commercial Loans

Commercial loans play a vital role in supporting business activity, financing expansion projects, trade operations, inventory acquisitions, and short-term working

[73] Ibid.
[74] Gatt (2024, 232–267).
[75] See, Consumer Financial Protection Bereau (2014).

capital requirements. They differ from personal (or consumer) loans in three fundamental respects, reflecting the distinct economic purposes, parties involved, and risk profiles of each category.

First, the parties to commercial loans are typically sophisticated commercial actors—such as corporations, financial institutions, institutional investors, and experienced professionals—who engage in arm's-length negotiations. For this reason, consumer protection regimes—such as the US' TILA, the EU Consumer Credit Directive, or analogous national laws—generally do not apply, or apply only in limited circumstances (e.g., when a small business owner personally guarantees a loan in a manner that triggers consumer-like protections). The terms of commercial loans are therefore negotiated freely between parties presumed to have comparable bargaining power, rather than imposed as standardized, take-it-or-leave-it conditions typical in consumer lending.[76]

Second, commercial loan agreements are substantially longer, more detailed, and more complex than those used in personal lending. These documents routinely include extensive representations and warranties concerning the borrower's legal status, financial condition, and business operations; affirmative covenants, requiring the borrower to maintain insurance, pay taxes, provide financial statements, and comply with laws; negative covenants, prohibiting additional indebtedness, asset disposals, mergers, or dividend distributions without consent); detailed financial ratio tests (e.g., debt-to-EBITDA, interest coverage, or liquidity ratios); reporting obligations; and precisely defined events of default. By contrast, personal loans—such as unsecured personal lines of credit or auto loans—rely on far simpler documentation, with fewer covenants and less intrusive monitoring, reflecting the lower complexity and smaller scale of the transactions.[77]

Third, the scope of security in commercial lending is typically much broader and more diverse than in consumer secured lending. A lender's security interest may extend to a wide range of business assets, including accounts receivable, inventory, equipment, machinery, intellectual property -such as patents, trademarks, and copyrights- contract rights, project cash flows, equity interests in subsidiaries, and even future-acquired property via after-acquired property clauses or floating charges.[78]

These distinctions are logical and functional in a commercial context, where transaction sizes are significantly larger, maturities are often longer, and lenders face greater exposure to business-cycle, operational, and market risks. They also rest on the reasonable presumption that commercial borrowers possess the financial sophistication, legal resources, and negotiating leverage necessary to understand, evaluate, and negotiate complex contractual terms. As a result, commercial lending law prioritizes contractual freedom, enforceability, and risk allocation over the paternalistic safeguards that characterize consumer credit regulation.

---

[76] Cole et al. (2015, 537) and Nation (2015, 181).

[77] Drucker and Puri (2009, 2635). See, Davies and Raczynska (2020).

[78] Heller et al. (2024, 379–392).

10.4.3 Syndicated Loans

Syndicated loans are sophisticated financing arrangements created by multiple banks collaborating. They consolidate resources to provide credit to a single borrower-usually for major needs. The law governing such loans outlines the rights and responsibilities of each bank involved, the structure of the collateral, if applicable, and the procedures followed step by step in case of default. The most important role, often, is that of the lead arranger, who is very influential, especially in validating the credit quality and tracking current risk. Several problems in regard to adverse selection and moral hazard could be reduced by means of some derivative tools, a credit default swap being one of them.[79] When the banks in a syndicate purchase protection through a CDS from the lead arranger, the onus on the lead bank to commit capital to the loan is reduced; hence, this can make bringing banks into the syndicate much easier.[80] This illustrates not only that syndicated loans are evolving but also that it is driven by both financial innovations and regulatory developments.

Syndicated loans involve a hybrid debt instrument, which is mostly preferred for massive corporate borrowings or governments. Syndicated loans involve a pool of lenders, including banks, coming together for providing a single borrower with a facility through a single loan agreement. This provides a hybrid system for bank lending and publicly traded debt, allowing participants to address huge demands for finances, which a single entity finds hard to handle. The borrower will enter into one agreement, but each bank in this case becomes a direct lender with a clearly defined promissory note. After closing, the agent bank becomes monitoring and handling the administration of loan functioning in relation to organizing interests, payments, and collateral on behalf of the syndicated banks. This ensures the effective avoidance of duplicative monitoring costs among participants in a loan syndicate. For the success of the syndicated loans, there is need for transparency in the information as well as the reputation of the managing bank. According to research, the result is better when the information is transparent; for example, the borrower has a credit rating or is listed. On the other hand, when the loan is riskier and the information is not clear, the managing bank signals its confidence in the loan by retaining more of the loan in its own book. Furthermore, it is argued that long-term loans are more easily sold compared to short-term loans in the market. Legally, these facilities are usually formalized by universally drafted agreements that conform to standardized documentation organized by bodies such as the Loan Market Association and the Loan Syndications and Trading Association. The agreements protect the facility by limiting the liability exposure of the managing bank to the member banks, except in cases where there has been

---

[79] Song (2011).

[80] Cortes, Tribo and Adamuz. (2020) and Dennis and Mullineaux (2000, 404–426).Reference 'Cortes et al. (2020)' is cited in text but not provided in the reference list. Please provide reference in the list or delete this citation.revised

deliberate negligence or gross negligence.[81] Summarily, the facility referred to as syndicated loans plays a crucial role in the financial industry, particularly among banks with set capitals, by providing a means to reduce risk that uses large loan facilities by removing them from individual balance sheets and providing access to additional aggregate funds.[82]

A syndicated loan is an interlocking web of contracts, separate yet intertwined. There is the main facility agreement between the borrower and the lenders; the agency agreement linking the agent with the lenders; the participation agreements that describe the sharing of rights among the lenders; the security documents, which establish and protect the collateral; and the guarantees or letters of credit supporting the borrower's obligations.[83] Generally speaking, syndicated loans are not regarded as securities, like bonds. They are purely contractual claims and, hence, are regulated by the law related to banking contracts. That said, in cases where participation rights are traded in the secondary loan market, they can actually become tradable instruments, and this starts to blur the line between banking law and capital markets law.

10.4.4 Loan Trading

Loan trading is when banks sell or transfer loans from their portfolios into secondary markets. In academic terms, it is a common way for banks to spread credit risk and manage their balance sheets in line with funding needs and regulatory limits.[84] Changes in this market suggest that banks do not treat credit default swaps (CDS) as simple replacements for selling loans; instead, they use CDS alongside loan sales to adjust their risk exposure.[85]

Prior research finds strong overlap between the two markets: loans to firms that trade actively in the CDS market are sold on the secondary loan market more often. Banks also often sell CDS protection as a way to make it easier to transfer or reduce their loan exposures. These findings suggest that loan trading is not a fixed legal practice; it changes over time as financial innovation develops and regulatory rules are revised. This arrangement means that credit risk can be transferred and kept under control by combining contractual assignments with hedging through derivatives.

10.4.4.1 The Secondary Loan Market

Secondary loan trading is when an existing loan, and the related credit risk, is sold by the bank that first made it to another investor. This market works differently

[81] See, Nazareth and Tahyar (2011, 145) and Deane and Chui (2025) and Marsh and Basta (2017, 1–6).
[82] Dennis and Mullineaux (2000).
[83] Sidorenko et al. (2023, 213–217), Keil and Müller (2019, 1269) and Jones (1999, 169).
[84] Gande and Saunders (2006, 1649–1684).
[85] Brigida (2022, 19–27) and Augustin et al. (2024).

from bond trading because it deals with negotiated loan contracts rather than standardized securities. Bonds are set up from the start to be sold to the public and traded in the market, while loans are usually private agreements between two parties or a lending group.[86] A loan can only be transferred if the contract allows it and the required regulatory approvals are in place. The market has grown quickly as firms try to manage regulatory capital under the Basel rules and as institutions look more to private credit. In practice, the legal issues in these trades vary a lot depending on how the transfer is structured.

The legal characterization of the transaction depends on whether the parties use an assignment, a participation, or a sub-participation, because each option affects privity of contract and whether voting rights are transferred. Apart from these structural choices, changes in the market suggest that financial institutions do not treat CDS as simple substitutes for selling these loans. Banks instead use these instruments as supporting tools to adjust and balance their risk exposures.[87] This pattern is clearest when loans to firms that are actively traded in the CDS market are more likely to be sold in the secondary market, and banks often support these sales by selling CDS protection to make the divestment easier. Overall, this interaction shows that loan trading is a legal activity that changes over time as financial innovation develops, and regulatory rules are updated.

10.4.4.2 Legal Mechanisms of Transfer

In loan trading, the legal framework mostly depends on the transfer method, and assignment is often the clearest and most straightforward way to transfer the loan. In a loan assignment, the current lender passes its rights and duties under the contract to another lender, and the borrower usually must agree to this unless the contract already removes that consent requirement. With this arrangement, the assignee steps into a direct legal relationship with the borrower and is treated as a party to the original loan contract.[88] This approach makes it clear who the lender of record is, but it can be slowed by the administrative work of getting consent or meeting required regulatory notice rules. Unlike an assignment, a participation lets the seller, or grantor, stay as the lender of record under the contract with the borrower, while passing the financial risks and returns of the loan to a third-party participant. Since the participant can bring a legal claim only against the grantor, not the borrower, banks often use this structure to limit their own risk without informing the borrower or setting off transfer limits in the loan agreement. This arrangement adds credit risk between the participant and the grantor because the participant is exposed to the risk that the bank, which remains the legal creditor, could become insolvent. Sub-participation adds another derivative step in which the original participation interest is syndicated and shared among several parties. These layered structures create more complex issues about privity of contract,

[86] Santos and Shao (2023, 249–272) and Colla (2011, 81–87).
[87] Kamstra et al. (2012, 1139–1181).
[88] Fabozzi et al. (2021) and Massa and Schmidt (2015).

confidentiality, and compliance with relevant regulations. These legal issues are especially clear when loans are sold to nonbank investors, such as hedge funds, whose goals may differ from those of traditional banks. Choosing between these mechanisms is not just an administrative detail; it is a legal decision that shapes how enforceable the parties' rights are, how clear the debt is, and how stable the credit relationship remains.

10.4.4.3 Regulatory Considerations

Loan trading is regulated through a mix of prudential rules and legal requirements that aim to keep markets stable and protect personal privacy. A central issue in these transactions is confidentiality. Transferring credit exposure often requires sharing the borrower's sensitive financial information, so it must be kept protected under banking secrecy duties and data protection law. Balancing investors' need for clear information with borrowers' right to privacy calls for clear contract terms that restrict access to proprietary information and prevent it from being shared without permission. Alongside confidentiality issues, KYC and AML rules place strict duties on assignees: they must confirm the borrower's identity and check that the funds used in the transaction come from a lawful source. This administrative layer becomes more complex because of Basel capital adequacy rules. When a selling bank reduces its risk-weighted assets to obtain capital relief, the investor buying the asset must still hold the required regulatory capital for the exposure it acquires. Market conduct rules add to the legal complexity in this market, especially when loans are tied to traded securities, since this can bring insider trading and market abuse rules into play. The secondary loan market is a hybrid space where the flexibility of private contract law sits alongside the strict requirements of public prudential oversight. This change reflects a wider shift in financial law: tools once seen mainly as routine banking products are now treated more like regulated legal entities, with rules aimed at keeping everyday business workable while also protecting the stability of the financial system.

10.4.5 Bond Issues

A bond is a type of debt where an issuer borrows money from investors and agrees to pay interest, usually in regular coupon payments, and then repay the original amount at the bond's maturity date. Bonds are not the same as loans because they are negotiable securities, which means investors can buy and sell them on secondary markets.[89] Issuing a bond shifts borrowing from a private loan arrangement to a form of public participation in the borrower's debt. In practice, the issuer and the investors do not deal with each other directly; a trustee or fiscal agent stands between them and acts on behalf of the bondholders to enforce their rights as a group.

[89] Choudhry (2006, 17–46).

Regulating bond issuances involves a legal framework that sits where corporate finance, securities law, and banking supervision overlap. In most cases, these instruments are regulated under strict legal rules, including statutes such as the EU Prospectus Regulation and related US securities laws.[90] The Securities Act of 1933 requires companies to provide detailed, accurate disclosures so investors can make informed decisions and markets remain fair and trustworthy.[91] In addition to general legal requirements, a bond issue must meet the listing rules of the exchange where it will be traded. Its main terms are set out in a trust deed or an agency agreement, which states the legal rights and protections of bondholders. Including restrictive covenants, such as limits on selling assets or taking on more debt, helps protect investors by setting clear boundaries on what the borrower can do during the life of the agreement. In the end, following these overlapping rules closely is necessary to keep trust in the system and to support the stability of global debt capital markets.

Background Information
Even with differences in legal jurisdiction and subject matter, all types of bonds rest on the same legal basics: a binding contract, the ability to transfer the instrument, and enforcement through established legal rules.

Bond types can be grouped in ways that show how varied they are, and the key factor is who issues the bond because that choice determines which legal rules apply. Corporate bonds are mainly shaped by private contracts and securities law, and firms issue them to raise capital.[92] By comparison, sovereign bonds are issued by states and often raise questions under public international law, especially when state immunity is at issue.[93]

Along with the issuer's identity, the instrument's structure and ethical aims also shape the range of legal issues that may apply. Convertible bonds are hybrid instruments that sit between debt and equity, so they raise questions about corporate governance and the rules that apply when the bonds are converted into shares.[94] Green and sustainable bonds, by contrast, are standard debt instruments that add ESG conditions, which means issuers must meet strict compliance duties, especially on how the raised funds are used.[95]

If a bond defaults, investor rights are enforced through legal procedures that aim to address individual claims while also limiting wider disruption to the financial system. A key part of this process is the trustee, who serves as a fiduciary for all bondholders as a group. The trustee's role is to reduce the risk that separate bondholders will bring individual lawsuits, which could create inconsistent outcomes

[90] ECB (2017) and Newman and Trautman (2021, 149–218).
[91] Schwartz (2019, 1069–1103) and Guttentag (2004, 123–196).
[92] Su (2025), Mizen et al. (2009), Kosi et al. (2025), and Guenster et al. (2025, 8–21).
[93] Bröhmer (2024, 182, 208).
[94] Huerga and Rodriguez-Monroy (2019, 4074) and Ang et al. (2025, 133–149).
[95] Hadas-Dyduch et al. (2022) and Curtis et al. (2023, 131–178).

and disrupt the market.[96] This shared approach is strengthened by collective action clauses (CACs), which allow a qualified majority of creditors to agree to restructuring terms that apply to all bondholders, reducing the risk that holdout creditors will block the recovery process.[97]

Cross-default clauses support these structural protections in the contract as a whole by treating a bond as in default if the issuer defaults on other debt, which ties the issuer's obligations together across its financing arrangements.[98] This interdependence means that if one part of the issuer's finances fails, it can prompt early intervention, and the governing law clause sets out clear jurisdictional rules for any later litigation or arbitration.

Recent changes in sovereign debt law, shaped by major disputes such as *NML Capital v. Argentina*, have raised new questions about creditor rights and the limits of state immunity. In Argentina, debt enforcement has shifted away from rigid, fragmented contract enforcement toward a more coordinated model of cooperative debt governance. This shift puts more focus on clear reporting of debt and on shared ways to resolve disputes, with the aim of reducing creditor lawsuits that could split the process into separate, uncoordinated cases.[99] Taken together, these reforms show a current legal view that prefers structured debt restructuring and stability in the wider system over forceful, stand-alone enforcement actions.

10.4.6 Risk Management and Legal Implications

Managing credit is, at its core, about assessing, measuring, and controlling risk. A loan contract involves two parties, but it operates within a framework of strict macroprudential rules designed to prevent one borrower's default from triggering broader financial instability or systemic stress. Hence, managing risk is not merely a prudent business choice; it is a binding legal requirement imposed on regulated financial institutions. Regulators generally categorize the principal risks inherent in lending activities into four main types, namely credit risk, liquidity risk, interest rate risk, and operational/legal risk. *Credit risk* is the fundamental risk that a borrower will fail to repay the loan or otherwise meet its debt obligations as agreed. The law addresses this through mandatory requirements for lenders to conduct thorough creditworthiness assessments (often referred to as KYC and affordability checks) and to properly perfect security interests in any collateral provided.[100] *Liquidity risk* arises when a bank is unable to meet short-term cash outflows because it funds long-term loans with short-term deposits or other volatile funding sources,

[96] Schwarcz and Sergi (2008, 1037–1073).
[97] Fang et al. (2021, 1–59) and Nakajima (2022, 100–138).
[98] Huang and Yin (2025, 215–225) and Choi et al. (2012, 131–179).
[99] Miller and Thomas (2007, 1491–1509), Weidemaier (2013, 123–131) and Reth (2015, 132–167).
[100] FCA (2017).

resulting in a maturity mismatch. This risk is mitigated through regulatory standards such as the Liquidity Coverage Ratio (LCR) and the Net Stable Funding Ratio (NSFR) under Basel III.[101] *Interest rate risk* refers to the potential adverse impact of changes in market interest rates on the economic value of a bank's assets, liabilities, or net interest income. It is particularly significant for fixed-rate and long-term lending portfolios, where future cash flows are contractually fixed while market rates fluctuate.[102] *Operational/legal risk* encompasses the risk of loss resulting from inadequate or failed internal processes, people, systems, or external events—including deficiencies in documentation, procedural failures, fraud, or adverse changes in laws and regulatory requirements.[103]

To ensure that banks exercise commercial prudence, the legal system reinforces internal risk controls through a multi-layered application of public law obligations.[104] Transparency and disclosure requirements serve dual purposes: they protect consumers by enabling informed decision-making and they promote market discipline by providing investors, counterparties, and regulators with sufficient information to evaluate and compare institutions' risk profiles. Lenders are required to furnish standardized information to borrowers and supervisory authorities, facilitating comparability of pricing, terms, and embedded risks. Minimum documentation standards are imposed to reduce legal risk: regulators mandate written agreements that clearly define events of default, the governing law, jurisdiction, dispute resolution mechanisms, and enforcement procedures. Increasingly, regulators treat undocumented loans, oral agreements, or poorly drafted credit facilities as material compliance failures.

Supervisory oversight is exercised through regular on-site inspections, off-site monitoring, stress testing, and asset quality reviews conducted by authorities such as the ECB, the US Federal Reserve, or BRSA. These exercises verify whether banks correctly classify loans (particularly non-performing loans—NPLs), maintain adequate provisions for expected and incurred losses, and adhere to prudential thresholds. A prominent recent example is the 2025 EU-wide stress test (coordinated by the EBA and paralleled by the ECB), published in August 2025. Covering 64 major EU banks (representing 75% of sector assets), the test subjected institutions to a severe adverse scenario featuring geopolitical escalation, trade protectionism, prolonged recessions, and sharp asset price falls. Aggregate results showed a CET1 ratio depletion of around 370 basis points (from 15.8% to 12.1% under CRR3 rules), driven primarily by credit losses (€394 billion cumulatively), yet the system ended with no widespread breaches of CET1 total SREP requirements and excess capital buffers of over €550 billion. This outcome confirmed enhanced resilience compared to the 2023 exercise (where depletion was 479 bps), owing to stronger starting profitability and capital positions—directly validating

[101] King (2013, 4144–4156).
[102] Onyiriuba (2017, 448). See also, Foos et al. (2022, 883).
[103] Butler and Brooks (2023, 1285–1304).
[104] Weber (2013, 1005–1074), Malik (2024, 266–289) and Suryadarma and Pujiyono (2025, 19–29).

the effectiveness of banks' loan classification, provisioning, and risk management practices under supervisory scrutiny.[105] Borrowers, in turn, are afforded clear legal avenues to challenge creditor conduct. Specialized commercial courts, financial ombudsmen services, consumer arbitration panels, and judicial review mechanisms ensure that creditors can enforce their rights only in compliance with fundamental procedural protections, including due process, fairness, and proportionality.

In the contemporary regulatory environment, the boundary between a private contractual breach and a public regulatory violation has become increasingly blurred. When a bank systematically fails to comply with standards—for example, by omitting affordability assessments, misclassifying NPLs, or engaging in reckless lending practices—the matter may escalate from a bilateral civil dispute to a serious breach of prudential rules. Such failures can trigger substantial administrative fines, mandatory remediation plans, removal of responsible management personnel, or, in extreme cases, revocation of the banking license.[106] Ultimately, risk management functions as the legal nervous system of the credit market. It imposes disciplined boundaries on the pursuit of profit, ensuring that private credit creation remains compatible with the stability, resilience, and soundness of the wider financial system.

10.4.7 Concluding Reflection on Loan Typologies

Loan types span a broad spectrum—from large-scale commercial syndicated facilities to everyday retail auto loans—and this diversity illustrates how credit law adapts flexibly to varying economic contexts, borrower profiles, and risk profiles. In basic terms, a loan transforms an element of trust into a legally enforceable commitment: one party agrees to repay a sum of money to another under defined terms that can be judicially enforced. This trust is far from an abstract concept; it is profoundly shaped by the social, economic, and regulatory conditions in which the relationship arises.

In consumer lending, legal rules function primarily as a protective safeguard. They impose obligations on lenders to provide clear, transparent disclosures (such as effective annual interest rates, total cost of credit, and repayment schedules) and impose limits on interest rates, fees, and aggressive collection practices. These measures are designed to mitigate the inherent imbalance of bargaining power between sophisticated financial institutions and individual borrowers, thereby preventing exploitation and promoting fair access to credit.

By contrast, commercial lending is predominantly governed by the principle of freedom of contract. Here, the law focuses on ensuring procedural precision—particularly in the accurate perfection of security interests—and on establishing clear priority rules for the distribution of assets in the event of default or insolvency. The

[105] EBA (2025).

[106] Giannopoulos and Kariofyllas (2025, 152).

emphasis is on enforceability, risk allocation, and the orderly resolution of competing creditor claims, rather than on paternalistic protections. This spectrum of loan structures plays a vital role in the financial system by efficiently spreading both risk and opportunity across participants. When the law delineates distinct categories for different transaction types—for example, treating a mortgage as an accessory right inseparably linked to the principal debt, or classifying a non-cash guarantee (such as a standby letter of credit or surety bond) as a contingent obligation—it facilitates more accurate valuation, pricing, and capital allocation.

For lenders, these typologies provide a practical roadmap for structuring transactions, planning enforcement strategies, and calibrating risk management. For borrowers, they offer a regulated and predictable pathway to access liquidity tailored to their needs and circumstances. Ultimately, loan typologies help ensure that the broad freedom of contract in commercial settings does not jeopardize financial stability. By enabling private debt to be clearly classified, systematically monitored, and effectively managed, they contribute to the resilience and orderly functioning of the modern economy.

10.5 International Banking Credit Agreements

10.5.1 Nature and Legal Foundations of International Banking Credit Agreements

International banking credit agreements constitute a central pillar of modern credit law. They take familiar domestic rules governing debt and extend them across borders, requiring the agreement to accommodate multiple—and often divergent—national legal systems simultaneously. These agreements are far more than simple contracts; they are sophisticated legal instruments that must harmonize domestic law, private international law, and international regulatory standards in a coherent and enforceable manner. At their foundation lies the principle of party autonomy: sophisticated commercial parties are generally free to select a well-established and predictable body of law—most commonly English law or New York law—to govern their rights and obligations and to define the framework for resolving disputes, whether through national courts or international arbitration. This choice promotes legal certainty, facilitates efficient enforcement, and reduces the risk of unpredictable outcomes in cross-border transactions.

Nevertheless, this autonomy is far from unlimited. Cross-border credit transactions are subject to overriding mandatory public international rules, including the Basel III capital adequacy standards, the FATF AML and CTF requirements, and international sanctions regimes (such as those administered by the UN, EU, US OFAC, or UK). These mandatory norms ensure that the pursuit of private profit does not compromise the stability, integrity, or security of the global financial system. In this dual capacity, an international loan functions both as a private contractual arrangement facilitating the cross-border movement of capital and as a public instrument that operationalizes and reinforces global financial governance standards. These transactions are typically structured through a suite of interlinked documents that, collectively, form a single coordinated legal and economic arrangement.

In a syndicated loan, for example, the Facility Agreement establishes the core terms of the credit facility—including amount, interest rate, maturity, covenants, and events of default. Complementary documents, such as the Agency Agreement and the Intercreditor Agreement, govern the relationships among the lenders and between the syndicate and the Agent Bank (or Administrative Agent). Additional structures—such as security trust deeds, parallel debt mechanisms, or collateral pooling arrangements—enable lenders to secure and enforce their interests across multiple jurisdictions through a unified legal vehicle, often a security trustee acting on behalf of the entire syndicate. Through these mechanisms, international banks and sovereign or corporate borrowers can efficiently allocate risk and returns across borders, transforming the loan from mere debt into a structured instrument for cross-border development finance, project funding, and global liquidity management.[107]

10.5.2 Governing Law and Jurisdiction

10.5.2.1 Choice of Law

In international finance, the choice of law clause determines which legal rules govern the interpretation, performance, and enforcement of the credit agreement, thereby enabling the parties to predict legal outcomes and better assess cross-border risks. Since these transactions typically involve parties from different legal systems, it is crucial to select a neutral and well-developed set of rules that is particularly suited to sophisticated commercial practice. As indicated, English law and New York law are by far the most common choices for international contracts. Parties tend to favour them because both systems place paramount emphasis on pacta sunt servanda—the principle that agreements must be kept as written—, offer an extensive body of commercial case law to guide interpretation, and provide creditors with clear, predictable legal rights that are rarely set aside without a sound legal basis. Additionally, the courts in London and New York possess deep expertise in complex financial disputes, issue reasoned judgments that contribute to legal certainty, and generally adopt a pro-enforcement stance toward valid contractual provisions.[108]

The validity and effect of these clauses depend on the applicable rules of private international law, most notably the EU Rome I Regulation (Regulation (EC) No 593/2008). Under Rome I, party autonomy is the fundamental starting point: a court will ordinarily apply the law expressly chosen by the parties, even if that law

[107] Gurara et al. (2019).

[108] Eisenberg and Miller (2009, 1475), Fountoulakis (2005, 306), and Cuniberti (2014, 455–517).

has little or no factual connection to the transaction.[109] This broad recognition of freedom of choice promotes legal certainty and reduces forum-shopping incentives in international finance. Nevertheless, this freedom is not absolute. If the parties fail to make a clear or valid choice of governing law, the court will generally apply the law of the country with which the contract is most closely connected—in lending agreements, typically the place where the characteristic performance occurs, which is often the country where the lender is established or has its principal place of business. This fallback rule ensures that the contract is always subject to a coherent legal framework and avoids the risk of it being left in a legal vacuum.

A significant limitation on party autonomy arises under consumer protection provisions. Article 6 of the Rome I Regulation reflects the principle that one party—usually the consumer—often has substantially less bargaining power than the other.[110] Even where a consumer credit agreement purports to be governed by foreign law, that choice cannot deprive the consumer of the mandatory protections afforded by the law of the country where the consumer has his or her habitual residence (provided the lender pursues commercial or professional activities in that country or directs such activities there). This protective mechanism prevents lenders from using choice of law clauses to circumvent local restrictions—such as caps on interest rates, rules on unfair terms, or safeguards against abusive repossession—and ensures that cross-border contractual freedom does not undermine domestic rules designed to promote social justice and consumer welfare. Recent CJEU jurisprudence reinforces this temporal focus on protection at the moment of contracting. In *AY v Liechtensteinische Landesbank (Österreich) AG*, the Court held that Article 6(1) does not apply where the professional did not pursue or direct activities to the consumer's Member State at the time the contract was concluded, even if such targeting occurs later during the contractual relationship.[111] The CJEU emphasized that retroactive application would undermine legal certainty, predictability, and the principle of party autonomy under Article 3, confirming that consumer protection under Rome I is assessed at contract formation rather than ex post.

10.5.2.2 Jurisdiction and Dispute Resolution

Choice of law determines which set of legal rules governs the interpretation and performance of the contract, while the jurisdiction and dispute resolution clause specifies where and how any disputes will be resolved and enforced. In international credit agreements, the parties must carefully decide whether to submit disputes to national courts—where proceedings are typically public—or to international arbitration, which offers greater privacy. Lenders frequently favour litigation in London or New York because these jurisdictions feature specialized commercial courts (such as the Commercial Court in London or the Commercial Division

[109] Volker (2011, 233–272) and Kuipers (2012, 35–36).
[110] Yuthayotin (2015, 219) and Rivoire (2025, 213–255).
[111] Case C-279/24. Judgment of the Court (Fourth Chamber) of 4 December 2025. AY v Liechtensteinische Landesbank (Österreich) AG.

of the New York Supreme Court) with extensive experience in complex financial matters. These courts can grant summary judgment, enabling a swift order for payment when the debt is clear and there is no genuine dispute of material fact. This procedural efficiency is highly valued in cross-border lending because it preserves liquidity, deters strategic defaults, and allows creditors to recover funds more quickly in undisputed cases.

In many cross-border contracts, however, the parties opt for international arbitration, most commonly under the rules of the International Chamber of Commerce (ICC), the London Court of International Arbitration (LCIA), or the United Nations Commission on International Trade Law (UNCITRAL). Arbitration is often preferred for its neutrality—ensuring neither party enjoys a home-court advantage—and its confidentiality, which protects sensitive financial information from public disclosure.[112] Moreover, the 1958 New York Convention on the Recognition and Enforcement of Foreign Arbitral Awards (ratified by over 170 jurisdictions as of 2026) facilitates the enforcement of arbitral awards in a far broader range of countries than most national court judgments, often making arbitration the more reliable option for cross-border enforcement.

Within the European Union, the Brussels Recast Regulation (Regulation (EU) No 1215/2012) provides a relatively streamlined framework for the recognition and enforcement of court judgments among Member States, generally without the need for exequatur proceedings and subject only to limited grounds for refusal (such as public policy or irreconcilability with a prior judgment).[113] A distinct set of legal issues arises when the borrower is a sovereign state, as rules on jurisdiction and enforcement may differ substantially from those applicable to private parties. In such cases, sovereign immunity doctrines (as discussed earlier) can restrict access to national courts or limit enforcement against state assets, often necessitating explicit waivers of immunity, choice-of-law clauses designating commercial-friendly jurisdictions, and arbitration provisions to circumvent immunity barriers.

10.5.3 Collateral and Security Structures

In international finance, collateral and security structures serve as an essential tools for mitigating losses in the event of borrower default, yet their effectiveness frequently hinges on compatibility with diverse, and often conflicting, national legal regimes. In common law jurisdictions, fixed and floating charges are used to secure debts against both specific assets and changing groups of assets such as inventory or receivables. In many civil law systems, by contrast, security is more often created through traditional pledges and mortgages, which typically require more formalistic steps and may be limited to identified, tangible assets.

[112] Noussia (2010).
[113] Whytock (2014, 113–124).

In syndicated financings, where several lenders share security interests, lawyers introduced the parallel debt mechanism to make the security easier to administer and enforce. Under this approach, the borrower treats the security agent as being owed a separate debt that matches the full amount owed to all members of the lending syndicate. This arrangement enables the security agent to take and enforce the collateral in its own name, thereby obviating the need for each bank to be listed separately as a mortgagee or pledgee in every local jurisdiction. The benefit of unified enforcement matters because it assures lenders that, in an insolvency proceeding, they can act together as a single cohesive group rather than pursuing fragmented and potentially conflicting individual claims.

Whether a security interest will hold up against third parties depends on perfection, that is, the required legal steps that put others on notice and render the interest enforceable against the debtor and competing claimants. Requirements vary by jurisdiction and may include such formalities as public registration, notarization, stamp duties or transferring possession through physical delivery. If these local filing or perfection requirements are not followed, the security interest may be treated as invalid or subordinated and thus may not be enforceable if the borrower enters bankruptcy. The UNCITRAL Model Law on Secured Transactions of 2016 seeks to align different national rules into a more predictable framework by promoting a functional approach to security interests, including unitary securities devices, electronic registration, and clear priority rules. However, adoption varies across states (with notable implementations in countries such as France, Belgium and several African and Latin American jurisdictions, but limited uptake in major common law financial centres).[114]

10.5.4 The Resolution of Credit Distress: Contractual Remedies and Judicial Recognition

At the end of a credit relationship, default and enforcement measures represent the primary mechanisms through which a creditor can assert and protect its rights. A contract often lists events of default that extend beyond mere missed payments. These typically include breaches of financial covenants, such as failure to maintain a required debt-to-equity ratio, the borrower filing for insolvency, and a cross-default clause that permits the lender to treat the loan as in default if the borrower fails to pay obligations to another major creditor. These triggers enable banks to intervene early, thereby preserving value before the borrower's assets are fully exhausted.

If a default occurs, lenders may pursue several remedies expressly available to them under the loan documents and applicable law. The strongest remedy is acceleration: this provision makes the entire unpaid balance (including principal, interest, and fees) due immediately, effectively turning a long-term loan into an

[114] Bazinas (2025, 1–16).

obligation payable on demand. Other common remedies include cancelling any unused portion of the credit line and requiring immediate repossession of the collateral.

> **Important**
> The validity of these actions depends largely on whether the prescribed procedures were followed carefully and consistently. In international practice, a default notice should be in writing, clear and specific, and served exactly as the contract's notice provisions require. Under English law, for instance, a default notice that is unclear may invalidate a later attempt to accelerate the debt, and it may also leave the bank open to a claim for damages for breach of contract.[115]

Enforcement of security interests is further governed by choice-of-law principles. The liquidation of a security is controlled by the *lex situs*, meaning the law of the place where the asset is located, so enforcement methods may vary depending on that location.[116] For example, a judicial sale is an auction run under court supervision, often used in civil law systems to ensure the process is open and to protect any remaining interest the debtor may have after the sale. By contrast, in many common law jurisdictions (and in certain commercial context under uniform commercial codes), a private sale may be allowed if the lender can show that the asset was sold at fair market value (often demonstrated through independent valuation or commercially reasonable procedures).

A further simplified enforcement method applies in the context of financial collateral. Appropriation is a streamlined method for dealing with financial collateral, such as cash or securities, under rules like EU Directive 2002/47/EC (the Financial Collateral Directive) and its national implementations. It allows the secured party to take ownership of the collateral and apply its value toward the secured debt, thereby avoiding the need to sell the asset first and reducing enforcement delays and costs.[117]

In cross-border cases, the process becomes even more difficult because courts must also recognize and enforce foreign judgments. A New York court order that seeks to seize assets located in Singapore or Turkey does not take effect automatically. To enforce it abroad, the requesting party generally must rely on the legal process in the foreign state, often through an applicable international treaty framework such as the New York Convention (for arbitral awards) or the 2019 Hague Convention on the Recognition and Enforcement of Foreign Judgments in Civil or Commercial Matters.

During recovery, banks must strictly follow AML rules to confirm that any seized assets are not the proceeds of crime; if they are, the collateral may be

[115] Beale (2017).
[116] Kieninger (2004, 16–17).
[117] Keijser et al. (2014, 429–458), Rusen (2007, 250–258), and Tot (2018, 37–72).

forfeited to the state rather than transferred to the bank. This obligation applies regardless of the enforcement jurisdiction and is reinforced by international standards (such as those set by the FATF) and national legislation (e.g., in Turkey under Law No. 5549 on Prevention of Laundering Proceeds of Crime). Failure to comply can result in severe regulatory penalties, criminal liability, or loss of the secured interest.

10.5.5 Sovereign and Interbank Lending

10.5.5.1 Sovereign Borrowers

When the borrower is a sovereign state, the lender–borrower relationship operates differently because the doctrine of sovereign immunity can significantly limit how creditors enforce repayment. States, unlike private companies, have long been protected by sovereign immunity that potentially limits suits against them in foreign courts and restricts when their assets can be seized. To address this gap, contemporary international loan agreements have shifted from basic debt documents to instruments designed to manage sovereign risk. The main legal tool here is an explicit waiver of immunity, where the state agrees to give up sovereign immunity so the debt can be treated as enforceable, and creditors can pursue claims in major financial centres such as London or New York. Such waivers—often combined with choice-of-law and exclusive jurisdiction clauses—are now standard in sovereign bonds issued to foreign investors, allowing courts in these jurisdictions to hear disputes and enforce judgments without the sovereign invoking immunity defenses (provided the waiver is properly drafted and the signing authority had the requisite power).

Recent UK jurisprudence underscores the importance of precise language in these waivers. For example, in *General Dynamics United Kingdom Ltd v The State of Libya*,[118] the Court of Appeal held that an arbitration agreement providing that any award would be "final, binding and wholly enforceable" constituted a sufficient written consent under s.13(3) of the State Immunity Act 1978 to waive immunity from execution against state assets in the UK (such as charging orders over London property), even without explicit "waiver" wording.[119] The decision affirms a broad, contextual approach to construing such provisions in commercial contexts, provided they demonstrate the state's intent to submit to enforcement jurisdiction—highlighting both the potential effectiveness of well-drafted clauses and the risks if language is ambiguous.

Sovereign lending is often most difficult during a crisis, when creditors have to coordinate how they will respond.[120] This section is shaped by two key clauses as pari passu clause and collective action clauses. Pari passu clause means the

---

[118] [2025] EWCA Civ 134.
[119] Webb (2025).
[120] Bunte and Kinne (2025).

sovereign agrees to rank all unsecured creditors on the same level, so no unsecured creditor is legally placed ahead of another.[121] The case of NML Capital v. Argentina is often cited in academic writing to examine sovereign debt enforcement and the limits of sovereign immunity. In the Argentina litigation (particularly the 2012 Second Circuit decision and related proceedings up to the US Supreme Court's 2014 ruling in Republic of Argentina v. NML Capital, Ltd.), holdout creditors pushed a narrow reading of pari passu to block payments to other bondholders, arguing that Argentina's selective payments to restructured bondholders violated the clause's equal treatment promise.[122] This interpretation stalled the country's attempts to stabilize its finances after the 2001 default and highlighted the potential pari passu clauses to empower holdouts in restructuring processes. Second, collective action clauses (CACs) were updated after problems caused by holdout creditors. In response, the IMF and ICMA promoted modernized CACs to make it easier for most bondholders to agree on a restructuring that applies to all. These provisions let a super-majority of bondholders approve changes to the bond terms, and once approved, those changes apply to all bondholders, including those who did not agree.[123] For instance, a 75% majority can approve a debt restructuring, and the agreed terms then become legally binding on creditors who dissented. This rule stops a single creditor from blocking a structured recovery plan and seeks to respect individual property rights while protecting the stability of the broader financial system. Post-Argentina reforms, including ICMA's 2014 enhanced CACs and single-limb aggregation mechanisms, have further strengthened these clauses by reducing holdout leverage and facilitating more orderly restructurings in new sovereign bond issuances.[124]

The legal framework for sovereign debt often reflects an ongoing tension between private autonomy and state sovereignty. From the lender's perspective, the aim is to have the loan treated as commercial rather than governmental, so the state cannot rely on diplomatic immunity as a defence. For a sovereign state, the main issue is how to raise funds from global capital markets while keeping enough control to govern and, if needed, restructure its debts during an economic crisis. Ultimately, this balance enables sovereign borrowers to remain within the global financial system as long as they comply with current norms in international credit law.

10.5.5.2 Interbank Lending

Interbank credit plays a central role in the global financial system because it enables banks to lend to and borrow from one another, ensuring that liquidity flows

[121] Olivares-Caminal (2009, 1217) and Weidemaier et al. (2013, 72).
[122] Newfield (2016, 175).
[123] Weinschelbaum and Wynne (2005, 47), Schwarcz (2017, 73), and Chung and Papaioannou (2021, 59–87).
[124] Gelpern and Powell (2023)

daily to where it is most needed.[125] In the past, these agreements were usually short-term, unsecured deals that relied on trust between the institutions involved. However, the systemic failures during the 2008 financial crises showed that this kind of trust can break down quickly under stress, prompting a fundamental shift toward greater reliance on collateralisation. Today, the interbank market therefore relies much more on collateral, with repurchase agreements (Repos) serving as the main tool.

A repo is a legal arrangement that combines elements of a sale and a loan: one party sells an asset and agrees to buy it back later, effectively functioning as borrowing cash with the asset as collateral. In a repurchase transaction, one bank sells securities, usually government bonds, to another bank and agrees in advance to buy the same securities back on a set date for a set price (plus and agreed interest component, often expressed as the repo rate).[126] In legal terms, a repo is treated as a sale in which title passes to the buyer, paired with a forward agreement to repurchase the same (or equivalent) asset at a later date, rather than as a standard secured loan. This distinction matters critically in insolvency. Since the buyer holds legal title to the securities, the buyer may sell them as soon as the seller defaults without being subject to automatic stays on enforcement. This can avoid the long court-imposed stay that often delays enforcement when the arrangement is treated as mere collateral in a traditional secured lending context.

In practice, most of these transactions are documented under the Global Master Repurchase Agreement (GMRA), primarily the 2011 version published by the International Capital Market Association (ICMA) in collaboration with SIFMA, to support consistent terms across countries and clearer legal outcomes.[127] This standard framework sets clear rules for margin calls: if the value of the original collateral falls, the seller must post extra securities (or cash) so the lender's safety buffer (haircut or margin) stays steady.

Under the Basel III framework, regulators have strengthened this market by introducing measures to mitigate counterparty and concentration risks by risk-weighting and large exposure limits. Risk-weighting means setting a specific capital charge for each interbank exposure so that the required capital reflects the probability that the counterparty may fail (with repos often benefiting from lower risk weights due to high-quality collateral, such as sovereign bonds).[128] On the other hand, large exposure limits cap how much credit one bank can extend to another. The aim is to reduce spillover risk, so that if one institution fails, its losses do not spread through interbank lending and trigger a wider chain of failures (for example, the Basel large exposures standard generally limits exposures to

---

[125] Reale (2022, 734–769), Castiglionesi and Eboli (2018, 1291–1334), and Craig et al. (2015, 99–111).

[126] Alexiou et al. (2025) and Cullen (2017, 85–116).

[127] ICMA (2023, 66–78).

[128] Blundell-Wignall and Atkinson (2010, 1–23).

25% of Tier 1 capital for most counterparties, with a stricter 15% limit for exposures between global systemically important banks (G-SIBs)).[129] In the modern interbank market, trust has been largely supplanted by a legal obligation backed by collateral, which helps preserve the international flow of money and maintain stability when market volatility is high.

10.5.6 Legal Proceedings in Cross-Border Disputes

In the final stage of a credit crisis, the focus shifts from managing contracts themselves toward strict procedural rules in court. In a cross-border dispute, the lender's main aim is to stop the borrower from moving or hiding assets while navigating several court systems that follow different rules and procedures. In practice, researchers and practitioners often employ fast, step-by-step methods to carry out this work. One efficient tool in undisputed debt cases is summary judgment, which is commonly used where the key facts are not disputed, allowing the court to enter judgment without holding a full trial. To preserve assets for enforcement, lenders may apply for a 'freezing order', a.k.a. Mareva injunction. This order stops the borrower from transferring or concealing assets, even if they are held abroad.[130] Such orders are particularly valuable in international context, as they can extend worldwide (often-termed worldwide freezing orders or WFOs) to prevent dissipation across jurisdictions, through their cross-border effectiveness depends on local recognition and cooperation.[131]

Successful carrying out these orders and collecting the debt across borders depends on recognition and enforcement, which act as the legal bridge between jurisdictions. Since a court order issued in one country is not automatically enforceable in another, lenders need to rely on international instruments, such as the 2019 Hague Convention on the recognition of enforcement of foreign judgments in civil or commercial matters. This Convention, which entered into force in 2023 and has been ratified by several states (including the EU (excluding Denmark), Ukraine, the UK (effective 2025), and Uruguay), provides a uniform framework for the recognition and enforcement of qualifying monetary judgments in civil and commercial matters, without re-examination of the merits, subject to limited grounds for refusal (e.g., public policy or improper notification).[132] Notably, however, it excludes interim measures such as freezing orders, insolvency proceedings, and certain other categories, limiting its direct application to final judgments.

When there is no formal treaty, enforcement depends on comity and reciprocity, meaning courts accord respect to decisions from other legal systems based on

---

[129] Pozdysev et al. (2023).
[130] Tajti and Iglikowski (2018), Yip (2024, 123–143) and Wordsworth and Wedder (2023, 247–277).
[131] Nicholls et al. (2024, 347–433).
[132] Webster and Packianatan (2025).

mutual regard. In many cases, this is facilitated through Letters Rogatory, which are formal requests for judicial assistance that ask a court in another country to help seize assets or collect evidence.[133] When a borrower fails completely, the case can move from a domestic process to cross-border insolvency, where the legal and practical issues become more complex. The UNCITRAL Model Law on Cross-Border Insolvency (1997) encourages courts in different countries to work together so that one corporate insolvency is managed as a single, coordinated process, rather than turning into a disorderly race to seize assets. Adopted in numerous jurisdictions worldwide, this Model Law promotes cooperation, recognition of foreign proceedings, and relief measures (such as stays on enforcement or asset preservation), thereby maximizing value for creditors and reducing fragmentation.

This type of coordination often includes collaboration with international bodies such as the IMF or the World Bank's StAR initiative, especially when asset tracing is involved. Ultimately, an international credit agreement should be judged not by the act of signing it, but by whether the lender can successfully manage cross-border procedural barriers and convert a court judgment into actual repayment.[134]

10.5.7 Collection of Receivables

10.5.7.1 Legal Nature of Receivables

In international banking, receivables are far more than mere accounting records; they are intangible legal assets that confer on a creditor an enforceable right to receive payment from a debtor. These assets are central to liquidity management and can be grouped into three main types based on the purpose for which they are used or the manner in which they are handled. First, primary receivables are the amounts a borrower owes directly to the original lender under the loan agreement, meaning the lender enjoys the initial legal right to collect payment from the borrower. Second, assigned receivables are claims that a creditor transfers to another party. This is often done to reduce exposure to nonpayment or to obtain cash more quickly. Third, securitized receivables are portions of debt that are grouped into a pool, transformed into tradable financial securities, and then sold to investors, often in international markets.

The rules for transferring these rights depend largely on whether the legal system follows civil law or common law approaches to the doctrine of assignment. In many civil law systems, an assignment does not take full legal effect against the debtor until the debtor has been notified. If no notice is given, the debtor may still pay the original creditor, and that payment will usually count as a valid discharge of the debt. This approach gives the debtor a clear level of legal certainty, since the debtor needs to know exactly who holds the claim and to whom the obligation

[133] Bassiouni (2008, 383–504).
[134] Ochnio (2021, 218).

must be performed. By contrast, common law systems recognise and treat equitable assignment as an accepted doctrine. Under this doctrine, an assignment can be valid between the assignor (seller) and the assignee (buyer) even if the debtor has not been informed. Such an assignment is equitable rather than legal until the debtor is formally notified. Until notice is given, the debtor is not bound by the assignment, and the assignee's priority can be lost if a later assignee (particularly one acquiring a legal interest) gives notice first. This distinction creates potential risks in cross-border transactions, as it means international banks need to be very careful with their notification procedures in order to ensure that their security interest in assigned receivables is properly perfected and remains protected against if other parties later assert competing claims.

10.5.7.2 Collection Mechanisms

When a credit obligation reaches maturity or goes into default, the law establishes an ordered set of collection methods that creditors can follow to recover the amount owed. These approaches range from negotiated agreements to court-ordered sale of assets, and each is shaped by statutory rules and contract terms designed to protect creditor rights while also promoting fair treatment of the debtor and safeguarding overall financial stability.

The simplest and most common method is voluntary payment, which is the main way a debt is recovered. It occurs when the debtor pays what is owed according to the agreed terms. In legal terms, this constitutes the ordinary performance of the contract, as a result of which the obligation is discharged and no further action is required. The voluntary payment doctrine holds that a person who pays money on their own choice, while knowing the relevant facts, usually cannot later seek a refund. An exception may apply if the recipient obtained the payment through fraud or by wrongfully causing economic pressure on the person who paid.[135]

A further non-judicial mechanism available particularly to banks is bank set-off, also called compensation. This is a unilateral right that lets a bank apply money held in a customer's deposit account to reduce or repay that customer's outstanding debt to the bank. This is allowed under banking statutes and pursuant to express contract terms, and it operates as an automatic repayment mechanism that does not require court proceedings.[136] When voluntary payment or set-off is not possible, judicial collection becomes necessary. This refers to the lender filing a lawsuit to recover the debt when the borrower does not repay voluntarily. The process ends with a court judgment that gives the prevailing party the legal authority to enforce the decision, for example by garnishing funds from bank accounts or ordering the selling of real estate at auction. In cross-border or complex commercial contexts, however, enforcing an arbitral award is often quicker than going through traditional court litigation. Under the New York Convention,

---

135 Flora (2012, 91–134).

136 See, Schroeder and Carlson (2019, 417).

arbitral awards are recognized and enforceable in 172 countries, which can speed up recovery of assets in jurisdictions whose courts generally support arbitration.[137]

Another common practice, especially for non-performing loans, is assignment to collection agencies. This means that a bank can transfer its unpaid receivables to a specialized recovery agency, which then seeks payment from the borrower.[138] Although the practice is legal, it is tightly controlled under data protection rules such as GDPR and AML standards to protect the borrower's privacy and to verify the source of the funds. At a more structural level, securitization can be understood as a planned way for the lender to exit its exposure by converting the loan into securities that can be sold to other investors. When the bank bundles its receivables into securities and sells them to investors, it moves the risk of nonpayment away from the bank and onto the investors. This gives the bank cash immediately, while investors take on the responsibility and risk of collecting the underlying payments.

Whatever mechanism is selected, lenders must comply with Debtor Protection Norms. These rules cover such matters as a ban on harassment, an obligation to keep information confidential, and a requirement that any recovery steps be proportional to the amount owed. In today's legal environment, a debt recovery approach that is aggressive or otherwise not compliant can trigger regulatory fines or even result in the voiding of a bank's claim, so collection activities have to stay within the limits of the law. Comparative insights from jurisdictions like Singapore underscore the value of targeted legislation in mitigating risks associated with informal and third-party collection practices.[139]

10.5.7.3 Cross-Border Debt Recovery

Domestic debt recovery is mainly handled through civil procedure. Cross-border debt recovery, by contrast, sits at the intersection between private law and the realities of international political economy.[140] In other words, when a lender tries to collect money from someone in another jurisdiction, they may run into limits that an ordinary court judgment does not address. These obstacles go beyond typical contractual or judicial issues and often stem from wider systems, shaped by a state's macroeconomic policies rather than by the borrower's own financial situation.

The legal and political obstacles most often discussed include the following. First, exchange and capital controls can pose a significant risk because a government may suddenly limit how money can be sent out of the country. If this happens, a local borrower may not be able to exchange local currency into the foreign currency needed to repay the debt. Second, insolvency moratoria can arise under local law, especially during a national financial crisis.[141] In these cases, the

[137] Kalaitsoflou (2021, 1–14).

[138] See, ECB (2017), Siraki and Yona (2021, 29–43) and Fell et al. (2021).

[139] Stanescu (2025, 364) Stanescu and Kepinski (2025, 393–420).

[140] Ontanu (2017).

[141] Gurinovich and Zhuravleva (2023, 39–49).

law may require a stay that temporarily prevents creditors from starting or continuing enforcement actions, primarily with the aim of preventing bank runs and reducing the risk of widespread failure across the domestic corporate sector. Third, political risk refers to infrequent but severe government actions, such as nationalization, seizing collateral, or imposing sudden capital controls, that can make a credit agreement difficult to enforce even when the contract is otherwise valid.[142]

To reduce these non-commercial risks, international lenders often rely on credit enhancement tools and insurance coverage. Entities such as the Multilateral Investment Guarantee Agency (MIGA), which is part of the World Bank Group, and national Export Credit Agencies (ECAs) offer political risk insurance.[143] In this regard, for example, Japan's Nippon Export and Investment Insurance (NEXI) is a state-backed export credit and investment insurer. In practice, it often acts as a backstop for Japanese companies investing in higher-risk areas, including parts of the energy sector. NEXI offers insurance for projects involving natural resources and often works with the Japan Bank for International Cooperation (JBIC) to support longer loan maturities and better financing terms when projects match Japan's national interests. Japan's legal approach often includes subrogation clauses in its international agreements, which allow one party to take over another party's claim under set conditions. After NEXI pays an investor for a covered loss, the law transfers the investor's rights and claims against the host government to NEXI. Transferring these rights to a state-backed body can deter host governments, because they may avoid regulatory steps that could trigger a direct legal dispute with the Japanese state. NEXI has a nation-based purpose and uses its PRI instruments to support Japan's overseas economic and industrial policy goals.[144]

However, when a crisis spreads through the whole system, disputes that might have been handled through individual lawsuits are often addressed instead through Multilateral Restructuring Frameworks. These are formal creditor clubs that organize joint action among lenders and a government facing financial distress. For example, the Paris Club is an informal group of official government creditors that meets to negotiate changes to the debt of a sovereign state, including rescheduling payments or, in some cases, cancelling part of the debt.[145] Similarly, the London Club is a forum for private commercial banks that work together when a country defaults on its debt. Its aim is to agree on a shared approach to restructuring so that one bank does not end up worse off than the others under the final plan.[146]

These mechanisms illustrate that, in international settings, debt recovery law is shaped not only by contract rights but also by diplomacy and the need to maintain stability in the wider financial system. Ultimately, a successful recovery depends on both firm legal enforcement and compliance with widely accepted international restructuring standards.

[142] Trebesch (2019, 421) Choi et al. (2012, 131–179).
[143] Williams (1993, 59).
[144] Papanastasiou (2021, 155–178).
[145] Mooney (2015, 91) and Cosio-Pascal (2010, 231).
[146] Kirchner and Ehmke (2012, 3) and Annamaria (2022).

10.5.8 Regulatory Oversight and Supervisory Cooperation

The last part of the international credit system is shaped less by private agreements and more by rules set and enforced by regulators. Since bank credit can move easily across national borders, oversight should not be limited to just one country. To address this challenge, financial regulators have built cross-border supervisory arrangements through MoUs and joint inspections, which allow timely data sharing and coordinated oversight of multinational financial institutions.

This cooperative approach is based on the Basel Core Principles for Effective Banking Supervision, which set out two main requirements as consolidated supervision and home-host coordination.[147] In regard to consolidated supervision, which means that the regulator in a bank's home country is responsible for supervising the bank as a whole, including all of its foreign branches and subsidiaries. The goal is to ensure that risks taken outside the home country are identified and measured at the group level, and that they are reflected in the parent company's balance sheet and overall capital position. When it comes to home-host coordination, it involves the routine exchange between the supervisor in the country where a bank is headquartered and the supervisor in each country where it operates. It aims to limit regulatory arbitrage by aligning oversight and sharing key information, so risk does not build up in parts of the bank that supervisors cannot see during the credit cycle.

To protect financial system stability, central banks and supervisory authorities apply a strict prudential checklist to all cross-border credit exposures. Each loan should be assigned a risk weight that matches the borrower's credit quality, and it should be backed by enough collateral to cover potential losses. Additionally, all cross-border flows are subject to strict AML controls, sanctions screening, and detailed reporting requirements.[148] At the global level, the FSB leads the macroprudential oversight of systemically important financial institutions (G-SIFIs).[149] By tracking how major lenders are linked across borders, the FSB can implement policies that reduce the risk that a default in one country spreads through the financial system and disrupts the world economy. In conclusion, the movement of private credit into public policy debates shows that, in the twenty-first century, international lending needs to be seen as part of global economic security.

10.5.9 Concluding Reflections

International credit agreements are not isolated legal documents. They help hold the global economy together by setting shared expectations for lending, repayment, and risk across borders. This section helps to consider these instruments

---

[147] BIS (2012).
[148] Ross et al. (2025).
[149] Knight (2015), Weber and Staiger (2014, 82), Walker (2013, 1–42) and Komarkova et al. (2012).

in two different ways. First, as a legal instrument, the agreement is the clearest expression of the globalization of private law. It brings common law and civil law rules together into one clear framework that makes legal outcomes easier to predict. It offers the certainty of hard law, grounded in *pacta sunt servanda*, so an investor based in one continent can reasonably trust that a borrower in another will be held to the agreement. Second, as a financial act, the agreement serves as a key part of the global financial system, helping money and trade keep moving across borders. This is not merely a transfer of money; it reflects how institutions formalize interdependence. When a bank lends across borders, it ties parts of one country's economy to another's, which can give both sides a reason to value peace, stability, and the rule of law.

Looking across past financial crises, from nineteenth-century sovereign defaults to the 2008 collapse, a clear lesson emerges for banking lawyers. Finance depends on both trust and legal rules: trust without law can lead to crisis, while law without trust can bring lending and markets to a standstill. This balance is critical. Relying on trust instead of enforceable law in lending can create the conditions for debt traps and predatory lending. If Basel III standards, AML rules, and disclosure requirements are not in place, profit seeking can push firms toward risky behaviour that builds economy-wide bubbles, and when those bubbles collapse, the social costs can be severe. Conversely, when people do not trust the legal order, lenders tend to pull back, and the result can be a credit crunch. When rules are too rigid, or when courts cannot consistently enforce even a basic loan agreement, investors tend to move their capital elsewhere. In short, trade and innovation rely on trust; when trust is absent, both tend to stall.

Chapter Summary

Chapter 10 provides a comprehensive examination of the legal and regulatory structures created to address systemic financial crises through the embedment of effective consumer protection features in the financial system. integrating robust consumer protection principles into the financial system. The chapter then reflects on the flaws in the antecedent pre-2008 doctrine of too big to fail with its costly taxpayer-funded bail-out packages. This failure led a global reform initiated by the FSB including all G20 major economies. The new rules focus on bail-ins, whereby losses of a failed bank are assigned to shareholders and creditors instead of taxpayers, which is conductive of preserving financial stability and market discipline. The FSB's Key Attributes of Effective Resolution Regimes (KAs) set the legal framework for resolution, stipulating that jurisdictions should have dedicated resolution authorities. The principle legal tools include but no limited to:

– Write-down and conversion powers, meaning the legal ability to immediately write down or convert a creditor's claim, including bail-inable liabilities, into ordinary equity shares.

- Bridging institutions are entities established as legal persons in order to take over the essential functions of a failing firm on a temporary basis to keep it running.
- Moratorium powers, which allow the regulators to stay certain transactions in order to prevent a run on the bank.
- Ring-fencing or separation are different legal forms that create a barrier between systematically important activities (such as infrastructure) and non-systemically important ones.
- An orderly liquidation program would mean that even when resolution is impossible, assets will be quickly and efficiently put on a market-based route for sale.

This chapter emphasises the Deposit Insurance Systems (DIS) as a key protection against bank runs. DIS provides a legal protection for a limited amount of retail deposits, thereby minimising contagion risk and harm to protected retail clients in case of resolution.

The last section connected financial stability and market integrity by focusing on consumer protection laws. This field is increasingly informed by behavioral finance, such as the realisation that consumers have cognitive biases (e.g., present bias, inertia). In this context, regulations like the EU's MiFID II (suitability and appropriateness), the US' TILA (focusing on disclosure), and nudge theory principles demand that financial institutions create an unambiguous unbiased environment for disclosing information through nudges as simple disclosures or default choices, such as opt-in or opt-out options, which may guide consumers to better outcomes.

Revision Questions

1. What is the basic difference between a state-led bail-out and a reform bail-in as it is used today in the sense of ripping through losses? Explain why the legal enforceability of the write-down and conversion power is key to the effectiveness of a bail-in regime.
2. Explain three specific legal powers that are necessary in order to meet the requirements of the KAs according to the FSB. Discuss how these powers maintain the provision of critical functions while a G-SIB is being resolved.
3. Examine the interplay between DIS and Resolution Authority in case of bank's failure. Discuss the reasons why the DIS should not apply to impose a greater cost on covered depositors in resolution that in ordinary insolvency ("no creditor worse off").
4. Describe how behavioural finance principles, including nudge theory, are applied in support of certain consumer protection laws (e.g., required simplified disclosure, default rules). Give an example of a nudge that is legal in investment/savings products.

5. Explain the role of MAC clause in loan agreements. Analyse how a declaration of financial crisis (such as sovereign debt distress or systemic event), shall active the legal right granted by MAC clause.
6. What is the legal significance of resolution authority sui generis being independent in terms of operations from the central bank and ministry of finance?
7. Explain what a G-SIB is. Describe how ring-fencing is able to safeguard the key domestic functions of a bank from problems arising with an international or speculative trading segment of the firm.◀

References

Ahmed F, Nizam K, Ahsan N (2024) Credit risk management and default risk: empirical evidence from United Kingdom. J Bus Educ Manage 3(2):95–110

Alexiou G, Pereira S, Rodrigues-Gomes V (2025) Repo collateral reuse and liquidity windfalls. European Central Bank, Frankfurt

Ang F, Tjwan G, Lianto A (2025) The mandatory convertible bond is an instrument to pursue dominant position among shareholders. Melayunesia Law 9(2):133–149

Andenas M, Fairgrieve D (2002) Misfeasance in public office, governmental liability, and European influences. Int Comp Law Q 51:757–780

Angeli F (2018) Usury and credit practices in the middle ages. Contabila Cult Aziendale 13(1):37–69

Annamaria V (2022) The role of Paris and London clubs: is it under threat? The centre for studies and research in international law and international relations online. Brill/Nijhoff. Leiden. https://doi.org/10.1163/1875-8096_pplrdc_A9789004373709_10. Accessed 31 Jan 2026

Atuahene S, Yusheng K, Benturn-Micah G, Aboagye A (2021) Impact of capital adequacy on banks' performance: considering the basel international regulatory framework for banks. ETIKONOMI 20(1):45–54

Augustin P, Subrahmanyam M, Tang D, Wang S (2024) Credit default swaps: a survey. Found Trends Finance 9(1–2):1–196

Baker C, Cohanier B (2025) The emergence of bills of exchange in the late medieval and early modern periods in Europe. Account Hist 30(2):341–362

Bamford C (2001) Directors' fiduciary duties and the approved persons regime. In: Ferran E, Goodhart C (eds) Regulating financial services and markets in the 21st century. Hart Publishing, Oxford

Barghouthi O, Bayyoud M (2016) Overview of the basel capital adequacy framework. Int J Finance Bank Res 2(3):102–115

Barth J, Miller S (2018) On the rising complexity of bank regulatory capital requirements: from global guidelines to their US implementation. J Risk Financ Manag 11(4):77

Bassan F, Rabitti M (2024) From smart legal contracts to contracts on blockchain: an empirical investigation. Comput Law Secur Rev 55:106035

Bassiouni M (2008) International criminal law, volume 2: multilateral and bilateral enforcement mechanisms. Brill, Leiden.

Bazinas S (2025) The UNCITRAl model law on secured transactions: preparation and implementation issues. Law Financ Markets Rev 18(1):1–16

Beale H (2017) Chitty on contracts: second cumulative supplement to the thirty-second edition. Sweet and Maxwell, London

Ben-Shahar O, Schneider C (2011) The failure of mandated disclosure. Univ PA Law Rev 159(3):647–749

Binder C, Lehner O (2019) The problem of heterogeneity within risk weights: does Basel IV contains solution? ACRN J Financ Risk Perspect 8(1):183–205
BIS (2010) Basel III: a global regulatory framework for more resilient banks and banking systems. https://www.bis.org/publ/bcbs189.pdf. Accessed 30 Jan 2026
BIS (2012) Core principles for effective banking supervision. https://www.bis.org/publ/bcbs230.pdf. Accessed 30 Jan 2026
BIS (2013) Basel III: the liquidity coverage ratio and liquidity risk monitoring tools. https://www.bis.org/publ/bcbs238.pdf. Accessed 31 Jan 2026
BIS (2021) Assessing the impact of Basel III: evidence from macroeconomic models: literature review and simulations. Basel Committee on Banking Supervision Working Paper
Blundell-Wignall A, Atkinson P (2010) Thinking beyond Basel III: Necessary Solutions for Capital and Liquidity. OECD J Finan Mark Trends 1:1–23
Bridge M (1996) Personal property law. Oxford University Press, Oxford
Brigida M (2022) Credit default swaps and bank safety. Appl Financ Lett 11:19–27
Bröhmer J (2024) State immunity and sovereign bonds. In: Peters A, Lagrange E, Oeter S, Tomuschat C (eds) Immunities in the age of global constitutionalism. Brill, Leiden, pp 182–208
Bubb R, Krishnamurthy P (2015) Regulating against bubbles: how mortgage regulation can keep main street and wall street safe-from themselves. Univ PA Law Review 163(6):1539–1630
Bunte J, Kinne B (2025) Strategic interdependence in sovereign lending. Eur J Polit Econ 89:102715
Busch D (2017) MifID II: Stricter conduct of business rules for investment firms. Capital Markets Law J 12(3):340–380
Butler T, Brooks R (2023) Time for a paradigm change: problems with the financial industry's approach to operational risk. Risk Anal 44(6):1285–1304
Cantu C, Gondo R, Martinez B (2024) Reserve requirements as a financial stability instrument. BIS Working Papers No 1182. https://iaefinance.org/wp-content/uploads/BIS-Working-Papers.-Reserve-requirements-as-a-financial-stability-instrument.pdf. Accessed 30 Jan 2026
Carlson M (2015) Lessons from the historical use of reserve requirements in the United States to promote bank liquidty. Int J Cent Banking 11(1):191–224
Castiglionesi F, Eboli M (2018) Liquidity flows in interbank network. Rev Financ 22(4):1291–1334
Cherednychenko O (2024) On the Bumpy road to responsible lending in the digital marketplace: the new EU consumer credit directive. J Consumer Policy 47:241–270
Cherednychenko O, Meindertsma J (2019) Irresponsible lending in the post-crisis era: is the EU consumer credit directive fit for its purpose? J Consum Policy 42:483–519
Childs P, Ott S, Riddiough T (1996) The value of recourse and cross-default clauses in commercial mortgage contracting. J Bank Financ 20(3):511–536
Choi S, Gulati M, Posner E (2012) The evolution of contractual terms in sovereign bonds. J Leg Anal 4(1):131–179
Choudhry M (2006) Bonds: a concise guide for investors. Springer, London
Chung K, Papaioannou M (2021) Do enhanced collective action clauses affect sovereign borrowing costs? J Bank Financ Econo 15:59–87
Cole S, Kanz M, Klapper L (2015) Incentivizing calculated risk-taking: evidence from an experiment with commercial bank loan officers. J Financ 70(2):537–575
Colla P (2011) Syndication and secondary loan sales. Theor Econ Lett 1(3):81–87
Consumer Financial Protection Bureau (2014) What you should know about home equity lines of credit. https://files.consumerfinance.gov/f/201603_cfpb_booklet_heloc.pdf. Accessed 30 Jan 2026
Cosio-Pascal E (2010) Paris club: intergovernmental relations in debt restructuring. In: Herman B, Ocampo J, Spiegel S (eds) Overcoming developing country debt crises. Oxford University Press, Oxford, pp 231–276
Craig B, Fecht F, Tümer-Alkan G (2015) The role of interbank relationships and liquidity needs. J Bank Financ 53:99–111

Cullen J (2017) The repo market, collateral and systemic risk in search of regulatory coherence. In: Chiu I, MacNeil I (eds) Research handbook on shadow banking. Edward Elgar, Cheltenham, pp 85–116

Cuniberti G (2014) The international market for contracts: the most attractive contract laws. Northwest J Int Law Bus 34(3):455–517

Curtis Q, Weidemaier W, Gulati M (2023) Green bonds, empty promises. North C Law Rev 102(1):131–178

Davies P, Raczynska M (2020) Contents of commercial contracts: terms affecting freedoms. Hart, Oxford

Day S (2005) Lines of credit and consumption smoothing: the choice between credit cards and home equity lines of credit. Bank of Canada Working Paper 2005–18

Deane S, Chui T (2025) 2025 updates to the LMA, APLMA and LSTA's green, social and sustainability-linked loan principles and guidance. https://www.deacons.com/2025/05/09/2025-updates-to-the-lma-aplma-and-lstas-green-social-and-sustainability-linked-loan-principles-and-guidance. Accessed 30 Jan 2026

Dennis S, Mullineaux D (2000) Syndicated loans. J Financ Intermediation 9(4):404–426

Denzel M (2025) International fairs as money, credit, and exchange markets, from the 12th to 16th centuries. In: Gaulin J, Rau S (eds) Fairs, cities and merchants: spatiotemporal analyses (14th-17th Century). De Gruyter, Leiden, pp 245–270

Dionysopoulos L, Marra M, Urquhart A (2024) Central Bank digital currencies: a critical review. Int Rev Financ Anal 91:103031

Dorman C (2012) Representations, warranties, and covenants: practical applications for commercial credit agreements. J Tax Regul Financ Instit 25(5):35–43

Dougherty C, Killen T (2020) Article 14 of Rome I and choice of law rules in cross border assignments. Butterworths J Int Bank and Financial Law

Drucker S, Puri M (2009) On loan sales, loan contracting, and lending relationships. Rev Financ Stud 22(7):2635–2672

Du B (2017) How useful is Basel III's liquidity coverage ratio? Evidence from US Bank holding companies. Eur Financ Manage 23(5):1–18

EBA (2025) 2025 EU-wide stress test. https://www.eba.europa.eu/sites/default/files/2025-08/0178b9c5-2f0d-42ee-8226-6fa0a87c0d6c/2025%20EU-wide%20stress%20test%20-%20Results.pdf. Accessed 30 Jan 2026

Eisenberg T, Miller G (2009) The flight to New York: an empirical study of choice of law and choice of forum clauses in publicly-held companies' contracts. Cardozo Law Rev 30(4):1475–1512

Ellias J, Fontenay E (2025) The credit markets go dark. Yale Law J 134:779–857

Espinosa V, Alonso-Neira M, Soto J (2023) The ethics of fractional-reserve banking system: a private property rights approach. Economies 11(9):221

European Central Bank (2017) Guidance to banks on non-performing loans. https://www.bankingsupervision.europa.eu/ecb/pub/pdf/guidance_on_npl.en.pdf. Accessed 31 Jan 2026

European Parliament (1999) The determination of interest rates. https://www.europarl.europa.eu/workingpapers/econ/pdf/116_en.pdf. Accessed 28 Jan 2026

Fabozzi F, Klingler S, Molgoard P, Nielsen M (2021) Active loan trading. J Financ Intermediation 46:100868

Fairweather K (2012) The development of responsible lending in the UK consumer credit regime. In: Devenney J, Kenny M (eds) Consumer credit, debt and investment in Europe. Cambridge University Press, Cambridge, pp 84–110

Fang C, Schumacher J, Trebesch C (2021) Restructuring sovereign bonds: holdouts, haircuts and the effectiveness of CACs. IMF Econ Rev 69(3):1–59

FCA (2017) Assessing creditworthiness in consumer credit: proposed changes to our rules and guidance. Consultation Paper No CP17/27

Fell J, Grodzicki M, Lee J, Martin R, Park C, Rosenkranz P (2021) Nonperforming loans in Asia and Europe—causes, impacts, and resolution strategies. https://aric.adb.org/pubs/nplresolutionstrategies/npls-in-asia-and-europe-causes-impacts-resolution-strategies.pdf. Accessed 30 Jan 2026
Feridun M, Özün A (2020) Basel IV implementation: a review of the case of the European Union. J Capital Markets Stud 4(1):7–24
Ferrari F (2020) Concise commentary on the Rome I regulation. Cambridge University Press, Cambridge
Ferretti F (2021) Peer-to-peer lending and EU credit laws: a creditworthiness assessment, credit-risk analysis or … neither of two? German Law J 22(1):102–121
Ferretti F, Livada C (2016) The over-indebtedness of European consumers under EU policy and law. In: Ferretti F (ed) Comparative perspectives of consumer over-indebtedness: a view from the UK, Germany, Greece, and Italy. Eleven International Publishing, Den Haag, pp 11–40
Flagg J, Hannon S (2023) An overview of personal loans in the U.S. finance and economics discussion series 2023–057
Flora C (2012) Practitioner's guide to the voluntary payment doctrine. South IL Univ Law J 37:91–134
Foos D, Lütkebohmert E, Markovych M, Pliszka K (2022) Euro area banks' interest rate risk exposure to level, slope and curvature swings in the yield curve. Euro Financ Manage 28(4):883–925
Fountoulakis C (2005) The parties' choice of 'neutral law' in international sales contracts. European J Law Reform 7:303–329
Freudenberg F, Imbierowicz B, Saunders A, Steffen S (2017) Covenant violations and dynamic loan contracting. J Corp Financ 45:540–565
Gande A, Saunders A (2006) Are banks still special when there is a secondary market for loans? J Financ 67(5):1649–1684
Gatt W (2024) Loan-to-value limits as a macroprudential policy tool: developments in theory and practice. J Econ Surv 38(1):232–267
Gebhardt J (1947) Pacta Sunt Servanda. Modern L Rev 10:159–170
Gelpern A, Powell A (2023) Sovereign debt restructuring: the need for a new approach. Inter-American Development Bank Discussion Paper No IDB-DP-1022
Geronimo R, Baclay F (2021) 2021 LIBOR phaseout and negative interest rates: some legal and contractual considerations. Philippine Law J 94(265–288):267–268
Giannopoulos V, Kariofyllas S (2025) When models fail: credit scoring, bank management, and NPL growth in the Greek recession. Int J Financ Stud 13(3):152
Gioia-Carabellese P (2016) Compound Interest and its validity (or invalidity) in the bank-customer relationship: the state-of-art of British Common Law discussed by virtue of a comparative analysis. Law Econ Yearly Rev 5(1):174–200
Glaeser E, Scheinkman J (1994) Neither a borrower nor a lender be: an economic analysis of interest restrictions and usuary law. https://www.nber.org/system/files/working_papers/w4954/w4954.pdf. Accessed 29 Jan 2026
Goode R (1975) The consumer credit act 1974. Cambridge Law Journal 34(1):79–130
Goodness S, Shan A, Oladele S, Stark B (2025) AI and credit scoring: assessing the fairness and transparency of machine learning models in lending decisions. https://www.researchgate.net/publication/390172601_AI_and_Credit_Scoring_Assessing_the_Fairness_and_Transparency_of_Machine_Learning_Models_in_Lending_Decisions. Accessed 30 Jan 2026
Griffith E (2007) Lenders and consumers continue the search for the truth in lending under the Truth in Lending Act and Regulation Z. San Diego L Rev 44:611–676
Grundmann S, Micklitz H-W, Renner M (2021) New private law theory: a pluralist approach. Cambridge University Press, Cambridge, pp 205–338
Guenster A, Jud R, Schwendner P (2025) Explaining new issuance premiums in the US corporate bond market. J Financ Data Sci 7(3):8–21
Gunnarsson E (2017) Default interest rates in international transaction: analyses of private law application. Eur Rev Private Law 25(4):765–788

Gurara D, Presbitero A, Sarmiento M (2019) Borrowing costs and the role of multilateral development banks: evidence from cross-border syndicated bank lending. J Int Money Financ 100(3):102090

Gurinovich S, Zhuravleva T (2023) The issue of moratorium on bankruptcy under unfavorable macroeconomic conditions. Econ Consultant 1:39–49

Guttentag M (2004) An argument for imposing disclosure requirements on public companies. Florida State Univ Law Rev 32(1):123–196

Hadas-Dyduch M, Puszer B, Czech M, Cichy J (2022) Green bonds as an instrument for financing ecological investments in the V4 countries. Sustainability 14(19):12188

Hardy D (1997) Instruments of monetary management. In: Balino T, Zamalloa L (eds) Instruments of monetary management: issues and country experiences. IMF

Hartlage A (2012) The Basel III liquidity coverage ratio and financial stability. Mich Law Rev 111(3):453–484

Hartley T (2011) Choice of law regarding the voluntary assignment of contractual obligations under the Rome I regulation. Int Comp Law Q 60(1):29–56

Heller D, Leitzinger L, Walz U (2024) Intellectual property as business loan collateral: a taxonomy of institutional and economic determinants. GRUR Int 73(5):379–392

Holton R, Turner B (1989) Max Weber on economy and society. Routledge, London. https://www.ecb.europa.eu/pub/pdf/scpwps/ecb.wp3147~6c60cabb50.en.pdf. Accessed 30 Jan 2026

Huang Z, Yin J (2025) Bond cross-default clauses and the degree of corporate earnings management. Adv Econ Manage Polit Sci 190(1):215–225Reference 'Huang and Yin (2025)' is cited in text but not provided in the reference list. Please provide reference in the list or delete this citation.adjusted.

Huerga A, Rodriguez-Monroy C (2019) Mandatory convertible bonds and the agency problem. Sustainability 11(5):4074

Hunt J, Richard S, Wallace N (2013) Rebalancing public and private in the law of mortgage transfer. American Univ Law Rev 62(6):1529–1586

ICMA (2023) The GMRA framework agreement as an example of standard documentation on the International REPO market. Actual Probl Russ Law 19(1):66–78

Ioannidou V, Pavanini N, Peng Y (2022) Collateral and asymmetric information in lending markets. J Financ Econ 144(1):93–121

Ivashina V, Vallee B (2025) Weak credit covenants. Manage Sci 71(12):9998–10021

Jamilov R, König T, Müller K, Saidi F (2025) Two centuries of systemic bank runs. https://users.ox.ac.uk/~econ0628/Bank_Runs_JKMS_Full.pdf. Accessed 10 July 2026

Janko C, Josep T, Maria A (2020) Are syndicated loans truly less expensive? J Bank Financ 120:105942

Johan S, Sudiro A, Gunadi A (2022) Do cross-default and cross-collateral clause fulfill the principles of justice and equality in loan agreement? (The case of Indonesia). Glob Bus Financ Rev 27(3):1–13Reference 'Johan et al. (2022)' is cited in text but not provided in the reference list. Please provide reference in the list or delete this citation.adjusted

Jones M (1999) Bankers beware: the risks of syndicated credits. N C Bank Inst 3(1):169–200

Kalaitsoflou K (2021) Exploring the concept of arbitral awards under the New York Convention. J Strateg Contracting Negot 5(1):1–14

Kamstra M, Roberts G, Shao P (2012) Does the secondary loan market reduce borrowing costs? Euro Financ Rev 18(3):1139–1181

Kasak A (2019) Is full preference for a secured claim in insolvency proceedings justified? Juridica Int 28:112–121

Keijser T, Kyrkousi M, Bakanos A (2014) Financial collateral: the legal framework of the European Union and UNIDROIT compared. Uniform Law Rev 19(3):429–458

Keil J, Müller K (2019) Bank branching deregulation and the syndicated loan market. J Financ Quantitave Anal 55(4):1269–1303

Kesuma A, Mahduf M (2023) The implementation of Pacta Sunt Servanda principle as a basis for making memorandum of understanding. Awang Long Law Rev 5(2):432–440

Khalifeh I, Benhmad F, Moussawi C, Tarazi A (2025) Net stable funding ratio: implication for bank stability in Europe. Global Financ J 67:101144

Kieninger E (2004) Introduction: security rights in movable property within the common market and the approach of the study. In: Kieninger E (ed) Security rights in movable property in European Private Law. Cambridge University Press, Cambridge, pp 6–38

King M (2013) The Basel III net stable funding ratio and bank net interest margins. J Bank Financ 37(11):4144–4156

Kirchner C, Ehmke D (2012) Private ordering in sovereign debt restructuring: reforming the London Club. Oxford University Comparative Law Forum. https://ouclf.law.ox.ac.uk/private-ordering-in-sovereign-debt-restructuring-reforming-the-london-club. Accessed 30 Jan 2026

Knight M (2015) Completing the G20's program to reform global financial regulation. https://www.cigionline.org/static/documents/no55_web.pdf. Accessed 27 Jan 2026

Komarkova Z, Hausenblas V, Frait J (2012) How to identify systematically important financial Institutions. https://www.cnb.cz/export/sites/cnb/en/financial-stability/.galleries/fs_reports/fsr_2011-2012/fsr_2011-2012_article_i.pdf. Accessed 31 Jan 2026

Kosi U, Franke B, Stoczek P (2025) Brexit and European corporate bond markets. https://papers.ssrn.com/sol3/papers.cfm?abstract_id=5389091. Accessed 29 Jan 2026

Kovacs L, Tertak E (2025) LIBOR: its inception, golden era and downfall. Econ Financ 12(2):137–165

Kuipers J (2012) EU Law and private international law: the interrelationship in contractual obligations. Martines Nijhoff Publishers, Leiden

Lambillon A (2026) The rise of sustainable debt. In: Walker T, Gramlich D (eds) The Palgrave handbook of sustainable finance. Palgrave Macmillan, Cham, pp 25–41

Lee J (2017) Should interest rates be regulated or abolished? The case for the abolution of usury. Western Australian Jurist 8:227–263

Levitin A (2024) The new usury: the ability-to-repay revolution in consumer finance. George Wash Law Rev 92(2):425–484

Levy K (2017) Book-smart, not street-smart: blockchain-based smart contracts and the social workings of law. Engaging Sci Technol Soc 3(1):1–15

Li N, Lou Y, Vasvari F (2015) Erratum to: default clauses in debt contracts. Rev Acc Stud 20:1638

Lima C (2023) Adhesion electronic contracts ("shrink-wrap" and "click-wrap") and the terms of use ("browse-wrap"). Braz J Law Technol Innov 1(2):108–153

Liu G, Molise T (2019) Housing and credit market shocks: exploring the role of rule-based Basel III counter-cyclical capital requirements. Econ Model 82:264–279

Loan Market Association (2019) Sustainability linked loan principles. https://www.icmagroup.org/assets/documents/Regulatory/Green-Bonds/LMASustainabilityLinkedLoanPrinciples-270919.pdf. Accessed 30 Jan 2026

Lonegrass M (2012) Finding room for fairness in formalism: the sliding scale approach to unconscionability. Loyola Univ Chicago Law J 44:1–64

Luhmann N (1988) Trust: making and breaking cooperative relations. In: Gambetta D (ed) Familiarity, confidence, trust: problems and alternatives. Basil Blackwell, Oxford, pp 94–107

Malik M (2024) Risk governance and regulatory adjustments in the public Commercial Banks of OECD. J Financ Regul Compliance 32(2):266–289Reference 'Malik (2024)' is cited in text but not provided in the reference list. Please provide reference in the list or delete this citation.adjusted

Marsh B, Basta T (2017) Loan syndications and trading: an overview of the syndicated loan market. In: Mellor T (ed) The international comparative legal guide to: lending and secured finance 2017. Stephens &George, London

Massa M, Schmidt D (2015) Insider trading in the bond market: evidence from loan sale events. CEPR Discussion Papers 10446

McCullough C (2016) Unconscionability as a coherent legal concept. Univ PA Law Rev 164:779–825

McNiece H (1946) The interest on interest rule in New York. St. John's Law Rev 20(2):71–79

Meaning J, Dyson B, Barker J, Clayton E (2021) Broadening narrow money: monetary policy with a Central Bank Digital currency. Int J Cent Bank 17(2):1–42
Menand L (2021) Why supervise banks? the foundations of the American Monetary settlement. Vanderbilt Law Rev 74(4):951–1022
Miller M, Thomas D (2007) Sovereign debt restructuring: the judge, the vultures and creditor rights. World Econ 30(10):1491–1509
Mizen P, Tsoukas S, Tsoukalas J (2009) How does reputation influence a firm's decision to issue corporate bonds? new evidence from initial and seasoned public debt offering. https://ideas.repec.org/p/not/notcfc/09-01.html. Accessed 29 Jan 2026
Mooney C (2015) A framework for a formal sovereign debt restructuring mechanism: The Kiss principle (keep it simple, stupid) and other guiding principles. Mich J Int Law 37(1):57–111
Nakajima K (2022) The international law of sovereign debt dispute settlement. Cambridge University Press, Cambridge, pp 100–138
Nation G (2015) Demand promissory notes and commercial loans: balancing freedom of contract and good faith. Nebraska Law Rev 94:151–192
Nazareth A, Tahyar M (2011) Transparency and confidentiality in the post financial crisis world—where to strike the balance? Harvard Bus Law Rev 1:145–193
Newfield D (2016) Pari Passu as a weapon and the changes to sovereign debt boilerplate after Argentina v. NML. Univ Miami Bus Law Rev 24(3):175–198
Newman N, Trautman L (2021) Securities law: overview and contemporary issues. Ohio State Bus Law J 16(1):149–218
Nicholls C, Bacarese A, Maton J, Scott R, Hatchard J (2024) Civil actions and remedies. In: Nicholls C, Bacarese A, Maton J, Scott R, Hatchard J (eds) Corruption and misuse of public office. Oxford University Press, Oxford, pp 347–433
Noussia K (2010) Confidentiality in international commercial arbitration: a comparative analysis of the position under English, US, German and French Law. Springer, Cham
Ochnio A (2021) The tangled path from identifying financial assets to cross-border confiscation. Deficiencies in EU asset recovery policy. Euro J Crime Crim Law Crim Justice 29:218–240
Odinet C (2021) Modernizing mortgage law. N C Law Rev 100(1):89–166
Olivares-Caminal R (2009) Understanding the Pari Passu clause in sovereign debt instruments: a complex quest. Int Lawyer 43(3):1217–1236
Onyiriuba L (2017) Bank risk management in developing economies: addressing the unique challenges of domestic banks through risk management. Academic Press, Cambridge
Papanastasiou T (2021) The implications of political risk insurance in the governance of energy projects: The case of Japan's public insurance agencies. In: Titi C (ed) Public actors in international investment law. Springer, Cham, pp 155–178
Parchimowicz K, Spence R (2020) Basel IV postponed: a chance to regulate shadow banking. Erasmus Law Rev 2:13–27
Pavlovich A, Sante T (2024) Banks' duties when providing advice and information. https://3vb.com/wp-content/uploads/2024/03/Banks-duties-when-providing-advice-and-information-w-029-1932.pdf. Accessed 30 Jan 2026
Pearce L (2008) Foakes v Beer and promissory estoppel: a step too far. King's Law J 19(3):630–636
Pereira J, Newton D, Paxson D (2003) Fixed-rate endowment mortgage and mortgage indemnity valuation. J Real Estate Financ Econo 26(2–3):197–221
Porras C, Boom W (2012) Information disclosure in the EU consumer credit directive: opportunities and limitations. In: Devenney J, Kenny M (eds) Consumer credit, debt and investment in Europe. Cambridge University Press, Cambridge, pp 21–55
Posner E (1995) Contract law in the welfare state: A defense of the unconscionability doctrine, usury laws, and related limitations on the freedom to contract. J Legal Stud 24(2):283–319
Pozdysev V, Svoronos J, Zyl R (2023) Challenges in supervising banks' large exposures. https://www.bis.org/fsi/publ/insights52.pdf. Accessed 30 Jan 2026

Pridgen D (2012) Putting some teeth in TILA: from disclosure to substantive regulation in the mortgage reform and anti-predatory lending Act of 2010. Loyola Consum Law Rev 24(4):615–639

Proksch L (1982) In praise of conditions subsequent. W Aust Law Rev 2:333–353

Purdue R (1941) The docrine of Foakes v. Beer in Washington. Washington Law Rev 16(1):42–48

PWC (2021) Green, social and sustainability (linked) bonds: the role of a verifier/certifier. https://www.pwc.lu/en/sustainable-finance/docs/pwc-green-social-and-sustainability-linked-bonds.pdf. Accessed 29 Jan 2026

Qian J, Strahan P (2007) How laws and institutions shape financial contracts: the case of Bank loans. J Financ 62(6):2803–2834

Ramadhani R (2020) Legal consequences of transfer of home ownership loans without creditors' permission. Int J Reglement Soc 1(2):31–37

Reale J (2022) Interbank market and funding liquidity risk in a stock-flow consistent model. Metroeconomica 73(3):734–769

Reth J (2015) Just your run-of-the-mill sovereign debt crisis: an analysis of Republic of Argentina v. NML Capital, Ltd. Maryland J Int Law 30(1):132–167

Rivoire M (2025) Party autonomy and the applicable law to the merits in intellectual property arbitration. Arbitration Int 41:213–255

Ross K, Geathy R, Elly B (2025) Investigating cross-border financial fraud and its detection challenges. https://www.researchgate.net/publication/388458518_Investigating_Cross-Border_Financial_Fraud_and_Its_Detection_Challenges. Accessed 20 Jan 2026

Rundo F, Stallo A (2019) A review of the main issues on the loan contracts: asymmetric information, poor transparency and hidden cost. Econo 7:91

Rusen G (2007) Financial collateral arrangements. J Int Commercial Law Technol 2(4):250–258

Russell J (2019) Unconscionability's greatly exaggerated death. University of California, Davis 53:965–1026

Sahlins M (2000) Culture in practice: selected essays. Zone Books, Brooklyn

Santos J, Shao P (2023) Investor diversity and liquidity in the secondary loan market. J Financ Serv Res 63:249–272

Schroeder J, Carlson D (2019) Three against two: on the difference between property and contract and the example of deposit accounts in bankruptcy. Emory Bankruptcy Dev J 35(2):417–508

Schwarcz S (2017) Sovereign debt restructuring and English governing law. Brooklyn J Corp Financ Commercial Law 12:73–103

Schwarcz S, Sergi G (2008) Bond defaults and the dilemma of the indenture trustee. Alabama Law Rev 59:1037–1073

Schwartz A (2019) Mandatory disclosure in primary markets. Utah Law Rev 5:1069–1103

Selmani B (2015) New perspectives on contractual law in the context of real contracts in the systems of international contemporary (roman) law. Euro J Interdisc Stud 3(1):142–151

Shahizam S (2023) Defending the orthodoxy: central bank money as liabilities: a reply to Will Bateman and Jason Allen "the law of central bank reserve creation" (2022) 85(2) MLR 401. MLR Forum 001. https://www.modernlawreview.co.uk/shahizam-bateman-allen. Accessed 19 Jan 2026

Sheard P (2013) Repeat after me: banks cannot and do not "lend out" reserves. https://www.hks.harvard.edu/sites/default/files/centers/mrcbg/programs/senior.fellows/2019-20%20fellows/BanksCannotLendOutReservesAug2013_%20(002).pdf. Accessed 10 July 2026

Shein A, Al-Dabbas N, Enizan A (2018) The role of the agent bank and the specificity of its legal status in the syndicate loan (a comparative study). J Polit Law 11(4):123–138

Shubhan M (2019) Deconstrucing simple evidence in bankruptcy petition for legal certainty. Indonesia Law Rev 9(2):66–108 Reference 'Shubhan (2019)' is cited in text but not provided in the reference list. Please provide reference in the list or delete this citation.Adjusted

Sidorenko M, Sidorenko T, Zhukov A, Averyanova V (2023) The legal nature and features of a syndicated credit (loan). In: Buchaev Y, Abdulkadyrov A, Regulina J, Khachaturyan A, Popkova E (eds) Challenges of the modern economy: digital technologies, problems, and focus areas of the sustainable development of country and regions. Springer, Cham, pp 213–217

Simmel G (2011) The philosophy of money. Routledge, London
Siraki Q, Yona L (2021) Factors influencing the recovery of non-performing loans in commercial banks: the case of Exim Bank. Eur J Bus Manag 13(14):29–43
Song W (2011) Financial innovations, credit default swaps, and syndicated loans. https://papers.ssrn.com/sol3/papers.cfm?abstract_id=1785844. Accessed 30 Jan 2026
Stanescu C (2025) An empirical evaluation of informal debt collection regulations in Singapore: fragmentation or complementarity? Singapore J Legal Stud 5:354–403
Stanescu C, Kepinski J (2025) Beyond soft law? evaluating the role of codes of conduct in regulating EU informal debt collection-evidence from FENCA members. J Consum Policy 48:393–420
Starkey M (2018) Credit creation theory of banking. https://shura.shu.ac.uk/23013/1/Starkey-CreditCreationTheory%28VoR%29.pdf. Accessed 15 Jan 2026
Su Y (2025) Perceived corporate individualism culture and corporate bond issuing costs. Int Rev Financ Anal 103:104191
Suryadarma F, Pujiyono P (2025) Implementation of prudential principles in risk management in digital banking business models. Devotion J Community Serv 5(1):19–29
Tajti T, Iglikowski P (2018) A cross border study of freezing orders and provisional measures: does Mareva Rulet he waves? Springer, Cham
Tot I (2018) Financial market Lex Mercatoria and its influence on the financial collateral directive. J Int Eur Law Econ Market Integr 5(1):37–72
Trebesch C (2019) Resolving sovereign debt crises: the role of political risk. Oxford Econ Papers 71(2):421–444
Tsintsadze K (2015) Mortgage as a means of guarantee. Eur Sci J 11(10):106–111
Tur O, Kravchyk M, Polonka I, Levytska O, Pshoniak M (2021) Theoretical problems of the legal nature of the loan agreements and its correlation with the credit agreement. Stud Appl Econ 39(6):1–13
Umeaduma C, Adeniyi A (2025) AI-powered credit scoring models: ethical considerations, bias reduction, and financial inclusion strategies. Int J Res Publ Rev 6(3):6647–6661
Vandenbrink D (1982) The effects of usury ceilings. Econ Perspect 6(1):44–55
Vaz D (1988) Four banking crises: their causes and consequences. https://elischolar.library.yale.edu/ypfs-documents/9629. Accessed 10 January 2026
Volker B (2011) Rome I regulation a -mostly- unified private international law of contractual relationships within-most- of the European Union. J Law Commerce 29(2):233–272
Vu A (2023) The impact of conventional and unconventional monetary policies on loan default risk—Evidence from UK peer-to-peer lending platforms. Int J Financ Econ 30(1):242–260
Walker G (2013) International financial instability and the financial stability board. Int Lawyer 47(1):1–42
Webb P (2025) Double waiver of immunity and ripple effects. ICSID Rev—Foreign Invest Law J siaf022
Weber R (2013) An alternative story of the law and regulation of risk management. Univ PA J Bus Law 15(4):1005–1074
Weber R, Staiger D (2014) Financial stability board: mandate and implementation of its systemic risks standards. Int J Financ Stud 2(1):82–102
Webster L, Packianatan T (2025) A new gateway for cross-border enforcement: Hague judgments convention comes into effect in the UK on 1 July 2025. https://www.finance-disputes.co.uk/2025/06/a-new-gateway-for-cross-border-enforcement-hague-judgments-convention-comes-into-effect-in-the-uk-on-1-july-2025. Accessed 10 Jan 2026
Weidemaier W (2013) Sovereign debt after NML v. Argentina. Capital Mark Law J 8(2):123–131
Weidemaier M, Scott R, Gulati M (2013) Origin myths, contracts, and the Hunt for Pari Passu. Law Soc Inq 38:72
Weinschelbaum F, Wynne J (2005) Renegotiation, collective action clauses and sovereign debt markets. J Int Econ 67(1):47–72
Werner R (2014) How do banks create money, and why can other firms not do the same? An explanation for the coexistence of lending and deposit-taking. Int Rev Financ Anal 36:71–77

Wessels B, Madaus S (2020) Rescue of business in Europe: a European law institute instrument. Oxford University Press, Oxford, pp 211–225
Whytock C (2014) Faith and scepticism in private international law: trust, governance, politics, and foreign judgments. Erasmus Law Rev 7(3):113–124
Williams L (1993) Political and other risk insurance: OPIC, MIGA, EXIMBANK and other providers. Pace Int Law Rev 5(1):59–113
Witzleb N (2023) Contract law in changing times: Asian perspectives on Pacta Sunt Servanda. Routledge, London
Wolff R (2018) E-Arbitration agreements and e-awards: Arbitration agreements concluded in an electronic environment and digital arbitral awards. In: Piers M, Aschauer C (eds) Arbitration in the digital age: the brave new world of arbitration. Cambridge University Press, Cambridge, pp 151–181
Wordsworth S, Wedder M (2023) On Arbitration: V. V. Veeder, selected writings and contributions to the development of law. Oxford University Press, Oxford
Yip M (2024) The mareva injunction and crypto fraud. In: Davies P, Tijo H (eds) Fraud and risk in commercial law. Bloomsbury, London, pp 123–143
Yuthayotin S (2015) Access to justice in transnational B2C E-Commerce: a multidimensional analysis of consumer protection mechanisms. Springer, Cham
Zaman M (2008) Usury (riba) and the place of bank interest in Islamic banking and finance. Int J Bank Financ 9(6):1–15
Zhifeng J (2022) Pacta Sunt Servanda and empire: a critical examination of the evolution, invocation, and application of an international law axiom. Mich J Int Law 43(3):745–801

Further Reading

Goodhart C (2011) The Basel committee on banking supervision: a history of the early years 1974–1997. Cambridge University Press, Cambridge
Subashree S (2024) Market minds: understanding behavioral finance concepts. Shanlax Int J Manage 11(1):162–168
Tarullo D (2008) Banking on Basel: the future of international financial regulation. Peterson Institute, Washington DC
Thaler R, Sunstein C (2009) Nudge: improving decisions about health, wealth, and happiness. Penguin Books, London
Cortés J, Tribó J, Adamuz M (2020) Are syndicated loans truly less expensive? Journal of Banking & Finance 120105942-10.1016/j.jbankfin.2020.105942

Payment Transactions and Financial Sources in International Trade

11

Contents

F. B. Erdem, *The Principles of International Banking, Finance and Investment Law*,
Springer Textbooks in Law, https://doi.org/10.1007/978-3-032-32505-1_11

Abstract

This chapter examines the instruments and financial sources used in international trade transactions. It begins by outlining various payment methods, including down payments and cash on delivery (open accounts). Cash against Documents (CAD) is explored in-depth, highlighting types like acceptance credit, documents against acceptance, and documents for payments. Prefinancing is also discussed as a key strategy to facilitate trade. The chapter further categorizes the sources of finance into short-term, medium-term, and long-term loans, providing an analysis of their roles and implications in international trade. These financial instruments and resources are essential for managing cash flows, mitigating risks, and ensuring the smooth execution of trade transactions in a global business environment.

11.1 Payment Instruments in International Trade

International trade payments instruments are structured establishments for discharging obligations from the crossing of goods and services across national boundaries. Each tool has an asymmetric and particular assignment of risk between buyers and sellers that is created through trade business arrangements, bank interactions, and the complexity of the financial system. Payment instruments are made in accordance with an ongoing trust relationship between parties, believed market usages, and where the financial market has matured in the applicable jurisdictions. Legally, payment instruments are governed by a combination of contract law, banking law, and customary practices for international trade transactions. International organizations, such as, the ICC and UNCITRAL have created rules, UCP 600 governing documentary credits and URC 522 governing collections, which develop baseline practices for international trade transactions throughout the world.[1] These sets of rules, while not necessarily binding unless referenced in a contract, create a quasi-legal framework which creates certainty and reduces costs of transacting across jurisdictions, which contributes to trading internationally.

[1] Hugo (2022, 32–33).

11.1.1 Down Payment

A down payment refers to an initial payment made by the buyer/importer to the seller/exporter of goods or services, signifying the buyer's good faith and undertaking for goods or services that have not yet been delivered. Typically, the down payment ranges from 10 to 50% of the contract value, but can vary depending on societal expectations and customs, aspects of the transaction itself, and the degree of trust between the parties.

11.1.1.1 Legal Nature and Framework

A down payment has legal status as only partial performance of an obligation under a contract; however, in international contracts such as the UNIDROIT Principles of International Commercial Contracts and the CISG Article 54, the buyer must take action to facilitate payment, such as obtaining permits to exchange currencies or banking approvals.[2] If the buyer terminates the contract due to the seller's inability to perform, the buyer may receive back their down payment, subject to local governing law. If the buyer is in breach of the contract and the conditions outlined in the contract don't provide otherwise, the seller may retain the down payment as liquidated damages or compensation.

11.1.1.2 Practical Applications

Down payments are often utilized when the exporter is looking for upfront working capital to fund raw materials procurement or commence production, in established buyer-seller arrangements, or customized orders where levels of production risk are higher. Down payments are common in the G20 economies for capital goods sales and are especially pronounced in Germany, Japan, and South Korea where machinery exports require significant pre-production expense. The OECD Arrangement on Officially Supported Export Credits governs the maximum allowable amount of down payment and the portion of the total credit that can be in the form of state-supported financing.[3] This measure encourages balancing state-supported export credits with non-supported credits and complying with international competitive rules in global marketplaces by reducing any potential advantage of state-backed financing.

11.1.1.3 Academic Discussion

Scholarly debates on down payments often focus on whether they serve a purpose of risk allocation in international trade contracts. Some academic critics suggest in cases of asymmetric trade relations—in particular in North-South trade relationships—down payments can be a source of harm to importers, potentially exacerbating liquidity constraints, and making it more difficult to access the market.[4] Others have argued down payments support contract enforcement because

---

[2] Osuna-Gonzalez (2005, 299–323).

[3] Mudde et al. (2024).

[4] Murray et al. (2012).

they signal a promise to pay, and are aligned with models from game theory based on relationships between principals and agents in international contracts.[5] More recently, academics are looking at how the use of escrow payments combined with blockchain-based smart contracts can provide increased security and transparency, particularly in the trade of digital invocation, where automated payments reduce reliance on trust.[6] Although these innovations present further options for payment on, there remain problems for the legal status of these agreements, and enforceability across jurisdictions; these issues are being addressed through a framework such as UNCITRAL's MLETR.

11.1.2 Cash on Delivery (Open Account)

The open account (cash on delivery or COD) is a relatively simple and trust-based payment option in international trade (which occurs when the exporter ships the goods and issues an invoice and the importer is committed to later pay typically at 30, 60, or 90-days—subject to their agreement).[7]

11.1.2.1 Legal Framework and Characteristics

The open account technique depends primarily on contractual trust and the enforceable payment obligations laid out under the governing law of the contract. The banks serve only a minimal role to facilitate the transfer of payment utilizing established methods (e.g., SWIFT). The exporter accepts considerable credit risk with the shipment of product made before such payment is made, with the possibility of non-payment or the buyer's insolvency. The CISG creates a framework for payments with the obligation to pay for open account transaction, specifically Articles 53–59, which states the buyer must pay the price at the time agreed by the parties and at the place agreed upon by the parties after delivery. In common law locations, including the United Kingdom, Canada, and the USA, additional principles of freedom of contract apply, along with UCC Article 2 in the USA governing payment obligations and delivery obligations. Civil law jurisdictions also codify similar principles in their national commercial codes in order to provide consistency in payment obligations.[8]

11.1.2.2 Commercial and Legal Risks

When exporters open account transactions, they face a significant risk of non-payment or buyer insolvency, in addition to difficulties enforcing a payment obligation across borders because of different legal systems and procedural laws.[9] To protect themselves, exporters may use credit insurance from companies, such

[5] Bridge (2019).
[6] Carr and Stone (2017).
[7] US Department of Commerce (2016).
[8] Mann and Roberts (2023).
[9] Arham and Sanjaya (2022, 72–74).

as Euler Hermes, Coface, or Export Development Canada (EDC) or engage in factoring or forfaiting of receivables and put the risk on their financial partner or the financial institution. Exporters can also obtain export credit guarantees from export credit agencies (ECAs), such as UK Export Finance (UKEF), Exim Bank of India, or Türk Eximbank. Credit insurance, factoring, forfaiting, and export guarantees all have their obligations determined by principles of private law, and principles public international law, including the OECD Guidelines for Officially Supported Export Credits, which place limitations on formally supported exports to reduce the potential for market distortion and promote fair competition.

11.1.2.3 Academic Discussion

Academic commentators on international trade often cite open account transactions as a risky transaction for exporters, especially in unpredictable markets or where legal systems are tenuous. Others proposed integrating blockchain-inspired smart contracts to automate payments based on digital ledgers, thereby reducing reliance on trust while executing payments as per MLETR. Innovative technologies align well with economic theories of relational contracting, which stress trust-based efficiency in repeated transactions.[10] In contrast, supporters of open accounts describe the role of the open account as a low transaction cost and effective means for stable and trustworthy bilateral trading relationships. The tension between risk and efficiency depicts a continuing debate between securing and facilitating trade finance, with suggestions for hybrid models that combine traditional tools with a digital element to address the modern challenges of trade.

11.1.3 Cash Against Documents (CAD)

Cash Against Documents (CAD) is an intermediate compromise that uses banks as intermediaries, paying for shipping documents. Unlike open accounts, CAD allows exporters to control goods until the exporter either receives payment or the importer accepts the goods because the importer, as a buyer, needs title documents (e.g., bill of lading) to take possession of the goods.[11]

11.1.3.1 Legal Nature

The foundation of CAD transactions is based on ICC's Uniform Rules for Collections (URC 522). URC 522 states in Article 2 as:

> a "Collection" means the handling by banks of documents as defined in sub-Article 2(b), in accordance with instructions received, in order to (1) obtain payment and/or acceptance, or (2) deliver documents against payment and/or against acceptance, or (3) deliver documents on other terms and conditions.

---

[10] Carr and Stone (2017).

[11] Law (2008, 71).

In practical terms, the exporter's process includes sending the commercial invoice and bill of lading to its remitting bank, which forwards those documents to the collecting bank located in the importer's country. Provided the importer pays (Documents for Payment) or accepts a bill of exchange (Documents against Acceptance), the collecting bank will release the documents to the importer. The bank acts as an agent, per the seller's instructions, and has no obligation to guarantee that the payment or acceptance will occur. The exporter retains ownership of the goods until the collection documents are released; creating a type of security interest under the principles of agency and mandate.[12]

11.1.3.2 Acceptance Credit

An acceptance credit occurs when the importer, or its bank, accepts a time draft (bill of exchange) drawn by the exporter, establishing a legally binding promise to pay at maturity.[13] The importer's acceptance of the draft provides a credit period to the importer and the exporter can discount the accepted draft with the bank and convert it to cash for immediate liquidity. Acceptance credits are subject to variations in UCP 600 or URC 522 depending on the instrument used[14]; however, acceptance credits are very common in financial centres in London, New York, and Tokyo. UCC Article 3 governs acceptance credits in the States, while the UK has the Bills of Exchange Act 1882. The acceptance creates a negotiable instrument, and the acceptance operates independently of the sales contract, creating a right to payment that is unaffected by disputes over the sales contract, unless fraud is proven- a standard recognized in UNCITRAL's Model Law on International Credit Transfers.[15]

11.1.3.3 Academic Discussion

The autonomy principle of acceptance credits is a key subject of academic discourse. Critics argue that the rigidity of the principle may invite fraud in opaque markets, and may reduce trust in jurisdictions where regulations may not contribute to regulatory and legal certainty.[16] Advocates argue that the same rigidity helps to maintain liquidity by making payment obligations independent of the disputes of the underlying contracts, which increases transaction reliability.[17] More recently, academics have debated how to use digital negotiable instruments to update acceptance credits, such as electronic bills of exchange, which is record-keeping technology that provides equivalent legal certainty, in particular under governing legislation such as MLETR.

[12] Tüfekçi and Ünal (2010, 333) and Kim (2021, 76).
[13] McCurdy (1922, 543), Goldby (2019, 59–84) and Längerich (2009, 87–88).
[14] Bergami (2009, 192).
[15] UNCITRAL Secretariat (1992, 3).
[16] Dolan (2007).
[17] Malek and Quest (2009).

11.1.4 Documents Against Acceptance (D/A)

Under Documents against Acceptance (D/A), the bank holding the documents will release the documents to the importer upon acceptance of a time draft obligating the importer to pay on a future date. This approach provides the importer with short-term credit, but also the exporter with a lawful instrument to demonstrate there is a debt. The exporter has rights under the bill of exchange, however, enforcement of those rights is subject to the applicable legal regime where the importer's business is legally domiciled. In many G20 jurisdictions, the 1930 Geneva Conventions on Bills of Exchange and Promissory Notes or other equivalent domestic laws govern the formal validity and enforceability of bills of exchange/drafts.[18]

Legal scholars highlight that the most problematic aspect of enforcement, which creates the biggest incentive for forum shopping and inconsistency in decision outcomes is under D/A, is enforcement of the agreements, which the academic literature notes is subject to jurisdiction variances. Proposals for further legal harmonization would be pursuant to UNCITRAL frameworks in order to promote uniformity with respect to the legal treatment and status of the bill of exchange.[19] Another emerging area of study is the growth in electronic bills under MLETR, as its efficiency potential creates issues of cross-boarder recognizing of electronic bills and establishing the digital form of the documents authenticity.

11.1.5 Documents for Payment (D/P)

Under Documents for Payment (D/P), the collecting bank only releases shipping documents once the importer has made full payment, providing additional protection for the exporter. The obligations of banks and the process involved in D/P collections are set out in the URC 522 Articles 4–6. Although D/P reduces the exporter's credit risk, it complicates transactions where goods have arrived at the importer's location.[20] The importer may refuse to pay, which could lead to demurrage charges and additional costs while the goods are in storage, or they may be unable to resell. Exporters of goods typically take out marine insurance to cover risks and pre-approved export guarantees.

While many criticize D/P for constraining trade in markets without sufficient access to credit, which limits the importer's ability to pay for the goods, it could be argued that these limitations may stifle their ability to engage in transactions where access to credit is scarce.[21] D/P proponents argue that the benefits of D/P security outweigh limitations, particularly in high-risk markets. Books and articles in the academic literature have recently catered toward supporting fintech solutions

---

[18] Voica (2011, 107–117). See also, Dorozynska and Dorozynski (2022, 21).

[19] Goode (2017).

[20] Bortoletti (2017, 190).

[21] Auboin (2007).

(real-time payments) for D/P to reduce the lag between payment and document release.[22] Fintech solutions for innovative D/P constructs represent a trend that demonstrates linkages toward enabling digital trade facilitation.

11.1.6 Prefinancing

Prefinancing (or pre-shipment financing) refers to interim funding to exporters for use to procure or produce and ship goods prior to receiving payment from the importer. Prefinancing plays an important role in enabling trade between sectors depending on the export destination, and specifically for exporters operating in and from developing economies faced with long production cycles, such as agriculture, textiles and manufacturing.[23]

Prefinancing is normally available through commercial banks, development banks, or ECAs and is subject to loan agreements, security arrangements, and assignment of export receivables. The international supervisory bodies set standards for instances of this type of financing, and more specifically, for treatment of the reverse flow of capital, credit risks associated with the execution of these kinds of arrangements, and regulatory treatment of capital substitutes, all with the common good of the credit market in mind. Examples of prefinancing can take the form of packing credit, advances against export orders, supplier's credit, and buyer's credit.[24]

From a strictly legal perspective, prefinancing has the characteristics of secured lending arrangements in that the prefinancing is secured by export receivables or collateral dealing with inventory, etc.[25] This arrangement is governed by some jurisdictional laws dealing with secured transactions or by UNCITRAL's 2016 Model Law on Secured Transactions. Exporters must comply with the laws associated with secured export credit, potential foreign exchange control regulations, anti-corruption legislation, and relevant environmental standards when prefinancing arrangements involve public or multilateral financing agencies. In addition to the above noted legalities, the WTO Agreement on Subsidies and Countervailing Measures (SCM Agreement) prohibitions govern state-supported prefinancing arrangements involving possible export subsidies, ensuring compliance with international trade norms. Finally, countries such as India (through EXIM Bank and RBI's export credit refinance schemes), China (through Sinosure and China Exim Bank), and Türkiye (through Türk Eximbank) have set up programs dealing with prefinancing during times of need, in a way that targets the liquidity of exporters while safeguarding bilateral and multilateral methods for exporters to remain competitive.

---

[22] Dalmia (2009, 145).
[23] Wu (2025, 4442) and Zhao and Huchzermeier (2018, 140).
[24] Bishop (2004, 138–140).
[25] Willsher (1995).

Scholarly discussions emphasize pre-financing's ability to resolve finance gaps for developing countries and the capacity of smaller exporters to achieve or maintain global competitiveness.[26] Opponents have suggested there may be distortions to WTO law whereby state-backed pre-financing might be treated as prohibited subsidies.[27] One can also contend the program encourages a degree of developmental equity by supporting exporters facing constraints to legally access credit; this justification is consistent with WTO's objectives to promote aid-for-trade. Research is also exploring potential for digitization of pre-financing, for example, through supply chain finance that uses blockchain technology, which can enhance transparency but will raise issues related to the fit of legal treatment for digital goods as collateral for secured transactions.

11.2 Sources of Finance in International Trade

International trade transactions are dependent on capital, and involve delayed payment processing between the shipment of goods and receiving proceeds. Exporters and importers generate liquidity and access working capital using various financing vehicles, categorized broadly into short-term, medium-term and long-term (or very long term) loans. Financial instruments mobilize trade, mitigate transaction risks and promote investment in export-oriented programs. Trade finance operates by using a legal framework that includes private commercial contracts, banking laws and regulations and international laws emerging from global institutions (IMF, World Bank, Basel Committee, OECD, WTO) with a focus on ensuring transparency, prudential regulation and non-discrimination.

11.2.1 Short-Term Loans in International Trade

Short-term financing, with maturities generally lasting up to a year, is used to finance a firm's working capital, to purchase raw materials or to bridge the time gap between the time of shipment and payment as per the sale terms. These loans play a critical role in ensuring ongoing access to cash flow regardless of geography in export and import trade. Short-term loans can be found in several forms, including export credit facilities, import loans, overdrafts, revolving credit lines, trade bill discounting, factoring and forfaiting.[28]

Short-term loans are subject to the contract law and banking regulations based on the law of the jurisdiction it is creating a loan agreement and, also, are subject to the influence of the Basel III Accord, as an international banking regulation. Under the Basel III Accord, banks that extend trade finance are required to take capital against credit exposures, but the short time between no more than one-year

[26] Auboin (2007).
[27] Ibid.
[28] Yakhshibaev (2011, 60–62).

duration and self-liquidating, that is what trade-facilitated loans are, allows banks to have preferential treatment regarding capital due to low-risk exposure.[29] These prudential requirements, as endorsed by the majority of G20 central banks, are meant to provide both stability and liquidity in international trade finance.[30] Consequently, short-term loans are most generally secured by a pledge or assignment of receivables presented through either domestic secured transactions legislation or through UNCITRAL's 2016 Model Law on Secured Transactions, letters of credit, and insurance coverage from export credit agencies (ECA).

The ICC's Uniform Rules for Demand Guarantees (URDG 758) and the UCP 600 provide uniform rules that indirectly cement short-term financing options. For example, if a bank discounts a bill drawn under a letter of credit, then the transaction is subject to the UCP 600 which protects all parties' legal interests. The OECD Arrangement on Officially Supported Export Credits captures both short-term (up to 2 years) and longer maturities of publicly supported financing to ensure that they do not distort competition or violate WTO law prohibitions on export subsidies.[31]

Legal challenges present in short-term financing include enforceability contracts and security interests across borders, conflict of laws (governing law clauses and jurisdiction clauses), regulatory compliance with AML/CFT regimes (FATF Recommendations) and compliance with sanctions regimes (such as US OFAC or EU restrictive measures). However, even with these legal challenges, short-term trade finance is still regarded as one of the safest and most resilient types of cross-border lending, with relatively low default rates historically, according to available industry data from Berne Union.[32]

Scholars have recognized the low default risk and stability of short-term trade finance, attributing its uniqueness to self-liquidation, and strong legal frameworks.[33] However, concern has been raised about how Basel III capital requirements have potentially limited the ability of banks to provide trade finance, especially in emerging markets, after the 2008 financial crisis.[34] A suggestion to reduce this burden on banks is the advancement of digital platforms that streamline the use of collateral issues.

11.2.2 Medium- and Long-Term Loans in International Trade

Medium-term loans (1–5 years) and long-term loans (beyond 5 years) are primarily used to finance exports of large-scale capital equipment, infrastructure projects, shipbuilding, energy and transportation contracts, and FDI projects. Unlike short-term facilities, these loans rely on long, complex legal documentation, a variety

---

[29] BIS (2017, 10) and Malloy (2021, 462–465).
[30] FSB (2013).
[31] Subedi (2012, 409).
[32] Bobillo-Carballo and Garcia (2025, 630) and Korinek et al. (2010, 15–20).
[33] Lastra (2015).
[34] WTO (2016).

of financial institutions involved, and in many cases states or quasi-states provide guarantees to minimize risk.

Medium- and long-term trade finance relies on a combination of private international law and public international law mechanisms. The loan agreement governing long-term finance is the primary contractual instrument and includes repayment schedules, interest rates, security arrangements and governing law clauses. Uniformity between jurisdictions is achieved through standardized documentation such as the Loan Market Association (LMA) standard loan agreements or the International Trade and Forfaiting Association (ITFA) standard loan agreements. Security on medium- and long-term loans includes mortgages on related assets (such as ships, aircraft and equipment), assignment of receivables to the lender (often in favor of a bank) and most importantly sovereign guarantees/insurance (from Export Credit Agencies) on the loan. The OECD Arrangement on Officially Supported Export Credits puts minimum interest rates and maximum repayment terms and minimum down payment requirements to prohibit unfair competition amongst G20 ECAs, and the WTO SCM Agreement prohibits other types of export credit subsidies. IMF Article VIII facilitates capital mobility, while UNCITRAL's Model Legislative Provisions on PPP aid in structuring long-term cross-border financing arrangements.[35]

Long-term trade finance entails sovereign default risk, volatility of exchange and interest rates, enforceability of contracts in foreign jurisdictions, and development of environmental and social standards. Some tools for mitigating these risks are political risk insurance (e.g., provided by Multilateral Investment Guarantee Agency (MIGA) or private insurers), arbitration clauses either under the ICC, LCIA or ICSID processes, and hedging instruments governed by ISDA contracts.[36]

Scholarly discussions pay attention to the geopolitical aspects of ECAs, especially in conjunction with plans like China's BRI, where the notion of strategic influence is seen as more important than fair competition.[37] Others address the role of ECAs in promoting export-led growth in developing countries, signalling the appropriate use of aid-for-trade.[38] Digitalization of long-term finance in trade finance through MLETR compliant platforms is noted as potentially disruptive, with work remaining to agree on cross-border legal recognition of digital assets.

11.2.2.1 Public and Private Actors in Medium- and Long-Term Trade Finance

11.2.2.1.1 Commercial Banks

Commercial banks are profit-oriented financial institutions that offer syndicated or bilateral loans under commercial terms. The term commercial banking is also used to refer to wholesale banking activities, generally aimed at large businesses and institutions, as opposed to retail banking, which focuses on individual clients, and

[35] Coppens (2014, 358–360).
[36] Jonasson and Papaioannou (2018, 86).
[37] Zhao (2025, 118).
[38] Yescombe (2014, 367–421).

investment banking, which focuses directly on capital markets. While the Glass-Steagall Act in the US established a legal distinction between commercial and investment banking activities, this distinction has lost its function over time.

11.2.2.1.2 Export Credit Agencies (ECAs)

ECAs assure guarantees, insurance or direct landing under proper circumstances since it is supported by the state treasury. Almost every country has ECA, i.e. US Exim, UK UKEF, Japan JBIC, China CDB, Germany KfW, India EXIM, Türkiye Türk Eximbank. These institutions aim to facilitate international trade, particularly by providing credit for exports. Their primary goal is to provide financing at suitable terms and costs, while minimizing political and commercial risks. This allows investors and exporters to obtain relevant loans from commercial banks based on policy guarantees.

11.2.2.1.3 Multilateral Development Banks (MDBs)

Unlike commercial banks, MDBs are established as non-profit organisations. Therefore, they can provide financing under more favourable conditions to support their primary goals of sustainable development and poverty reduction. Furthermore, on account of their often AAA credit ratings, they can borrow from international financial markets at low costs, creating affordable financing sources for borrowing countries. For instance, namely, the WB, Asian Development Bank (ADB), or EBRD co-finance trade and infrastructure projects.

11.2.2.1.4 Institutional Investors

Institutional investors are legal entities, such as foundations and associations, established to achieve a specific purpose. Investment decisions affect the legal entity and, consequently, the individuals who benefit from them. Therefore, their investments should be less risky than those of individual investors. Insurance companies, pension funds, aid funds, investment funds, portfolio management companies, social security institutions, personnel trusts, and investment partnerships are among institutional investors.

11.2.2.2 Examples from G20 Economies

11.2.2.2.1 The US

The EXIM Bank offers medium- and long-term guarantees on capital goods exports in accordance with the Articles 3 and 5 of the Export–Import Bank Act of 1945 for negotiable instruments and credits.[39]

11.2.2.2.2 The UK

UKEF supports exporters with long-term buyer's credit facilities in compliance with OECD and WTO obligations.

[39] Levit (2004, 65).

11.2.2.2.3 Japan

The Japan Bank for International Cooperation (JBIC) and Nippon Export and Investment Insurance (NEXI) co-finance long-term industrial and infrastructure exports.

11.2.2.2.4 China

The China Development Bank (CDB) and China Exim Bank provide global short and long-term project loans against collateralised guarantees, especially under the Belt and Road Initiative (BRI), utilizing bilateral treaties and sovereign guarantees.[40]

11.2.2.2.5 Germany

Euler Hermes and KfW IPEX-Bank operate under EU banking supervision and provides guarantees and refinancing options available for exporters, increasing availability of short-term trade finance.[41]

11.2.2.2.6 India

As instruments of trade diplomacy, the EXIM Bank and other government supported lines of credit to both African and Asian nations appear to be part of India's strategy in trade. Besides, RBI's Export Credit Refinance Scheme provides concessional funding for pre-shipment and post-shipment credit.[42]

11.2.2.2.7 Türkiye

Türk Eximbank provides medium and long-term buyer's and supplier's credit facilities under the auspices of the Turkish Treasury.[43]

11.3 Conclusion

The dynamics of payment transactions and the funding that informs the international trade are the pillars of modern global trade; they spawn trans-jurisdictional transactions, which could be assured, legally safeguarded and economically effective. The interactions between the legal system and financial system have been connected in this chapter in a multiple of risk-allocation mechanisms and how trade-finance mechanisms will be incorporated into a future globalised economy have been noted. This being the case, an understanding of the interplay between these legal and financial mechanisms and commercial realities is necessary.

International trade finance architecture is based on commercial realities, but the complexity of the legal frameworks allows goods and services to be funded

[40] Kern and Reinsberg (2022, 1–14).
[41] Dawar (2020, 382–384).
[42] Ahmad (2016, 33–41).
[43] Akarsu et al. (2024, 1316–1323).

transcendently of distance and jurisdiction. Global trade is in the world of perpetual transformation; in order to ensure sustainability in a more digitalized world that is required by ESG demands and geopolitics, the law should be constantly reformed to find a balance between innovation and regulation. Therefore, it is crucial to understand all the relevant mechanisms to navigate and form the international future of trade finance. This need of flexibility is especially acute in the functioning of payment systems where the freedom of the contract is reasonably balanced against the control of the regulations.

The international trade payment system works at the border of the autonomy of the private law and the control of the public authority; the parties have a lot of freedom to structure payment and finance using such tools as the letters of credit, collections, or prefinancing loans if and only if parties address AML regulations verbatim, CFT, and sanctions. Institutions such as the UCP 600, URC 522, URDG 758 and MLETR provide harmonized frameworks to increase predictability and decrease transaction costs. Within these harmonised frameworks, certain foundational legal principles play a central role in ensuring the reliability of trade finance transactions. The principle of autonomy, separating the obligations imposed on the bank from disputes arising from the underlying contract, further supports a predictable, reliant, and continuous flow of trade, in accordance with court decisions across G20 jurisdictions. Continuing on this legal predictability, trade finance instruments are structured to address different financing needs across a spectrum of time horizons.

Working-capital requirements are based on securing short-term debt instruments with receivables and other assets, and the Basel III considers them low-risk assets in case of minimal default risk; Basel III does not classify receivables as assets. Capital-intensive projects are also financed by medium- and long-term debt instruments secured by ECA and MDB and regulated according to principles provided by OECD and WTO to prevent distortive subsidies. Nevertheless, these privately funded arrangements are not independent; they are progressively influenced by the international law by the state. The Article 8 of the IMF prohibits international payments, whereas the SCM Agreement regulates export credits and similar tools in order to filter against distortive subsidies. The focus on trade finance imports to help nations withstand global crises is highlighted by G20 action plans on global crises, including the 2008 financial crisis and the COVID-19 pandemic. At the same time, technological developments are transforming the operational premise of trade finance. A shift to electronic documentation - efforts are being made by the MLETR—to the G20 memberships, including Singapore and the UK, to improve efficiencies but legal characteristics such as negotiability and cross-border enforceability are questioned. Distributed-ledger technology, as well as blockchain, offers increased transparency, thus disrupting the legal status quo of the concepts of possession and endorsement. Simultaneously, technological innovation is being displayed and a more normative commitment to sustainability and the principles of responsible finance.

ESG criteria have started to be enshrined within the trade-finance industry by legal frameworks, such as the EU Sustainable Finance Taxonomy as well as the Equator Principles. These frameworks presuppose due-diligence requirements on lenders and other providers of financial services, in the course of their decision-making procedures. All of these changes are indicative that the future of international trade finance will be tuned on the convergence of legal certainty, technological innovation, and regulation that is sustainable.

Chapter Summary

This chapter presents a comprehensive legal and commercial analysis of payment instruments and sources of finance in international trade, emphasizing upon the imperative nature of payment instruments in managing risk, maintaining cash flow, and ensuring certainty in international trade dealings. As numerous of you will recall, trade finance is based on a wide range of payment instruments, with different levels of trust and risk distribution between the importing and exporting companies, as their core component. At the one extreme of this spectrum, down payments have the effect of providing an early showing of good faith, which grants the exporter immediate working capital, and it forms part of legal performance of the contract. On the other end of the spectrum, however, there are the open account transactions, also known as cash on delivery (COD), which exposes the exporter to risk by far, because the goods are delivered and the invoiced long before receiving payment, in most cases a 30 and 90 day period. This structure relies a lot on the execution of legal corrective measures and contractual trust. In between these two paradigms, there is also the cash against documents (CAD) that makes the banks their middlemen in the process and the exporters can hold on to shipping documents until payment or acceptance is received as per the International Chamber of Commerce Uniform Rules of Collections (URC 522). In this model, the documents can either be issued against immediate payment (D/P) on which the exporter is provided with the highest possible level or against acceptance (D/A) when the importer accepts the time draft or the bill of exchange and hence receives a short-term credit. In addition to these payment systems, prefinancing, also referred to as pre-shipment financing, is a system where the exporter is offered a short-term loan by the commercial banks or export credit agencies to purchase or produce goods before shipment, which is technically a type of secured loan facility

Simultaneously, the trade finance providers are normally separated based on their tenor, hence indicating diverse financing requirements and risk profiles. The short term loans are typically those that have a maximum duration of one year and are mainly used to finance working-capital needs as well as fill any payment lag. They are granted favorable regulatory treatment by the Basel III due to self-liquidating nature and relatively low risk of default; these facilities are more often designed as factoring, receivables or revolving credit lines. On the contrary, large and long-term financing, the one-year to five years and above, is essential to capital-intensive exports, massive infrastructure projects, and complex investment projects. Such deals require complex legal paperwork based on LMA guidelines, carefully arranged security agreements in the form of mortgages or receivables assignments, and subject to typically involve government participation in the form of export credit agencies or multilateral development banks. Such financing should be made in accordance with the OECD Arrangement on Officially Supported Export Credits to allow fair competition and prevent distortive subsidizing. By and large, the legal landscape of trade finance remains defined by unremitting compliance requirement pertaining to the AML/CFT regimes and the international sanctions, whereas the ongoing digitalisation, especially the use of such tools as MLETR, and incorporation of ESG requirements are increasingly defining the future architecture of the trade finance contracts and their management.

The chapter concludes with the assertion that the legal structure of trade finance requires the constant adherence AML/CFT regimes, sanctions and dynamic regulatory norms. Besides, the move to digitalization, which has been exemplified by the MLETR, as well as the rise of ESG factors are reshaping the future of trade finance contracts.

Revision Questions

1. Draw a diagram to demonstrate the allocation of risk spectrum of three payment instruments, i.e. on open account, down payment, and D/P bu the exporter. Explain the reason why it is the legal concept of contractual trust that is of maximum importance in the open account arrangement.
2. Spot the differences between D/P and D/A based on the chronology of the importer to make payment. Identify the mechanism that causes the formation of a negotiable instrument, such as a Bill of Exchange or Time Draft, and indicate the international rules according to which the bank participates in the process of collecting.
3. Discuss the reason why trade finance loans with maturities less than one year tend to be of low risk and are accorded preferential capital treatment under Basel III standards. Describe also the legal procedures required to procure such loans.
4. What is prefinancing, otherwise referred to as pre-shipment financing? Explain its legal nature as a kind of secured lending and comment the part the use of international agreements in limiting state-sponsored prefinancing, including the World Trade Organization Agreement on Subsidies and Countervailing Measures (WTO SCM Agreement).
5. Discuss why ECAs and MDBs are required to support the provision of medium and long-term trade finance. Scrutinise in which ways ECAs activities are limited under legal constraints under the OECD Arrangement on Officially Supported Export Credits.

6. Analyse the main legal issue for an exporter prefers D/A when the importer defaults on the accepted draft. When is the enforceability of this debt diverse according to the jurisdictions?
7. Within the context of international trade finance, define two major legal compliance requirements, including those related to AML and sanctions, that banks need to integrate in their own procedures of issuing short-term loans.◄

References

Ahmad A (2016) EXIM Bank of India's export financing strategies: an analysis. Res J Econ Bus Stud 5(8):33–41

Akarsu O, Aldan A, Torun H (2024) Heterogeneity and nonlinearity in the relationship between rediscount credits and firm exports. Borsa Istanbul Rev 24(6):1316–1323

Arham H, Sanjaya U (2022) Potential legal risks arising in cash on delivery (Cod) payment mechanism in E-commerce applications. Indonesian J Law Policy Stud 3(1):72–85

Auboin M (2007) Boosting trade finance in developing countries: what link with the WTO? WTO Staff Working Papers ERSD-2007–04

Bergami R (2009) UCP 600 Rules—changing letter of credit business for international traders? Int J Econ Bus Res 1(2):191–203

BIS (2017) Basel III: finalising post-crisis reforms. https://www.bis.org/bcbs/publ/d424.pdf. Accessed 14 Dec 2025

Bishop E (2004) Finance of international trade. Elsevier Butterworth-Heinemann, Oxford

Bobillo-Carballo E, Garcia A (2025) Trade finance gap: why credit risk mitigants are not applied. Global Pol 16(4):630–643

Bortoletti F (2017) Drafting and negotiating international commercial contracts: a practical guide, with ICC model contracts, International Chamber of Commerce

Bridge M (2019) The sale of goods. Oxford University Press, Oxford

Carr I, Stone P (2017) International trade law. Routledge, London

Coppens D (2014) WTO disciplines on subsidies and countervailing measures: balancing policy space and legal constraints. Cambridge University Press, Cambridge

Dalmia S (2009) Financial supply chain. McGraw-Hill Professional, New York

Dawar K (2020) Official export credit support: competition and compliance issues. J World Trade 54(3):373–395

Dolan J (2007) The law of letters of credit: commercial and standby credits. Aspen, Boston

Dorozynska A, Dorozynski T (2022) The role of export credit agencies in trade financing. Lodz University Press, Łódź

Financial Stability Board (2013) Overview of progress in the implementation of the G20 recommendations for strengthening financial stability. Report of the Financial Stability Board to G20 Leaders. https://www.fsb.org/uploads/r_130905c.pdf. Accessed 14 Dec 2025

Goldby M (2019) Electronic documents in maritime trade: law and practice. Oxford University Press, Oxford

Goode R (2017) Goode on commercial law. Penguin, London

Hugo C (2022) The impact of the COVID-19 pandemic on international trade, with specific reference to the role of trade documentation. In: Watney M (ed) The impact of Covid-19 on the future of law. University of Johannesburg Press, Johannesburg, pp 27–52

Jonasson T, Papaioannou M (2018) A primer on managing sovereign debt-portfolio risks. IMF Working Paper WP/18/74

Kern A, Reinsberg B (2022) The political economy of Chinese debt and international monetary fund conditionality. Glob Stud Q 2:1–14

Kim S (2021) Payment methods and finance for international trade. Springer, Cham
Korinek J, Cocguic J, Sourdin P (2010) The availability and cost of short-term trade finance and its impact on trade. OECD Trade Policy Working Papers, No. 98, OECD Publishing, Paris
Längerich R (2009) Documentary credits in practice. From & Co, Glostrup, Denmark
Lastra R (2015) International financial and monetary law. Oxford University Press, Oxford
Law J (2008) Oxford dictionary of finance and banking. Oxford University Press, Oxford
Levit J (2004) The dynamics of international trade finance regulation: the arrangement of officially supported export credit. Harvard Int Law J 45(1):65–182
Malek A, Quest D (2009) Jack: documentary credits: the law and practice including standby credits and demand guarantees. Bloomsbury, London
Malloy M (2021) The emerging regime of international financial services regulation. NC J Int Law 46(2):439–472
Mann R, Roberts B (2023) Smith & Robertson's business law. Cengage, Boston
McCurdy W (1922) Commercial letters of credit. Harvard Law Rev 35(5):539–592
Mudde P, d'Ambrieres H, Dornel A (2024) Social infrastructure and the OECD arrangement on officially supported export credits: an analysis of current regulations, prevailing challenges and potential amendments. UK Export Finance Independent Report
Murray C, Timson-Hunt D, Holloway D, Dixon G (2012) Schmitthoff: the law and practice of international trade. Sweet and Maxwell, London
Osuna-Gonzalez A (2005) Buyer's Enabling Steps to Pay the Price: Article 54 of the United Nation's Convention on Contracts for the International Sale of Goods. Journal of Law and Commerce 25(6):299-323
Secretariat UNCITRAL (1992) Note by the UNCITRAL Secretariat on the UNCITRAL model law on international credit transfers. Uniform Law Rev 20(2):3–27
Subedi S (2012) Textbook international trade and business law. The People's Public Security Publishing House, Hanoi
Tüfekçi H, Ünal C (2010) International payment methods. Marmara Üniversitesi Hukuk Fakültesi Hukuk Araştırmaları Dergisi 16(3–4):327–351
Voica I (2011) Bills of exchange and promissory notes—comparative perspective. Juridicial Tribune 1(2):107–117
Willsher R (1995) Export finance: risk, structures and documentation. Palgrave Macmillan, London
WTO (2016) Trade finance and SMEs: bridging the gaps in provision. https://www.wto.org/english/res_e/booksp_e/tradefinsme_e.pdf. Accessed 15 Dec 2025
Wu A (2025) Support a financially constrained supplier with order financing and refundable non-refundable advances. J Ind Manage Optim 21(6):4441–4473
Yakhshibaev G (2011) Sources of short-term finance and investment opportunities. Eur J Bus Econ 2:60–62
Yescombe E (2014) Principles of project finance. Academic Press, Cambridge
Zhao L, Huchzermeier A (2018) Supply chain finance: integrating operations and finance in global supply chains. Springer, Cham
Zhao M (2025) Geopolitical impacts of China's Belt and Road Initiative: opportunities and risks across Asia, Africa, and Europe. Adv Econ Manage Politics 164(1):118–127

Further Reading

Auboin M (2007) Boosting trade finance in developing countries: what link with the WTO? WTO Staff Working Papers ERSD-2007–04
Carr I, Stone P (2017) International trade law. Routledge, London
Dawar K (2020) Official export credit support: competition and compliance issues. J World Trade 54(3):373–395

Hinkelman E (2008) Short course in international payments: letters of credit, documentary collections and cyber payments in international transactions. World Trade Press, Traverse
Kim S (2021) Payment methods and finance for international trade. Springer, Cham
Shadikhodjaev S (2021) The WTO agreement on subsidies and countervailing measures and unilaterism of special economic zones. J Int Econ Law 24(2):381–402
US Department of Commerce. (2016) Open Account, https://beta.trade.gov/article?id=Trade-Finance-Guide-Chapter-5-Open-Account
Zhao L, Huchzermeier A (2018) Supply chain finance: integrating operations and finance in global supply chains. Springer, Cham

The Legal Ground of Debit and Credit Cards

12

Contents

Abstract

This chapter outlines the legal framework and operational aspects of bank and credit cards. It starts by introducing the card payment system, detailing the procedural flow and relevant laws. It identifies key parties, including the card

F. B. Erdem, *The Principles of International Banking, Finance and Investment Law*, Springer Textbooks in Law, https://doi.org/10.1007/978-3-032-32505-1_12

scheme owner, issuer, holders (both primary and additional), guarantors, and acceptors. The chapter also reviews popular payment systems like MasterCard, Visa, Union Pay, Diners Club, TROY, and American Express. It explains the function of interbank card centres, including ATM networks and real-time gross settlement systems. The rights and obligations of involved parties are described, alongside procedures for dispute resolution and evidence. Finally, the chapter addresses internet banking, debt restructuring, and disputes related to debit and credit cards.

12.1 Introduction

The legal provisions concerning banks and credit cards are currently a field of law that has experienced some of the fastest development within modern financial law. These instruments are not merely means of payment; instead, they form a two-sided market, where the interests of the consumer, the merchant, as well as the banks, are evenly weighed through a complicated system of contracts. In legal terms, a payment transaction using a credit card consists of a two-level process.

With the evolution of the financial sector from offline terminals to online banking and real-time gross settlement systems, the role of regulatory authorities has expanded from facilitating transactions to maintaining the stability of the overall system and safeguarding consumers. This chapter discusses the rights and obligations of the different stakeholders in the industry, the impact of international regulatory frameworks such as the IFR and PSD2 on the specific issues of debt restructuring and dispute settlement in the card industry. It also discusses the best possible models for balancing innovation and security in the emerging world of card industry through comparisons of the different models within various regions, including the U.S. Durbin Amendment and the Chinese QR code revolution.

12.2 Card Payment System

The card payment system is a two-sided market and is provided with a complex regulatory framework. The primary purpose of the system is that it is aimed at the management relationship between the card holders and the contracted merchant, as well as the cost–benefit analysis.[1] In fact, from a legal perspective, the card transaction is not a single transaction but an intricate two-step contract mechanism.[2] The process begins with the conclusion of a framework contract that determines the long-term rights and obligations between the Bank and the Card Holder. By virtue of the contract, the Card Holder gives the bank with every use of the POS

[1] Tosza (2009); McAndrews and Wang (2012).

[2] Maria Raquel Guimarães (2012),

device, consecutive mandates to pay the money to their business and also charge their accounts. The Payment Service Directive 2 (PSD2) is the response of the European Union that brought about the Strong Customer Authentication (SCA) Standards in efforts to ensure the security of these directives.

The transaction must pass through certain security and risk management processes according to the instructions provided by the European Central Bank.[3] The initial security and risk management process is Authorization. The POS machine (Terminal) sends a request to the issuing bank of the card (Issuer) through the payment system (Switch). At this technical level, the AI system Transaction Risk Analysis (TRA) is engaged to analyse customer trends and stop any incidence of money fraud. The second security and risk management process is Clearing. Clearly, this is where the flow of financial information from the two banks occurs. The final security and risk management is Settlement. Clearly, this is where the money is transferred from the two banks to the merchant bank Acquirer.[4]

> **Important**
> There is currently greatest debate in the law surrounding card transactions with regard to the rules surrounding the Interchange Fee. The IFR (Interchange Fee Regulation), applicable to EU member states, imposed a cap on fees in 2015 (0.2% for debit cards and 0.3% for credit cards).[5]

In card payment systems, the commissions charged are calculated not only on the basis of the cost incurred but also in a manner that ensures maximum participation of both sides in the system. The end result is a tipped pricing system where consumers are tempted by rewards, and the charges are primarily shouldered by the merchants.[6] Even though regulations may look good on paper, they can, in essence, have a negative effect on consumers. If the charges or fees that the merchants or financial institutions impose on the consumer are lowered, it does not affect the product cost, and the extra revenue is simply pocketed away by the retailer. Simply stated, it is extra money to the seller and not to either the bank or the consumer. Not to be disregarded is that fact that consumers who are wealthy and have high-priced transactions are not charged any bank fees due to maintaining high balances within their accounts, whereas low-income consumers who have low balances within their bank accounts pay a certain set of fees and expenses each month.[7]

In terms of best practices from G20, one of the earliest governments to take action in this area globally was the RBA, who made their first move in the area

[3] European Central Bank (2015).
[4] Tompkins and Olivares (2016); Herbst-Murphy (2013).
[5] ECB (2015).
[6] Garcés and Lutes (2018).
[7] Ibid.

of Card Payments in 2003.[8] The RBA intervened as they believed that Interchange Fees were too high for the free market. Therefore, they introduced a new methodology for determining interchange fees which was referred to as Cost Based Benchmarking. This meant that banks now had to calculate their interchange fees using only the direct costs of processing transactions (for example, software/hardware costs for transaction authorisation); therefore, the RBA was successful in reducing costs for Merchants, but ultimately this led to reduced rewards points (Miles, cash back, etc.) and increased annual fees for cardholders, which is documented as an example of the delicate balance point of regulation.[9]

In the US, this scenario occurred as a result of legislation enacted in 2010, referred to as the "Durbin Amendment", that was included in the Dodd-Frank Act. The Durbin Amendment placed a strict upper limit (approximately $0.21 plus 0.05% of the transaction value plus an additional $0.01) on the amount of money that Large Banks could charge for Debit Card transactions.[10] The intent of this change was to provide consumers benefits; however, the unintended consequences of this legislation resulted in large retailers saving millions of dollars without passing that savings on to Consumers in the form of lowered prices for products. Additionally, in an attempt to offset this loss in earnings, banks introduced charges for some free services related to bank accounts, thus raising the cost associated within banking, especially for those in low-income households and thereby posing a threat of financial exclusion.[11]

The European Union, through its so-called oversight standards, as described by the ECB 2015 guidance, ensures that all steps involved in the transaction are subject to tight oversight. The EU's strategy encompasses not only minimizing commissions but also ensuring maximum security for payments with PSD2. In the above discussion, although the UK, as an EU member until 2020, now continues with its pre-Brexit IFR (debit 0.2%, credit 0.3%), the UK Payment Systems Regulator (PSR) adopts an independent and dynamic vision.[12] Especially since Brexit, as major players Visa and Mastercard increase their cross-border transaction costs, the PSR has increased its control over costs involving such transactions to incorporate transparency. The UK, although commending projects for innovation by banks for projects such as open banking, adopts tight oversight strategies to minimize costs incurred during cross-border transactions.

Turkey, on the other hand, is trying to strike a balance between the cost pressure of an international payment network (Visa/Mastercard) and local payment systems like TROY. The rates within the Turkish context are periodically revised by the Central Bank of the Republic of Turkey based on the middle ground that protects both the businesses and the sustainability of the banking system.[13]

---

[8] Gans and King (2003) 462–472.

[9] Stillman et al. (2008); Morris et al. (2022).

[10] Mikula (2024) 67.

[11] Ibid 68–70.

[12] Adeyemi (2019) 47–53; See also, European Commission (2023).

[13] Kayalıdereden and Çetiner (2018) 67–75.

Brazil has one of the most advanced card payment systems in the Latin America region. However, the main challenge in this regard was that some banks and processors had dominated the market for a considerable time. Nevertheless, to overcome the abuse of market power problem, the Central Bank of Brazil (BCB) imposed a cap on the commissions that need to be charged on debit cards from 2018.[14] What is unique in the Brazilian market is that the purpose of this regulation is not only to reduce prices but also to develop competition on both sides of the two-sided market (that is, both the cardholder and the merchant sides) making it simpler for new fintech firms like Nubank to enter the market.

China's approach to card payment systems has been a world apart from the Western model entirely. The Chinese government supported the only existing card system for a long time, which was named UnionPay, a government-backed system that was in place as the only system in the country for a long time. The interesting thing about China, however, is not how the card payment systems are regulated but how a "QR based mobile payment solution" such as Alipay or WeChat Pay skipped the system entirely. The Chinese government was then able to utilize these digital payment methods to reduce the high fees with card systems to as low as 0.45% commissions for banks.[15]

Canada is treading a different route to ensure that it is protected from the destructive effects of harsh regulation. The Canadian government was in agreement with Visa and Mastercard that a voluntary commitment was preferred to regulation. In a voluntary commitment mechanism, the card schemes were asked to maintain interchange fees below a certain threshold for small businesses, and in exchange, the government was asked not to intrude in the system. The soft regulatory mechanism is believed in the literature to strike a delicate balance in which banks can continue their loyalty cards reward schemes for consumers and ensure that small businesses do not go over-budget.[16]

South Korea is one country with one of the best usage rates for cards. The regulatory framework is highly interventionist and tiered commission system. The tiered commission system is highly beneficial for small businesses, in which the lower a business's annual turnover, the lower the commission rate it pays. The tiered commission system is believed in the literature to have the potential drawback that the cost will eventually be passed on through consumer loans or service charges.[17]

> **Important**
> The current systems display a move from static rules to dynamic analysis, as is apparent in security standards, a document published by ECB in 2015. AI can prevent fraudulent activities in seconds by analysing decisions based upon the location where a transaction is

[14] Veronese and Bertran (2023) 1–25.
[15] He and Sappideen (2008)168–174; Klein (2019); He (2022).
[16] Department of Finance Canada (2018).
[17] Financial Services Commission (2018).

happening, identity and even biometric details (e.g. fingerprints etc.), thereby preventing a completed transaction.[18]

12.3 Commonly Used Card Payment Systems

Card Payment Systems operate by utilizing two different operational models: four party (Open) systems and three party (Closed) systems. This means that the structure of the fees associated with using each of the two models will depend upon the respective regulatory environment in which they operate.[19] At this time, most credit card systems operate under the Open model, and the largest players in terms of market share are Visa and Mastercard. They do not directly issue cards to customers. Instead, they create the framework for operation for each issuer bank to license the use of the brand name and products of the Credit Card System, and the underlying infrastructure for technology and payment processing. Visa has become known as being very strong in terms of consumer acceptance, along with being one of the first companies to effectively implement digital and secure transactions; while Mastercard has become known as being focused on technology and B2B initiatives.[20] In Europe, the Multilateral Interchange Fees (MIFs) are currently being monitored by competition authorities as an area of concern, as they are perceived to affect competition by restricting or inhibiting competition through the regulation of MIFs under the EU Interchange Fee Regulation (IFR) and the European PSD2 regulations.[21]

UnionPay, the state-backed giant in China, is one of the largest global card brands based on number of transactions. It dominates the Asian Region; and is benefiting from the regulatory advantage of being state-backed in China,[22] but is trying to compete on a global basis, with the card networks of Visa/Mastercard, through the WTO regulatory structure.

Two prominent players in the three party model (closed system) of payment processing are Diners Club and American Express. As the issuer and acquirer, both are focused on serving high-income customers and corporate travelers. They are well known for their premium reward and benefits programs. Closed systems are exempt from interchange fee restrictions, or IFRs, as there are no interchange fees between two banks as a result of a closed system.[23] Closed systems provide regulatory arbitrage opportunity for both companies to collect higher commissions.

[18] Zouaoui and Naas (2025) 55; Faisal et al. (2024) 181–197.

[19] Mariotto and Verdier (2017) 307–349; Rysman and Wright (2014) 303.

[20] Chandel et al. (2024) 41.

[21] See also, Matteis and Giordano (2014) 85–95; Morra and Vangelisti (2021); See also, Vihuto (2025) 487.

[22] Jingrong and Jigeer (2025) 259–274.

[23] Marianne Verdier (2006); OECD (2006); Degennaro (2006) 27–42.

The Turkish government has been developing an indigenous payment system called TROY to minimize its heavy reliance on other countries' payment systems. It can quickly and efficiently address the needs of the local markets. For instance, it supports installment payments. It does not charge any licensing costs to banks since it does not require any licenses from abroad.[24] RuPay from India[25] and Elo from Brazil,[26] like TROY from Türkiye, are considered models that are supported by their countries' governments to overcome the global duopoly controlled by Visa and Mastercard. Seemingly, this localisation trend is becoming widespread across the G20 countries.

> **Important**
> The European Central Bank has established a standard for member states to follow with respect to surveillance techniques and standards. Accordingly, all card schemes must have an AI-based system to assess transaction risk and provide strong customer authentication (SCA).[27]

12.4 An Interbank Network (ATM Consortium) and Real-Time Gross Settlement (RTGS)

Interbank networks are cooperative models of collaboration that facilitate various financial institutions in providing their customers services through an integrated system. An ATM Consortium is the strongest example of such models, as it handles retail payment traffic through shared terminal and POS networks. In retail payment systems, such as the ATM Consortium, the Deferred Net Settlement (DNS) system has been generally used. Although the DNS system lessens the liquidity requirements of banks, the risks associated with such systems are substantial until the final settlement of the payment at the end of the day.[28]

RTGS systems are systemic infrastructure on which gross settlement of payments is done; that is, every transaction is processed individually. Although it was first introduced in the 1980s, it took just 30 years to become global commonplace.[29] Such systems are designed for high-value payment settlements. The most important legal benefit that RTGS has is the finality of settlement. It means that once a transaction has been confirmed in an RTGS system, it cannot be reversed. This is the most foolproof defense against the possible propagation of systemic

[24] Kayalıdereden and Çetiner (2018) 67–75.
[25] Tuli and Mittal (2025); George et al. (2023) 117–126.
[26] Madjov (2023).
[27] Deb (2019) 33, 48.
[28] Guo et al. (2015).
[29] Bech et al. (2017).

risk, particularly in the case of bank runs. The bank runs in March 2023 have clearly illustrated the necessity of real-time information on payments.[30]

The main drawback for conventional interbank transaction systems is their relatively high cost, particularly for international payments involving correspondent banking. The TARGET2 system, operated in Europe, is one of the latest developments based on RTGS technology. The instantaneous settlement of transactions in RTGS systems forces banks to greatly rely on central bank reserves, that is, they utilize their liquidity.[31] The application of algorithms for preventing "gridlock" situations, as well as automated queue management, is as significant as a legal requirement for operation in RTGS systems such as TARGET2.

Important
A joint report by the Bank of Canada, the Bank of England, and MAS in 2018 says that by combining RTGS systems along with CBDCs and DLT in cross-border payments among different banks, it will enhance "payment-versus-payment" systems and will ensure that risks are minimized altogether.[32]

In legal terms, though retail systems such as ATM consortia are more concerned with customer convenience, RTGS systems are known to be the backbone of banking systems that ensure "payment certainty." Combining these systems together has enabled even retail payments to be accomplished within RTGS times for faster payments.[33]

12.5 Rights and Obligations of Card Scheme Owner, Card Holders and Card Acceptors in General

In the context of card payment transactions, the relationship between the contractual parties is not only technical but complex, as it entails a contractual network. This contractual network and the terms of engagement are ensured through incidental agreements. This entails that the contractual agreement between the parties has to be processed through an approval process that is dependent and independent of the framework agreement at the same time. Thus, the legal protection has to be operative at the time of contract and at the transaction process as well.

[30] Cipriani et al. (2024).

[31] Bakšys and Sakalauskas (2009).

[32] Bank of Canada, Bank of England and Monetary Authority of Singapore (2018).

[33] Guo, Z., Kauffman, R. J., Lin, M., & Ma, D. (2015). *Near Real-Time Retail Payment and Settlement Systems Mechanism Design*. SWIFT Institute Working Paper.

12.5.1 Obligations of Card Scheme Owner

It is the responsibility of card scheme operators as well as issuing banks to ensure that there is reliability as well as functionality within the system. The ECB has placed great emphasis on ensuring that operational continuity as well as security policies are within the responsibility of card scheme operators as well as issuing banks.[34]

12.5.1.1 Card Issuance

It is the obligation of the issuer to print the card securely, either in physical form or virtually, and to deliver the card to the cardholder. In the absence of agreement to the contrary, the time of delivery of the card marks the time when the legal obligation arises.[35]

12.5.1.2 Determining Limit

It is an obligation of the bank to establish the level of expenditure, which must be determined based on a review of the financial position of the customer.

12.5.1.3 Make a Statement of Account

The banking institution is mandated to periodically disclose statements regarding all transactions to the card-issuing institution. Clearness within these documents is mandatory for the promotion of consumer rights.[36]

12.5.1.4 Unfair Use and Insurance of the Card

In case the card gets lost, stolen, or used illegally, the issuing company needs to shield the card and minimize the losses as soon as possible when notified. In some systems, there is a type of protection provided for unauthorized transactions up to a specified limit, which might be covered or insured.

12.5.1.5 Other Obligations

Serving as a 24/7 notification service for cardholders and ensuring the privacy of the data being used in the system are also very important tasks.

12.5.2 Obligations of Card Holders

Under a bank credit card facility, cardholders are supposed to observe certain guidelines regarding the use of the credit limit or deposit given to them.

---

[34] ECB (2008).

[35] It is an obligation of the bank to establish the level of expenditure, which must be determined based on a review of the financial position of the customer.

[36] Flora (2017).

12.5.2.1 Security Precautions

Cardholders must keep their cards as well as securities, such as PIN number protection, safe. Nevertheless, allowing others to use or operate cards constitutes gross violation of contract.[37] If the cardholder uses his/her PIN or any secured information such as CVV or password with others or lets his/her card lie around somewhere, financial losses incurred due to fraudulent transactions might have to be borne by the cardholder himself/herself and will not be insured.

12.5.2.2 Prompt Notification

In case the card gets lost or stolen, the cardholder needs to report to the issuer. Processing payments for illicit goods or services, a suspected money-laundering transaction, or a specified list of prohibited transactions that are clearly defined by the card schemes (such as adult materials or gambling) will result in the instant cancelation of the merchant agreement and substantial fines.

12.5.2.3 Repayment Obligation

The basic obligation is to repay funds to the bank for costs incurred, as reflected on the account statement, by its due date. In cases where this type of transaction is effected, any kind of fee that is applied has to be disclosed, and the consumer has to be made aware of it before the transaction occurs. This is in addition to following the laws in the area in which the card is being used (such as state law in the US or consumer laws in the EU).

12.5.3 Obligations of Card Acceptors

Card transaction-acquiring merchants have obligations to both the bank and the customer.

12.5.3.1 Honor-All-Cards (HAC) Rule

The merchant must accept any legitimate card bearing the merchant's logo. They cannot ask for cash payment for any transactions involving an amount below a predetermined level. Also known as the HAC rule, the first most common infringement of the law takes place when some kind of cash-only policy or refusal to accept cards below a certain amount takes place. Harsh contractually agreed penalties ensure compliance. However, the other side of the same coin reveals the Bill of Rights in the role of a pressure relief valve for the HAC rule in its impact on the cost of the rule. In other words, the HAC rule secures the "pay anywhere" factor for the consumer but also harms the merchant. From a purely legal point of view, the rule finds itself walking a thin line in both safeguarding competition and maintaining things in the right gear. Within the last few years of the last millennium, the law relaxed the rules considerably. These days, it is possible for the merchant

---

[37] Tjandraningsih (2024).

to ease the restriction to accept high commission credit cards but no debit cards or vice versa.[38]

> **Important**
> In the US, the anti-trust disputes involving Visa and Mastercard since the 2000s contested the HAC and anti-steering policies on the argument that they hinder competition. Agreements provided the merchant community with a limited flexibility to surcharge or switch to more expensive cards. However, nowhere in the US courts was the compulsory acceptance of both credit and debit cards ruled upon. Across the Atlantic, the 2015 Interchange Fee Regulation in the European Union set a ceiling on the interchange fees per card type used by consumer cards to reduce expenses and enhance competition. Although it moved the needle a bit by exempting commercial cards, the regulation failed to require the merchant community to be given a direct right to individually accept or decline a given card type.

12.5.3.2 Verification

As part of a given transaction, the business must check for the cardholder's signature at the back of the card or have the cardholder physically sign a paper receipt. They must also uphold any required authentication criteria for a given system—such as obtaining the proper PIN code for a chip and PIN transaction or adhering to restrictions and verification protocols for contactless transactions. This process goes a long way to reduce any risk of fraud and allow for compliance with card association regulations (Visa, Mastercard, etc.), failing which can lead to significant liabilities for the business.

12.5.3.3 No Surcharge Rule

Traditionally, most places prohibited merchants from charging more for card transactions. Evidence from the Australian Retailers Association's note is that in some areas, this is no longer the case, as costs can now be passed on more transparently. This is a vertical lever that is controlled by payment networks and affects merchants. When it comes to economic logic, its primary purpose is to optimize its own profits and, through that, indirectly sponsor cards. Once this rule is implemented, everything that is spent on cards will be incorporated into price through bloat, and there will be a cross-subsidy that will support cards. Those who don't use cards will pay for rewards.[39]

[38] Rochet and Tirole (2008); Reserve Bank of Australia (2005) 40–49.

[39] The abolition of the surcharging rule would cause a shift away from costly reward schemes towards fee competition, and thus a change in competition within networks from reward schemes to fees would ensue. In this regard, a new "legal and economic era" would emerge, potentially allowing for a "more efficient financial system and a higher level of overall social welfare. See, Schwartz and Vincent (2006) 72–102.

12.5.3.4 Transaction Integrity

Merchants are required to enter accurate data into the system while also not storing customer card information without authorization. The merchant must express all details of a payment in the system—involving amount, date, and credit card number—with precision. The slightest mistake or omission will increase the risk of chargebacks, placing the merchant at risk. Moreover, to comply with PCI DSS requirements, the merchant is advised not to store the credit card details of the consumer, including the full magnetic stripe, CVV/CVC, or the PIN number, unless with the consumer's express authorization. The merchant should remove the details after a successful payment. Failure to comply with these regulations leads to possible fines, cancellation of the acceptance agreement, or even additional audits by the card schemes.

12.6 The Use of Bank and Credit Cards in Internet Banking

The internet has caused a sea change in the way we interact with banks and credit cards, and finance has been shifted from physical counters to internet browsers. While this increases speed and ease of access, it has also introduced new responsibilities on the online front. In traditional banking, credit cards represent a physical means of making payments; on the internet, they represent data, which travels along a "virtual credit card" and a "payment gateway." Users are primarily accessing the internet for transactions such as withdrawing money and querying statements, but some transactions, such as clearing credit card debt and obtaining statements, are expected to rapidly shift to the online environment.[40]

Internet banking is now at the very centre of core banking operations such as payments through cards, money transfers (RTGS/NEFT), and smart card management. Here, the card serves simply as an authorization instrument that is processed through the internet banking facility. Having said that although internet banking is no radical departure for conventional banking from an administrative perspective (consider deposit insurance), regulations are now becoming stringent. A technology-intensive paradigm regulatory regime is required because cybersecurity threats also loom very large.[41] This is because online banking fraud/scams such as phishing, skimming, and other practices are on the increase and banks are faced with the obligation to adhere to security policies.[42] These policies within the banks are not simply internal policies but consumer protection regulations.

[40] Sandhu and Arora (2020).

[41] Saghir (2021).

[42] Kavita (2021).

12.7 Debt Restructuring of Credit Cards

Debt restructuring for credit card debt is a targeted intervention that helps to alleviate the pressure on debtors incurring financial distress while also ensuring a sound management of Non-Performing Loans by banks. However, debt restructuring goes well beyond debt maturity management; it indeed involves a careful balance of debtor conduct and liquidity constraints.

> **Important**
> A large-scale field experiment carried out by Dobbie and Song (2016) showed that the simple act of writing down the actual amount of the debt payment was much more effective in improving the rates of payment than lowering the amount of the minimum payment due.[43]

Credit card debt structuring issues are most commonly associated with that can broadly be described as the democratisation of credit. Technology and finance innovations, such as credit scoring and automated underwriting, in the credit industry have lowered the barriers for entry into the credit industry. This paves the way for riskier and formerly unqualified debtors to gain access on a wider scale. As a result, more households have more unsecured debt in their portfolio than was the case in the past, as well as more difficulty in paying these debts. This is why debt restructuring is more common.[44] This broader lending has revealed a remarkable, persistent pattern in household finance: the credit card debt puzzle. For many households, consumers juggle heavy, high-interest card balances while keeping a large cash cushion in checking or savings accounts with little to no yield. The basic driver behind this seemingly irrational combination is a deep-seated liquidity desire-to cover vital expenses that cards won't finance, such as rent, utilities, and groceries. Because consumers must maintain this cash buffer, aggressive strategies to divert every available dollar toward debt repayment can backfire.[45] They become depleted of ready cash for daily living needs and end up slipping into delinquency or default. While debt restructuring typically provides short-term relief by lowering required minimum payments, it comes with an important trade-off (unintended negative effect). By extending the overall repayment period significantly, it leaves the borrower exposed to default risk for a much longer time. This prolonged exposure to future financial shocks or even strategic default can partially or fully offset the initial benefits of the restructuring.[46] However, an important tenet of modern

[43] Dobbie and Song (2016).
[44] Livshits et al. (2016).
[45] Telyukova (2013).
[46] Agarwal et al. (2015).

debt reconstruction programs has continued to be the mandatory minimum payment floors that are enforced. Such payment floors have proved to be an important means for preventing borrowers from falling into an even deeper debt hole. In summary, a successful credit card debt restructuring process is not merely a mathematical extension of the debt's maturity; It is the management of the dynamic relationship between the borrower's liquidity needs,[47] strategic default risks,[48] and market entry conditions.[49]Telyukova 2013 is cited in the text but is not given in the reference list. Please provide a full reference or delete the citation from the text.added

12.8 Disputes Arising from Debit Cards and Credit Cards

Disputes involving credit and debit cards occupy the most intricate boundary of the consumer-issuer relationship. The leading cause of disputes regarding unauthorized transactions, such as card duplication fraud and cyber data theft, is fraud.[50] For example, based on data collected by the Consumer Financial Protection Bureau (CFPB), complaints regarding credit cards are the main component of overall complaints filed by consumers. Debt Collection, in which the card debts are no longer repayable, is among the areas where complaints are most common. Typically, consumers complain either about miscalculations in the amount due, known as billing errors, or unlawful collection practices.[51] In most cases, the legal way to handle a card issue entails the use of a chargeback system. When notification of a dispute is made to the banks, they freeze the transaction associated with the problem.[52] Another thing worth considering is the fact that 'pay-by-bank' credit transfers and other real-time payments, having appeared as new alternatives for traditional card payments, are also likely to influence the system of dispute resolution. Even if credit cards have been known to enjoy a strong position in terms of customer protection thanks to legislation like the Truth in Lending Act, the absence of reversal rights in real-time payments, also referred to as payments originating from bank accounts, might bring about changes in this context.[53]

Chapter Summary

A complex set of contracts governs card transactions, distributing risk and liability among issuers, cardholders, and merchants. The implementation of

[47] Telyukova and Wright (2008).
[48] Dobbie and Song (2016).
[49] Livshits et al. (2016).
[50] Consumer Financial Protection Bureau (2025) 80.
[51] Ibid.
[52] Ibid 102.
[53] Ibid 190.

requiring an electronic signature under PSD2 and SCA, instead of traditional form agreements, is a global trend to enhance the security of transactions and protect customer data privacy. At the heart of this design lies the two-sided market: the interchange fee and pricing schemes are designed to attract the maximum number of agents, although they usually cross-subsidise different consumer groups.

Across the globe, regulators are shifting from rigid and prescriptive and 'one size-fits-all' rules to more dynamic, data-informed supervision. The EU's IFR and the US's Durbin Amendment aimed to lower the costs faced by merchants with fee caps, but data shows that savings rarely pass through to consumers in practice. Bank service fees are essentially a net gain, as the drop in interchange revenue is backed up with new service fees, which can price out low-income users and creates paths to exclusion. In an alternate scenario, China has the QR-based system while Turkey has TROY. These cases show that local innovation and leapfrogging could potentially avoid entirely traditional card rails to create payment landscapes that are much more competitive.

The system is shored up by strong back-end rails like RTGS and TARGET2, which make settlement final and protects the financial system from a domino effect. As the industry moves towards Pay-by-Bank and real-time payments, we are going to need to consider chargeback rights and dispute resolution in new legal terms. In the end, the future of card payment law has to try to balance a'pay anywhere' attitude with the protection of the most vulnerable players in the financial ecosystem against fraud and crushing debt spirals.

Revision Questions

1. Explain the legal difference between a framework contract and successive mandates in card payment transactions, and account for why that distinction makes a difference as far as liability is concerned.
2. Define two-sided markets in card schemes. Looking ahead, how does tipped pricing shift the incentives between merchant participation and consumer participation?
3. Weigh the costs of the Durbin Amendment in the United States against its unintended consequences and determine whether it actually delivered on its promise to help low-income consumers.
4. Compare and contrast the different roles of Authorization, Clearing, and Settlement, and then consider how AI and Transaction Risk Analysis change the distribution of legal responsibility for issuers.
5. What are the key legal and financial implications of Deferred Net Settlement (DNS) contrasted with Real-Time Gross Settlement (RTGS) systems?

6. Exactly what does "Honor-All-Cards" mean, and in view of new regulations that have recently "untied" it in jurisdictions such as Australia, how have long-standing merchant responsibilities changed?
7. Analyse the No Surcharge Rule from an antitrust perspective. Does the prohibition of surcharging really redistribute funds from cash to credit card holders through the process of cross-subsidization?
8. According to Dobbie and Song (2016), for what reasons are debt write-downs potentially more effective at solving the excess demand problem than a minimum payment reduction?
9. As the industry shifts from physical to "virtual data" cards in online banking, banks' obligations on consumer protection and cyber security are influenced in what way?
10. Consider the regulatory approach taken by Canada and compare it to South Korea's more aggressive approach. Does a tiered scheme offer more protection to small businesses?◂

References

Adeyemi A (2019) A new phase of payments in Europe: the impact of PSD2 on the payments industry. Comput Telecommun Law Rev 25(2):47–53

Agarwal S, Chomsisengphet S, Mahoney N, Stroebel J (2015) Regulating consumer financial products: evidence from credit cards. Q J Econ 130(1):111–164

Bakšys D, Sakalauskas L (2009) Simulation of automated real-time gross interbank settlement. Technol Econ Dev Econ 15(1):123–135

Bank of Canada, Bank of England, Monetary Authority of Singapore (2018) Cross-border Interbank Payments and Settlements: Emerging Opportunities for Digital Transformation. https://www.mas.gov.sg/-/media/MAS/ProjectUbin/Cross-Border-Interbank-Payments-and-Settlements.pdf. Accessed 8 January 2026.

Bech M, Shimizu Y, Wong P (2017) The Quest Speed PaymS. BIS Quarterly Review.

Chandel S, Kaushik V, Kumar V (2024) Harnessing Artificial Intelligence for Strategic Advantage: A Case Study of mastercard's Innovations and Applications. Comput: J Appl Comput Sci Intell Technol 4(2):41–60.

Cipriani M, Eisenbach T, Kovner A (2024) Tracing bank runs in real time. Federal Reserve Bank of New York Staff Reports.

Consumer Financial Protection Bureau (2025) The consumer credit card market. https://files.consumerfinance.gov/f/documents/cfpb_consumer-credit-card-market-report_2025.pdf. Accessed 8 January 2026.

Deb S (2019) Towards a cyber-security roadmap for digital payments: best practices and recommendations. Obs Res Found 33:48

Degennaro R (2006) Merchant acquirers and payment card processors: a look inside the black box. Fed Reserv Bank Atlanta Econ Rev 91(1):27–42

Department of Finance Canada (2018) Backgrounder: new voluntary commitments from payment card networks. https://www.canada.ca/en/department-finance/news/2018/08/backgrounder-new-voluntary-commitments-from-payment-card-networks.html. Accessed 8 January 2026.

Dobbie W, Song J (2016) Debt relief or debt restructuring? Evidence from an experiment with distressed credit card borrowers. Princeton University

ECB (2008) Oversight framework for card payment schemes—standards. https://www.ecb.europa.eu/pub/pdf/other/oversightfwcardpaymentsss200801en.pdf. Accessed 8 January 2026.

European Central Bank (2015) Annual report. https://www.ecb.europa.eu/pub/pdf/annrep/ar2015en.pdf. Accessed 8 January 2026.

European Commission (2023) Payment services: revised rules to improve consumer protection and competition in electronic payments. https://ec.europa.eu/commission/presscorner/detail/el/qanda_23_3544. Accessed 8 January 2026.

Faisal N, Nahar J, Sultana N, Mintoo A (2024) Fraud detection in banking leveraging AI to identify and prevent fraudulent activities in real-time. Non Hum J 1(1) 181–197

Financial Services Commission (2018) FSC Reforms Card Processing Fee Rates. https://www.fsc.go.kr/eng/pr010101/22195?utm_source. Accessed 8 January 2025.

Flora H (2017) Legal protection against credit card holder customers in the perspective of Law No. 8, 1999 on Consumer Protection. South East Asia J Contemp Bus, Econ Law 12(4):1–8.

Gans J, King S (2003) A theoretical analysis of credit card reform in Australia. Econ Rec 79(247):462–472

Garcés E, Lutes B (2018) Regulatory intervention in card payment systems: an analysis of regulatory goals and impact. https://papers.ssrn.com/sol3/papers.cfm?abstract_id=3346472. Accessed 8 January 2026.

George S, Hovan George, T Baskar (2023) RuPay card: revolutionizing india's payment ecosystem. PartnS Univers Int Innov J 1(2):117–126.

Guimarães M (2012) The debit and credit card framework contract and its influence on European legislative initiatives. https://indret.com/wp-content/themes/indret/pdf/892_en.pdf. Accessed 8 January 2026.

Guo Z, Kauffman R, Lin M, Ma D (2015) Near real-time retail payment and settlement systems mechanism design. SWIFT Institute Working Paper 2014-004.

He L (2022) Mobile Payments in the U.S. and China. Master Thesis, MIT Sloan School of Management.

He L, Sappideen R (2008) The payment system in China. J Int Bank Law Regul 23(3):168–174

Herbst-Murphy S (2013). Clearing and settlement of interbank card transactions: a mastercard tutorial for federal reserve payments analysts. Consumer Finance Institute discussion papers 13–02, Federal Reserve Bank of Philadelphia.

Jingrong L, Jigeer S (2025) Third-party payment regulation: analysis of risks and legal mechanisms in China. J Digit Technol Law 3(2):259–274

Kavita D (2021) Analysis of internet banking along with legal aspects in India. Kurukshetra Law J 11:113–129

Kayalıdereden D, Çetiner M (2018) Monitoring national payment schemes: some global practices and Turkish payment scheme—troy. J Bus Digit Age 1(2):67–75

Klein A (2019) Is China's new payment system the future? https://www.brookings.edu/wp-content/uploads/2019/05/ES_20190617_Klein_ChinaPayments.pdf. Accessed 8 January 2026.

Livshits I, MacGee J, Tertilt M (2016) The democratization of credit and the rise in consumer bankruptcies. Rev Econ Stud 83:1673–1710

Madjov S (2023) Popular payment methods in Brazil—the iGaming Industry Perspective. https://env.media/wp-content/uploads/online-gaming-payment-methods-in-brazil-env-media.pdf. Accessed 8 January 2026.

Mariotto C, Verdier M (2017) Who pays for card payments? A general model on the role of interchange fees. Rev Netw Econ 16(3):307–349

Matteis A, Giordano S (2014) Payment cards and permitted multilateral interchange fees (MIFs): will the European commission harm consumers and the European payment industry? J Eur Compet Law Pract 6(2):85–95

McAndrews J, Wang Z (2012) The economics of two-sided payment card markets: pricing, adoption and usage. Federal Reserve Bank of Richmond Working Papers 12-06.

Mikula J (2024) Banking as a service: opportunities, challenges and risks of new banking business models. Kogan Page
Morra C, Vangelisti M (2021) Digital payments market: standardization and coopetition. https://www.uer.it/jeanmonnetchair/euinno/wp-content/uploads/2020/09/Digital-Payments-Market-Intervento-30-Settembre.pdf. Accessed 31 Jan 2026.
Morris J, Zywicki T, Manne G (2022) The effects of price controls on payment-card interchange fees: a review and update. International Center for Law and Economics White Paper 2022-03-04.
OECD (2006) Competition and efficient usage of payment cards. https://www.oecd.org/content/dam/oecd/en/publications/reports/2007/10/competition-and-efficient-usage-of-payment-cards_26446813/10ab4e54-en.pdf. Accessed 8 January 2026.
Reserve Bank of Australia (2005) Reform of the EFTPOS and visa debit systems in Australia. https://www.rba.gov.au/payments-and-infrastructure/debit-cards/consult-doc-feb05/pdf/consult-doc-feb05.pdf. Accessed 8 January 2026.
Rochet J, Tirole J (2008) Tying in two-sided markets and the honor all card rule. Int J Ind Organ 26(6):1333–1347
Rysman M, Wright J (2014) The economics of payment cards. Rev Netw Econ 13(3):303–353
Saghir W (2021) The online age: the shift from traditional banking to online banking in the UK. Financial Law Review 23(3):63–76
Sandhu S, Arora S (2020) Customers' usage behaviour of e-banking services: interplay of electronic banking and traditional banking. Int J Financ Econ 27(2):2169–2181
Schwartz M, Vincent D (2006) The no surcharge rule and card user rebates: vertical control by a payment network. Rev Netw Econ 5(1):72–102
Stillman R, Bishop W, Malcolm K, Hildebrandt N (2008) Regulatory Intervention in payment card industry by the reserve bank of Australia. https://www.rba.gov.au/payments-and-infrastructure/payments-system-regulation/past-regulatory-reviews/review-of-card-payment-systems-reforms/pdf/review-0708-pre-conclusions/cra-28042008-2.pdf. Accessed 8 January 2026.
Telyukova I, Wright R (2008) A model of money and credit, with application to the credit card debt puzzle. Rev Econ Stud 75(2):629–647
Tjandraningsih D (2024) Credit card holders and users as a means of payment in legitimate commercial transactions. Int J Educ Manag Sociol 3(6):341–353
Tompkins M, Olivares A (2016) Clearing and settlement systems from around the world: a qualitative analysis. Bank of Canada Staff Discussion Paper, No. 2016–14.
Tosza K (2009) Payment card systems as an example of two-sided markets—a challenge for antitrust authorities. In: Munich Personal RePEc Archive. https://mpra.ub.uni-muenchen.de/23822/1/MPRA_paper_23822.pdf. Accessed 8 January 2026.
Tuli K, Mittal S (2025) India's payment revolution: can UPI and rupay challenge visa and mastercard? https://ink.library.smu.edu.sg/cases_coll_all/522. Accessed 8 January 2026
Verdier M (2006) Retail payment systems: what can we learn from two-sided markets?. MRPA Paper No 2606
Veronese D, Bertran M (2023) Fintechs and traditional banks: regulation, competition, and cooperation in Brazil. Rev Direito GV 19:1–25
Vihuto L (2025) Effective U.S. interchange fee regulation that will ensure consumer welfare based on the European Union's IFR. Southwestern Journal of International Law 31(2):487–510
Zouaoui H, Naas N (2025) Credit card fraud detection and risk management strategies: a deep learning-based approach for EU banks. Res Pap Econ Financ 9(1):55–80

Further Reading

European Union (2018) Payment Services Directive (PSD2)
Evans D, Schmalensee R (2005) Paying with plastic: the digital revolution in paying and borrowing. MIT Press

Geva B (2021) The law of electronic funds transfers. Matthew Bender Elite Products
Goldby M (2013) Electronic documents in maritime trade: Law and practice. Oxford University Press
Law J (2008) Oxford dictionary of finance and banking. Oxford University Press
Malloy M (2021) The emerging regime of international financial services regulation. N C J Int Law 46(2):439–472
Mann R, Roberts B (2008) Smith & Robertson's business law. Cengage Learning
Rochet J, Tirole J (2003) Platform competition in two-sided markets. J Eur Econ Assoc 1(4):990–1029
Telyukova I (2013) Household Need for Liquidity and the Credit Card Debt Puzzle The Review of Economic Studies 80(3):1148-1177 10.1093/restud/rdt001

13 Methods of Resolution of Securities Investment Disputes in Comparative Law

Contents

F. B. Erdem, *The Principles of International Banking, Finance and Investment Law*, Springer Textbooks in Law, https://doi.org/10.1007/978-3-032-32505-1_13

Abstract

This chapter examines the state of investor-state dispute resolution in depth, focusing on the emergence of investment arbitration as an important development in international law. It investigates the intricacies and needs for reform within the Investor-State Dispute Settlement mechanism (ISDS). It proposes a dispute settlement à la carte system, which establishes a Multilateral Investment Court alongside other forms of dispute resolution, all contained within one multilateral institution. The author employs a comparative institutional design approach to analyse the flexibility and legal certainty across the different international dispute systems and introduces a new dataset regarding state compliance with arbitral awards to improve future empirical research in investment dispute settlements.

13.1 Introduction

Disputes amid investors and states have become a crossing point between economic order and sovereignty. In these cases, the foreign investors pursue remedy against the host countries due to the failure to fulfil the norms of protecting these investors. Such disputes have become increasingly common in the last decades because of the globalisation of the capital and the proliferation of BITs.[1] Previously, the foreign investor engaged in diplomatic channels or domestic courts to resolve the dispute, yet these two forms did not reduce the miscarriage of justice. The ISDS clauses have altered this since the investors can access dispute resolution institutions that are impartial.[2] This process aims to instil confidence in the investors, which can invoke the undertaking against expropriation; unfair treatment; the breach of the investment protection; and other forms of breach.

Although there has been a certain controversy around ISDS, sceptics of ISDS argue that it circumscribes states' regulatory powers with regard to public health measures, and increasingly financial stability measures.[3] For instance, invest disputes have brought attention to ISDS' investment dimension because they concern a dispute between a private party or a number of investors, challenging a state's action during an economic or financial crisis, which initiates debate over the balance between suggested private rights and public interests. Lately, there have been some changes within the ISDS system to fix some of these complaints. According to a report recently released by UNCTAD recently, there were over 1,400 known cases of ISDS as of 2025, and of these cases, the majority had occurred within the

[1] Dewi and Afriansyah (2019, 151–172), Kollamparambil (2016), and Oscarsson (2022, 55–56).
[2] Crynes (2023, 182) and Ciocchini and Khoury (2018, 976).
[3] Lavdari and Lavdari (2024, 62).

last 15 years.[4] This conveys the significance of implementing systemic changes to the ISDS process.

For added complexity, a layer of securities investments has been introduced into ISDS disputes presented in this paper. Securities include stocks, bonds, and derivatives; such instruments include portfolio investments or non-controlling stakes in companies or ventures as opposed to foreign direct investment (FDI), which involves building/ investing in a factory through construction or otherwise. The disputes are normally structured around actions exercised by a state upon financial markets, such as a reorganization of public debts, or a regulation centred on a trade of a financial instrument. Moreover, a state-FDI obligation typically in ISDS terms may clash with national regulations on securities, presented through disputes on sovereign debt bonds and stock donations or stakes given for privatized state sectors.[5]

Against this backdrop, change has been gaining momentum. UNCITRAL's WG III has been playing a crucial role in meetings in 2025 reviewing a set of proposals relating to procedural improvements, focusing, amongst others, on a standing mechanism of dispute resolution.[6] The EU, too, has been pushing forward a vision of a Multilateral Investment Court (MIC) in an effort to move forward from ad hoc arbitration, aiming at a more institutionalised dispute resolution mechanism, complete with permanent judges as well as appeal rights. This corresponds to a concept called 'dispute settlement a la carte' which provides menu options regarding each available method made available in a streamlined clearance mechanism among a reduced selection.[7] The involved actors could then have a chance to consider an option based on speed, dispute resolution through a mediator based on a common ground, and finally, an appeal decision from the judiciary when a precedential decision was needed in an effort to have common ground regarding adaptability versus predictability.

Based on a comparative approach, the current chapter will discuss the different methods pursued by various jurisdictions to resolve different disputes related to securities. This has been achieved through the analysis of different case studies. This includes the ICSID disputes, the disputes resolved under the U.S. FINRA Arbitration procedure, the post-Achmea regime within the EU framework, and the domestic systems applicable to Canada as well as the EU. This does show the advantage through the efficient resolution of disputes using arbitration methods. Also, since this chapter explores the theme of compliance data, there has been plenty of voluntary compliance in the awarding of arbitrations, despite some concerns over their enforcement, e.g. politically sensitive matters. For example, there have been studies showing states complying with most of the awards rendered by the ICSID.[8]

---

[4] UNCTAD (2025).

[5] Goldman (2017) and Wilson et al. (2023, 249). Also see, Maffett et al. (2025, 269–309).

[6] UNCITRAL (2025).

[7] Schill and Vidigal (2019, 311–341) and Schill and Vidigal (2021, 220–263).

[8] Pauwelyn (2015, 767).

The aim of this chapter is to demonstrate a broader basis to consider these kinds of mechanisms, perhaps instilling a degree of respect for the dynamic process of international investment law. In particular, the current chapter commences with the mechanism of ICSID arbitration. This is one of the oldest most recognized forms of dispute settlement within the remit of international investment. Operating under the WB framework, ICSID has managed the resolution of hundreds of disputes, many of which have had a component concerning securities.[9] In order to ensure the fullest consideration within the examination of judicial mechanisms, essential examples will chart the manner within which particular courts signify the notion investment within the financial framework—examples which will provide future precedent within these kinds of disputes. Regional and domestic divergences will then be identified to reach the stages of derivation and synthesis.

13.2 International Securities Investment Disputes Subject to ICSID Arbitration

13.2.1 General Framework of the ICSID Arbitration System

The ICSID was established in 1966 by the Convention on the Settlement of Investment Disputes Between States and Nationals of Other States (a.k.a. the Washington Convention). ICSID is a sister organization within the WB Group and functions as a forum for alternative dispute resolution in investment disputes arising from foreign investors and host states. It is meant to ensure a non-politicized investment dispute resolution process, where a case is now brought by investors rather than through diplomatic channels. The ICSID arbitration is consent-based and loosens the consent of both parties.[10] This is often given by a BIT, a multilateral agreement such as the Energy Charter Treaty, or an investment agreement in general. Once the arbitration begins, it is governed by formal rules for constituting a tribunal, presenting evidence, and issuing an award. The award is final and binding, and in accordance with Article 54 of the Convention, it has to be recognized and enforced by the member states as if it were a decision by a domestic court.[11] This recognition and enforcement is a significant benefit of ICSID as an arbitral body compared to others.

The notion of investment is one of the pivotal elements within ICSID jurisdiction. In the context of Article 25 of the Convention on the Matter of Jurisdiction of ICSID, the dispute has to be connected to the investment, but the definition is left ambiguous, requiring that these questions are dealt with on a 'case by case basis' by the tribunals. In the area of securities investments, the determination of whether the particular type of investment made is actually an investment under Article 25 is made on the basis of risk duration and the contribution to the economy of the host.

[9] Franck (2023, 349–403).
[10] Reisman (1989, 743).
[11] Bermann (2020, 311–344) and Reinisch (2022, 1470–1515).

A wide reach has resulted in some debate on how the reach applies in the area of financial crisis situations, specifically within the area of the necessity defence that has been applied by state representatives.[12] There has been recent data to reflect the popularity of ICSID jurisdiction. Over 1,058 cases have been registered by June 2025.[13] Disputes involving securities are but a subset. They often relate to allegations of expropriation based on changes to the laws and default on repayment of debts. These disputes signal the balancing between protection for investors and the rights of states to regulate their economies, and this already has been a theme involving substantive and institutional reforms.

13.2.2 Libananco v. Turkey

Difficulties in jurisdiction over indirect ownership of securities-an example-is Libananco Holdings Co. Limited v. Republic of Türkiye.[14] In that case, the Cypriot company Libananaoco alleged that it indirectly owned shares of the Turkish energy companies Çukurova Holding and Kepez Elektrik. The claimant asserted that the Republic of Türkiye expropriated Libananco's assets in violation of both the Energy Charter Treaty and the Türkiye-Cyprus Bilateral Investment Treaty. The Respondent argued for lack of jurisdiction, asserting that Libananco is nothing more than a shell company owned and controlled by Turkish nationals lacking in "foreign investor" status under the treaty. The tribunal held extensive hearings regarding ownership of the investments, and it pursued an inquiry into the corporate veil and the beneficial owner of the investments. The tribunal denied the claims in 2011 based on a determination of a lack of sufficient evidence of bona fide foreign ownership. The tribunal emphasized that what is required is an actual substantive owner whose existing ties to the investments are not merely formal title. The Libananco Holdings case emphasizes broader themes in disputes about securities. An investment may be indirect, and the reliance on intermediaries makes it problematic to distinguish ownership and proof of nationality.[15] The case also has procedural implications for bifurcation of jurisdiction and merits phases that could streamline what might otherwise be complex procedures in arbitration. In short, the case represents one example where a tribunal invoked treaty objectives while, at the same time, maintaining investment protections from foreign nationals as well as abusive forum shopping.

---

[12] Exelbert (2016, 1243–1279).

[13] ICSID (2025).

[14] ICSID Case No ARB/06/8 (Official Case No) IIC 506 (2011).

[15] Tanzi (2020, 57–75).

13.2.3 Postova Banka and Istrokapital v. Greece

Poštová Banka, a.s. and Istrokapital SE v. Hellenic Republic[16] examined whether sovereign bonds could be considered protected investments. The claimants in this case were a Slovak and Cypriot entity that held bonds issued by the Greek government. The bonds were affected by the 2012 debt restructuring connected with the Eurozone crisis.[17] The claimants stated that this was expropriation in breach of the Greece-Slovakia BIT. Greece objected to jurisdiction on the grounds that bonds were commercial deals and not an investment under the ICSID case law and the BIT. This objection was upheld in 2015 by the tribunal because bonds that were openly traded in the market did not have an investor-state relationship that could qualify them as an investment. The tribunal distinguished the bond from project investments on the basis that no territorial relationship and economic contribution were considered. The implications of this decision place it firmly on the side of conservatism in relation to financial instrument valuation in relation to the regime of ISDS, thereby narrowing the ambit of protection afforded to financial investments in order to avoid inundating arbitration tribunals with claims, most of which may arise in relation to sovereign debt.[18] The arbitral outcome might influence future claims by investors through changes in the way claims can be brought, possibly through other means such as judicial claims through domestic courts and human rights tribunals. This decision may feature in broader talks about reform being considered in 2025 when the UNCITRAL Working Group deliberates on the manner of coming up with precise definitions on qualified investments.

13.2.4 Enron v. Argentina

Enron Corporation and Ponderosa Assets, L.P. vs. Argentine Republic[19] arose from a financial crisis that engulfed Argentina in 2001. Enron argued that currency devaluations and a freezing of prices by Argentina affected its investment in the distribution of natural gas, amounting to a violation of fair and equitable treatment, in contravention of the U.S.-Argentina BIT. The tribunal ordered damages in favour of the claimant in 2007, concluding that there was a violation of treaty standards because there were insufficient grounds for a defence in light of an economic crisis.[20] The enforcement of this award became contentious and was raised by Argentina on grounds of necessity under customary international law. The proceedings before the annulment committee were partially successful, with the final arbitration award remaining valid. In Enron, it can be seen how economic emergencies challenge to the ISDS mechanism are and how there is a delicate

---

[16] ICSID Case No. ARB/13/8 (2013).
[17] Chevry (2016, 169–172).
[18] Grund (2017, 86) and Mitsou (2016, 687–721).
[19] ICSID Case No. ARB/01/3 (2004).
[20] Frutos-Peterson (2008, 164–174).

relationship between the expectations and rights of foreign investment and states' sovereignty. The two ICSID decisions have been influential in consideration on regulatory freedom[21] and culminated in new treaties and neo-liberal investment treaties containing specific provisions for issues related to public policy.

13.2.5 Evaluation

ICSID arbitration has been tried time and again on the threshold of the ambit of jurisdiction in relation to claims concerning securities investment: the Libananco case raised the threshold of indirect shareholding, while the Postova Banka case showed uncertainty as regards the contours of government bonds as an investment; the Enron case showed the limits of state intervention in times of crisis. These cases reflect that a uniform application of investment law against financial markets is far from realistic, and it needs the incorporation of more flexible dispute resolution mechanisms which would be better attuned to the realities of each country's or region's economy and the nature of the dispute. Thus, the "dispute resolution à la carte" approach discussed later is intended to overcome the rigid restrictions of ICSID and further develop a more heterogeneous model of resolution.

13.3 Resolution of Securities Investment Disputes Through Arbitration Under FINRA in the US

This section examines the arbitration process involving securities investment disputes, specifically arbitration conducted through the Financial Industry Regulatory Authority (FINRA). This section traces the evolution of arbitration through Supreme Court cases, describing the process by which there was an eventual display of understanding by the judiciary about an arbitration-friendly and FINRA-friendly system. This section relies on academic views as part of an approach to offer appropriate academic context relevant to those undertaking study associated with Comparative Investment Law. The use of academic journals through referencing and footnotes is done as appropriate to offer points of reference regarding citations related to legal journals, as well as confusion studies.

13.3.1 General Framework of the FINRA Arbitration System

In the US, it appears that the regulation of disputes resolution in securities transactions is, in essence, a matter related to private law. The primary agency involved in playing this regulatory role is FINRA, which resulted from a combination of

[21] Staden (2011, 210).

the National Association of Securities Dealers (NASD) and NYSE arbitration systems in 2007. FINRA is a private, autonomous self-regulatory organisation (SRO), which oversees dispute resolution process as it pertains to conflicts arising from securities transactions initiated between broker-dealers of securities, as well as those initiated by investors.[22] The element of having a SRO monitor the entire securities market, in conjunction with a dispute resolution service having a focus in a specific field, aiming at expediency, makes it a very efficient dispute resolution mechanism.

The FINRA arbitration in question is mandated by the broker-dealer group members that operate in American capital markets. This is part of the membership agreement. In practice, nearly every contract entered into with an investor will include a section which allows for arbitration in case of disputes. What is more, the investor will not look for redress from federal courts but through FINRA contra panels.[23] These panels will, in general, be composed of three persons, one serving as the chairperson, one representative of the industry or a financial business, and the third a representative of the public or other interest to support impartiality and diversity.

The FINRA arbitration process complies with the FAA of 1925, and federally balancing federal legal arbitration outweighs arbitration-based impartiality. FAA affirms the reliability of arbitration contracts and narrows the list of salient topics for judicial review of arbitration awards to fraud and misconduct claims.[24] However, up until the mid-twentieth century, federal courts showed remarkable scepticism of the propriety of using arbitration in disputes related to securities laws. This came to a culmination in *Wilko v. Swan*, creating one of the most restrictive anti-arbitration positions in US law for the next three decades.[25] Scholarly analysis generally states that this sovereignty can be placed in the greater context of interest in investor protection as the financial markets grew, seen at the time as unsuitable for enforcing the federal securities regulations.[26]

FINRA Arbitration-itself evolving-illustrates its assurance to bring fast and cheaply made resolutions to participants, despite facing scrutiny along the way around transparency and enforceability. For example, the academic literature notes FINRA's flexibility to address modern challenges, including its use of technology for virtual hearings and improvements it has made to its discovery processes to speed the proceedings along.[27]

[22] Brodsky (2020, 10–14).
[23] Turk (2025, 389).
[24] Horton (2018, 367).
[25] Phillips (2017, 1965–1742).
[26] Giovine (2022, 993–1032).
[27] Blankley (2021).

13.3.2 Wilko v. Swan (1953)

This first substantial landmark decision by the US Supreme Court on arbitration agreements in the context of securities law. Wilko, the plaintiff, sued the broker-dealer Swan & Co., for fraudulent sales under the Securities Act of 1933. The broker-dealer had invoked an arbitration provision in the contract between the two sides to keep the case from going to court. The Supreme Court invalidated the arbitration provision, stating that it did not offer investors sufficient protection because arbitrators could not be held accountable to judicial review for legal error so that investors might suffer. Therefore, arbitration was contrary to public policy for it to keep investors from statutory protection and the judicial review of their statutory rights.[28] It left arbitration flat from securities, too lose close to 30 years, and the ultimate creation of a framework for the judiciary have self evidence: to see that statutory protections would be delivered just as was expected after Sarbanes–Oxley. Some scholars claimed that Wilko is outdated and of course much of it is because today is shaped by post-depression era where some reforms occurred to bump up the role of federal government in enforcement.[29]

> **Important**
> The *Wilko v Swan* made a disproportionate priority to investors protection, and thus not taking account of some of the efficiencies that arbitration would provide. This resulted in Wilko setting precedence would be slowly undermined in future decisions. The case provides an example of the underlying conflicts between the contractual autonomy and regulatory imperatives according to the interpretation within the context of a financial law.

13.3.3 Scherk v. Alberto-Culver Co. (1974)

Scherk v. Alberto-Culver Co. was a slight exception to the anti-arbitration tone of *Wilko*. The same case saw the American based Alberto-Culver company engage in a stock-transfer deal with the German investor Scherk that provided that future disputes should be adjudicated by use of arbitration. Nevertheless, even with the arbitration provision, the plaintiff eventually attempted to remain in arbitration and initiate claim in court in the US. The court, in contrast to *Wilko*, eventually accepted arbitration, with the need of predictability and stability of international trade, and added that arbitration clauses in international commercial contracts were unpractical and unnecessary on many occasions. The case itself restricted the strict anti-arbitration position of *Wilko* to domestic dealings and defined the necessity

[28] Gaitis (2006, 1–63).
[29] Taylor (1987, 203–228).

of different considerations in the cross-border securities dealings.[30] According to such scholarly reviews, *Scherk* has been of great importance to the US arbitration jurisprudence as it helps in uniting the domestic securities policy to the demands of international commerce. It has been observed that the ruling had an effect on subsequent decisions and formed the basis of the idea of a policy based system on a federal basis which is more amendable to arbitration because it showed the level of sophistication of the international parties.[31] To that end, *Scherk* comes in handy when studying how globalisation is influencing the national laws at the domestic level.

13.3.4 Dean Witter Reynolds v. Byrd (1985)

Dean Witter Reynolds Inc. v. Byrd was a momentous one and served as a significant overturn of the way Federal Arbitration Act (FAA) was interpreted to have supported arbitration. The Court concluded that in the event that a federal securities action is mixed with a claims based on state-laws, the resulting mixed claims have arbitrable disputes that require to be resolved through arbitration. The Supreme Court stressed the fact that the FAA demands the rigid enforcement of arbitration provisions, and sometimes, the contractual independence with respect to the discrepancies in the results of the arbitration and a court. All this weakening the protective strategy outlined in *Wilko* and thus, simply reinforced one more pro-arbitration trend in federal law.[32] Scholars generally pitch *Byrd* as abolishing the mutual conception of intertwining, where courts had before gone to hold arbitrary disarmed arbitration to prevent the different outcomes. Byrd is mostly seen to explain the pre-emptive influence of the FAA in the mixed-claims field as it promotes the wider usage of arbitration. Byrd as an example is one of the pedagogical illustrations of an emerging jurisprudence that reinstates the conflict between statutory rights and contractual obligations.[33]

13.3.5 Shearson/American Express Inc. v. McMahon (1987)

Shearson/American Express Inc. v. McMahon highlighted that arbitration had the wide application to issues which arose under the securities law.[34] In the case, the plaintiffs claimed that their broker-dealer had engaged in unfaithful acts and that they were suing them in the federal court, but a contractual arbitration clause sent the case to the National Association of Securities Dealers (the now Financial Industry Regulatory Authority). The Court determined that arbitrability is

[30] Jalili (1975, 738–757).
[31] Giberson (1975, 491–503).
[32] Force (1986, 131–142).
[33] Fox and Dautaj (2019, 1–51), Siffert (2022), and Freer (2009, 113–117).
[34] Bedell et al. (1987, 2) and Hoellering (1987, 153–156).

bestowed by the Securities Exchange Act of 1934, at the same time placing boundaries on it by being critical of *Wilko*. Its arguments depended upon the development of the contemporary arbitration institutions and institutional structures like FINRA that the Court considered was adequate to protect investors, hence confirming an effective trial to take place. The *McMahon* ruling recognizes the advances that arbitration has made in protecting against fraud but significantly diminished judicial distrust and effectively made arbitration the pre-eminent tool of dispute resolution in the securities sector of the financial services industry. The case has emerged as a landmark case study on research in the field of investor-broker relationship, wherein the Court held that arbitration was a good public policy and has indicated that the federal and state policies support arbitration.[35] Finally, *McMahon* explains how the Supreme Court has reformulated their doctrine of arbitrability to the changing market complexities.

13.3.6 Rodriguez de Quijas v. Shearson/American Express Inc. (1989)

Rodriguez de Quijas v. Shearson/American Express Inc., cleared the way to overrule *Wilko*. The Court ruled that the action before the 1933 Securities Act, can be forced into arbitration, and investors can waive the right to litigation under the contractual provisions. This decision supported the arbitration institutionalization, and arbitration bodies have become more professional: arbitrators are less affiliated to parties, they are less inadequately constrained, and are more specialised, which means that they provide sufficient protections to investors. In turn, the argument by *Wilko* about the vulnerability of investors was invalidated.[36] This decision made pro-arbitration characteristics permanent in American jurisprudence, in the twenty-first century, and cemented the supremacy of FINRA. The analyses by the scholars explain *Rodriguez de Quijas* as a progressive advancement of the case law which creates an improvement in efficiency of dispute resolution at the possible loss of access to justice. It demonstrates judicial pervasiveness to the law and practice in the industry.[37]

13.3.7 Evaluation

The process of resolving securities disputes through arbitration in the US has developed over roughly fifty years, moving through several court decisions to reach its current iteration. The anti-arbitration era heralded by *Wilko*, was definitively closed by *Rodriguez de Quijas*, when the Supreme Court welcomed arbitration

[35] Katsoris (1988, 361–387).

[36] Steinberg (1996, 1503).

[37] Stone (1999, 931–1036) and Wallace (1990, 1199–1251).

agreements as part of federal public policy.[38] The success of FINRA comes from the fast resolution time, low cost, and specific expertise in the sector. There are still criticisms about the independence of arbitrators, no appeals process, and the compulsory presence of investors in the arbitration process, particularly concerning retail investors. Nevertheless, the US model is a case in point of the effectiveness of institutionalized private arbitration in capital market disputes and could offer models to the international systems.[39]

13.4 Settlement of Securities Investment Disputes According to EU Law

This section discusses the framework for resolving securities investment disputes in the EU, which has a different approach from traditional ISDS systems. It will look at the changes to the EU investment policy and practice following the 2009 Lisbon Treaty. It will consider the impact of the *Achmea* decision and review how ADR systems are deployed in EU practice. It will note the importance of the EU throughout this period of implementation and its ambition to create a MIC, in the context of other reforms. Written in an academic but approachable tone, this discussion is suitable for undergraduate and master's level students and provides sources of authority but also provides paths for further inquiry and additional research. The delivery of these themes is eventually presented in an organized way, where each sub-section ought to progress according to the earlier discussion in order to present a clear picture of as well as continuity when examining the EU practice in relation to securities disputes.

13.4.1 Framework for Investment Disputes in the EU

Investment dispute resolution in the EU has developed significantly, since the Lisbon Treaty took effect on November 1, 2009. Prior to this treaty, disagreements were mostly the responsibility of BITs between EU member states. The Lisbon Treaty conferred the European Commission with competence over foreign direct investment, leading to a single EU investment policy that was intended to protect investment and support the internal market. This change creates a more consistent resolution framework for investment disputes, both for disputes between EU states (intra-EU) and for investment relations with third states such as Canada, Singapore, and Vietnam.[40] Securities investments, which include instruments such as shares, bonds, or derivatives, are addressed in the EU white the principles of

[38] Gross (2016, 171–186).
[39] Black (2014, 412) and Gross (2016, 171–186).
[40] Moloney (2023) and Georgaki and Papanastasiou (2019, 209–226).

free movement of capital (Article 63 TFEU) and free provision of financial services.[41] These principles benefit investors by allowing them to carry on business in each member state without undue restriction, while disputes are adjudicated in accordance with EU Law, focussing on integration and consistency in regulation.[42]

The EU's stance stands apart from the conventional ISDS framework which is primarily based on ad hoc arbitration. EU institutions have criticized ISDS for undermining democratic accountability, for curtailing states' ability to regulate for the public good, and for challenging the autonomy of the EU legal order.[43] Such critiques are grounded in concerns about transparency and consistency, eventually leading to the historic Achmea decision, which redefined intra-EU investment arbitration. Scholarly writing has emphasized the EU's movement toward a public-law oriented framework that trades arbitral flexibility for judicial oversight in order to preserve uniformity in the law across member states.[44]

13.4.2 The Achmea Ruling and the End of Intra-EU Arbitration

The Achmea BV v. Slovak Republic case (C-284/16), decided by the Court of Justice of the European Union (CJEU) in 2018, represented a major turning point in the EU approach to investment dispute resolution. The case emerged when Achmea, a Dutch company, challenged Slovakia's limitations on foreign investors in the health insurance sector (slovenská generalizacija) under the Netherlands-Slovakia BIT. An arbitral tribunal under the UNCITRAL arbitration system, acting much like ICSID, issued a ruling in favour of Achmea. Slovakia then sought to annul the award in German courts, arguing that the decision was contrary to EU law, which required a reference to the CJEU.[45]

The CJEU ruled that intra-EU investment arbitration was incompatible with EU law. Its reasoning was based on the idea that arbitral tribunals cannot interpret EU law and this could violate the autonomy and coherence of the EU legal order, especially because arbitral awards are not subject to judicial review by the CJEU. The Court indicated that disputes in the context of the EU's internal market must be resolved by national courts or judicial bodies of the Union, to ensure compliance with Union law.The ruling effectively invalidated intra-EU BITs, moving toward a process of terminating those treaties. After Achmea, the European Commission asked EU member states to terminate intra-EU BITs. The result is the substitution of arbitration with national courts or mechanisms at the EU level for disputes between member states. Academics have noted that Achmea's ruling now reinforces the sovereignty of EU law, but at the same time it limits investors' access to neutral forums for arbitration, which raises questions about whether investors

[41] Bermann (2012, 397–445).
[42] Basedow (2021, 643–660).
[43] Lenk (2015, 10).
[44] Gáspár-Szilágyi (2021, 682).
[45] Korom (2022a, b, 110–115).

are adequately protected in the EU. For students, Achmea demonstrates the tension between international arbitration and regional legal integration, which is a key question in today's discussion of investment law.[46]

13.4.3 EU Law Approach to Securities Investments

Securities investments take on special significance at the EU level due to their role in upholding the integrity of the EU internal market. Their safeguarding is governed primarily by the MiFID II and by the framework of the Capital Markets Union (CMU), whose objectives include increased transparency as well as investor protection and market efficiencies (Directive 2014/65/EU, 2014). Adopted in early 2018, MiFID II governs the standard requirements for investment service providers to provide a fair and transparent process for resolving disputes, and ensures safeguards for investors.[47] In Article 75, MiFID II requires member states ensure access to effective ADR systems for investor complaints. ADR systems typically take the form of 'financial ombudsmen' or independent mediation, which provide a no-cost, accessible avenue to resolution outside of a court of law or tribunal. Unlike mandatory arbitration system such as ICSID or FINRA, the ADR systems in the EU context are fairly tailored with regards to investor recourse to court or tribunal systems. Examples include:

- Germany: The Bundesanstalt für Finanzdienstleistungsaufsicht (BaFin) governs the securities markets, and, for complaints from investors, the "Ombudsmann der privaten Banken" (ombudsman for private banks) provides mediation and binding decisions.[48]
- France: The Autorité des Marchés Financiers (AMF) operates a mediation unit for investor dispute resolution, focusing on rapid and amicable resolution.[49]
- Netherlands: The Klachteninstituut Financiële Dienstverlening (KiFiD) acts based on a hybrid model that entails mediation, and arbitration for financial disputes.[50]

The common elements of this approach are accessibility, as well as fairness, as each one advances the EU investor protection framework while ensuring access to courts. According to the academic literature, EU ADR systems provide a balance between efficiency and safeguarding rights, whereas arbitration imposes a binding decision in other jurisdictions.[51] This approach, which is an express regulatory

[46] Lavranos (2018).
[47] Busch (2017, 340–380).
[48] Huertas (2024).
[49] Autorité des Marchés Financiers (2023, 46).
[50] Hendrikse and Rinkes (2007).
[51] European Parliament (2025).

choice by the EU, signals a more general approach to embedding dispute resolution in regulatory policy to be in accordance with principle of the Internal Market.

13.4.4 EU's MIC Initiative

Commission, since 2015, has constructed the Investment Court System (ICS), which is a permanent court intended to replace ad hoc arbitral panels.[52] The ICS was introduced first into the EU-Canada Comprehensive Economic and Trade Agreement (CETA), and later in agreements with Singapore and Vietnam. Key features of the ICS include permanent judges, appeals and transparency. Rather than arbitrators appointed by the parties, the ICS employs judges who must adhere to strict ethical rules and standards of impartiality. There is an ability to appeal from incorrect legal determinations during the initial case, which addresses a significant complaint with representative arbitration—the inability to correct errors. In addition to that all proceedings will take place in public which aids accountability and reinstalls public confidence.[53]

Alongside its work on the ICS, the EU has promoted a global MIC through the UNCITRAL working group III. By 2025 these discussions were progressing with consultations with stakeholders shaping the proposed organization of the MIC as it would co-exist with other systems such as ICSID and ad hoc arbitration.[54] The MIC is consistent with the vision of "dispute settlement à la carte," allowing parties to choose the dispute settlement system that best fits the dispute, whether arbitration, mediation, ombudsperson or court.[55]

Scholars have eulogised the MIC for its potential to standardize the resolution of investment disputes and recognize the democratic deficits that ISDS creates. Opponents highlight the challenge of achieving a globally and democratically sufficient consensus and collaboration with other legal traditions.[56] For students, the MIC provides a great example of the EU as a leader in reforming global investment law, balancing the need for institutional consistency while providing the option of flexibility.

13.4.5 Evaluation

The EU framework for investment disputes (especially dealing with securities) is conceived as an institutional and public law approach, rather than an arbitration-centred ISDS model. The EU's framework aims to protect investors while maintaining states' regulatory space and democratic accountability, in last

[52] Sennekamp and Vertessy (2025).
[53] Shirlow (2025), Irvita and Asriani (2025, 27), and Cravens (2024, 1089–1091).
[54] UNCITRAL (2025).
[55] Schill and Vidigal (2021).
[56] Tussupov (2022, 175–179).

having mainly been a feature of the EU's integrationist project.[57] The Achmea decision narrowed the avenues by which investors could request neutral forums by abolishing intra-EU arbitration, but will favor the coherence of EU law overall.[58] The proposal for a MIC, in conjunction with new ADR mechanisms, intends to retain the same flexibility enjoyed in arbitration, while focusing on judicial oversight and providing an avenue for substantive appeal in suit of legal certainty. For dealing with securities disputes, the EU provides a unique multi-layered protection framework: national courts for formal litigation, financial ombudsmen for informal and inexpensive resolution, EU regulatory authorities for oversight function post dispute, and with an eye to a MIC in the future for formal and expansive dispute resolution worldwide. The framework aims to straddling liability, flexibility and accountability in the investor's space–and represents a model possibility for jurisdictions. Academics have noted that the EU's approach is a progressive model from traditional ISDS, however, the efficacy is contingent upon implementation and international cooperation.[59]

13.5 Resolution of Securities Investment Disputes in Different Countries

This part outlines a comparative analysis of the way securities investment disputes are resolved in different countries to bring to the forefront the institutional diversity, as well as the divergences in legal theories and social/moral values surrounding law. It uses the case examples of the United Kingdom, Germany, Japan, and Turkey to demonstrate how different legal systems achieve a balance between investor protection, the interests of the state in regulating the market, and efficiency in procedural matters.

13.5.1 The UK

The UK employs a rigorous framework for the resolution of securities investment disputes that draws on a mixture of the courts, private arbitration, and the ombudsman system. As part of British law, the primary sources supporting investor protections are the Financial Services and Markets Act 2000, as well as several other rules and regulations implemented by the FCA.[60] The UK also has Financial Ombudsman Service (FOS), which provide the primary resolution mechanism for complaints initiated by individual investors. The FOS can make binding decisions that are only subject to judicial reviews on the merits. So the regulatory scheme

[57] Nasirli (2025, 1–4).
[58] Collet (2021, 690–694).
[59] Lenk (2020, 62–91), Reinisch (2016, 761–687), Zarate (2018, 2765–2790), and Faccio (2023, 625–643).
[60] Moloney (2023).

can provide certainty for both the investor and the market.[61] What is more, for more complex and institutional matters involving multiple parties, the parties may use the London Court of International Arbitration (LCIA) or other forms of ad hoc arbitration through the price of using arbitration clauses in the contracts used in these international transactions. Both mediation and arbitration were regulated to adaptative and flexible in outsourcing the resolution of disputes to experts in the field of using alternative dispute resolution techniques.[62] In light of these, the UK model prioritizes investor protection while providing legal predictability and flexibility, making it a preferred choice for international investors who often designate London as their arbitration seat in contracts.[63]

13.5.2 Germany

In Germany, a dispute concerning the investment of securities is handled under the supervision of the BaFin, which enforces compliance within financial markets.[64] BaFin acts as both a regulator and an overseer of disputes related to banks, broker-dealers, and fund managers by setting the governance for investors' objections to preserve the integrity of the marketplace.[65] Businesses in the private banking sector also prefer independent ombudsman such as the 'Ombudsmann der privaten Banken' to resolve disputes as inexpensively and quickly as possible for retail investors.[66] However, it is worth noting that in high-value or complex disputes, German federal courts are engaged even though arbitration is also considered. Germany's hybrid system combines state supervision with private dispute resolution options, attempting to strike a balance between state access to regulatory authority and investor access to dispute remedy.

13.5.3 Japan

Japan's resolution of disputes arising from securities investment is centered on the JSDA Dispute Resolution Center within the country's strong regulatory structure governing securities and investments.[67] The JSDA offers relatively inexpensive and quick means for both individual and institutional investors to resolve their differences through mediation and binding arbitration.[68] Parties maintain the ability to appeal decisions to either national or regional courts, although the JSDA's

[61] FCA (2024).
[62] Born (2020).
[63] Ibid.
[64] BaFin (2024).
[65] Moloney (2023).
[66] BaFin (2024).
[67] Arner and Taylor (2009, 488–513).
[68] Ali (2013, 92–108) and Maeda (2022, 92–93).

decisions are final, meaning the courts act as a check on the arbitral decision.[69] In this regard, the Financial Instruments and Exchange Act (FIEA) provides a strong investor protection framework and supports the arbitration and mediation of the JSDA to ensure the stability of the securities markets.[70] Japan's framework incorporates expert arbitration and state oversight and consequently balances investor protection with market regulation.[71]

13.5.4 Comparative Assessment

When these countries are compared, some consistent themes can be observed. First, it is demonstrated that most countries key to this analysis have hybrid models, integrating a combination of arbitration and state oversight, including Germany, and Japan. Second inference, in particular, both the UK and the US focus on the importance of speed and cost efficiency in arbitration, utilizing institutions like LCIA and FINRA, as they are focused on procedural efficiency. Besides them, international arbitration systems such as ICSID, FINRA or LCIA provide confidence by assuring protection of investors, while national courts provide the same assurance for the protection of public good and state regulatory authority.[72] On the basis of what has been covered hitherto, the "dispute settlement à la carte" model is one of the most reasonable approach, since there is a model of adjudication or oversight from which the parties can choose; in this model parties have a choice of courts, arbitration, mediation or an ombudsman, depending on the type of problem the parties face.

13.6 Conclusion

Disputes between investors and states, especially disputes concerning securities investments, are becoming more and more important in international economic relations. This raises important issues about how to balance investor protections against the regulatory authority of the state. This chapter has studied the resolution of investor-state securities disputes from the comparative law perspective, focusing on situational nuances with regards to institutional differences and distinct legal paradigms across various frameworks. On the international level, ICSID arbitration provides a binding and generally accepted pathway for resolving disputes dealing with securities. The cases of *Libananco, Postova Banka*, and *Enron* demonstrate some of the challenges in safely piecing together an inclusion of these types of investments in ICSID's legal definition of investment as it relates to ownership and indirect ownership, state performance bonds and other sovereign obligations,

[69] Arner and Taylor (2009).
[70] Japan Securities Research Institute (2022).
[71] Ibid.
[72] Baaij (2019, 161) and Vassileva (2024, 46).

and the interplay of state authority and state investment in times of crisis. All of these cases illustrate the need for more flexible and nuanced dispute resolution mechanisms for securities investments to help balance investor rights with state sovereignty.[73]

In the US, securities arbitration within FINRA is informed by decisions in the US Supreme Court, Wilko v. Swan to Rodriguez de Quijas, that swung US policy to be more arbitration-friendly. FINRA offers speed and cost savings, but is subject to criticism around arbitrator independence and limitations on appeals.[74] The EU follows a public law model as exemplified by the Achmea decision that ended intra-EU arbitration, while creating avenues such as financial ombudsmen and the MIC in the future. This model creates a means to protect investors, while preserving state autonomy to regulate and the democratic accountability of those regulations.

By comparing the UK, Germany, Japan, and Turkey, we can see hybrid structures that incorporate mediation, ombudsmen, arbitration, and courts. By preserving the regulatory jurisdiction of the state and ensuring protections of the investor, these structures ensure legal predictability and flexibility.[75] These systems are well-supported by figures regarding compliance of states to arbitral awards with over 90% of the states complying voluntarily even though, at times, there is a delay in enforcement.[76] The evidence supports a model of "dispute settlement à la carte" which provides a responsive multi-layered model, in which the parties have options—judicial, arbitral, mediation, or ombudsman models. This approach establishes investor protection and maintains state regulatory authority over time by offering additional options which promote an investor's rights and protection, such as ICSID, FINRA, members of the EU ombudsman, or national courts to resolve substantive securities investment disputes in a modern way.[77]

Chapter Summary

Chapter 13 provides an extensive review of the various legal schemes available to resolve disputes that arise from the investment of funds into securities. The chapter discusses the relationship between the competing interests of protecting the investor and regulating the host country through ISDS arbitration. ISDS has received considerable attention since the introduction of Article 54 of the ICSID Convention, which allows foreign investors to file a formal complaint against the host country if there is an alleged violation(s) of the BIT between the two countries. The analysis was also supported by the fact that the definition of what constitutes

[73] Salacuse (2021).

[74] Stipanowich (2011, 125) and Nelson (2015, 592–594).

[75] Moloney (2023).

[76] Rogers et al (2025) 50(2).

[77] Kaufmann-Kohler and Potestà (2020, 8–10).

an investment continues to be vague as evidenced by court cases such as Libananco v. Turkey, where a higher level of proof was required for a foreign national wishing to make an indirect investment in Turkey through a foreign subsidiary. Similarly, *Poštová Banka v. Greece* determined that sovereign bonds that are publicly traded are generally not eligible for ISDS so any potential claims would be limited to those related to the reorganisation of sovereign debt. Enron v. Argentina provides another type of conflict between an investor's reasonable expectation of receiving "fair and equitable" treatment and a host country's ability to assert a defence of necessity due to a financial crisis.

In terms of dispute resolution between investors and US brokers (depositories or securities dealers), the principal framework for these disputes is FINRA arbitration, which is expressly permitted by the FAA. Litigation, however, became the primary means of resolving disputes related to securities dealers and their clients (an investor). In the past decade, arbitration clauses have gained significant acceptance due to a perception of efficiency, cost-effectiveness, finality and, most importantly, that the outcomes could not be challenged. In relation to the EU regulatory framework for dispute resolution, the CJEU ruled in the case of Achmea that BIT between EU member states and the respective provider/source cannot co-exist with the EU's regulatory framework, effectively dismantling the ISDS regime within the EU. Currently, the EU appears to be moving towards a more quasi-public law-based framework, through its MiFID II directive, which mandates that the regulatory authorities (such as Germany's FOS and BaFin) must provide their retail investor clients with an efficient, low-cost and streamlined mechanism to resolve disputes. It also outlines a broad framework for EU member states to adopt reforms to provide a greater level of services for their investors. As part of these proposed reforms, EU member states have established permanent judges, an appellate mechanism and much greater levels of transparency than that historically available with ad hoc international arbitration mechanisms.

Following this analysis, there is a strong agreement that a flexible dispute resolution model à la carte is the preferred approach, allowing the parties to select a mechanism (e.g. courts, FINRA, Ombudsman, MIC) that is best suited to their needs. These methods aim to strike a reasonable balance between predictability and uncertainty.

Revision Questions

1. Discuss the meaning of the *Poštova Banka v. Greece* on the sovereignty of the question of sovereign debt instruments under the ICSID jurisdiction. How was this decision a conservative interpretation of the legal definition of in investment in financial markets?

2. Discuss the *Achmea* Ruling by the CJEU by stating which reasons the CJEU gave to find that intra-EU investment arbitration could not coexist with the EU law, and by what institutional form does the EU now posit new encourage the alternative?
3. Compare and contrast the role of the US jurisprudence on securities arbitration by considering two cases, *Wilko v. Swan* with the conclusion taken in *Rodriguez de Quijas*. Trace the main factors that contributed to this legal evolution including efficiency and institutional quality.
4. Discuss the case in the *Enron v. Argentina*, the expectation of investors under an investment treaty bilateral protection and application of the necessity defense by the state. What has this case contributed to the incorporation of express carve-outs of public policy measures in the new investment treaties?
5. Name two fundamental features of ADR programmes, including ombudsman programmes, required in the EU by MiFID II of retail investors. Look at this system in comparison to the mandatory arbitration model of FINRA considering the access of the investor to justice.
6. What does dispute settlement à la carte mean? Explain why this multi-layered model, incorporating courts, arbitration, and MIC, has been seen as a more successful model in solving complex securities investment disputes compared to a single system which is rigidly based like the traditional ICSID.
7. Name and describe two main aspects of the suggested MIC that are aimed at mitigating the negative consequences of the conventional ad hoc ISDS arbitration: judicial oversight and judge selection.◄

References

Ali S (2013) Consumer financial dispute resolution in a comparative context: principles, systems and practice. Cambridge University Press, Cambridge

Arner D, Taylor M (2009) The global financial crisis and the financial stability board: Hardening the soft law of international financial regulation? University of New South Wales Law Journal 32:488–513

Autorité des Marchés Financiers (2023) Annual report 2023. https://www.amf-france.org/sites/institutionnel/files/private/2024-08/2023_amf_annual_report.pdf. Accessed 31 Jan 2026

Baaij C (2019) Hiding in plain sight: The power of public governance in international arbitration. Harv Int Law J 60(1):135–180

BaFin (2024) Annual report 2023. https://www.bafin.de/SharedDocs/Downloads/EN/Jahresbericht/dl_jb_2023_en.pdf?__blob=publicationFile&v=3. Accessed 31 Jan 2026

Basedow R (2021) The EU's international investment policy ten years on: The policy-making implications of unintended competence transfers. J Comm Mark Stud 59(3):643–660

Bedell S, Harrison L, Harvey S (1987) The McMahon mandate: compulsory arbitration of securities and RICO claims. Loyola Univ L Rev 19(1):1–38

Bermann G (2012) Navigating EU Law and the law of international arbitration. Arbitr Int 28(3):397–445

Bermann G (2020) Understanding ICSID article 54. ICSID review Fore Invest L J 35(1–2):311–344

Black B (2014) The past, present and future of securities arbitration between customers and brokage firms. In: Markham J, Gjyshi R (eds) Research handbook on securities regulation in the United States. Edward Elgar

Blankley K (2021) FINRA's dispute resolution pandemic response. Arbit L Rev 13(2)

Born G (2020) International commercial arbitration. Kluwer Law International.

Brodsky S (2020) FINRA arbitration of customer/broker-dealer disputes: an overview for the uninitiated. Comm Busi Litig Comm 21(2):10–14

Busch D (2017) MiFID II: stricter conduct of business rules for investment firms. Cap Mar L J 3:340–380

Chevry J (2016) Poštová banka, a.s. and ISTROKAPITAL SE v. Hellenic Republic, ICSID Case No. ARB/13/8 (*Poštová banka* v. *Greece*). Wor Tra Rev 15(1):169–172

Ciocchini P, Khoury S (2018) Investor state dispute settlement: institutionalising "corporate exceptionality." Onati Soc Leg Ser 8(6):976–1000

Collet P (2021) The current European Union investor state dispute settlement reform: a desirable outcome for investment arbitration? Int L Polit 53:689–701

Cravens S (2024) Off the record: transparency challenges in judicial misconduct and discipline. Ca W Res L Rev 74(4):1053–1105

Crynes V (2023) Mapping the evaluation of legitimacy: arbitration clauses in investment chapters of American International Free Trade Agreements. Penn Sta J L Int Aff 11(1):182–228

Dewi Y, Afriansyah A (2019) Dispute settlement mechanism in Bilateral Investment Treaties (BITs). Yuridika 34(1):151–172

European Parliament (2025) Alternative dispute resolution. https://www.europarl.europa.eu/RegData/etudes/BRIE/2024/757639/EPRS_BRI(2024)757639_EN.pdf. Accessed 31 Jan 2026

Exelbert J (2016) Consistently inconsistent: what is a qualifying investment under Article 25 of the ICSID convention and why the debate must end. Ford L Rev 85(3):1243–1279

Faccio S (2023) Investment contracts and the reform of investment arbitration: towards sustainability. ICSID Rev Fore Invest L J 38(3):625–643

FCA (2024) Annual report and accounts 2023–24. https://www.fca.org.uk/publication/annual-reports/annual-report-2023-24.pdf. Accessed 31 Jan 2026

Force R (1986) Doctrine of intertwining: a dead-end after—Dean Witter Reynolds, Inc. v. Byrd, The. J Disp Res 11:131–142

Fox W, Dautaj Y (2019) The life of arbitration law has been experience, not logic: Gorsuch, Kavanaugh, and the Federal Arbitration Act. Card J Conf Res 21(1):1–51

Franck S (2023) Reforming World Bank dispute resolution: ICSID in context. Mich J Int L 44(3):349–403

Freer R (2009) Forgoing American arbitration policy: judicial interpretation of the Federal Arbitration Act. In: Hay P, Vekas L, Elkana Y, Dimitrijevic N (eds) Resolving international conflicts. CEU Press, pp 113–117

Frutos-Peterson C (2008) Enron corporation and Ponderosa Asset, L. P. v. Argentine Republic (ICSID Case No. ARB/01/3) Annulment Proceeding Decision on the Argentine Republic's Request for a Continued Stay of Enforcement of the Award. ICSID Rev Fore Invest L J 23(1):164–174

Gaitis J (2006) Unraveling the Mystery of Wilko v. Swan: American Arbitration Vacatur Law and the Accidental Demise of Party Autonomy. Pepperd Dis Res L J 7(1):1–63

Gáspár-Szilágyi S (2021) Between fiction and reality: the external autonomy of EU Law as a "Shapeshifter" after opinion 1/17. Eur Pap 6(1):675–692

Georgaki K, Papanastasiou T (2019) The impact of achmea on investor-state arbitration under intra-EU BITs: a treaty law perspective. Pol Yearbook Int L 39:209–226

Giberson F (1975) Case note: arbitration of international securities transactions—Scherk v. Alberto-Culver Co. Bos Col Ind Comm L Rev 16(3):491–503

Giovine P (2022) Arbitration and FINRA's customer code: a tailored approach to when a forum selection clause may supersede FINRA Rule 12200. Ford L Rev 91(3):993–1032

Goldman M (2017) International investment law and financial regulation: towards a deliberative approach in international investment law and the global financial architecture. In: Tams C, Schill S, Hofmann R (eds) Int Invest L Glob Fin Archit. Edward Elgar, pp 57–88
Gross J (2016) The historical basis of securities arbitration as an investor protection mechanism. J Disp Res 171(1):171–186
Grund S (2017) Enforcing sovereign debt in court—a comparative analysis of litigation and arbitration following the Greek debt restructuring of 2012. Univ Vienna L Rev 1:34–90
Hendrikse M, Rinkes J (2007) The new Netherlands Financial Services Complaints Tribunal (KiFiD): complaints settlement in the financial services market in the Netherlands. Uitgeverij
Hoellering M (1987) Shearson/American Express v. McMahon: Broadened Domain of Arbitration in U.S.A. J Int Arbit 4(3):153–156
Horton D (2018) Arbitration about arbitration. Stanf L Rev 70:363–441
Huertas M (2024) BaFin concerned about rise in 2023 in number of regulated complaints in respect of german financial services firms. https://legal.pwc.de/en/news/articles/bafin-concerned-about-rise-in-2023-in-number-of-regulated-complaints-in-respect-of-german-financial-services-firms. Accessed 31 Jan 2026
ICSID (2025) ICSID releases caseload statistics for the 2025 fiscal year, with expanded data insights. https://icsid.worldbank.org/news-and-events/comunicados/icsid-releases-caseload-statistics-2025-fiscal-year-expanded-data. Accessed 31 Jan 2026
Irvita M, Asriani A (2025) Transparency and accountability in the justice system: building public trust and justice: the role of public trust in fair law enforcement. Priv Soc Sci J 5(4):26–40
Jalili M (1975) International arbitration—Scherk v. Alberto-Culver Co., The Exemption of International Contracts from the Wilko Doctrine Voiding Agreements to Arbitrate Securities Disputes. Loy Univ Chic L J 6(3):738–757
Japan Securities Research Institute (2022) Securities market in Japan 2022. Japan Securities Research Institute
Katsoris C (1988) Securities arbitration after McMahon. Ford Urb L J 16(3):361–387
Kaufmann-Kohler G, Potestà M (2020) Investor-state dispute settlement and national courts: current framework and reform options. Springer
Kollamparambil U (2016) Bilateral investment treaties and investor state disputes. ERSA working paper 589. https://econrsa.org/wp-content/uploads/2022/06/working_paper_589.pdf. Accessed 31 Jan 2026
Korom V (2022a) Intra-EU BITs in light of the Achmea decision. Cent Eur J Compar L 3:97–117
Lavdari F, Lavdari X (2024) Effects of Investor-State Dispute Settlements (ISDS) on Foreign Direct Investment (FDI) Flows. Poli Persp 21(2):61–95
Lavranos N (2018) After Achmea: The need for an EU investment protection regulation. https://legalblogs.wolterskluwer.com/arbitration-blog/after-achmea-the-need-for-an-eu-investment-protection-regulation. Accessed 31 Jan 2026
Lenk H (2015) Challenging the notion of coherence in EU foreign investment policy. Eur J Leg Stud 8(2):1–20
Lenk H (2020) The EU investment court system and its resemblance to the WTO appellate body. In: Gáspár-Szilágyi S, Behn D, Langford M (eds) Adjudicating trade and investment disputes: convergence or divergence? Cambridge University Press, Cambridge, pp 62–91
Libananco Holdings Co. Limited v The Republic of Turkey (2011) ICSID Case No ARB/06/8 (Official Case No) IIC 506 (2011)
Maeda T (2022) How are the disputes settled in Japan's financial ADR? statistical analysis of the determinative factors in the facilitation and conclusion of settlements in FINMAC mediation. Jap Comm Arbit J 3:91–104
Maffett M, Milone M, Rao W (2025) 'The impact of foreign investors' challenges to domestic regulations'. J L Econ 68(2):269–309
Mitsou A (2016) Greek debt restructuring and investment treaty arbitration: jurisdictional stumbling blocks for bondholders. J Int Arbitr 33(6):687–721
Moloney N (2023) EU securities and financial markets regulation. Oxford University Press

Nasirli F (2025) Balancing investor protection and sovereignty: the evaluation of bilateral investment treaties and investor-state dispute settlement in international investment law. West Eur J Hist Eve Soc Sci 3(5):1–4

Nelson W (2015) Take it or leave it: unconscionability of mandatory pre-dispute arbitration agreements in the securities industry. Univ Pennsyl J Busin L 17:573–618

Oscarsson C (2022) Exchanging bilateral investment treaties and investor-state dispute settlement for the acquis communautaire: a three-stage analysis of the effects for investors, the level of investment protection and for the flow of foreign direct investment on the internal market. Master Thesis, Stockholm University Faculty of Law

Pauwelyn J (2015) The rule of law without the rule of lawyers? Why investment arbitrators are from mars, trade adjudicators from Venus. Am J Int L 109(4):761–805

Phillips L (2017) If it quacks like a duck: the financial industry regulatory authority and federal jurisdiction. Washing Lee L Rev 74(3):1965–1742

Reinisch A (2022) Article 54'. In: Schill S, Malintoppi L, Reinisch A, Schreuer C, Sinclair A (eds) Schreuer's commentary on the ICSID convention: A commentary on the convention on the settlement of investment disputes between states and nationals of other states. Cambridge University Press, Cambridge, pp 1470–1515

Reinisch A (2016) Will the EU's proposal concerning an Investment Court System for CETA and TTIP lead to enforceable awards?—The limits of modifying the ICSID Convention and the nature of investment arbitration. J Int Econ Law 19(4):761–687

Reisman M (1989) The breakdown of the control mechanism in ICSID arbitration. Duke L J 4:730–807

Rogers C, Childress III D, Coe J et al (2025) Complying in the shadow of the award. Yale J Int L 50(2)

Salacuse J (2021) The law of investment treaties. Oxford University Press, Oxford

Schill S, Malintoppi L, Reinisch A et al (2022) Schreuer's commentary on the ICSID convention: a commentary on the convention on the settlement of investment disputes between states and nationals of other states. Cambridge University Press, Cambridge

Schill S, Vidigal G (2019) Designing investment dispute Settlement à la Carte: insights from comparative institutional design analysis. L Prac Int Cour Trib 18:311–341

Schill S, Vidigal G (2021) Investment dispute settlement à la Carte: a proposal for the reform of investor-state dispute settlement. In: Elsig M, Polanco R, Bossche P (eds) International economic dispute settlement: demise or transformation? Cambridge University Press, Cambridge, pp 220–263

Sennekamp P, Vertessy P (2025) TIPP: important step forward on "Investor-state Dispute Settlement" (ISDS). https://www.businesseurope.eu/wp-content/uploads/2025/02/2015-00364-E-e4c-1.pdf. Accessed 31 Jan 2026

Shirlow E (2025) Transparency in investment treaty arbitration: past, present, and future. J Int Dis Settle 16(3):idaf019

Siffert D (2022) Recent developments in arbitration: articles from the conference presented by the Center on Civil Justice at NYU Law School. Center on Civil Justice at NYU Law School

Staden A (2011) Towards greater doctrinal clarity in investor-state arbitration: the CMS, Enron, and Sempra Annulment decisions. Czech Yearb Int L 2:207–226

Steinberg M (1996) Securities arbitration: better for investors than the courts. Brooklyn L Rev 62:1503–1533

Stipanowich T (2011) Revelation and reaction: the struggle to shape American arbitration. Yearb Arbit Med 3:125–199

Stone K (1999) Rustic justice: community and coercion under the Federal Arbitration Act. Nor Carol L Rev 77(3):931–1036

Tanzi A (2020) On judicial autonomy and the autonomy of the parties in international adjudication, with special regard to investment arbitration and ICSID annulment proceedings. Leiden J Int L 33(1):57–75

Taylor C (1987) The arbitrability of federal securities claims: Wilko's Swan song. Univ Miami L Rev 42(1):203–228

Turk M (2025) FINRA arbitraion as financial regulation. Alabama L Rev 77:389
Tussupov A (2022) Corruption and fraud in investment arbitration: procedural and substantive challenges. Springer
UNCITRAL (2025) Working Group III: investor-state dispute settlement reform. https://uncitral.un.org/en/working_groups/3/investor-state. Accessed 31 Jan 2026
UNCTAD (2025) Recent trends in investor-state arbitration cases. https://unctad.org/system/files/official-document/diaepcbinf2025d4_en.pdf. Accessed 31 Jan 2026
Vassileva R (2024) Investment arbitration and the rule of law: how transparency impacts on domestic accountability. In: Andenas M, Heidemann M (eds) Commercial contract law and arbitration: from assignments to unfair terms. Routledge, pp 46–77
Wallace P (1990) Securities arbitration after McMahon, Rodriguez, and the new rules: can investors' rights really be protected? Vander L Rev 4(4):1199–1251
Wilson T, Banens Y, Sharif S (2023) ISDS and States' Ability to Deal with Financial Crisis. J Int Arbitr 40(3):245–262
Zarate J (2018) Legitimacy concerns of the proposed multilateral investment court: is democracy possible? Boston Coll L Rev 59(8):2765–2790

Further Reading

Karton J (2020) International arbitration as comparative law in action. J Dis Res 2:293–325
Korom V (2022b) Intra-EU BITs in light of the Achmea decision. Cent Eur J Comp L 3(1):97–117
Rogers C (2025) Donald Childress III, Jack Coe, Christopher Drahozal. Complying in the shadow of the award. Yale J Int L 50(2):174–221
Schreuer C, Schill S, Malintoppi L, Reinisch A, Sinclair A (2022) Schreuer's commentary on the ICSID convention: a commentary on the convention on the settlement of investment disputes between states and nationals of other states. Cambridge University Press, Cambridge
Vadi V (2010) Critical comparisons: the role of comparative law in investment treaty arbitration. Denv J Int L Pol 39(1):67–100
Vassileva R (2024) Investment arbitration and the rule of law: how transparency impacts on domestic accountability. In: Andenas M, Heidemann (eds) Commercial contract law and arbitration: from assignment to unfair terms. Routledge, pp 46–77

Current Debates on Emerging Trends

14

Contents

F. B. Erdem, *The Principles of International Banking, Finance and Investment Law*, Springer Textbooks in Law, https://doi.org/10.1007/978-3-032-32505-1_14

Abstract

In the last past half-century, the worldwide financial services sector has developed into one of the largest consumers of IT products, while regulation consistently lags behind. Since the 2007–08 financial crisis, there has been a slow but gradual development of financial regulation, particularly in the US and the EU. Importantly, an increasing number of regulatory obligations are creeping up on financial service providers. Policymakers are employing compliance and disclosure obligations to change commercial incentives and business models. The phenomenon of universal banking has encountered attempts at regulatory or mitigating supervision through ring-fencing obligations and increased regulatory capital requirements. In relation, regulatory initiatives were enacted to limit system risk due to the widespread use of collateralized debt obligations by financial service firms—one of the main elements of financial contagion, due to the fundamental decoupling of credit risk from its origin.

14.1 Topical Issues on Finance Law

In this subsection, we will examine the recent topics that have been at the heart of conversations in finance law. Although enrolment in our studies is designed to examine the topics noted below, that list can expand as new developments occur.

14.1.1 Sustainable Finance

Sustainable finance is in essence a type of financing aimed at supporting economic growth, while mitigating environmental impacts, and fulfilling obligations to achieve international commitments on climate and sustainability. The effects of global warming are more apparent today than ever before. The most recent report from the United Nations Intergovernmental Panel on Climate Change (IPCC) highlights the scale of the threat posed to human beings. The report explains the erratic seasonal average temperatures, higher numbers of wildfires, changes in ecosystem dynamics, floods, droughts and incidence of diseases caused by climate and its alteration have increased. Such changes threaten ecosystems and justify staggering declines to economic and social stability. Reduced agricultural production and availability of water along with soil erosion damage the economic bases of human wellbeing.[1]

The financial system is on two paths with climate change. On the one hand, it creates additional harm to the environment, as investors look to invest in carbon-heavy activities. On the other hand, it has an enormous opportunity to redeploy capital to sustainable, low-carbon sectors. This has produced ongoing global efforts to green financial systems, especially after the 2015 Paris Climate Agreement that set out ambitious objectives for limiting increases in global average temperature and to adopt development that is climate-resilient.[2]

The EU has been a vanguard in developing regulatory frameworks to embed sustainability in finance. Following the 2018 Sustainable Finance Action Plan, the EU put in place several of its cornerstone pieces of legislation. The most important example is the 2020 EU Taxonomy Regulation, which provides a regulatory classification system for environmental activities that are sustainable.[3] The taxonomy allows investors, companies, and policymakers to know which economic activities contribute to climate mitigation or adaptation and do not cause significant harm to other environmental objectives or goals.[4] It also supports a common language across the EU, supporting transparency and limiting greenwashing—where misleading claims damage reputation and trust.[5]

Another significant development is the Corporate Sustainability Reporting Directive (CSRD), which expands on the Non-Financial Reporting Directive. The CSRD requires large and listed companies to provide more detailed information on their environmental and social impact. The main aims of these requirements are to increase accountability, to ensure sustainability information is comparable and reliable and ideally made available to investors and stakeholders.[6] Together, the EU Taxonomy and CSRD form the basis of the EU's sustainable finance framework and work in complete harmony with the goals of the European Green Deal.

A related undertaking is the EU Green Bond Standard (EUGBS) which establishes strong standards for green bonds issued in the EU. Green bonds are a means to finance green projects (e.g., renewable energy, energy efficiency, sustainable transport), and the EUGBS aims to provide a degree of investor assurance through stipulations which require clarity on how proceeds will be spent, environmental verification and/or reporting obligations.[7] By increasing consistency of practice in relation to green bonds, the EU hopes to encourage investment into sustainable projects and to limit misleading environmental claims.

---

[1] Marbaix et al. (2025, 318) and Fatemi and Fooladi (2013, 101).
[2] Clark et al. (2018, 345–346).
[3] Hurk and Klooster (2024, 17).
[4] Lucarelli et al. (2020, 6460).
[5] Dempere et al. (2024, 1–14).
[6] Martinčević et al. (2024, 317–327).
[7] Smolenska (2025, 8).

Other parts of the world, outside the EU, have also made significant progress on sustainable finance. For instance, the UN has introduced the Principles for Responsible Banking and Principles for Responsible Investment, aiming to align banks and businesses with the UN SDGs. Likewise, the UK, Japan and Canada have started their own taxonomies or roadmaps on sustainable, sometimes modelled on the EU.[8]

Sustainable finance embraces related concepts such as ESG investing, impact investing, and climate finance. ESG investing incorporates non-financial factors—such as carbon emissions and labour practices, and governance—into the investment process. Impact investing goes further and requires that the social and environmental benefit can be measured in addition to financial returns. Climate finance factors in funding and financing to address, mitigate, or adapt to climate change; and in many international contexts such as the Green Climate Fund.[9]

Adopting sustainable finance is not without challenges. Greenwashing, or organizations claiming to be "green" without any meaningful or verifiable benefits, is a persistent concern. In addition, regulators and international bodies are countering greenwashing with standardized approach (for example, through the IFRS Foundation), increased disclosures, and rigorous audits. Another issue is data availability and quality: credible and truly comparable sustainability data is essential for addressing and evaluating risks and making decisions, but many markets struggle with inconsistent disclosures and issues regarding verification.

There is also a lively discussion around the role of central banks and supervisors in promoting sustainability.[10] Discussion is whether including climate risks in the monetary policy and the regulation of stability, or about the jeopardy overstepping mandates. The Network for Greening the Financial System (NGFS), consisting of more than 100 central banks and regulators has become an important forum for sharing best practice and continuing to develop tools to assess financial risks related to climate.[11] This network illustrates ways on how cooperation can begin to turn intangible ideas into mechanisms that can be deployed.

In conclusion, sustainable finance is a paradigm shift in the way the world does finance.[12] It demonstrates that economic growth and environmental protection are not mutually exclusive, but interdependent. Through a range of instruments such as green bonds, sustainability-linked loans and ESG metrics markets are redirecting capital towards a low-carbon, inclusive economy. However, realizing this potential will require policy coherence, a clear standard and global harmonization as practices continue to emerge.[13] Seemingly, and more sustainability is becoming the

[8] Lombardi et al. (2023, 7–11).

[9] Kalinowski (2024, 281–296), Lokuwaduge and Silva (2022, 149), and Lagoarde-Segot (2024, 101397).

[10] Dikau and Volz (2021, 107022).

[11] Dias et al. (2024, 10).

[12] Ryszawska (2018, 219).

[13] Niekerk (2024, 11–14).

defining feature of modern finance and policy, thus shaping regulations, strategies and the long-term health of the global economy.

14.1.2 Behavioural Finance

Trade decisions frequently do not conform to rationality due to heuristics, emotional impulses, and social pressure. When these individual actions are aggregated at the market level, there are often plausible explanations of financial anomalies that traditional theory cannot completely describe. Behavioural finance is an interdisciplinary area that combines concepts from psychology, economics, and sociology to explain how feelings and cognitive flaws influence financial decision-making. It directly confronts the classical economics' homo economicus—the idea of a perfectly rational investor making decisions to maximize utility based only upon all available information.[14]

Traditional finance, at its essence, is based in the Efficient Market Hypothesis (EMH), which argues that asset prices respond instantaneously to all available information, and continuous profitability from the market is impossible. However, real-world events such as speculative bubbles, panic-driven overreaction, and persistent mispricing provide evidence that markets are not perfectly efficient. Behavioral finance was developed to explain these situations in psychological terms and would provide a coherent model for why investors and markets may act irrationally.[15] This has provided a useful bridge between theoretical models and the unpredictable/unknown in the real world.

Cognitive biases are at the heart of behavioural finance, which are systematic deviations in judgment that warp the allocation of information. Prominent in this realm is Prospect Theory, introduced by Daniel Kahneman and Amos Tversky, posits that people judge outcomes as relative to a reference point, commonly the status quo, rather than in absolute terms. People exhibit loss aversion whereby the discomfort of losses is felt more intensely than the same amount in gains. Therefore, an investor may retain an asset that has lost its value to avoid the implication of a loss—or divest any value-gaining asset too soon. This is commonly referred to as the disposition effect. From my analytical experience with investor portfolios, experienced investors tend to amplify poor outcomes at times of erratic price movements.[16]

Overconfidence bias is another widely felt effect in behavioural finance, where an investor's assessments of his or her own experience or forecasting ability may be inflated. Thus, overconfidence will lead to excessive risk-taking and trading activity and volatility in the market. This leads to confirmation bias, where an investor will seek out information that supports the investor's ideas, while rejecting

[14] Illiashenko (2017, 29–30) and Subashree (2024, 162–168).
[15] Li (2024, 244–245) and Fakhoury (2020, 19–23).
[16] Kahneman and Tversky (1979, 1–50).

evidence that contradicts, which may create echo chambers with unexplained price fundamentals.[17]

Herding behaviour is another key principle for understanding the behavioural finance proxies. In moments of uncertainty or volatility, investors often choose to imitate those around them, rather than analysing the situation on their own. This imitation can lead to trend-following behaviour, and result in bubbles, followed by crashes.[18] In the classic example of the late-1990s Internet or dot-com bubble, many participants became victims of collective overoptimistic behaviour, accompanied by the overconfidence bias, that led to rampant and widespread overvaluation of dot-com company stock. Similarly, the 2008 global financial crisis reflected collective overoptimism and overconfidence with respect to the behaviour of different mortgage-backed securities, which eventually led to significant overvaluation of global stock markets and bubbles in the US housing market.

There are other biases as well, in behavioural finance. Mental accounting is the tendency for people to assign different values to money based on its origin or intended purpose, even though money is assumed to be fungible economics-wise. For example, a person might engage in extremely reckless gambling behaviour after winning a windfall gain, while engaging in more conservative behaviour with earned income. Anchoring bias is when individuals over-rely on initial data points, like historical prices, even when those data points are not relevant.

Behavioural finance also raises interesting legal or regulatory questions. Traditional regulation or financial laws are premised on the belief that actors are aware, rational, and informed. However, behavioural finance suggests evidence to the contrary (e.g., biases). It is also interesting to know that regulations and legal policies have been developed to apply "nudge" strategies, or provide interventions that raise awareness and promote better choices, while still respecting and protecting individual autonomy. Richard Thaler and Cass Sunstein popularized "nudges," which might include automatic enrolment in pension plans or explaining risks in other formats. For me, these nudges seem humane since they embrace our weaknesses.[19]

Behavioural insights redefined consumer protections in finance by requiring more communicative disclosures of risk to counteract framing biases. In corporate governance, behavioural insights contribute to the reduction of executive overconfidence or boardroom groupthink. While behavioural finance creates helpful descriptions of irrationality but does not have the mathematical sophistication and predictive power of traditional models (more often creating a description of only a specific context) there is an increasing body of evidentiary support that has brought the adaptations into finance practice.[20]

In summary, behavioural finance broadens our understanding of financial processes by applying human psychology to the mix of actors. It reminds us that

[17] Rabbani et al. (2024, 1–17), Boussaidi (2022, 3360), and Michailova and Schmidt (2011, 21–22).
[18] Roekel and Smit (2022, 499).
[19] Thaler and Sunstein (2009).
[20] Davies and Brooks (2017, 542–560).

markets are not just based on algorithms, but on actors who are emotive, biased, and socially influenced. By adopting these realities, investors, regulators, and the institution can create a more stable and equitable financial ecosystem. Behavioral finance demonstrates an important truth: that true market efficiency will require not only data but understanding of the humans who construct meaning from the data.

14.1.3 Digital Finance

Digital finance represents the convergence of digital technologies with financial services, transforming the way individuals and organizations access, manage and transfer money. Digital finance includes innovations such as online banking, mobile payments, digital lending, cryptocurrencies and blockchain, as well as many other fintech services. In my expert opinion, having followed this evolution through the years, the development of digital finance has changed the financial services markets by substantially lowering transaction costs, increasing efficiencies, and expanding services to populations frequently excluded from services offered in traditional systems.

The origins of digital finance began in the late twentieth century with the digitalization of banking, which began with electronic tables, the credit card and electronic transfer, the growth of digital finance has seen explosive growth in development, rate of adoption and innovation, due to widespread access to the internet, smartphones and data analytics. Digital finance now expands beyond traditional banks; it has developed a community of digital users and providers including payment gateways, P2P lending platforms, robo-advisors and neobanks that are entirely digital.[21]

One prominent aspect of digital finance is that it focuses on providing financial inclusion. With mobile applications and fintech, billions of people in developing nations have entered formal financial ecosystems for the first time. A case in point is M-Pesa in Kenya, which I have studied carefully; it illustrates how digital platforms have enabled everyday users and small businesses to transact safely, cheaply, and at a distance with no physical bank, thereby increasing inclusion. Inclusion in finance allows underdeveloped nations to reduce poverty, increase entrepreneurship, and promote equality of gender, as providing finance begins to open new sectors of economic activity.[22]

Big Data and AI are another pillar as they are able to enable better credit assessments, fraud detection, and unique product offerings. For example, digital lenders can offer credits using unconventional data such as mobile phone usage and e-commerce use, where individuals may be excluded by traditional credit metrics.

[21] Murinde et al. (2022, 102103).
[22] Omanga and Dreyer (2017, 207–227).

Also, robo-advisors broaden access to wealth management services by using algorithms to provide a more affordable investment service thereby widening access to different forms of financial products.

Nonetheless, the growth of digital finance introduces new regimes of regulation and ethics. Privacy of data, cybersecurity, consumer protection, and algorithmic fairness are at the forefront of policy objectives. With growing access to online transactions, the protection of personal information and financial data is of utmost importance and cybercrime, identity theft, and hacks are serious risks that affect both individuals as well as systems and networks. Globally, regulators are trying to balance the challenges of encouraging innovation while maintaining stability and this balance become femur in some emerging markets, especially those where regulatory oversight is minimal.

From a legal perspective, digital finance raises complex questions of jurisdiction, liability, and regulation. Digital finance's cross-border or global nature challenges national laws and jurisdictional authority, to the extent that questions arise about which national authority controls the regulation of cross-border payments, exchanges of digital currencies, or crypto constructs. Various jurisdictions have developed domestic frameworks, such as the EU's Digital Finance Package and the MiCA regulation, that streamline rules on digital assets. Central banks have also been exploring and testing CBDCs, which are digital sovereign currencies for the purpose of more efficient payments, lowered costs, and to expand financial inclusion, while simultaneously raising ethical issues on consumer privacy and consequences of policymaking.

In closing, it is anticipated that digital finance is one of the most transformative developments in finance. Leveraging technology has increased efficiency, and transparency, and extended reach, making opportunities available to many. We must continually keep pace with the changes required of the regulation of the risks introduced by these new developments.

14.1.4 Project Finance

Project finance is a specific financing mechanism used for large-scale ventures that require significant capital, and the repayment of the project debt is primarily based on the cash flows generated by the project, rather than the broader financial wherewithal of the project sponsors. It is a methodology used primarily in sectors like energy, transportation, telecommunications, natural resources and infrastructure, and relies on the concept that a special purpose vehicle (SPV) will be formed to create a separate legal identity to isolate the project assets and risks from the project sponsors' other assets and liabilities.[23]

A defining characteristic of project finance is the limited or non-recourse nature of the finance, meaning lenders' claims extend only to the revenues and assets

[23] Sainati et al. (2020, 243).

attributed to the project, and not to the sponsors' broader asset base.[24] As a result, extensive due diligence is conducted, as lenders' returns depend on the project's commercial viability, technical and construction feasibility, and regulatory stability. Complexity is further increased because numerous parties, including the project sponsors, lenders, such as commercial banks or development institutions, contractors, suppliers, and regulators are involved in any project finance transaction. Each party is also bound to one another by interrelated contracts, such as loan agreements, offtake contracts, construction agreements, and operation contracts that assign responsibilities and risk to one another to assist in the bankability of the project. For example, an offtake agreement secures a buyer of the project output, such as electricity or commodities for predictable cash flows to service the lenders' repayments.

The process of allocating risk sits at the center of project finance. Risk is allocated to the party that is the most capable of managing it; contractors take construction risk, operators take operational risk, and sponsors or offtaker take market risk. Legal factors and regulatory environment are paramount in providing a stable investing environment for capital providers, but the importance of these factors is most pronounced in PPPs which combine public goals and objectives with private capital and efficiency.[25]

Project finance provides the benefit of accessing a large amount of capital, allocating risk across parties, and developing state owned or public infrastructure outside of public budgets. However, project finance entails relatively large transaction costs, long and complicated negotiations, and exposes all parties to political or regulatory changes, particularly in emerging market economies. In my opinion, project finance as a discipline-most importantly its emphasis on precision, anticipation, and contingency management-captures the same spirit reflected in the global commitment to financing sustainable infrastructure.

Ultimately, project finance represents an advanced mechanism for developing capital heavy strategic developments by linking investing to future cash flows. The process relies upon a robust contractual framework, optimization of risk, and legal certainty. As the demand for infrastructure well as the demand for energy for clean sources accelerates, project finance remains an important vehicle to achieving sustainable economic integration.

14.1.5 Equipment Finance

Equipment finance consists of methods for a business to finance the acquisition of equipment, vehicles, and technology without meeting the cost of the asset up front. This keeps working capital available for other strategic objectives. Additionally, it

[24] Farrell (2003, 548).
[25] Demirel et al. (2022, 155).

is especially beneficial in capital intensive industries like manufacturing, construction, agriculture, transportation, and healthcare to achieve the desired operational outcome while spreading the cost of the asset over time. Equipment finance typically occurs by means of an equipment lease or an equipment loan. When it is an equipment lease, the equipment funder (lessor) purchases the equipment and subsequently leases it to the business that will use the equipment (lessee) in exchange for recurring lease payments. Equipment leases can be operating leases, where ownership of the asset and any associated risks remain with the lessor until lease termination, or finance leases, where ownership risk and ownership benefits shift to the lessee. At the end of the leasing period, the lessee has the option to either; return the equipment, extend the lease, or outright purchase the asset based on the lease terms. In contrast, an equipment loan allows the business to purchase the equipment outright, while securing the loan by using the very equipment purchased as collateral.[26] As payments are made to retire the loan, ownership transfers at the end of the loan period. This is a better option for firms who will require long-term use of the asset, such as those who need specialized manufacturing equipment.

Legally, equipment finance relies on contracts that describe the payment terms, responsibilities for maintenance, insurance requirements, and rights and obligations in the event of a default. Because of the importance of documentation to the avoidance of litigation, accurate documentation is critical in avoiding disputes about ownership or repossession. Financial institutions also have to comply with accounting and regulatory rules about asset recognition, depreciation, and disclosures. The advantages of equipment finance include improving cash flow, tax advantages of being able to deduct your lease payment or depreciation, and access to innovative technology that would otherwise be prohibitive. The downsides could include extra costs in the long term as a result of interest and lease premium, and being stuck in the middle of the lease with technology that is already outdated, especially in fast-moving industries.

In summary, equipment finance provides businesses with a dynamic opportunity to get access to key assets and preserve the required liquidity to maintain the health of the business. When properly structured to deliver against required operational capacity, this can lead to improved innovation and competitiveness no matter the industry or size. In a changing economic environment, this asset acquisition strategy will remain important for businesses looking to stay fluid and equipped with both the required tools and tangible left over cash flow.

14.2 Topical Issues on Banking Law

In this section, we will examine some of the more salient issues that are currently influencing the conversation in banking law. The issues reflected here are for the most part current, but are likely to change as conversations evolve in response to

[26] Schroth (2010, 325).

the rather rapid developments inspired by the topics discussed below. To speak personally, as I have followed the changes regarding bank regulation since the 2008 financial crisis, the shift to, and—more importantly—the regulation and supervision of technological innovation, is clearly one of the main challenges facing modern banking systems looking to balance innovation with the stability necessary for the public good today.

14.2.1 Fintech and Digital Banking

FinTech clearly encompasses new methods of delivery for financial services that are enabled by digital technologies and allow for enhanced and automated delivery of financial services and products. This type of technology includes a range of developments including digital banking, mobile payments, P2P lending, robo-advisory, crowdfunding platforms, as well as blockchain-enabled products. Over the past decade, financial technology development has transformed the way individual and institutional customers deal with financial resources, disrupted traditional banking, and driven, even required, significant deliberation and discussion regarding the law and policy regarding banking generally and banking law specifically. Considering the transformative nature of fintech globally, the acceleration of fintech as a means to engage with financial systems has driven new opportunities for customers, while regulators work feverishly to remain engaged with the speed of the change.

Digital banking, a primary result of fintech, offers consumers financial services solely through online platforms or mobile applications, completely eliminating the need for physical branches. This business model on average reduces operational costs to below those needed to support physical banking operations and allows digital banks to lower fee structures, provide higher interest rates, and customize services. The most important it will help advance financial inclusion by reaching unbanked and underbanked consumers, especially in areas with very few banking opportunities.

Fintech also assists SMEs by providing alternative funding mechanisms. Crowdfunding and P2P lending sites allow entrepreneurs to engage with investors directly, thereby circumventing traditional intermediaries. Further, payment and e-wallet services facilitate both domestic and international transactions with greater speed and lower costs.[27] Nevertheless, the rise of financial technology introduces real challenges. Regulatory agendas are now dominated by data protection, cybersecurity, and consumer rights issues. As the finance sectors continues to digitize, it becomes increasingly unclear where banks stop and financial technology companies begin.[28] Regulators will have to rethink oversight of financial firms and the risks they may introduce to the financial ecosystem or regulations of the industry

[27] Coakley and Huang (2020, 1–18) and Fenwick et al. (2018, 103–131).
[28] Adegbite (2025, 6).

to safeguard against systemic risk[29] that can spread rapidly across interconnected platforms.

In conclusion, fintech and digital banking have the potential to reform financial systems by introducing efficiencies, improving accessibility, and promoting competition. However, they also pose unique threats—such as data breaches and disruption of financial markets—and need appropriately agile regulatory frameworks to respond to change.

14.2.1.1 Regulatory Responses to Technological Innovations

Regulatory measures have historically been instrumental for the stability of a financial system, and for establishing trust and integrity. However, with the rise of fintech and digital banking, regulators have had to reconsider conventional approaches to addressing new risks and behaviors introduced by technology. Unlike conventional banks, many fintechs have operated and still operate outside the defined regulatory perimeter, resulting in gaps in oversight and consequential systemic risks.

To address these gaps, regulators in various jurisdictions are exploring a range of initiatives, the most salient being regulatory sandboxes. Sandboxes provide a controlled environment for fintech companies to launch new products and services in a supervised environment, enabling regulators to examine new technologies the opportunity to innovate in controlled environments. The sandbox has been established and embraced by many regulators across the globe beginning with the UK's FCA and Singapore's MAS for future innovation.

At the European level, the EU's Digital Finance Package offers a consistent framework for digital financial services. Among the components contained in this package, the MiCA provides rules for issuers and providers of cryptocurrency, and the Digital Operational Resilience Act (DORA) sets strict cybersecurity specifications for financial institutions.[30] The PSD2 requires that banks share customer data with licensed third parties through secure APIs, which will enhance competition and innovation while maintaining customer protection. Each of these steps represents a more nuanced approach to regulation, ensuring that new technologies can promote progress and innovation without undermining financial stability. In the US, regulations remain more fragmented and siloed, with agencies such as the SEC, CFTC, and OCC independently overseeing tenets of fintech, including securities and payment-related guidelines.[31] Nevertheless, there are increasingly collaborative processes occurring between agencies, particularly as the separation between finance and technology continues to blur. On the global scene, organizations such as the FSB and Basel Committee on Bank Supervision are issuing recommendations related to risk management frameworks for fintech, cybersecurity, and digital assets, maintaining an element of international consistency. In

[29] Buckley et al. (2020, 40).
[30] Lannoo (2023, 539).
[31] Grennan (2025).

my view, this global coordination is necessary to ensure that there are consistent international standards that are reflective of the fintech, which operates across borders. Allowing national regulators and supervisors to develop their own regulatory frameworks will only lead to regulatory arbitrage opportunities on the part of fintech players who can transfer their operations within regulatory gaps.[32] In sum, there is an evolution of regulatory approaches to fintech to balance innovation with systemic integrity. Initiatives such as sandboxes and regulatory frameworks like MiCA and DORA signal a positive shift in action, even though there are still issues associated with keeping oversight in lockstep with the pace of change.

14.2.1.2 The Political Economy of Financial Crises

Fintech and digital banking exist within larger economic conditions and the issues of financial crises, where innovation may lessen or worsen systemic risks. The political economy perspective demonstrates the interplay of this and how that relates to policy, market behavior, and impact on society.

Digitalization provides the potential for increased efficiency, transparency, and access to information. These processes could address prior inefficiencies that led to instability. For example, data analytics in real time allows for better monitoring of risk. Additionally, however, rapid innovation—especially in areas like crypto-assets and DeFi and algorithmic trading—can also contribute to increased volatility.[33] All these are operating much faster and at greater scale than ever before, and they may put stress on the system and escalate shocks during stressful periods. Furthermore, the established involvement of Big Tech into the financial world brings up new potential problems of concentration of data and privacy, and systemic reliance on digital systems which I also brought up in my policy work as a potential "too big to fail" in a new form. The 2008 crisis highlighted how complexity and lack of oversight can turn into a global crisis. While there may be different forms, fintech operates in ways that could replicate these issues once again, especially in dealing with emerging patterns such as speculative dynamics in crypto. There has already been talk recently about some stablecoin failures not having sufficient regulatory supervision to prevent damaging downward cascades after failure. The question from a policy perspective might be "will we see fintech bridge to the real economy or is this just more dependable finance coupled with speculative aspirations?".

To achieve this balance, coordination will be required from central banks, regulators, and competition authorities. Governments should be cognizant of the macroeconomic effects of fintech, such as implications for the monetary policy transmission mechanism or interdependencies between economies across borders. For example, a cybersecurity incident or a technology system failure in one jurisdiction can affect the rest of the world through interconnected digital platforms. I have seen this modelled in some stress tests and it is frighteningly plausible. Solid

[32] Calomiris and Mason (2004, 5–27).
[33] Aramonte et al. (2021, 22).

international cooperation, within the context of a forum like the FSB, will be necessary to ensure that standards are aligned and to avoid crises that may not start domestically. To summarize, the political economy of financial stability or crises has shown that fintech can play both roles, of stabilizer and amplifier of risk, and policymakers will have to harness the benefits while mitigating its negatives, to ensure that innovation remains compatible within the framework of economic stability in an increasingly global digital world. This will require not just regulation that reacts to FinTech, but rather thinking ahead of regulation that can forecast how technology will shape systemic risks.

14.2.1.3 Risk Management in Financial Markets: Assets and Liability Management

Risk management continues to serve as the foundation of financial soundness, a reality that remains true today—despite the ever-present and increasing pace of digital transformation. In traditional banking, asset and liability management (ALM) focuses on mitigating risks associated with interest rate, liquidity, and capital adequacy. While these core concepts continue to exist in the fintech and digital banking landscape, they must confront new risks arising from a technology-first operating model.[34]

Since digital banks rely on technology and data, their operational risks are heightened and can include system outages, data breaches, and hacking or cyberattacks. Effective ALM has expanded to include not only management of the balance sheet, but also digital resilience—the ability of an institution to remain operational and to preserve its critical functions when impacted by significant technology disruptions.[35] As an example, the EU's DORA, or Digital Operational Resilience Act, promotes comprehensive ICT risk management and incident reporting.[36]

Another key area of concern is liquidity management. Digital banks often have a thinner physical footprint and reduced capital cushions, which exposes them to increased risks related to sudden withdrawals or market volatility. However, advanced analytic techniques and tools, particularly in real-time data monitoring, can reduce those risks through more accurate forecasting and stress testing. It can be said that working with a neobank that utilized an AI-based liquidity model to navigate higher periods of volatility, which highlights technology's emerging role on the ALM front.[37]

Reputational risk has also become more potent in today's digital world, where a single security breach, or even a bad customer experience, can greatly erode customer confidence in a very delicate matter of time, compounded by social media's vast reach. As a result, transparency, comprehensive data protection, and ethical governance, are key parts of any risk strategy.[38]

---

[34] Ciaponi et al. (2021, 50–67).
[35] Ahmed et al. (2024, 133).
[36] Alugoju (2024, 15–21).
[37] Walker and Morris (2021, 43).
[38] Perera et al. (2022, 28).

In conclusion, fintech and digital banking will reshape the risk management landscape to incorporate traditional ALM thinking, while navigating a world of digital resiliency. It should also be emphasized that while technology supports risk monitoring, inherent risks from tech implementations must be properly managed and respond to our ability to refresh our thinking and capabilities as global risk managers. In these circumstances, a successful path shall include marrying innovative risk technologies with sustainable risk governance practices, and institutional culture to remain responsible and resilient in an ever-increasing digital space.

14.2.2 Open Banking

Open banking entails a broad change in financial services, allowing people to securely share their bank account information with a third-party organization under an agreement with their bank using a standardized digital interface, usually an Application Programming Interface (API). It shifts the current system away from the traditional banking system where data was locked in, and heavily controlled by banks, toward a more transparent, competitive and customer-focused system. Arguably, open banking redefines the relationship between individuals, banks and the technology firms, inasmuch as it creates a framework for data portability and customer agency.[39]References 'Grabowski (2024), Billiam et al. (2022), Oh et al. (2024), IntechOpen (2025), Johnson and Scott (2019), Korejo et al. (2021), Turner (2012), Nabilou (2019), and Geva (1992)' are cited in the text but not provided in the reference list. Please provide the respective references in the list or delete these citations.All adjusted

The essence of open banking is rooted in the concept of data ownership. Banks allow customers to give third party organizations permission to access their account information, including account data, transaction history or payment data in order to provide customized services to the customer.[40] Open banking services range from personal finance software to budgeting apps to payment apps to investment apps and more. In promoting competition, open banking allows for the development of technology firms that develop products that designed to go up against the lethargic and often impeded traditional bank systems.

The EU took the lead on the topic with the PSD2, which has been applicable since 2018. This regulation obliged banks to allow licensed third parties using customer consent to access data in a secure manner. The PSD2 has introduced two new players to the environment—Account Information Service Providers (AISPs) which can allow the aggregation of data and provide a singular view of finances, and Payment Initiation Service Providers (PISPs) that allow customers to make direct payments using third-party apps.[41] This has lowered barriers to entry and

[39] Mohammed (2019, 31–43).
[40] Babina et al. (2025, 4–5).
[41] Grabowski (2024, 173–183).

increased consumer transparency accompanied by in unison with the wave of fintech innovation.

Worldwide, open banking is also gaining traction.[42] The UK's Open Banking Implementation Entity (OBIE), uses standardized APIs to promote interoperability and layering[43]; similar standards recently have evolved in Australia, Singapore, and Brazil.[44] All of these areas are heading towards "open finance" in which data is being shared around insurance, investments, and pensions. Open banking brings a set of challenges in scope of the privacy and cybersecurity realm. Sharing sensitive data, regardless of financial, opens up across several players has real implications around authentication, encryption, and how consent is obtained.

From a consumer perspective, open banking enables improved management of their finances, more personalized products, and added convenience given integrated platforms. From a bank perspective, open banking promotes collaboration and innovation but also puts competitive pressure for banks to be more agile and tech-enabled as the fintech operate. From my experience, traditional banks often struggle with the concept of openness and those that choose to lean into it will benefit competitively. The banks also must find the right balance between innovation and consumer trust, as once a consumer's trust is breached, the results are immediate. Overall, the concept of open banking facilitates a transformation to more inclusive and innovative forms of finance. Open banking promotes the consumer's participation in finance, and competitiveness among banks as it relates to deposit-taking and lending products.But ultimately, the success of open banking relies on legal schemes, strong data protection and the trust of the public.

14.2.3 Shadow Banking

Shadow banking refers to the performance of financial activities outside the traditional banking system and traditional regulation and oversight. Shadow banking includes hedge funds, money market funds, and a specific category of fintech platforms, and facilitates credit intermediation outside the placing of financial control occupying the central position of commercial banks.[45] Shadow banking emerged after decades of financial liberalization and deregulation, and has been accelerated by globalization and deregulation of capital controls. These transitions opened new opportunities for financial activities to occur outside the banking system. It created an environment for decentralized financial activities—repo markets, securitization, and over-the-counter derivatives—that occurred outside of the traditional banking system. Unlike traditional banks, shadow banks are better situated to fund long-term assets with short-term liabilities. This behaviour is efficient but also raises additional vulnerability for financial market instability. Considering the collapse

[42] Billiam et al. (2022, 67–88) and Oh et al. (2024, 7187).
[43] Colangelo and Khandelwal (2025, 4).
[44] Ibid., 5.
[45] Hasman and Samartin (2022, 101039) and Irani et al. (2021, 2182).

of Lehman Brothers in 2008, it was clear that there was an amplification of the mortgage crisis, which was also intensified by shadow banking's dependence on short-term funding.

Shadow banks have unique advantages. By investing in government and corporate bonds, derivatives, and other instruments, they provide liquidity to traditional banks and will fund high-risk, high-reward projects the banks would prefer to avoid. This flexibility helps to stimulate innovative and competitive sectors; typically benefiting consumers by providing additional financial products and potentially lower borrowing costs. For instance, shadow banking can enable SMEs to access capital that traditional banks viewed as too risky, helping to facilitate economic growth in financially disenfranchised sectors

At the same time, the absence of regulation invites systemic risks to increase. The opaque nature of shadow banks and their propensity to fund short-term liquidity can lead to a liquidity crisis, or "run," if either depositors or investors lose confidence. If depositors suddenly want their money back, and many depositors make the request at the same time, their financial institutions could be forced to sell illiquid assets in fire sales at depressed values, leading to a broad market instability. The 2008 global crisis demonstrated how non-performing loans, excessive leverage and unregulated shadow banking can cause contagion on a global scale, which we shouldn't forget with the experience of DeFi becoming increasingly common.[46]

The discussion surrounding shadow banking has largely been around regulation. As its structure is decentralized and its supporters argue that too much regulation will limit their innovation, others argue for regulatory measures to limit risks associated with shadow banking. The "too big to fail" concept, which protected most of the large financial institutions in the wake of the 2008 financial crisis, may decline as the shadow banking system distributes risk across a larger number of participants.[47] However, with the dispersion of risk also brings the challenge of monitoring and regulating individual companies, which could still cause systemic risk. Therefore, global institutions, like the FSB, are looking at solutions that allow for increased monitoring of risk exposures in shadow bank institutions.

In conclusion, shadow banking is clearly a complex means of adapting the global finance landscape to the new realities of the finance sector. It brings new jets of innovation and liquid resources to the global finance climate, but it also brings risks as there is no regulatory oversight. Its participation in the 2008 financial crisis shows how such institutions can add to systemic risks if not managed carefully. I have spent a lot of time discussing this with my colleagues as more scrutiny, balance, and oversight are required. As the financial comes to grips with the change global finance that is taking shape, there are benefits and tricky challenges of shadow banking that requires constant scrutiny to ensure that it contributes to an economic environment that supports stability rather than undermines it.

[46] Allen (2023, 966–968).
[47] Buckley et al. (2016, 277–354).

14.2.4 Money Laundering

ML, which in the Watergate context of the 1970s remained a colloquialism, is actualized in complex legal spheres that involve layers.[48] Essentially, ML consists of the exploitation where dirty money, or money derived from criminal activity, is made clean in order to conceal the source of said money while integrating said money back into the financial circuit. It is a crime that is not committed in a single instance but in a continuous manner that seeks to evade detection, confiscation, or seizure. Although definitions vary from country to country, they are all traced back to international standards, which provide a common standard for all nations. For example, the United Nations Convention against Transnational Organized Crime (Palermo Convention) has equated ML with the conversion or transfer of property, which is known to be the proceeds of crime, with the intent of disguising its origin or to avoid legal punishment for a person who is related to the crime.[49] At the regional level, the EU defines ML as intentionally masking the true character, origin, location, or ownership of property resulting from criminal activity. It further recognizes that money laundering may also occur despite the fact that the criminal acts, which resulted in the property, occurred in another EU member country or third countries. In the US, the Bank Secrecy Act of 1970 and the Money Laundering Control Act of 1986 are examples of early legislative measures enacted, which targeted the practice itself and focused on money transactions that attempt to mask the source and/or ownership of criminal profits.

Legally speaking, the process of money laundering consists of these three stages, which are placement (exfiltration or introduction of the illicit funds into the system), layering (routing these funds through layers of transactions), and finally, integration (laundering these funds as good old-fashioned honest-clean capital).[50] This systematically links money laundering to its predicate or source crimes, such as drug smuggling, corruption, or fraud, as without these crimes, the claim for laundering would be baseless.

Typically, AML statutes are anchored on two fundamental aspects of mens rea and actus reus in order to place the blame on the guilty party. In simpler terms, basically, at the beginning of the evaluation process, there has to be prior knowledge or reasonable cause on the part of the perpetrator that the funds came from unlawful activities. Then, the appropriate act has to manifest the guilty intent to alter, mix, or conceal the genuine identity of the objects or properties involved.[51] The current legal system has expanded the scope of liability to include wilful ignorance or recklessness, particularly for the financial sector and DCOs. They can be held liable for not turning in suspicious transactions despite not being part of the

---

[48] Korejo and Said (2021, 727) and Schneider and Niederlander (2008, 391).
[49] Korejo and Said (2021, 725–736) and Cantorias (2009, 45).
[50] Georgieva (2020, 24).
[51] Korejo and Said (2021, 730).

initial crime. The point is that compliance has come to realize that it is not merely a technicality but a legal necessity that has roots based on public law.[52]

14.2.4.1 Historical Development of AML Frameworks

The evolution of AML laws has kept stride with the development of crime, which has changed from local smuggling to global financial crime.[53] The earlier AML regulations date to the 1970s and 1980s and were primarily fuelled by illicit trafficking and organized crime. The US' Bank Secrecy Act of 1970 provided the foundation: requirements for record keeping and reporting. But then came an international push via the 1988 Vienna Convention and the 1989 creation of the FATF, propelling AML to the worldwide stage.[54] A second generation that integrated AML with CTF rules began to emerge following 9/11. The US PATRIOT Act (2001) further expanded due diligence and reporting. An effort to standardize AML/CTF rules began in Europe through Directives.[55] The present day, with its technological revolution, has brought along the third phase of AML, which includes a risk-based approach with technology solutions, also known as RegTech. The scope of compliance has widened to include fintechs, cryptoasset service providers, as well as non-bank financial entities.[56]

14.2.4.2 The Economic and Legal Rationale for AML

ML is more than a negative thing for a single individual; it is a danger to the entire international financial system. Therefore, rules under AML are not suggestions; they are essential for the health of the financial system as a whole. Dirty money circulating within the financial system causes it to become clouded, affecting the rate of exchange and creating unfair trade practices.[57] Money launderers are not just looking to make a buck; instead, they launder their funds and then invest them in a respectable company, affecting the market rate and driving out regular businesses, which unbalances the entire market. ML is also considered to relate to another negative phenomenon, which is tax evasion, resulting in lower government funds and a weaker public service system.[58]

Consider the financial system as a public good that the rule of law should protect.[59] Banks are not only retailers that offer credits and accept deposits; they are also guardians of the integrity of the financial system. The legitimacy of banks derives not only from legal mandate but also from public confidence. In realizing that laundered finances are used to fund grave crimes such as terrorism, drug trafficking, among other crimes, an effective antidote to money laundering has the

52 Tiwari et al. (2020, 271–303) and Korejo and Said (2021, 725–736).
53 Isolauri and Ameer (2023, 426–468).
54 Turner (2015, 547–559).
55 Arnone and Borlini (2011, 226–271).
56 McCarthy (2022, 186–199).
57 Korpela (2025, 65–80) and Roomen and Jonge (2024).
58 Storm (2013, 1437).
59 Ilgen (2018, 95–112).

symphony of breaking the cycle of crimes by not allowing its proceeds to finance further crimes. Even worse, those who acquire financial influence can undermine the rule of law by exerting political influence through corruption.

14.2.4.3 The Legal Relationship Between AML Compliance and Corporate Governance

AML compliance is no longer a backroom task but a core, unavoidable piece of modern corporate governance. In today's legal environment, compliance acts as the risk-management face of governance which helps the financial institutions to practice prudence, transparency, and ethical integrity. It is within this evolution of the AML regime that compliance, from being a technical side job, came to the very core of legal accountability and corporate responsibility. Globally, boards bear the ultimate legal responsibility for an institution's AML framework. This governance mandate encompasses a number of core responsibilities. The board is required to officially sanction robust AML policies and ensure these policies match a risk-based legal methodology. Additionally, it is their responsibility to ensure that internal monitoring systems are appropriate and to ensure that staff training is ongoing to empower personnel to identify complex money-laundering schemes. It is also a significant governance requirement to oversee that SARs are filed appropriately with regulators, as failure to report can generate direct liability.[60]

In case that implementing agency gets involved in money laundering, they are not simply fined for these infractions. Rather, they may be subject to a range of enforcement actions, including but not limited to significant financial penalties, being forced to implement independent compliance monitors, or even having them revoke their charters. Today's legislation sometimes reaches beyond the corporate structure, allowing district attorneys to prosecute executives who turn a blind eye to illegal conduct within a corporation. In fact, a continued disregard for AML regulation may be viewed by the judiciary as a display of management ignorance, mismanagement, or even a breach of a corporation's fiduciary responsibility to its shareholders and the public.[61] Against this background, a proper AML compliance program is more than a nuisance as a key to a stable financial system.

14.2.4.4 The Three-Stage Model of Money Laundering and Legal Implications

ML typically unfolds in three distinct stages: placement, layering, and integration. The first stage, known as placement, involves introducing dirty money into the financial system for the first time. Since large cash deposits or purchases can easily trigger detection, primary preventive measures include KYC rules, mandatory reporting of large or suspicious cash transactions, and strict limit on cash-based activities. Criminals may attempt to place funds by depositing cash into bank accounts, buying high-value goods (movable or immovable property), or using

---

[60] See, Çemberci et al. (2022, 1020–1032) and Castro et al. (2025, 1–30).

[61] See, Dunaway (2025, 255) and Pollman (2019, 2013).

cash-intensive businesses. Then follows the layering process, which is a very complicated series of financial transactions intended to reduce any trail which might lead back to the crime committed. This is where banks have the responsibility for transaction monitoring, Enhanced Due Diligence (EDD), or finding out who actually owns the beneficiary. Funds might jump between different accounts, or offshore territories might enter the equation, or a trade-based ML scheme might be employed. Thirdly, in the integration phase, the money goes back into the legal system as if it originated from a genuine source. The legal mechanisms used in this phase include asset tracing, seizure, and reporting of suspicious investments. The funds are usually invested in property, valuable commodities, and capital in business ventures, and it is almost impossible to distinguish between laundered money and clean money. This occurs at the junction between criminal law and administrative law. A process like ML is a criminal offense that has consequential criminal law charges against those involved. On the other hand, the banking or financial institutions involved in this process also have responsibilities stemming from administrative law such as maintaining files and being audited.[62]

14.2.4.5 The Preventive Legal Architecture of AML

AML laws both punish and prevent at the same time. They obligate the financial institutions and specified non-financial businesses to become the frontline protectors against financial crimes. The objective of forming the preventive system is obvious: to prevent the misuse of the banking and financial system to launder criminal funds.

An integral part of this preventive measure is Customer Due Diligence (CDD), which entails customer identity verification, discovering the ultimate beneficial owner, and comprehending the reason for each and every transaction. Simplified customer due diligence is applied in cases where the risk of money laundering is low (e.g., government bodies or low-value payments); enhanced due diligence is mandatory for high-risk customers, for instance, politically exposed persons or persons from high-risk jurisdictions.[63] Continuous monitoring and tracking are another important lines of defence. It is necessary to monitor all transactions throughout the relationship with a customer to ensure that everything is in line with the customer's risk profile and source of funds. Continuous monitoring enables early detection of any deviating patterns.[64] The financial institution record-keeping obligation is closely related to monitoring and tracking because financial institutions must maintain all customer information and records of transactions for a certain period of time to facilitate 'follow the money' analysis.

Lastly, SARs are important for firms to report any suspicious transaction that appears to be related to money laundering or terrorist activity to the financial intelligence units (PPATK in Indonesia). This is monitored by relevant authorities to

[62] Georgieva (2020, 23–37), Vlcek (2024, 35–48), Reuter and Truman (2004, 25–43), and Arman and Nendi (2023, 353–363).

[63] Chitimira and Munedzi (2023, 53–62) and Pol (2020, 1–22).

[64] Harras and Salahddine (2025, 73–85).

ensure that it is in line with international best practices regarding FATF recommendations and the principles of the Basel Committee. This is monitored by OJK or Bank Indonesia.[65]

14.2.4.6 Challenges in AML Enforcement

The struggle with ML today is also ensnared in a complex matrix. While the world is seeing more laws being crafted to deal with the problem, the complexity inherent in the structure itself makes it difficult for effective anti-money laundering to function. Where globalization, global transactions, and digital payments continue to go untracked, it dampens the effectiveness of transparency within the financial sector. Shell companies, combined with complex trusts that are set up to hide beneficial holders, continue to confound regulators who are trying to follow the money for illicit activities. Throw in cryptocurrency and decentralized finance, so that a regulatory gap is further stretched beyond the reach of central regulation. Without the momentum of global cooperation, along with regulatory laws that are country-specific, a regulatory gap beckons global money launderers to take advantage of the vulnerabilities. Getting past all that now requires effective information-sharing pipelines, which would involve global MoU, for instance, between central regulators, banks, and regulatory law enforcers.

All in all, AML regulation has now become an integral part of the wider oversight and corporate governance framework. It imposes a substantial burden on financial institutions by entrusting them with the primary responsibility—traditionally held by the state—of ensuring the integrity of the financial system. Banks and other obliged entities now serve as frontline gatekeepers, actively preventing the entry and circulation of illicit funds.

14.2.4.7 Final Observations

The global regime to combat money laundering has developed from soft-law instruments and international treaties that have increasingly strengthened to make up a binding regulative framework at the national level.[66] At the core of it all is the FATF, established in 1989 through the G7, which is the central driver of global AML/CTF regulation. Its 40 action items, drawn up in 1990 and subsequently reviewed a number of times, with the last revision completed in 2012, form a comprehensive policy approach to combating ML.[67]

The FATF's advice pertains to a broad spectrum of issues such as making money laundering and terrorist financing crimes; performing customer due diligence and maintaining records; reporting suspicious transactions; controlling non-financial businesses and professions; and encouraging worldwide cooperation, mutual legal aid, and seizure of proceeds of crime. Even if these rules are not binding on countries in a legally obligatory fashion, they have become binding de facto by virtue

---

[65] Sunarmi and Lubis (2022, 103–116).
[66] Pursiainen (2022, 135–172).
[67] Gathii (2010, 1–20) and Pavlidis (2021, 765–773).

of peer reviews and the reputational risk of a country being identified as a non-cooperative country. The FATF employs a 'name and shame' tactic in this manner because this has become a worldwide enforcement tool.[68]

The UN framework is reinforced in the following key treaties, which are inter-connected: the 1988 Convention against the Use, Possession, and Transfer of Illicit Drugs for Non-Medicinal and Scientific Purposes in the Vienna Convention, the 2000 Palermo Convention, and the 2003 Merida Convention against corruption. These conventions collectively require that states make the crime of ML illegal, establish financial intelligence units (FIUs), and cooperate in the international investigation process as well as in the recovery of assets. Thus, the global AML system represents a mix between criminal, administrative, and public international law to make the integrity of finances a collective responsibility in the international system.

14.2.5 Transfer of Electronic Funds

Electronic fund transfer is essentially a matter of transferring money electronically—fast, secure, efficient, and streamlined. These payments work through interbanking networks, Swift, EFT, and other frameworks, governed by tight regulatory principles. EFT, in a legal regulatory context, deals essentially with verifying payments, safeguarding information, validating consumer identities, as well as combating fraudulent practices. Its analysis in the study of Lehmann explores its relevance to implementing global financial instruments, together with their regulatory legal frameworks.

14.2.5.1 The Evolution of Electronic Payments

The EFT system represents the most far-reaching change in the law of banking since negotiable instruments first emerged. Its precursor harks back to the 1870s, when Western Union began moving money without requiring the physical presence of people, and over time it has grown into the immediate transfer of funds across digital networks, abolishing settlement times. The leap accelerated with ARPANET in the 1960s, a forerunner of the internet, and when Stanford Federal Credit Union became the first bank to offer online banking in 1994, banking moved from brick-and-mortar halls to cyberspace. This technological upheaval compelled traditional principles of payment to extend into cyberspace, bringing along hordes of pressing legal questions. The laws today undertake electronic data messages as valid payment orders, but we still do need new rules about how payments are authorized, how data integrity is guaranteed, and cybersecurity is managed. Cross-border transfers introduce jurisdictional confusion, and who bears responsibility for mistakes or fraud is still one of the central questions regarding the future feasibility of the digital financial system.

[68] Young (2019, 122–141) and Otudor and Bagheri (2023, 1289–1301).

Whereas the increasing adoption of digital payment methods has led to a point where trust is now based on technological infrastructure that is secure—and requires, for example, biometric security. The emergence of platforms like PayPal, which allows people to transfer funds via an email, and Square, which allows small businesses to accept payment even using a smartphone, has made financial inclusion a reality. However, they pose a regulatory dilemma.[69] The new law, thus, accommodates the online world by redefining the traditional understanding of the banking sector to keep up with the anonymity of the online world.

14.2.5.2 Legal Foundations

EFTs function in a corridor where law, contacts, and international standards intersect. At the domestic level, you will notice a few bread-and-butter frameworks. These include the United States Electronic Fund Transfer Act (EFTA) of 1978, which protects consumers in debit card transactions, ATM transactions, and direct deposit transactions; the PSD2 aims to increase competition, security, and innovation within payment services; and the United Kingdom's Payment Services Regulations of 2017.[70] Aside from law, the nature of the relationship between customers and financial institutions is governed by contracts. The agreements contain the service terms, which include fees, the cap on liability for unauthorized transfers, and the procedure for reversing an error. These agreements are the private law framework underlying EFTs and permit contracting parties to obligate themselves within the framework established by mandatory law, with respect to authentication and use practices.

International norms have great significance regarding cross-border funds transfers. Bodies such as SWIFT have implemented standardized messaging patterns that maintain confidentiality and efficiency for interbank communication. The UNCITRAL Model Law for Electronic Commerce from 1996 provides a good starting platform; it states that online transactions must be equivalent to paper-based transactions and therefore maintain a standardized environment for everyone concerned with global commerce and finance. With these joint guidelines at work, an electronic funds transfer becomes a valid and legal transaction as soon as the customer signs off on it via a safe and secure authentication mechanism—imagine multi-factor checks that verify the intention and prevent fraud. The bank will follow this mandate in good faith and complete it as soon as possible without unnecessary delay. Finally, to maintain transparency at all levels, it is imperative to ensure that this electronic funds transfer has a way to record and trail the transaction correctly.

Large money transactions between different banks are actually the motor that fuels the global financial engine. This is supported through a network of book transfers and communication wires. Of course, from a very basic perspective, any financial transaction could actually be settled through just adjusting one's debit

[69] Jindal (2023), Geva (2020). See also, Pacifici (2015, 90–115) and Liu et al. (2015, 372–391).
[70] Raiwa-Rietbroek (2020).

and credit records if both sides of that transaction held accounts within the very same bank. This is not, however, the case when dealing with two separate institutions. Today, these transactions go through very wide electronic conduits. The messaging is handled by SWIFT, netting and clearing by CHIPS, while Fedwire is responsible for the instantaneous settling of the payments. SWIFT, known fully as the Society for Worldwide Interbank Financial Telecommunications, is not a money transfer facility but a communications facility exclusively set up for the purpose of transferring money instructions among banks. The society is based in Belgium, with an identity-verification system for the sender and the receiver done through encrypting algorithms.

In the land of large-value payments connected with the US dollar, two systems dominate: Fedwire and CHIPS. Fedwire, operated by the Federal Reserve, is a Real-Time Gross Settlement (RTGS) system-every individual transfer is treated and settled separately in real-time central bank money. CHIPS, operated by the New York Clearing House, handles nearly 95% of all international dollar transfers, and its new architecture provides for real-time final settlement through the constant matching and netting of payments multilaterally throughout the day. The contrast is straightforward: Fedwire is immediate and final; CHIPS offers added efficiency in liquidity by allowing the net positions at the end of the day to determine settlement.[71] These systems are underpinned by a robust legal framework and conditions of participation. Prior to 1991 the United States had no federal legislation for such transfers but today, Sect. 4A of the Uniform Commercial Code is the principal federal law applicable to large-value fund transfers. That section addresses, among other things, the question of who is liable if a transfer goes astray or is executed in error, the contractual impact of the payment, and when settlement becomes final. Federal Reserve Regulation J supplements that law by adopting UCC 4A's rights and responsibilities for Fedwire participants.

The running of these systems is covered by a legal framework and a set of uniform participation agreements. Before 1991, there was no federal trade law in the U.S., although currently the UCC Sect. 4A has become the key legal basis for massive funds wire transfers. Section 4A of UCC regulates who bears responsibility for unauthorized or allegedly erroneous transfers, payment rights under commitments, as well as when finality of payment can occur. Federal Reserve Regulation J adopts UCC Sect. 4A provisions of the rights and responsibilities of Fedwire participants.[72] In recent years, efforts to combat money laundering and technology advances have altered how such systems function. Starting 1996, new regulations mandate that payment messages must have sender and recipient details for the entire process—a mechanism known as the "travel rule." Or, where records were stored only on microfiche and where past search retrievals were difficult, now banks such as Chase Manhattan can access history from years back with merely a keystroke. In sum, the global financial system remains fast and secure because

[71] US Congress (1995, 28).
[72] US Congress (1995, 120).

of three pillars: SWIFT's messaging language, the sound consensus networks of Fedwire and CHIPS, and protective laws such as UCC 4A. This is more than an efficiency mechanism—it is a key governance tool in overseeing risks in the system and monitoring financial frauds.[73]

14.2.5.3 Regulatory Standards and Consumer Protection

Banks have enforced two-factor verification and strict customer verification procedures in an effort to prevent unauthorized fund transfers. Based on EU PSD2 rules, banks have been directed to maintain secure electronic communications and incur liability for any unauthorized or fraudulent transactions unless it is proved that there is customer negligence. Similarly, U.S. Regulation E protects consumers from unauthorized electronic debits if they notify their banks about any irregularities in time. Such liability-sharing reflects a concept of risk distribution, in which banks and customers demonstrate reasonable diligence.

In view of the personal and financial information dealt with in EFTs, a failure to comply with GDPR has serious implications for banks. Data has to be processed in a legal manner. Encryption of that information has to be done. Data has to be transferred only to countries that have adequate safeguards. Data breach could result in a fine or license loss.

14.2.5.4 Legal Characterization of Electronic Transfers

14.2.5.4.1 Payment Finality: When Does Payment Occur in an Electronic Transfer?

The timing of an actual completion of an electronic funds transfer is dependent upon a legal interpretation of "payment finality." On a fundamental principle of "receiver finality," a "payment is final as soon as the recipient bank accepts it and is bound to the creditor." The payer no longer has a unilateral right to rescind a mandatorily transferable instruction once the creditor bank has credited funds to the beneficiary's account or notified the creditor, which is a sign of legal finality. This has been stipulated in various norms, such as the EU Finality Directive (98/26/EC), primarily to reduce risks in case of bankruptcy situations.

There is a very important difference between these new digital assets: e-money and stablecoins. E-money refers to regulated digital money issued by authorized institutions. It usually provides a 100% fiat-to-cash money-back guarantee. On the other hand, stablecoins are market-oriented private assets. In any case, these legal systems are intended to ensure that debts are finally cleared when it comes to payment transactions.[74]

14.2.5.4.2 Errors, Fraud, and Reversal

Erroneous or fraudulent transfers put the law in a very nuanced region where property rights, unjustified enrichment, and banking laws converge. Conventional

[73] Ibid., 20, 28.

[74] See, Geva (2003, 33–59; 2009, 633–677).

notions within restitution theory have a hard time adjusting to accommodate awards that have to be carved differently, particularly with eft payments. Cases and the law classify various rules of liability regarding the nature of the transfer. In the case of unauthenticated transfers where the customer's payment instruction actually reached the bank without the customer's consent–for instance, through forgery–normally the bank will incur the loss since the bank acted without authority. However, in these scenarios, the bank does not have the authority to debit the customer's account but may still recover the funds through restitution.[75]

Concerning the issue of mistaken transfers, a cause of action for money had and received may be available to recover the money on the basis of the recipient's unjust enrichment. The important factor is that the transfer of the money is a result of the mistake causing the recipients' unjust enrichment, which is itself negated by the mistake that impinges the sender's subjective intention to make the transfer. When it comes to fraud, particularly APP scams, the person who is a customer is tricked into making the payment instruction. In this case, the "push" payment takes place when the customer instructs the bank to make a payment to a third party. The bank's liability is questioned in the context of the duty of care and system security.[76]

▶ **Important**

Case Study: Philipp v Barclays Bank UK plc [2023] UKSC 25

This case represents a precedent in suits involving APP fraud victims against their banks. Mrs. Philipp was deceived by fraudsters who fraudulently presented themselves as police and financial auditors. She consequently paid £700,000 in two sums to an account in the United Arab Emirates. Mrs. Philipp sued Barclays claiming the bank had a quincecare duty. Finally, the Supreme Court held that the Quincecare obligation did not apply to APP fraud. The bank's primary obligation and duty were to carry out their client's clear and unequivocal instructions. As put forward by Mrs. Philipp, her instructions were given to the bank in person and with knowledge, and so it was no business of the bank to suspect them to be fraudulent and breach her instructions. While the Court did not dismiss the bank's fall-back claim, 'retrieval duty,' attempting to recover the money once it knew about the fraud, it pointed out that such a possibility was highly unlikely.[77]

---

[75] Booysen (2024, 149–158) and Shum (2025, 43–69).

[76] Shum (2025, 43–69).

[77] Philipp v Barclays Bank UK plc [2023] UKSC 25; Booysen (2024) and McIlroy and Sethi-Smith (2023, 513–516).

14.2.5.5 Cross-Border Transfers and International Regulation

Cross-border electronic fund transfers stand at the junction of numerous legal systems, in a complicated interaction whereby several countries' laws might apply all at once. The basic question sounds simple: which law—originator's, intermediary's, or beneficiary's-should apply to a transfer throughout its stages of initiation, transmission, and completion? Accordingly, the technical and procedural aspects will usually be subject to the law of the place where the payment system is situated (*lex loci* operationis). Contracts, on the other hand, will be governed by the law which the parties have selected (the proper law of their contract). Nevertheless, the more familiar concept of lex loci delicti-that is, the law of the place where a tort is said to have taken place-manifests some persistence, particularly in Australian and English claims with tort-like character. The application of this principle commonly gives rise to misgivings about certainty and predictability, since it may prove difficult to specify the exact location of a digital "tort".[78]

The global aspect of international payments indicates there could be other ways in which disputes can be settled rather than visiting the courts. According to Haryanto, financial scandals abroad, as well as the regulation gap in international payments, may hamper the ability of financial consumers in seeking justice. It can be seen here that in the aspect of financial consumer protection, there is a potential for regulatory competition when seeking enforcement abroad, thereby calling for more stringent financial regulation internationally.[79]

In transnational disputes involving different nationals from different states, the impasses tend to revolve around who will govern the matter—and where the matter will be tried—"the seat of court" and the issue of the autonomy of the respective parties. A critical aspect of transnational arbitration that the national court shall recognize the agreed framework if the award is to be enforced.[80] However, within regions involving public policy, such as payment systems, the landscape changes. In such cases, local consumer safeguards or the need to abide by AML/KYC laws might qualify as overriding mandatory laws, leading to a possible conflict between the contractual parties' choice of law and the law applicable to them.

Electronic money transfers are closely monitored as a means to ensure the integrity of the international finance system. In the focal point of the finance system oversight is Recommendation 16, which is also known as the 'Travel Rule', introduced by the FATF. This ensures all fund transfers contain information regarding the origin and the receiver to ensure the flow of money can be traced from cover to cover.[81] The current regime prefers a risk-based approach over a broad, generic solution. This has been reinforced in a conformity guide published by the European Banking Authority's document numbered EBA/GL/2022/05, stating that a senior AML/CFT Compliance Officer ought to be assigned and risk management

[78] Pietriche (2015, 1–38).
[79] Haryanto (2024, 339–348).
[80] Goode (2001, 19–39).
[81] Stanley and Buckley (2016, 1–24).

ought to be integrated into operations. This is a process that is both a KYC and CDD procedure that analyses conduct.[82]

The incorporation of AML/CTF requirements might give rise to a challenge within financial inclusion. A very stringent approach to de-risking might force genuine customers to resort to informal transactions, particularly within low-income sections, thereby increasing the number of account closures. The current regulatory model strikes a balance between ensuring security and ensuring that the financial sector remains open, using innovations in technology such as digital identity and real-time tracking.

14.2.5.6 Digital Transformation and Emerging Instruments

The shift to digital finance has enabled fund transfers that reach beyond classic bank wires and card payments. One of the most disruptive of these is instant payments, real-time reconciliation systems, transfers built on blockchain, distributed ledger technology, central bank digital currencies, and stablecoins. These innovations alter the way liquidity is managed by allowing payments to be cleared within seconds, reducing costs in cross-border transfers, and providing enhanced access to financial inclusion. They also challenge us to consider, anew, entrenched legal conceptions relating to money, payments, and reconciliation. One of the current hot issues is whether a digital token-whether crypto assets, stablecoins, or CBDCs-constitutes "electronic money" for the purposes of existing laws. Taking the European Union as an example, the definition of electronic money in the Electronic Money Directive 2009/110/EC is a prepaid reservoir of value that can only be issued by an authorized electronic money institution. Second, regulators and scholars continue to diverge upon whether this definition captures a blockchain-based token or whether a completely new category of legal classification is required.[83]

Despite the many different technologies for moving money that we have at our disposal, the basic legal principle has remained the same all this time. It is the continuity of function principle. In simpler terms, a payment system will qualify no matter the technology it employs if the end result is the debtor's final discharge of the debt. It's no different principle than what has been practiced from the time of the Romans to the present-day systems for payments. It's all based on the ideology of technological neutrality.[84] So when making a standard bank transfer, a real-time payments network transaction, or a stablecoin transaction facilitated by the use of the blockchain technology, if the transaction leads to the final discharge of the debt, it's considered a payment. The debt is settled, and the risk has changed.

14.2.5.7 Concluding Observations

The transition from cheques to EFTs reflects the general trend in banking law—moving from paper-based formalities to the fast-paced world of electronic

[82] Shahin (2013, 109–118).
[83] See, Moloney (2014), Zetzsche et al. (2021), and Nabilou (2019)
[84] Reed (2012) and Guimarães (2012).

payments. The goals do not change, however—the search for certainty, integrity, and accounting. Both systems illustrate how the law adjusts with technology but retains its core meaning. The foreign check is based on signature verification and in-person delivery; the wire transaction relies on encryption coding. Each situation has trust as a foundation—the legal recognition of an obligation fulfilled. In conclusion, it seems that the above discussion of the legal treatment of payments instruments is significant to a fundamental issue of financial law. Money is not simply a means of economics; it is a function of confidence and is constructed as a confidence or a hope as illustrated above.

Chapter Summary

Chapter 14 examines a fundamental paradigm shift in modern finance: the mandatory integration of ESG factors into financial decision-making, governance, and regulation. This development expands the focus of finance beyond profit-driven metrics to explicitly incorporate environmental and social externalities. Essential concepts and legal foundations are covered. In terms of the legal impetus, the foundation is rooted in international agreements (e.g., Paris Agreement, UN SDGs) and the legal recognition that fiduciary duties of fund managers must now be interpreted in light of long-term sustainability risks. In this context, the concept of sustainable finance (SF), refers to the process of incorporating ESG considerations into investment decisions—resulting in increased investments in sustainable activities—is playing an increasingly central role. The feasibility of sustainability finance is directly related to how investors evaluate ESG criteria, which constitute a non-financial risk and opportunity framework utilized by investors. These include environmental (climate change, pollution), social (labour rights, diversity), and governance (board structure, corruption) considerations.

The Regulatory Architecture: Focus on the EU Model. The European Union's Sustainable Finance Action Plan represents the most advanced global framework in this domain. The concrete manifestation of this general framework is based on fundamental regulations that define sustainable economic activities and classify financial products accordingly. The EU Taxonomy Regulation serves as the core legal instrument establishing a binding, science-based classification system that defines which economic activities qualify as environmentally sustainable, such as those related to climate change mitigation and adaptation. This regulation provides a standardized framework for sustainable finance. The SFDR imposes mandatory transparency requirements on financial market participants, such as asset managers, regarding the integration of sustainability risks and adverse impacts (e.g., PAI) into their processes. It also establishes legal distinctions among financial products, including Article 6, 8, and 9 funds. For these classification and transparency obligations to be meaningfully implemented in financial markets, corporate reporting must also be strengthened accordingly. The NFRD and the CSRD require large companies to disclose specific non-financial and sustainability information. This disclosure supplies essential data for financial institutions to comply with the SFDR and the EU Taxonomy Regulation.

In terms of systemic and prudential risk integration, three types of risks have been argued as climate-related financial risks, physical risks and transition risks. As per climate-related financial risks, it is required for banks and insurers to implement management strategies. In this regard, physical risks refer to direct economic losses resulting from climate change events, such as floods and droughts while transition risks encompass financial risks that emerge from the transition to a low-carbon economy, including stranded assets and policy changes. It has also been noted that regulation on green banking involves central banks and prudential authorities, such as the BCBS and the NGFS, integrating climate-related risks into supervisory processes, including Green Stress Tests and potentially capital requirements under the Green Basel model. Climate risk is increasingly recognized as a source of macro-prudential and network risk. Accordingly, the chapter also touched on the legal liability for greenwashing activities, which mislead customers about a product's sustainability credentials. Strict disclosure rules (e.g. MiFID II) create a basis for legal liability for misrepresentation, fraud, and breach of fiduciary duty.

Review Questions

1. Distinguish between physical risk and transition risk within the context of a commercial bank's balance sheet. Furthermore, construct an argument for why prudential supervisors—such as central banks—should treat climate risk as a significant source of systemic or macro-prudential risk.
2. Define the EU Taxonomy Regulation and identify its principal legal objective. In your analysis, explain how this framework serves to mitigate market fragmentation and combat the phenomenon of greenwashing. Critically assess the evolution of the legal construct of fiduciary duty, specifically regarding the obligations of care and loyalty. How have substantial jurisdictions adapted these duties to mandate the consideration of ESG (Environmental, Social, and Governance) factors?
3. Explain the legal distinctions between Article 8 Funds ("light green") and Article 9 Funds ("dark green") as classified under the Sustainable Finance Disclosure Regulation (SFDR). Elaborate on the enhanced disclosure requirements expected of Article 9 Funds.
4. Define the term "greenwashing" in a legal context. Enumerate and analyze at least two legal bases—such as fraud, breach of contract, or securities law violations—upon which an investor might initiate litigation against a financial institution for the deceptive representation of its sustainability profile.

5. Present a policy-driven argument for the potential integration of environmental factors into the programming of a Central Bank Digital Currency (CBDC). What are the legal implications of such programming, particularly concerning privacy rights and monetary neutrality?
6. Describe the functional relationship between corporate disclosure mandates, specifically the NFRD and CSRD, and the ability of financial institutions to comply with SFDR and EU Taxonomy requirements. To what extent does the quality and standardisation of ESG data represents a primary challenge for legal compliance?◄

References

Adegbite M (2025) Data privacy and data security challenges in digital finance. J Dig Secu Foren 2(1):6–19

Ahmed F, Hussain A, Khan S, Malik A, Asim M, Ahmad S, El-Affendi M (2024) Digital risk and financial inclusion: balance between auxiliary innovation and protecting digital banking customers. Risks 12(8):133

Allen H (2023) DeFi: shadow banking 2.0? Willi Mary L Rev 64(4):919–968

Alugoju N (2024) Digital Operational Resilience Act (DORA). Int J Comp Eng Technol 15(6):911–921

Aramonte S, Huang W, Schrimpf A (2021) DeFi risks and the decentralisation illusion. BIS Quart Rev: 21–36 https://www.bis.org/publ/qtrpdf/r_qt2112b.pdf. Accessed 31 Jan 2026

Arman M, Nendi I (2023) Money laundering: a three step secrete game. J Soc Sci 2(3):353–363

Arnone M, Borlini L (2011) International anti-money laundering programs: empirical assessment and issues in criminal regulation. J Mon Lound Cont 13(3):226–271

Babina T, Bahaj S, Buchak G et al (2025) Customer data access and fintech entry: early evidence from open banking. J Finan Econ 103950

Booysen S (2024) The bank's duty of care as payment agent. Sing J Leg Stud 149–158

Boussaidi R (2022) Implications of the overconfidence bias in presense of private information: evidence from MENA stock markets. Int J Financ Econ 27(3):3660–3678

Buckley R, Arner D, Zetzsche D, Selga E (2020) Techrisk. Sing J Leg Stud:35–62

Buckley R, Avgouleas E, Arner D (2016) Reconceptualising global finance and its regulation. Cambridge University Press, Cambridge, pp 277–354

Calomiris C, Mason J (2004) Credit card securitization and regulatory arbitrage. J Finan Serv Res 26(1):5–27

Cantorias M (2009) Anti-money laundering/combating financing of terrorism: a Philippine perspective on a donor-driven initiative. Arel L Pol Rev 10(1):42–61

Castro F, Leonori L, Giorgio S (2025) A comprehensive review of literature on compliance function post-basel iii. J Finan Reg Comp 4:1–30

Clark R, Reed J, Sunderland T (2018) Bridging funding gaps for climate and sustainable development: pitfalls, progress and potential of private finance. L Use Poli 71:335–346

Chitimira H, Munedzi S (2023) Overview international best practices on customer due diligence and related anti-money laundering process. J Mon Laund Cont 26(7):53–62

Ciaponi G, Dalbon F, Fabris P, Frigero C, Longobardi E, Lucernati R, Pattarello I, Repetto E, Terrizzano F (2021) Reputational risk for financial institutions: a proposal of quantitative approach. Risk Manage Mag 16(2):50–67

Coakley J, Huang W (2020) P2P lending and outside entrepreneurial finance. Eur J Financ 29(13):1–18

Colangelo G, Khandelwal P (2025) The many shades of open banking: a comparative analysis of rationales and models. Inter Pol Rev 14(1):1–23

Çemberci M, Başar D, Yurtsever Z (2022) The Effect of institutionalization level on the relationship of corporate governance with money laundering activity: an example of the BIST corporate governance index. Borsa Istanbul Rev 22(5):1020–1032

Davies G, Brooks P (2017) Practical challenges of implementing behavioral finance: reflections from the field. In: Baker K, Filbeck G, Ricciardi V (eds), Financial behavior: players, services, products, and markets. Oxford University Press, Oxford, 542–560

Demirel H, Leendertse W, Volker L (2022) Mechanisms for protecting returns on private investments in public infrastructure projects. Int J Project Manage 40(3):155–166

Dempere J, Alamash E, Mattos P (2024) Unveiling the truth: greenwashing in sustainable finance. Front Sustain 5(1):1–14

Dias D, Chalwe-Mulenga M, Chamas T, and Alonso T (2024) Exclusion risks in climate-related financial regulation: an analytical framework. https://www.cgap.org/sites/default/files/2024-12/WP_Climate%20Regulation_Complete.pdf. Accessed 31 Jan 2026

Dikau S, Volz U (2021) Central bank mandates, sustainability objectives and the promotion of green finance. Ecol Econ 184:107022

Dunaway D (2025) Uncovering red flags in the silver state: recognizing and expanding the corporate duty of oversight in Nevada. Nevada L J 26(1):255–287

Fatemi A, Fooladi I (2013) Sustainable finance: a new paradigm. Glob Financ J 24(2):101–113

Fakhoury S (2020) Market efficiency vs. behavioral finance. Proche-Orient, Études En Manage 32:13–31

Farrell M (2003) Principal-agency risk in project finance. Int J Project Manage 21(8):547–561

Fenwick M, McCahery J, Vermeulen E (2018) Fintech and the financing of SMEs and entrepreneurs: from crowdfunding to marketplace lending. In: Cumming D, Hornuf L (eds) The economics of crowdfunding: startups, portals and investor behavior. Palgrave Macmillan, Cham, pp 103–130

Fox D, Green S (2019) Cryptocurrencies in public and private law. Oxford University Press

Gathii J (2010) The financial action task force and global administrative law. J Prof Law 197:1–20

Geva B (2003) Settlement finality and associated risks in funds transfers—when does interbank payment occur? Penn State Int L Rev 22(1):33–59

Geva B (2009) Payment finality and discharge in fund transfers. Chic-Kent L Rev 83(2):633–677

Geva B (2020) Electronic payments: guide on legal and regulatory reforms and best practices for developing countries. Osgoode Legal Studies Research Paper. https://papers.ssrn.com/sol3/papers.cfm?abstract_id=3631155. Accessed 8 July 2026

Georgieva N (2020) Concept, definition and characteristics of the money loundering phenomenon. J Proc Manage New Technol Int 8(2) 23–37

Goode R (2001) The role of the lex loci arbitri in international commercial arbitration. Arbitr Int 17(1):19–39

Grennan J (2025) FinTech regulation in the United States: past, present, and future. Cambridge University Press, Cambridge

Guimarães M (2012) The debit and credit card framework contract. https://indret.com/wp-content/themes/indret/pdf/892_en.pdf. Accessed 30 Jan 2026

Harras M, Salahddine M (2025) Tracking financial crime through code and law: a review of regtech applications in anti-money laundering and terrorism financing. Corpor L Govern Rev 7(3):73–85

Haryanto J (2024) Cross-border enforcement of consumer banking law. West Sci L Hum Rig 2(4):339–348

Hasman A, Samartin M (2022) Leaving the darkness: the emergence of shadow banks. J Financ Stab 61:101039

Ilgen F (2018) Financial stability as a global public good and relevant systemic regulation as a problem of collective action. In: Philippe Bance (ed) Providing goods and commons toward coproduction and new forms of governance for a revival of public action. CIREC, pp 95–112

Illiashenko P (2017) Behavioral finance: history and foundations. Visnyk Nat Bank Ukraine 239:28–54
Irani R, Iyer R, Meisenzahl R, Peydro J (2021) The rise of shadow banking: evidence from capital regulation. Rev Fin Stud 34:2181–2235
Isolauri E, Ameer I (2023) Money laundering as a transational business phenomenon: a systematic review and future agenda. Crit Perspect Int Bus 19(3):426–468
Jindal N (2023) The evolution of digital payments and its impact on the economy. https://www.researchgate.net/publication/374550077_Evolution_of_Digital_payments_and_its_impact_on_the_Economy. Accessed 8 July 2026
Kahneman D, Tversky A (1979) Prospect theory: an analysis of decision under risk. Econometrica 47(2):263–291
Kalinowski T (2024) The green climate fund and private sector climate finance in the global south. Clim Pol 24(3):281–296
Korejo M, Said R (2021) The concept of money laundering: a quest for legal definition. J Mon Laund Cont 24(4):725–736
Korpela S (2025) Between a rock and a hard place: managing the conflict between anti-money laundering and financial inclusion. J Mon Laund Cont 28(7):65–80
Lagoarde-Ségot T (2024) Greenwashing and sustainable finance: an approach anchored in the philosophy of science. Cur Opin Environ Sustain 66:101397
Lannoo K (2023) Regulating crypto and cyberware in the EU. In: Adamski D, Amtenbrink F, Haan J (eds) The Cambridge handbook of European monetary, economic and financial integration. Cambridge University Press, Cambridge, pp 539–552
Li W (2024) Analysis of financial market efficiency. Int J Glob Econ Manage 2(2):244–253
Liu J, Kauffman R, Ma D (2015) Competition, cooperation and regulation: understanding the evolution of the mobile payments technology ecosystem. Elect Commer Res Appl 14(5):372–391
Lokuwaduge C, Silva K (2022) ESG risk disclosure and the risk of green washing. Australasian Accoun Bus Fin J 16(1):146–159
Lombardi F, Stocchetti Lina Strandvåg Nagell Hanna Biro (2023) The EU sustainable finance taxonomy's spillover effects on international classification mechanisms for sustainable economic activities. https://bellona.org/assets/sites/3/2023/10/The-EU-Sustainable-Finance-Taxonomys-spillover-effects-on-International-classification-mechanisms-for-sustainable-economic-activities-1.pdf. Accessed 31 Jan 2026
Lucarelli C, Mazzoli C, Rancan M, Severini S (2020) Classification of sustainable activities: EU taxonomy and scientific literature. Sustainability 12(16):6460
Marbaix P, Magnan A, Muccione V et al (2025) Climate change risks illustrated by the Intergovernmental Panel on Climate Change (IPCC) "burning embers." Earth Syst Sci Data 17:317–349
Martinčević I, Primorac D, Dorić B (2024) Corporate Sustainability Reporting Directive (CSRD): obligations, challenges and requirements for companies. Enter Res Innov 10(1):317–327
McCarthy J (2022) The Regulation of RegTech and SupTech in Finance: Ensuring Consistency in Principle and in Practice. Journal of Financial Regulation and Compliance 31(2):186–199
McIlroy D, Sethi-Smith R (2023) No point preventing fraud? Philipp v Barclays Bank. Butterworths J Int Bank Finan L 513–516
Michailova J, Schmidt U (2011) Overconfidence and bubbles in experimental asset markets. Kiel Working Papers 1729
Moloney N (2004) EU securities and financial markets regulation. Oxford University Press
Murinde V, Rizopoulos E, Zachariadis M (2022) The impact of the FinTech revolution on the future banking: opportunities and risks. Int Rev Financ Anal 81:102103
Omanga J, Dreyer J (2017) Innovation and financial inclusion in Kenya: A case study of M-PESA. In: Yüksel Ü (ed) Christiansen B. Technological integration as a catalyst for industrial development and economic growth, IGI Global, pp 207–222
Otudor L, Bagheri M (2023) Legitimacy of power exercised by FATF under international law. J Fin Cri 31(6):1289–1301
Pacifici E (2015) Making PayPal pay: regulation E and its application to alternative payment services. Duke L Technol 13:90–115

Pavlidis G (2021) Financial action task force and the fight against money laundering and the financing of terrorism: Quo Vadimus? J Fin Cri 28(3):765–773
Perera S, Jin X, Maurushat A, Opoku D (2022) Factors affecting reputational damage to organisations due to cyberattacks. Informatics 9(1):28
Pietriche R (2015) The ascendancy of the Lex Delicti: the problematic role of theory in Australian choice of tort law rules. Melbourne J Int L 16:1–38
Pol R (2020) Anti-money laundering: the world's least effective policy experiment? Together, we can fix it. Pol des Prac 3(1):1–22
Pollman E (2019) Corporate oversight and disobedience. Vanderbilt L Rev 72(6):2013–2046
Pursiainen A (2022) The FATF and evolution of counterterrorism asset freeze laws in the Nordic Countries: we fought the soft law and the soft law won. In: Karjalainen K, Tornberg I, Pursiainen A (eds) International actors and formation of laws. Springer, Cham, pp 135–172
Rabbani M, Azam Q, Hawaldar I, Aljalahma R, Dsouza S (2024) Does an overconfidence bias affect stock return, trading volume, and liquidity? Fresh insights from the G7 Nations. Cog Econ Fin 12:1–17
Raiwa-Rietbroek I (2020) Electronic payments: consumer policies and practices in EU and US law. PhD Thesis, Universiteit van Amsterdam
Reed C (2012) Making laws for cyberspace. Oxford University Press, Oxford
Reuter P, Truman E (2004) Chasing dirty money: the fight against money laundering. Peterson Institute for International Economics 25–43
Ryszawska B (2018) Sustainable finance: paradigm shift. In: Bem A, Daszyńska-Żygadło K, Hajdíková T, Juhász P (eds), Finance and sustainability, Springer, pp 219–231
Roomen T, Jonge B (2024) Balancing privacy and public interest in the fight against illicit financial flows: lessons from an European case study. J Econ Criminol 5:100093
Sainati T, Locatelli G, Smith N, Brookes N, Olver G (2020) Types and functions of special purpose vehicles in infrastructure megaprojects. Int J Proj Manage 38(5):243–255
Schneider F, Niederlander U (2008) Money laundering: some facts. Eur J Law Econ 26(3):387–404
Schroth P (2010) Financial leasing of equipment in the law of the United States. Am J Compar L 58:323–352
Shahin W (2013) Compliance with international regulation on AML/CTF: the case of banks in Lebanon. J Mon Launder Cont 16(2):109–118
Shum N (2025) Authorised push payment fraud: theorising a loss allocation model. UCL J L Jurisprud:43–69
Smolenska A (2025) The constitutive role of law in sustainable finance. Ind L J:dwaf026:1–20
Stanley R, Buckley R (2016) Protecting the west, excluding the rest: the impact of the AML/CTF regime on financial inclusion in the pasific and potential responses. Melboure J Int L 17:1–24
Storm A (2013) Establishing the link between money loundering and tax evasion. Int Busin Econ Res J 12(11):1437
Subashree S (2024) Market minds: understanding behavioral finance concepts. Shanlax Int J Manage 11:162–168
Sunarmi D, Lubis T (2022) Implementation of customer due diligence principles on financial service companies in preventing and eradicating criminal action of money laundering in medan. Jurnal Mercatoria 15(2):103–116
Thaler R, Sunstein C (2009) Nudge: improving decisions about health, wealth, and happiness. Penguin, London
Tiwari M, Gepp A, Kumar K (2020) A review money laundering literature: the state of research in key areas. Pac Account Rev 32(2):271–303
Turner N (2015) The financial action task force: international regulatory convergence through soft law. New York L Sch L Rev 59:547–559
van den Hurk A, van der Klooster I (2024) The European Commission's sustainable finance action plan and other international activities. In: Busch D, Ferrarini G, Grünewald S (eds) Sustainable finance in Europe: corporate governance, Financial Stability and Financial Markets. Springer, Cham, pp 17–95

US Congress (1995) Information technologies for control of money laundering. Government Printing Office
Young S (2019) Policing and prosecution of money laundering. In: Valsamis Mitsilegas, Saskia Hufnagel and Anton Moiseienko (eds) Research handbook on transnational crime. Edward Elgar, pp 122–141
van Niekerk A (2024) Economic inclusion: green finance and the SDGs. Sustainability 16(3):1128
van Roekel G, Smit M (2022) Hard behaviour and the emergence of clusters. Spat Econ Anal 17:499–519
Vlcek W (2024) Let's talk about layering: money laundering, anti-money laundering, and digital surveillance. Brown J Wor Aff 31(1):35–48
Walker T, Morris L (2021) The handbook of banking technology. Wiley
Zetzsche D, Annunziata F, Arner D, Buckley R (2021) The Markets in Crypto-Assets Regulation (MiCA) and the EU digital finance strategy. Cap Mark L J 16(2):203–225

Further Readings

Busch D, Ferrarini G, Hurk A (2021) The European Commission's sustainable finance action plan and other international initiatives. In: Busch D, Ferrarini G, Grünewald S (eds) Sustainable finance in Europe: corporate governance, financial stability and financial markets. Palgrave Macmillan, Cham, pp 17–95
European Commission (2019) Regulation (EU) 2019/2088 (The Sustainable Finance Disclosure Regulation—SFDR)
European Commission (2020) Regulation (EU) 2020/852 (The Taxonomy Regulation)
Ryszawska B (2018) Sustainable finance: paradigm shift. In: Bem A, Daszyńska-Żygadło K, Hajdíková T et al (eds) Finance and sustainability, Springer, pp 219–231
Smolenska A (2025) The constitutive role of law in sustainable finance. Ind L J:dwaf026
Grabowski M (2024) Account Information and Payment Initiation Services and the Related AML Obligations in the Law of the European Union. FinTech 3(1):173-183 10.3390/fintech3010011
Nabilou H (2019) Central Bank Digital Currencies: Preliminary Legal Observations. SSRN Electronic Journal 10.2139/ssrn.3329993
Billiam B, Lastuti A, Handayani T (2022) The Urgency of Open Application Programming Interface Standardization in the Implementation of Open Banking to Customer Data Protection for the Advancement of Indonesian Banking PADJADJARAN. Jurnal Ilmu Hukum (Journal of Law) 9(1):67-88
Oh S, Gyongchan, Chung G, Cho K (2024) New Sustainable Fintech Business Models Created by Open Application Programming Interface Technology: A Case Study of Korea's Open Banking Application Programming Interface Platform. Sustainability 16(16):7187
Mohammed B (2019) Api "application Programming Interface" Banking: A Promising Future For Financial Institutions (international Experience). Le Revue des Sciences Commerciales 18(2):31-43

FSC
www.fsc.org
MIX
Papier | Fördert gute Waldnutzung
FSC® C083411

Kolibri 360 GmbH
Ferdinand-Jühlke-Straße 7
99095 Erfurt, Deutschland
produktsicherheit@kolibri360.de